ALSO BY NEAL GABLER

An Empire of Their Own:
How the Jews Invented Hollywood
(1988)

WINCHELL

WINCHELL

GOSSIP, POWER AND THE CULTURE OF CELEBRITY

NEAL GABLER

ALFRED A. KNOPF   NEW YORK   1994

THIS IS A BORZOI BOOK
PUBLISHED BY ALFRED A. KNOPF, INC.

Grateful acknowledgment is made to the following for permission to reprint previ-
ously published and unpublished material:
The American Play Company: Excerpts from the letters of Damon Runyon. Reprinted
by permission.
Donnelley Library, Lake Forest College: Excerpts from the letters of Frank Hause.
Box 17, File 7, Patterson Papers. Reprinted by permission.
Dutton Signet: Excerpts from *My Last Million Readers* by Emile Gauvreau, copyright
© 1941 by E. P. Dutton & Co., Inc. Reprinted by permission of Dutton Signet, a
division of Penguin Books USA Inc.
The L. Wolfe Gilbert Estate: Excerpts from "Mrs. Winchell's Boy" by L. Wolfe Gil-
bert (1932). Reprinted by permission of Mrs. L. Wolfe Gilbert on behalf of the
estate.
Kate Hadley Baker and Nicholas John Hadley: Letter of their grandfather George
Washington Hill. Reprinted by permission.
The Jean and Alexander Heard Library, Vanderbilt University: Excerpt from "The
Sharpshooters" by Grantland Rice. The Jean and Alexander Heard Library, Special
Collections, University Archives, Vanderbilt University.
Irving Caesar Music Corporation: Excerpt from "Papa, We've Got to Move Uptown"
by Irving Caesar. Reprinted by permission of Irving Caesar Music Corporation.
Mrs. Marcy Levine: Excerpts from the letters of Ed Sullivan. Reprinted by permission.
New York Daily News: Excerpts from "Flash! –30– For WW" by Ed Wilcox (*New
York Daily News*, March 2, 1969), copyright © 1969 by New York Daily News, L.P.
Reprinted by permission.
Jane White Viazzi: Excerpts from the letters of her late father, Walter White. Re-
printed by permission.
Mrs. Ed Weiner: Letters of her late husband, Ed Weiner. Reprinted by permission.

Frontispiece and First Part Title photos, Rose Bigman Collection.
Second Part Title photo, courtesy of Hal Layer.
Third Part Title photo, Bill Mark.

Library of Congress Cataloging-in-Publication Data
Gabler, Neal.
  Winchell: gossip, power and the culture of celebrity / by Neal Gabler.—1st ed.
    p.   cm.
  Includes bibliographical references and index.
  ISBN 0-679-41751-6
    1. Winchell, Walter, 1897–1972.   2. Journalists—United States—Biography.
I. Title.
PN4874.W67G33   1994
070'.92—dc20
  [B]   93-44259
            CIP

Manufactured in the United States of America
First Edition

For my beloved daughters, Laurel and Tanne,

*And for all those who stand outside the
corridors of power and privilege*

What is the end of fame? 'tis but to fill
A certain portion of uncertain paper:
Some liken it to climbing up a hill,
Whose summit, like all hills, is lost in vapor.

GEORGE GORDON, LORD BYRON,
Don Juan

Contents

*A photographic insert of 8 pages will be found following page 172,
and an insert of 16 pages following page 396*

Introduction

In the end, few really remembered, fewer cared. His daughter Walda was the only mourner at his funeral, and a memorial service held six weeks later on what would have been his seventy-fifth birthday attracted only 150 guests, many of whom drifted out before the eulogies ended. There were front-page obituaries, but they portrayed him as a relic long past his prime. An attempt by friends to rename the traffic island in New York's Times Square after him and erect a monument there met with bureaucratic indifference. Nothing he left behind seemed to endure. His name faded—the name he had worked so hard to burn into the public consciousness.

By the time of Walter Winchell's death a friend admitted that trying to explain him to a generation unfamiliar with him "would be like trying to explain Napoleon to the second French generation after the Napoleonic wars." But for more than four decades Walter Winchell had been an American institution, and arguably one of the principal architects of the culture. By one estimate, fifty million Americans—out of an adult population of roughly seventy-five million—either listened to his weekly radio broadcast or read his daily column, which, at its height in the late thirties and forties, was syndicated in more than two thousand newspapers; it was, according to one observer, the "largest continuous audience ever possessed by a man who was neither politician nor divine." It was said that when he switched papers in New York, two hundred thousand readers followed him, and one report attributed nearly half the readership of the Hearst newspaper chain to Winchell's column. Presidents courted him, and government officials of America's foreign enemies castigated him by name. Hit songs were written about him, and Hollywood coaxed him to star in two movies, both of which were box-office successes. For a time you could walk down any street on a warm Sunday night at nine o'clock, when his broadcast aired, and hear his disembodied voice wafting from open windows, giving ghostly validation to his own slogan: "Winchell . . . HE SEES ALL . . . HE KNOWS ALL."

He had first come to public attention in the twenties as the Bard of Broadway, a glib, wisecracking young columnist on the New York *Graphic* whose life and writing seemed perfectly synchronized to the rhythms of the Jazz Age. "It was his contribution," drama critic and raconteur Alexander Woollcott wrote approvingly of Winchell's early effect on American journalism, "to go on strike against the vast impersonality which, at the time of his advent, was deadening the American newspaper into a kind of daily Congressional Record." He wrote in a smart, slangy prose that no less an expert than H. L. Mencken credited with having enlarged the American vernacular. Couples didn't get married in Winchell's column; they were "welded," "lohengrinned," "Adam-and-Eveing it." They didn't have fun; they "made whoopee!" They didn't have babies; they had "blessed events." And when they got divorced, they were "Reno-vated" or "phffft!" Movies were "moom pitchers" and movie lovers were "cinemaddicts." Legs were "shafts." Passion was "pash." Debutantes were "debutramps." Jews were "Joosh." It was a vigorous style, personal and pungent, and as early as 1929, *Vanity Fair* was reporting that Winchell had "inspired more burlesques of himself than any writer since Hemingway."

But if his vivid prose helped transform the style of journalism and made him a popular curiosity, what made him a national phenomenon was gossip. In 1925, at a time when the editors of most newspapers were reluctant to publish even something as inoffensive as the notice of an impending birth for fear of crossing the boundaries of good taste, Winchell introduced a revolutionary column that reported who was romancing whom, who was cavorting with gangsters, who was ill or dying, who was suffering financial difficulties, which spouses were having affairs, which couples were about to divorce, and dozens of other secrets, peccadilloes and imbroglios that had previously been concealed from public view. In doing so, he not only broke a long-standing taboo; he suddenly and single-handedly expanded the purview of American journalism forever.

But he did not just invent the modern gossip column. He became an opinion-maker largely because he understood, as no one else then seemed to, the bitter subtext of the gossip he purveyed. Having grown up in poverty himself, attention-starved, and nursing deep resentments against his social betters, he understood that gossip, far beyond its basic attraction as journalistic voyeurism, was a weapon of empowerment for the reader and listener. Invading the lives of the famous and revealing their secrets brought them to heel. It humanized them, and in humanizing them demonstrated that they were no better than we and in many cases worse. Or as Winchell once put it to an associate, "Democracy is where everybody can kick everybody else's ass." Adding, "But you can't kick Winchell's."

Writing in 1933 with an appreciation for Winchell's impact on society, Woollcott predicted that historians would some day label the era "the Age of the Two Walters, Lippmann and Winchell." In making this declaration, Woollcott recognized that Lippmann, the sage political columnist, and Winchell constituted not only the extremes of American journalism but, far more important, represented the combatants in a war for America itself in a period of dynamic social change, a war over who would finally set the nation's cultural agenda. On one side was Lippmann, the patrician, reasoned and moderate, the urbane elitist, the counselor to the mighty and skeptic of the rationality of the popular will, the embodiment, by temperament if not birth, of the embattled American aristocracy. On the other side was Winchell, the plebeian, flip and intemperate, the urban scamp, the voice of the disenchanted and disenfranchised and the champion of democracy, the embodiment of the ascendant American masses.

To challenge the mature, elitist, bookish culture of Lippmann, which had dominated American life for more than a century, Winchell had helped inaugurate a new mass culture of celebrity—centered in New York and Hollywood and Washington, fixated on personalities, promulgated by the media, predicated on publicity, dedicated to the ephemeral and grounded on the principle that notoriety confers power. This culture would bind an increasingly diverse, mobile and atomized nation until *it* became, in many respects, America's dominant ethos, celebrity consciousness our new common denominator.

Most of his detractors seemed deaf to this Whitmanesque strain in Winchell's raucous music; in time they would complain that he vulgarized and trivialized everything he touched, especially after he had made the seemingly improbable leap from gossipmonger to political commentator. But Alistair Cooke, at the time the American correspondent of the British magazine *Listener*, observed the appeal firsthand when he visited Winchell's radio broadcast, which was then emanating from the columnist's vacation spot in Miami Beach, Florida. "I was astonished at what I saw," Cooke wrote.

It was a small studio and possibly a hundred people were in there. They were all the shapes of the immigrant poor in that sunny land. . . . Winchell had something for them that he would never have for you and that I never dreamed of. He was the promise of American freedom and uninhibited bounce; he was Americanism symbol ized in a nose-thumbing at the portentousness of the great; he released them for fifteen minutes once a week from the fear of oppression; he was the defender of the American faith.

Over the years, Walter Winchell would lose his reputation as a populist who had once heralded an emerging new social order, lose his reputation as a charming gadfly. He would be remembered instead, to the extent that anyone remembered him at all, as a vitriolic, self-absorbed megalomaniac—an image indelibly fixed by Burt Lancaster's performance as gossipmonger J. J. Hunsecker in the 1956 film *Sweet Smell of Success*, which everyone assumed had been inspired by Winchell's life. He would be remembered spewing bile, picking fights, destroying lives through his column. That would be the image that would finally stick.

It would stick, in part, because of the public's own ambivalence toward the culture of celebrity, even as the culture continues to flourish. It would stick because of what was perceived as Winchell's own political wrongheadedness in the fifties, when he seemed to turn his back on his thirties populism and embrace the fashionable Red-baiting conservatism of the time; the image of Winchell as a journalistic Joseph McCarthy, slashing and burning his way through the American left as he had once slashed and burned his way through the right, would become almost as powerful an image as Lancaster's in *Sweet Smell*, and it seemed to wall off anything he had done before, anything he had been.

And it would stick, finally, because Winchell *was* often as vindictive, cruel, egocentric, paranoid, selfish, cheap and thoroughly reprehensible as his detractors portrayed him as being, though these qualities had once been part of his waggish appeal too. "He was truly a 14-carat son-of-a-bitch, no doubt about it," critic John Crosby wrote in his obituary of Winchell. "He looked like a cross between a weasel and a jackal and he was indeed a bit of both." George Jessel, a childhood friend and later an enemy, said, "He can be as warm as the first night of a love affair and as cold as the first night in a theater." (Winchell printed the remark in his column.) "There are bleeders and there are not bleeders," commented another acquaintance trying to characterize him. "You could jab him with anything."

Though he was capable of great kindnesses, Winchell did nothing to discourage the darker impressions of himself; if anything, he seemed to promote them. Even in his autobiography, which was written shortly before his death and which one might have expected him to use to rehabilitate his reputation, he snarled at the ingrates who had forsaken him. "I want them all to know that I've wearied of the mutual deception," he wrote.

I have forgiven, but I don't have to forget. I'm not a fighter, I'm a "waiter." I wait until I can catch an ingrate with his fly open, and then I take a picture of it.

When some heel does me dirt (after I've helped him or her) I return the compliment some day. In the paper, on the air, or with a bottle of ketchup on the skull. I don't make up nasty things to write about them. I wait until they get locked up for taking dope or pimping and then I make it Public. Vindictive? You're gahdamb'd right! You Botcha Me, I Botcha You!

But by the time he wrote these words, the grudges that had once made headlines seemed as petty and irrelevant as the former king of gossip himself. Once the plucky Prince Hal of American journalism and then its Richard III, he had become its ranting King Lear.

It was Dorothy Parker who once quipped, "Poor Walter. He's afraid he'll wake up one day and discover he's not Walter Winchell." After a melodramatic existence that tacked through a Dickensian childhood, vaudeville and tabloids, divorce, tragedy, suicides, betrayals, threats and mental illness, Parker's prophecy was borne out. Winchell's life became a paradigm of what one might call the tragedy of celebrity. He lived by fame and died by neglect. He assumed a public persona only to find that the persona assumed him. And when the show finally ended its run, he was left in costume but with no role to play and nothing inside himself upon which to draw. He awoke to find that he was no longer Walter Winchell. He awoke to find that he was no longer anybody.

And yet, despite its tragic emptiness, few lives are more instructive of the forces that shaped mass culture in America than Walter Winchell's. Because he changed American journalism, examining his life enables us to understand better the evolution of the media in this century. Because he both effected and symbolized the changing of the cultural guard in this century, examining his life enables us to understand better the challenge that mass culture issued to high culture in America. Because he helped create a culture of celebrity, examining his life enables us to understand better the symbiotic relationship between the public and the famous. And because he lived the cycle of celebrity himself, examining his life enables us to understand better the mechanism by which one achieves fame and loses it, the things one gains by being famous and the things one sacrifices.

After Winchell's death, a friend eulogized him extravagantly but not without truth: "Winchell's primary objective is to explain the 20th century to his millions of readers. The fact is, however, that historians will be unable to explain the 20th century without understanding Winchell."

To do so now is the aim of this book.

PART ONE

WALTER WINSCHEL

What rage for fame attends both great and small!
Better be damned than mentioned not at all!
—JOHN WOLCOT

CHAPTER I

The Curse

As Chaim Weinschel made the long journey from Russia to the United States, he carried within him an implacable darkness of spirit. "Life has not always shown me a smile," he would write. "I feel like the human being who hears steps over his grave as he listens to the conversations of the living, who's trying to throw off the earth that covers his grave and remove the stones at its head, only to realize that he is powerless. . . ."

Born in Minsk in 1834, the son of a rabbi named Baruch who, in Chaim's words, "was loved by everyone who knew him and had seen his way of life," Chaim had been trained to follow his father's righteous path. Baruch Weinschel had sacrificed for his son. He had bribed authorities to save Chaim from military conscription and had pawned the family furnishings to provide him an education. Baruch eventually settled in Bialystok, where he served the Jewish community for thirty years and where he died, greatly honored, at eighty-five in 1890. Chaim became an itinerant cantor, a religious singer, riding the circuit through western Russia and Poland, wherever a congregation needed a spiritual leader to conduct its services, from Kovno to Kolo to St. Petersburg to Grajewo to his father's Bialystok to Suwalki.

But despite a powerful voice that could "amaze" the congregation, Chaim "cursed the day they put the cantorial hat on my head to serve in the holy task." He lived in a nimbus of gloom, racked by doubt and stalked by misery. He married a young woman named Hannah who bore him two daughters, but she died in 1869, possibly in childbirth. Chaim was inconsolable. "My heart is as ripped as my clothes," he wrote. "I was like a shadow oppressed by the grief that burdened me." At the urging of concerned friends, he began to write poetry, invariably lachrymose verses about his own misfortunes, and these became his only succor. "Grief stands in front of me as a wall / If I remember you, my pen, my sadness is relieved."

Hannah had been dead less than a year when Chaim, doubtless needing a mother for his infant girls, remarried. Fannie Sweri was only nineteen, a plain, pious, unlettered girl sixteen years her husband's junior. Within a year she had borne him a son, Jacob, but neither the marriage and children nor an apparently growing reputation seemed to lift Chaim's despondency. "Where am I going?" he wrote one midnight in Bialystok in 1880 as he prepared to leave for an assignment in St. Petersburg. "What am I doing?" And always the most important question: "Tell me, my hope—will my pact with sorrow be broken now?" An invitation the next year from a congregation in America seemed to offer the answers he sought. "With a happy heart I prepared for my trip / My hope was like my right-handed shadow / Telling me that [in] going the money is ready and / Only good will welcome you."

With Fannie, his two daughters from his first marriage and four children from his second, Chaim Weinschel set out for America in August 1881, intending to alter his destiny at last. In America, Chaim believed, he could soar above the prosaic. In America, he believed, he would break the pact.

IN YIDDISH, "Weinschel" literally means "sour cherries," and there was a time when those who bore the name were likely to be vintners. But through elisions and compressions the name could also be translated as "fine" (*fein* for *wein*) and "school" (*shul*), or "fine student," which is probably how it came to be applied to the Weinschel clan. The Weinschels were scholars. They disdained manual labor and extolled the life of the mind. Chaim himself, no mere religious pedant, had been described by a colleague as a "wise man," and when he collected his poems for publication, the colleague wrote him that it "is justly expected that by your valuable book you will acquire such fame as to rate your name among the great modern poets." "You are praised by both young and old," Chaim told himself in his journal. "Who does not enjoy your prayers?"

The Weinschels, soon numbering nine with the birth of a son in 1883, settled on East Broadway on the Lower East Side of New York City, where a small cluster of Russian Jews was already collecting that summer in flight from the pogroms. In those first few years of the great Russian emigration, before the Lower East Side was ghettoized, East Broadway was a broad boulevard with spacious sidewalks and handsome homes where the Jewish immigrant intelligentsia would assemble to debate religious issues, and Chaim's circular kitchen table became the center for one particular group of scholars from Russia and Poland.

He relished their esteem, but if he had come to America expecting it to end his pact with sorrow, he was to be bitterly disappointed. America brought him only additional discouragements and new sorrows. What he wanted from his new country, what he wanted from life, was regard—not just from his religious *landsmen* but from the larger secular community as well. Why not a "great poet," as his friend had predicted? Why not a literary immortal? What he found instead was a country hard and pragmatic, one that scorned his ethereal intellectualizing as much as he scorned its stolid industriousness. "[T]his isn't the country for people like you to soar on the wings of imagination," he wrote an immigrant friend in commiseration. "Knowledge is not honored here. . . . All wisdom is useless. Dear friend, don't try to be smart here."

He attempted to adjust. By the mid-1890s he was variously Hyman or Herman Weinschel or Weinschiell, and he had moved his family north to Harlem, which was then, before masses of Russian Jews began swarming there, "the province of only the exceptional immigrant," in the words of one historian. Clearly Chaim believed himself to be among the exceptional. And his children believed it of themselves too. But unlike Chaim the moody dreamer, they had no interest in the life of the mind and no desire for regard. What they wanted, what they fully expected as if it were their natural entitlement, was gentility.

In this George Weinschel, the second son, was the model for his generation. In 1911, after years of clerking in brokerage houses, he had landed a seat on the "Curb"—a stock exchange literally situated on the curb of Broad Street in the Manhattan financial district. Though the Curb was known more for its tumult than its gentility, the Weinschels accounted George a "big man on Wall Street" and a source of great pride. By this time Hyman Weinschel was long gone, dead at sixty-six of chronic pneumonia on New Year's Day 1901, and George had become not only the model but the undisputed family leader to whom all the others deferred.

Nowhere was his authority more evident than in what happened to the name "Weinschel." The children, quite possibly chafing at its overt Jewishness and foreignness, had never seemed entirely comfortable with it; they would haphazardly drop the first *e* or the *s* or the *c* one year, only to restore it the next, and there were periods when three given family members were simultaneously using three different spellings. It was George who first Anglicized it to "Winchel"—the name of a fellow clerk—no doubt appreciating the English origins it suggested. Fannie adopted it the year after her husband's death, and soon all the rest, save George's older brother, Jacob, were "Winchels."

But the burnished name couldn't hide the reality that the Winchels' gentility was as much a delusion as their father's literary pretensions. George—despite his limousines, his bespoke suits, his servants and his fashionable Seventh Avenue apartment that had once belonged to the Guggenheims, despite even his snobbish wife who wouldn't ride in their new car until the chauffeur put on his cap—was really just a fun-loving and high-spirited man who made and then lost several fortunes and whose motto was "Life is a lemon and you've got to squeeze out as much juice as you can."

Max, five years younger than George, was known primarily as a good dancer and an excellent cardplayer. "The minute you saw Max Winchel, you knew you were going to have a good time," said a relative. But she added that "anyone who was knowledgeable would say he was stupid." After working in his mother's candy and cigar store and then briefly as a conductor, he landed a job through George in a brokerage on the Curb, where he remained until his death, in total obscurity except for a minor trading infraction which earned him a fine and a small notice in the newspapers.

Their older sister Dora was as doleful as her brothers were blithe, but no more genteel. Too high-strung to hold a job, she nevertheless became hysterical at the mere mention of marriage, despite her family's best efforts to arrange one for her. Instead she spent her life supported by George, caring for her mother, and, after Fannie died in 1928, attending funerals—whether she knew the deceased or not. "All the society people in New York used to keep a seat for her in all the churches," her niece remembered. In 1936 she was committed to the Bellevue psychiatric hospital. She died two years later at the age of sixty-six in the Manhattan State Mental Hospital on Wards Island.

Rebecca Winchel found herself in a loveless, unhappy marriage to a health-conscious sweater manufacturer who once insisted she walk two miles when she left the hospital after an operation. Three children and two separations later, he died suddenly, leaving his widow $40,000, which her brother Max promptly invested in the stock market. She lost it all in the crash of 1929 and in true Winchel fashion was treated thereafter with withering contempt—ironically, by the very man who was responsible, Max.

It was the youngest of the Winchels, Beatrice, or Beatty, as she was called, who came closest to fulfilling her family's lofty ambitions, and she did it through gambling. An attractive, elegant and independent woman—she finished high school at a time when it was rare for women to do so—Beatty married Billy Koch, a top lieutenant of America's pre-eminent bookmaker, Frank Erickson. "When you talked about Billy Koch," said one of the Winchels, "you were really talking about somebody." Money flowed easily for the Koches. For the Koch children, there were governesses, private schools, horseback riding lessons and expensive boarding camps in summer.

It was, however, neither literary achievement nor gentility that was to be the Winchel legacy. Rather, the legacy would be the pretension itself. Many years later, as his aunts and uncles were passing into their dotage, Walter Winchell would see the lyricist Irving Caesar in some Manhattan nightspot and insist he sing an old song Caesar had written about the daughter of a Lower East Side Jewish family with aspirations for something better.

> *Living in the third floor back, what can you expect,*
> *All the classy people turn me down.*
> *They knock me down.*
> *Where we live you know it's true,*
> *Chances for romance are few.*
> *Papa, we gotta move uptown*
> *With trees around. . . .*
>
> *We'll settle down uptown in a very expensive flat.*
> *We won't stop at that. You can bet your hat and*
> *your overcoat.*
> *We'll have a list to bring new visitors to our*
> *floor.*
> *A maid to say "Come in" when they knock on the door.*
> *The furnishings must be the best which could be*
> *found.*
> *I must have an atmosphere to catch which boys*
> *around.*
> *Living in a neighborhood filled with stables isn't*
> *good.*
> *Papa, we gotta move uptown.*

"Winchell loved this song," Caesar remembered, though the songwriter couldn't possibly have known why. He couldn't have known that it was the story of Walter's own family. He couldn't have known that he had described Walter's inheritance of the curse of expectation.

II

Among the Winchels, everyone hated Jacob. "The rest of the family wanted nothing to do with him," said his niece Lola. His brother George's family regarded him as "stupid," and George once remarked that he wasn't sure he could ever bring himself to attend Jake's funeral. Though he was charming and attractive and shared the affectations of his siblings—he wore spats, carried a cane and on occasion called himself Jack de Winchel—Jacob undermined any impression of gentility by the foul-smelling cigars he smoked, the ostentatious clothes he wore and the awful jokes he told—all of which deeply embarrassed his family.

His offenses were only compounded by his selection of a spouse. Jacob had probably met Jennie Bakst sometime in 1895 on the Lower East Side, where his father officiated in a synagogue at 12 Pike Street. Jennie's younger sister Rose had been married there by Chaim on January 1, 1896, and the Baksts were living in the building which housed the synagogue, so Jacob and Jennie certainly had had opportunities to see each other.

Morris Bakst, Jennie's father, had brought his family from Russia in 1890. The name "Bakst" derived from a small town in Lithuania, but most of the family, including Morris, changed it to Baxter once they had settled in the United States. It was one of the few concessions they made to their new country. Unlike Chaim, who petitioned for citizenship as soon as he could, Morris Bakst never became a U.S. citizen, and neither did Jennie. They clung instead to the old ways. The Winchel children, despite having a cantor for a father, quickly abandoned the obligations of keeping kosher. (For years after her husband's death, Fannie Winchel would hunt through her children's iceboxes searching for bacon, which is proscribed by kosher dietary law.) Jennie Bakst, on the other hand, was an observant Jew. And while the Winchel children bore no trace of an accent, Jennie and her family spoke with an unmistakable one and would always grapple with English. Rose never even learned how to read.

Perhaps the biggest difference between the Winchels and the Baksts was that the latter were simple, unassuming people of limited skills and ambitions. There were four Bakst children. Frank remained in New York and worked at menial jobs most of his life; Dorothy married a gentile and was essentially read out of the family for having done so. (By contrast, Max Winchel had married a gentile and none of the Winchels cared.) Rose married an executive in a tobacco company and moved South.

Of the four, Jennie was the most self-possessed and assertive, though the haughty Winchels saw her as comically self-involved and aggressive—a compulsive talker. (George used to call her "Becky Sharp" after the self-centered heroine of Thackeray's *Vanity Fair.*) What everyone, even the Winchels, did grant was that she was lovely. A neighborhood girl described her as a "beautiful, stately woman, with raven-black hair and soulful blue eyes." Photos show her as petite with high cheekbones, a full mouth, a rounded little chin. Her skin was smooth and fair, contrasting with Jacob's dark good looks. They made a handsome couple.

They were married by Chaim on May 14, 1896, in his new synagogue, Congregation Nachlath Zevi, in Harlem. Jacob gave his age as twenty-four, Jennie as nineteen. The newlyweds moved into a small apartment in a squat three-story building at 116 East 112th Street between Park and Lexington Avenues, just a few blocks from Jacob's parents' apartment on 106th Street. Eleven months later, on April 7, 1897, Jennie gave birth there to a son. Jacob's younger brother George provided the name: Walter. Walter Winschel.

He was an extremely attractive child. He had large blue eyes, a thin, almost feminine mouth, a sharp little nose and the delicate, rounded chin of his mother. His complexion, like hers, was exceedingly fair, and it would remain so unusually pink and soft that throughout his life people remarked upon it. Jennie cut his blondish hair in a long bang across his forehead; later he swept it to the right just over his eye in what was nearly a "peekaboo." Only the ears seemed oversized, and it wasn't until he reached his teens that he grew into them.

The Winchels believed he favored their family, and most especially his aunt Dora. Jennie liked to believe he favored her, as he did increasingly as he neared adolescence. She adored him and dressed him in stylish suits and knickers that almost dandified him. (He didn't get his first pair of long pants until he was fifteen.) An aunt said of Jennie's relationship to Walter, "She used to butter his bread and put it in his mouth."

And yet, whenever as a grown man Walter reminisced about his childhood, it was never the maternal affection he recalled, never much happiness of any sort. What he remembered was the deprivation he suffered, the times he went unfed, unclothed, and neglected. And he remembered not just the poverty, for the poverty seemed not even the worst of it; his sensitivity sharply honed by the Winchels' condescension to his father, he remembered most of all the abuse that accompanied the poverty from people who felt superior to him—people who insulted and reviled him because he was poor. And he related these tales of mistreatment so matter-of-factly that at least one friend would nearly be moved to tears as he listened. "Horrible cruelty was the way of the world. He knew no other."

The Winschels were indeed poor. At the time of Walter's birth Jacob was a shirtmaker working with two brothers from the Lower East Side named Lapidus who owned a clothing store at 42 Walker Street, just below Canal Street in a warehouse district of lower Manhattan. But he barely earned a living. The family was so poor that they were constantly on the move, presumably to dodge the rent-collector or take advantage of the rent reductions that landlords often offered new tenants as an inducement. From the apartment on East 112th Street where Walter was born, the Winschels moved to 25 East 103d Street, at the corner of Madison Avenue, just a block from Central Park, two blocks from the New York Central Railroad, which ran up Park Avenue and amid empty parcels of land soon to be filled with other apartment houses. One year later they moved again, this time to a five-story tenement at 113 East 100th Street, across from the car barns of the Metropolitan Street Railway and as close to the abject, working-class section of Harlem as any Winchel ever ventured.

It was in this apartment on May 20, 1900, that Jennie gave birth to her second child. Once again George Winchel provided the name. Algernon he called him, with typical Winchel pretentiousness, though even Jennie was befuddled by it. "Walter I like," she would say. "But what's with this Algernon?"

The Winschels weren't long on 100th Street either. Before Algy had turned two, they had decamped for another five-story tenement on a largely undeveloped block between Fifth and Madison avenues on 106th Street near Central Park. Within a year, they were gone again. The building at 15 East 117th was also five stories, but there were only six families living there, and the area, three blocks south of Mount Morris Park, was reasonably nice. With Jennie's father as a boarder, this would be their home for the next three years—a brief interlude of stability in their otherwise hectic, unsettled life.

It was during this period that Jacob left the Lapidus brothers and went into business for himself, selling silk for women's undergarments. But a partner soon made off with the bolts of cloth, and Jacob hadn't the resources to fight. "My pop wasn't much of a businessman, but he was a hell of a pinochle player," was the way Walter would later put it to a friend, suggesting that his father was really the victim of his own shiftlessness.

Bumping haplessly from job to job, Jacob would cadge money off his brother George or his brother-in-law Billy Koch. Billy's son, Howard, remembered Jacob appearing uninvited every Sunday before dinner, always with a new get-rich-quick scheme if only Billy would advance him the money. "Here's Uncle Jake again" became a family refrain. The Winchels saw him in his dapper suits, living far beyond his means as they themselves were, trying to maintain a pretense of success, but nothing could mask his desperation. Jacob Winschel was a failure. He reminded them of who they really were and how little removed they themselves were from disaster. He was their nightmare.

And Jacob knew. However insouciant he may have seemed in his weekly forays for money, he knew he was a failure. It was humiliating for him to be scraping by while George and Max were making their way on the Curb. It was humiliating to beg for their handouts. He was the eldest, five years George's senior, yet George was the family chieftain, the one who had even named Jacob's own children with Jennie's blessing, while Jacob himself was ostracized. In his own view, he was not shiftless. In his own view, he had been the victim of bad luck and ill timing, and it was in moments like these—when he was forced to confront his failure and beg for money—that his humiliation would flare into resentment.

What aggravated that sense of resentment, what brewed the storm within the Winschel family, was that Jennie was no more sympathetic to her husband's plight than were his siblings. "There was nasty talk," remembered Beatty Koch's daughter, Lola, speaking of family gossip about quarrels between Jennie and Jacob. The wife of Jennie's nephew Willie said, "He never made the mother a living—I'll put it like that." Jacob would agree that his wife's open hostility was the product of his business misfortunes. "My wife has been most dissatisfied with me for the reason that I am not as good a provider or [*sic*] as she has observed other husbands to be." In the best of times, he later admitted, he never earned more than $1,600 a year.

But there was more to the Winschels' tension than financial distress. There was also Jacob's infidelity.* "My father was always attractive to women—a real lady killer," Walter would write with some pride. The adultery ripped the family apart no less than the poverty since Jennie, neither long-suffering nor forgiving, often responded to her husband's misbehavior by disappearing—usually with the children, occasionally without them. By some accounts, Walter and Algy were shuttled from one relative to another, even split up and boarded out to strangers

---

*Lyle Stuart in his 1953 exposé *The Secret Life of Walter Winchell* (New York: Boar's Head Books) asserted that Jacob was a child molester and that this was obviously a formative element for Walter—especially when Walter witnessed Jacob being beaten by a policeman for wooing a fourteen-year-old neighbor. If true, this would force one to reevaluate Walter's entire childhood. But there is no evidence, documentary or otherwise, that substantiates this charge, and Stuart himself told me, "I don't believe it's true. . . . It was as scurrilous as the stuff he [Winchell] does."

while Jacob gallivanted and Jennie sewed piecework to make ends meet.

In the fall of 1905, when Walter was eight and Algy only five, Jennie moved in with her sister Rose in Danville, a moderate-sized tobacco and cotton mill town of fifteen thousand in the Virginia Piedmont. As Walter recalled it unsentimentally in his autobiography, his mother took Algy while he remained behind with Grandma Fannie in New York. It was unlikely, however, that Jennie would have taken Algy and left Walter. Algy annoyed her. Unlike Walter, he was pinch-faced, with a high forehead, beetle brows and a wide mouth curled into an expression of perpetual dyspepsia that made him look like a gunsel in a gangster film. "Algy was pathetic," said his cousin Lola.

It was much more probable that Jennie took both boys, possibly intending to leave Jacob for good, and a gap in Walter's education of fifteen months—from October 1905 to January 1907—coincides with the time Jennie spent in Danville. Exactly what Walter and Algy did during this year is impossible to determine; there is no record of either attending school there. What Walter seemed to remember from this period were his Aunt Rose's "delicious chawklit and coconut cakes" and the nickel she gave him each day.

But Danville was only a respite from the domestic storm, not an escape. Dressing Walter like "a little bitty" so he could get on the train for half-fare, Jennie returned to New York that winter of 1906–07, this time to still another apartment—the sixth in nine years—in a six-story building at 55 West 116th Street, between Lenox and Fifth avenues in their old Harlem neighborhood, now on its way to becoming a Jewish ghetto. And she returned to Jacob.

It was shortly after their return that Jacob gave up his foundering silk company. For the next two years he clerked, but once again his financial prospects failed to improve. To help out, Walter took on a series of jobs: running errands at the local butcher shop, delivering the Harlem *Home News* and the New York *Evening Journal*, peddling subscriptions for the *Saturday Evening Post* in front of the subway kiosk at 116th Street and Lenox (hoping, futilely, to win a pony) and on rainy days holding an umbrella over detraining passengers for a nickel.

In a childhood of unrelieved poverty, hard work, dislocation and parental discord, the incident Walter seemed to remember most vividly, almost fondly, was an accident. As he told it in one version—and he loved telling it so much that he kept telling it throughout his life with embellishments and variations—he was chasing a ball during a game of punchball when he was struck by a trolley. "That is how I became a Broadway columnist," he would quip. "I was kicked in the head by a horse when I was young." In another telling, he was sledding down a hill at 110th Street and Manhattan Avenue when he swerved to avoid a drunk, spun into the street and was struck by the wagon, opening a three-inch gash on his leg. Terrified, he ran blocks looking for help, but nurses chased him off their stoops. Finally he staggered into a drugstore, where a kindly policeman calmed him and called an ambulance to take him to the hospital. He received three stitches—his family couldn't afford a painkiller—before his grandmother Fannie collected him. The *Evening Sun*, he said, even reported the incident, marking his first appearance in a newspaper.

What seemed to make the episode so memorable for Walter was not the terror or the pain or even the nurses' anger as he sought their help, but that he had gotten attention. In a life of poverty and neglect, in a life where his parents were increasingly preoccupied, that is what he most craved, what he most needed. The questions he now asked himself were how and where a poor boy might find attention in Harlem. And though he was shy and insecure, he found the answer directly across the street from his apartment building in the Imperial Theater.

Owned by two brothers named McKibbon, who prided themselves on discovering talent, the Imperial was, in its day, one of the leading show-places in Harlem. By 1909, its day had long passed, and its name had become ironic rather than descriptive. "[T]he carpets in its aisles were frayed from the scuffling of many shoes," remembered one of Walter's neighbors, "its orchestra consisted of one piano whose ancestor must have been a tin can, and everyone in the neighborhood knew by heart exactly what its four faded backdrops looked like." It had fallen so steeply that the McKibbons had even converted it from a vaudeville house into a movie theater.

None of this made any difference to Walter. Already he was practicing to perform—pounding iron strips into the soles of his shoes and tap-dancing on the bathroom floor until the neighbors ordered him to desist. At school, he would rehearse for classmates. "I can still remember the way I felt when the other kids watched me dancing," his longtime ghost-writer Herman Klurfeld quoted him. "It was a kind of exciting, breathless feeling."

The only way to get onstage at the Imperial was to be a "song plugger"—someone who sang new tunes before the movie started and led the audience in a community sing. (Pluggers were called that because their object was to sell sheet music for the songs they sang.) Late in 1909 Walter and a classmate named Jack Weiner convinced the McKibbons to give them a chance. For the McKibbons, the risk was low: just ten cents per song on Sunday and five dollars for the week according to one performer, nothing according to Walter. Ushering was a throw-in.

But before the pair got started, the son of the Imperial's new cashier also approached the McKibbons looking for a job. Another victim of poverty, tiny George Jessel had been furloughed to Harlem to live with his maternal grandparents, and he frequently serenaded the customers at his grandfather's tailor shop. Now that his mother was working at the theater, Jessel also hatched the idea of plugging songs there. As Jessel later recounted it, one of the McKibbons told him that he had hired two other boys just the day before but thought the three of them might be able to form a trio. The owner then summoned Walter and Jack Weiner and negotiated a merger. A photo at the time shows Jessel, almost exactly a year younger than Walter and a full head shorter, staring seriously and somewhat diffidently at the camera, while Walter, hand casually in his pocket and wearing a flowing tie, striped knickers and a key fob, strikes a much more confident pose. He was already preening.

Billing themselves as the "Little Men with the Big Voices," Weiner the tenor, Walter the alto, and Jessel the baritone took the stage name of Leonard, Lawrence and McKinley, the Imperial Trio.* Because of the Gerry Society, an organization that watchdogged children working in the theater, the trio couldn't perform on the stage; instead they sang in the small piano pit, where Phil Baker, later to become a famous comedian, accompanied them. Daytime audiences received the trio generously. However, the evening audiences, wrote Jessel, resented them as an intrusion on "a great deal of heavy necking (and other things), which was the main reason for going to a movie in those days, particularly in that neighborhood with its lack of motels and crowded tenement bedrooms." The trio often found themselves dodging "pickles and other assorted garnish from the local deli" until the McKibbons hired a neighborhood ruffian named Harry Horowitz to keep order. Five feet tall and "the ugliest guy I ever saw, with sneaky little orbs" and "more pimples and acne than any of us," in Walter's description of him, Horowitz would later gain notoriety as "Gyp the Blood," one of the assassins of the gambler Herman Rosenthal.

At the Imperial, Walter got attention, but not because his voice was particularly good—he was only a middling singer—or because he understood stagecraft. He was the star of the Imperial Trio because he was attractive. Mildred Luber, a neighbor, remembered watching him there with Jennie and Algernon. He was "dressed in blue serge knickers pulled far down below the knees," she recalled thirty years later, "his hair cut 'Buster Brown style,' and with a collar after that worn by the same comic-

---

*When he was famous, Walter usually told interviewers that the trio consisted of himself, Jessel and Eddie Cantor—an obvious attempt to revise his past and make the Imperial Trio seem far more impressive than it really was.

strip character." The effect was "very romantic. For Walter Winchell was a very handsome boy—blond, slim, with finely chiseled features."

Jessel called him the "heart throb of 116th Street," and Walter concurred. "No lady killer or any of that stuff," he wrote in his autobiography. "I just liked girls." In one story, which was repeated in nearly every profile of Winchell during his heyday, his partners took the stage while he was occupied in the balcony with a girl. As Jessel told it, he and Weiner were singing "I Dream in the Gloaming of You" when he realized that Walter wasn't going to appear. So Jessel stopped and informed the manager, who, in turn, dispatched Gyp the Blood to fetch him. "Winchell spent the rest of his life getting even with me," Jessel wrote earnestly after the friends had had a falling-out. For his part, Walter later denied it had ever happened: "I missed the performance because I was sore at my partners about something or other. Maybe I was too busy selling papers." Years later, however, he would recall a girl named Ruthie Rosenberg sitting in the balcony of the Imperial after school to hear him sing or tell a few jokes between songs.

It was a happy interval, but it was to be short-lived. Jessel's recollection was that the Imperial Trio were fired for reasons of economy. In one account, Walter learned that they were about to be terminated and made a preemptive assault by asking for a raise. When the manager dismissed them instead, Walter allegedly wheeled on Weiner and yelled, "This is your fault. I told you the jokes are lousy." Years later, Weiner said in his own defense that "Winchell talked too fast. He talked us right out of that job."

Fortunately, a song plugger named Leo Edwards had heard the boys and mentioned them to his brother Gus, a singer/songwriter who was then forming a new vaudeville revue featuring child performers. A few weeks after their firing, the Imperial Trio regrouped in Tin Pan Alley to audition and won a spot in the upcoming show. It was to be called *Gus Edwards' 1910 Song Revue*, and it was to be Walter Winschel's passport out of Harlem.

Not all the Winchels approved of Walter's leaving school for vaudeville; no doubt they feared he would end up like his father, aimless and broke. But Walter, having also witnessed his father's futility, was adamant that show business was the way he would avoid his father's fate. "Ever since I was a little boy," he recalled,

I had a great suspicion that the commonly known ways to fame and fortune were the bunk. I even charged my family with conspiracy, when at a meeting of sixteen uncles and fourteen aunts [obviously hyperbole], I was informed that the only way Mrs. Winchell's little boy could ever be famous was by practicing "early to bed and early to rise" and the golden rule. Look at the milkman, I childishly argued, where would he be today if he ever listened to such advice. . . . When my grandmother seized her knitting instead of offering an answer I knew that I had them tied in knots. From then onward I decided that I would be different. I would attain success by going to bed late and getting up later. . . .

The story seems improbable, since the Winchels were not a particularly close-knit family. But it was almost certainly an accurate reflection of how Walter felt at the time: angry, independent, rebellious, eager to get on with his life. School held no attraction for him; when he was famous, he liked to brag that he had been the "school dunce." Even if he had been studious, his year in Danville with his mother had effectively put him a year behind, and at P.S. 184 he had been left back in Grade 5B twice and Grade 6A once, meaning that his classmates were now more than two years younger than he was.

In the end, he may have been too emotionally insecure for school, too sensitive and needy underneath the tough-street-kid carapace he wore. A teacher once mildly reprimanded him and he raced home in tears. On another occasion he had secured a pass to the Alhambra Theater and brought it to school to show off to his envious classmates. Before long he had concocted the story that his father was *manager* of the Alhambra. When his classmates found out otherwise and began taunting him, he was so humiliated, or so the story goes, that he stayed away from school for three weeks.

To the extent he was remembered by the teachers at P.S. 184, it was, he said, "as a boy with perfect manners" who "always doffed my cap." To the extent Walter remembered the school, he remembered a Miss O'Donnell, his sixth-grade teacher, "a robust looking brunette" who kept him after school to kiss him full on the lips, though another time, musing about having had to repeat the grade, he wrote, "Maybe she really cared." By June he had been expelled, almost certainly for truancy. (In his last semester he was present only forty-six days and absent twenty-eight.) But by this time he was already appearing with Gus Edwards.

In 1910, it wasn't unusual for boys Walter's age to quit school and go to work, though in later years he would often make it sound as if it were. In 1914, the year Walter would have graduated from high school, less than 12 percent of seventeen-year-olds earned a diploma, and as late as 1925 the dropout rate from fifth to sixth grade was 10 percent, with another 10 percent dropping out between the sixth and seventh grades. What was far more unusual than his leaving school was his leaving home, leaving Harlem. Harlem, however, would never leave him. His friend Ernie Cuneo believed that Walter's childhood "had left him with four inches of scar tissue around his heart, and with a heart full of fear, instead of some love, the fear of being broke." That is why, Cuneo said, Walter became such a compulsive worker, repeating on many occasions his own axiom: If you want a helping hand, take a look at the end of your arm. "[W]hat was regarded as a cynical statement by him was in fact the story of a boy who *worked* his way up."

His childhood in Harlem had made him antagonistic, suspicious and resentful. Some people said it had made him incapable of caring about anyone or anything save himself, all of which he readily admitted. Speaking before a charitable group some fifty years later, Walter told them:

> I met the world and all comers at catchweights on the Harlem and other New York streets as a newsboy. . . . The only thing in my corner (when I was 12) was the corner lamp post. . . . Any tenderness I may have developed is entirely due to the cold iron and steel in that lamp post.
>
> A lot of people are going to psychiatrists these days to find out what they want [he concluded]. From my childhood (with the Gus Edwards' School Days Act when I was 13) I knew what I didn't want. . . . I didn't want to be cold. I didn't want to be hungry, homeless or anonymous.

III

They called Gus Edwards "the Dago." A wiry man with a narrow face, thick black hair, and dramatically dark eyes, Edwards had actually been born in Poland in 1868 of German and Polish parents and had grown up in Poland and Russia as the borders shifted. At thirteen he decided to join two brothers who had emigrated to America, but having no passport, he drove cows across the Russian border into Poland, then ran as fast as he could "without so much as a farewell look toward Russia." He came over from Rotterdam in steerage, passing the voyage by singing on deck while wealthier passengers tossed him coins.

In New York, he worked as a tobacco stripper at a cigar factory, but he was always singing for his fellow workers and eventually pestered his way onstage. Soon he was writing his own songs. While entertaining at an Army camp during the Spanish-American War, he met Will Cobb. With Edwards composing the melody and Cobb the lyrics, they wrote "I Can't Tell Why I Love You but I Do." It was the first of a string of hits that would make Edwards one of the country's most popular songwriters: "By the Light of the Silvery Moon," "In My Merry Oldsmobile," "If I Was a Millionaire," "Look Out for Jimmy Valentine" and, perhaps the most enduring of them all, "School Days."

In 1905 Edwards married Lillian Bleiman, a former actress, and with her assistance rapidly became his own cottage industry. While continuing to write songs for stage plays, he began producing vaudeville acts: the Blond Typewriters, the Messenger Boys (with a young Groucho Marx), and a children's vaudeville he called Kid Kabaret (which launched Eddie Cantor). He had no children of his own, but his shows obviously compensated. Most of his discoveries were poor kids, as he had been. "They were talented youngsters," his wife remembered, "that Gus had recruited from ferryboats, street corners, alleys and wherever youngsters happened to be singing or dancing." One joke at the time ran: "Here comes Gus Edwards. Hide your children."

Walter Winschel, Jack Weiner and George Jessel joined Edwards's *Song Revue* for rehearsals in April 1910 and opened six weeks later, on June 10 at the Hudson Theater in Union Hill, New Jersey. By vaudeville standards it was an extravaganza. The program lasted forty-two minutes with five scene changes, more than a dozen songs, and a cast of twenty-eight including Edwards himself. *Variety*, the entertainment trade paper, called it "without a doubt the largest offering from a scenic view point that variety holds."

The curtain rose to reveal seven newsboys, among them Walter, shooting craps in the Bright Light District and breaking into "Dear Old East Side" before seguing into "If I Was a Millionaire." In the next scene, on an Italian street set, Edwards and a young soprano named Lillian Boardman, accompanied by the children in peasant costumes, sang "Rosa Rigoletto." For "Look Out for Jimmy Valentine," in which Walter had a featured role, the cast dressed as burglars and crept down the aisles. Edwards then performed a medley of his hits, the blue stage curtain emblazoned with his crest parting to reveal tableaux that illustrated the songs. The finale, "On the Levee," was a white-face minstrel show. "I was one of the kids who helped decorate the stage with bales of cotton and all those beautiful girls," Walter recalled.

Though the show earned an enthusiastic reception in Union Hill, the performances there amounted to a tryout before hitting New York City, where the booking agents for the vaudeville circuits were headquartered. Getting a booking on one of the circuits was the only real security in vaudeville, but Edwards arrived in New York only to discover that the larger agencies had little interest in "kid" shows. After a spate of rejections he finally persuaded the Hammerstein Theater to book the act. Then he braced himself for the audience's reaction.

"What an ovation on opening night," Mrs. Edwards recalled years later. "A dozen curtain calls and Gus taking bow after bow with his talented babes screaming with glee because we were 'in.' " The reception was the same at nearly every performance: three encores and four curtain calls at one show, five encores at another and, by one report, "the applause did not subside until Gus, gasping for breath, made a neat speech." The reception proved equally enthusiastic on the road. In Chicago, the reaction was so tumultuous that Edwards had to take the stage again and promise to return the following year before the crowd would quiet. One reviewer accurately prophesied, "It will attract business in any town."

For Walter, the success of the *Song Revue* meant $15 a week and the promise of relief from the abuses he had suffered by being poor. But it was only a promise. After contributing $5 each week to his mother and after covering his own expenses, there was virtually no money left, not even for necessities. He would always remember playing in Springfield, Massachusetts, with Edwards when the air was brisk and chilly and he hadn't an overcoat. He was warming himself over a grate when a girl in a song-and-dance act motioned him in and offered him an old coat that her partner was going to toss away. Walter gratefully accepted the gift. But just as she was shortening the coat her partner returned, saw Walter and "flew into a terrible rage." He began screaming at the boy, calling him a "dirty little beggar."

There was another promise too: the promise of emotional security. In joining the troupe, he had escaped his own unstable family for a surrogate family that was designed, if only as a business proposition, to be harmonious and efficient. Mrs. Edwards always traveled with the company, clucking maternally over her wards, and she was especially fond, or so she said, of Walter. "You probably never knew it," she would later write him, "but you were my favorite long before you became the famous W.W.— your personality—even as a young man you were at the time you joined us[,] was outstanding—and you appealed to me very much."

And while Gus himself complained in mock exasperation about his charges—"Personally, I am in favor of an act of the Legislature authorizing an official spanker with every theatrical company employing children"—he also served as a father figure to them. One writer, watching him with his troupe before a performance, remarked that "the solicitude Edwards showed for every one of his boys and girls was only matched by the friendliness of the boys and girls for each other."

But for Walter Winschel the promise of camaraderie was broken by a single incident. A few weeks into the tour, at the Warburton Theater in Yonkers, New York, Walter was playing tag backstage with another of the boys, little Georgie Price, when Price accidentally broke a prop vase and then told the manager that Walter had done it. Walter was immediately dismissed. Despondent, his world suddenly shattered, he sat in the gutter outside the theater, his head buried in his arms, and wept. Irene Martin, one of the revue's featured performers, saw him and asked what was wrong. When Walter told her he had been fired, she ordered him to get ready for the show.

As Walter later learned, Irene was close to Mrs. Edwards. "When Irene told her that I was dismissed, she gave her husband the Old What For...," wrote Walter of Mrs. Edwards's response. But Walter, vengeful even then, could never forgive either Georgie Price or Gus Edwards for the injustice done him. More than thirty years later, when Edwards was ill and broke, his wife wrote Walter asking his help and still apologizing about the vase. It did not soften Walter. When a press agent representing Edwards asked Walter to place an item in the column on his old mentor, Walter allegedly said, "Go tell that SOB to go —— himself!"

The show, with Walter back in the fold, was booked for a solid year on the Orpheum vaudeville circuit, traveling from Chicago to California and back again. (To get reduced children's fares on the train, it was said that Edwards dressed all the boys in knickers, until a conductor spotted Jessel smoking a cigar.) But whether it was his disillusionment over the vase incident or his natural wariness, Walter had already disengaged himself from the other members of the company, including Jessel. Most of the fourteen-year-old's attentions during the tour were now focused on beautiful eighteen-year-old Irene Martin, the girl who had intervened to save his job. With Martin's smile, he said, "the whole world lighted up.... I carried one of her valises. I ran errands for her.... I worried so much that someone might molest or bother her that I became her self-appointed G-man." Wherever she stayed, he would take a room and sleep outside her door to ward off harm.

Though she reciprocated only with kindness, Walter cried when they parted at the end of the season.* She would be off to another show while he returned to Harlem that summer of 1911, to his family's new, and what would prove to be its last, apartment, at 125 West 116th Street, a narrow railroad flat on the fifth floor of one of eleven tenements on the block, next door to an undertaker who stacked his coffins on the Winschels' stoop. Walter rejoined Edwards that fall and spent the next

---

*When she married another vaudevillian several years later, Walter was jealous. Decades later in Los Angeles, he met an acquaintance of Irene's who suggested he call her. He tried repeatedly and left messages with the woman who answered her phone but never heard from Irene. Seeing the acquaintance again not long after, he recounted his efforts to contact his old "love." "She wants you to remember her as she was," he was told.

two seasons in new editions of the *Song Revue*. Though Edwards had made only minor alterations, mainly adding songs and moving "By the Light of the Silvery Moon" to the climax, the response didn't diminish. "There is not a member of Mr. Edwards' big company, from the star himself down to the clever children who are big factors in the success of the act, who does not make good as a singer and dancer," enthused one reviewer that year, proclaiming the show "the hit of the season" and predicting a record audience.

After three seasons, though, Walter was still essentially an extra. Georgie Price, who did imitations of stage and vaudeville stars, and diminutive Lila Lee, who sat atop the piano while Gus played, were the stars who stole the show while Walter languished anonymously in the chorus. Though he had no alternative plan, by the summer of 1913 he seemed ready to leave the show. He was sixteen, his career was stagnating, he was getting too old to play a newsboy, and as a supernumerary he had never received the attention he so badly desired.

As it turned out, the decision was made for him after the *Song Revue* closed at the Hammerstein Theater in New York and Edwards was forced to reduce the company for the road. Walter was offered a job in *School Days*, another Edwards act, but he latched on instead with singer Kitty Gordon, belting songs from a box while she changed costumes. Here was a chance for him to solo, to be the center of attention, only he went terribly off key at one performance and fled the stage in acute embarrassment just as he had once fled his classroom. He never returned to the act.

Temporarily out of show business, he took a job as an office boy with the Remington Typewriter Company, but his boss, "a young man who was marvelous material for a second Lieutenancy, made me unhappy," and Walter left "before I got caught stamp collecting." Another job with the American Felt Company ended just as quickly. Office jobs, he quickly realized, "bored the hell out of me." So back he went to the rehearsal hall where Edwards's *School Days* was being readied for the summer-fall season. He arrived just as one of the boys was balking at his role. A few days later, Walter got the part. He would play Ritchie Cross, the "tough guy."

Walter himself was anything but tough. He was so nervous his first week out in Schenectady, New York, that he provoked a fight at the local pool hall because, as he later told the road manager Roy Mack, he felt he had to seem tough all the time to hold on to his job in the show. Mack was small and jug-eared with arching eyebrows and a round little mouth that gave him a supercilious look; in the act he played O. Bostonbeane Harvard, a snooty milquetoast whom Walter bashed with a rolled-up newspaper. Though not much older than Walter, Mack now took him under his wing. Walter, who had never planned beyond the next season, even began thinking that he might become a road manager like Mack. Eventually, when Walter complained about being the lowest-paid member of the act, Mack appointed him assistant manager, with a $5 raise which he paid out of his own pocket, "as Edwards would not give anyone a raise." Together they would break the sets and pack the show for the train ride to the next town. Between performances, they wrote songs— Mack the music, Walter the lyrics. For the first time in his life Walter was focused. He had an ambition.

And, that summer of 1914, he also had love. Nellie and Dolly Cliff were two petite English orphans in the nine-member company, but Walter hadn't had much to do with either of them until he was paired with Nellie in a number called "Here Comes My Rover." For the song the boys would get down on all fours and paw the air while the girls put dog collars around their necks. At one performance—in Lowell, Massachusetts, on July 4, Walter would always remember—Nellie "chucked hers at me and struck me on the nose." Walter cursed, and Nellie stormed off the stage, demanding that he be fired.

As he often did when he felt desperate, Walter left the theater and began to weep. Then he went to Nellie's dressing room and stood outside the door, rehearsing an apology. He happened to overhear Nellie tell Dolly that she would die for Lux, a soap and washing powder, so Walter immediately raced out to get it. The next day a mollified Nellie sat next to him on the train. "You know, you're a nice boy," she told him. "You have nice features, too. And you'd make a nicer appearance if you did something about those pimples." Walter was so embarrassed by his recent outbreak of acne that he slathered his face with medications for years "because Nellie liked me a little."

Nellie was a lovely girl. She had wide dimples, an engagingly broad smile and long brownish blond ringlets that framed her square face. And, unlike Irene Martin, she was no cold, unattainable object. She had an effervescence about her; one acquaintance said she danced when she walked. Walter was so infatuated that he scarcely had time for anything else but Nellie, including his duties as assistant manager. He loved entertaining her. Between performances Roy Mack would play "Oh, For the Life of a Fireman!" on the piano, and Walter, singing and "doin' my funny imitation" would make Nellie and Dolly "holler with laughter." It was, Walter said, "a beautiful time in my young life."

The courtship took place on hot dusty trains, in dressing rooms and boardinghouses, at the Greek diners where the thespians invariably ate. There was no money for anything else. On nonworking days, which was any day the troupe was traveling or was laid over, no one got paid, and because each performer bore the cost of his or her own Pullman berth, all but the highest-salaried, like the Cliff sisters, were always strapped for funds. To his acute embarrassment, Walter looked like a vagabond. His pants had a hole in the seat, and he claimed he never went out without a raincoat to cover it, even on the sunniest of days.

As the *School Days* troupe moved West, after making the Delany Time vaudeville circuit through New York and spending a few weeks on the small Gus Sun circuit in Ohio, Walter decided to stage a strike. There was a week's layoff after the performances in Stockton, California, and Walter told Mack he was going to stay. "Either you were pretty broke or I had refused to advance you some money or general disgust" was how Mack later reasoned it. How serious the threat was, with Walter so deeply smitten by Nellie, is hard to say. But he told Mack that he had landed himself a job on the Stockton *Record* as a reporter, and when Mack, incredulous, checked it out, he found that Walter *had* indeed somehow managed to sell himself as a newspaper reporter.

Now Mack tried to call Walter's bluff by heading off to the train station without him. Walter didn't budge, and in the end, Mack—mainly, he said, because he would have been obligated by California law to pay Walter's fare back to New York—talked him out of quitting and gave him another small raise to load the baggage. That ended the revolt, but it was the first time Walter had indicated any interest in journalism.

The reason seventeen-year-old Walter had wanted the raise was that he had decided to marry Nellie and had even introduced her to his mother, who approved. What disrupted their plans was the outbreak of war in Europe. Nellie and Dolly had a brother back in England and felt they should return home to be with him during the hostilities. Between performances in Baltimore Walter mournfully accompanied Nellie on a shopping expedition for the young man who, Nellie said, was just about Walter's size. Using him as a model, she selected a complete wardrobe. Later that evening, at a farewell party for the Cliff sisters, Nellie presented Walter with a brown paper package. It was the wardrobe, and with it a large brown trunk embossed with Walter's initials. "Wear these," she told him, "they will keep you remembering me."

They bade farewell the next day at Grand Central Station, pledging their troth to each other as the train pulled out, fully expecting to be reunited once the war ended.

NEARLY TWO MORE YEARS passed before Walter returned to New York—two years on the road with *School Days* and away from Nellie. He was so pale and haggard after the tour that on the train from Philadelphia to New York he sat on the sunny side of the car with his face pressed against the window, desperately trying for a last-minute suntan to make himself more presentable to his parents.

For the summer hiatus in 1916 Edwards had given him a job at 1531 Broadway in Edwards's music publishing offices. At night, Walter and Harry Ruby, a pianist who later became famous as the writer of "Three Little Words" and "I Wanna Be Loved by You," plugged songs. Though he was still assuming that Nellie would return and they would be married, Walter's plans remained vague. When they had been touring the West, he, Mack and another member of the company, Dave Seed, had toyed with the idea of forming their own act, the Whoopee Trio, but by the fall he was back for his third season in *School Days*, his sixth season on the vaudeville circuit.

On the road again, he was miserable, pining for Nellie. "[W]hy[,] he even cried," recalled a friend, "and his one thought in life at that time was to get to England[,] for that was where his sweetheart was going and he would not be happy until he was reunited with his lady love." But Nellie hadn't written him in months, and he now began unburdening his soul to a pretty sixteen-year-old who had joined the act as a replacement and who seemed eager to console him.

By June 1917, with the show on summer hiatus, Walter was once again at loose ends. He and Mack had composed a patriotic song for *School Days*, drumming up support for the recent American intervention in the Great War, and they had found a small Pittsburgh music company to publish it. Walter spent most of that summer plugging the tune, called "Follow the Flag," and finally persuaded the orchestra leader at the Palace Theater in New York, the most important of the vaudeville houses, to play the song as an exit march. "The bugle's call to arms has sounded round the USA," it began.

> *Uncle Sam is calling for us all.*
> *He's in a plight.*
> *He has tonight*
> *To help humanity.*
> *Now is there one among you who will stall?*
>
> *Follow the flag you love and do your duty.*
> *Don't be afraid to go and fight the foe.*

Walter was so excited to hear it played that his *School Days* confidante thought "he would have a stroke." But it didn't take him long to realize that the song wasn't going to be a hit, and his enthusiasm for songwriting quickly waned. Instead he went to work for his father, who, with George

Winchel's backing, had formed another new company to import and sell silk. Walter lugged a trunk filled with bolts of silk and satin from theater to theater, hoping to convince the chorines to buy a few yards and make their own undergarments. "[A]s W.W. was a young and handsome fellow in those days," wrote his *School Days* friend, "he had little or no trouble selling his silk."

Still almost totally directionless, he wangled an invitation from Mack to help out at a summer resort in upstate New York where Mack had headed during the layoff. Mack had struck a deal with a vaudevillian named Billy Dale to run a casino in Kenosha Lake called Rosenzweig's Waterfalls—entertaining, waiting tables, tending bar. Walter was taken on as a handyman with room and board as salary, but he lasted only one night, claiming "[h]e couldn't stand the noise of the crickets and frogs."

Back in New York that fall of 1917 he continued to drift, finally through with *School Days* but without anything to replace it. Calling himself with some exaggeration a "light comedian," he began visiting booking agents, but this effort didn't pan out either, and it began to seem to him more and more likely that he might be heading down his father's road to oblivion. Only one option seemed to remain. His pretty *School Days* confidante had been entreating him to form an act with her. The girl's name was Rita Greene, and by this time she and Walter had fallen in love.

IV

Rita and Walter had first met back in late 1913 or early 1914, when *School Days* was appearing at Fox's Audubon Theater in New York and Rita stood outside the stage door asking how she might join the show. They met again three years later when she was pulled from another Gus Edwards revue to replace a departing performer in *School Days*, and Walter, as assistant manager, coached her through rehearsals.

Born in Manhattan on January 26, 1900, she was the eldest of three sisters. Her father, James Greene, was a sensitive, donnish Irish Catholic schoolteacher who was given to severe bouts of depression. When Rita was still a child, he suffered a nervous breakdown, and the girls and their mother were sent to live with his sister on Staten Island. He recovered, but could never return to teaching, and he became a placid, almost recessive presence in the Greene household while his wife, in her granddaughter's words, was "the ruler of the roost."

Without paternal supervision, Rita as a child was a hellion. She hated school and found every possible way to avoid it. Once, despite her parents' injunctions against it, she took a trip up the Hudson River on the Day Line without telling anyone and threw her mother into a panic. Her greatest love was dancing, and that is why she was outside the Audubon Theater that winter day, hoping to find a spot in the chorus of a vaude-ville show, though she was only thirteen at the time, stood well under five feet and weighed less than ninety pounds. "I'm small but mighty," she used to say.

Eventually she did hook on with Gus Edwards, joined *School Days* and consoled the moping Walter over Nellie Cliff. Theirs wasn't love at first sight, but "sympathy being kin to love," Rita would write, "before I knew it I fell in love with him, and he fell in love with me." Nellie Cliff was largely forgotten now.* Sailing back to New York from Florida that June with the company when the season ended, Walter natty in a straw floater, and Rita comely in a long flowing shift, they were clearly moony about each other and dreaded being apart, which is why Rita had pressed Wal-ter about forming an act.

When she first broached doing a "double act" together, "the idea of the thing," she remembered, "almost scared him to death." All he could say was, "What can I do [?]" He tried convincing her to rejoin *School Days*, but Rita flatly refused and joined another act instead, the *Moore & Megley Revue*, while Walter dithered. They were both so miserable apart that she soon quit and was back in New York, trying to sell him once again on the idea of an act and trying to boost his sagging confidence. He was young, she told him. He was handsome. He cut a good figure on-stage. And his voice, though he was no longer a tenor or alto, still wasn't half bad. Finally, with no other prospect before him, Walter surrendered.

Taking command, Rita borrowed money to buy an act for them—novices usually didn't develop their own acts—then found an agent to represent them. The agent's name was Sam Baerwitz, a Russian immi-grant who had worked his way up the ranks of the legendary William Morris agency before leaving to open his own firm. He provided them with an old drop, or background, and paid them a straight salary while he got his share from the theaters, "which helped us no end," Rita said, "for we were both young and all we really had was ambition."

They called themselves Winchell & Greene. Rita claimed to have added the second *l* to Walter's name because she thought the name looked unfinished otherwise, though Walter later circulated the story, of-

---

*Many years later Walter would find Nellie once again—working as a cleaning woman for an acquaintance of his. She was suffering from colon cancer and was indigent, and though she asked that Walter not be told, he was informed anyway. He arranged for her care and she thanked him profusely, but the two never saw each other.

ten repeated, that it had once been misspelled with two *l*'s on a marquee and he decided to keep it because it looked better. (The problem with this tale is that Walter always dated the error to 1919 in Chicago, whereas they were actually being billed as Winchell & Greene long before then.) In another story, Walter credited his Uncle George with having planted the idea years before when Walter visited George's office and noticed an extra *l* on his uncle's name on the glass door. George "explained that the signpainter had made a mistake, but that it wouldn't be fatal." Again, Walter liked the way the name looked and remembered it. Whichever story is true, he was now Walter Winchell—a name so alliterative, so aesthetically balanced, so crisp, that in later years many of his enemies would assume he had simply made it up.

Baerwitz booked Winchell & Greene at a theater in Astoria, Queens, where the Loew's vaudeville circuit broke in new acts. At first, Walter was so frightened he barely moved, but he practiced constantly between performances, gradually gaining enough polish and confidence that in a few weeks he was singing a solo number and making patter while Rita changed costumes. After several more weeks at "break-in" theaters, they got a booking at Loew's American at 42nd Street and Eighth Avenue in Manhattan. Over the next few months they appeared in theaters throughout greater New York and up and down the eastern seaboard until Loew's sent them on the road to Canada.

At the time there were, by one estimate, twenty thousand vaudevillians in the United States, but only eight to nine thousand of them were regularly employed. According to another, even gloomier estimate, there were ten thousand vaudeville performers, but only eight hundred of them had regular work. Salaries were generally paltry, as Walter himself had discovered: $20 a week for a single at one typical theater in Brooklyn, $40 for a double. Moreover, out of that salary you had to subtract not only train fares and expenses but the commissions for both the circuit on which you were booked and the agent who booked you—what the performers derisively called a "double dip." ("That's like paying the butcher a commission to shop at his store," said Walter.) But for those chosen few who did succeed in getting long-term bookings on one of the better circuits, the rewards could be considerable. At one booking office, acts averaged $93 per week on the small-time circuits, usually in America's backwaters, and $427 for those who made the big time—this in 1919, when the average manufacturing wage was $1,293 a year.

Rita and Walter played the "small time," a term coined by a *Variety* reporter to describe the downscale circuits where performers either persevered in the hope that they might be discovered and ascend to the big time or had already made the big time and were now in their descent.

Whichever they were, small-timers were constantly being reminded that they were second-raters, and Walter later recalled "a dirty crack posted by stagehands in the wings of the house at Butte, Montana. It flippantly reminds the 'smallies' that the reason big-timers never have use for bathrobes 'is because they don't have to wait around between performances.' "

To add to their ignominy as small-timers, Rita and Walter were also what was called a deuce act. Deuce acts occupied the second spot on a vaudeville bill, one of the least desirable since the audience was often still arriving while the deuce performed. Most deuces on the small time, Walter said, "suffered the same agony and humiliation." The job of the deuce act was to "settle" the audience and prepare it for the show to follow, though Walter cracked with some truth that being second in vaudeville "meant that your act wasn't good enough for tardy customers."

Just how good or bad Walter and Rita were in those early months is a matter of some dispute. Watching them rehearse in her parents' apartment, Aunt Beatrice's daughter Lola thought they were "terrible." And as bad as they were in the living room, she said, they were even worse onstage. Another who remembered them from that period was only slightly more charitable: "He was a fair actor, with bright chatter, but not 'big time' caliber."

But Walter had been steadily improving and had conquered his early jitters, and other reviewers, if not exactly effusive, nevertheless found Winchell & Greene quite satisfactory. "Both have good voices, and are conscientious workers," wrote one. "Miss Green [sic] is a nimble and graceful dancer, while Winchell is not far behind her in this respect." Another said they "made a decided hit with their comedy chatter and songs, putting much 'pep' in their clever act." And a third called them "as attractive a couple as is to be found in a 'double.' They are refined, talented and strive successfully to please."

The act, called *Spooneyville*, was rudimentary by the standards of big time. It opened with Rita perched on a brick wall, where Walter approached her. After some comic patter, they launched a duet, then wandered to a bench for a "spooney bit" and delivered another song. While Rita changed costumes offstage, Walter made some wisecracks and sang a war song before giving way for Rita's "eccentric" solo dance. They closed with another duet and danced off into the wings. The whole performance lasted twelve minutes.

Good or not, Winchell & Greene worked steadily through the spring of 1918, partly by default. The war had decimated the ranks of vaudevillians, for even though entertainers were classified as being "engaged in a useful occupation" and thus exempt from service, hundreds had enlisted. Walter never even mentioned the war, but playing benefits that spring in Canada for wounded troops, some of them terribly maimed, he suddenly decided to enlist and convinced some Canadian officials to help him. (Always a performer, he told Rita he wanted to join the Canadian Air Force because he liked their uniforms better than the drab ones back home.) It was only by claiming that airplanes terrified her that Rita was able to persuade him to postpone his enlistment until they returned to New York.

Once back in the city, Walter enrolled on July 22 as an apprentice seaman in the Naval Reserve Force. It wasn't a particularly dangerous assignment—his only wound was self-inflicted when he accidentally burned his nose with sealing wax while trying to overhear a conversation his superiors were having about women—and there was virtually no chance of his being sent overseas. While Rita danced in local nightclubs, Walter, a two-finger typist, worked from nine to five in the New York Customhouse in lower Manhattan as a clerk and errand boy for Admirals Johnson and Burrage. In the evening Walter would go to Rita's apartment on 22nd Street for dinner, then head up to his parents' Harlem apartment to sleep. Occasionally Aunt Beatrice invited them for one of her soirees, and occasionally Rita's mother sprang for tickets to the Palace, but these were about the only interludes in a period of dull routine.

As far as his duties went, Walter was perfectly competent, and by August he was promoted from landsman to yeoman. Five weeks later he was called up for active duty, and a month after that he was assigned to sea duty on the USS *Isis,* a small vessel the Navy had commandeered from the Coast and Geodetic Survey to patrol the harbor. Though he never discussed how he felt about his naval service, he did like wearing the blue uniform, and Rita even speculated that is why he joined the Navy rather than the Army. Like a costume, it seemed to give him a new assurance. "Winchell was probably one of the few men in the Navy who could strut sitting down," remembered a fellow seaman. "He always acted as if he was about to make a stage entrance or exit."

As it turned out, he was to wear the uniform for less than five months. On November 11, 1918, the armistice was declared, and on December 5, he was released from active duty with, he was to brag, perfect marks for proficiency, sobriety and obedience. There was never any question that he would return to vaudeville after his muster from service. "It never dawned upon him that any other fields of endeavor might be entered into," Rita later wrote, "for where in any business could you sleep until noon and more or less live your own life as you saw fit, all of which appealed strongly to W.W."

But the winter season of 1918–19 was a particularly difficult one on the vaudeville boards. An epidemic of Spanish influenza had begun ripping through the East in October, closing theaters and sending performers scurrying back to New York in retreat. One trade paper reported that the flu had forced the layoff of five hundred acts, and by November, as it swept across the country, leaving millions dead, it had even crowded war news off the front pages. In Chicago the health commissioner ordered that tickets not be sold to anyone "suffering from coughs or colds," and in the city's suburbs, the militia patrolled the streets, breaking up gatherings of any kind. By late November the shuttered vaudeville houses were slowly beginning to reopen, but then a second wave of the flu, just as serious as the first, slammed the nation, darkening the theaters once again. In many cities only the drugstores remained open.

For Walter and Rita professionally, the one positive note was how slowly the armed services were moving to discharge their fellow vaudevillians. Once the epidemic had passed, this opened a small breach for Winchell & Greene. They resumed at a dilapidated theater, misnamed the Grand Opera House, at 23rd Street and Eighth Avenue in Manhattan. Rusty from the layoff and embarrassed by the venue, they decided to ease themselves back in—wearing old clothes rather than their good costumes and cutting out Rita's big dance solo. After their first performance even they realized they were awful. Rita blamed the orchestra and the theater. Walter, suddenly snappish, blamed Rita for cutting her dance and not flirting with the audience the way she used to. As these recriminations were flying, the assistant manager knocked on their door. Walter, just quipping, cracked, "Yeah, we're packing." But the assistant manager said, "Okay, Winchell, here's your pictures."

Walter was stunned. Not since the Imperial had he been canceled, much less canceled from a place like the Grand Opera House. For the next few weeks, jobless and overcome with his old feelings of inadequacy, he loitered in front of the Palace, "hoping to meet a friend rich enough to invite me to join him across the street for a cup of coffee and a sandwich. It was all so damn frustrating and humiliating."

Most humiliating was trying to catch on again. Booking agents, he complained, "considered you only after you could tell them: 'Come up to Proctor's on 125th Street the last half of the week after next. I have a showing there.' " But "[a]s a rule they stalled you until you 'went out and got a rep' and then they were willing to 'handle' you. Many a time I used to pull that alibi that most 'hams' use today when you catch them at their worst. 'Oh, don't tell me that you caught me at that performance!' I used to howl. 'You should have been in last night when we knocked them for a goal!' " But no matter how casual he may have seemed later, he never forgot the sting of their neglect.

By January, he and Rita were back on the boards in New York, Connecticut and Massachusetts, playing the Poli circuit—a small-time route even by the standards of small time. As the season wore on, they gradually edged west, reaching Chicago late that February. They arrived in the midst of a wintry blast that was threatening to paralyze the city. A friend of Walter's named Jo Swerling (later a prominent Hollywood screen-writer) was a reporter on the Chicago *Herald-Examiner* and had been as-signed to cover the blizzard. Between performances, Walter begged him for a chance to help, and Swerling finally assigned him to go to the Illi-nois Central Station and report back. "I told him of the great crowds, women, children, this and that," Walter would remember happily. "And on the first page of the paper next morning I thrilled seeing less than the paragraph I phoned him—included in the general story." It was Walter's first newspaper article.*

In later years, whenever Walter told the story of his first journalism as-signment, he usually said that he was tired of vaudeville at the time and was considering becoming a newspaperman anyway. But aside from his brief sit-down strike in Stockton years before, there is no evidence that Walter had ever thought about becoming a reporter, and in any case he had absolutely no training in journalism, save visiting newspaper offices to finagle publicity for the act. But this time he left Chicago with a press card authorizing him as a traveling correspondent—a gift from another staffman on the *Herald-Examiner*. And he left with something else: His newspaper aspirations had been "aroused."

THAT SUMMER, WORK WAS scarce. The best Winchell & Greene could do was a few weeks on Loew's New York circuit and a few more at some of the smaller theaters owned by vaudeville impresario B. F. Keith. Weary and dispirited after two seasons of "chairwarming in offices and rebuffs and rebukes," Walter grumbled that the New York booking agents were never going to give them a fair shake, and he devised a plan that he said would determine their future once and for all. As Walter laid it out to Rita, first they would sharpen the act, then, saying good riddance to New York, they would somehow make their way to Chicago and try to impress the western booking agents there in hopes of getting themselves a long engagement on one of the western circuits where the competition wasn't as fierce as back east.

Fortuitously, Walter had no sooner hatched his scheme than Sam

---

*It is possible that Walter's memory failed him when he called it a massive snowstorm. On March 1, 1919, the Chicago *Herald-Examiner* headlined 45-MILE GALE SWEEPS CITY, com-plete with an account, in the eleventh paragraph, of how the storm was affecting railroad traf-fic. This may have been Walter's item, but the snow was probably his embellishment, since the paper reported "there will be little snow, but a high wind & sharp drop in temperature."

Baerwitz, their agent, phoned with a distress call: One of his acts had canceled and Winchell & Greene were to take their place—a "disappointment," as it was known in vaudeville parlance. The new booking, on Loew's southern circuit, originated in New Orleans and snaked through Kentucky to St. Louis. But the best part was that it ended at the McVickers Theatre in Chicago, precisely where Walter wanted to be.

The trip north from New Orleans was tense. Walter had gotten hold of a week-old issue of *Variety* in which the Chicago critic Jack Lait had blasted another "double act" for doing the same song Walter had added to *his* act, a flag-waving anthem called "Friends." Remembering that the Irish patriot Eamon De Valera had recently visited Chicago, Walter quickly revised the lyric on the train: "And so I say—from Broadway to Long Island . . . From lowland up to highland—*if we free Ireland*—we'll be *the best friends* the Irish ever had!" Meanwhile, with President Wilson sailing to Europe to iron out the postwar peace treaty, Walter borrowed some topical gags from a team called Craft and Haley, which was booked solidly back east and freely lent the material.

RITA: I was just thinking that the man I marry must be capable of being President of the United States!
WALTER: Oh, ["I intoned with a Pained Expression"] then I won't do!
RITA: Why not?
WALTER: Because ["I groaned, winking at the audience"] I get seasick—so easily!

Another gag, designed to appeal to World War I veterans, was the one that "Really Did It," according to Walter.

RITA: What is your idea of a good time?
WALTER: ["To which I deadpanned"] Watching a boatload of second lieutenants sinking!

There was a ten-day layover between their engagement in St. Louis and their show in Chicago. To tide them over, Walter booked them in a few small theaters in the Southwest where they were the only act on the bill and where at least one of the theaters still used oil lamps for footlights. Walter sold the tickets himself and flirted with the girls who looked "longingly" at him. Along the way Rita came down with the grippe and was running a high fever, but the anticipation of Chicago was so great that she went on anyway. "I felt instinctively," she later wrote, "that after we played the McVickers Theatre in Chicago, all would be well." At their next-to-final stop, a three-day engagement in Indianapolis, she spent the entire time washing their costumes in the hotel sink and pressing them in preparation.

Waiting in Indianapolis the night before their Chicago opening, Walter and Rita shared their trepidations. Walter knew that if the act failed now he was finished in show business, and he realized that he had made no provision for doing anything else. They calculated that they had managed to save just enough money to get them back to New York—"where we intended to leave the aches of the profession to braver hearts," Rita said. Arriving in Chicago the next morning, August 4, 1919, in the middle of a blistering heat wave, they were so nervous they couldn't eat. "[O]ur knees were shaking," wrote Rita. "[E]ven my hands were shaking, and we both tried to appear nonchalant, for neither of us wanted to let the other know how nervous we really were. . . ."

Just as they were about to go onstage—at eleven forty-eight that morning, Walter remembered fifty years later—a new crisis arose. The fire inspector advised them that their "drop" hadn't been properly fireproofed and that it would cost them an additional ten or twelve dollars to make it acceptable. (Walter had had it done in St. Louis to save money.) On the verge of his biggest moment in vaudeville Walter exploded, yelling that the fireproofing was a racket. He was in the middle of his tirade when their music started, and he and Rita raced onstage.

What happened next was remarkable. Rather than fluster them, the argument had so preoccupied them that they sailed flawlessly through the act. By the time they hit their second dance break, the "applause was deafening," and when Walter closed with his joke about the second lieutenants, the "roof went off the theater, as show folks used to exaggerate. We got six bows." Returning to their dressing room, flushed with victory for the first time in their careers, Walter asked Rita to marry him. "[I]t will be the perfect finale to the struggle that just ended," he told her.

Rita demurred. It wasn't the first time that Walter had broached marriage, but Rita had always insisted that they have at least a year's work lined up before she would consider it. Even now, despite their apparent triumph, she knew the only reaction that really counted was the booking agents'. Walter looked outside to the alley to receive their verdict. It was choked with agents begging to sign them. He took full advantage of the moment, savoring how the tables had turned from just a few weeks ago. He wore his " 'tallest millinery' when I went out to see them for I had never tasted of success before and that moment of being high hat gave me my biggest thrill. Here I was really snubbing booking agents!"

They were, Rita agreed, "bewildered with offers." They chose to go with Bheeler & Jacobs, a distinguished Chicago-based agency, and signed a two-year contract. By Friday, they had landed forty-eight weeks of work on the Keith western circuit and then were promptly offered another forty-eight on the Pantages circuit. This meant that they had nearly two years of solid work and, since the second offer had come directly from the Pantages's Chicago manager, that they didn't have to pay a commission to an agent for that tour. They had been bringing in $125 a week, with Baerwitz giving them $80 to split. Now they would be making $250 a week. They were ecstatic.

The only question that remained was marriage. Walter proposed every day that week in Chicago—"twice a day in fact." Now, her condition met, Rita agreed but added one new stipulation. She made Walter promise that they would eventually leave show business before show business left them. Walter was so giddy he readily accepted. "If I would only marry him[,] he felt sure he could conquer the world."

They were married at the City Court in the County Building in Chicago on August 11, 1919, a week to the day after their triumph. After paying their hotel bills, having a celebratory dinner and putting away enough for their fare to Rockford, Illinois, their next stop, they had no money left for a ring. Rita had been keeping an emergency fund of $40 in case they "brodied"—vaudeville slang for "flopped." Now she dipped into it for her wedding band. The couple's only wedding gift was $100 worth of Liberty bonds Aunt Beatrice sent them.

Though they had no money, they affected style. Walter, now twenty-two, wore a wide-brimmed hat, a tight suit with the cuffs riding up well above his ankles and a broad cravat with a stickpin. Completing his outfit was, usually, a vest with a watch chain and fob. His overcoat, with a dark velvet collar, seemed to smother him. His hair was now parted down the middle and slicked straight back. She, only nineteen, was a small beauty, even in her frayed dresses and oversized bonnets. She had high cheekbones and large green eyes with a cascade of brown tresses. "The boy is slim, good-looking and possessor of a good voice," said a reviewer of their Chicago appearance. "His partner is a cute little girl with the heels of a frisky filly."

They spent that fall and winter in the Midwest—in places like Collinsville, Illinois, and Bay City, Michigan—small-time still but with marquee billing now. By spring they had joined Road Show No. 151 on the Pantages circuit—owned by the Greek-born theater magnate Alexander Pantages—which routed them through Minneapolis, then north across Canada, dipped south again to Montana and west to Washington State, nipped up to British Columbia, then dived south once again through Oregon and into California until they zagged east to Utah, Colorado and Missouri.

These were exciting times for the newlyweds, full of adventure. Walter later remembered the time in Denver when "I had my head almost knocked off by three gorillas for talking out of turn." Or the time in Salt Lake City when Bob Knapp of Knapp and Cornalla tried to steal Rita from him. Or in Butte, Montana, when the girls in the troupe went horseback riding and returned so sore they couldn't dance that evening. Or the prostitutes in Missoula who flirted from the box; the ferry ride between Oakland and San Francisco when he would watch the sun setting over the bridge; the fragrance of oranges in the train because the troupers "thrived on them"; the engagement in Colorado Springs where "we went so good we were shifted from second to 'next to closing' for the first time in our lives."

But the most notable event of the tour was a gift from Rita. And that summer it changed their lives.

V

She had given it to him after they had struck west from Minneapolis toward Winnipeg. Still nursing the journalism bug he had caught in Chicago, he had begun submitting short columns, a mix of one-liners, news and admonitions, to *Billboard*, a weekly vaudeville trade paper. In February it published one of his columns under the title "Stage Whispers" by "The Busybody." In March it published three more columns with the same title and by-line. In April, it published two more, and at the bottom of the second, for the first time, were the initials W.W.

By now the columns were being written on a Corona portable typewriter—the gift from Rita. They were clearly modeled on similar chatty backstage columns in *Variety*, the New York *Clipper* and other trade publications, and they weren't terribly imaginative; but they did have a voice and signature all their own. "Most actors are married, then live scrappily ever after" ran a typical contribution. "Seen outside of Cleveland movie theater: 'Geraldine Farrar supported for the first time by her husband,'" went another. Other items were topical. He was especially amused by the recent imposition of Prohibition. "Populace very gloomy," he reported. "No wonder with everybody out of spirits—News item. Whaddaya mean, everybody?" Still other items griped about the treatment of vaudeville performers. And others were personal: a note to Nellie and Dolly Cliff to contact the column ("they will learn something to their advantage"); a joke that the Palace was doing away with the deuce spot altogether; a lament, "When will I play the 'better houses'?"

In May he stopped submitting to *Billboard*, having moved on to a new literary project. Enthralled by his typewriter, he had now begun chronicling the various escapades of his own troupe and posting the typewritten sheets backstage under the title "Daily Newssense." Though he was only playing at being a reporter, Walter exerted himself in this little hobby to find out what was going on, and his fellow performers, seeing their names in print, began to take note. Soon he was waking up early and hieing himself to the basement of the theater where he hunched over his Corona and rapped out "Newssense." Some days he even wrote a second edition.

Rita was always his first audience—he would read every word to her—and seeing how much he enjoyed the attention, she encouraged him. She understood that it was Walter's way of winning the starring role in his company that he could never win onstage, his way of gaining attention. And for a novice, Rita had to admit, he was good at it. He had a fine ear and a facility for language, and from his years in vaudeville he had learned a breezy patois and a brisk rhythm that allowed him to whittle a wisecrack to its essentials. And he *was* a busybody. "He used to be pretty good in digging up the dirt on people," recalled one vaudevillian. "Anything that was supposed to be secret, everybody would find on the theater bulletin board, where Walter had scrawled it."

Occasionally a subject took offense. When he wrote that "Bill J. and Ernestine O'B. are making whoopie," Bill J. allegedly decked him. But Walter so enjoyed the little fuss now being made over his sheet that nothing could deter him. By the time the troupe reached the West, Rita was making her sightseeing excursions alone while Walter was engrossed in "Newssense." When they left for the next engagement, he always left a copy for the company that followed. Just to give them a laugh. Just to let them know that Walter Winchell had been there.

But if Walter's quest for attention was being satisfied, his other insecurity remained: money. The train fare for the Pantages circuit from Chicago cost $155.27, $201 with the side jumps the troupe was required to make. Rita sent home $10 each week to her parents, and Walter, reluctantly and only at Rita's insistence, sent $10 to his. With the remainder, after expenses, he rushed to the post office whenever they reached a new town and bought a money order made payable to him. The plan was to return to Chicago and open an account there when they had saved $500—their nest egg for the time when they would leave vaudeville.

Walter monitored their finances with despotic vigilance. "In those days that bank book was Winchell's bible," remembered Rita, "it was a regular mania with him, and I was forever hearing the 'don't do' as far as spending money was concerned." To save money, she always laundered their clothing in the hotel basin with a ten-cent washboard, and when her nightgowns wore out, Walter gave her his pajamas to wear, even though they hung ridiculously on her tiny frame. He never bought her gifts for her birthday or Christmas. Instead he would hand her a check in front of the company, then privately convince her to tear it up because they needed the money for their future. By the time they left for their Western swing that spring, their clothes were so threadbare that Rita said they looked like "orphans in a storm." Only then did Walter finally relent, buying two suits for himself and letting Rita get an outfit for herself, though he also pressed her to have her mother, an excellent seamstress, make her two new dresses.

Rita claimed she was forbearing through all this sacrifice; she loved Walter deeply, and she believed he was only saving for them. But just before their Western trip they had an awful row in Detroit when Rita insisted on sending for her mother—her father had gotten a job with the railroad so the fare was nominal—and Walter had to dig into their savings for her room and board. Seething, he fixed on an old starched collar of his that he said Rita had let go yellow. "I got the first taste of W.W.'s temper," wrote Rita. From that point on, Rita had Walter send out his clothes for laundering while she continued to wash her own. But of course, even Rita understood that none of this was about collars or laundry. It was about Walter's almost pathological obsession with money and his dread of poverty.

THOUGH RITA had no way of knowing it at the time, her deliverance from show business would come from an eight-page vaudeville trade paper called *The Vaudeville News*, the first issue of which was rolling off an old printing press at the Palace Building in New York that April just as Winchell & Greene were heading into Canada. The paper, brainchild of impresario Edward Franklin Albee, was the product of a long, costly and heated battle for the very soul of vaudeville, a battle that had begun nearly twenty years before when Albee and his chief rival among booking agents, F. F. Proctor, joined forces to monopolize all vaudeville bookings between them under the banner of a new organization called the United Booking Office. Incensed by the usurious commissions proposed by the UBO, performers had quickly joined the battle by forming an association of their own called the White Rats, after a charitable English organization.

Over the next decade, warfare between the UBO and the Rats became a seemingly permanent feature of the vaudeville world. In 1920, seeking to deliver a deathblow to the Rats, Albee formed a cooperative association of vaudeville managers and performers called the National Vaudeville Artists and required performers to join on penalty of unemployment.

At the same time he rented a building across from the Rats' headquarters on 46th Street from which he monitored their activities. With Rats members unable to work, their association finally collapsed. (As a last measure of revenge, Albee took control of their old headquarters and refurbished it as the new seat of the NVA.) NVA membership swelled to more than twelve thousand, all of whom were required to pay the $10 dues, perform at NVA benefits and buy ads in the NVA programs.

The Vaudeville News was the NVA's house organ, distributed by theater managers free of charge. In a front-page editorial in its first issue, Albee proclaimed the paper's purpose: "to help cement the relationship of artist and manager and make for a better, happier condition in vaudeville by clean, constructive, cooperative methods," and its masthead, somewhat disingenuously, featured a handshake meant to represent comity between management and artist. Thanking contributors in advance, Albee wrote, "With their continued assistance we will soon have a newsy, entertaining little publication."

Walter later claimed that a Tacoma theater manager had mailed a copy of the "Daily Newssense" to *The Vaudeville News* that June, but it was actually Walter himself who sent it on, as he had sent his contributions to *Billboard*; only now Walter wrote in his cover letter that he was thinking of leaving vaudeville to try his hand at journalism. Came the response the next week from the *News'* editor, Glenn Condon:

> We knew of course that you were an actor, and must say that you show an unusual aptitude for the newspaper profession. I really cannot quite agree with your judgment in wanting to leave the vaudeville profession for the writing game. Newspaper men as a class are the poorest paid professional people in the world, and very few writers ever receive an income equal to the average salary of a performer. However, once you get the "bug" it is hard to get away from it, as is evidenced in your own case.

Telling Walter he would be "using most of the items in this under your name in our current issue," Condon concluded, "Hoping to hear from you frequently, and trusting that you will find time to contribute some items from the coast in addition to those appearing in your little paper." "That was the start," Condon later said, "of six months of calls and visits to my office by Walter."

As reproduced in the June 11 issue of *The Vaudeville News*, Walter's "Newssense" filled nearly three columns. "Devoted to interests of goodfellowship, companionship and the like" ran its banner. "Fearless editorials written to bring closer those estranged." Though it still didn't venture much beyond other, similar trade gossip, Condon called it "one of the cleverest things of the kind that has ever come to our notice." Some of it was shameless pandering to the NVA, which Walter had obviously included to improve his chances of getting his paper published. The rest was essentially the same mix as his "Stage Whispers" columns for *Billboard*. One long section picked up on a current craze: You tell 'em ——, I'm —— (e.g., "You tell 'em ouija, I'm bored"). Other items reported news: "Bothwell Browne appearing at the Moore-Orpheum here is ill abed with inflammatory rheumatism." A new department, "Merciless Truths," provided aphorisms: "A fool says, 'I can't.' The wise say, 'I'll try.' " "The lucky gambler is the one who doesn't gamble." "Father and Mother are kind, but God is kinder."

Walter answered Condon's letter by dashing off new columns for the *News*, which the editor, who had a staff of one, happily accepted and published under the title "Pantages Paragraphs." By the July 16 issue Walter had added a second column to the first, an expansion of his "Merciless Truths." Everywhere he went now, he carried a *Vaudeville News* shoved into his pocket or tucked under his arm. Some disgruntled performers felt he had become too closely identified with the *News* and the NVA, that he was really an "Albee spy," and Walter had even been warned that stagehands sympathetic to the Rats might drop a sandbag on him during the act. (He made sure to check with the theater manager about his safety.) He was, in fact, providing so much copy that by August 13 his photo was appearing beneath his by-line, and he was beginning to feel that his columns were the most important departments in the paper, even though he wasn't earning a cent for his contributions.

"One wonders how and why actors and actresses become actors and actresses," he wrote in his July 9 column, clearly pondering his own future now that he was being regularly published. "[S]urely the saying 'he was born for the stage' doesn't really mean what it implies." Canvassing his own company, Walter found that "Rita Greene aspired to make hats and the like, but she, too, 'couldn't control her limbs,' and now she kicks them high while appearing with Walter Winchell. I edit a paper for the members of the show, entitled 'The Newssense.' Once someone told me that I would make a good editor, and I believed him."

Though Rita had already determined that they would set Walter up in a vaudeville agency of his own once the tour ended, and though he was hedging his own bets by commissioning a playwright named Lawrence Grattan to write a new act for them, there seemed little doubt that had Walter had the option, he would have left vaudeville that summer and become a journalist, so gratifying was the attention he was getting. "I wanted to be a newspaperman and kept 'wishing so,' " he recalled. But now another opportunity suddenly presented itself, and with it a whole new dilemma. While Walter was in Los Angeles late that July, the *News* gave him an assignment to interview Alexander Pantages, the head of Walter's circuit. "I have met many magnates in show business," he exaggerated in his cover story, "but none more democratic than Alexander Pantages, into whose private office I was ushered as soon as I presented my card."

Walter had naturally taken along copies of "Newssense," and Pantages, an illiterate ex-grocer, was impressed. On the spot he offered Walter a job in his press bureau at $60 a week—substantially less than he and Rita were making on the stage, but it was the first real alternative to vaudeville Walter had ever had. "[Y]ou might be something ten years from now if you join me," Walter would recall Pantages saying. "You probably will still be a song-and-dance man ten years later if you stick to trouping."

Pantages couldn't have realized how sensitive a nerve his comment struck. No doubt with his father in mind, Walter had increasingly come to fear what would happen to him if he remained on the. boards. "I felt somehow I wasn't good enough and that when I couldn't knock them out of their seats with my dance routines any longer . . . it would be too late to start all over again in some other profession." He doubted that he and Rita would ever advance beyond the small time, however regular the work, and he shuddered that "unless you 'connect' in a big way, old age will find you a burden on someone or in some institution."

Still, Rita urged him to reject the offer and pursue their original plan in New York. Walter countered that he might not get an offer like this again, that the money wasn't to be taken lightly, that he would still be associated with the theater, and reiterated that he wasn't sure they would ever make the grade. In the end, Rita prevailed. Playing on the Winchel in him, she got him to concede that if he didn't at least try to succeed in New York, he would always wonder whether he would have made it there. So he declined the offer and continued with the tour.

By now the attention he was getting for his dispatches in the *News* appeared, on the surface at least, to have worked a change in him. He seemed to project a new self-assurance. One vaudevillian described him as "cocky"—a kid who was "going places." Yet beneath the cockiness he continued to suffer doubt. "What people thought bothered him a great deal," Rita admitted, "what they said worried him, for in his heart of hearts he always took himself very seriously, and needed constant reassurance that he was good, that he had ability, that he mustn't let things get him and that things would come out for him, and that someday he would be a success, you had to repeat this over and over until it finally made an impression upon him."

"The unpardonable sin," he closed one of his "Pantages Paragraphs," was "being found out."

THAT SUMMER, Rita cracked. In August she and Walter had traveled through southern California, visiting warships and military aircraft at the bases in San Diego and making a jaunt to Tijuana, before moving east to Utah. By September they were mired in Texas, doing four shows a day in a series of stale cracker box theaters in the baking southwestern summer. It was then that Rita began spiraling. After a year of being continuously on the road, she was homesick and tired of the routine. She wanted out. "Her state of mind was low," Walter wrote. "She was depressed day and night. . . . I kept telling her, 'We have only one more month, honey,' but that didn't help at all. Her feeling for the act was gone." "I can't go on, Walter," she begged him, "please take me home."

Bowing to her wishes, Walter wired Pantages for a release on the ground that his wife was too ill to continue. Pantages granted it, provided they remain until St. Louis and that once Rita recovered, she and Walter would obligate themselves to play the four weeks they owed him. Happy to comply if it meant a respite, Walter and Rita finished their Texas swing and continued on to New Orleans, with Walter making his weekly submissions to the *News* and Rita counting the days when she would be back with her family in New York.

What they would do once they got there was still undecided. Even as the time neared, Walter was planning for the act and behaving as if they would resume after a short hiatus. In Dallas he had met up with a light comedian named Howard Langford who played a double with his wife, Ina Fredericks, and Walter had asked Langford to write him a new act. Pantages had already scheduled their return for November 21 in Chicago, but Walter wrote Langford that he hoped "to postpone the date so as to rehearse the new act. Then while in Chi I will show the act for half a week (the new one) and see what the bookers say." He closed by telling Langford to take his time in rewriting their show and "that we are tickled sick with our new chance to 'get over.'"

At the same time Walter was also pressing his case with Glenn Condon, *The Vaudeville News* editor, to give him a job. Condon kept deflecting him. He obviously wanted Walter's copy; after all, it was free. A job was something else. Walter felt that if he kept submitting, Condon would eventually succumb. "I expect to conduct a news column only," he wrote Langford, "but I feel the column of truths ["Merciless Truths"] is already identified with the sheet and he may offer me some jack to continue."

Walter was not, however, leaving things entirely to chance. After deciding to suspend his "Merciless Truths" while he and Rita took their sabbatical, he wrote Langford asking for assistance. "About a week from now send a letter to the editor of the News asking why M.T.s are not running. In this way mebbe he will think it is valuable to the sheet and offer me cash to write, savvy? If you can get anyone else to do it I will appreciate it." And he added, "Let your wife sign her name to the letter, not you, but also the team name." In another letter shortly after, he asked them to hold off. He had a "new idea." He was going to try to get their letter placed in *Variety* where it (and he) would get far more exposure.

Walter's indecision over his future was now also complicated by a surprising new development: As they neared the end of their tour, he and Rita were receiving the best notices of their career. "Winchell & Green [*sic*] are a youthful couple possessing all the attributes for the better houses," Jack Josephs wrote in *Variety* after their San Francisco performance. O. M. Samuel, reviewing their New Orleans appearance that October for the same publication, said, "Winchell and Green [*sic*] stopped proceedings in second position. Most of their matter is of the sure-fire sort and is planted just right. Miss Green is a looker in abbreviated togs, while Winchell is improving right along as a light comedian." Even Walter was shocked; he enclosed the notice in a letter to Langford with the comment that having seen them in Dallas, Langford probably wouldn't believe it was the same act.

That very week, buoyed by the reviews, Walter received Langford's script for the new act and immediately began making suggestions—asking for additional gags, prompting him for a "match song" ("you strike me and I'll strike you"), requesting more explicit stage directions when Rita made her costume change and recommending they add a dance. ("Personally I believe if we do a little dancing we are in a better chance to get away from two spots.") "We have every confidence in you and the act you've sent us," Walter wrote, suddenly not sounding like a man who was thinking of abandoning the profession. "I feel it fits us perfectly and we should have a good break with it. That's just how confident I am." And he reminded Langford of a promise to send him a letter of introduction to Myron Bentham, one of the most prominent vaudeville agents.

They left St. Louis that October in high spirits, wrote Rita, "two minds but with a single thought, the future of Walter Winchell, but little did I know or think that it was the beginning of the end. . . ."

"WALTER ('MERCILESS TRUTHS') WINCHELL of Winchell & Green [*sic*] returned to the city after an absence of nearly eighteen months," *The Vaudeville News* reported the next week. "From personal observation, we are of the opinion that Walter seemed very glad to return to his 'hum town' and the [NVA] club, and renew acquaintance with the many friends he left behind when he took Horace Greeley's advice to 'Go West.' " Glenn Condon had many opportunities to observe personally Walter Winchell those first few weeks. Almost immediately upon his return, Walter visited Condon in the two-room *News* office on Broadway next to the Palace Theater. "I've got $1,500 to invest in Walter Winchell, Inc.," he told Condon, meaning the nest egg he and Rita had saved. Walter proposed to pay himself $25 a week if Condon kicked in another $25 for a six-month trial period, during which Walter could determine "whether I had any business in the newspaper racket."

Condon, a big, affable, baby-faced fellow with a bowl haircut—he had been a yellow journalist in Tulsa before joining Albee and had once been fired on the front page for embellishing a story on a gunfight—claimed that the *News* was already being printed at a loss and he couldn't possibly afford another employee. But Walter was persistent—persistent because he was desperate, desperate because there was nothing else waiting for him except the prospect of months more on the road. Goaded by Rita, he continued campaigning for a job, socializing with Condon and his wife nearly every night those first weeks back, until Condon's resistance began to melt and he promised to raise the issue with Albee.

Even with this concession, Walter was dissatisfied and impatient. Though he had been back less than a month, his euphoria was already waning. "[H]e was eager and anxious," remembered Rita, who kept trying to buck up his flagging spirits, "and although I know he has waited for the outcome of many more important decisions since this time, I doubt whether any job or any decision has ever been so important to him as the getting of the job on the Vaudeville News."

Finally, on November 17, Condon wrote Albee about his new friend:

Sometime ago you told me to look around for a young fellow to break in as my assistant on the Vaudeville News. I now have a young man whom [sic] I think is the ideal person for the place.... His name is Walter Winchell. He is twenty-three years of age, married and has had newspaper experience. He has also been in vaudeville several seasons and I find, on investigation, that he has a splendid reputation, is a thoroughly loyal NVA, and his general character is A-1....

He is highly desirous of improving his position, and is bent on staying in the publishing game, as he does not care for the stage.... He is at liberty now and I should like to make a deal with him this week....

At the bottom of the page, Albee scrawled only two words: "How much?"

Three days later, Walter wrote Langford in a gush of elation about "a wonderful proposition" to be the assistant editor of *The Vaudeville News.*

I have accepted, believing that the future of such a position holds remarkable things for me (if I show 'em what I'm made of) and has unlimited possibilities.

You no doubt don't blame me, because you have heard me mention that I would love to become a figure in the world, preferably in the news game. I have always had an inclination to want to be in it, and at last I've had my wish granted. Of course the money is not a hell of a lot, and I know I cannot save [crossed out "as much as we both did"] but the fact is that any day may bring more wonderful things. . . .

Still hedging, he said, "I also realize that when I tire of this (if I do) I can always go back to being an ordinary actor, can't I?" And he closed by asking if he could keep the script for the new act "as you can never tell when the bug will hit me to go back."

Talk of going back, though, was Walter's fear talking; he would never return to vaudeville. But neither would he forget what vaudeville had inculcated in him. "Mr. Winchell's rise may seem meteoric to the casual observer," journalist Heywood Broun would write when Walter was first taking New York by storm with his column, "but when his life and works are considered in Freshman English classes a hundred years hence, the wise professor will point out that the years he spent as a small-time hoofer constituted a period of preparation. He did not drop his pumps for his pen until his message had taken form within his soul." Walter had spent his entire adolescence and then his young manhood, from thirteen to twenty-three, on the vaudeville hustings—his changing, contingent vaudeville family substituting for his real one, his *School Days* act substituting for his formal education, his stage persona substituting for some more fundamental and authentic identity.

Vaudeville educated him and imbued him with its values, which anticipated the values of mass culture. Emerging after the Civil War out of what were then known as "concert saloons" and flourishing at a time when America was first beginning the difficult transition from an agrarian society to an industrialized nation, vaudeville provided, in one historian's words, "a kind of theatrical laboratory for experimenting with the new culture that clashed with Victorianism." Vaudeville was incautious, unselfconscious and liberated; it valued idiosyncrasy and novelty in its performers and exposed audiences to different cultures, new values and a fresh, exuberant, often irreverent style; it was a "kid game for men in their kid moments," said critic George Jean Nathan.

Vaudeville made Walter an entertainer for life and in life. Growing up in vaudeville as he did, he not only absorbed its diversity, its energy, its nihilism, and then deployed them in his journalism, but learned how to create his journalism *from* them: journalism as vaudeville. In the end, then, Heywood Broun was right: It was vaudeville that formed the message within Walter Winchell's soul. It was vaudeville that forged him.

And that included vaudeville's dark side as well as its bright one. Walter would always remember the anxiety of playing "a half-filled house on a dead matinee in some hick town" and not being certain "there wasn't some scout for a big producer out front." He would remember "when every three days or a week meant 'having to make good' all over again . . . for some theater manager, whose opinion mattered." He would remember "counting on the mediocre orchestras (of five or maybe six) to play your tempo correctly." He would remember the "cellar dressing rooms," the "unsteady engagements" and the " 'phony' booking office representatives" who were actually stenographers and office boys sent to cover his act.

Above all, he would remember the audiences: the customers who threw coins at the performers, the ones who waited outside the stage door to throttle him for some flip remark he had made onstage, the ones who "gaped up at you—mouths wide open and eyes colder than a headliner's stare" with their " 'go ahead and make me like your act!' attitude." George Jessel always believed that Walter failed in vaudeville while he, Jessel, succeeded because Walter could never establish the proper relationship with the audience. "We who were successful had learned to love our audiences," Jessel said. "And when we loved 'em, they knew it. It was something you couldn't put your finger on, but they knew it. Walter's trouble was that he didn't like the audience. He was afraid of it and so he wanted to outsmart it, to convince himself he was sharper than they were. He didn't love them and they could sense it."

Jessel was right. Walter had always been afraid of the audience; he had always protected himself against it, even as he craved its attention. He once said that he had had the opportunity to play the Palace, the crowning achievement for a vaudevillian, but had declined because he was terrified of flopping and ruining his career forever. In elaboration, he composed a ditty which he said summed up why he left vaudeville: "I would rather click on second in a smallie town like Dallas, than be flopping at the Palace on a Monday matinee!"

For Walter, vaudeville had provided, as his Harlem childhood had, a lesson in fear, humiliation and resentment, and he brought those to his journalism too. "It was a good apprenticeship," he was to say, "being rebuked and rebuffed by critics, stagehands, house managers and baggagemen. And, of course, audiences." But whereas in vaudeville he would always be subservient and marginal, the new promise of journalism was that he could become, as he wrote Langford, a "figure in the world."

For anyone who knew the Winchels, this was a familiar refrain, echoing the sentiments of Chaim Weinschel, just as Walter's lament about vaudeville echoed his grandfather's lament, so many years before, about his religious duties. In weighing show business against journalism, Walter was really unwittingly reenacting his grandfather's own struggle between his unsatisfying religious position and the literary life he so desperately wanted. In choosing journalism, Walter had a chance to gain the recognition his grandfather had never received. In choosing journalism, he had a chance to lift the family curse of expectation and disappointment. Chaim Weinschel had demanded that attention be paid.

Now, at last, it would.

CHAPTER 2

Newsboy

W ALTER WINCHELL ARRIVED IN New York in the fall of 1920 on the cusp of what may have been the most self-consciously epochal period in American history, a decade during which many of the social, economic, political and demographic forces that had been building momentum since before the turn of the century finally tipped the national balance and during which a style was devised to signify the changes. An agricultural country gave way to an industrial one, a rural society to an urban one, until by decade's end sixty-nine million Americans—56 percent of the population—lived in cities, up from forty-two million at the beginning of the decade. A homogeneous population gave way to a more heterogeneous one, with more than a million immigrants entering the United States in 1920 and 1921 alone. And a country whose principles had long been sternly pragmatic gave way to one caught up, as an analyst described it, in a "revolt against dullness."

In some precincts that revolt exploded into what seemed by mid-decade to be a binge of distraction, self-involvement, heedlessness, even hedonism. "If all the Armenians were to be killed tomorrow," wrote George Jean Nathan, a member of the so-called Smart Set that would help establish the decade's tenor, "and if half of Russia were to starve to death the day after, it would not matter to me in the least. What concerns me alone is myself and the interest of a few close friends. For all I care the rest of the world may go to hell at today's sunset."

But there was another, less highly publicized revolt being waged in the twenties besides the one against dullness. For the ever-increasing number of minorities, immigrants, urbanites and working poor, people who didn't go to nightclubs or make smart chat, the twenties meant self-assertion, not self-absorption. It meant that for the first time they would have to be reckoned with as a cultural force, that to them, as to Winchell, attention would have to be paid.

To some Americans this was a terrifying prospect, and perhaps no single issue so engaged the minds of the decade as the question of whether democracy could still work once the genteel elites no longer exercised control. Most intellectuals had their doubts. Walter Lippmann in *Public Opinion* believed that in a world as vast as ours, one in which events could no longer be directly apprehended by the public, the ordinary citizenry would not be well informed, dispassionate and rational, and he concluded that public opinion could be managed only by a "specialized class," a kind of intellectual aristocracy. H. L. Mencken in *Notes on Democracy* inveighed against the "inferior man" loaded with prejudices, and concluded, "I have never encountered any actual evidence that *vox populi* is actually *vox Dei*. The proofs, indeed, run the other way." As Edmund Wilson interpreted Mencken, he believed "it is the desire on the part of the peasants to rob the superior classes of rewards unattainable by themselves or to restrain them from the enjoyment of activities that they are unable to understand."

The object of all these discussions was to rescue America from the perils of cultural democracy that the twenties had suddenly unleashed. And perhaps no single figure over the years would so come to embody both the possibilities and the dangers of that democracy as Walter Winchell.

HE BEGAN at *The Vaudeville News* like a tornado. Even after he and Rita moved from her parents' house to their own apartment on 117th Street in Harlem, he spent virtually all his time either at the *News'* fifth-floor office at 1562 Broadway or directly down below on the sidewalk outside the Palace Theater gathering news and gags for his column from the unemployed vaudevillians who loitered there. Once a week, while Rita and Mrs. Condon, the editor's wife and a former vaudevillian herself, manned the office, Walter delivered the papers to agents and managers throughout the Palace Building. (He would always remember the ones who tossed the bundles in the wastebasket.) When he wasn't out on his rounds or delivering papers, he dusted the desks or filed the mail. "I was office boy, errand boy, and Star Reporter," he said later.

But he loved it, couldn't get enough of it, and each night after he left the office, still humming with energy, he headed to the National Vaudeville Artists' Club on 46th Street, where the local vaudevillians congregated in the evenings. Usually he spent the entire night there, mixing and gabbing. "Times Square and all of Broadway have not the Bohemian atmosphere that the N.V.A. affords at midnight," Walter wrote glowingly at the time. He was soon spending so much time at the NVA that Rita decided she would have to pass her evenings there as well if she were ever to see him. But even after they would return home, near dawn, and Rita would attempt to sleep, Walter would often rouse her to read her a poem of his or a witty new saying for the column, and "if you didn't listen you were liable to be kicked playfully out of bed. . . ."

He called his new column "Broadway Hearsay" and himself Broadway's "Fax" collector. " 'Hiy, Hiy!' yells Harry Burns, of Burns and Frabito, as the 'Fax' collector pounds the pavement on the G.[reat] W.[hite] Way where the red trolleys kiss Times Square good-bye," began a typical item. " 'I wan you should poot in your paper dat I haf bought more pallons 'cause soon in mine howse I 'spect a leetyle a one. You catch me, keed?' Which means that Harry will soon be buying new shoes or roll somebody for them."

It was the same sort of column he had contributed to the paper while he was on the road, but now that he was being paid for his submissions, now that he was a professional journalist, he felt new pangs of inadequacy. He feared that Condon was going to fire him and felt certain that Condon would be perfectly within his rights to do so. (Condon, later, didn't disagree.) He became so discouraged that he even flirted with the idea of dispensing with prose altogether and becoming a photographer instead, borrowing money from his uncle Billy Koch to get a Graflex, but he realized he was no good with the camera either and gave it away.

What brought him through this brief crisis and bolstered his confidence was the way he now found himself being treated. Among vaudevillians everyone read the *News*, and to them it hardly mattered whether his column was brilliant or not. They realized that a mention in a column, *any* column, was a form of free publicity and that a columnist, *any* columnist, was someone to be courted. Walter basked in their attention, and Rita bitterly recalled how "he could go into minute detail of what people said about him, how he was doing, what a wonder he was, life was just one grand compliment for W.W."

But having vaudevillians toady to him wasn't enough to soothe his insecurities. Walter also began campaigning to be popular, and given the hours he kept and the rounds he made, one could hardly avoid him around Broadway. Walter didn't enter a room; he invaded it, tossing off greetings, slapping backs, telling anecdotes while his eyes scanned for someone else to accost. And while there were those who found him too eager to please, too obvious and even obnoxious in his glad-handing, most on Broadway saw him for what he was that first year at the *News*: an unsophisticated, ambitious, driven young man working hard to get ahead.

That wasn't the way Walter wanted to be perceived. He would have much preferred to be viewed as a young man of substance on Broadway, less a go-getter than someone who had already arrived. Maintaining appearances, however, was costly, and Walter was still earning only twenty-five dollars a week, which meant that he was obliged to draw heavily on the nest egg. After eight months in New York the fund had dwindled to $100, and Walter with Rita's approval had used that to join the Masonic lodge into which many of his fellow vaudevillians had already been inducted. It was another brick in the wall of status he was building for himself.

He had resisted asking for a raise because he feared that Condon might fire him instead and destroy everything. But Rita now demanded that he ask or she would either ask herself or force Walter back to the stage until they had built a new nest egg. Condon griped about Walter's request, but within a few weeks Walter's salary was doubled to $50.

It was still nowhere near enough for the clothes he required, the dues, the lunches and nightly dinners at the NVA, not to mention the rent. Each day he rationed Rita one dollar and two cigarettes before leaving for work, even though she told him she resented being treated like a child. Realizing he would need much more money, he set out to convince Condon to take ads for the *News*. Walter would do all the soliciting so there would be no additional staff, and in return he would take a 20 percent commission. Condon was aghast at the proposal. The *News* was a free newspaper and a house organ, he said. Albee would never countenance ads. But Walter was a hustler and a tireless advocate. Within weeks he had gotten Condon to propose the deal to Albee, who surprisingly accepted.

If Winchell had been a familiar figure on Broadway before, he became ubiquitous selling ads. "He was kind of a pest," said one Broadway denizen, "and yet you didn't mind him, and if you could spare five or ten dollars you bought his ad and helped him write a couple of sentences about you." No one on Broadway worked harder. He was always knocking on doors, scurrying, pressing, pushing, gabbing, always in a hurry, always promoting himself—all day long and deep into the night. He barely slept, fearing he might miss something. The "later it grew the more interesting the conversation," Rita noted, "and W.W. enjoyed his friends and company so much that it was next to impossible to get him home at a decent hour."

"I go the pace that kills," he wrote in one of the poems for his column. He began another:

> *I have always held a hatred for the men*
> *Who make little effort to attain the heights;*
> *With contempt I've written of them with my pen,*
> *For I loathe the lazy loafers who dodge fights!*

One contemporary remembered his standard greeting: "What do you know that I don't know?" Bernard Sobel, a theater press agent, recalled Walter's waving hello to him though he didn't have the slightest idea of who Walter was. "I saw a young man who reminded me of a college youth, his features regular and attractive, his smile genial and his manner so intimate that I took it for granted that we knew each other."

Walter was beginning to feel that he was among the winners now. Though he still complained about his finances, he was soon earning $150 a week on his commissions in addition to his base salary at a time when the average twenty-five-year-old cub reporter on a metropolitan newspaper was making $25 a week and a thirty-five-year-old reporter was making $50. More important, the Broadway regulars recognized him and congratulated him on his doggerel. ("It didn't dawn on me at the time that they were giving me a line because they wanted a plug," he wrote later.) He and Glenn Condon joined the Cheese Club, a group of Broadway insiders. He became the treasurer-adjutant of the NVA's American Legion post. He was asked to perform at an NVA benefit and was called onstage to sing during a tribute at the Friars Club. In an environment that valued personalities, young Walter Winchell was becoming one. "Nighthawk of the Roaring Forties'/Is my reputation now," he wrote in an ode both to Broadway and to himself:

> *Times Square to Columbus Circle,*
> *Seems to take to me somehow.*
> *Feel assured that I'll defend you*
> *If somebody tries to harm;*
> *Right or Wrong I will befriend you!*
> *I've surrendered to your charm.*
> *No one loves you more than I do,*
> *For you've tolerated me;*
> *Street of Streets! I bow before you;*
> *You have made a man of me!*

II

The explosion came on March 1, 1922.

By the end of their first year back in New York, Rita, restless and unhappy over Walter's parsimony, returned to the stage with a girl named Bernice Blair. "Two Sweet Things—Plus" they called their act, which traveled the small-time Gus Sun circuit that winter. That Christmas Walter, in a letter to Kris Kringle in his column, was lamenting, "I have a wife and money too, but I'm a sad old bloke. . . . We have most ev'rything at home 'cept something running 'round, so take a hint, old fellow, from this very lonesome hound. . . . justify my faith, dear sir, by bringing us a baby!"

Walter's life, however, left very little time for a baby. It left little enough for Rita. "I was a newspaperman, and I gave the job almost twenty hours a day," he wrote in his autobiography. He admitted that Rita had cause to feel neglected. As he described that night of March 1, "There was a minor quarrel, and one day Rita left a bundle for me at the NVA Club. . . . There was no note in the bundle. I took the hint." Thus his marriage ended.

Rita, however, would describe the evening much differently. It was very late, and she was talking with some friends in a room upstairs at the NVA Club when the phone rang. The operator told her that Walter was waiting downstairs for her and wanted to go home now. Fearing something was wrong for Walter to want to leave so early, she immediately headed downstairs, but when she saw that he was perfectly fine, she told him she wanted to stay and asked him to join her. As they stepped out of the crowded elevator, Walter suddenly slapped her. "Don't you stick out your tongue at me," he snapped. "I saw you through the mirror."

Rita headed directly for her friends' room. Walter followed her inside and again demanded she come home. "When I get good and ready," she said. "I shall never forget that night if I lived [sic] forever," she would write of what happened next. "I was sitting on a bed and W.W. just reached his arm out and pulled me up from my seat, gave me a general pushing and slapping around, in front of these people. . . . " Though bristling, Rita said she had enough presence of mind to get up and leave rather than retaliate. During the taxi ride home, Rita lacerated him, warning that she would not permit herself to be abused. The next morning she moved to her mother's house. She returned to their apartment the day after, but Walter had already left. Three days later he asked that his clothes be sent to the NVA Club.

It was to be a strangely unresolved separation, not at all the sudden break Walter made it out to be. He kept begging Rita to come back to him. He even "appropriated" money from the ad revenues he collected for the *News* to support his wooing; that Easter, for the first time Rita could remember, he bought her gifts, two silk nightgowns and a bouquet of white roses. She responded coolly, questioning the sincerity of his efforts. She had come to believe the only way she could save her marriage was by establishing her independence. So that summer she decided to form a new act, this time with a friend named Jewell DeVoie. When the act, "Jovial Juveniles," attracted the attention of several agents and won first-class bookings, Walter was delighted and even helped Rita wade through the offers. In October he went to Philadelphia to give them pointers on their closing number, and when he mentioned that he hadn't sold the front-page ad for next week's *News*, Rita generously took it to repay him.

Walter insisted he loved her and told his cronies that he was at a loss without her. Rita believed it was merely a ploy for sympathy. When she played Baltimore, he wrote, "There's a guy in the heart of Maryland with a gal that belongs to me," though Rita insisted she was still faithful to him. Meanwhile, Walter's Aunt Beatrice, in whom Rita had confided, argued that he would come to his senses and advised her not to do anything precipitate. She and Rita both believed that Walter, however swell-headed he might have become, wasn't bad—just discombobulated by his newfound recognition and not quite sure how to handle it.

Rita spent the next season, 1922–23, on the road, steadily moving west. She kept in touch with Walter through phone calls and letters, and when the tour concluded in Chicago that June, she returned to New York, fully expecting that she and Walter would iron out their disagreements and resume their married life together.

It was, however, to be an uneasy truce that summer. Though the two saw each other almost every night at the NVA Club, Rita lived with her mother while Walter boarded at the club. Neither dated. On the road she had heard rumors of Walter's being unfaithful, of weekend revelries at mind-reader Norman Frescott's house out on Long Island. Walter dismissed such stories as gossip ("Now Mrs. W., you know little Walter better than that") and continued to profess his love for her. But they both seemed uncertain.

As the summer drew to a close, they were no nearer to a reconciliation, and Rita prepared to tour again. She was to open with Jewell late that August in Brooklyn. But seeing the dilapidated condition of the theater, she canceled the engagement and arranged to meet her mother that afternoon in the city instead. They were strolling up Broadway when, at 48th Street, Rita spotted Walter, his back to her, with a beautiful young woman who was "busily smoothing W.W.'s face with her pretty hands." As Rita approached, she heard the young woman murmur to Walter, "Your wife." All Walter could do was stammer to Rita that he thought she was in Brooklyn performing.

Rita hired a lawyer to arrange a legal separation and a financial settlement. But still the odd marital stalemate dragged on, with neither party willing to effect either a clean break or a rapprochement. Rita hadn't given up hope that the marriage could be salvaged, and Walter went on writing lovelorn verses in his column:

> I like to think no more my love you'd spurn,
> That is—if you came back (of course, you won't);
> I like to think that you want to return—
> I like to think so even though—you don't.

They continued to correspond. "Letters exchanged by two estranged souls have a tendency to cause the blues," Walter wrote her in December 1923. "But yet, there's something nice about writing to bad little girls, I think." The separation payments and the legal fees, he said, were really hurting, especially since he had borrowed large sums for her in the wake of their breakup. "I'm sure you understand that a ten spot every week for ten weeks not including uncle Morris Plan* who gets that and more makes quite a dent in the old income," and he asked if she might get her lawyer to desist for the time being. "Although you are several hundred miles away from me, I feel you by me constantly. . . . Every minute I imagine hearing you say: 'I'll put you in jail! I'll get even with you, Walter!' " He decorated the margins with little pen drawings: a ten-spot, Rita chasing him with a knife, Rita crying and smiling.

By March, the second anniversary of their separation, he was gently dunning her for the payments on the old *Vaudeville News* ad, but admitted it "gave me an opportunity to communicate with you to find out if you were still alive. . . . " Not having heard from her for weeks, he had heard rumors that she had found someone she liked, that she was planning on divorcing him secretly in Chicago, that she had been drinking too much. He didn't believe any of it and had even been planning to surprise her in Chicago before thinking better of the idea. "You and I are so far apart that we don't even realize it ourselves," he wrote her. "We are just like a great many other people who just drift away from each other and Time

---

*The Morris Plan was a loan program in which participants were obligated to repay in weekly installments.

makes us forget even more. You say I am crazy. Well, maybe I am. I'm crazy from a lot of grief that nobody knows about. Nobody, Rita, not one single little body knows."

Meanwhile, his family was also drifting away. Walter's marriage had become a casualty of his desperate and ultimately successful attempt to become a figure in the world, at least the circumscribed world of Broadway. His parents' marriage would be a casualty of Jacob's inability to make it in the world. It had been unraveling almost from the time it started, frayed by Jacob's hapless efforts to be a Winchel and by Jennie's frustration. On January 28, 1919, it had finally come apart. "To let out my terrible temper, I tore both curtains off from the front windows," Jacob wrote Walter a few days after the blowup, "and not alone that, but wait till you hear the other terrible thing I done, listen, I tore both shades too and when I came home I found all my clothes nicely packed up." By June, Jennie had brought suit for a legal separation. Some two years later, after sending her brother to investigate a rumor that Jacob was now living with another woman, Jennie filed for divorce. It was just two months before Walter and Rita's quarrel at the NVA.

THE GRIEF of which Walter had written Rita had actually begun at the NVA Club the May after their separation. As he told it, he had received a tip late one night that a young showgirl boarding at the club had adopted a baby. Thinking this might make a good story and without considering the time, he bolted up the stairs to her room and knocked on the door. In one version of the story, she asked sleepily from behind her closed door who was there, and when Walter introduced himself, she told him to go away, that he had awakened her and the baby. Chastened, Walter went to the lobby and wrote her a note of apology. According to another account, the girl appeared at the door with the sleeping child and told him to interview the child. This time Walter retreated, leaving a note: "Sorry. It was rude of me to break in on you at such a late hour. But I really wanted to interview *you*."

Walter's story about the baby appeared in the May 5, 1922, issue of the *News* with a photo of the child and a drawing of the young woman in a fur piece and fur hat and holding a bouquet of flowers. "The parents of little Angeline, aged 3, could not afford to bring her up as they would like to," it began. "Miss Aster, who, like the child's parents, is a vaudeville artist, became attached to the baby, and obligated herself to 'mother' Angeline. Miss Aster is 17 years old and one of the prettiest girls in the N.V.A."

But the truth was that Walter had not met Miss Aster for the first time that night. She was one of a group of girls who dined nightly at the NVA

Grill, and as Rita recollected it, she always seemed to have a smile for Walter. Since he was an inveterate table-hopper—"he never sat through his meals without getting up a half dozen times," said Rita—he often stopped to chat with her. Watching Walter's effusive greeting to Miss Aster one evening, Rita mentioned that if anything should happen to their marriage, she believed he might be attracted to her. Walter again declared his devotion and told her that all his pleasantries were for the sake of his business.

The "Miss Aster" was June Aster, at the time teaming with Olive Hill in a "high kick" specialty act named Hill & Aster, and she was a slender, leggy, reddish-blonde dancer whose "grace and beauty," Walter said, "drove all the guys nuts," including, he admitted, him. She had been born in Brookhaven, a sleepy, genteel village founded by wealthy merchants in the hilly piney woods of southern Mississippi. Brookhaven was the kind of town, said one guide, "where ladies never made calls without hats and gloves, where the blinds were drawn for afternoon siestas, where streets were unpaved and shadowy with the arching branches of live oak trees, and where the daily arrival of the train and the mail were events to be anticipated."

Because June's mother was a Hoskins, she was part of Brookhaven's aristocracy. Her great-grandfather, James A. Hoskins, had married Elizabeth Ann Whitworth, whose father had founded Whitworth College, the oldest women's college in the state, in 1858. Hoskins himself, said the local newspaper, the Brookhaven *Leader*, had done "more for the growth and prosperity of Brookhaven than any of its early residents" by helping to complete the railroad and build the town's first sawmill. James Hoskins had two sons, James and Isaac, who maintained his father's sawmill until it burned down in 1884. Mamie, June's mother, was Ike's daughter.

Mamie Hoskins was short and thin with fiery red hair and a temperament to match. A family member recalls her as very theatrical, "always acting in shows in Brookhaven and cutting up." Another said she had a dry wit, for which the Hoskinses were known, and a streak of rebelliousness, for which they weren't. According to family lore, nineteen-year-old Mamie found herself pregnant, and the Hoskins men, armed with shotguns, made the suitor marry her. As the Brookhaven *Leader* tersely reported it, "M. C. Magee and Mamie Hoskins were married on Monday night [July 20, 1903] and left at once for St. Louis." Elizabeth June Magee was born ten weeks later on September 6.* By this time Maximil-

---

*June always lied about her age, even to her family, shaving off two years. When she met Walter, she was actually nineteen, not seventeen, as he thought, though it is unlikely that Walter ever learned the truth.

lian Magee had already departed. (He would in fact be married three times before he was twenty-six.) June never knew him.

Though Mamie had obviously scandalized the proper Hoskins family and become its example of the wages of sin, she hadn't lost her verve or surrendered her theatrical ambitions. She passed them on to her daughter and to Elizabeth McLaurin, a cousin who lived with them. The three of them formed a singing act, touring the backwaters of the South as part of Earl and His Girls.

Their theatrical aspirations evidently became much more serious after 1915, when they hit the vaudeville trail—Mamie, June and Elizabeth performing, Mamie's aunt Jennie making the costumes and chaperoning. Like Walter's vaudeville adolescence, June's was to be a rootless and unstable existence. Somewhere along the way Mamie hooked up with another entertainer named Guy Aster. Whether or not she and Aster ever married—"She may have led the family to believe they were married because she didn't want it known that she had been 'foolish' twice," suggested a relative—they had a child, whom she named Mary Rose. Aster departed; Mamie told Mary Rose that he had died, but Mary Rose said, "I didn't believe it." In time the baby was recruited into the act too, now known variously as the Aster Sisters or May and June Aster or Mamie Magee or even as Gil Mack and His Girls, depending, apparently, on Mamie's mood at the time, who happened to be aboard or what show they had hooked up with.

Eventually June struck out on her own, just as Walter had with Rita. Mamie and Baby Mary Rose continued touring together and became enough of a minor phenomenon that a drugstore in Memphis even named a sundae for the little girl. Not long after June met Walter, Baby Mary went to Hollywood to make her first motion picture, and it was probably Walter who reported it for the *News*.

Though he was newly separated, Walter had tried currying favor with June ever since his noninterview with her, and he seized every opportunity to see her, even misreporting in the *News* that mail was being held for her at the NVA Club just so he could pretend to assist her. The reason was that at their encounter over the interview, he had fallen in love with her voice. "She had such a sweet voice," he told his cousin Willie. He began tracking her engagements, taking the train to wherever she was playing and showing up at the stage door with flowers. But June was having none of it. When a friend of hers told him that she already had a boyfriend, Walter was so despondent he said, "I couldn't eat, sleep or laugh at the funniest comedians in show biz." He was hopelessly smitten.

He was also married, albeit in a rather peculiar and ill-defined way, and while he was absolutely infatuated with June, his professions of love for Rita were not necessarily lies. A victim of the twenties' changing moral values, he was clearly confused, shifting between the roles of suitor and husband, living a double life, hoping that the situation might resolve itself without his having to do anything, and never firmly opting for one outcome over the other.

How June felt about the situation is impossible to say. Walter insists she kept spurning his advances, asking him, when he cornered her on the street one day, if they could just be friends. But she let him follow her that August to Atlantic City, where she and Olive Hill were performing; there were photos in the *News* of them on the beach, "[t]wo popular young members of the N.V.A.," and there were two separate items about Hill & Aster's appearances—both the photos and the items no doubt arranged by Walter, who also ran his own photograph from Atlantic City in the *News*.

As Walter always told it, theirs was a whirlwind courtship. No more than a few months passed, he was to say, before he finally wore her down, as he always seemed to do to his prey when he really campaigned for something. "If you go for anybody," he told an interviewer a few years later, "you go for them. You want to marry." So he and June, he said, impulsively raced off to the courthouse one day for a municipal wedding. The date he always gave was May 11, 1923. There was only one problem with this story: he hadn't yet divorced Rita.

III

While the private Walter Winchell was brooding over his domestic crisis, the public Walter Winchell also faced a dilemma. He had received an offer from another paper, he told Rita nervously when he called her for advice. It was a real newspaper, not a trade paper like the *News*, but the pay was less than he was earning now, on which he could barely make ends meet. He also found himself gripped all over again by the old apprehension that if he accepted the new job he wouldn't be able to succeed in this bigger journalistic arena. "[H]e couldn't afford to fail, or so he thought," Rita remembered.

The paper, yet to be launched, was to be called the New York *Evening Graphic*, and it was the creation of a remarkable character by the name of Bernarr Macfadden. He had been born Bernard McFadden in Mill Spring, Missouri, in 1868 to an alcoholic father and tubercular mother. He spent most of his childhood as an indentured servant to a series of cruel taskmasters. Small and sickly, he ran off to St. Louis when he was twelve and began weightlifting to improve his health, winding up with a physique so beautifully sculpted that according to one of his five wives, he would often stand in front of a mirror admiring it. Over the years he ran health salons, sold exercise equipment, lectured, wrestled, even founded a planned community dedicated to health; but it was one magazine, *Physical Culture*, that provided the keystone of what was to be his empire and another, *True Story*, that made him his fortune, estimated to be as much as $30 million at its height.

To most who knew him personally, he was a crackpot. Edward Bernays, the renowned public relations consultant, said that Macfadden once proposed to walk barefoot from his office on 65th Street to City Hall to demonstrate the benefits of healthy living, and when Bernays dissuaded him from that idea on the ground that he would be ridiculed, Macfadden suggested they send a nude statue of his eleven-year-old daughter across the country as an example of what his health principles had done for his own children. His main nemeses were doctors. He excoriated them as quacks and recommended that people forgo their ministrations. There was no illness that couldn't be prevented through physical exercise and proper nutrition and none that Nature couldn't cure. "Doctors are taboo," he told his wife.

His vehemently dogmatic views had horrifying and heartbreaking consequences when the Macfaddens' infant son Byron suddenly began convulsing. Macfadden's wife begged him to call a doctor, but he plunged Byron into a scalding sitz bath instead. The baby died moments later in his mother's arms. Another child, a daughter from an earlier marriage, had a congenital heart defect, but her father insisted she exercise. She died too, Macfadden declaring to his surviving children, "It's better she's gone. She'd have disgraced me."

A macho blusterer, an illiterate, a libertine, a narcissist with the hawkish profile of a warrior and long, wild hair, Macfadden nevertheless harbored one large and ridiculous ambition: He wanted to be President of the United States. He already had a sizable fortune. What he needed now was a vehicle to promote him. Macfadden's wife at the time suspected it was Fulton Oursler, the supervising editor of Macfadden magazines, who planted the idea that they begin a tabloid newspaper to harvest his ambition. "Money is power," Macfadden would declare at home. "But it takes newspapers to direct that power if a publisher expects to get anywhere politically."

According to Oursler, it was Macfadden's idea to start a tabloid, and though Mrs. Macfadden portrayed Oursler as her husband's Cardinal Richelieu, scheming to ride him to power, Oursler himself said he ap-

proached the enterprise with trepidation. He "knew that there were degrees of sensationalism as there are degrees of fever. Macfadden had no
checkrein of good taste to hold him back, and I considered it the gravest
part of my duty to provide such a brake upon his ardor for the appalling
and the lurid."

His new paper, Macfadden announced in August 1924, would be "surprising." Other papers he said were like factory-made shoes—"all alike,
made in the same mold, controlled by the same old-time worn-out prejudices." They smelled, he said, "of the literary machine-shop or the cemetery." The *Graphic* would operate by an entirely different principle.
Dedicated to "the masses not the classes," it would present human interest stories rather than hard news and not only present them but, like his
True Story magazine, present them in the first person.

Long before the public announcement, Walter had heard about the
launch of the *Graphic*, originally to be called *The Evening Truth*, from his
friend Norman Frescott, the vaudeville mind-reader, who was also a good
friend of Oursler's. Walter implored him to phone Oursler on his behalf
that very moment. Frescott protested that it was too late at night to call,
but Walter wasn't to be denied. Frescott arranged an introduction at the
NVA Grill, where Oursler, somehow under the mistaken impression that
Walter was the playwright Winchell Smith, kept calling him "Mr. Smith"
until Walter finally corrected him.

In agreeing to meet Walter, Oursler couldn't have known what he
was getting himself into. Just as Walter had done with Glenn Condon
when he set his sights on the *News* job, he now began calling Oursler morning, noon and night, once at 2 a.m., to convince him that
the *Graphic* would need a Broadway columnist and that he was the perfect candidate. Oursler thought the items in Walter's "Broadway Hearsay" in the *News* were "nothing to write to Chaucer about," but there
was something appealing about the way Walter presented them. "It was
personal. It was intimate." Oursler had even submitted a few poems
of his own to the column which Walter had rejected. "I knew then,"
Oursler allegedly said, "he would make a good editor for our drama
pages, etc."

Like Condon before him, Oursler eventually capitulated to Walter's assault, introduced him to the paper's editor at the NVA Grill and closed
the deal. For Oursler, Walter's real value wasn't the column so much as
the pipeline he seemed to have. "From my talks with him I soon realized
that he knew more about the goings-on and the goings-off of Broadway
than anyone I had ever met," Oursler later wrote. "It was my understanding that he would constantly be giving tips to the City Desk." The offer
was $75-per-week salary for a column and drama criticism, plus a 15 per-

cent commission on all the theater advertising he sold.* But Oursler, who obviously didn't know Walter very well, believed the salary was really irrelevant to him. "[W]hat meant everything to Winchell was that he could have a daily column."

Still, there was that fear of failure. Having won the job with his tenacity, he was now in a quandary, as he explained to Rita, of whether to take it. "Winchell was scared about it," said Glenn Condon. He and Condon spent all day pacing up and down Fifth Avenue while Walter deliberated. At one point he asked if Condon would become his agent, promising him 10 percent of his earnings for the next one hundred years. Finally Condon ended the debate. "Look, Walter," he said, "as of now you're fired." "That's how he moved over," Condon recalled, "he couldn't make up his mind so I had to do it for him."

His Aunt Beatrice tried to talk him out of accepting, and offered to send him to journalism school instead. Walter pondered the offer and approached Herbert Bayard Swope, the highly respected editor of the New York *World*, for his advice. As Walter remembered it, Swope said, "Walter, you've had four years' experience as a newspaperman. If you and a journalism graduate walked in the door this minute, I'd hire you."

However terrified he was at the prospect of moving to a daily newspaper, Walter had won enormous goodwill among the Broadwayites as amiable, bright and industrious, and now they offered to come to his assistance. "Are you going to handle the theatrical advertising on the 'Evening Truth'?" wrote Walter Kingsley, a Keith circuit press agent and himself a fixture on Broadway. "If you are, count us as your allies with copy, for you are a good kid and regular and I don't know of anyone who stands better on the Rialto or along Tin Pan Alley."

In his four years on the *News*, twenty-seven-year-old Walter had ingratiated himself so well among his Broadway brethren that a hundred of them threw him a testimonial dinner two days before the *Graphic*'s launch. One news account said it "proved beyond question of doubt that he is one of the most popular figures on Broadway." Oursler admitted he was "astonished at the gathering. The room was filled with Broadway celebrities including Fred Stone, George Jessel, Eddie Cantor, Al Jolson, Jimmy Walker. . . . " Twenty-two performers rose to give him testimonials, which, said one account, "Winchell deserves. And more," and then presented him with a gold cigarette case. Oursler made a sentimental speech that had everyone "dissolved in tears" and promised that Walter

---

*Or so said Oursler. Walter later indicated that he got no advertising commission on the *Graphic*.

would be given a free hand to run the theatrical department on the paper. But it was Jimmy Walker, then a New York state senator, who made the most lasting impression of the evening. "Walter, as a dramatic critic and knowing every manager, actor and playwright in this town who will naturally expect undeserved boosts, you must make your choice," he intoned dramatically. "You can keep your friends and be a failure—or lose them and be a success." It was advice Walter would often quote as his career ascended.

THE ANTICIPATION of the *Graphic* in journalistic circles was immense, not because anyone imagined the paper would be good but because no one could imagine how awful it might be. "We couldn't envisage," said one journalist, "one [paper] made up of the ingredients of muscles, bare feet, out-thrusted chests and raw vegetables, or mistakes in love and life—before and after." Only two test runs were scheduled early that September before publication was to begin on September 15. After the second dress rehearsal Macfadden was so pleased he returned to his home in Nyack that evening, examined his nude body in the mirror and then proclaimed to his wife that it would be a propitious time for them to conceive a son.

The next day the *Graphic* made its first appearance, with Macfadden prophesying in ads "A Newspaper with a New Idea. . . . It will flash across the horizon like a new comet." The staff gathered that morning in the musty city room on the fourth floor of the old *Evening Mail* building to receive its marching orders from the health faddist. Hoisted atop a desk by some reporters and compositors, Macfadden looked, to one employee, like an Indian, "his gestures and bearing having some quality of the Noble Savage," and he spoke in a unique dialect that struck the observer "as a combination of Old Scotch and Choctaw."

"We are going to publish a newspaper," he told them, "which will publish Nothing but the Truth. . . . We will have it on the cover. Be ready to fight for the Truth to the last ditch. We are not going to have a paper governed by any secret power. It will be of the people, by the people and for the people." Telling them that with their assistance the "people themselves will write a great deal of this paper," he then launched into an attack on "medical ignorance," "prurient prudery" and the "contaminations of smallpox vaccine." (In time, critics said the *Graphic* was "for fornication and against vaccination.") With the staff cheering he was carried to the elevator, and the presses began their "rumble."

An inaugural editorial, titled "We Are of the People" and illustrated with a cartoon of a man with "Graphic" across his chest leading a phalanx of common citizens, sounded the same themes. "The common people are the salt of the earth," it began. "They are the great rank and file that make up this nation. . . . [W]e just want to be recognized as one of the folks." But the real point came later in the editorial, and it wasn't about populism; it was about entertainment. "We intend to interest you mightily," it said. "We intend to dramatize and sensationalize the news and some stories that are not news. But we do not want a single dull line to appear in this newspaper."

If sensationalism was what Macfadden was promising, he more than delivered. The headline that first day shouted: SHE GAVE UP ART FOR A BARONET and I KNOW WHO KILLED MY BROTHER, and on page two, a motion picture actress who was depressed over losing a suit against a producer declared, MY FRIENDS DRAGGED ME INTO THE GUTTER. PRINCE TELLS ME JUST WHY IT IS HE'S SO SAD went another story, this one on the Prince of Wales. ALWAYS COUNT YOUR CHANGE, ran an advice column. And in the fifth column ran this announcement: BROADWAY GOLD PAVED FOR WALTER WINCHELL. There were other stories that week about a divorcing couple, an eloping heiress, an unmarried mother, a broker who absconded with one million dollars and a pastor who claimed to have poisoned two parishioners.

The reaction was swift and predictable. After the *Graphic's* first week, *Time* magazine, itself just a fledlging, adjudged it "hardly a newspaper," to which the *Graphic* spikily retorted, "We are not a newspaper in the accepted sense. . . . The *Graphic* will try to be more the *maker* than the *follower* of fashions." *Editor & Publisher*, a leading newspaper trade weekly, surveyed one issue and found on the front page "only three inches that did not relate either to murder or rum running." Other features it disapprovingly noted were a "stock market discussion without quotations," a daily sermon, a love diary, a bedtime story, an article on how to play the ukulele, another on physical culture and "Broadway gossip by Walter Winchell." The New York Public Library stopped carrying the paper after six weeks. Even an irate reader of Walter's wrote asking, "[I]f you're so clever why aren't you on a regular paper?"

There would come to be a standing joke about the *Graphic* reporter whose mother begged him to leave the paper and return to his old, more respectable job: piano player in a whorehouse. But for Walter, his personal insecurities aside, having a daily column in a newspaper, regular or not, was nearly all that one could ask from life. Citing some scathing criticism of the *Graphic* by H. I. Phillips of the *Daily News*, Walter quoted the columnist Franklin P. Adams: "Our advice to young men about to enter journalism is to enter it if possible, for any other business or profession seems to us like shooting craps for no stakes. But to the youth we must add: 'Any friends you must consider as just so much velvet.' " Walter had the quote, which echoed Jimmy Walker's advice, pasted on the wall over his desk.

IF WINCHELL was fearful despite campaigning so hard for the job, it was in part because the field of columning was already so crowded, the competition so stiff. Columnists were everywhere. The *Tribune* had Percy Hammond on the theater, Burton Rascoe on publishing and Don Marquis writing humor pieces in the guise of archy the cockroach—"the goddam biggest cockroach you ever saw"—who tapped out the column by leaping on the typewriter keys. When the *Tribune* and *Herald* merged, Alexander Woollcott, pundit, raconteur and curmudgeon, took his column of wry observations there. The *American* had humorist Bugs Baer and political commentator Roy K. Moulton. The *Post* had Christopher Morley on literature and Russel Crouse on amusements. The *Morning Telegraph* had a half dozen columnists, including Helen Green on slang. The *Telegraph-Mail* had S. Jay Kaufman's "Around the Town." The Sunday *World* had Ring Lardner, Milt Gross's "Looie, Dot Dope" about the Bronx, Frank Sullivan, Karl Kitchen on theater, Laurence Stallings and Lloyd Mayer on the latest doings of the younger set. And the *Morning World* had, in Walter's estimation, the "crack" columnists: Heywood Broun and Franklin P. Adams, a sour-tempered autodidact whose "Conning Tower," a compendium of poems, aphorisms, criticisms, witticisms and reflections, was the most highly regarded of them all.

For Walter the immediate challenge was staking out his own territory—because other journalists wouldn't stand for anyone trespassing on theirs, and neither would readers. "This newcomer, who shook in his hoofing shoes in awe of all the 1924 Mighties, figured the only way to fight extinction was to prepare his own menu, and let the other fellow's dishes alone," Walter would write of his days just before the *Graphic's* introduction. "Broadway was unexplored copyland and besides it was the only area he knew."

There had in fact been columns at the periphery of Broadway—ones like S. Jay Kaufman's that occasionally reported Broadway news or Benny Holzman's in the *Mail* that reprinted press releases. But no columnist outside the entertainment trade papers had made Broadway his exclusive domain. No columnist had burrowed himself in its folkways, its language, its fads, its opinions, its quips, jokes, tales, grievances, failures and triumphs—above all, its personalities. None had, probably because no editor was sure readers would care about this alien and insular enclave.

Other daily columnists ruminated about events and ideas in general circulation. Some, like O. O. McIntyre, even presented themselves as representatives of the common man—McIntyre, the small-town boy from Plattsburg, Missouri, taking a wide-eyed view of the big city. What columnists as disparate as the erudite FPA and the gaping McIntyre shared was a certain nineteenth-century regard for language—for the well-turned phrase, the polished sentence, the literary allusion, the rhetorical flourish. FPA even had a regular department chiding fellow journalists for their grammatical errors.

But Winchell's new Broadway column had little to do with his readers' daily experience, and it had no pretensions whatsoever to literary merit—no reverence for grammar, high-blown prose, intellectual palaver or edification. Walter was an entertainer, and that was what he sought to be in his column. "Other columnists appealed to the highbrows," Walter's editor wrote of the columnist's alter ego in a novel based on the *Graphic* experience. "I would try a column run for the masses in their own vernacular."

"Your Broadway and Mine," as he called the column, debuted on September 20, 1924, with a poem that expressed Walter's trepidation about taking on the "Mighties" among the columnists, and concluded: "It's hard to be a youngster, in the learning / Beginners, as you know, must go through hell." But having displayed his humility, he then served notice to his rivals by criticizing them for having stolen from his old *Vaudeville News* column without giving him credit: "For seasons we have wished that the boys would give us the ethical by-line when borrowing from our department. . . ." He included a gag from humorist Fred Allen—"If there is such a thing as reincarnation in vaudeville, could the Hunchback of Notre Dame come back as a straight man?"—and had another gag about sufferers of the sleeping sickness epidemic: "While I was in a certain small time theater last night I noticed they were all in the house." He ended his column with an explanation of why torch singer Sophie Tucker had left the *Vanities* (she wasn't allowed enough time to sell her songs) and promoted a dancer named Ed Lowry who quit the *Ritz Revue* because the producers wanted him to do comedy and play the clarinet rather than dance.

Walter entered the *Graphic* offices that first night buzzing with energy. "The place vibrated to his gait," remembered one staff man to whom Walter immediately introduced himself. "It was our first meeting but one would have thought he had known me all his life. . . . He came up in a way that made one feel important and pleased." The offices themselves were in an open loft partitioned by frosted glass. Cubicles were assigned by rank; the highest-ranking staff members got the ones in the rear. Walter as the lowest-ranking member on the paper—a Broadway character, not even a journalist—was given an old rolltop desk out in the open near the sports department and about halfway between the managing editor's cubicle and the city desk. Anyone getting off the ancient, clanking elevator which led from the bowels of the pressroom to the city room practically bumped into Walter's desk. Since there was no receptionist, the desk became the depository for most of the paper's deliveries, and Walter spent the evenings after his rounds plowing through the detritus so he could clear the top and write his column.

His editor described him sitting at his rolltop, "a hunched figure with a white lean face of deceptive humility, looking up occasionally, startled." He worked with "frenzied determination." Another co-worker said he had a "lean hungry look but he was young and so ambitious that when you watched him crouched tensely before his typewriter, he reminded you of a five pound sack into which ten pounds of humus had been pounded. You looked at him and expected something to give at any moment."

Much of what seemed like single-mindedness was actually anxiety, which Walter ascribed to his vaudeville experience, when each day brought new pressures to make good. He admitted now to "stage fright" and was always soliciting suggestions for improving the column. On Sundays he remained at the *Graphic* until three or four in the morning, scouring the last editions of the competition to reassure himself that his own copy was fresh. To his fellow workers he was always cordial, but he seldom fraternized.

After work he vanished in the direction of Broadway to forage for column material at the NVA Club or at a bustling chophouse on West 48th Street called LaHiff's—after its proprietor, Billy LaHiff—where the Broadway cognoscenti usually gathered. These were centers of theatrical Broadway—the Broadway of show people, chorus girls, prizefighters, restaurateurs, journalists, even politicians like Jimmy Walker. Walter knew this Broadway intimately. But there was another Broadway—the Broadway of speakeasies and gangsters and idle playboys hunting for good times—about which Walter was almost completely ignorant. He couldn't glad-hand his way through this Broadway. He needed guides.

Because Broadway was an open and tolerant community of exhibitionists, self-promoters and gossip-mongers, and because Winchell was clearly a young man on the rise who could provide publicity, guides readily presented themselves to him. The first was named Sime Silverman. Silverman, with his raspy voice, unmanageable chestnut hair and perpetual cigarette, was one of Broadway's most familiar figures; he was also among its most powerful. Born in upstate New York to an iconoclastic money broker, he had entered the family business as a bookkeeper, but the pull of show business proved irresistible. He eventually took jobs at two entertainment trade papers, then, with a $2,500 loan from his father-in-law, decided to start one of his own. *Variety* debuted on December 16, 1905, and stumbled through its infancy. The field was already crowded with more than a half dozen other trades, and Silverman's debts were enormous—sheriffs parked out in the office so often that everyone assumed they were employees—but *Variety* had a lively, irreverent appeal, not unlike Walter's, and within a year it was outselling *Billboard* and the New York *Clipper*, its two chief competitors.

At the time he met Walter, Silverman had been Broadway royalty for nearly twenty years, with a sense of noblesse oblige toward newcomers trying to make their way. Toward Winchell he assumed an attitude that Silverman's biographer called "almost paternal." He escorted Walter to nightspots, introduced him to celebrities, advised him on how and what to write, lent him money when he needed it, even gave him tips for the column. ("My best tipster" Walter called him.) When Walter asked Silverman why he gave away items that just as easily could have appeared in *Variety*, Silverman answered, "Walter, I give you tips to use so I can jack up my staff for being scooped."

It was Silverman, too, who introduced Walter to the woman who would become another of his mentors. Walter had reported that the bouncers at a nightclub owned by the racketeer Larry Fay subdued unruly customers by socking them with a fistful of quarters, and that one unlucky drunk had been knocked down a flight of stairs. Silverman called to tell Walter the story was false, and offered to take him to the club to get the real story from its hostess. Walter feared he might be beaten up, but the hostess, a loud, amply proportioned, overdressed, brassy blonde by the name of Texas Guinan, greeted him warmly and explained that the injured man was an obnoxious drunk who had been cursing and shoving other patrons. "A couple of the boys went to reason with him, to quiet him down," she continued. "Do you know what he did? He pulled a gun! So we *had* to go to work on him." Walter apologized. "From that time on, I was one of her best friends," Walter said, and he was soon stationing himself in her club each night from midnight to 6:00 a.m., the way he had at the NVA Club, while Texas schooled him in the ways of the rich, rambunctious Broadway she inhabited. He called her club his "fort."

No association could have proved more profitable for Walter in his first months at the *Graphic*. In those days Texas Guinan was the sun around which all of Broadway seemed to orbit. She had been born Mary Louise (Cecilia) Guinan on a ranch in Waco, Texas, in 1884, but a family friend dubbed her Texas, and the name stuck. A skilled horsewoman and an independent soul, she spent most of her adolescence traveling in Wild

West shows before trying the legitimate stage and then, at the invitation of cowboy star William S. Hart, the movies. Starring as a cowgirl in a series of two-reelers, she became widely known as the female Hart and won a following that included President Harding and the Prince of Wales. But she was an incurable romantic, and her Hollywood career ended when she followed her leading man back to New York, where she continued to bounce between vaudeville and the movies.

In 1922, during an engagement at New York's Winter Garden Theater, she was enjoying an after-theater repast at the Beaux Arts Café when someone suggested she sing. "I didn't need much coaxing, so I sang all I knew," she remembered. "First thing you know we were all doing things. Everybody had a great time." The café's owner was so impressed by the conviviality she inspired he promptly hired her as the greeter, and, dyeing her brown hair a bright yellow, she assumed a new career: hostess.

It was a year later as hostess at El Fey—owned by horse-faced Larry Fay—that Texas became the Queen of the Nightclubs. El Fey was less than splendid—just a narrow, crowded, smoke-filled room decorated sparely with colored hangings. The tables were tiny and crammed together. The dance floor scarcely accommodated a dozen people and even those kept colliding, though a jazz band blared away anyway. When the band wasn't playing, there was a roving quartet; asked once if this was sufficiently grand for her entrance, Texas said, "It depends how many quarts are in the quartet."

It wasn't the setting that made El Fey the hottest club in New York; it was the hostess. At forty, Texas was no longer conventionally beautiful. She was large, wore too much makeup and jangled with far too much jewelry. Edmund Wilson described her as a "prodigious woman, with her pearls, her glittering bosom, her abundant beautifully bleached yellow coiffure, her formidable rap of shining white teeth, her broad bare back behind its grating of green velvet, the full-blown peony as big as a cabbage exploding on her broad green thigh. . . ." But Texas "had something that made everyone feel instantly at ease and ready for a good time," remembered Sophie Tucker. That was her talent. The customers would pound their silverware on the tables, the trumpets would blast a flourish and out would come Texas braying, "Hello, sucker!" "There was something in that 'Hello, sucker!'" wrote veteran newspaperman Jack Lait, "which softened up a man and made him what she called him." Then she'd sing in her deep-throated voice:

> *Let's turn this into a whoopee place and have a lot*
> *of fun,*
> *And if we sing about you, why don't get up and run.*

*We'll sing about the Broadway folks, and anyone you
choose.
It'll save you then from buying the Graphic, Mirror
and the News.*

Technically, Texas's job was to serve as mistress of ceremonies for El
Fey's ribald floor show. "This little girl is new: give her a hand," Texas
commanded her patrons, coining a popular phrase for the national lexi-
con in the process. More accurately, she was a spirit—in host Nils T.
Grandlund's description, "the spirit of after-the-war, the spirit that says:
'Come on, fight it out. It may be life, it may be bitter, but laugh at it, you
old fool.' " This was certainly a source of her enormous appeal, and it was
something she imparted to Walter. But equally appealing, and no less a
part of Walter's repertoire, was a kind of cynical honesty she provided
that was attuned to the contemporary urban mood. "It was as if, elevated
to fame by a world suddenly gone cockeyed," one observer wrote, "she
had taken her fortune as a measure of the world's moral aberration."

IF TEXAS Guinan served as a maternal figure showing Walter the demi-
monde, and Sime Silverman as a paternal figure making him contacts and
teaching him a sort of sophistication, Mark Hellinger served as Walter's
fraternal guide, offering him companionship as Walter made his nightly
rounds. Hellinger had grown up on Park Avenue, the first child of a self-
important Orthodox Jewish Hungarian attorney who disdained other
Eastern European Jews and of a rich Polish mother whose family had
taken the improbable name of Rinaldo when one of her ancestors joined
the circus.

Despite this rather genteel upbringing, Hellinger was an insurgent who
seemed to design his life to antagonize his strict, conservative father.
Having been expelled from one school and flunked out of another, he began writing advertising copy, but he dreamed of becoming an actor or a
playwright or a reporter, anything that would put him in the thick of the
Broadway action. Through a friend of his mother's, he got a job at an entertainment trade paper called *Zit's Weekly* and promptly began inundat-
ing Phil Payne, the editor of the *Daily News*, with clippings until Payne
finally hired him as an entertainment reporter at $50 a week.

Hellinger looked as if he belonged on Broadway. He was painfully slim
and sharp-featured and so self-conscious about his looks that he had had
all his stained snaggleteeth pulled when he was eighteen and replaced
with a set of gleaming white dentures. Even as a young man—he was five
years younger than Walter—he exuded a weary confidence, his walk

stooped, his head cocked, his voice clipped. He spoke in slang, always tipped big and wore dark blue shirts and white crepe ties because he said the Broadway names never wore white. "His conscious effort," wrote his biographer, "was always to sound hard-boiled, disillusioned."

He met Winchell in the bathroom at the federal court building in Manhattan when both were covering a trial there—Walter gave him a bum tip—and they hit it off so well they became virtually inseparable. "If Hellinger comes, can Winchell be far behind?" Broadway denizens joked. "The gintellectuals," said Walter, "named us the Damon and Pythias of Broadway." Making the rounds together each night, they exchanged items, shared confidences, waited up together for the first editions of the *News* when Hellinger was given his own weekly column and swore that whichever of them died first, the survivor would devote an entire column to him.

There was spirited rivalry between them—Hellinger once got Walter drunk and left him in Central Park to beat him to a story—but never jealousy. When Percy Hammond, the hulking, pear-shaped drama critic of the New York *Herald-Tribune* known for his acidulous intelligence, praised Walter—"He is young, fearless, sophisticated, and he combines a pungent news-sense with good Broadway taste, endurance and a forthright style of prose expression"—Hellinger was the one who enthused for his friend. "I was happy. I was happier than if it had been written about me," Hellinger wrote Walter the morning of Hammond's tribute. "Hundreds, thousands, millions in the bank couldn't buy a thing like that. It was written by the greatest of them all. It is only an inkling of the praise and joy that are rushing your way at a hectic pace."

Hellinger was right. Winchell was becoming a novelty. His name and exploits were cropping up in other columns with greater and greater frequency. He initiated the idea for a contest to determine the "Mayor of Broadway," and S. Jay Kaufman promptly conducted a poll in his column. He wrote a song at Nedick's orange drink stand one night, then raced to LaHiff's to sing it to Damon Runyon and "the other illiterati of the Main Stem, who lauded the idea" and noted it in their columns. There were several accounts in the columns of how a gangster named Two-Gun Murphy escorted Walter to some of New York's roughest speakeasies, where the young columnist witnessed one act of violence after another, not realizing that the tour was a practical joke staged by his friends. Wrote one reporter after this flurry of activity: "If Walter Winchell ever gets a flat tire or loses his pencil what'll that fornograph [the *Graphic*] do?"

But, among general readers, Winchell was generating interest less because of his exploits than because of the way he was exploiting language in his column. The gradual migration of newspaper offices northward from Park Row to the Times Square area, the opening of the new Madison Square Garden nearby, and the proliferation in the quarter of speakeasies defying Prohibition had created in the twenties a new enclave around Broadway of journalists, gamblers, sportsmen and bootleggers, all joining the showpeople who were already there. Out of this enclave had emerged a distinctive patois that was a form of self-identification, and Walter, borrowing heavily from the show business shorthand in which he was so well versed, quickly became, as one speech professor later put it, "the dictator of contemporary slang."

On its face this might have seemed a relatively minor achievement, not a likely foundation for real popularity, were it not for the fact that language in the twenties was assuming a new and energizing role in the culture. Like so much else in the decade, slang was a form of cultural democracy; it was a way for the disenfranchised to reclaim their language from the genteel elites. Slang aerated English and in doing so created a new language, a kind of subversive tongue that was especially attractive to young urban Americans. To know which words were in vogue, to know what "scram" meant and "palooka" and "belly laughs" and "lotta baloney" and "pushover," was like being part of a secret society—one from which the arbiters of good taste were obviously excluded. For these readers, then, language wasn't just a means of expression; it was a nose-thumbing, a fashion, an entertainment, a way of showing one was in the know when being in the know was an important differentiation.

Walter often said that he had adopted slang as protection against his own deficiencies in grammar; with slang he felt he could say anything without feeling inadequate. But slang was obviously more than a defense mechanism for him. It was practically keyed to his metabolism. Since vaudeville, it was the way he chose to talk, the way he was most expressive. "I'm an alleged representative of Broadway," Walter told *Editor & Publisher*, "and the mob I mix with express themselves in the argot of the 'Canyon.' That's the language I savvy better than any other," adding that "most four syllable words are over my head." What he didn't say is that slang put *him* ahead of the curve. Slang gave him importance.

Recognizing its appeal, he worked as painstakingly as a lexicographer, collecting new phrases and coining his own, until what had begun as a column subheading, "Slanguage," soon permeated every paragraph of his column. People began to read Winchell for his new coinages the way fans read the sports section for the latest scores. In Winchell, Broadway was the "Main Stem," "Coffee Pot Canyon," "The Incandescent Belt," "Mazda Lane." Speakeasies were "sotto voce parlors" or "hush houses," and liquor was "giggle-water." A mistress was a "keptive." Newspapermen on Park Row were "Park Rowgues." An oriental dancer was a "torso tosser," a "hip flipper" or a "thigh grinder." Every day brought newly minted words, and the words themselves became an objective correlative for the syncopated rhythm of the twenties. "My idea is to play you as the coming poet of Broadway," one editor wrote him while asking Walter to slip him some pieces. It was an astonishing idea.

IV

Walter's editor may have been right that "No paper but Macfadden's tabloid could have nursed such a prodigy," if only because no respectable paper would have hired him in the first place. Even among tabloids, the *Graphic* was legendarily unrespectable.* Though it had long since given up on its idea to convert all the news into first-person accounts—the editor had even tried to get President Coolidge to write one—it had become, if anything, more outrageous as time went on. Scantily clad women were a staple; the only instruction one *Graphic* editor received upon his hiring was that "The boss wanted sex on every front page, big gobs of it. On the inside pages he expected it to be spread out like butter over canapés." Next to sex, Macfadden loved contests best, and the *Graphic* ran dozens of them, sometimes several simultaneously: crossword puzzle contests, joke contests, a contest to pick yourself out of a crowd photo, a contest for the best letter on "why I grew a beard," and an Apollo-Diana contest which offered a reward to selected men and women of athletic physiques who married each other and had children.

The paper's lonely hearts column evolved into a Lonely Hearts Club which sent dozens of the lovelorn streaming into the office and hectoring any employee who would listen to their plaints. (They joined dozens of health faddists who also made pilgrimages to the office, one of them ripping a telephone book in two, another hanging from a pipe by his hair.) To demonstrate to advertisers how popular the hearts column was, Macfadden arranged Lonely Hearts Balls and attracted so large a crowd at Madison Square Garden that loudspeakers had to be rigged outside to accommodate the overflow. The column and the balls were discontinued when one "member" wound up murdering another, but the demand was so great that the column was reinstated, only to be killed again when

---

*In 1927 the New York Society for the Suppression of Vice attempted to close down the *Graphic* on the grounds that it was a violation of the penal code to publish and distribute a newspaper made up "principally of criminal news, police reports of criminal deeds, or stories of deeds of bloodshed, lust and crime." In dismissing the charges, Judge Martin J. Healey admitted that some might find the paper "disgusting" and "not what we believe should be printed. . . ."

an unsophisticated editor innocently listed men looking for other men.

The *Graphic's* major investigative crusade was to prove that the Miss America contest was rigged. When Broadway producer Earl Carroll, one of those allegedly implicated in the scheme, called to demand a retraction on threat of a half-million-dollar lawsuit, the editor screamed, "Piker!" and told Carroll he couldn't make the front page of the paper with any suit less than $1 million. The paper was sued by another aggrieved party after it had successfully campaigned to save two accused murderers named Greco and Carillo from the death penalty. Having no photo of the men, editors used a picture of actor Leo Carrillo instead.

The *Graphic's* most notorious contribution to journalism, aside from Walter himself, was the "composograph." Composographs were essentially composite photos. Pictures of actual individuals were spliced with those of models, or the faces of actual individuals were put on models' bodies, with the result that the *Graphic* could provide a photograph of virtually any event, whether a photographer was present or not. The first of these was a composograph of the Kip Rhinelander trial at which wealthy playboy Rhinelander was seeking an annulment of his marriage to Alice Jones on the ground that Jones hadn't told him she was a Negress. Jones had been ordered to bare herself in court to show her skin color. The *Graphic* found a model to reenact the scene, and the composograph was born.

"Newspapers have not yet recovered from the old *Graphic* days," a former *Graphic* editor wrote in the mid-thirties, taking account of the ways in which the paper debased journalism. But in fact the *Graphic*, including Walter, was part of a journalistic upheaval so profound that it amounted to a revolution from which newspapers never recovered: the tabloid revolution.

The first modern American tabloid, the *Illustrated Daily News*, debuted in New York on June 26, 1919, the inspiration of Chicago *Tribune* publisher Joseph Medill Patterson, who had been introduced to tabloids in England during the war. The *Daily News* was distinguished chiefly by its size, half as big as a full paper, and by its heavy reliance on photographs, but a rival editor fingered the real difference between it and New York's seventeen other daily English-language newspapers: it operated "on the psychological principle that, no matter what his background or education, a man is governed by his emotions."

Like the old yellow press of the 1890s, which had since grown nearly as gray and respectable as its more traditional confreres, the *Daily News* employed a formula of screaming headlines, lurid tales and plentiful illustrations to build a huge following. Within a year and a half it was showing a profit; within four, at the time Walter went to work at the *Graphic*, it had the largest circulation of any paper in the country at 750,000 readers. A year later the number had risen to just under 1 million. (The *Graphic*, by comparison, had a circulation of roughly 250,000, though it carried less advertising than the *Post*, which had only 35,000 readers.) By then the *Daily News* had been joined by William Randolph Hearst's *Daily Mirror*, launched in June 1924 with the promise to be "90 per cent entertainment, 10 per cent information," and by Macfadden's *Graphic*, which debuted that fall—an assault of tabloids on more delicate journalistic sensibilities.

"Why do most journalists dislike the N.Y. tabloids?" Walter asked in his column, and then gave the answer. "Because they have 1,600,000 circulation in Greater N.Y." It was true, much to the distress of more sober journalistic observers, that the tabloids had rapidly attracted nearly 40 percent of the readership of New York's papers. The only consolation one could find in this situation was that while the population in the metropolitan area increased by 128,000 in the first half of the decade, newspaper circulation rose by almost exactly the total circulation of the tabloids, allowing fretful critics to announce that at least the tabloids hadn't drawn readers from real newspapers, hadn't in fact drawn real readers at all.

But this was small comfort to the journalistic establishment. While a tiny minority of observers believed the tabloids had actually provided a necessary tonic for an enervated journalism and while others praised them for being "of the people instead of trying to be above the people," the vast majority of journalists deplored them. Their readers were "semi-literate," carped one. "[O]nly a sharp lowering of the IQ of a newspaper was necessary to make it attractive to a hitherto unexploited portion of the great metropolitan rank and file," sniped another. "It is difficult to believe that one half of the population of the world's greatest metropolis is one hundred per cent moron," wrote a third, but that was the only conclusion he could draw from the popularity of tabloids.

Many critics cast their opposition in moral terms. The tabloids struck at the very fiber of the American soul, contributing to widespread degeneracy, they said. They filled impressionable heads with drivel. They degraded the "taste of their readers and set up wholly fictitious standards." E. E. Cummings, writing in *Vanity Fair*, blamed them for a current of infantilism in American life, and journalist Aben Kandel warned, "If this appetite is not curbed, a tabloid a day will soon be a national drug habit."

At least one defender believed that the uproar over the menace of the tabloids was really just the old conservative order yowling once again over something beyond its control. "It is a skirmish in the war traditionalism is waging to block liberalization of education, music, art, dress, literature," he wrote. "It is the protest of the static against the movie; the drab expressing distaste at the dramatic; the ghostly dead moaning at the ways of the quick." This may have been true in the larger culture. But to the journalistic establishment, the antagonism had a special edge. For it, the tabloids threatened the fundamental tenets of respectable journalism and all the things these tenets symbolized: objectivity, order, reason. They threatened the practice of journalism itself.

Even, or especially, their publishers realized that the function of the tabloids wasn't to dispense news, provide information or allow readers to comprehend their world, which had been among the traditional functions and obligations of the newspaper. The tabloid really wasn't a *news*paper at all, but rather an entertainment medium, and as such it had far more in common with the motion pictures than with journalism. Like the movies, the tabloids were primarily visual; no less an authority than William Randolph Hearst declared, "The success of the tabloid is largely PIC-TURES." One didn't read a tabloid, one watched it, and the images, as one analyst noted, soon became as familiar and iconographic as anything on the screen: "Shaggy Einstein was the symbol of intellectuality; fierce-featured Toscanini was the artistic temperament personified; Hemingway was the artist as adventurer; Gertrude Stein the artist as incomprehensible."

But perhaps an even greater affinity between the tabloids and the movies than the visual one, and an even greater threat to the old journalistic order, was the narrative one. Tabloids told stories. Day after day they presented their readers with serials—real-life soap operas complete with stars, melodrama, lurid details and cliffhangers. The juicier the plot elements, the bigger the story, in a reversal of the revered idea, seldom breached since the decline of the yellow press, that events dictated the news, the newspaper didn't dictate events. "There was a time when a reader of an unexciting newspaper would remark, 'How dull is the world today!' " historian Daniel Boorstin succinctly summarized the change four decades later. "Nowadays he says, 'What a dull newspaper!' " That was the legacy and to most journalists the danger of the tabloids.

Anyone reading the tabloids then would have found the twenties an endless stream of mayhem and debauchery, obviously because these sorts of things provided the most vivid story elements, the best entertainment. Especially lurid murder trials, like the Hall-Mills trial in New Jersey, in which an heiress was tried after the bodies of her minister husband and his choir singer mistress were found on a deserted lover's lane, or the Snyder-Gray trial, in which a corset salesman and a suburban housewife were tried for bludgeoning her husband to death with a sashweight, became the tabloid equivalents of motion-picture blockbusters.

For comic relief there was the long-running saga of an eccentric real estate speculator named Edward West Browning. Browning first came to the tabloids' attention when his wife ran off to France with her dentist, and the lonely fifty-one-year-old millionaire placed a newspaper ad for a young girl to adopt. The winner out of twelve thousand applications was Mary Louise Spas, the sixteen-year-old daughter of Bohemian immigrants living in Queens. Soon, however, the tabloids were reporting that Mary was older than sixteen and not as demure as she let on. The next day the headline in the *Daily News* proclaimed: I WANT TO GO HOME. The day after that, back in her parents' house, Mary allegedly drank a bottle of iodine in a suicide attempt, though "Daddy" Browning, as he was now called, believed it was faked. The same day Browning dropped his claim to be her legal father when it turned out Mary was actually twenty-one. All this in only five days.

Once the tabloids had developed a character, there were usually sequels. In Browning's case the sequel concerned a teenager named Frances Heenan whom Browning married after meeting her at a high school sorority dance he had organized. Meanwhile, the *Graphic* contracted with Miss Heenan, now known as Peaches, to give a running account of her new life with Daddy Browning. Far from objecting, Browning seemed to enjoy the publicity. To keep up the momentum, the *Graphic* convinced him to buy a gander, a rare African honking gander, it assured him, which, to the delight of photographers, he now carried with him wherever he went. When Peaches, pleading a nervous breakdown, returned to her mother and filed for a separation, the *Graphic* paid her another thousand dollars for the story. "Honk Honk. It's the Bonk" was the caption of one composograph of Peaches, Daddy and the goose in their bedroom, presumptively about to engage in the strange sexual practices that Peaches divulged. She eventually wound up in vaudeville—a celebrity created by the tabloids.

To the tabloids' antagonists, it was these daily melodramas that made the papers a potpourri of idiocy and degeneracy. "Distort the world, until its news is all murder, divorce, crime, passion and chicanery," reproached one critic describing the tabloids.

To the poor struggling upward present the paces above as tenanted by witless millionaires and shallow adventuresses, contemptible yet glorious in their spending. Sentimentalize everything, with cynicism just beneath. In place of the full life, or the good life, or the hard life of experience, fill the mind with a phantasmagoria where easy wealth, sordid luxury, scandal, degeneracy, and drunken folly swirl through the pages in an intoxicating vulgarity.

But taken altogether in just this way—not simply the headlines and the featured melodramas—the various elements of the tabloids, including

Walter Winchell, provided something more than mindless entertainment for their readers. They purveyed a cosmology, an attitude toward the world which was every bit as rich as the cosmology of the traditional press. In place of cool reason, heated passion. In place of the primacy of world and national events that presumably determined the readers' own destinies, trivial and salacious events, a "drama of life" as one called it, that reflected a world gone mad. In place of faith in the objective and verifiable, the subjective and provisional that ceded no higher truth. (Mystery was always a major component of the tabloid: Who did it?) In place of facts marching in neat ranks down the page and conveying the essential orderliness of things, a jumble of words and images conveying the essential disorderliness. This was the tabloids' message: chaos.

And their readers, however much they were demeaned as morons, almost certainly knew it. Largely working-class and, by one estimate as much as one-third women, the tabloid readership self-consciously embraced this view as its own alternative truth set against the truth of the wealthier and more powerful custodians of the social order represented by the conservative press. "To be seen reading *The New York Times* is a stamp of respectability," that paper had once advertised. But to be seen reading the *Graphic* or the *Mirror* or the *Daily News* was a stamp of disreputability, and the readers, like the papers themselves, bore it proudly as an assertion of their own power.

All this made the tabloids a battlefield in the twenties' ongoing cultural war. And because Walter Winchell was not only in the tabloids but of them, he was inevitably drawn into the conflict. But not yet. Not until gossip.

WINCHELL NO more invented gossip than he invented slang. The old "penny press" of the early nineteenth century had carried news of family strife and scandal, and in the 1880s a New York patent attorney named Louis Keller launched *Town Topics*, largely to establish a pecking order in high society now that the Gilded Age had added nouveau riche industrialists to the aristocratic Old Guard, but also to document their behavior—the bawdier the better. "When someone tells us a long story about mice in China, culled from the Encyclopedia Britannica, we are bored," a *Topics* ad later admitted. "When we hear of Mrs. Brown's latest indiscretion we are thrilled."

In the early twenties a wily operator named Stephen Clow hit upon the brilliant notion that since gossip was most often derogatory, individuals might pay him not to be gossiped about. Clow's *Broadway Brevities and Social Gossip* had a circulation of only four thousand, but the editor wound up coercing such financial stalwarts as banker Otto Kahn, railroad magnate W. Averell Harriman and yeast king Julius Fleischmann into giving him money or taking out ads in return for his not printing their names and foibles. It worked until one enraged victim lodged a criminal complaint, and Clow and three of his associates were brought to trial for using the mails in furtherance of a criminal scheme.* "I know of few things meaner than to threaten publicly to blast the lives of private individuals by the publication of their social or moral errors," pronounced the judge in sentencing the publisher to six years in prison and a $6,000 fine.

Where Clow had led, the general press was obviously loath to follow. Society columns, often called gossip, were really less gossip than reports of who had attended which party and what they wore. Anything more would have been regarded as unseemly by the traditional press. But even if the press hadn't been restrained by its own sense of decorum, the law hovered menacingly. In 1890 then Harvard law professor and later Supreme Court Justice Louis Brandeis had written a highly influential article in the *Harvard Law Review* decrying gossip and arguing for a legally enforceable right to privacy. As the courts continued to grope their way through the issue—and they continued to grope for decades—even the tabloids trod lightly where rumor and innuendo were concerned, obviously fearing legal action. The rule of thumb, as enunciated by the *Daily News'* Joseph Medill Patterson, was "no private scandal or private love affairs" unless they came to trial in a divorce action, thus becoming part of the public record.

Yet the media themselves were exerting an almost inexorable pressure toward gossip by engendering a fascination with personalities. In the movies, magazines and the tabloids, personalities were sales devices; once the public became aware of these personalities, its curiosity was insatiable. With the interest in place, all that was needed to cross the line to gossip was someone with the audacity and nerve to begin writing frankly about the various private doings of the celebrated—someone who would defy the taboo. That was where Winchell came in.

Less than three weeks after he started his column, Walter had in fact begun running a few mild items that might have qualified as gossip, if just barely: "Edna Wheaton and Bert Gordon were married last week," "The Ray Hodgsons had another baby day before yesterday," "And don't say that I told you, but Amy Frank of 'Vanities' is stuck on Charlie Morrison." The idea for a more daring gossip column, he sometimes said, came from Texas Guinan. An inveterate gossip herself—Damon

---

*Charges of blackmail or extortion were not brought because that would have required the victims to testify about the specific nature of the rumors. For the charge of mail fraud, witnesses needed only to identify letters sent to them by Clow and his associates.

Runyon described her alter ego, Missouri Martin, as a woman who "tells everything she knows as soon as she knows it, which is very often before it happens"—Texas sat with Walter nightly, drinking coffee, chain-smoking and providing him with a running commentary on her customers' activities. One night she mentioned that Mrs. Vanderbilt was going to have twins. Walter admitted he hadn't the slightest idea who Mrs. Vanderbilt was. "Why don't you make a note of it for the column, you fool!" Texas razzed him. He did, and Mrs. Vanderbilt had her twins two weeks later.

Walter also gave another version of how his gossip column was born. In this account, he had gotten a tip that Imogene Wilson and Frank Tinney, two popular vaudeville headliners with a long and tangled romantic history, were going to reconcile, and he brought it to his editor to have it vetted for publication. The editor refused, saying that Walter had no verification. A week later the item appeared in another paper and Walter was furious. Meanwhile, Walter received two more items—one on the notoriously bibulous John Barrymore taking the pledge not to drink, then winding up drunk the very next night, and another on Irving Berlin's elopement with heiress Ellin Mackay—but his editor still insisted Walter verify the stories before they could be published. "If you got a tip over the phone from some half-witted schoolboy, you'd rush ten reporters out on motorcycles," Walter fumed.

"I was giving them hot news, and the dumb bastards were throwing them on the floor," Walter said years later. But he kept collecting the items nonetheless, scribbling them on little scraps of paper which he stuffed into his pockets, until, stuck one day for a column, he gathered the items, sneaked them past his editor and ran them with an apology for his breach of taste. "This news feat," the veteran editor Stanley Walker wrote half-jokingly, "marked one of the greatest advances in journalism since the first transatlantic cable."

Headed "Mainly About Mainstreeters," the new column stunned everyone. "People could scarcely believe what they saw in print," remembered one Broadwayite. "All the old secrets of personal sex relations—who was sleeping with whom—were exposed to the public gaze. Only *Broadway Brevities* and *Town Topics* had been purveying that sort of information up to then. If Winchell were to keep on talking this frankly, no one would be safe. A fellow wouldn't be able to escort a girl across the street without having everyone think that . . . The buzz of comment and criticism and alarm spread from Broadway to Park Avenue."

Since it appeared on Monday, readers took to calling it simply "the Monday column," as distinguished from his columns of anecdotes, gags and slanguage that ran the other days of the week. And it was soon typographically distinguishable from those columns too. "Mainly About Mainstreeters" began with the gossip arrayed in large blocks. On June 6, 1927, the Monday column's name was changed to "This Town of Ours," signifying that Walter was expanding his scope beyond Broadway, and its format was changed so that items were now separated by ellipses, or "three dots," as Walter preferred to call them. Graphically the dots gave the column a jazzy, almost musical look; items now seemed to cascade down the page, each with its own urgency. (Ben Hecht said he wrote "like a man honking in a traffic jam.") At the same time Walter modified his prose, paring each item to its bare essentials—occasionally to not much more than subject and predicate. The effect was that of a high-velocity montage of snapshots, a fragmentary new journalistic form that mirrored the modernistic experiments in high literature then being conducted by Gertrude Stein, Hemingway, Céline and others.

As for the danger of libel actions that had deterred everyone else from gossip, Walter finessed the problem by using deliberately cryptic slang. To say a man was "that way" about a woman gave a reader a clear impression of the situation but left Walter with other defensible interpretations. Similarly, "blessed event," "on the merge" or "on the verge," "sealed," "this-and-that-way," "uh-huh," "curdled," "Adam-and-Eveing it" and "on fire"—all of which Walter coined—conveyed and obfuscated at the same time.

As to what had motivated him to begin writing gossip, the most Walter ever said was that he saw it as a way of avenging himself on his editor. But the real explanation may have simply been that Walter loved gossip— loved hearing it, loved writing it, loved printing it, loved getting reactions to it, loved the attention it elicited, loved the way it seemed to turn him into an incorrigible rascal, loved the sense of omniscience it bestowed. "Winchell reacted almost physically to gossip," his ghostwriter Herman Klurfeld would write, "and seemed to purr with delight when he had a particularly juicy item. . . . He was as fascinated and unself-conscious as a four-year-old gravely making mudpies." His ethics, he proudly boasted, never permitted him to reveal a source and required him to exert "every effort not to involve a married man or woman with another person. Our record is pretty good." With those exceptions, virtually everything else was permissible.

Not surprisingly, the journalistic Old Guard was enraged by the affront to privacy, but the avidity with which the Monday column was devoured by readers left no doubt that Walter had tapped into the American psyche, into something beyond voyeurism, even if it would always be difficult to define precisely what it was he had struck. Part of it was the general interest in anything that had to do with the new class of celebrities. Part of it may have been attributable to urbanization. Sociologist Louis Wirth had distinguished between the concept of *community*, where individuals knew one another and were bound by ties of kinship and neighborhood, and the concept of *society*, where secondary relationships increasingly supplanted primary ones. As the twenties transformed America from a community into a society, gossip seemed to provide one of the lost ingredients of the former for the latter: a common frame of reference. In gossip everyone was treated as a known quantity; otherwise the gossip was meaningless. In gossip one could create a national "backyard fence" over which all Americans could chat.

Like slang, gossip also made one feel knowing, ahead of the curve. And like the tabloids in which it first appeared, it could be a means of wreaking vengeance in a country that prided itself on its social mobility and provided very few outlets for class antagonism. It could serve, said one approving editorial more than six decades later, "as justice in a corrupt world." The rich, the powerful, the famous and the privileged had always governed their own images. Now Winchell, with one act of defiance, had taken control and empowered his readers. No one was safe from the Monday column. It was the ultimate revenge for the humiliation he felt he had suffered.

V

The somber-faced *Graphic* editor who kept thwarting Walter was named Emile Gauvreau, and "from the very beginning[,] September 15, 1924," Walter was to say, "Gauvreau was opposed to me." "I think Gauvreau was jealous of him and wanted to keep him way in the back of the tabloid so he would not become highly visible or popular," public relations man Edward Bernays said. Several times Bernays suggested that Walter's column, easily the tabloid's most popular department, be moved nearer the front of the paper, but Gauvreau kept vetoing the idea. Bernays believed that Gauvreau knew he "would be overshadowed if Winchell became famous and popular."

While it certainly seemed true that Gauvreau was envious of the attention his young columnist was getting, his intense, almost pathological hatred of Winchell seemed to have much deeper roots. This cheerless, cynical and bitter man had had a childhood in New Haven, Connecticut, that had been, if anything, worse than Walter's in Harlem. When Gauvreau was five years old, his father, a French-Canadian who liked to reminisce about his role in putting down a separatist rebellion, angered a group of drunks, who retaliated by dragging a cannon to the Gauvreau home and firing. Little Emile was so severely injured by the blast that he spent a year in a wheelchair and walked with a pronounced limp thereafter. At school his classmates taunted him as a "freak" and goaded him into wrestling another student, a hunchback whose hump prevented him from being pinned. His tormentors, Gauvreau remembered, "burst into a savage jeering, a depraved howl of laughter, whose hardness of heart I couldn't believe was possible among human beings."

He began his newspaper career at the age of fourteen, when he got a job at the New Haven *Journal-Courier* because his family desperately needed the money. During the war he moved to the more highly regarded Hartford *Courant*, a rock-ribbed Republican newspaper whose editor inculcated in Gauvreau a hatred of the yellow press and its practices. Eventually Gauvreau became managing editor of the paper, but when he began a campaign to expose Connecticut doctors who had received their degrees from a diploma mill, he was fired. The same day, February 3, 1924, his infant son died of pneumonia.

Job-hunting in New York the next month, he happened to board at a hotel across the street from the Macfadden offices and decided to introduce himself. He was taken immediately to see Fulton Oursler, then already planning the *Graphic*. Oursler took him to see Macfadden. With his abhorrence of doctors, Macfadden was impressed by Gauvreau's campaign at the *Courant* and asked him to join the *Truth*, as the paper was then being called.

The *Graphic* soon revealed an intractable division within Gauvreau: One side of him wanted to sin, and the other needed to pay penance. On the one hand, Gauvreau was a stern moralist who was forever upbraiding transgressors, especially Walter, and talking ruefully of the painful compromises he had had to make in editing the *Graphic*. "I was part of that strange race of people," he would say, "aptly described as spending their lives doing things they detest to make money they don't want to buy things they don't need to impress people they don't like."

On the other hand, Oursler, who harbored the same reservations about the paper as Gauvreau, accused him of being among the *Graphic*'s worst offenders. The editors, Oursler wrote, "behaved like the sons of clergymen suddenly on their own in the midst of the world. That blunder of mine [hiring Gauvreau], more than anything else, made the *Graphic* the crazy thing it was, a daily nuisance of vigor and bad taste. . . ." Gauvreau's own wife thought the *Graphic* was her husband's "rebellion against hypocrisy, strait-laced New England puritanism. It was a kicking over of the traces." But a staff man strongly disagreed with this assessment— "Gauvreau's heart was involved with the paper"—and Gauvreau himself quoted favorably an analysis that George Sylvester Viereck, a poet and one of the paper's advisers, had made of him. "You are pouring out all your passion, tenderness, all you have to give, all your love, vitality and libido into jazz journalism to escape from the realities of life. This enables you to give vent to all these base instincts—lust and savagery and crime—which dwell like Apaches in the subcellars of your mind, without assuming responsibility for your escapades."

A large portion of his guilt Gauvreau displaced onto Winchell. Very early on, Walter became a symbol of Gauvreau's own compromises, of the bargain he had struck with the tabloid world and with his own less admirable impulses. That may be the only explanation for Gauvreau's obsessional hatred of the columnist. Walter was as much a part of his thoughts, he admitted, "as though he had been a design woven into the editor's mind." Gauvreau even went on to write a novel about him, *The Scandal Monger*, in which he portrayed Walter as a poverty-stricken dynamo who "bludgeoned his way out front," and a ruthless self-promoter with "an utter lack of a sense of ethics."

Yet at the same time that Gauvreau was heaping on Walter all the sins of tabloids as well as all of his own, he was living through him. Gauvreau was a power-fetishist. His office had paintings, books, even a bust of Napoleon, and Gauvreau, short and dark with a deep cleft in his chin, often had a forelock of hair strategically curled on his forehead as his hero had. It was said he paced his office like Napoleon and struck Napoleonic poses, his hand stuck in his jacket. There were those who said he actually believed he was Napoleon's avatar.

But if he was Napoleon, his army was Walter Winchell. Loathing Walter, he nevertheless always took credit for having created him, and in his novels at any rate boasted through his alter egos that he would use the popular gossip columnist as the instrument of his own triumph: "crowning himself king of Broadway, Monarch of the Main Stem, with all the sycophants kneeling at his feet in homage." "He'll smell out the rats in their vile holes, so I can dangle them in the faces of my greedy public," snarls the French-Canadian editor William Gaston in *The Scandal Monger*, speaking of his gossip columnist. "A swell business, my fine bastard, and you, Gaston, are its most artful practitioner."

Only in his fantasies, however, would Gauvreau ride Walter to power. In real life he was one of fortune's losers, which could only have exacerbated his resentment of a comer like Walter. Gauvreau had fallen in love with an ambitious young opera singer and had maneuvered her into the Metropolitan Opera, only to find himself cuckolded as soon as he left the love nest for which he was paying. "I was the only one on the paper who didn't know," he grieved, telling the story over and over again for years like the Ancient Mariner. Another time, during his row with Earl Carroll over the Miss America contest, his enemies placed him in a compromising situation with a young woman in a negligee and only his political connections saved him from an embarrassing trial.

But even if Gauvreau hadn't been as feckless as he was, his dreams of power through Walter would have been chimerical. Walter detested Gauvreau every bit as much as Gauvreau detested him. He harped cruelly on his deformity, calling him a "cripple," and mused on whether it was Gauvreau's "defect" that "accounts for their [the managing editors'] extreme bitterness on and off the paper." By some accounts he once heaved Gauvreau down the stairs, though Walter claimed the feud had gone on as long as it had only because "it is dangerous in New York to strike an antagonist who wears spectacles or who is otherwise handicapped." Gauvreau once even hinted, without actually naming him, that Walter had asked gangland contacts to murder the editor.

Still, it was much more a matter of seething tensions between the two than outright warfare—until the Shubert affair. Jacob and Lee Shubert were two of the most powerful and tyrannical Broadway producers and theater owners in New York. For years they had wreaked vengeance on drama critics who dared disparage their shows, and in 1915 they had even won an injunction barring Alexander Woollcott from their theaters after he had called a farce of theirs "not terribly amusing." They were especially offended by the *Graphic*'s policy of inviting guest critics, ordinary theatergoers, to accompany Walter and review their shows. "As I do not approve of this system of criticism, nor do I want it," the Shuberts' general manager, C. P. Grenaker, informed the paper, "I must decline to give you additional seats for our openings."

Had the Shuberts only left well enough alone, Walter might not have become the *Graphic*'s only critical voice, but they hadn't, and he did. He brought to the task the same irreverence he brought to the column and a dogged populism that, editorialized the *Graphic*, did more "to show up the bunk of theatrical criticism than any drama reporter in a decade." When taunted by another critic with the remark, "Only those who have been written about sarcastically know the sorrow it causes," he retorted with the story of the columnist who "never prepared a roast, rap or disparaging comment on any one or anything, and was suddenly replaced by writers who do."

Walter conceded he wasn't a very good critic no matter how high he ranked on *Variety*'s box score correlating reviews with box-office success or failure. When fellow critic John Mason Brown solicited Walter for some pieces of criticism for an anthology, Walter wrote back, "I really don't think any of my regular reviews are any good at all," and sent on only one, his deadpan demolition of a lavish Ziegfeld musical called "Smiles":

The greatest and most marvelous and grandest and stupendous and most thrilling and most colossal and most wonderful show that ever had been produced in the whole, wide world is "Smiles." . . .

What a show! The great book by William Anthony McGuire was so funny throughout the entire proceedings that bluebloods, and even the anemic, fell right into the aisles laughing and laughing and laughing.

As for star Marilyn Miller, her dancing "so excited the auditors she stopped the show 18 times. Perhaps it was 19 times, we lost count, so thrilled were we at it all." The scenic design, particularly a Chinese set, was "too much for one pair of eyes," and the girls "are more beautiful than any Mr. Ziegfeld has collected; he sure is a wonder."

He had run afoul of the Shuberts at first not because he was lambasting their shows but because they felt he was ridiculing them personally. Both prideful men, they demanded to be referred to as the "Messrs. Shubert," not "Jake and Lee," as Walter had taken to doing. "One is named Lee and the other Jacob," instructed General Manager Grenaker in a huffy note, to which Walter replied, "All I ask is to let me write my column and give me a pass now and then. I will give your firm publicity in return. I get no advertising AT ALL so let me clown when I'm in the mood."

The Shuberts were not amused. By March 1926 they had pulled their advertising from the *Graphic*. Walter called Lee Shubert daily until Shubert finally promised to place "all special announcements on Shubert productions such as opening ads, closing ads, big copy, etc.," but he had not delivered and Grenaker was giving Walter the "runaround." When Walter wrote that singer Al Jolson, then performing in a Shubert production, was "complaining of his pipes already," Grenaker fired off a telegram once again warning that the *Graphic* would not get Shubert advertising unless Walter behaved. "Am I to write what I think or call his bluff?" Walter wrote Macfadden. "I want your backing and if you take my only weapon away from me, I'll be helpless."

Macfadden agreed with Walter that "we should not allow them to bulldoze us," and advised that Gauvreau and Walter come to some accommodation with the Shuberts. An uneasy stalemate continued, though Walter would always assert that Gauvreau was maneuvering behind his back to use the situation as a pretext to get him fired. Even so, he kept up a steady barrage of jokes about the Shuberts and criticisms of their plays. "I made the terrible mistake," he quipped, obviously unbowed, "of panning fifty-four of their [the Shuberts'] shows, when it appears they produced only fifty-two of them."

The showdown came on January 11, 1928. Walter received a telephone call notifying him that the "Shuberts feel you are unfriendly to them and their interests," and banning him from all thirty of their theaters—clearly an impediment for a drama critic. The *Graphic*, apparently at Macfadden's instruction, leaped to Walter's defense with a full-page editorial warning the Shuberts that "this paper is staffed by nothing but Winchells!" and advising the producers to "read Mr. Winchell's remarks and to profit thereby. . . ." Meanwhile, other theaters began following the Shuberts' lead, even posting detectives at the door to keep him out. "Walter very likely will soon find himself a critic always dressed up with no plays to go," one newspaper punned.

Walter enjoyed the controversy. Barred from *The Buzzard* at the Broadhurst, he said he slipped around to the stage entrance posing as a reporter from the Bronx *Gazette* and watched from the wings. "Fun, no end!" he exclaimed in his column. As for the Shuberts, Walter now intensified his little attacks. "You get weary being barred from the Shubert theatres. You miss the splendid exercise you got walking out on their shows." Or "A certain critic has been barred from all Shubert openings but he isn't worried. He will wait three nights and go to their closings."

While Walter sniped, Gauvreau was trying to arrange a truce that would "placate them, keep you happy, and secure their advertising." He suggested that they simply assign another critic to review the Shuberts' shows. "I am trying very hard to save you from embarrassment so that you will have the proper spirit to keep up your very fine column," he wrote Walter in conciliation. Grenaker was adamant: no Winchell. Winchell was equally adamant: no other reviewer. Oursler backed him, but Walter thought Gauvreau was still too eager to capitulate.

In the meantime, the feud was becoming a cause célèbre. "Everybody in town is talking over the nocturnal tables of Walter Winchell's feud with the Shubert boys," one paper noted. Mutual friends—among them Mayor Jimmy Walker and New York *World* editor Herbert Bayard Swope—were now lobbying the Shuberts to desist. "You are making a mistake," they cautioned, "he is unknown, except around Texas Guinan's. But the hullaballoo over the ban will make him appear more important than he is!" Walter wasn't really unknown by this time—he was already the author of the Monday column and master of slanguage—but he was to say that the Shubert contretemps "taught me that the way to become famous fast is to throw a brick at someone who is famous."

That November, after ten months of squabbling, Walter sued for peace, offering to stop his personal digs at the Shuberts if they dropped their ban. The Shuberts countered by demanding that he promise not to pan their shows. "I won't crawl," Walter told them, and took up arms again. The Marx Brothers were opening in a new show named *Animal Crackers* which included a character modeled on Walter—Wally Winston of the *Evening Traffic*. Walter had publicly vowed to see it on opening night. The Shuberts assigned nine press agents and two detectives to patrol the doors and make sure he didn't.

Opening night Harpo Marx stuck a beard on Walter with mucilage and shoved a Hotel Algonquin towel up his back to make a hump. (Walter remembered passersby pointing at him and roaring with laughter as he sat in a cab.) The "hunchback" easily slipped past the lookouts and into the Marxes' dressing room, where he was now made up to look like Harpo. Standing in the wings undetected, he watched the entire show and wrote a review, though Gauvreau wouldn't run it.

It wasn't until four years later, when Al Jolson refused to appear on the opening night of his new show *Wunderbar* unless Walter was permitted to sit in his regular spot, that the ban was lifted. Then Walter, incorrigible to the end, panned the show, and the ban was immediately reinstated. But by that time he was bigger than the Shuberts. By that time he was bigger than almost anyone.

VI

Writing a Broadway column, Winchell became synonymous with Broadway in the twenties. He was called the "Boswell of Broadway" or its Samuel Pepys, the "North Star of Broadway" (in Percy Hammond's tribute), the "Mayor of Broadway," the "Bard of Broadway." He seemed to own Broadway. Alma Sioux Scarberry, a *Graphic* reporter, remembered dancing with actor Tommy Meighan at a Metro-Goldwyn-Mayer ball on Broadway when Walter interrupted to ask what she was doing there. "Covering," she said. Walter snapped, "You can't. Don't cover anything on Broadway. Broadway is mine!" The next day he told Gauvreau that he had seen her drunk at the party. "He was making Broadway 'mine,' as he said ... and it was," recalled a *Graphic* staff man. "It became so completely his Broadway that he could give it to America...."

The Broadway Winchell gave America was something strange and fantastic that would take its place beside the tabloids, slang and gossip as an expression of the decade. "[E]very race in every age has picked out some one street, one square, one Acropolis mount or Waterloo Bridge to celebrate its most glowing literature," wrote columnist and critic Gilbert Gabriel. "Let it be known to the Americanologist of 3000 A.D. that we New Yorkers idolized a strange, boomerang-shaped, nightly fiery thoroughfare of broken hearts and blessed events, which we called Broadway. That will explain us."

Physically, Broadway was New York's longest street, extending some eighteen miles from its source at Battery Park on Manhattan's southern tip up north through Union Square where it veered west and then shot up north again through the West Side, Harlem, Washington Heights, and on up to the Broadway Bridge at Manhattan's northernmost finger. The stretch from just below 42nd Street, however, at what was known as Times Square, after the New York Times building there, to 59th Street was its heart. Here, in what one visitor described as a "suffusion of floods of soft electric light," legitimate theaters alternated with dance halls, clip joints, nightclubs, speakeasies, diners, newsstands. And all this populated each night by an extraordinary menagerie, as Gauvreau would scornfully observe, of "actresses, night club wenches, doctors playing the market with the money they raked in from venereal treatments, underworld politicians, racketeers interested in the collection of high art, gamblers, the occasional virgins who were considered among the underprivileged."

To almost everyone in the twenties, even those in the American heartland who would never visit it, Broadway was more than New York's theater district; it was as much a mythical city as Hollywood, and made nearly as strong a claim on the national imagination. Hollywood was balmy and languorous; Broadway was a place where the pace never slackened, the lights never dimmed, the crowds never thinned, the revelry never stopped—a place where all the hedonistic energy of the age could roar. Hollywood symbolized glamour; Broadway symbolized freedom.

And it was no less a magical city for its inhabitants. For them Broadway was a form of living theater, highly self-conscious and highly stylized; in fact, the imaginary city of Broadway evolved in the twenties *because* it was theater, and it was theater because it had attracted a set of largely rootless, dissatisfied people, people without families or commitments, people whose lives could be fulfilled by the nightly rituals of saloon-hopping and flagrant display, people who had nothing else to do and nowhere else to go—people like Walter Winchell. "Broadway was to me where everybody who felt rejected where they grew up would come," confessed one press agent. "Because nobody felt rejected on Broadway. Everybody was accepted there. We didn't care how rich you were or what your background was. What we cared about was did you have a [story], were you anecdotal." On Broadway these denizens collected nightly in their costumes and played their roles. The gangsters looked like gangsters with their dark shirts, garish ties and droopy felt hats. Texas Guinan looked like a speakeasy hostess. The chorus girls looked like chorus girls, the gamblers like gamblers, the society swells like society swells and the newspapermen like newspapermen.

Whether the reality of Broadway came first and this image then followed or the image came first and the Broadwayites felt compelled to conform to it, is difficult to say. Certainly Walter in his daily dispatches helped shape the idea of Broadway for his contemporaries; his friend Ernie Cuneo compared what Walter did for Broadway to what Mark Twain had done for the Mississippi River. Later generations, however, were more likely to think of this mythical city as the sole invention of another of its inhabitants: Damon Runyon.

Runyon's Broadway was winsome; the man was anything but. A drunken father, a wild and unrestrained childhood, a peripatetic career as a newspaperman that took him from Pueblo, Colorado, to San Francisco and back again, had all taken their toll on Damon. He arrived in New York in 1910 to work on Hearst's *American*, an aloof, cynical, bilious man and a caustic drunk. Acquaintances called him "Demon" with good reason. Few men were as self-absorbed. Though his glasses eerily magnified his blue eyes and his complexion was always sallow, he was a peacock who spent an hour each day dressing himself and another hour preening in the bathroom. He had dozens of suits color-coordinated not only down to his socks but even to his typewriters. "If you happened to meet Damon three different times in a single day," remembered sportswriter Bill Corum, "it was not unusual to see him in as many costumes, complete to hat, suit, and shoes." He wore suspenders bearing his own profile.

His wife, a former society editor of the *Rocky Mountain News*, bore him two children, but he seldom saw them. "Give a woman a couple of kids and she'll let you alone," he told a friend. His son remembered him as a "fierce fellow"—an impression "heightened by the constant storm warnings from the womenfolk, 'Don't bother your father.' " By 1920 he had abandoned them all, and his wife turned to alcohol. She was to die eleven years later in a drunken stupor; their children went to live with her mother in Washington State while Damon continued his nightly performance as Broadway's resident cynic.

But however cruel and steel-hearted he was to his family, his darkling vision of life gave him a certain cachet on Broadway, where cynicism and misanthropy were the respected attitudes and where his bragging that he wrote for money, not sentiment, only enhanced his status as journalistic royalty: a newspaperman's newspaperman. It was as an author of fiction, though, rather than as a journalist, that his reputation soared. The subjects of his stories were what Runyon knew best: the guys and dolls who inhabited Broadway. By romanticizing them, and in romanticizing them immortalizing them, he became Broadway's man of letters too—a distinction Walter would never hold and one he greatly respected.

Awed by Runyon, Walter was tickled when the great man modeled a character after him. "Damon Runyon, darnim, has prepared a magazine article in which the villain is a tabloid critic named Walter Winchester,"

Walter boasted in a column in January 1927. The character was actually called "Waldo Winchester" in the first of Runyon's Broadway tales, "Romance in the Roaring Forties," and for whatever reason, it wouldn't appear until July 1929 in *Cosmopolitan*, but Walter had obviously served as the inspiration. "This Waldo Winchester is a nice-looking young guy," Runyon wrote, "who writes pieces about Broadway for the Morning Item. He writes pieces about the goings-on in night clubs, such as fights, and one thing and another, and also about who is running around with who, including guys and dolls."

In the story, fast-talking Waldo strikes up a romance with Miss Billy Perry, a chorine at Missouri Martin's Sixteen Hundred Club and the girlfriend of gangster Dave the Dude, who happens to be in the Bahamas on business at the time. When the Dude returns to find Waldo kissing his girl, he socks him, only to watch Billy minister to her fallen lover. A few weeks later in a gesture of sacrifice, the Dude grabs Waldo off the street to take him to the Woodcock Inn on Pelham Parkway to marry Billy. Waldo is miserable. He may love Billy, but it just so happens that he is already married. (Did Runyon know about Walter's own predicament?) Nevertheless, the ceremony proceeds. Waldo and Billy are about to exchange vows when there is a commotion at the door, and in bursts Waldo's wife, circus acrobat Lola Sapola, who socks the Dude and flings Waldo over her shoulder "like he was a sack of oats." As the Dude recovers, Billy pledges her love to him, and the ceremony continues with the new bridegroom.

Written by a transplanted Coloradan for whom New York would always be exotic no matter how long he resided there, Runyon's stories were as fanciful and fabricated as the actual Broadwayites were. His was a Broadway of tough-talking, swindling, showy, licentious, eccentric, quintessentially twenties folk with a perspective no larger than the next bet, meal, romance or show. The characters were caricatures who spoke in their own highly distinctive argot. They were "Runyonesque." Emotionally they may have been Runyonesque too, as hollow as their author, but Runyon himself wrote that his breezy, slangy, nonjudgmental prose was itself a moral judgment, like Texas Guinan's detached merriment. "By saying something with a half-boob air, by conveying an air of jocularity," he said of his work, "he gets ideas out of his system on the wrongs of this world."

It was difficult to say what Runyon felt those wrongs were. While Fitzgerald plumbed the tragic depths of the Jazz Age, examining its ambivalence toward the money and the verve that enlivened it, Runyon, no less a twenties writer, skated over its shiny surface where there was no tragedy, only comedy, some sentiment and occasional rue—unless that *was* the real tragedy: that, like so many others on Broadway, he had lost the capacity to feel and was left only with the capacity to perform.

Winchell was much more overtly ambivalent about the street than Runyon was and contributed another, contrasting vision of Broadway. "With one hand it bestows, and with another it takes away. . . . It yields to all men what they have the strength to take, and then, like the water that is drawn from the sea, Broadway takes its own again." "It is a hard and destructive community even for those who 'click.' . . . What you accomplished last season doesn't matter. 'What have you got now?' is the incessant query." "The popular maxim is 'Every man for himself' and 'Knife the other fellow before he knives you,' " he wrote. "What can you 'get' on the other fellow?" the gossip king asked. "What do you know about him? Is he doing anything he'd be ashamed of, and how much is there in it for me?" "It is vicious, merciless, selfish and treacherous," he concluded.

Nor did Walter spare himself in this account. He was anxious to get ahead too. "The reason why the Broadway character usually acts selfish, untrue and indifferent toward his friends," he told a high school journalist in an analysis with obvious application to himself, "is that he is desperate for recognition. Our Broadwayites experience so much bitterness trying to crash the heavens, they go to extremes to make good. . . . I have personally experienced many difficulties with the Broadway gang who were envious of my success and tried to shove their elbows in my way. I merely retaliated with my own elbows and continued on my way."

The slang, the gossip, the Broadway gags and anecdotes had all accreted—accreted until Walter Winchell, in just a few years on the *Graphic*, had become a name. "One day he was a nobody," recalled a Broadway ticket broker, "and the next time you looked, everybody was reading his column and around Broadway you had to decide whether to fear him or favor him." But not just on Broadway and not just in New York. "[Y]ou are a very much admired young man in the said city of Detroit," a press representative wrote him. "I was repeatedly asked the color of your hair, eyes and eyebrows. Further than that the polite Detroit maidenhood goeth not in inquiry." Even O. O. McIntyre, whom Walter often twitted as "the very Odd McIntyre," wrote him from a San Francisco vacation, "I hear you widely quoted on the coast and many inquire about you." The Chicago *Evening Post* said he was so "widely quoted in the big city that there's hardly a conversation among folk who know things that he isn't mentioned" and added that a friend of Walter's claimed "Winchell is always desiring to prick himself with a pin to see whether it isn't all a dream."

Most of the sudden attention was the result of syndication, first by the

Graphic and then, in the early fall of 1928, by the Central Press Association, a Cleveland-based agency, which introduced the column to major
metropolitan areas with a heavy advertising blitz and brought it to dozens
of new papers. (FPA, by comparison, was carried in six.) "According to
the gossip syndicates," editorialized the Louisville *Herald-Post*, "Winchell
is the high man in the outlying districts," permitting him to claim "a
truly national audience." "There are those who affect not to understand
his daring flashes," it continued. "But to understand Winchell is a test of
Americanism, no less than to be able to explain the Constitution."

The national recognition both thrilled and scared Walter. On the one
hand, where once he had hunched over his desk lost in his own world, he
now bustled into the office brandishing his column and read it aloud.
"When he did this he'd put his head almost against mine, holding the
copy a few inches from my eyes," remembered one staff man. "He had
to have undivided attention and even the ringing of the telephone had to
wait until he had finished. His voice carried throughout the building and
sprinkled fine saliva on my face." When a copy editor ribbed him that his
column was "lousy," Walter moped until he caught on. If the criticism
was intended seriously, Walter would never solicit the person's advice
again.

On the other hand, the attention convinced Winchell he could not let
up for fear of losing his competitive edge. Offers were coming from all
quarters, and Walter hardly refused any of them even though he was already overworked. In August 1927 he signed with Simon & Schuster to
write a book. *Cosmopolitan* wanted to talk to him "about doing some
things for us." H. N. Swanson, the editorial director of *College Humor*,
kept pressing for stories on "young people in picaresque and picturesque
situations in the Big Town," and when Walter didn't respond to this suggestion, pressed him to do a series to be called "Broadway Biographies,"
though not necessarily on real people. ("Like all editors," admitted
Swanson, "I am pretty much afraid of libel.") Walter was also contributing articles to *Judge* and *Life*, a humor magazine, and when *Life* folded,
he promptly agreed to a monthly column for the *Detroit Athletic Club
News*. Even *Vanity Fair*, the most sophisticated of magazines, solicited
him. *VF* editor Donald Freeman, Walter wrote, "played me up as being
a 'somebody.' . . . And to make sure I would be accepted and not ridiculed, Donald Freeman polished my pieces of drivel, embroidered them
with big words." When the offers finally overwhelmed him, Walter
farmed out assignments to his friends, keeping the fee and repaying the
favor with column items.

An even better gauge of his popularity than how much he was being
asked to write was how much was written about him. *Editor & Publisher*

had run two articles on Walter in 1928. John O'Hara, then at *Time*, was working up a piece on columnists and wrote Walter, "[I]f ever I can find you, I want certain information which has been holding up the yarn." *The Outlook and Independent* ran a long profile, and Robert Benchley, one of the original Algonquin wits, wrote an encomium in *The New Yorker* calling Walter "one of the phenomena of modern newspaper writing. . . . Within a year, Winchell has become an institution, both as a personal reporter and a compiler of folk-sayings. People buy the *Graphic* who never knew it existed before and hide it between sheets of their *Evening Post*. His words and the words of the people he quotes are taking their place in the national language. . . ." According to another *New Yorker* item, Walter had also inspired a two-hour debate in one of the "shadier night clubs" over whether he was a stylist or not. Walter arrived during the discussion, but, wrote Heywood Broun, "that didn't help much because he kept shifting his ground and taking now one side and then the other."

Amid all the accolades describing him as the spirit of the urban zeitgeist, Walter called himself a newsboy: "A newsboy is a citizen immature in everything but nerve, who posts himself conspicuously in a public place and shrills so relentlessly as to menace the stoutest eardrums for a radius of several blocks." Asked by an interviewer if he had ever dedicated himself to anything, he answered, "[T]o exposing the phoney," then added, "but I'm a phoney myself, and the best phoney on Broadway, because I admit that I am."

He began cultivating the image of gadfly, always picking fights, trying to goad targets into counterattacking him. One of his more incongruous vendettas that fall of 1928 was aimed at St. John Ervine, a novelist and playwright and the celebrated drama critic of the London *Observer*, who had accepted a one-year appointment on the *World* to replace the departing Alexander Woollcott. Walter immediately began baiting Ervine, "not only to fill my column," he admitted, "but to get some attention from this distinguished visitor." Walter always referred to him as St. Yawn Irksome. Ervine's mild retort was to call Walter Little Boy Peep. It was only after Ervine had returned to England that he derided Walter, who, he said, "looked like an over-grown choir boy who had taken to bad ways in the vestry," and tweaked him as "the darling of the pseudo-intellectuals in New York."

Not everyone viewed Winchell's popularity with the same equanimity as did the Algonquin crowd. Walter himself reported that producer Morris Gest had cornered him one night at the new St. Regis Roof Café and "out of a sky as blue as Mineralava," asked him, " 'Tell me, Winchell. What is going to happen to America if people like you are successful?' Not a little amazed we stammered: 'I don't know what you mean. Please don't be sarcastic.' 'I'm not,' he thundered, 'if people like to read the slang you write and the junk you prepare and publishers pay you for that stuff, what is going to happen to art, literature and intelligence?' "

This had been Lippmann's fear too, and in an election year that pitted conservative Iowa-born Herbert Hoover against New York Governor Al Smith, the derby-hatted, cigar-smoking eastern urbanite, the fear assumed a force and poignancy inspired, wrote Lippmann, "by the feeling that the clamorous life of the city should not be acknowledged as the American ideal." Walter Winchell *was* New York. He *was* the clamorous force of the twenties; that was one reason he had suddenly been seized by so much of the populace that year. "Whether used as a warning or as an example," said the *Literary Digest* the next year, "the success of Walter Winchell as a newspaper man makes him a notable figure." But which it was to be, warning or example, was yet to be determined.

VII

The great revealer of other people's secrets had one large secret of his own: He had still not resolved the situation with Rita and June, though he seemed to behave as if he had. After her encounter on Broadway with Walter and June in August 1923, Rita was off on tour again and Walter still plaintively wrote her, despite the fact that he and June were now living together. (He told Rita he was living with a friend named Jack and had then moved back into the NVA.) They had taken an apartment in the Seventies, far beyond his means with his Morris Plan installments, his support payments to his mother and his weekly stipends to Rita, but Walter couldn't bring himself to admit to June that he hadn't as much money as she thought. (Rita had no way of knowing that this was the reason for his letters begging her to restrain her attorneys dunning him for support.) Instead he borrowed from *The Vaudeville News*' ad income, just as he had for Rita.

In October he had a new expense: June had a baby. The story the Winchells told was that June was shopping along 49th Street one morning when she saw a thin, sickly woman sweeping the sidewalk and surrounded by a hungry brood of children. June asked if the woman wanted help with one of her babies. "Oh, I wish you would," the mother told her. "You must love children to want to do that." June gave the woman her address and phone number and Walter's office address and number and promised to bring the infant by every day. Then she took the baby home and, as Walter told it, surprised him.

There would always be those who suspected that the baby hadn't been adopted this way, that she was Walter and June's natural child, and they had concocted the story to cover her illegitimacy. These skeptics pointed to a family resemblance as proof, and suspicions were only fueled by June's refusal to adopt the child formally—because she never wanted the child to find out she wasn't theirs, she said.

The Winchells' was the more likely scenario. As her custody of Angeline had demonstrated, June liked caring for infants (Angeline was eventually returned to her parents). Her own strange, peripatetic childhood had given her a chronic longing for a family, and she frequently volunteered at an adoption agency called State Charities Aid, providing foster care for infants until permanent homes could be found for them. The emaciated six-week-old infant she had brought home that October morning, however, was unlikely to find a new home. June took her to Dr. Curley, a prominent pediatrician, who suggested she be returned: she was sick—a heart ailment. Instead, June resolved to nurse the child back to health.

The baby's name was Gloria, and Walter, a man of few real attachments, absolutely adored her as he had adored no one else in his life. "I don't recall her ever crying the way most babies cry," he wrote in his autobiography. "She never screamed or shrieked, never disturbed my sleep. I often washed and changed her diapers, took the chill off her bottle, and shoved the nipple into her rosebud mouth around 6:00 a.m. when I came in from doing the Broadway night places just as Gloria was about to wake up—so that June could slumber a little longer. I knew she had been up hours before, feeding Gloria. I was a Very Good Daddy. Ask Junie."

Gloria never was returned to her mother; no one ever said why. Instead, with "pablum and the other baby food that you feed infants with a spoon—and so much Love," Walter said, "Gloria grew up strong and healthy." True to June's word, she never told anyone the child wasn't theirs. Gloria was always treated as if she were.

Yet, much as he loved her, the addition of Gloria intensified the financial pressures on Walter, who was then still at *The Vaudeville News*. The Winchells were living now in a furnished apartment over LaHiff's Tavern, where Damon Runyon, Jack Dempsey, Bugs Baer and other notables had all once lived. June had found it and hadn't bothered to inform Walter about the rent—June, like Rita, took care of business—but when he learned it would cost them $150 a month, he informed June they would have to leave. In what was probably Walter's very favorite story, one he would tell "at least a million times" over the years, he approached genial Billy LaHiff to give notice. "Justaminnit," said LaHiff in Walter's version. "How about making it one twenty-five?" Walter said it was still too steep for the salary he was making on the *News*. "Can you afford a hundred?"

LaHiff asked. Walter said he thought he could manage that. "Okay, then," said LaHiff. "It's a hundred a month. Just promise me you won't take that baby's carriage from in front of this building—it's the only sign of respectability it has!" Elsewhere Walter said that when "I didn't know where the rent was coming from or the next meal—Billy LaHiff 'carried' me and my brood for nearly a year."

Gloria grew into a beautiful little girl—tall for her age and lanky, with straight blond hair in a pageboy cut, a fragile triangular face, large blue eyes and a broad smile. Almost everyone described her as angelic, and these admirers meant not only in appearance but also in temperament. Walter's affection for her was genuine and deep. He made a point of phoning her each evening from the office to bid her good night, occasionally passing the receiver to a deskmate who remembered a "caress in her gay voice."

By Walter's own admission, it wasn't much of a family life even before he moved to the *Graphic*. He got up in the afternoon, was out all night, returned to feed the baby and then go to sleep. Sometimes weeks would pass without his having any time with June; she often was sleeping when he came home and out shopping when he woke up. And if Walter was largely an absentee father, June herself was not exactly the epitome of Victorian domesticity, Walter's assertion that her "respectability was Topic A around the NVA Club" notwithstanding. Like Nellie Cliff and Rita before her, she had grown up wild, stubborn, and rebellious. Like them, she had been a lifelong performer, without a father or anyone else to discipline and anchor her. Exhibitionism was her way of getting attention, even love. Once she and her partner Olive Hill were arrested in Atlantic City for refusing to wear stockings on the beach. On another occasion Walter's Aunt Beatrice had seen her in a nude revue and told Rita, but Walter insisted she had only done it on a dare.

Walter had to protect her honor, since by this time everyone assumed that June was his wife. Many of his acquaintances hadn't even known Rita, and those who had naturally thought that she and Walter had divorced. For her part, June had given up her career to care for Gloria. In any case Walter always introduced June now as Mrs. Winchell. Only Rita seemed oblivious of the situation, both because she never seemed terribly curious, perhaps fearing what she might discover, and because Walter constantly lied to her, denying that he was involved with anyone else.

Still, Walter was painfully aware that his relationship with June was illicit. He wrote her when he was at *The Vaudeville News*:

Supposing, sweetheart, I were lying lifeless in a shroud,
And there were grieving relatives and others by my bier.

*Would you come forward from the mourners, unashamed, and
    proud,
But broken-hearted—weep a little—so they all could hear?*

*I really think it would be tactless of you if you did.
They'd question and embarrass you and your right to be there,
And from the dismal chamber where I'd lie, I'm sure they'd bid
You leave the place—and that would be too much for you to bear.*

He concluded, "They wouldn't understand our kind of love—they never do!"

Early in 1925, Rita was introduced as Mrs. Winchell to a woman who insisted they had already met in Atlantic City. "Don't you remember, I held your baby," Rita quoted her as saying. Rita immediately phoned Walter at the *Graphic* for an explanation, but Walter just scoffed, and Rita obviously wanted to believe him. Still, she warned that "I had no intention of handing him over on a platter to anyone, blonde, brunette or redhead, he was married to me for better or worse and as I had gone through the worst I was going to be there for some of the better...."

Then, that summer, thumbing through the *Daily News*, she saw a photograph of "Mrs. W. Winchell, making a cradle of sand for daughter, Betty,"* taken at the ocean on Long Beach, Long Island. Once again Rita demanded an explanation from Walter, and once again he waffled. But she insisted that if he could support June and a child, he could certainly afford to support her, and she had their separation agreement reinstated.

What Walter thought he was doing is impossible to say. He may have been hoping to stave off Rita from getting a divorce so that he wouldn't have to pay alimony, which was sure to be larger than the ten dollars she was getting each week in their separation agreement. No doubt he was also trying to protect himself now that he was beginning to succeed. No one appreciated better than he the power of gossip. A scandal was the last thing he wanted, especially since he had dug his own grave by letting everyone think that he and June were married. What would the smart folk on Broadway say if they knew he had never gotten a divorce, if they knew there was another Mrs. Winchell? How would he be ridiculed? His career, he felt, was precarious under the best of circumstances. It could never survive this. Then, too, Rita was the one person who knew just how insecure he really was. What would she reveal if he were to tell her that he was living with June? So he continued to pretend, with astonishing

---

*One has to assume this is a reporter's error, since the child certainly appears to be Gloria.

immaturity, that nothing was wrong. And that is what he kept telling Rita.

Moreover, he had recently seen the bloodletting of divorce firsthand in his parents' breakup. His mother still lived in the old Harlem apartment at 125 West 116th Street with Algernon, now a bookkeeper, and a young boarder from Poland. His father, now calling himself Jacko, had moved in with a new "wife" named Adlina (sometimes Adelina) Laino, a recent arrival from Puerto Rico twenty-two years his junior. Adlina, her younger sister Mary and Jacko ran a store selling ladies' silk underwear. The Winschels had been apart for five years, but Jennie's hostility always seemed fresh. She despised Jacob. Without the slightest provocation she would break into denunciations of her former husband, prompting George Winchel to bark, "What did I pay for the divorce for if you're going to keep talking about him? Do you want him back?"

While her bizarre marital minuet continued, Rita happened to brush past June in a drugstore that fall of 1926, and what she saw appalled her. June was obviously pregnant. The next day she phoned Walter and advised that "he was in a position whereby a divorce was about to become an absolute necessity." Walter, however, was still denying everything. Full of skepticism, Rita left for a vaudeville engagement in Chicago. "I felt instinctively from reading his column that a blessed event of great importance was about to take place." When she saw an item in his column late in March announcing that "Mr. and Mrs. ??" expected a blessed event, she knew the reference was to Walter and June and immediately returned to New York.

She arrived on April 1, 1927, and began phoning all the hospitals where she thought June might have gone. None of them had a Mrs. Winchell as a patient. Then she remembered a sanitarium where theater people often went. She phoned and discovered that June wasn't there either, but only because all the beds were filled; she had been sent on to the Park West Hospital. When Rita called there, her suspicions were confirmed.

Walter, meanwhile, had been contriving to have his Aunt Beatrice break the news to Rita, and even when Rita and Walter met the next day and she pressed him for information, he said nothing about a baby, only about work. Rita didn't let on she knew, but she was boiling. Aunt Beatty counseled her to wait and let Walter work it out. Rita was nearly hysterical. "[T]he more I thought of the situation at hand the more strained I became," she wrote, "from the way I felt one would have thought that I was the direct cause of a tragedy. . . ."

Finally she decided to have it out with Walter. They met one evening, and Rita told Walter she knew about his new baby. For Walter the announcement seemed to bring relief, releasing him from three years of tension and anxiety. After all the backing and filling, he was now bold, almost insolent. "His bravado," wrote Rita, "was sickening." He began ranting that kings had had illegitimate children, though Rita reminded him that while he was becoming increasingly popular, he was no king and had to live by the same moral rules as everyone else. It was only when he realized that Rita wasn't going to exact revenge, wasn't going to try to ruin him, that he calmed down and was willing to discuss their options.

Obviously he wanted to keep the divorce secret. Secrecy, after all, was the whole point. A friend of his at *Variety* suggested that Rita obtain the divorce in Chicago, far from the glare of New York. As for the financial terms, Walter wanted to reach an agreement before either of them went to attorneys. He proposed to pay some alimony and post a bond to guarantee the payments for five years. But when Rita said the bond was inadequate and insisted on getting the divorce in New York, Walter refused, and the situation dragged on still further.

In the meantime, there was the new baby, born on March 31, 1927. Walter and June wrestled with a name. Her birth certificate said "Eileen Joan Winchell." Two days later Walter came up with one of his word-weddings, Walda, for "Waldarling," though nearly everyone thought it another instance of Walter's own egomania. In May he was still debating. "If you had a new baby girl," he asked in his column, "would you name it Eileen or Joan?" A reporter that fall called her Patsy.

Eventually he and June settled on the name Walda and settled into a new apartment in the sizable Whitby at 325 West 45th Street in the theater district. A neighbor, Bernard Sobel, would remember dropping in on Walter each day around noon. " 'Bills, rent, bills, rent,' he'd lament while June toiled away [with] the children, a lovely-looking mother, patient and capable." He worked doggedly and complained constantly, yet he had gotten his $200 raise from the *Graphic* that Christmas and had enough money to hire a West Indian nursemaid for the girls. "In the background of all his first efforts was a wind-blown clothesline full of diapers," Alexander Woollcott wrote of Walter's stay at the Whitby, "and the only fellow scribe toward whom I ever saw him vindictive was a plump and mincing bachelor who lived in the same apartment house with Winchell and who complained to the janitor that he could not get to his monastic flat without barking his shins on the darned old Winchell perambulators which cluttered up the hall. Winchell, as I recall, was planning to kill him."

A year after Walda's birth and Rita's confrontation with Walter, the Winchells finally agreed on their divorce. They would file the action on Staten Island, across Upper New York Bay from Manhattan, where it was likely to escape notice. Walter offered to provide Rita with a lawyer; she refused, preferring to choose her own. She would, however, instruct him to accept Walter's proposed financial settlement: thirty-five dollars a week beginning immediately. Walter would arrange for the witnesses—they would have to testify to adultery—because he feared Rita still might double-cross him. He was terrified that he was being set up.

"I do trust it is done quickly," Walter wrote Rita's mother, who had asked him for theater tickets. "You see I have no protection that it will ever be done at all, except a promise. The thing can be prolonged and postponed indefinitely now that I have admitted my alleged guilt, which you know was done purely to give a name to my baby to keep in accord with the so-called moral code of our America." He asked her not to tell anyone about his marriage. "Of course if publicity comes, let it come. When you have a child you love as I love mine you don't really give a damb [sic] what happens." It was the first time in the entire episode that Walter expressed concern for anyone other than himself.

The hearing was held on the unseasonably cool, rainy morning of June 4, 1928. By prior arrangement, Walter didn't appear, but an acquaintance of both June and Rita's testified that Walter had called June "Mrs. Winchell" and that she had seen them together in their nightclothes caressing. (Also by prior arrangement, June's name was not to be mentioned in the courtroom. The corespondent was identified only as "a woman whose name is unknown to plaintiff," though June's friend slipped and the name had to be stricken from the record.) Next to testify was Mark Hellinger, who also said he had met a "Mrs. Winchell" and seen Walter and her in intimate circumstances. The court then confirmed Rita's financial agreement with Walter and granted an interlocutory decree for divorce.

That evening Rita telephoned Walter, who was waiting to hear the disposition. Everything had gone as planned, and she assured him that nothing had leaked to the press. Then Walter offered her theater tickets to see Helen Hayes in *Coquette*, warning her it was a very depressing play. Rita went anyway. "I was not in the mood for laughter."

The divorce became final in September. For Rita it was to be the trauma of her life. Her family believed she loved Walter still, would in fact always love him. She never remarried, never even had a serious relationship with another man. Occasionally over the next year she would run into Walter on Broadway, and he would regale her as always with his latest exploits. Several times she asked him whether he had gotten around to marrying June, but Walter told her he hadn't yet—he was very busy just then, and their plans kept getting postponed. In the end they never did get married, most likely because Walter was just too afraid that someone might find out about Walda's illegitimacy and his own odd double life.

Indeed, there were enormous demands on his time now. In November he needed minor surgery. And in December Mamie, June's mother, died from pneumonia after a stage appearance in Reading, Pennsylvania. June brought the body back to New York for burial. Baby Mary Rose, who was with her mother when she died, stayed with Aunt Jennie and then another aunt until June got her. She moved in with Walter, June and the children at the Whitby, adding another mouth to feed and another responsibility for Walter, a man who hated responsibility.

As the decade drew to a close, Walter had a new wife, a new family, new fame and status. He had arrived with the twenties, a scared but eager young man, untested in a new profession, nervously riding the tide of merriment, a creature of the times. He was leaving the twenties as one of its architects and its symbols.

CHAPTER 3

Surviving

NOW HE NEEDED A NEW PAPER.
Ever since the Shubert dispute, Walter's relationship with Gauvreau had
been deteriorating from what was already a state of belligerence. When
Walter complained that correspondence was stacking up on his desk
and asked for occasional assistance, Gauvreau quashed the idea. When
he asked for a salary increase after adding a syndicated series on vaudeville to his duties, Gauvreau refused, saying he "didn't want the damned
stuff in the paper." When Walter put in for expenses of $10.80 incurred
covering a story, Gauvreau vetoed it, saying it was a food receipt and
Walter should have eaten at home. And even aside from these constant,
nagging indignities, Walter was beginning to feel that he had outgrown
the *Graphic*.

At the same time there was no lack of suitors waiting to woo him away.
The *Daily News*, the *Morning World*, William Randolph Hearst's *Journal*
and its sister paper the *Mirror*, had all made inquiries about his availability. But while the *World* and even the *Daily News* might have seemed too
restrictive for the kind of journalism he practiced, he had no such qualms
about Hearst. The son of the discoverer of the Comstock Lode silver
mine, Hearst had grown up a rich, aimless, headstrong rapscallion. After
being expelled from Harvard for a practical joke, then having been read-
mitted and flunked out, he surveyed his father's numerous holdings and
decided to ply his talents on the San Francisco *Examiner*, where, by
launching a crusade against safety violations of the Southern Pacific Rail-

road, he doubled circulation in the first year. By 1895 he had come to New York, bought the *Journal* and begun journalistic warfare against Joseph Pulitzer's *World*—a war that was to end with massive circulations for both papers and a flamboyant new style of news presentation labeled the "yellow press" after a mischievous comic strip street-urchin known as the Yellow Kid.

Like Walter's contributions to journalism, Hearst's were usually castigated by the press establishment. Detractors said he had introduced sensationalism and distortion into the news. Less jaundiced observers saw his main innovations as placing the story function of the newspaper above the information function and elevating reporters to the role of stars. For *New Yorker* press critic A. J. Liebling, however, Hearst's legacy was not so much what he did with his newspapers as how he acquired them. He would be remembered "as the man who introduced the use of big money into the newspaper business"—the one who demonstrated that "a man without previous newspaper experience could, by using money like a heavy club, do what he wanted" with no apparent regard for tradition or taste.

What he wanted, it seemed, was to shape American opinion in the mold of his own idiosyncratic political philosophy, which was one part populism and one part conservatism. To this end he created a formidable press empire. In 1920 he owned twelve daily newspapers in eight cities. By decade's end he had twenty-six papers in eighteen cities, with a total circulation of roughly five million. In their peak years in the early thirties, Hearst papers represented 12 percent of total daily circulation in America and 21 percent of Sunday circulation. And that may underestimate his influence; the percentages were double those figures in most of the large urban areas where Hearst's blunderbuss journalism found its natural constituency.

In the past, Walter had been loath to move from his situation at the *Graphic*, which, if untenable, was at least predictable, and he had used any offers he received only to leverage up his salary and his freedom at the paper. Now, however, Walter was seriously considering proposals. If the enervating battles with Gauvreau and the ever-falling status of the paper (falling while Walter's status was rising) weren't reasons enough to leave, there was also Walter's belief that the *Graphic* had reneged on a promise to raise his salary to $300 a week plus 50 percent of its gross revenue from the syndication of his column.

It was a sign of just how badly other papers wanted Walter that they were willing to negotiate in the spring of 1929 even though his contract with Macfadden had two more years to run. William Curley, the managing editor of Hearst's *Evening Journal*, asked sportswriter Bill Corum, a

mutual friend, to arrange a meeting with Walter. Curley offered Walter
a signing bonus, $500 per week, and 50 percent of the gross syndication
revenues for his column. In "reprisal" against Gauvreau, Walter accepted
the first week of April. A reporter interviewing him the day he signed the
contract found him "jubilant." In announcing the deal, *Editor & Publisher*
reported, "It is believed to be the first time any newspaper man has
signed a contract to be effective at such a distant date."

So now began the wait. Outraged by Walter's lame duck status,
Gauvreau instructed the "letters to the editor" department to stop running any favorable mentions of Walter and to feature instead letters that
attacked the columnist's credibility. Meanwhile, Walter hired Arthur
Driscoll, a prominent Manhattan attorney, to see if he could find any
loophole in the Macfadden contract that might win him early release.
That incensed Gauvreau even more. "My secretary has informed me that
you offered her one-thousand dollars to procure for [*sic*] her the original
copy of your contract with Macfadden," he wrote Walter in May. "I am
informed on legal authority that this is attempted larceny." Driscoll fired
back that if Gauvreau didn't immediately retract his accusation of larceny,
Walter would sue him for libel.

Now, or so Gauvreau later claimed, Walter shifted the attack to
Macfadden. He began phoning the health-faddist in the middle of the
night and shouting imprecations at him. During one call at four o'clock
in the morning, according to a story Gauvreau heard but never verified,
Walter supposedly accused Macfadden of having eaten a planked steak
bathed in Worcestershire sauce followed by a baked Alaska while he was
supposed to have been in the middle of a two-week fast. Macfadden had
never really appreciated Walter anyway; like Gauvreau, he resented being
upstaged by his employee, and his wife said he found the column a "daily
preparation of unintelligible jargon" and "wondered what made people
talk about it." As Gauvreau told it, he received a call from Macfadden the
morning of May 29 and was ordered to fire Walter.

But before breaking the news to Walter, Gauvreau called Louis Sobol
into his office. Sobol was a diminutive young man with a balding, bulb-
shaped head, a rather pronounced nose, thick horn-rimmed glasses and a
pencil-thin mustache. He had been a small-time Connecticut newspaper
reporter before moving to New York to work on *Automotive Daily News*,
a Macfadden trade journal, although he admitted his "chief claim to dubious prestige" was having ghosted pieces for Queen Marie of Romania
during her widely publicized American tour. "Do you think you can handle Winchell's job?" Gauvreau asked him. When Sobol said he could,
Gauvreau ordered him to tell Walter of the firing.

"Winchell stared at me in disbelief," Sobol remembered. "He fiddled
with some clips on his desk and then, rather subdued for him, asked,

'When did he tell you that?' " He was silent for a few moments before erupting, then grew silent again, "unlike the self-confident, vehemently assertive chap those of us on the *Graphic* and folks generally around Broadway had come to know. . . ." Walter went to Gauvreau's office for a confirmation and returned five minutes later, handing Sobol some press releases he could use for the column. "See you later," he waved as he left. He never stepped into the building again.

Now, with Walter unexpectedly at liberty, a fight broke out within the Hearst ranks for his services. William Curley at the *Journal* had signed him up, but Arthur Kobler, the publisher of Hearst's tabloid *Mirror*, which was in much more dire straits at the time, wanted him too. Hearst decided that the *Mirror* would get Walter until the end of his *Graphic* contract, which had been due to expire on May 18, 1931, and the *Journal* would get him afterward.

Though the *Mirror* had a checkered past, it was still an improvement over the *Graphic*. For one thing, being tied into the Hearst syndicate, called King Features, meant a whole new magnitude of readership— millions more than the *Graphic* syndication afforded. For another, it disinfected Walter from the taint of the Macfadden press. No more of those laborious articles about physical culture and advice to the lovelorn that cluttered the pink pages of the *Graphic*. The *Mirror* took its sensationalism straight. Its credo, stated daily on the editorial page, was Thomas Jefferson's self-evident truths: "that all men are created equal, that they are endowed by their Creator with certain inalienable rights, that among these are Life, Liberty and the pursuit of happiness," though it was the pursuit of happiness that seemed to interest the *Mirror* most.

By one account the *Mirror* had spent more than $50,000 to ballyhoo Walter's defection—"When New York sophisticates and thousands of others want to enjoy the best column in New York . . . they read Winchell," trumpeted an ad—but his first column for the *Mirror* ran on June 10, 1929, without fanfare, just a silhouette of Walter on the front page with his signature and "Page 18" underneath. Nor did Walter himself acknowledge the move. "The Sig Thayer (Emily Vanderbilt) romance has wilted already," he began, and then ran through several dozen more items of marital hijinks ("As soon as they get their respective decrees Sonny Whitney and Mrs. Edgarton Warburton will be sealed"), of misdeeds ("One of the better known moom pitcher execs welched on a 100 grand roulette loss last week") and anticipated births ("The Frederic McLaughlins [Irene Castle] anticipate another blessed event"). Had he been nervous about switching papers? Mark Hellinger asked. "Not at all," said Walter. "It was just as if I had closed in Bridgeport and opened in Danbury."

Within months, in fact, he was joined by Hellinger, who had been told by the *Daily News* to write gossip or leave. Hellinger, who preferred writing "novelettes" about life in the city, left. And there was soon to be another defector to the *Mirror*, one whose arrival solved one of the mysteries that had been gnawing at Walter since his own departure from the *Graphic*: Why had Gauvreau let him leave? Everyone knew that Walter was responsible for a considerable portion of the *Graphic*'s circulation. So how could Gauvreau have let him go when Walter was contractually obligated to stay for two more years? To Walter there had always been a "smell" about it.

And then, to Walter's astonishment, Gauvreau joined the *Mirror* as its new managing editor. As Gauvreau later told it, he had long suspected that the *Graphic* couldn't keep hemorrhaging money and survive; consequently, he had kept open lines of communication with Arthur Kobler. One Sunday morning, Kobler arrived unannounced at Gauvreau's door in a limousine and drove him out to Hearst's opulent Long Island estate. While Kobler, Gauvreau and Hearst breakfasted and then uncrated furniture, the press magnate grilled Gauvreau about the *Graphic*. "You have created an awful nuisance," Hearst said. The three subsequently went shopping for art in Manhattan. Whatever the exact nature of the test, Gauvreau evidently passed it. Over lunch at the Ritz-Carlton the next afternoon, Kobler proffered him a five-year contract, and when the editor hesitated, Kobler stuffed a $10,000 bonus check in his pocket. "We're going to be happy together," Kobler said. "We're going to get out a great tabloid and do splendid things."

Walter suspected that this wasn't the whole story, and it probably wasn't. He discovered that Gauvreau had not gotten permission to fire him from Macfadden's chief, O. J. Elder, who was in Europe at the time and who, upon his return, told Walter how unhappy the firing had made him. Walter also thought it strange that when he went to Gauvreau's office after Sobol's announcement the editor already seemed to know Walter was going to the *Mirror*, not the *Journal* as originally planned. What Walter later heard was that Kobler had struck a deal with Gauvreau to release Winchell, which Kobler evidently assumed would kill the rival tabloid, in return for Kobler's buying Gauvreau's worthless *Graphic* stock for $80,000 and hiring him as editor of the *Mirror*. Macfadden was furious. "Gauvreau sold me out," he told an interviewer years later. "Gauvreau fixed it so that I'd fire Winchell. . . . We didn't have much chance after that at the *Graphic*."

IN CHANGING papers, Winchell wasn't quite as sanguine about things as he told Hellinger he was. Working for the *Mirror* created new expectations and, as always with Walter, new fears of failure. The reporter who interviewed him the day he jubilantly signed his Hearst contract also described him as tense and insecure and betraying "in a hundred ways the fear and anxiety of the *arriviste*":

> He is still sensitive about ridicule [the reporter wrote]. He is taut and self-conscious of his role all the time. He cannot relax. He seems to be eternally vigilant, fearful of missing something. He seems to have no privacy, no retreat to which the human being Walter Winchell can sometimes find shelter. He is constantly betraying a nervous, horrible fear of losing his punch, of being discarded as a vogue.

For Winchell it always came back to the same theme, one which had been bred in the bone: The fates were fickle, success was short-lived; one had to work beyond endurance, beyond exhaustion, to stave off the inevitable descent. "If the gossip doesn't materialize," he admitted then, "people forget." So he worked hard to fill the column's insatiable maw or, more accurately, its maws, since the format changed each day and no single type of material would satisfy them all.

The Monday column, of course, was for gossip. Tuesday's and Thursday's columns, the ones that most resembled his early columns at the *Graphic*, featured gags, puns, poems and anecdotes arranged in two columns. Wednesday's column, which he called "Portrait of a Man Talking to Himself," contained observations and animadversions. Friday's column, which he had devised one day when he was strapped for material and decided to run his log of calls and memos, was labeled "A Columnist's Sec'y Jots Down a Few Notes." Saturday's column was a list of arcane facts: "Things I Never Knew Till Now."

His office in the *Mirror* building on 45th Street was a grim cubicle on the third floor, all its available floor space filled with newspapers and magazines, the walls plastered with photographs. In practice he occupied the room only in the early hours of the morning. Most of the time it was the redoubt of his secretary, Ruth Cambridge. Young, effervescent and strikingly pretty with thick chestnut hair, Cambridge was a former showgirl from Pittsburgh who had been steered to Walter's cubicle by mutual friends. Though he insisted he couldn't really afford his own secretary, Cambridge convinced him when she picked up the phone and began fielding calls, including one from an angry column subject who was threatening retaliation. She could neither take dictation nor type, and her schedule was irregular (lunch breaks could take hours), but she was unfazable and self-confidently chipper and she was so attractive that press agents haunted the office just to flirt with her.

While Ruth held down the office, Walter foraged for gossip, jokes, slang—anything to fill the maws. He described his life as a "tough racket." "My beat is the Main Stem and environs; my hours are often twenty-four a day. They telephone me from as far as Chicago and Denver, and I don't count a day productive unless I've seen and talked with fifty or sixty of those 'in the know.' " One night at Reuben's delicatessen he complained to Hellinger that he couldn't get any sleep. "Edison only slept four hours a night," Hellinger riposted, "and he invented the electric light." "Yeah, but he didn't have a column to write," said Walter.

That October, just four months after Walter joined the *Mirror*, the stock market crashed, fatally weakening the economy, effectively ending the twenties and creating new anxieties for Walter. All the high times and mirth, the sharp and lively cultural warfare, the bohemianism, the hedonism, the egotism, the bold cynicism, the *spirit*, were snuffed. "All over the country people were sitting around in stunned bewilderment just as I was," wrote madam Polly Adler, "trying to understand what had happened to all that money. One minute you were kinging it on top of the world and the next you were flat on your behind in the street." "It was borrowed time anyhow—the whole upper tenth of a nation living with the insouciance of grand ducs and the casualness of chorus girls," F. Scott Fitzgerald was to write in his own valedictory to the twenties.

Walter's reaction to the crash, at least publicly, was extremely cavalier. On Black Tuesday he quoted an Eddie Cantor joke: "The situation is so terrible that when a man goes into a smart hotel these nights and asks for a room on the 17th floor, the clerk says, 'For sleeping or jumping?' " The next day he quoted Cantor again that if investors wanted to recoup their losses, they should buy National Casket (this drew howls, he said, at Dave's Blue Room) and quoted Heywood Broun's political gibe: "I only wish that those people who said they wouldn't vote for [Al] Smith because business would suffer were up to their necks in Montgomery-Ward [stock]!"

But however lighthearted he may have seemed, it soon became apparent to him that in terminating the age, the crash had destroyed the spiritual wellspring of his column; it had dampened nightlife and dimmed the luminosity of Broadway from which Walter drew his inspiration and to which he was inextricably linked in the public mind. So for Winchell the issue was less whether the economy would survive than whether his image would survive the end of the twenties. He had been whelped by the decade. His manner, morals, dress, attitude, even his prose style, were products of the period. He was, rhapsodized one writer before the full impact of the Depression hit, "the spirit of this mad jazz age. Like the times, he is brilliant, enthusiastic, keyed to the highest pitch, successful— with the faults of our day and all its glamor." The very week of the crash Walter had posed for photographer Edward Steichen at the behest of

Vanity Fair; in the photo, published that January, he sat on a stool and lit a cigarette, his silhouette cast on the wall behind him: an icon of twenties insouciance.

But Walter knew these were no longer times of insouciance. He just didn't know how he would adjust. So he plunged ahead, hoping to make up in energy what he lacked in direction. A friend said that being with him was like being with "human electricity." He smoked furiously, gabbed incessantly, scribbled quickly (usually with a stubby pencil on the back of envelopes or on a folded square of newsprint) and drummed the table with his fingers on the rare occasions when he wasn't talking. He walked fast, airily, like the dancer he once was, but the jauntiness was gone; the pressure of making good at the *Mirror* had driven it out. Old friends suddenly found him peevish. When Walter asked if he might put his name on an article press agent Bernard Sobel had written and Sobel refused, Walter exploded. "He cursed me," wrote Sobel, "and said something ugly about getting even." For weeks Walter wouldn't speak to him or mention him in the column, until Sobel finally relented. Another time he motioned to Louis Sobol at the Club Abbey, and Sobol, tired and prickly with the flu, snapped, "You want me, come over here." It triggered, said Sobol, a "coolness between us that lasted for years."

His own assessment of himself at the time was that he was "unquestionably the town's most conceited peasant" and that when he praised other columnists, "you can tell that he isn't sincere. . . ." He admitted it was harder to do the column than in the past when he was unknown because "I didn't know the well-knowns intimately" then and "I could write what I liked about them." Now they came to him with their scandals, trying to exact promises that he wouldn't publish what they told him. "You can't have friends and write what people like to read about them," he said, echoing once again the advice Jimmy Walker had given him. But when he asked himself if he boiled when he was attacked, he "thundered (as he is very primadonnish and highly strung)" that "[w]hen people dislike me they have damn good reasons!"

Yet it was an odd sort of self-importance he had acquired at the *Mirror*. He wasn't arrogant, and was anything but smug. Whatever he demanded was for the column. It was the column that was important, the column that had to be served and read and respected. Walter never deluded himself that he had any popularity or power independent of the column; if anything, he believed that were he to lose it, he would immediately lose everything. Winchell was only the column's instrument, important only insofar as the column was. That was why the column had to be tenderly nurtured each day. It was the column that gave Walter Winchell life, not the other way around.

II

And if he stopped moving, if his desperation lessened, would it all evaporate? "Gotta have excitement," Walter wrote in 1930. "Gotta have a reason for being incessantly charged with zip . . . Never believed that theory that too much work laid a guy low . . . It's a short life at most . . . That's why I want to crowd all of it in before some kid with a new idea comes along." He was constantly searching for new ideas of his own—anything that would keep him in the vanguard, anything that would make him seem fresh, anything that would give the impression he was moving forward. And in 1930, less than a year after joining the *Mirror*, he found one: He was going to go on the radio.

By 1930 radio was, much to the consternation of the press barons, no longer a novelty. While newspapers had been devastated by the crash, with advertising revenue plummeting in its aftermath, radio actually enjoyed a 90 percent increase in ad revenue during the first two years of the Depression, and a committee formed by the American Newspaper Publishers Association to analyze the threat of the new medium concluded that radio was newspapers' "greatest competitor."

None of this, however, deterred print journalists from signing on for radio programs, and Walter, with his vaudeville training, his rapid-fire delivery and his already well-defined puckish persona, seemed a natural for the new medium. As early as January 1928, when Walter was still at the *Graphic*, Bernarr Macfadden had asked public relations adviser Edward Bernays to investigate the possibilities of getting the columnist on the air, "as Mr. Winchell is very popular, and could talk on Broadway and New York plays, about which he is a unique authority." Nothing came of this particular inquiry, but Walter made an appearance in the fall on a special broadcast boosting humorist Will Rogers's mock presidential candidacy—Walter called for a more entertaining House of Representatives with some girls and a stage erected in the Capitol building—and was singled out by one radio critic for seeming "more at home before the mike than any newspaperman we have ever heard." In January 1929 he made a special appearance over forty-two stations on the National Broadcasting Company network conducting a tour of Broadway, with, in one critic's description, "deprecating yet loving gestures." Over the next few months he made several guest appearances on singer Rudy Vallee's radio program (at $250 per shot), and by the fall he was MC'ing Alexander Woollcott's show and doing occasional interviews. But he was still searching for a program of his own.

What probably happened that spring of 1930 was that the advertising agency for the Saks & Company department store devised a fifteen-minute program of gossip and a guest interview for Walter to air on Monday nights at 7:45, and that William Paley, head of the Columbia Broadcasting System—who was then actively courting agencies and sponsors to bring their programs to CBS rather than the more established NBC—convinced them to place it on his WABC flagship station in New York. As for Walter, he was so eager to please that he willingly submitted his script for vetting by the sponsor: "Let me know as soon as possible what to delete, if anything."

"Before Dinner—Walter Winchell" debuted on May 12, 1930, boldly listed among the radio highlights in the *Mirror*. (Within a few weeks it was renamed "Saks Broadway with Walter Winchell.") "I introduce myself to you as New York's most notorious gossip," Walter began modestly, "in case you have never read my drivel in the *Daily Mirror* or the other papers with which I am associated. I'm the 'Peek's Blab Boy' who turns the Broadway dirt and mud into gold, a terrible way of making a living, perhaps, but some people are radio announcers. They have called me a lot of things, too numerous to mention now, and what will you call me if any of the gossip I offer this evening concerns you, won't really matter."

It wouldn't matter, he said, because he was just then locked in a highly publicized feud with Ethel Barrymore that would drown out any other criticism. Calling all tabloid columnists "rock men," in an interview with the Sunday *World* on April 27, Miss Barrymore had reserved her harshest criticism for Walter. "It is a sad comment on American manhood that Walter Winchell is allowed to exist," she told the *World*. "And the worst of it is, not that he is published here [New York], but his stuff appears all over the country."

Never one to take a hit without firing back, Walter immediately attacked the *World*'s interviewer, a disgruntled playwright whose last effort Walter had panned, for allegedly distorting Barrymore's remarks. But when Barrymore wired the interviewer that she had indeed made these disparaging remarks about Walter, he attacked her too. "[Y]ou may rest assured that she is in a lather because we have printed many things about her. According to our files of several months ago we wrote: 'Ethel Barrymore will not make any Paramount Pictures, her screen test not being so hot!'" On radio, Walter crowed, "[I]t is a pretty good advertisement and I need publicity also, considering that I am supposed to be somewhat of an exhibitionist ... With a little luck, perhaps, Miss Barrymore's argument might help me to greater profits [...] [W]hen the other editors hear about Walter Winchell they might be deceived into believing that I am important. ..."

Not even radio was enough. On one show that June, Walter announced that he had been engaged to star in a movie short. "And he isn't going to be seen as the villain, either," he reported. "He will be the hero who burns down a school so that the kids can have more time to put the black mustaches on pretty girls [*sic*] billboard faces."

Filmed in July at the Vitaphone studios in Queens, *Bard of Broadway* was a disposable eleven-minute vignette, significant chiefly for being Walter's first screen appearance and for bearing witness to how fully formulated his Broadway persona already was. The movie opens at Mrs. Williams's School for Girls, where the matronly schoolmistress tells her teenage charges that she "does not tolerate smoking, drinking or any other form of weakness." Tuning a large radio receiver at the front of the classroom to a broadcast of Professor Lovejoyce on the "Elizabethan era and its refining influence on the twentieth century," Mrs. Williams instructs the girls to take notes and then leaves the room. No sooner has she left than one of the girls, smoking a cigarette and reading Winchell's column, suggests they find something "torchy" on the radio. Discovering Walter's broadcast, they crowd the receiver, secret conspirators in the revolution against gentility.

Looking small and boyish at the microphone, despite streaks of silver in his hair, Walter delivers a discourse on Broadway, "the double-crossroads of the world," where "there are broken promises" for every light. When Mrs. Williams returns and asks for a summary of the lecture on Queen Elizabeth, one of the girls says, "She made so much whoopee she didn't even have time to have a blessed event!" But another of the girls tattles, and Mrs. Williams promptly expels the transgressors, all of whom then conspire to meet that night at the Alpine Casino, where "Winchell gets the lowdown on the high hats."

That evening at the casino with two of the girls dressed as male escorts, the group asks the maître d' if they might be introduced to Walter Winchell. When Walter is informed, he decides to play a little joke on them. He asks the maître d' to seat him next to the girls and call him "Mr. Smith." Naturally one of the students, the pretty blond troublemaker (Madge Evans), asks him if he knows Winchell, and Walter sneers, "Oh, that Winchell is always stirring things up." He is still jesting when the club is raided by the police and the girls are carted off to jail.

At the police station the girls and Walter are both unmasked—"Always on the job when the story breaks," says a policeman—and Walter pleads the girls' case. "O.K., Walter. I'll take your word anytime," says the officer in charge. Now Walter offers to get them reinstated with Mrs. Williams, but the girls are incredulous. How could he? "She doesn't know Mrs. Winchell's bad little boy, Walter," he smiles. "He has a way of doing things, even when it seems impossible." At that moment the police drag in Mrs. Williams, who is decked out in a gown and carrying a feather fan, obviously having been caught making whoopee herself. If she will reinstate the girls, Walter says, he won't embarrass her in print. Mrs. Williams agrees, and the film ends with the blonde asking Walter for his autograph. "You can have my name anytime you want to," he says. "For keeps."

Like Runyon, he said he did it all for the money, did it because the exigencies of living made it necessary. By July, with *Bard of Broadway* completed and still another month to go on his radio contract, he was tired and restless and itching to get out of New York to see June and the girls, who had decamped to Hollywood for the summer. "Maybe if I could get out of the radio deal," he confessed in his column, "I could scram to H'wood and see June and the kids, miss 'em so." Addressing an item to Walda and Gloria, he wrote, "Daddy loves you so . . . Daddy is making pennies . . . Huh, huh, lotsa pennies, pussycats, so mamma can travel in drawing rooms."

Hoping to win his escape, he had submitted compilations of old column material to Kobler to run in his absence, but Kobler rejected the columns and warned him that he would be suspended without pay unless he provided new material. "I agree with you that you should have a vacation and certainly a vacation with full pay," Kobler wrote him after Walter made a veiled threat to stop writing, "but both you and I owe a holy obligation to over five hundred thousand fans. . . . Fortunately for you, you have a constitution of iron, and I often marvel at the amount of work you can do, but I would suggest that instead of writing for five or six magazines and doing moving pictures, that you defer this and write twelve extra columns in advance so that you may fully enjoy your vacation without depriving readers of what is coming to them." And Kobler closed with some advice "of an older man with more experience than you have. Don't ever threaten. That is bad business. But, if you try to get even with me it will please me very much because I think you owe me a hell of a lot." Meanwhile, Gauvreau forbade Walter to go to Hollywood. "I would advise you to stay here and cover Broadway as usual."

So Walter stayed in New York, moping in a room at the new Lincoln Hotel, camouflaging his impotence in the face of the *Mirror* edicts by pretending he didn't want to leave the city after all "for fear I'll miss something." When his family finally returned the first week of August, Walter was noticeably euphoric. "Walda, 3, was so cute with her excited tale of 'the hot hot' that came on the train with her from California [. . .] 'I come home to my daddy, and never leave him no more 'cause I, he baby, love him all much, my poor, poor daddy' . . . Her gorgeous hair and eyes are just like June's ... And Gloria, beautiful Gloria ... I can see her ten years from now when she's 16 ... Wonder if I'll amount to anything ten years from now?"

The next week the family escaped again from the sweltering city heat, this time to Atlantic City, and Walter was still stuck in New York, thinking wistfully of them. "Maybe if I told everybody where they could go to—then I could get on a train and see Walda running up and down like an Indian without any top on ... I see those Club Abbey gals every night without any tops on ... But what's that? ... Copy, merely copy ... Copy, however, that turns into paragraphs ... Paragraphs that turn into columns and columns that turn into gold ... Gold, pretty gold—to turn the wolves away from Walda's and Walter's door."

Angry that he had been forced to stay in New York even after his radio program ended on August 4, and no doubt taking Kobler's dare, Walter began circulating feelers that he might be available to another paper when his contract expired the following May. "I had dinner with Winchell last night," *Daily News* managing editor Frank Hause wrote the paper's publisher, Joseph Medill Patterson. "He assured me he would like to work for The News. He contends that the *Mirror* offered him $1,000 (?) a week and all syndication rights. I am of the opinion that The News could get him for one-half or $500 a week." Hause was scheduled to go on vacation, but he regarded the matter as urgent enough for him to stay and arrange a meeting for himself, Patterson and Winchell.

It was a thorny situation. Walter wanted more power and more money, but he was afraid that the *News*, which was already running three gossip columns, might try to trim his sails. The *Mirror* couldn't really afford to let him go, but neither did it want to grant him the freedom he wanted and that it had just denied him. The *News* knew that getting him would be a terrific coup, one that would wound the *Mirror* as mortally as his defection had wounded the *Graphic*, but it was only prepared to get him at a price and all along thought it was outmaneuvering him. "Winchell is trying to give us the rush act," wrote one *News* executive after Walter reported that the *Mirror* had tendered him a new offer. "Mr. Hause said not to pay any attention to all the things that Winchell would say."

But the *News* had outsmarted itself. When Hause contacted him in early September, Walter informed the *News* editor that he had already signed a contract with Kobler that would make him one of the highest-paid journalists in the country. Walter had played each side against the other and emerged the victor.

"It's a regular Horatio Alger story!" Walter gloated. "And I wish I wasn't the one on the spot, so that I could write the story myself about some other guy." The new five-year contract would pay him $121,000 a year, double his old salary. Moreover, he had signed a new radio contract for $1,000 a broadcast with the Wise Shoe Company, which billed him reasonably as "New York's Highest Priced Reporter." There were those who might grouse that he wasn't worth any of this, but Kobler, who resented Walter's popularity nearly as much as Gauvreau did, wasn't being charitable. The *Mirror's* circulation had climbed from 430,000 to 585,000 in Walter's first year there. The new contract was the price of keeping him and presumably the new readers.

With his contract freshly signed, he returned to the radio on September 9, once again on station WABC, all ajitter. "There is a wallop in the breathlessness and nervousness that grip you waiting for your guest star to show up," he had written a few days before. "The crowding in of several sentences in the few minutes allotted ... The problem of keeping from faltering or stumbling over a swift sentence, a syllable or a scoopee containing too many s's ... It will be a thrill, again, to hear that heart-thumping march-tempo'd 'Give My Regards to Broadway' ... The tap on the shoulder from the time-keeper signalling 'one minute to go' ... All of which hastens the blood thru my veins and keeps me from getting bored with myself." He opened the program: "It is a great kick for me at least, this giving you the lowdown on the big heads." He closed another broadcast: "I remain that very conceited Winchell Person who has gone slightly deaf—the result of so much applause, you know."

For all his blatant self-promotion, Walter was indeed the recipient of swelling applause that fall. When he appeared at the premiere of *Bard of Broadway* later that September in the Winter Garden Theater, a record audience cheered at his introduction and again at his first appearance on screen—"instantaneous, general and sincerely enthusiastic." "To report that Walter is a popular young man in the theater," added the observer, "is to pull one's punches plenty." The only damper for him was the decision by Wise Shoes that December not to pick up the radio program because, its operating director reluctantly wrote Walter, the board of directors hadn't approved a radio budget and there were no additional funds to divert. Ordinarily Walter might have panicked at this kind of news, but he had been so overworked that he seemed to regard it more as a commutation than a setback.

Now he could spend time with his neglected family. In December, two days after his final broadcast, he and Gloria were on a train to Florida for his first Miami trip—they were to meet June and Walda, who were riding down on a bus after a minor train accident in Stafford, Virginia—to get "some of that sunshine that everybody appears to think is good for the body." "It will be a thrill being alone with Gloria," he wrote on the trip. "Getting acquainted with her, after all these years [. . .] I can see myself being a nurse and cutting her food into tiny slices for her, and seeing that she gets to bed by 7."

But even on the rails with his beloved daughter, Walter felt the column asserting its priority and disturbing his peace. The maws had to be fed, the public served. "Wonder how it would feel if I ever could get one of those 'holidays' where I didn't have to be bothered with pencils, typewriters, paragraphs, drivel, columns and the other things that floor you!" But all he could ever do was wonder since he was already the column's victim. The maws were devouring him.

THOUGHTS OF avenging the slights he had suffered before fame struck were never far from Winchell's mind. He often remembered his vaudeville days when he was a nobody scrambling for recognition. Sometimes he daydreamed about revisiting the small towns where Winchell & Greene had flopped a decade earlier—revisiting them not as a celebrated columnist but incognito, observing the citizenry for a day or two with his cold eye and then writing them up in the column.

His biggest dreams were about the Palace Theater. The Palace was the vaudeville pinnacle where the best of the big-timers played, and it was the place outside which Walter had loitered with the other out-of-work vaudevillians when times were hard and he needed company and a handout. "All the years of playing the hick towns, getting the rebuffs and the humiliations and hoping that someday you'll play the Palace," he told an associate years later. "It's difficult for people who weren't part of the old vaudeville days to understand. But for me, playing the Palace was better than being elected to the White House."

By 1930 the grand old Palace was gasping in the general collapse of vaudeville as the motion picture increasingly took the place of live performers. The Depression only accelerated the decline. With the introduction of the talkies, the Palace was losing as much as $4,000 a week—in flush times it had shown a yearly profit of $800,000—and its management, in one last effort to resuscitate it, was desperately shuttling in headliners, sometimes three or four on a single bill. As often as not, headliners who once appeared shortly after intermission were now closing the shows just to keep people in the house.

Another innovation vaudeville managers had instituted was hiring newspaper columnists as masters of ceremonies. It wasn't that newspapermen were necessarily good or even adequate performers, but they provided free publicity in their columns, and they often attracted entertainers whom the theater could never afford in salary but whom the columnists could afford in generous column mentions. Heywood Broun, the rumpled wit of the *World*, appeared at the Palace early in 1930. Mark Hellinger, following Broun's lead, made appearances in Queens and Manhattan that summer. Walter was originally scheduled to play the Palace beginning June 28, but something interfered—possibly preparations for *Bard of Broadway* or just his overwhelming workload or nerves—and his debut was postponed indefinitely.

In January, however, shortly after Walter's return from Florida, the Palace renewed the offer at $3,500 a week, and this time Walter promptly accepted, then fretted over having done so. However much he wanted vindication, the Palace Theater was still daunting. Rita, who knew how much appearing at the Palace meant to him, called him at the office to wish him luck and found him a "nervous wreck." The Palace, for its part, did everything it could to soothe his fears, teaming him with Harry Richman, a popular and handsome crooner, and singer Lillian Roth. His friends also offered their support, many of them—Texas Guinan, Jimmy Durante, Rudy Vallee, Irving Berlin, Bugs Baer and Hellinger—making appearances onstage during the week.

As for the show itself, Walter read telegrams, acted in blackout sketches (in one he played a lover discovered by Richman as a cuckolded husband, in another he played a cuckold himself who jumps out of the closet dressed as a Salvation Army Santa Claus), heckled Richman from a box, did a brief soft shoe ("[T]he audience started to howl with glee," wrote one reviewer, "and when it was over they howled for more") and in the finale served as the base of a human pyramid with everyone piling on him. "That's Winchell under there!" they shouted joyfully.

Nothing, however, could disguise Walter's initial discomfort. Despite a thirty-five-second ovation when he appeared, the "daily columnist was scared out of his blue serge suit almost at the start of the opening matinee," said *Variety*. Another reviewer in the same issue wrote, "His nervousness was not assumed to make the public think him a shy, unpretentious fellow; it was real agony, translated into clenched hands and short, jerky movements," and ended, "Add simile: As scared as Winchell." In a review of his own, also for *Variety*, Walter called himself "another freak attraction . . . His appearance is oke—he has a natty tone about him . . . But he is hardly big time material. He simply won't do."

By midweek, his appetite destroyed by nerves, he had dropped four and a half pounds; by week's end, seven. "I'll never do this again for twice the coin," he averred in his column but admitted, "I would have been a chump to spurn all those 'coconuts.' . . . It will pay for the bride's and the kids' holiday at Miami Beach." Still, for all Walter's grumbling, the appearance was an unqualified success, avenging his vaudeville career once and for all. His first show set a house record, his first weekend set a weekend record, and he just missed Eddie Cantor's week's record set over New Year's. His 249 congratulatory telegrams broke still another Palace record. ("If you are as good on the stage as you are in your column," wired George S. Kaufman, "please cancel my seats.") Most gratifying was the reception by his Broadway confreres. "They went out of their way to give me a break, which is something I certainly never gave any of them," he wrote halfheartedly. "Remorse set in when I heard that reception . . . I've been such a rat."

Before the week ended, the Palace was asking him to extend his appearance, but Walter declined. Shortly after the close, producer Charles B. Dillingham approached him to do a summer revue, and Publix theaters offered him $5,000 a week for four weeks—two each at the Paramount Theaters in Manhattan and Brooklyn. He declined these too—as much as it must have pained him to do so—but later in the year, another producer, E. Ray Goetz, asked him to appear in a new musical by Cole Porter and Herbert Fields, and evidently under pressure from Kobler, who saw it as an opportunity to publicize the *Mirror*, he reluctantly accepted—so reluctantly that even the reports announcing the signing included the possibility of his reneging.

This time June put her foot down, and Walter wrote Kobler begging off the show because it "threatened my otherwise placid home life." "Mrs. Winchell, who asserts she has waited ten years for me to give her some companionship, is fed up with not getting any," he wrote. "That my joining a show or taking on any extra work only robs her of me, and she has told me in no uncertain terms that if I go with any show and overwork myself more than I am doing now, . . . she would not only throw a bomb right under your chair, but would take the babies and leave me. I would rather not irritate her. She has been patient with me for a long time." He practically beseeched Kobler for a release from the Goetz commitment. "My family and my health deserve some serious thought before it is too late," he warned.

Survival was very much on Walter's mind that winter of 1931. His professional survival as he saw it—and as Kobler and Gauvreau encouraged him to see it—depended on his continuing to go the pace that kills. On the other hand, there was the very real matter of Walter's physical and emotional survival—sleeping only a few hours, racing from club to club, pounding away at the column and the articles and until recently the broadcasts, making the appearances. While Kobler and Walter himself were strapping him to the rack of the column, June was encouraging Walter to disengage. These countervailing forces obviously agonized him, pitting as they did his professional life against his personal life, enforcing the fact that he couldn't have both (at least not as he perceived his job), and he was becoming physically and emotionally drained.

Back in October 1930 his personal physician had advised the *Mirror* that a vacation was "mandatory," but Kobler and Gauvreau had held him off until December, and even then compelled him to submit columns from Florida. By January, after the Palace appearance, the doctor told Walter that he "should leave the city at once," but Walter, obviously protecting his flanks, offered to continue writing the column, provided that no mention was made of his being out of town. Gauvreau warily responded that "the matter of your health has been a matter of grave concern to me for six years," and offered to confer with Walter about it. When Walter pressed the issue again a few days later, Gauvreau reluctantly conceded, warning that if he didn't return in two weeks, "The *Mirror* shall reserve the privilege of employing a ghost writer to carry on your column. . . . " Gauvreau knew there could be no more dire threat to Walter. But by this time Walter was so exhausted, Ruth Cambridge informed Gauvreau, that he couldn't leave the city no matter how badly he wanted to.

When he was able to depart a week later, he headed once again for Miami Beach. He had first gone there at the instigation of a bright young press agent named Steve Hannagan who had been hired to publicize the area and who calculated that Winchell describing Miami Beach's attractions and its personalities, rhapsodizing over its weather and lauding its creature comforts, could make of it the same sort of mythical city the columnist had made of Broadway: Broadway South, another island of splendor in hard-times America.

The Winchells stayed in the penthouse of the Roney-Plaza Hotel, Miami Beach's swankiest hostelry. It sat upon six palmy acres along the ocean on three blocks of private beachfront. It boasted an Olympic-size swimming pool, tennis courts, a putting green, nightly dancing and shopping, all enfolded in what it advertised as "pleasant privacy." The hotel building itself was tall and L-shaped in a style once labeled "Mediterranean eclectic," since the brickface was smooth and sand-colored with the junction of the L topped by a Romanesque cupola, and there were accents of Spanish Colonial Baroque, Tuscan Villa and Venetian Gothic in the ornamentation. Walter called it a "sample of heaven."

The Roney-Plaza would have been an ideal place for relaxation if Walter had been capable of it. Instead, he manned the phones and the wires and trolled the Miami clubs, collecting column material while June and the girls frolicked on the beach. As badly as he desired to get away, he was uncomfortable far from Broadway, far from the action. (Before Miami, Walter had "vacationed" in Long Beach, Long Island, or in Atlantic City.) The only way for him to relax, ironically, would be for him to draw

the action south with him—the press agents, the celebrities, the journalists, the nightclubbers. In time he would. "Winchell was very important
in making that season there," said a press agent who migrated to Miami
when Walter occupied the Roney. In time Miami Beach became
Winchell's own kingdom.

But that winter there was another beleaguered figure ruling Miami
Beach. A mutual friend, quite possibly New York gang chief Owney Madden, had asked Walter if he wanted to meet the chief of the Chicago
crime organization, Al Capone, and Walter leaped at the chance. Taken
out to Capone's fortress mansion on Palm Island connected to Miami
Beach by a causeway, Walter found the gang leader playing cards with his
cronies. Capone waved them off and invited Walter in. "The size of Al-
phonse was what impressed me more than anything about him," Walter
recalled. He spotted a large automatic pistol in one of the gullies on the
table where the poker chips were kept. "I don't understand that," Walter
said, making conversation. "Here you are playing a game of cards with
your friends, but you keep a gun handy." "I have no friends," Capone
snapped. Walter found Capone visibly "glum" over charges that he had
evaded income taxes, and when Walter asked him why he didn't just pay,
Capone insisted that all his wealth came from presents.

Walter apparently enjoyed Capone's company. He made three visits to
Capone's "shack," as he called it, and was rewarded with a racing card full
of winners. "[A]nd what long shots!" He also won $16,000 in two nights
at the roulette and dice tables. "I am feeling better," he wrote Gauvreau
after two weeks away, "and when I come back I will try and be a good
boy, but remember I am not promising!" Even so, Walter was concerned
over the continuing acrimony between him and Kobler. "I am still wondering why the last tiff with Mr. Kobler started. Until I find out the reason I will sulk. Don't tell me it is because I lost my temper. What was the
reason for making me lose it? . . . Sometimes I think you prefer having
Kobler and I [sic] mixing it up—to prove to him that I am all you told
him I was."

IF WALTER had learned anything from his incipient breakdown, it certainly wasn't evident. Rather he returned from Miami refreshed and recharged and ready for the wars, and he threw himself into the fray with
the same desperate energy as before and heading for the same fate. His
moaning the previous winter about radio notwithstanding, by summer he
was back on the air for La Gerardine, a preparation that created waves in
a woman's hair without a permanent. Advertising man Milton Biow wrote
Walter a few days later, outlining an aggressive push Biow was planning

for La Gerardine. "I want you to feel, Walter, that you are not merely talent in a broadcasting campaign, but an integral part of a great sales campaign." And he added, "I know that you will write to all your friends in the newspaper world, whether they carry your column or not, about your series of broadcasts, so we'll get the largest amount of newspaper advertising."

For Walter, however, the product being sold was less La Gerardine than Walter Winchell. Having had only limited success with Saks and Wise and even then only in the local New York market, Walter wanted to conquer radio as he had the papers, and he was willing to suffer restraints he would never have tolerated from the *Mirror*. "I wont [*sic*] submit offensive stuff," he promised Biow shortly after his first innocuous broadcast on September 15. "I know better. I like the job and the G—and I don't mean a string on a violin!"

Walter still complained about the grind as if he weren't the one ultimately responsible. "I am now leaving my office at 5:10 a.m.," he wrote Biow. "I could collapse so awful do I feel. Nothing to eat. Little sleep, had to do a review, my Sat col'm and this broadcast." But celebrity had to be stoked, stoked constantly, or it would be extinguished. He said he had been offered $10,000 for three weeks' work in a movie and asked Biow to arrange to broadcast from Hollywood, and he was now reconsidering the E. Ray Goetz musical that June had prevailed upon him to exit earlier that year.

Meanwhile, La Gerardine was thrilled with the new broadcast. "[W]e insisted that Walter Winchell be sold as 'the world's greatest columnist,' " the company's general manager gushed after the first program, "but after hearing you broadcast last night, I've written a letter to each of our eighty salesmen instructing them not only to sell you as a great columnist, but as a great radio personality." He prophesied that Walter would build a radio audience equal to that of his newspaper readership, and La Gerardine salesmen were soon reporting a dramatic rise in purchases of the tonic, especially on Wednesdays and Thursdays, after the Tuesday night broadcast.

Walter was far more critical. June listened devotedly every Tuesday, and together she and Walter would meticulously critique the broadcast. After one show, he wrote Biow, June had concluded that "I talked too deliberate and slow (I thought so, too). I'm a racy talker and must speak fast to get the breathlessness of my stuff over. . . . I want to cooperate, but let's have speed, zip, pep."

Walter's own criticisms notwithstanding, one impressed listener was George Washington Hill, maverick president of the American Tobacco Company. At the time the gaunt, beetle-browed Hill was sponsoring a one-hour musical program on Tuesday, Thursday and Saturday nights over the NBC radio network. Called "The Lucky Strike Dance Hour," it featured big bands from across the country with B. A. Rolfe, a jovial, bald, rotund bandleader, as master of ceremonies. As Walter later told it, Hill, apparently looking to add some kick to the program, ordered his advertising agency to sign Walter as Rolfe's replacement. One NBC executive said that the choice of Winchell "startled the town."

The problem was that Walter was already under contract to La Gerardine on WABC, the local CBS station. But Hill, an eccentric autocrat who wore large sombreros at the office and personally chose the musical selections for his program by forcing the NBC president to dance to them, was not to be denied. If La Gerardine didn't want to release Walter, Hill offered to pay them $35,000 to let Walter appear on "The Lucky Strike Hour" every Tuesday, Thursday and Saturday at ten o'clock for a four-week trial period while Walter continued to host the La Gerardine show at 8:45 on Tuesdays. It was an unprecedented arrangement, both because of the money involved (Albert D. Lasker of American Tobacco's Lord & Thomas & Logan ad agency called it the "first baseball player deal in radio history"), and because of Walter's duties as "the first commercial air doubler."

If King Features had given him national visibility as a journalist, Walter realized that "The Lucky Strike Dance Hour" had the potential to make him a star. This was precisely what Hill had had in mind in engaging him. The thirties were an "age of sound"; radio performers rivaled movie stars in popularity, and surpassed them in their intimate relationship with their audience. The number of radio receivers had skyrocketed from eight million in 1928 to eighteen million just four years later (by comparison, daily newspaper circulation had dipped 7 percent to thirty-six million over the same period), but those numbers only hinted at the cultural implications of radio. As the country seemed to disintegrate under the stress of the Depression, radio provided a bond and a balm—the sense of shared culture to which the gossip column had also contributed. "Sound helped mold national responses," according to one analyst, "it helped create or reinforce uniform national values and beliefs in a way that no previous medium had ever before been able to do," and it would be as much through the sounds of the era—through the hiss and crackle of the imperfect sound of the talkies, the sonorities of Franklin Roosevelt, the songs of the Dust Bowl and the melodies of the Depression—as through anything else that the period would be remembered.

Radio was the power that helped unify America, and the NBC radio network was the power behind radio. Its fifty stations stretched from New York to Los Angeles, offering Walter an even larger audience than syndication had. Yet, as always, the prospect that so tantalized Walter also frightened him. As always, he was haunted by the possibility of failure, by the possibility that if he did fail, he would destroy his new aura of invincibility and ruin his career, by the possibility that he would finally be found out to be talentless. He debuted on November 3—he was introduced as "the one and only Walter Winchell, whose gossip of today becomes the news of tomorrow"—nervous and contrite but surprisingly candid about his motives. "[M]y skin is thick," he said. "As the Honorable Ham Lewis of Illinois said to the editor of a famous New York daily—'notice me, for Heaven's sake, notice me. If you can say something good, say it; but, in any event, say *something.' Notice me!'"

Nor was he being anything other than honest in expressing his fear in having graduated from La Gerardine to Lucky Strike. "This alleged heart of mine is actually thumping and bumping all over the studio," he told his listeners, "because I realize I am part of what certainly will prove to be one of the greatest radio entertainments—an air show that must attract millions of ears. It excites me, of course, to be in the show. . . . It all sounds so Big-Timey to me." He began his second broadcast thanking his listeners for their criticisms and soliciting more. "I have been in long trousers long enough to know that sticks and stones may break your bones—but slams only prove that you are not being snubbed."

It was not by any means all Walter's show. His assignment was to introduce the orchestras and the station identification ("Here's that fellow with the chi-MES," he would say of NBC's trademark three-note scale) and to deliver two gossip breaks of roughly five minutes' duration each. The program's primary appeal was still its music and its "magic carpet" gimmick of zipping from an orchestra in one city to a second orchestra in another, and it was this that earned the show its encomiums as "one of the greatest steps forward in radio entertainment on record." Plans were soon being made to connect orchestras from Buenos Aires, Havana and Montreal, and in December "The Lucky Strike Dance Hour" featured the first transatlantic broadcast of an English dance band on a sponsored program.

But if Walter was not the central attraction yet, he was making his presence felt. Under B. A. Rolfe, the program had been criticized for its lack of spontaneity. "He was continually under wraps," wrote *Graphic* radio columnist Jerry Wald, "and every note played, every cymbal crashed, was passed on pompously by a board of directors." With Rolfe gone, the program was still choppy, Wald believed, but Walter energized it and provided it with a unifying personality and perspective. "It's a known fact that the red-faced gossiper's chattering is holding up the whole feature on his frail shoulders. He has something interesting to offer."

He went about his radio business with the same sort of imploded energy that had drawn comment in his early days at the *Graphic*. One visitor said he was so intent on his work that he required an extra announcer to stand beside him during the show and depress his shoulder when it was his turn to broadcast. He smoked constantly and dashed about the studio asking people what they thought of the broadcast and telling them about letters he had received. Even after he was renewed for four more weeks that November, he took nothing for granted. When Louis Sobol, who had recently moved to the *Journal* from the *Graphic*, planted an item with Bide Dudley of the *World* that Lucky Strike had made him an offer, Walter detonated, firing off letters to American Tobacco and to Jerry Wald at the *Graphic* asking them to refute the implication that he would soon be replaced. To Sobol, he wrote: "That was certainly third-rate trying to even a grudge with me. . . . Get a big radio contract, all the more power to you, but don't try to do it the way you tried in the *Journal* on Monday." Sobol remonstrated that Lucky Strike had only signed him to a retainer in case anything happened to Walter, but this didn't appease Walter. Their feud, already hot after Sobol's apparent snub, boiled.

Sobol was undoubtedly telling the truth. By mid-December, with Walter's second four-week contract nearing an end, *Radio Guide* reported that he would soon be forced off "The Lucky Strike Dance Hour" unless La Gerardine relented. Already he was quibbling with La Gerardine both over the censorship of his broadcast and over the provision that he secure the guest star for his program each week and pay him from his own salary. "I am glad, Walter, to have done this for you," Raymond Spector of the Biow agency wrote him when Spector landed singer Morton Downey for the show in October, but warned, "perhaps that is the end of the rope of my talent contact."

Even if he hadn't been unhappy, the idea of being forced to relinquish the national "Lucky Strike" for the local La Gerardine was unthinkable, especially since his La Gerardine contract still had thirty-seven weeks to run. But, again, one could never underestimate George Washington Hill. Hill, whose father had also been president of American Tobacco, lived for one thing: to sell his Lucky Strikes. It was an obsession more than a profession. And Hill believed that Walter in his eight weeks on the air had helped sell cigarettes. Hill wanted Winchell. La Gerardine wanted $55,000 to release him. By December 20 a deal had been struck. Walter signed a new contract at, *Radio Guide* said, $3,000 a week, putting him in the lofty company of radio stars Morton Downey, who got $5,000 a week from Camel cigarettes, Kate Smith, who got $4,000, and Bing Crosby, who got $2,000. Knowing the publicity value of a salary, Walter sent the magazine a correction: he was actually getting $3,500 a week.

"I don't know how to say what I want to say," he wrote American Tobacco's ad agency, Lord & Thomas & Logan, the week of the contract.

Maybe you will understand if I get right to the point like this. Thanks. Thanks for everything. I mean my new contract. It's [*sic*] generous contents and what you have done to elevate me—lifting me from a circulation of 602,000 (the *Mirror*), and an estimated six million among my syndicated newspapers—to the greatest circulation of them all: the Lucky Strike Dance Hour tuner inners.

I am the happiest boy in town right now and, of course, you gentlemen must know that. You have brought the day nearer to me when I won't have to strive so much, and maybe get that vacation I've been looking forward to since 1910. . . .

Frankly, I was apprehensive at first when I started the Lucky Strike Dance Hour. I feared that the people in the smaller towns would be opposed to me and my "gossip." To my amazement they appear to like me. I attribute this to the fact that such a representative and dignified organization as the American Tobacco Company sponsored me.

"If anything happens to me now," he closed, "it will be my fault I feel sure."

There remained only one barrier between him and the possibility of stardom: La Gerardine wouldn't release him until he found a replacement. He immediately thought of Hellinger and dangled the salary in front of him, but Hellinger declined, saying, "I wouldn't be a Winchell imitator for $10,000 a week." Next he recruited Sidney Skolsky, a local gossip columnist and friend of Walter's, but Skolsky's voice didn't register properly for radio when he auditioned. He finally enlisted the young gossip columnist at the *Graphic* who had been tapped to replace Sobol there. Ed Sullivan was stiff, but he had good contacts and had done some MC'ing, and La Gerardine found him acceptable. After a two-week hiatus, the program returned that January with a new title, "Broadway's Greatest Thrill," and its new host. As a result, Walter would always take credit, not without justice, for having launched Ed Sullivan's radio and television career.

MONEY. If it was always about fear of failing, at some level it would also always be about money: about securing the present against the harms of the past. With his new Lucky Strike contract, he was making an almost unconscionable salary—$6,000 a week by one estimate—but he was generally frugal, allowing himself surprisingly few luxuries for a man of his means. Since the fall of 1929 he and June had lived comfortably but not extravagantly in a five-room suite at the Hotel Park Central at 55th Street and Seventh Avenue; he also maintained a room two floors below where he could sleep daytimes undisturbed. Late in 1930 they moved to the new Lincoln Hotel, a tall buff-colored building at Eighth Avenue and 44th Street, where Walter had stayed while his family was in California that summer. The Winchells moved back to the Hotel Park Central late in 1932, but they still lived unostentatiously. Walter bought his suits from Earl Benham, a former vaudevillian turned clothier, and as always dressed nattily and tastefully but within his means. His only jewelry was a gold wristwatch that Hellinger had given him on his birthday and a ring with a blue stone which he described only as a recent gift. His sole indulgence was a Stutz Bearcat automobile that he acquired after signing his Wise Shoe contract in the fall of 1930.

While most of his frugality stemmed from childhood deprivations, part of it was the claims made upon him. In November 1929 he had voluntarily increased Rita's weekly stipend to $50; when she notified him in July 1931 that she was contemplating legal action to increase the amount again, he agreed to pay her $75 every Monday so long as he lived. As for his other familial responsibilities, Jacob Winschel had retired from the women's undergarment business and was now dependent on doles from his sister Beatty and from Walter. Walter was also supporting Jennie after his brother Algernon, a credit manager, married in November 1929 and moved out of his mother's apartment. Walter assumed the rent and sent her a weekly allowance—later he ensconced her in an apartment in the Hotel Franconia at Central Park West and 72nd Street—but he never begrudged her these things. Whatever his childhood adversities, he loved Jennie and was always attentive to her, making a point of stopping by her apartment no matter how demanding his schedule and occasionally taking her to lunch at Lindy's with the Broadway wise guys. For her part, Jennie, whom everyone now called "Grandma Jinny" after Walda's and Gloria's name for her, remained independent. "She went around a lot by herself, and she'd say she liked her own company," recalled one relative.

Walter also lent money to other journalists when the Depression tightened its fist around them, including FPA, whom he had never even met. "Cast your bread upon the waters, I once read, and sometimes you get back angel food cake," Walter wrote. "All of them helped fill my column with quips and advance news about their intimates—which newspaper exec was on the Way Up or Out and so on." This way Walter feathered his own nest, his column, and subtly exerted his power. But when Gauvreau accepted a salary cut out of solidarity with Hearst, who was taking a beating during the Depression, and recommended that Walter do the same, Walter laughed at the idea. Money was for safety, and it was for power. It was never to be surrendered out of symbolic gestures of solidarity. Years of poverty had taught him that.

III

At NBC, the idea was fame. Now that he worked for Lucky Strike, the idea was to make of Walter Winchell a star whose popularity would rub off on the cigarettes the way Walter believed the dignity of the American Tobacco Company had rubbed off on him. Walter represented the modern, the breathless, the indomitable, the glamorous. So would Lucky Strike. "Hill wanted me to help build a radio audience for Winchell, who was unknown except to readers of his syndicated newspaper column," public relations counsel Edward Bernays later wrote, underestimating somewhat Walter's level of public recognition. "I planned to build him as if he were an institution."

With this commitment from Hill and infused with confidence, Walter began "The Lucky Strike Dance Hour" that January under his new contract. He was talking faster and hitting harder. And he was acting less like the continuity between orchestral segments than like the star of the program. Critics approved. "To the thrill furnished by the competition in the musical portion of the program," reported the Portland *Oregonian*, "Winchell adds the thrill of suspense. You listen not because you admire him, but because you expect each night his egotism will overreach itself, plunging [him] up to his neck in trouble."

But Walter was still his own severest critic. "It sounded monotonous, even to me," he told an interviewer a few years later. "Too many blessed-eventings, heartings, reno-vatings, elopements, twoings; too many movie people and *flash-flashes*. Needed highlights. Something." Walter said he had discovered the missing element himself, but George Washington Hill also closely monitored the broadcasts and soon advised Walter that he knew what was missing: humor.

There had always been an element of humor in Walter's columns; besides the jokes, he had always planted his barbs with a grin that for most readers, if not for the subjects themselves, softened any sense of malice. Though an egomaniac, he also had a self-deprecating wit, and he never hesitated to make himself the butt of his own gibes. Now he had to find a way to bring some of that to the radio. Walter remembered that before they both joined the *Mirror*, he and Mark Hellinger had waged a mock feud in their columns, stopping only when readers began taking their sallies seriously. Now Walter decided to begin a new mock feud on the air. And the first target that came to mind, he said, was Ben Bernie.

Bernie was a banana-nosed, nasal-voiced band leader who had a more or less permanent engagement at the Sherman House's College Inn in Chicago, where he broadcast over local radio. Walter knew him from the days when Bernie had played New York—they had actually written a song together—and liked him. He now phoned Bernie and told him he was going to take a crack at him and asked Bernie to fire back in kind. "I just had some swell scrambled eggs," went a typical Bernie gag. "Gosh, if only Winchell had come in, I'd have had ham and eggs." To which Walter riposted on his show, "Old fooph Bernie needn't worry about ever running for President, 'cause how could you get that nose on a two-cent stamp?"

Over the months—and then years—hundreds of these juvenile insults flew back and forth. It was a measure of Walter's popularity that Bernie practically parlayed their feud into full-fledged stardom. Soon Pabst Blue Ribbon Beer was sponsoring Bernie on his own national radio show, Paramount Pictures was flying him out to Hollywood for a film, and his salary escalated to $6,500 a week for the broadcast and $7,000 for personal appearances. He even hired a young writer just to craft his insults.

Some listeners never caught on, just as some readers had never caught on to the Winchell-Hellinger feud. They couldn't understand why two men would engage in this sort of nasty banter if they didn't mean it, and they deluged the sponsors with letters asking them to desist. No doubt realizing the damage a truce would inflict on his own career, Bernie nervously wired Albert Lasker of the Lord & Thomas & Logan ad agency to lobby for the continuation: OFFSETTING THIS SMALL MINORITY OF CHRONIC OBJECTORS ARE THOUSANDS OF LISTENERS WHO WAIT EAGERLY FOR WINCHELL'S GIBES AND WHO REALIZE THE RAILLERY IS ALL IN JEST. Despite this plea, a year after it started the feud was temporarily suspended by the sponsors, prompting Walter to muse in the column, "Don't tell me that we've both been that 'deep'—unfunny or harsh!" But if the feud confused some listeners, especially those outside the big cities where this sort of banter was acceptable, it also launched a trend. Other mock feuds followed—Jack Benny and Fred Allen, W. C. Fields and Charlie McCarthy, Bob Hope and Bing Crosby—enlivening the airwaves by parodying show business competitiveness and helping dissipate the much more serious tensions and anxieties loosed by the Depression.

WHILE WALTER and Ben Bernie jousted, George Washington Hill had been supervising the entire Winchell campaign approvingly. "I am, myself, as great an enthusiast over timely gossip as you are," Hill wrote Walter early in February, offering what he called some "constructive criticism" but also demonstrating surprising acuity about the functions of gossip.

I think it is the modern trend and the modern thing that builds reputations and businesses. The psychology of the American public is not interested in what has happened, so much as they are interested in those happenings which point out what is going to happen. On the other hand, there seems to be a danger, and I say this from your personal point of view, of too much enthusiasm in connection with news, to the end that one runs the risk of getting the reputation of being destructive. Therefore, I think that in your programs, you have been consciously, or unconsciously, very wise of late—because to me your programs exemplify thoughtful consideration of four major points.

Hill said he noticed that Walter didn't speak ill of anyone unless the person's reputation was already "nil"; that Walter was more and more drawing a "moral" from the tales of misbehavior he told ("This seems to be building you in the eyes of your public . . ."); that Walter was including a few "heartthrob" items in the broadcast, which "builds in the public mind the consciousness that you, too, have a real heart"; and that Walter made as many kindly references to individuals as he made negative ones. Walter gratefully acknowledged these letters and responded with toadying letters of his own.

Walter had reason to be grateful. As he had hoped, "The Lucky Strike Dance Hour" extended his popularity far beyond New York and far beyond the newspapers, and it established him as a national icon. When he began introducing orchestras with the slogan "Okay, America," the phrase instantly became a national catchword, and Hill quickly incorporated it into his Lucky Strike advertising. By the spring of 1932 there were 45,000 billboards of Walter in a tuxedo riding his microphone stand like a broomstick with the legend "OK—America!" underneath, scattered throughout 18,886 cities. National magazines presented full-page ads of Walter trilling, "Luckies are kind to your throat . . . I KNOW." When a skeptical stockholder asked at a meeting if the money on Winchell was well spent, a company representative answered that American Tobacco had done a telephone survey of five hundred respondents in six cities each week and found that "not only is our program successful, but it is one of the most popular on the air." Sixty percent of all radio listeners on the Tuesdays, Thursdays and Saturdays Walter broadcast were tuned to his show.

In the past there had been journalists who had attained celebrity—the dashing Hearst reporter Richard Harding Davis, for one—but it had always been a function of their journalism, of the stories they reported and of their own exploits in reporting them. Winchell was a different kind of phenomenon. He was not a star reporter. He was a journalistic entertainer—a radio star, a stage star, even a minor movie star. There were now songs about him,* ads featuring him ("His infallible taste in correct pocketwear is comparable only to his instinctive flair for topical tattle," ran a handkerchief spot in *Vanity Fair*), stories about him, soon plays and movies about him. Envelopes bearing nothing but his picture were routinely delivered to the *Mirror*.

And there were now imitators of him. Louis Sobol had succeeded Walter at the *Graphic* and then, in July 1931, moved to Hearst's *Journal*, but Sobol was a sentimental and timorous man, not a true challenger, and Walter kept him under control. "Why do you go into places when I do?" he would ask, and Sobol would respond feebly, "Walter, I don't know when you're going to be here." Sobol's replacement at the *Graphic*, Ed Sullivan, was something else again. Sullivan would later become the wooden, cadaverous, pickle-faced host of a popular Sunday television variety show, but once he had been a ruddily handsome high school athletic star in Westchester County outside New York City. Upon graduation he had drifted into sportswriting, landing on the *Graphic*. An ambitious but lazy man, Sullivan was described by one staff member as "getting more use out of a chair than anybody else connected with the place." With his carefree attitude, Sullivan was so popular with his fellow writers that they elected him sports editor when an opening developed, but a new managing editor replaced him, and he floated in a kind of limbo until Sobol left for the *Journal*. Sullivan was offered the Broadway column as a sop. He accepted largely because it got him a $50 raise.

"It's only fair to warn Eddie, of course, that his home life from now on is a thing of the past," Sobol wrote in his valedictory column. "He'll be coming home anywhere from 5 to 8 in the morning. He'll be coming

---

You can talk of Shakespeare or Eugene O'Neill
They may have great appeal
But when you talk of writers
This is how I feel
There's just one for me
I'm sure you'll agree
Who knows more about you than you do
Be it sorrow or joy?
It's that gadabout guy
We're madabout—Mrs. Winchell's boy.
("Mrs. Winchell's Boy" by L. Wolf Gilbert and Abner Silver, Marlow Music, 1932)

home worn out, tired, grouchy and resentful at the world in general. He'll toss around in bed wondering what in the world he'll use for a column the next day." But Mrs. Sullivan shouldn't worry, he said. "They'll only mean that Eddie is a good Broadway columnist. Only good Broadway columnists act that way."

Sullivan, however, was not in a fraternal mood when he wrote his first column on June 1, 1931. Titled "The Maimed Stem," the column blasted his rivals. "I feel, frankly," he said, in what seemed an obvious dig at Walter,

> that I have entered a field of writing which offers scant competition, a field of writing which ranks so low that it is difficult to distinguish any one columnist from his road companies.
>
> Other writers, in other departments of a newspaper, must hoist themselves by their own bootstraps; the Broadway columnists have lifted themselves to distinction by borrowed gags, gossip that is not always kindly and keyholes that too often reveal what might be better hidden.... *I charge the Broadway columnists with defaming the street.*

Later that week he continued the barrage. "To my former associates in the field of sports writing," he wrote, "I must report that THIS is a soft-touch in an unusually responsive arena ... While all my columning contemporaries are fuming and fretting at my invasion, one of them has even carried his personal alarm into the two-column measure of his daily piece. This particular fellow has never had much competition. He's got it now. I have not decided whether to chase him over the right field fence or the left field fence.

"This, however, is purely a matter of route, and immaterial."

It turned out that the fellow he was referring to was Louis Sobol, who had counterattacked that week by writing, "[E]mpty vessels make the most sound." At a theater opening a few nights later Sullivan, possessed of a choleric temper, grabbed Sobol and threatened him. Of course, it was one thing to pick on Sobol and quite another to pick on Walter Winchell.

Winchell and Sullivan had had a testy relationship ever since their time together on the *Graphic*. Sullivan often told the story of how Walter, at his wits' end over the constant squabbles with Gauvreau, had asked Sullivan to intervene with O. J. Elder, a friend of his and a ranking Macfadden executive. On a fishing trip with Elder the next week, Sullivan did.

A few days later, an enraged Gauvreau called Sullivan into his office and demanded to know why he had gone over his, Gauvreau's, head. As

Sullivan told it, he explained to Gauvreau that he had simply told Elder what a shame it was that the editor and Winchell were always at logger-heads. "When he finally cooled down, he said, 'All right, now, who do you think told me about your going to Elder?'" And when Sullivan said he just assumed it was Elder, Gauvreau told him it was actually Winchell. Gauvreau then called Walter in and, again according to Sullivan's version, Walter, white with fear, sheepishly admitted having told Gauvreau, but said that Gauvreau had forced it out of him. "Walter, what can I do with a cringing coward like you?" Sullivan snarled. "If I hit you, you might get hurt; if I spit in your eye it will be coming down to your level." (Walter denied that any of this ever happened.)

The night after his first Broadway column appeared, Sullivan said he arrived at Reuben's Delicatessen and found Walter there. Sullivan was voluble, but Walter was uncharacteristically quiet before finally cutting in. "Did you mean what you wrote today?" he asked Sullivan. Sullivan hedged, saying that he was merely trying to make a big entrance. When Walter said that he accepted this as an apology, Sullivan exploded. "I got so mad," he later said, "I grabbed him by the knot in his necktie and pulled him over the table, right on top of the cheesecake. 'Apologize to you?' I said—'You son of a bitch, I did mean you and if you say one more word about it I'll take you downstairs and stick your head in the toilet bowl.'" Then, said Sullivan, Walter got up and slunk out.

These were terrific stories, dramatic evidence of Sullivan's power, but he told them only years later, when Winchell's own power was in decline. In 1931 almost no one, certainly not a fledgling columnist, treated Winchell that way. In fact, several weeks after his debut Sullivan was writing Walter, grumbling good-naturedly that Walter hadn't tossed him any bouquets over his scoops but had instead bristled when Sullivan cor-rected a "wrongo," and singing Walter's praises. "Your Monday column still fills me with respectful amazement," he wrote flatteringly. "It's gor-geous great. Where you get it, I don't know but as I pay better dough, I believe your operatives, with the possible exception of Dorothy Parker, will see the error of their ways and get on the Sullivan bandwagon."

If Sullivan was hoping to curry favor, Walter was having none of it. Walter knew it was a cutthroat business, and he was deeply suspicious of everyone. Paul Yawitz, a young staff writer at the *Mirror*, remembered Walter's telling him he was going to Detroit. Yawitz absently said that he was glad. *Why* was he glad? Walter insisted on knowing. He demanded credit for his gags, coinages and innovations and did battle against any-one who denied it as if the slights were a conspiracy against him. "Won-der why it is every time a word becomes popular some publicity-hungry abba-dabba breaks into print with his argument that it isn't new, at all?"

Walter complained in 1931, when his coinage of "whoopee" was being challenged by a professor. "Whoopee, the Dr. told the Times, was at least 300 years old . . . He never would explain why the edition of the dictionary waited 300 years before including it under the W's. Or W.W.'s."

He had no sense of proportion. While he steadily attacked journalistic heavyweights like O. O. McIntyre, accusing him of stealing from the column, of using improper English, of recounting a "true" story that turned out to be the plot of a recent Broadway hit, he was equally hard on the flyweights. A screed by an M. Glebowitz in the Yiddish-language *Jewish Daily Forward*—"Broadwayites fear him as they would a conflagration"— which chided Walter for having implied that Larry Fay had given Texas Guinan an automobile for sexual favors, drew his wrath even though the number of people who had read it was minuscule compared with the number of people who now read the charge in his column. "Apparently, Mr. Glebowitz cannot read our 'English' as well as he can read the language he writes," Walter fumed.

> The line in question was printed here in this manner: "Larry Fay has sold his $38,000 car, which once belonged to the Belgian King, to Texas Guinan for $2,000." What we meant to say, Mr. Glebowitz, if we didn't make it clear, was that Larry Fay has sold his $38,000 car, which once belonged to the Belgian King, to Texas Guinan for $2,000.

It was all so precarious, he believed. There were so many who wanted to see him fail now that he had risen, so many who wanted to make him an object lesson in hubris once they had built him up. "The big idea now is to wreck Walter Winchell," he complained to *Variety*'s Sime Silverman, his longtime mentor, when the paper suddenly began censuring him for various and sundry offenses, including his having formed a corporation allegedly to avoid taxes. ("That's a pip—maybe I would wind up in jail, thanks to an old friend," he wrote Silverman.) At the same time Walter was oblivious of the insults he issued. A young press agent had written some jokes for an act Mark Hellinger was doing at Loew's State Theater in Manhattan. That night Walter wrote: "Many years ago when a yokel came to the Big City, we'd sell him the Brooklyn Bridge. Now we sell him tickets to see Mark Hellinger at Loew's State." The press agent was furious. How could Winchell write that about his friend? But when he went to Hellinger's office to commiserate, Hellinger instead picked up the phone and called to thank Walter for the plug. "Winchell thinks if you mention him it's a break," explained Hellinger. "Winchell would be upset if I didn't thank him."

IV

With Walter Winchell's popularity that winter of 1931–32 had come an issue: the "Winchell problem." Almost everyone recognized that Winchell had created a new and highly imitated form of journalism—so much so that press observers were now regularly referring to the "new journalism" when they discussed his effect on their profession. Almost everyone recognized that he had expanded the purview of news into the most private behavior of public personalities and that in doing so, he had torn down not only the long-standing barrier between the private and the public but the barrier between marginal gossip sheets like *Broadway Brevities* and *Town Topics* and the daily newspaper, making it nearly impossible to tell where to draw the line.

Traditionalists were appalled and not a little frightened. Winchell was an entertainer certainly, but was he, they asked, really a journalist? And if he was a journalist, had his gossip compromised journalistic integrity beyond repair? The Code of Ethics adopted by the American Society of Newspaper Editors said, "A newspaper should not invade private rights or feelings without sure warrant of public right as distinguished from public curiosity." By that standard, the answers seemed self-evident. "[H]e is fond of calling himself a newspaper man, but he will be a wise-cracking, gossiping trouper as long as he lives," wrote one critic, who nevertheless admitted to reading Winchell's column daily. "[H]e outdoes the yellow sheets in prodding impudent fingers into intimacies which any gentleman would consider deserving of privacy." "When Winchell discusses the personal affairs of actors, musicians, nightclub performers, cabaret rounders, no one is much concerned because many of these people court such publicity," said another, drawing a new distinction, "but when Winchell gets down into the financial district and talks so carelessly, so cruelly, often so inaccurately, about people below Fulton Street, his flippancy and misstatements can ruin careers. . . . Winchellism throws mud upon the institution of journalism." Incensed by a "swarm of Winchell imitators" cropping up on the radio, the motion picture studios, under the leadership of film industry czar Will Hays, petitioned the Federal Radio Commission to stop them. Walter said he welcomed an investigation but added that the studio press agents were the ones who were feeding him material.

In January 1932 Marlen Pew, the respected editor of *Editor & Publisher*, weighed in with his pronouncement on the practice of gossip. "The talk of the columnists is borrowed from gigolo society and is about as responsible as the chatter one might hear over cups in a night club," he wrote.

"In fact, much of the stuff is faked or guessed. Other matter is dirt no respectable writer would put on paper. . . . It is a dirty business." But Pew was confident that "every such column carries the germ of its own self-destruction. We have been seeing them come and go for thirty years, usually passing out by the libel route, though occasionally some more violent form of control is exercised by outraged victims. These columns, we daresay, belong in certain mediums. . . . They disconcert us mainly when we see them tucked away, like a secret cabinet of sin, in some newspaper which makes pretenses of virtue."

Some of the soul-searching even came from quarters once friendly to Walter. New York *World-Telegram* columnist Heywood Broun had been an early admirer of Walter's, and when Broun had run for Congress in 1930, Walter served as master of ceremonies of the candidate's fund-raiser and recruited most of the talent. Walter even carried a wallet that Broun had given him as a token of friendship. But when Broun received a letter from a woman saying she had been sinned against by Winchell and asked how she could get redress, Broun began musing on ethics. "A great tradition is being smutted over," he wrote in his column. "Some may say that the brilliant young commentator on the passing scene has merely adapted the small town paper practice to the needs of Broadway. That is an insufficient argument. Who wants New York to have the same sort of underground wires which make small towns so mean and so petty?" As Broun saw it, former *World* editor Herbert Bayard Swope's rule was the correct one: that only private issues which were matters of court or official record should be made public. In any case, good journalistic practice demanded verification. "Mr. Winchell prints the tips. He uses not only what he knows but what he thinks he knows." "There used to be a thing called private life," Broun lamented. "Some people like it very much. A man or a woman ought to have the right to say 'I love you' or 'I don't love you' without first turning up the carpet to see if any tabloid is represented around the premises."

Walter leaped to his own defense the next day, taking exception to Broun's categorization of him and especially to Broun's complaint that he listed who was dining with whom. "He confuses me with the ladies who report such trivia." He did have his own code of ethics, Walter insisted. He was not like others who "never pause to separate the names of the married men who might have told their squaws that they were going to be late on business . . . so the list comes out and there is hubby's tag under the name of a doll that perhaps his wife has heard things about."

Even so, Walter was pulling his punches against Broun until the following week, when the issue was joined by the reporting of Mayor Jimmy Walker's personal life. Every journalist knew that the lively Walker, a Roman Catholic married to another Roman Catholic who would not grant him a divorce, was having a torrid romance with a young Broadway actress named Betty Compton. Walker never hid it from them. But there had been a long-standing gentlemen's agreement among reporters that no one would publish anything about the affair. When Compton shocked the city by suddenly marrying actor Eddie Dowling in the spring of 1931, she returned from her Cuban "honeymoon" and told Walter that she had been drugged by political confederates of Walker's and steamrollered into the marriage, but she begged him not to publish anything about her plans to seek a divorce. As hot a story as it was, Walter kept her secret, and her romance with the mayor was soon renewed.

Now, a year later, the gentlemen's agreement seemed to be unraveling as word of the affair began leaking into the press, though no journalist wanted to take responsibility for the breach. Instead, the *Mirror* self-righteously editorialized against reporting about the mayor's private life, prompting Broun to attack the inconsistency of a newspaper editorializing thus while printing in the same issue a news story "filled with a considerable amount of innuendo." Editor Burton Rascoe, writing a series for the Detroit *News*, then attacked Broun for indulging in the same sort of subterfuge as the *Mirror*: "[T]o attack Mayor Walker's private life while trying to appear to defend it from attack is a bit thick." Walter now attempted to enter the fight by reprinting Rascoe's charges in his column and adding a few new ones of his own. But Gauvreau nixed the column, saying Walter couldn't use the space to indulge his "personal prejudices." So Broun, in a gesture of journalistic solidarity, ran it unexpurgated in the *World-Telegram*.

In his piece Walter claimed that all these newsmen solemnly invoking ethical standards were hypocrites. "As if this or that newspaper cares a continental about ethics, as they are so amusingly called—in these wild days of thefting each other's circulation ideas, plans and all the other malaaaarkey that passes for tradition—haw!" The *Herald-Tribune*, the *Evening Telegram* and *Time* magazine, he said, had all made insinuations about Mayor Walker while pretending to be above such prattle. "I remember them well," Walter wrote, "for I chuckled long and loud at the time, when I thought how these same goodies (who belittle the tabloids) grabbed and front-paged what they must have termed a news-beat." And in a left-handed defense of Broun, he said, "All Broun did was keep mentioning it after all the others had decided it was none of their business."

Though the issue of the public's right to know, which Walter's column had raised, was obviously an important one, the debate just as obviously wasn't terribly rigorous, at least outside legal circles. That was largely because it was never really the ethical debate it purported to be. It was, like the conflict over the tabloids themselves, a cultural debate. Traditionalists believed that certain things just weren't done by decent people, including decent journalists. Certain proprieties had to be maintained. Revealing romances, divorces, anticipated births, illnesses, financial exigencies—all of which Walter did—whether ethical or not, was unseemly, ungentlemanly.

On the other hand, Walter's defense of gossip wasn't in any way philosophically based either. It wasn't an issue of First Amendment protections or the unimpeded flow of information. It was personal and intuitive: him against them, outsiders against insiders, democrats against cultural royalists. In his mind it was all a matter of the journalistic establishment trying to maintain its control against usurpers like him. "How they have groaned about me—these old-fashioned fogies," he wrote. "How they cried for publishers to dismiss me . . . And when they failed there, they penned their own versions of their imaginations hoping it would 'blow the man down!' . . . Yes, indeddy . . ."

For all the labels of hypocrisy he pasted on others, however, Walter was stung by the charges of knavery. Privately he always called himself a reporter, not a gossip. "While a lot of people say I'm a dirt-disher," he wrote Lucky Strike's ad agency after signing his new contract, "I have always been a reporter of chiefly news—with my name signed to my drivel, so that anyone who wanted to know who 'wrote that terrible thing' could put the finger on me, as we Broadway vulgarians always say." He made a similar comment to Stanley Walker, the *Herald-Tribune* editor, who was preparing a chapter on Walter for a book and had called him a "mogul scandalmongerer." "I wish you would call me something else, Stanley," he protested in a letter. "I don't consider it scandalmongering . . . I strive so hard to get news. The only thing that annoys me is that most of the boys—who try to do what I do—go in for scandalmongering." After Marlen Pew's assault in *Editor & Publisher*, Walter frantically phoned Bernays for advice on how to control the damage. Bernays advised him to do absolutely nothing. The squall would quickly pass.

But Walter was incapable of heeding Bernays's advice. The attacks by Pew, appearing as they did in the leading journalism trade paper, were particularly nettlesome, and Walter needed to do something, though what he did only added credence to Pew's charges that he was a thug and bully. Through his sources, Walter had learned that Pew had once been jailed for criminal libel for accusing a corrupt Philadelphia politician of bribing a juror. (The case was never tried.) The incident had been elaborated upon in the *National Republican* newspaper in an effort, Pew said, to intimidate him into desisting from criticizing misleading Republican press releases on the Teapot Dome scandal, but opponents had also accused him of conducting a vendetta against then-President Coolidge. As Walter related the events in his column in January 1933, a full year after Pew's criticism of "gigolo journalism," Pew had been *convicted* of libel and had drawn the wrath of the Republican party for his intemperate attacks on the President. Consequently, "he is hardly qualified to appoint himself as dictator of American journalistic ethics."

"A great many people have suffered injury and indignity at the hands of Walter Winchell in recent years," Pew answered in his own column in *Editor & Publisher,*

but few have stepped forth to call his bluffs. He is considered by some an American untouchable. To sue him is to touch pitch. . . . Among racketeers he is a hero. Respectable people flee from such menaces as Winchell and not without reason. Better to ignore his libels than wallow. In one respect this is sensible, because Winchell is now so thoroughly revealed, thanks to a few courageous playwrights, magazine writers, columnists and others, that the public must discount his daily blather almost entirely.

"Winchellism," as Pew called the practice of gossip, was endangering "the good name of journalism," and now Pew himself had been put "on the spot." "I could sue him and doubtless make it stick," but "my hide has thickened during the jazz age," and the editor merely sought now to set the record straight. "I have more interesting things to write about in this space," he ended, "but some good will come of this week's installment, aside from personal allusions, if the editors of the land get a better view of the real meaning of Winchellism."

Two days later, Walter twitted Pew for filling a whole page defending himself: "When a man takes more than 5 minutes denying anything—he *must* be guilty!" Two days after that he framed the fight as one between a "veteran of the Old-Fashioned School of journalism and an upstart representing the New School." "[E]very time a controversy arises about the old-time journalism and the new—I am selected as the concrete example of 'Stop Selling These!' " he wrote. "Some fun!" After throwing a new and incongruous charge at Pew—that Pew had called a policeman to arrest a noted attorney who, while inebriated, had accosted a woman on the subway and that Pew then had failed to appear the next day in court—he challenged the editor to "match my public life as a newspaperman, with his." "Here's his chance," Walter dared. "Has he anything on me? If so, print it, sweetheart. It is also a grand opportunity to other enemies to help him show me up as a schemer, an on-the-cuff guy,* or a hotel bill grafter, as the legends go ... I may be a naughty boy, but I'm not a naughty-naughty one ..."

But Pew—now called "Peeyew" in Walter's column—didn't respond, and the skirmish turned one-sided with Walter taking frequent, gratuitous shots at Pew. The Old-Fashioned School of journalism seemed to know it couldn't win by getting into a fight with a bare-knuckles scrapper. The New School couldn't fight any other way.

FOR THE Old School it didn't end with ethics. There was also the matter of image. Now that Walter Winchell was the most famous American journalist, he was regarded by many as the model of how journalists looked and acted. Broadway and Hollywood had accepted and amplified this impression, so that journalists were typically portrayed as Winchell clones: fast-talking, wisecracking, cynical, fedora-hatted snoops without scruples. Journalistic traditionalists who had spent their lives trying to elevate the status of their profession were furious and blamed not Hollywood or even Charles MacArthur and Ben Hecht, whose *The Front Page* had contributed mightily to the image before the advent of Winchell; they blamed Winchell. When Warner Brothers released *Five Star Final*, a picture about an amoral, sensationalist newsman, Marlen Pew raged at it as "one of the evils that oozed out of the *New York Graphic* office, thanks to the Winchell and Gauvreau journalistic gangsters."

Walter was no less concerned about the scabrous image that was now circulating, even as his behavior gave it credence. When two young exnewsmen approached him with the first act of a play they had written about a famous gossip columnist who double-crossed an unwed mother for a scoop, Walter "nearly plopped." "You don't think any columnist ever did or would do a thing like that?" he said, again protecting his reputation. "Say anything else but that, please! That's horrible." The authors assured him that their hero would redeem himself in the end, but Walter realized that he would be sullied by it anyway. Even before it landed on Broadway on February 12, 1932, the play, called *Blessed Event* and advertising itself as "The Lowdown on a Broadway Columnist," was purchased by Paramount Pictures for the movies, its main appeal apparently being the extent to which it capitalized on Walter's growing notoriety.

"Alvin Roberts [the gossip columnist] is a curious figure," said one

---

*Being "on the cuff" meant getting things gratis. Most of the Broadway columnists were on the cuff at nightclubs and restaurants.

critic, "funny as monkeys in the zoo are funny, naive, impervious to criticism, bold, daring, alternately good-hearted and inconsiderate, ruthless in his search of vital statistics for a 'punch' for his column, possessed of a strange code of morals and a growing megalomania as his notoriety increases." Brooks Atkinson of *The New York Times* called it "both vulgar and funny. . . ." "Founded on the Broadway career of Walter Winchell, it is America's private joke." Another critic, feigning shock that Winchell "hasn't taken the precaution to have his individuality copyrighted," called it "the biggest advertisement he has ever had from someone else."

In reality, as the authors must have anticipated, Walter was the biggest advertisement for the play, and on opening night he was as much the object of attention as *Blessed Event* itself. Alexander Woollcott reported that "several members of the audience were suffering from conjunctivitis, brought on by the strain of trying to keep one eye on the play and the other on Walter Winchell." Another observer said Walter "squirmed and blenched and betrayed all the familiar symptoms that go with a sense of guilt." To which Woollcott cried, "Nonsense! Winchell's emotions at 'Blessed Event,' if any, were probably an ingenious and gratified surprise at finding himself, at thirty-five, already recognized as enough of a national institution to be made the subject of a play." In his own column Walter sniped that he gave a better performance in his seat than anyone onstage. Nevertheless, he went to see it at least twice.

That signified his dilemma. Respect, if not respectability, was important to him. When the prestigious literary magazine *Scribner's* ran a piece on him in February 1931, describing the column as the "most widely read, the most frequently quoted, and the most stolen from of any column" and describing Walter himself as the "unsurpassed . . . satirist of this going-to-hell civilization," he was so delighted that for years he carried it with him in a special binding, reading it to others at the slightest provocation.

Yet however much he desired respect and however viciously he reproved those like Pew who he believed had maligned him, there was the other side of Walter Winchell which actively promoted his image as a wholly unscrupulous journalistic gangster—his ear to the ground and eye to the keyhole. "[T]hat's merely a pose on my part," he once boasted of this persona. "So that people won't think I'm a columnist." He opened another column with the story of an irate husband who arrived at the police station to confess that he had just shot Winchell for printing things about him in the Monday column. " 'Veriwell,' said the desk sergeant indifferently, 'but you're in the wrong place. They pay rewards down at headquarters.' " "Whenever you complained about an item," remembered Oscar Levant, "he said, 'I'm a shitheel.' " Meanwhile, a brochure for King Features publicizing Walter's syndication called him "The Angel Lad, The Devil Man"—a description that seemed to capture the division within Walter between the journalistic trailblazer he wanted to be regarded as and the puckish rogue he hated to surrender, between the respect he desired and the revenge he needed to wreak.

He loved to tweak the newspaper establishment. *The New York Times*, Walter reported, had set up an internal committee to see who was leaking information to him, and when he published a story about the *World*'s spending forty-five dollars a minute for a transatlantic call to the wife of an aviator named Dieudonne Coste and it turned out she spoke only French, the embarrassed *World* began an investigation to unearth Walter's source. "Well, I guess I won't rate a pass to heaven, after all." Walter chuckled. "I'm a bad boy, that's what I am. . . . All the time making cracks."

Even Congress got into the act. Representative William Sirovich, a physician, a onetime playwright, and in 1932 the chairman of the House Patents Committee, announced that he had received letters from aggrieved theatergoers denouncing New York drama critics and fingering a conspiracy, launched at the Algonquin, to predetermine which shows to praise and pan. The ringleaders, said Sirovich, were George Jean Nathan and Walter Winchell, and he asked both of them to come to Washington to explain themselves. Walter refused, saying that he "never went out of town to cover a show, a circus, or a carnival" and then that he wouldn't go because "I saw some of the Congressman's other shows on Broadway."

Like most of Walter's squabbles, this one quickly fizzled. Late in January, however, two weeks after Pew's first attack and just a few days after the brief contretemps with Broun, a new controversy erupted that would testify both to Winchell's reputation as a cultural pariah and to his status in a growing community of celebrity much disapproved of by the old social and journalistic establishments. The roots of the controversy stretched back to May 1926, when Broadway producer Earl Carroll was tried and convicted for perjury for having lied about hosting a party in which a young showgirl named Joyce Hawley took a nude dip in a bathtub of champagne. Walter had attended the party and testified before the grand jury, but he claimed to have stonewalled: "No one was ever going to say of me that my testimony helped send Carroll to Atlanta [penitentiary]."

Nevertheless, Carroll had gone to Atlanta, and he had returned to Broadway nursing a grievance against Winchell, evidently believing that Walter had betrayed him while testifying before the grand jury. Walter hadn't, but neither had he helped matters by blasting each of Carroll's subsequent shows and printing a quip credited to George S. Kaufman and Groucho Marx: "What did you think of Earl Carroll's 'Vanities'?"

asked Kaufman. "I'd rather not say," replied Groucho. "I saw it under bad conditions—the curtain was up!"

The night of January 30 more than one hundred New York and Hollywood notables gathered at the Central Park Casino—a posh restaurant that Mayor Walker had erected, it was said, for his assignations with Betty Compton—to fete producer-financier A. C. Blumenthal and his actress wife, Peggy Fears. "[T]he nicest party I ever crashed," Walter called it. Singer Morton Downey provided the entertainment, then introduced actor Billy Gaxton, who, in turn, introduced several movie stars before asking Earl Carroll for a few words. "Mr. Carroll seemed strangely pallid as he took the floor," Mark Hellinger observed. Walter believed he was "charged to the gills" when he spoke. Carroll made some "gracious and charming" remarks. Then he paused and fixed his gaze on Winchell. His voice quivering, he said, "Walter, in each gathering there must be a serious note. You have been saying things about people in your column for years. I wonder if you, yourself, can really take it?"

Walter later admitted he was "handcuffed." "Go ahead, it's OK," Walter shouted back. Carroll wet his lips. "There are some wonderful people here," he said, "and I don't think you are fit to be with decent people." "If there had been a bomb dropped on the building," remembered one guest, "it would not have had more effect. There was complete silence." It was broken by producer George White, who shouted, "Walter, I'm ashamed of that. I apologize for him." And to the accompaniment of boos and catcalls, Carroll raced from the room.

Now the crowd demanded that Walter make a speech. "Don't lose your head," Mayor Walker whispered to him. "You've got the judge and the jury with you. Be smart. Make it sweet and short." So Walter arose and used Dorothy Parker's line: "Will somebody please open a window? The room stinks with celebrities." This won him an appreciative laugh and defused the tension. Meanwhile, Carroll broke down and wept in the foyer. Later that evening he phoned Mayor Walker to apologize and sent his regrets to the Blumenthals.

"This important incident in social history might have ended there," Marlen Pew sneered in the next issue of *Editor & Publisher*, "had not Mr. Solomon, the restaurateur, muscled in." Solomon, the custodian of the Casino, had his own gripe against Mark Hellinger for having called the place too "high-hat." Now, as the party was breaking up, Solomon announced loudly that he agreed with Carroll and thought the same thing applied to Hellinger. On the gravel path outside the restaurant escorting guests to their limousines, Solomon shouted one last blast: "Winchell and Hellinger are not fit to associate with decent people—that goes."

By Monday the Carroll incident had become one of those minor events that had all New York talking. Hellinger and Sidney Skolsky at the *News* had both written their accounts ("As always, he was once more the victim of his own craving for sensationalism," Hellinger said of Carroll), and Ed Sullivan jested in a note to Walter, "If you let me know who's fighting at the Casino next week I would like to make my reservations in advance." Though this seemed no less a "personal prejudice" than Walter's tiff with Broun, Gauvreau was not about to stop Walter from writing a column about the incident since he had had his own run-in with Carroll back in 1926 over the Miss America fraud. "If you want to say that he attempted to frame an editor with a gang of crooked private detectives," Gauvreau wrote Walter, "bribed an assistant district attorney who was fired for his part of it in the editor's presence, go ahead."

In fact, Walter was wary of being framed himself. Since the episode three friends of Carroll's had approached Walter in the course of one evening, trying to reconcile the antagonists. One of them, Renee Bonnie, who had once been mobster Dutch Schultz's girl, asked Walter to come to her apartment, but he hung up on her. "I am trying hard not to get into a spot which they are obviously attempting," he wrote Gauvreau and his secretary, Ruth Cambridge, with surprising solemnity. "However should anything happen to me bury me from Campbell's [Funeral Home] but only let my family in there—I dont [sic] want anybody else!" Writing to editor Stanley Walker a year later, he said, "If I wanted to use the gangster people I know to fight my battles for me, that is one time I certainly could have taken advantage of it. I fought my own battles right along however." But he admitted, "Carroll was certainly entitled to a scolding of me. I treated him pretty mean for many years."

In his column on February 2, Walter began to even the score. Identifying Carroll as "formerly of Pittsburgh, but more recently of Atlanta," he recounted the incident at the Casino complete with Carroll's crying jag afterward. The next day he took up the cudgels again. "Mr. Carroll said that I was not fit to associate with decent people, meaning, of course, decent people like himself." For ten years, Walter cheerfully confessed, he had lambasted Carroll, and Carroll had suffered the abuse, even saying hello to Walter when they met. "He turned the other cheek, which shows you what a damn fool he is . . . I knew he was never sincere in his howdys, but I didn't care" because, Walter said, for him it was all sport—a way to keep up interest in the column. "I am putting on a show myself," he freely acknowledged, "or did you know that? . . . I must change my show every day . . . And keep my audience interested and so often my star act is Earl Carroll." If the roles had been reversed, however, and Carroll had been abusing him, "I would break your head with a loaded mineral water bottle or break the bottle on your conk! . . ."

In the end, as Walter understood so well, the whole affair was just another entertainment, another spur for circulation. (Kobler even invited Carroll to retaliate in the *Mirror*.) But for Pew it illustrated once again the dangers of the new journalistic order that Winchell represented. Walter was one of the creators of a "new culture" which "circles about the Broadway column, babbles an audacious brand of illiteracy, sets up a new concept of decency in human relations and has as its bugle call the Bronx razz." Moving from the Carroll incident to a condemnation once again of Broadway gossip, Pew fastened on a recent item in Walter's column— "The best known film magnate attempted suicide last week"—and suggested that this pernicious item "contained no truth, but was just one of those spontaneous hunches that may easily pour from an undisciplined brain onto a permanent printing surface when stirring copy is feverishly needed, and nobody is reading manuscript." "I have no stomach for the job of regulating the journalistic morals of the white light paragraphers," he said, "being perfectly willing to let Broadway sewage find its own way to the sea."

LIBEL WAS the magic incantation of the Old School to topple the new one. And libel was the dread of the gossip columnists themselves—all except Winchell. Anyone who wanted to sue him, he joked, should get in line, and he would always brag that no one had ever won a judgment against him. There were many comers. Stephen Clow, the old editor of *Broadway Brevities* who had returned from prison to resume his duties at the revived paper, sued Walter late in 1930 for $250,000 over a report that *Brevities* would soon cease publication. Novelist Georgette Carneal sued him when he asserted that another writer had authored one of her books. (Walter's attorney argued, haplessly, that Walter had attacked not the author but the book.) Lady Nancy Cunard filed a libel suit against him for stories he had written about her while she was gathering material in Harlem for a book.

In a column on November 25, 1931, Walter related the story of a young caricaturist who was fired by an ad agency back in 1927, when he was three hours late for work because his wife was having a baby. Four years later the old boss, "shabbily attired with a sad face," slunk into the office of the caricaturist, now head of an art department himself. "I know I was a rat to do that to you," the man said, "but I've lost my job. I have no money and my wife is having another baby." As Walter told it, the caricaturist gave the man a job. But now the former boss brought suit against Walter for calling him a "rat" and won a $300 judgment. "The word is used in objurgation and has come to be regarded as an opprobrious epithet," the court declared.

The same week as the column about the caricaturist, Walter broadcast on "Lucky Strike" that he had read that Prince and Princess Matchabelli were being investigated by the government for helping the Soviet Union.

I wonder if they are in league with the Reds? I say, I wonder— because I know that Prince Vasili, a nevview of the Czar[,] is now working for the Matchabellis who are in the perfume racket now, times being what they are. And anyway—any kin of the Czar (who was murdered by the Revolutionists you know) certainly doesn't want to help them now. I know I wouldn't. The Czar's nevview, they would have me believe, brought with him all the secret formulas for perfumes that were in the Romanoff tribe. But as Mack of Moran and Mack would say, "Ah wouldn't like it even if it wuz good!"

Five days later the Matchabellis brought suit against Walter for his remarks and asked for damages set at $1 per listener.

The suit made all the papers, but the complaint included remarks that Walter had not used in the broadcast; they had appeared instead in a news story in the *Mirror* the day before the program. "You had all been afraid I would involve you in a suit," Walter wrote Gauvreau, "and here you have involved me in one." The Matchabellis amended their suits in December and again in January and then eventually settled without damages. But the publicity, Walter said, "pained me very much." "Obviously the Matchabellis never heard my broadcast," he wrote Stanley Walker afterward, still defending himself as unassailable. "I never made any settlement, nor have I ever reconciled myself with these people when the opportunity was presented. . . . Of course—they were looking for some publicity—and they got it."

But if Walter had escaped largely unscathed from the lash of libel, another episode soon revealed that it wasn't because he was particularly cautious or cagey. Back in 1929, about a month after he had joined the *Mirror*, he was sitting at his typewriter in the city room and racing to finish a column when a man named Michael Picard approached him. Talking "very swiftly and hurriedly," Picard explained that he had just gotten married and that his wife either worked for or had worked for or knew (Walter couldn't remember which) Gus Edwards, who had given him Walter's name, and that he was looking for a break. Picard was selling memberships in what was to be an "exclusive" club called the Fleetwood Beach Club on Long Beach, Long Island, and he wanted to add Walter's name to those of other notables like George Jessel and Eddie Cantor who had joined the board of governors. Walter demurred on the grounds that he might have to write about a club member, but Picard was so persistent that Walter finally agreed, just to get rid of him and get back to the col-

umn. Later Walter said that Hellinger had also badgered him into lending his name to the Fleetwood because, unlike so many other country
clubs which prohibited Jews, it was to be non-discriminatory.

A few days later a young *Mirror* reporter named Nathan Zalinsky
stopped by Walter's office to thank him for the invitation to join the
Fleetwood, while admitting he was concerned about the cost. Now Walter realized that it wasn't an exclusive club at all but that his name was
being used to solicit names he believed were selected from the phone
book. A few nights later, as Walter told it, he got a call from Mayor
Walker informing him that the club was run by gangsters and asking
what Walter's name was doing on the Fleetwood letterhead. Walter immediately fired off a registered letter demanding his name be removed,
but he got no response. Then, at 3 a.m., while he was composing his column at the *Mirror*, three men entered his office—"immaculate appearance, fancy duds, clean shaven, boots shined, and nails manicured"—and,
calling themselves "friends of friends," began interrogating Walter on the
Fleetwood. When Walter again demanded that his name be removed
from their stationery and solicitations, the men told him it was staying.
"We've invested a lot of dough in this thing, and you behave yourself."

Even if Walter hadn't had mob contacts of his own, he did have his
column. The next morning, November 23, 1929, his opening ran: "If I
were king I would throttle the swift-talker who got me to consent to
serve on the Board of Governors for the planned Fleetwood Beach
Club," and he said the enterprise "is being worked along the lines of another 'racket' to which I am opposed, and I hope others won't invest in
the damb [*sic*] thing because our names are being prostituted." After the
column appeared, Walter received a visit from Picard and his partner,
Sam Zack, obviously agitated. Restraining themselves from taking a
punch at Walter, they asked why he had written what he had, and when
he explained that he was committed to exposing rackets "for the benefit
of the public," Zack, as Winchell told it, said, "Well, I will sue you and
take you for all you have got, you son of a bitch." Zack's version was different. He claimed Walter had boasted that "he writes anything he wants,
there is nobody who can stop him, he gets paid to do anything he wants
on that damn thing, and he pointed to the typewriter. . . . That was his
opinion and that was all that was important; he was the Great Winchell."

On January 24, 1930, Picard and Zack filed suit against Walter and the
Mirror for libel. Thus began a long legal odyssey—Walter said the case
dragged on because no attorney wanted to represent the Fleetwood for
fear of Walter's reprisals—that revealed much more than Walter must
have liked about his methods and his motives. The case went to trial on
December 18, 1933, in New York Supreme Court in Manhattan. As

Fleetwood saw it, Walter was not a civic crusader, exposing fraud where he found it. Rather he had been slighted when Eddie Cantor demanded he be removed from the board of governors. "Imagine playing cards at the club," Cantor was said to have told one of the Fleetwood's organizers, "and telling my wife I visited a sick friend and that bastard Winchell would put it in the column the next day that I had lost a fortune gambling at the club." Or "[i]f I dance with a woman at the club, it would be inferred in the column of Winchell that I put my hand up her clothes. . . ." Cantor said that if Winchell and Hellinger weren't thrown off the board, he and Jessel would resign. "Am I not as good as [Bugs] Baer, Hellinger, [Harry] Hershfield and the rest?" Walter allegedly whined before taking arms against the Club. (Cantor, however, testified in Walter's behalf.)

More, Fleetwood's attorney accused Walter of snobbery. He had been angry when Nathan Zalinsky joined the club, angrier still when he heard that a plumber had joined. That "so disgusted him," declaimed the attorney, "this man of high social standing, a man who thought he is too big, too exclusive to associate with a common plumber, that so disgusted him that he went out and wrote this rotten article." The charge was baseless, and Walter, rightfully incensed, snapped, "If you are trying to make me look like a snob, Mr. Mackey, please don't, because I am not like that."

But if Walter Winchell was no snob, the trial revealed that he was also not the careful reporter of facts he often claimed to be. Under cross-examination, Walter, wearing smoked glasses, admitted that his accusations were based on no hard evidence, only a conversation with an insurance executive who had been approached to become the club's president and unfounded rumors about the unsavory backgrounds of the club's principals. On the stand he could neither substantiate the charges nor even remember who spread them. (The phone call from Mayor Walker had now faded from memory.) The best he could muster was that the organizers were "dishonest" and "I didn't want to be associated with those fellows." In the end the article was an act of pique over the fact that his letter of resignation had gone unacknowledged. "[T]hese men that write columns on the papers, particularly those men who are employed to put over a scandal and bring out distasteful things," roared the Fleetwood attorney in summation, "they get to feel they are king; they get to feel that if they are offended, off with his head."

After four days of trial and five and a half hours of deliberation, the jury returned a verdict in favor of the plaintiffs and awarded them $30,000 from the *Mirror* and $2,500 from Walter for malice. (Walter blamed the histrionics of the plaintiffs' attorney for the loss.) Appeals prolonged the case for another eighteen months until the judgment was finally halved and affirmed in May 1935.

But that was not the end of it. After the ruling by the Court of Appeals, Arthur Kobler came to Walter's office and said he expected him to pay half the $15,000 judgment against the *Mirror*. Astonished and outraged, Walter packed his things and left the office. "I just got lost. To hell with all of them." A representative of Hearst phoned to assure him that everything would be taken care of if only he would return, but Walter refused. He was on strike.

One afternoon during his protest he sneaked into the Stork Club for a sandwich and was waylaid by Jack Lait of the *Mirror* and Hearst syndication chief Joseph Connolly, who had claimed all along that he sided with Walter. (Someone had tipped them off that Walter was coming.) While the three chatted, a waiter handed Walter a phone. Hearst was calling from his San Simeon estate and wanted to know why Walter had stopped writing. "I just found out, boss, that I am responsible for half the liabilities at the *Mirror* but not half of the profits," he said he told Hearst. Hearst chuckled and asked what he wanted them to do. "I could never again, Chief, go to a typewriter and feel free to report the news worried that I might have to pay a hefty sum and have no money," said Walter. And when Hearst asked again what he wanted, Walter said he wanted "a letter from you holding me blameless from damages. . . . Why should I, Chief, be held to blame for stuff my bosses O.K. for publication?" Hearst asked that Connolly be put on the line and instructed him to place the requested clause in Walter's contract immediately.

So ended Walter's strike and any possibility of his ever having to pay a libel judgment. In its own tortuous way, the Fleetwood case had brought him this freedom and had proved Pew and the other defenders of the journalistic faith wrong. No court, no law, could stop Winchell now.

V

Even before his manumission from libel, Winchell's power spelled trouble at the *Mirror*.

Arthur Kobler, its publisher, was a short, florid man with white hair, moist gray eyes and a bulbous nose. Favoring tailored suits, pince-nez and a yellow snakeskin-handled cane and sporting an ample paunch, he might have been mistaken for a *Mittel*-European diplomat, but he was instead deep in the world of yellow journalism and tabloidia, having managed Hearst's *American Weekly* Sunday magazine supplement for years before taking over the *Mirror* in a complicated transaction that not even veteran Hearst watchers fully understood. (Kobler had bought the paper, then sold it back to Hearst.) His main interests were art and women, whom, one staffer opined, he pursued with far more avidity than he ever showed toward his newspaper.

From the time he joined the *Mirror*, Walter had found himself at odds with Kobler. Walter was a star rather than an employee; he was irreplaceable. Nevertheless, Kobler, like Gauvreau, felt obliged to remind Walter that the publisher was still the boss, even if the reminders were often capricious and even if the net effect was to annoy Walter rather than bring him in line. Much of their conflict, then, seemed to have little to do with Walter's column and much to do with Kobler's asserting his own prerogatives in a test of wills—in this case between the traditional newspaper hierarchy from which Kobler derived his authority and a new order that was every bit as daunting to the structure of a paper as Walter's column was to a paper's ethics.

At the beginning, Gauvreau was still the instrument of Kobler's revenge when Gauvreau wasn't inflicting vengeance of his own. It was Gauvreau who deducted $227.68 from Walter's paycheck for telegraph and telephone tolls when Walter was filing from Miami in the winter of 1930. And when Kobler in January 1931 ordered that a section of Walter's column called "Recommendations for Diversion Seekers" be killed because it gave "publicity to night club entertainers who got into the paper without paying a penny for advertising," it was Gauvreau who delivered the message to Walter, bringing the two into "open battle" once again. Walter was so vituperative protesting the action on the phone that Gauvreau demanded that henceforth they communicate only in writing. Walter was also forbidden to enter the editor's office.

Later that year a new irritant arose. Walter had been asked by Gauvreau to submit his column the day before publication, and Walter had acceded. But now Gauvreau was slicing so much out of it—for fear of libel, he said—that Ruth Cambridge had to scramble to fill the column by deadline. Walter asked Kobler to ask Gauvreau to read the proof earlier. Failing that, Walter said he would simply deliver later. "I used to like to annoy him," Walter later said of Kobler, "because I knew he was a pushover for irksome teasing and had phone operators listen to my conversations. I know this sounds childish, but it was fun. . . ."

No sooner had the censorship issue arisen than Kobler raised a new one. On his "Lucky Strike" show Walter had broadcast that two bodies found in northern Canada might be those of the French aviators Charles Nungesser and François Coli, who had been lost four years earlier attempting to cross the Atlantic. Kobler thought this was totally irresponsible, and he waited at the *Mirror* office until midnight to tell Walter so.

According to one account, the confrontation made the famous telephone scene in *The Front Page* where the reporter excoriates his managing editor "look like last year's straw hat in comparison." Kobler began yelling and banging on the desk. One report said he carried Walter's typewriter into the hall and smashed it. Walter screamed back at him. "He told him what he could do, where he could go and to do things that are utterly impossible," went another report. Kobler then threatened to hit him, and Walter replied that if Kobler did, he'd better call an undertaker. Kobler left Walter's cubicle, slamming the door behind him. A few weeks later, early in December, Kobler removed Ruth Cambridge from the payroll and ordered Walter to pay for all the daily papers he received. Walter responded this time by sending a bill for a news story he had submitted. In the midst of all this, Gauvreau was writing his novel loosely based on Walter. Walter threatened to resign unless it was suppressed, and the two skulked around the city room "exchanging malevolent glares."

Matters worsened that January, when the *Mirror* launched a Sunday edition with all of its regular columnists except Winchell, who demanded that he be paid a thousand dollars for the additional column and that Ruth Cambridge be reinstated on the *Mirror* payroll. Kobler refused. For a time the publisher thought of holding one of Walter's daily columns for Sunday, but Saks and Ipana toothpaste had contracts guaranteeing that their ads run next to Walter's column. Another rumor had Walter agreeing to write the Sunday piece if Kobler agreed never to speak to him again, but when Kobler accepted, Walter allegedly reneged. In the end Kobler hired Lee Mortimer, a young reporter from the "amusements" section, for the Sunday piece.

Seething over Mortimer's Sunday column and no doubt fearful that it was trespassing on his franchise, Walter once again sicced his attorney, Arthur Driscoll, on the *Mirror*, accusing it of breaching his contract by publishing a column substantially similar to his. Kobler answered by locking Walter and Ruth Cambridge out of the *Mirror* offices. Walter now screamed breach of contract again and began hunting for a way to leave the *Mirror* and join the *Daily News*. Under this threat Kobler relented, discontinuing Mortimer's column and ending the lockout but restricting Walter and his secretary to their own office. In his last column Mortimer said that Walter had "cluttered up the air waves" and called him an "aspirinated columnist."

One rumor had Kobler selling Walter to the *American*, but when Walter confronted Gauvreau and Kobler with this, they both denied it. "Ignore all silly rumors," Gauvreau wrote. "Don't be pediculous." He added in postscript: "How could you leave without me? I wouldn't stand for it. This is a common-law marriage." Walter was not assuaged. *Variety* reported that Driscoll was "itching to go into court and place on the record . . . how it treats a star reporter responsible for much of its circulation. . . . No reason is known by newspapermen why Winchell is subject to so much irritation," the article said, "unless it be enviousness over Winchell's rapid rise to a national figure and his much larger earnings." For all his newfound fame, he was clearly unfulfilled. He wrote:

I am perched for the moment moderately well upon the slippery rungs of the ladder called success, and it isn't nearly as jolly as I had been led to suppose. The initial sensation in undoubtedly exhilarating. One stands for the moment enchanted in the gaudy flare of having been shot out of the vast herd of nobodies into a somebody. . . .

The ego soars off in a wonderful joy ride; one's eyes brighten; one's pulse quickens; one's step lightens. . . .

A month or two of this toxic drug, and then the ego comes home to roost, the ground firm under one's feet, and there is today to get through and tomorrow—and the day after—crammed from morning to night; aye, and far into the night to think up, create and invent wordage so that the checks will keep coming in.

His blood pressure was low, he was perpetually nervous and he still couldn't sleep. Comparing a photo of himself before he had joined the *Graphic* with another taken after he had joined the *Mirror* six years later, he remarked that his hair was now prematurely silver where it had once been dark. "You get old-looking too fast in this racket." And for all his outward confidence, he was still filled with self-doubt. "He thinks his stuff is terrible," an interviewer said. "When anyone likes it enough to tell him so, he doesn't believe it."

Most of all, he was dissatisfied with the demands of the column. "There must be a time in your career when you do not have to do things," he wrote in April 1931. "I'm a loafer, at heart, I know . . . But you can't be a professional loafer . . . Not in this town, sir . . . Unless you never get hungry." "[O]h, the weariness that follows the two hours or more searching every letter for a nugget you can use!" he complained while discussing the rigors of preparing his column. "The chief trouble with columning daily is that your most affectionate admirers are fickle . . . They demand that your stuff be better than it was yesterday [. . .] Which is too tough a verdict." When another interviewer asked where he thought he would be in ten years, he told her, "Dead. I'll not live that long."

Though he was only thirty-four, increasingly he spoke of retiring. It was, he seemed to realize, his last chance to disengage from the column before it completely overtook him, his last chance to preserve himself. He would leave the paper in five years, he told one reporter in 1931, and write when he chose. "I want a few more years' time yet—so I can get enough practice at columning to learn how to throw anything into type and be two weeks in advance like an expert," he said. In another column, in February 1932, he dreamed of writing only once a week so he could spend time with the children and June. "She's been waiting a decade to go away with me—and if I had any moxie I'd chuck the whole routine and go somewhere with her and the children and laugh a little." If it weren't for June, he admitted, he never would have had his success. "And when I tell her that, she dismisses it with a shrug and tells me that nothing else matters but me—not even the kids."

June was, in fact, remarkably supportive of Walter under trying circumstances. "She has never, ever done anything to distract me," he told an interviewer, adducing as evidence of her thoughtfulness that she wouldn't even attend the theater if she had a cough, for fear of disturbing other playgoers. For her it was a lonely existence with Walter seldom home. He once recounted an episode of finding himself at 5:14 one morning at the corner of Broadway and 52d Street when the city was absolutely empty and sepulchrally quiet. Unnerved, he raced home to the Park Central and collapsed in the foyer, before being roused by a bellhop and helped upstairs. June refused to open the door. "It can't be Mr. Winchell," she insisted, "it's yesterday yet!"

That Walter loved June, there was no question. Whether he was faithful to her was something else. *Broadway Brevities*, locked in one of its frequent tussles with Walter, kept accusing him of philandering. "Gee! It's that sob column on how much I miss the wife and kiddies," *Brevities* spoofed, "and how they tug at my heart strings even when I'm mugging some blonde in the back room of the Club Jason [. . .] Mustn't mention girl-friends' names too often . . . The gang gets wise." Letters in his office files seemed to substantiate the charges, though it was entirely possible that the correspondents were women fantasizing about Walter and not real romantic interests. One woman, describing her search for a "dream man," wrote: "I believe my search is near ending. . . . I hope our contact will prove interesting and agreeable." Another said, "What particularly depresses me is the fact that I'd found a friendship that promised to be ideal, and phfttt—it went. But who cares about that?" A third woman asked, "Why haven't I heard from you? I bet the answer's funny," and told him she would need the job he promised her.

In any case, Walter's first love wasn't women. His mistress was the column, and she left little enough time for anything else, including his beloved daughters. "Can't golf, fish, swim, fly in planes, play piano, cook, or even ice skate!" he once said, but he added that he had his family to compensate. "My family comes first with me every time," he boasted, and at the time meant it even if his dedication to the column betrayed his words. It grieved him that he knew he neglected Walda and Gloria, that he often had only a half hour each morning to play with them, at one point even forcing himself to get to bed at 3 a.m. instead of six to extend his time with them. He hated to rush into Childs restaurant to grab dinner with them and then rush off again.

It was partly in compensation that he began doting on the children in the column. "Gloria is a beautiful child, whose face, someone once remarked, seemed as though it had been chiseled from marble by a genius," he wrote in one typical entry, which also described how devastated she had been when Olympic swimming champion and movie star Johnny Weissmuller had told her to eat her spinach and carrots so she could grow up faster and they could be married and then she found out Weismuller had gotten married to someone else. "Gloria broke down and wept furiously . . . She hasn't been the same since." "That Walda of mine hands me the heartiest chuckles," he wrote in another column, meditating on her photograph and Gloria's in his office. "For without the likenesses on the office walls of Gloria and Walda—the ache of missing them would be too much to take . . . Their pretty faces and their affection for me offsets all the other trivia that comes up in a week. . . ."

"I only want to live long enough to see Gloria and Walda grown into girlhood," he wrote in another column early in 1932. "And have the necessary stuff to get them beautiful frocks, and furs and things that girls seem to like so much."

Some readers, wanting gossip, resented these columns. Some thought they were nauseatingly self-serving. Westbrook Pegler, a sportswriter on the Chicago *Tribune*, devoted one of his own columns to a blistering parody of Walter's "Portrait of a Man Talking to Himself." He began:

> Oh, how I love my beautiful darling wife and kiddies. I am one of the best husbands in the world. And fathers, too. Some husbands and fathers keep these things in the bosom of the family, but it is a business with me, and I blab it all over the good white paper.
>
> Hell, sweetheart. Here is a kiss for you. I am selling this kiss to the customers for three cents a copy; ten cents on Sundays [. . .] Hello, Shirley, darling. Your papa sends you a kiss. Your papa loves you. Papa loves baby. Isn't that original, darling?

Ernest Hemingway, writing to editor Arnold Gingrich, derided Pegler's parody and defended Winchell. "You should be a better writer than the

man you parody," said Hemingway, "and not just try to establish a moral
superiority. Pegler is a better writer but not 1/100th the newspaper man
Winchell is. Winchell is the greatest newspaper man that ever lived."
Writing a sports column, Hemingway believed, was easy. "But this
bloody Winchell has to function six days a week and if on his off days,
which are very obviously days of rest, he wants to put in a lot of sentimental crap about his family it is o.k. with me. Look what he does on
Mondays."

The best evidence of Walter's devotion to his daughters was the money
he lavished upon them when he was so stingy with himself. They were
privately educated. They received dance lessons at the Ned Wayburn
New York Institute of Dancing. They spent at least one summer at Camp
Tekakwetha near Lake George in upstate New York, and in winter they
went to Florida. All these things required substantial funds, and Walter
always justified his negligence by appealing to his need to make money.
"If you really care anything about the three of us you'd do something
about it!" he quoted June as saying about his workload. " 'But I can't do
anything about it,' I say back. 'If I do not hustle around tonight for the
next paragraph, then what? Don't you see, honey? Paragraphs! Things!
Stuff! To keep them from saying things. If I start getting careless, where
is the coin coming from to pay for those fancy skirts, and your dressy
feathers on Walda's collar, and the very "smart" and fancy 19-dollar-
dresses for Gloria and so forth?' "

But it was, in truth, more than the money. Even as he realized that the
column was overtaking him, Walter needed it, needed the excitement and
the pressure if only to feel that he was not stagnating. Nor was it something he could slough off at the end of the day; it was a part of him. Once
he was talked into spending a weekend in the country. In the morning he
was awakened by the birds and blinded by the sun. "I guess my own artificial routine of living is best, after all," he concluded. Another time he
got three columns ahead, then found himself restless. "I thought, I remember at the time—'Gee, it must be terrible to be [jobless] and have
nothing to do with yourself—but sit in the movies and wonder where
the next meal or job is coming.'. . . The very thought gave me the shudders . . . I just couldn't be idle—a fight, a controversy or anything—
something to do!"

And there was a column of Franklin P. Adams's he had clipped at
roughly this time about the strange attraction that journalism held. "You
might suppose that the thrill of hearing things a few hours sooner than
your fellows would soon pass away," Adams wrote, obviously speaking for
Walter as well as himself. "Some of us never find it has passed. We always seem, at our work, to be closer up against the life of our time than

anywhere else, nearer its center and more in its confidence." But within the romance lay the mystery. "Or perhaps it is for none of these sound and plausible reasons [we love journalism] any more than it is for sound assignable reasons that men fall in love." So it was for Walter Winchell.

FINALLY, IN April 1932, he crashed.

It had begun with Kobler—with the niggling disputes, with the removal of Ruth from the payroll and the cutting off of his private office phone and the dunning for tolls for the stories he filed outside the office. And it had continued with a small item in the middle of his Monday column on February 8 that was to apply new pressures. "Five planes brought dozens of machinegats from Chicago Friday," it ran, "to combat the Town's Capone . . . Local banditti have made one hotel a virtual arsenal and several hot-spots are ditto because Master Coll is giving them the headache . . . One of the better Robin Hoods has a private phone in his cell! . . . Haw!"

"Master Coll" was Vincent Coll, a vicious young rogue gangster nicknamed "Mad Dog" who was terrorizing both the public (he had killed a child while attempting to gun down an enemy) and his rival mobsters. He had kidnapped Owney Madden's friend and partner Frenchy Demange to extort money from Madden. After Demange was ransomed, for a reported $40,000, Madden apparently declared he had had enough. So Coll, by arrangement, was in a drugstore on 23rd Street when he was called to the phone booth. And as he took the call, three gunmen entered and pumped more than sixty bullets into his body before vanishing into the night. That was February 8—the night of the day that Walter had predicted Coll's demise.

Walter had known Madden for years; it was Madden who had given him his Stutz Bearcat, though Walter insisted on sending the gang leader a check as payment. As a protégé of Madden's, Walter had enjoyed the protection of the mob. Occasionally, however, there were reported death threats, presumably from other gang chiefs he had offended. When Paul Sweinhart, the editor of *Zit's Weekly*, reported that a "certain daily newspaper columnist will be bumped off in six months," everyone just assumed he meant Winchell. A Philadelphia newsman wrote: "We hereby notify Walter Winchell that he's likely to be shot any day now." *Time* magazine said there were rumors that Walter had placed the names of would-be assassins in a safe deposit box. At the time Walter himself joked to the *New Yorker*'s Robert Benchley: "DEAR BOB SEE YOU AT THE NEW YORKER THEATER TONIGHT[.] DON'T WORRY ABOUT ANYTHING AS I HAVE JUST BEEN KILLED[.]"

Of course nothing had ever happened. Why? "Very simply—Winchell could make money for them. Big money," said his friend and crime reporter Robin "Curley" Harris, meaning that Walter could plug the mobsters' nightclubs. But his prediction of the Coll murder had sent a shock wave through the mob ranks, not so much because Walter had broken a confidence, though that was bad enough, but because he would almost certainly be questioned by the district attorney. All of this was complicated by the fact that Madden at the time was fighting the parole board, which wanted to return him to Sing Sing for parole violations. Walter knew immediately that he was in trouble. "I turned green. I was sick to my stomach," he later told an interviewer. "I learned later that Coll had a list of names in his pocket when he was shot—names of people he intended to murder. Mine was on it." The next day two confederates of Coll's emerged from hiding and were killed.

On Tuesday, at the NBC radio studios, Walter received a phone threat to stop publishing stories about Broadway gangsters and racketeers or he would be "taken for a ride." He received another threat three hours later at his hotel suite and another by mail on Wednesday. The next day he appeared at the 47th Street police station with two private guards provided by "Broadway friends," presumably Owney Madden, and asked for protection. Officers described him as "nervous and in genuine fear of his life," and they provided him with the additional guards.

On Monday, a week after the murder, Assistant District Attorney George M. Carney subpoenaed Walter to testify before a grand jury investigating Coll's death. Walter was now roiling with terror. "He stayed up all night," recalled Curley Harris. "He thought he was going to be exposed." He arrived at the courthouse early the morning of February 16 and brushed past the gang of reporters. After an interminable wait Walter finally testified for about twenty minutes, then left just past noon, telling photographers, "I'm no heel; I'll stand up to be shot." In fact, on advice of counsel, Walter said he refused to divulge his source—it was later revealed to have been Texas Guinan—but he admitted to Stanley Walker, "I lost seven more pounds, I think, testifying before the grand jury that time."

As Walter related it to Curley Harris afterward, he had been dealt with much differently from the way he expected. He had expected to be treated like a criminal. Instead the authorities greeted him as if he were a visiting celebrity. "The members of the grand jury—they all got around Walter," Harris said, "and he gave most of them [theater] tickets. . . . So by the end, he'd been there fifteen minutes [actually twenty] and he owned the whole place." His only regret was that the *World-Telegram* reported him being "curt" to his fellow reporters. Walter apologized in his column that he hadn't slept for twenty-nine hours, he was anxious to get home and he was legally prohibited from discussing grand jury proceedings, but he had always vowed to be civil with reporters because "so many people we had to meet and interview years ago—were not civil or courteous."

Coll's killers were never found, Walter's source was not revealed until many years later, Madden was ultimately remanded to Sing Sing, and eventually the issue of Vincent Coll subsided. (One later, unverified account claimed that Madden had spared Walter only after he had extorted $90,000 from him.) But Walter had been emotionally drained by the episode. He was dispirited and irritable. He wanted desperately to get away, but he was enchained by contracts and obligations.

Then, on April 16, after his "Lucky Strike" broadcast, Winchell collapsed in the studio, suffering what reports called a "nervous breakdown." Details were vague. "They said it would happen for a long time," wrote radio columnist Jack Foster in the *World-Telegram* two days later, speculating on whether Walter would be able to return for his next broadcast. "I, for one, hope he is back at the microphone soon, for he gave vitality and speed to radio."

Reports, however, were soon circulating that Walter was seriously ill and confined to his suite at the Lincoln Hotel, where he was being attended by his physician, and that he would not be returning anytime soon. One account said his doctor had ordered him to take a month's vacation. Louis Sobol was to take over the broadcasts, and Paul Yawitz, who had been writing the Sunday column, was to assume the daily column.* For one commentator, at least, it spelled the end of the Winchell phenomenon. "He was dragged out of the place into the quickest oblivion that perhaps ever engulfed a man whose name was so well-known," he wrote. "Within 48 hours the wolves had torn him to pieces, leaving him not a vestige of anything. . . . Wherever he is now and whatever he's doing, he faces the prospect when and if he recovers, of starting completely over again." Several days after the breakdown, editor Herbert Bayard Swope wrote him: "I hope the reports of your illness are exaggerated. It's too bad you had to smash up just as you were going so well."

What really had happened? Everyone wanted to know, and the answers ranged from Walter's being mentally and physically exhausted to his having been shot and paralyzed. Walter remained mum, leaving for California with his family to convalesce. But a year later he explained the truth

---

*To get the assignment, Yawitz had submitted a sample column with fictitious names, and it had accidentally been published—proving that the form of gossip was more important than its content.

to Stanley Walker. The breakdown "was a trick on my part to get out of all contracts," he said, warning Walker not to print this information if Walker thought Walter could get sued. "I was fed up with fighting my publishers and editors who were horsewhipping me and killing my column every day by removing choice bits at the last moment. So I decided to take a rest—the first in eleven years."

Walter admitted it was "painful" for him to feign illness, and he didn't feel comfortable until he debarked in California. Announcing that a small nerve at the base of his brain had become temporarily numbed and saying he was taking the "sun cure" at his doctor's insistence, he checked into the Hotel Biltmore in Santa Barbara. "It's great to have been ill," he proclaimed to an interviewer. "I'm getting a chance to become acquainted with my wife and family." To George Washington Hill he wrote that he was feeling much better thanks to Santa Barbara.

But the sun cure didn't last long. Within days the Winchells had left Santa Barbara and landed at the Ambassador Hotel in Los Angeles, where Walter immediately threw himself into Hollywood nightlife. Though he had been reporting on Hollywood for years, it was the first time since his vaudeville days that he had actually been there, and he was dazzled by the differences between this world and his own Broadway universe. "I'm utterly amazed by Hollywood's round of entertainments," he told an interviewer. "Hollywood's parties outdistance those on Broadway or any place else in the world." As for the Hollywood celebrities, he liked them because "they aren't demanding. They're letting me rest. They are considerate enough not to push and prod me into going places merely so they can gratify their curiosity." While in Santa Barbara, he had received hundreds of invitations from stars eager to meet him, he said, and had received hundreds of calls since arriving in Los Angeles but without anyone attempting to obligate him socially.

Could he live and work in Hollywood? He certainly liked the glamour, which, he said, exceeded that of Broadway. "Nowhere in the East is there so enchanting a rendezvous as the Coconut Grove in Los Angeles ... Where the celebrated of the screen and even the lesser prominent sip and sup and stay up until almost 12:30 in the morning [. . .] And swap loves almost daily." But Hollywood gossips were required to turn major stories of divorce or romance over to the city desks. "And often without a byline ... I would rather perish first." In any case, he believed his writing and broadcasting would suffer in California. "I'd be handicapped by public opinion and by censorship. In New York I can say what I want about Hollywood, and by the time it has soaked in out here, those involved have cooled off." An old New York friend, then an MGM story editor, Sam Marx, remembered Walter always had his "eyes out" when he visited the studio commissary for anyone he might have insulted. "He always took the most circuitous route to the table."

He had no sooner landed in Hollywood than he was being courted by studios as well as stars. Referring to him only as "one of the most famous newshounds in the big town," Louella Parsons had earlier written that he was scheduled to appear in a movie called *Beau Peep*. *Variety* reported that both Columbia and Universal were pursuing him to star in a picture and that Columbia had offered him $50,000, but Walter, negotiating for himself, was holding out for $100,000. MGM had apparently also entered the bidding, but by mid-May Walter had concluded a deal with Universal for a picture titled *Okay America*, to start shooting on June 6 and to be based on Walter's own career.

Originally he had been scheduled to recuperate for a month. He had already been gone that long when he made his agreement with Universal, which threatened to keep him out for at least another month. George Washington Hill was getting restive, wanting to inaugurate a new format for the "Lucky Strike Dance Hour" of three rotating hosts and saying, reasonably, that if Walter was healthy enough to make a movie he should be healthy enough to fulfill his broadcast obligations.

Oddly enough, Walter was feeling restive too. Though he was enjoying California, he was all too aware of how rapidly the wheel of celebrity turned. "They'll forget you," Sime Silverman had warned him when Walter departed New York. Furthermore, new rumors were flying that Walter had decided to retire. Another rumor called him despondent because he had allegedly been on the verge of a scoop in the kidnapping of aviator Charles Lindbergh's baby and the kidnapper had double-crossed him. "Winchell—" he said of himself, "the guy who for years said almost everything about everybody—couldn't stand the rumors and legends he heard out there." He decided to hasten back to New York "at the hottest time of the year" to "prove that all these things were not true."

Universal, already preparing *Okay America*, was shocked, but Walter had agreed to star in the film only pending a satisfactory negotiation; he had not signed a contract. Two hours before his scheduled departure Universal executives arrived with a certified check for $25,000 as an advance payment on $50,000—the amount Walter had already refused from Columbia. They promptly raised their offer to $60,000 plus 10 percent of the picture's profits. Walter held firm. He said he wanted $100,000 in advance. What he really seemed to want was to get back to Broadway.

And so Walter left for New York on May 21 to reclaim his throne. (Lew Ayres ultimately played Walter's role in *Okay America*.) He told a reporter in Chicago that he planned to rest a little while longer when he got back to the city, but June wagered that he would be back to the column the next day, and she was very nearly right. He had become an emotional bulimic—gorging himself on work, then purging himself as he did on his California trip, then gorging himself again. "Walter Winchell. Now—Completely recovered from his recent illness will resume writing his famous and inimitable column," declared a *Mirror* advertisement on May 27, just days after his arrival.

He returned to the paper on June 1, after nearly six weeks away, with the snarl still in his voice. Broadway was as "dull as ever," he wrote. "Those groups of nobodies, however, are still sitting around complaining about those who get the juicier breaks—or telling those who are clicking how it ought to be done." As for the rumors of his retirement, "That's why I came back. I figured that if I hurried home I'd make thousands of people a little ill. They had me paralyzed in both legs, dead, shot by gangsters, run out of town by them, and all sorts of wild reports."

As everyone on the *Mirror* soon discovered, the rumors of Walter's demise had been greatly exaggerated, and he moved quickly to reassert his authority. Paul Yawitz lost Walter's "famous show-window" but was given the consolation of a small column of his own. Bernard Sobel, who had taken the drama critic's position, was less fortunate. "He [Winchell] was in perfect health and straight away took his place as first critic, making me automatically a second-stringer," Sobel remembered. Now Walter began waging "guerilla warfare" against him, having Kobler tell Sobel what to do and what not to do. "If I wrote one sort of column, I was told to change it," Sobel said. "It was an encroachment on Winchell's premises."

Two weeks later Walter resumed the Lucky Strike broadcast, but the series suffered from the changes made in Walter's absence. "I cannot see any reason, as a critic, for applauding the present series," wrote *Radio Guide* three weeks after the new format's debut. There were hints that the program would undergo another revamping, but by that time Walter had suffered another collapse and had been ordered by his physician to rest. At least that was Walter's story. Kobler, less charitably, insisted that Walter had gone out of town on private business and he, Kobler, hadn't any idea when he might return.

In late August, two weeks after this second (putative) collapse, there were stories that Lucky Strike was planning to "struggle along" without him. "We want Walter Winchell back on the air again or we change from Luckies to some other brand of cigarette," wrote an irate listener. "That is what my friends want me to write you and they mean it. . . . Remember, this is not the only spot in the world that feels that way." Walter, however, had delivered his last broadcast for American Tobacco.

· · ·

HIS CONVALESCENCE was short-lived. In the vise of his bulimia, he was soon engorging himself again. Within a month he signed to appear in and assist in the production of thirteen one- or two-reel film shorts. By October he had concluded a deal with the Andrew Jergens company, manufacturer of Jergens hand lotion, for a fifteen-minute weekly radio broadcast on Sunday nights over the NBC Blue network.* The "Jergens Program," as it was first called, debuted on December 4, 1932, with Walter's salutation "Good evening Mr. and Mrs. United States, Cuba, Canada and Alaska!" He confessed that he had missed the "excitement that goes with radio" during his months off the air and that he was "breathless and keyed up to an exciting pitch." He renewed the feud with Ben Bernie—his ears remind you of a taxicab "with both doors wide open!"— then glided into gossip. "This is where I peddle my papers." Later he recommended plays and books, read a brief story and answered letters. He closed, "And so until next Sunday evening at the same time, then—I remain—your New York correspondent, who has come to the conclusion, after seeing some of the latest motion pictures, that the wrong actors— are out of work!"

It had been a strong performance—energetic, dramatic, riveting. The advertising manager of the Jergens company wired: ALL EXECUTIVES IMMENSELY PLEASED . . . YOU HAVE SET A HIGH MARK TO SHOOT AT IN THE FUTURE. The only dissenter among a raft of favorable reviews seemed to be Ed Sullivan, who wrote Walter apologizing for some remarks that had been construed as criticism but then going on to say that Walter hadn't selected the best items from his column for the broadcast and that Walter's "written stuff had a certain impertinent air to it that made it great reading and that your broadcast that night lacked it." Still, for all their professional rivalry, Sullivan said he didn't want it to affect their friendship. "[Y]ou are the only one for whom I hold a sincere personal and professional respect."

The challenge, Walter seemed to realize now that he was free from the distractions and interruptions of "The Lucky Strike Dance Hour," was to translate the column into the terms of radio. He couldn't simply read the column aloud. He had to find aural equivalents for the column's pitch, for its breathlessness, its ellipses, its abrupt shifts, its drama. He had to refine his "voice" and convey a radio persona like his newspaper persona. And he had to devise new segments that could provide variety and pace. It was the challenge of providing a whole new format and approach—there were

---

*NBC had two networks: the Red, which was the more prestigious and over which "The Lucky Strike Dance Hour" was broadcast, and the Blue.

no antecedents for this sort of program, except his own early efforts—just as he had at the *Graphic* with his column.

What did the listeners hear? They heard the clack of a telegraph ticker at the top of the show and also in between the items—a sound that was to become as closely identified with Walter Winchell as his trademark salutation to "Mr. and Mrs. America and all the ships at sea," which he incorporated into the broadcast in 1934 and retained thereafter. The clacks meant nothing in Morse code, though they suggested that the news was hot off the wire. "The Big Idea is for sound effect," Walter admitted, "and to set the tempo." He also said it helped him catch his breath.

They heard Walter's voice, the timbre high and clipped like verbal tap shoes, racing at nearly two hundred words per minute. (His scripts were a mess, evincing the visual urgency that the broadcasts bore aurally. He scribbled over words, crabbed notes into the skinny margins, pasted old copy over new.) "My voice goes up exactly one octave on the air," he told a friend. "I want to create as much excitement as a newsboy on the streets when he yells, 'Extry, extry, read all about it.' After a while—most people don't notice this—my voice settles down to normal."

They heard an effluence of romance, marriage, divorce, the effect of which was like that of a sexual fantasia. In Winchell's broadcast, marriages seemed to have the life expectancy of a mayfly. Divorces seemed commonplace and unexceptional—this at a time when they were anything but in the ordinary experience of Americans—and new romance was always in the offing. Indeed, Reno, where the wealthy hied for a quick divorce, and Yuma, where they hied for a quick, unobtrusive wedding, were the program's twin capitals. It was as if there existed a single massive celebrity *ronde* of partners continually coupling and uncoupling. Sometimes, in fact, Winchell's romantic carousel spun so fast that a divorced couple remarried each other; once he reported that Henry Fonda and director William Wyler were both aspiring to remarry the former wife of both, actress Margaret Sullavan.

It all seemed mildly but excitingly illicit—this world Winchell hurled each Sunday night into the teeth of Depression America. It was a glamorous world governed by none of the ordinary rules of behavior or responsibility. It was a world where romance was a euphemism for sex and where each listener was a voyeur, vicariously enjoying the suggestion of perpetual sexual availability of these stars, celebrities and socialites who changed lovers, husbands and wives like clothes. And it was Walter's presentation that made it seem so. By piling one item on another and by wrenching them all from any context, he created a new context: a dizzying and disorienting bacchanalia, almost prurient in its appeal. Once

Broadway's Boswell, Walter Winchell was now, on the "Jergens Program" and in the Monday column, becoming America's Ovid too.

VI

It was the greatest tragedy that was ever to befall him, and it so rent his life that he was never quite the same again. He had noticed it initially a week after his first broadcast for Jergens lotion. "Gloria had walked across the parlor on her heels with outstretched arms, as though to make me her prisoner," he wrote in his autobiography. "She giggled as she teased: 'I'm gonna get my daddy and let him take me to breakfast!' " But at the breakfast table she didn't eat and complained that she didn't feel well. "The doctors and specialists said pneumonia. . . . The doctor slept on a sofa alongside her oxygen tent." On a wet, gray Christmas Eve morning in the Winchells' suite at the Hotel Park Central, eleven days after the onset of her illness, nine-year-old Gloria Winchell died. The clock read 7:50 a.m., Walter noticed. "Every time I wake up," he wrote later, "it always seems to be 7:50 in the morning or night. Thirty-six years later, it still makes me think of her." "Stardust" was playing on the radio.

"The sympathies of friends are comforting indeed, even though they do not erase the terrors that come in the night when slumber is stubborn and you think you hear the baby you miss in the room," he wrote a friend who had sent a note of condolence.

> You talk about those of us who have had some good breaks being ready to sacrifice everything to keep our babies well. Twice before, when Gloria was six weeks old and when she was five, she was gravely ill with pneumonia, and when I was getting $25 per week, the doctor saved her. Now, when I can afford eight doctors at a time, scores of oxygen tanks and all the other things, that coin couldn't buy me when we wanted so much. . . .
>
> She was such a lovely little girl; I never saw her cry, and the third day she was sick, when Mrs. Winchell and I realized she was in danger, my tear ducts opened wide and Mrs. Winchell, for want of something to say to Gloria under the glass tent, said "Poor Daddy cried when he heard you were so sick" and Gloria said, in amazement "He did? Why I didn't know daddies cried!"

June was devastated. She had neither slept nor eaten through most of Gloria's illness. When she was told that Gloria had died, she ran frantically to the window and attempted to leap. Walter caught her by her hair and nightgown and pulled her from the windowsill. "She said her heart was broken," remembered a friend of June's. "She would have killed herself if it weren't for Walda." The funeral service was held at Campbell's Funeral Home, at Broadway and 66th Street at two in the afternoon on December 28. Afterwards Gloria was interred in a receiving vault at the Woodlawn Cemetery, where her body would remain for the next thirty-five years. Walter was unable to bury her.

She had been, with Walda, the love of Walter and June's lives, and with her passing the family foundation was rocked, its cracks more evident than ever before. June, unable to shake her grief, left with Walda for Florida shortly after the funeral. Walda's own response to her sister's death was, according to a later assessment, "unusually severe and enduring." Walter and June found themselves incapable of telling their surviving daughter the truth, so they told her instead that "Sissy has gone to camp," even though Walda, then five, said she realized it was too cold for her sister to be at camp. During the funeral she was packed off with a strange nurse. Weeks passed before she was finally told the truth—with, it turned out, terrible consequences.

While June tried to escape her pain in Florida, Walter inured himself to his by diving back into his work. "With my numerous activities I manage to get through the daytime all right," he wrote a friend. But any chance he might have had to decouple himself from the column and pull himself from its maw was now irretrievably lost. He generally hid his grief. Though he immediately suspended the column, the night after Gloria's death he delivered his broadcast without mentioning his personal tragedy. "I couldn't have said it," he wrote later. "It would have made me choke." A week later, on New Year's Day, he opened the broadcast with a story about Greta Garbo's applying for a passport. He closed the broadcast with: "To you, you, you, and you, from Border to Border and Coast to Coast—Mrs. Winchell and I thank you so very much from the depths of what's left of our hearts."

But however well he seemed to cope, he found, he *sought*, reminders of Gloria everywhere. A reader in Johannesburg, South Africa, had sent him an ebony and gold mourning ring which he never removed, not even when he washed his hands. (One day, years later, he injured his hand and was forced to remove it; the ring disappeared, and Walter suspected that June had taken it. "It makes me sad," she had told him.) On his desk he kept a small white shoe of Gloria's. He always touched it now before he began to type his column. Her photo was on his wall, and he made certain that flowers were regularly sent to her crypt. Subsequent Christmases, he said, were always "faked."

"He never got over her, never got over her," recalled a friend. "He carried her memory to the grave." "I met him long after she was gone, but he brought her up every now and then," confirmed Walter's longtime associate Herman Klurfeld. "He said he missed her. How beautiful she was. . . . He could cry easily—about children. He wouldn't actually weep, but you would see he would well up. . . . Anything involving children touched him very deeply." "The only tragedy in my life," Walter wrote a year after her death, "was the 'going upstairs' of Gloria. She was an inspiration to me and I'm afraid I will never get over her going."

On January 2 he resumed his column, again without mention of Gloria. But on January 4 he made his grief public with a poem:

> *The Garden of Verses and all of her toys*
> *Had been placed in an orderly row.*
> *The dollies and tea things had all been arranged*
> *For a Christmas night "party," you know.*
>
> *"Right after the broadcast, now please hurry home,*
> *Or the tea will get chilled," she had said.*
> *"My dolls will be hungry and weary for sleep*
> *And they should be early to bed."*
>
> *Oh, Little Boy Blue, whose tin soldiers faithful*
> *Hold their vigil with never a noise—*
> *Please send a few of your trustiest guardsmen*
> *To watch over Gloria's toys.*

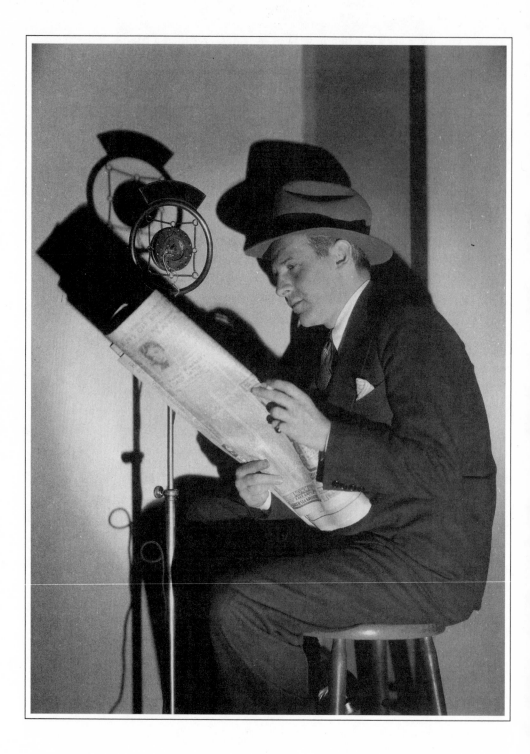

PART TWO

W.W.

Fame sometimes hath created something of nothing.
—THOMAS FULLER

CHAPTER 4

Filling the Void

FOR MANY AMERICANS, THE GAY times of the twenties ended with the crash. For many others, they ended when the full severity of the Depression finally set in several years later. But for Walter Winchell the good times ended with Gloria's death. Her passing came as an awful fulfillment of Walter's own deeply held belief that life was beyond one's control, that everything was provisional. For years he had worked indefatigably, almost literally without rest, with the promise that he would soon be able to retire to his family, to the one security he could know. Gloria's death had now broken the promise and driven him back into his work, where he could fend off insecurity only with hell-bent energy.

With June and Walda having escaped to Florida, leaving Walter to his despondency, he invited Curley Harris to room with him. Harris, a young red-haired *Daily News* crime reporter, was cocky, gregarious and well connected with the Broadway crowd—the sort of fellow Walter himself had been a decade earlier. A self-confessed "fresh kid," he readily accepted Walter's offer. They lived companionably in a two-room bachelor apartment at the Park Central. He and Harris kept similar hours: out during the night, sleeping during the day. Sometimes, Harris remembered, Walter brought a girl to their quarters. Most of the time, however, they went their separate ways, Walter immersing himself once again in his grueling routine of six columns and one broadcast each week and, by the first week of February, acting in a new film short for Universal called *I Know*

Everybody and Everybody's Racket, despite the fact that he had broken his ankle.

"No heroics," Walter said he cautioned the screenwriters this time. "Make the other fellow a smarty. Keep me in character—let me be the chump, which I am." That, he said, is what the public wanted. They are "not satisfied with knowing that a 'Weisenheimer' (a columnist or New Yorker) has one pedal on a banana peel.... People like it better knowing that the 'wise guy' has both feet on one!"

Based on a story by Mark Hellinger, the short starred Walter as himself, bored with New York nightlife, wearily offering to squire a pretty out-of-town news reporter around the nightspots because "I know everybody and everybody's racket." After a whirlwind tour Walter introduces the young lady to some gangsters, who continue her education. Sometime later the gangsters return—without the girl and, they soon realize, without their wallets. Patting himself down, Walter discovers his watch is gone. They have all been conned. The picture, bragged Walter, "did more to offset the legends about Broadwayites being so smart—than any other trick."

But Walter's busyness that January and February could not distract him from thoughts of Gloria. When James Carroll, a screenwriter, wrote a poem about his own dead infant daughter, Walter published it and then added "Poor fellow ... He's missed so much!" At the same time another correspondent was sending him reminders not only of Gloria but of how much animosity and envy Walter had stirred. These reminders came in the form of daily postcards with insults in green ink. Each was signed "the Old Copyreader." On one card, received just two days after her death, was pasted a news photo of Gloria with "RETRIBUTION?" written below it. The same man was apparently firing off letters to any essayist, columnist or editor who had remarked favorably on Walter. Walter suspected Gauvreau until a new postman who had been collecting the cards for mailing happened to read the one on Gloria and decided to contact Walter.

"We know the identity of the ambusher, the sniper or the hit-and-runner ... None of his groans matter, really," Walter bristled in the column. Claiming he didn't yet know what he was going to do with the information, he decided, "[O]fficial proof is best to make him ashamed of himself before the audience (who will be amazed, they won't easily associate 'anonymous letters' with him), so famous is he...." "I thought I'd die from the thrill when the investigators told me that the distinguishing mark on my favorite anonymous letter writer's machine was an 'M,' " he wrote a week later. "Such irony! Because—up to that time, I couldn't really believe that the lad I suspected could find the time to send me or editors all over the country such stupid comments [. . .] I never dreamed I affected him that terribly. . . ."

Three days later, Hearst wrote Kobler complaining about Walter's using the paper for his "personal antagonisms" and ordering the publisher to take "definite" action to stop Walter's campaign against the letter writer. In this, however, Hearst was merely attempting to protect one of his highly valued properties—a man who had been much bothered by Walter's little gibes in the column. As Hearst no doubt knew, the address the postman had given Walter was a new residence at 290 Park Avenue that had but a single occupant. That occupant was one of the Hearst *Journal*'s most popular syndicated columnists, O. O. McIntyre.

BY THE SECOND week in February, Walter had managed to escape New York himself and join his family in Miami Beach. "The scenery between here and Miami Beach is most depressing—broken down shacks, debris, rubbish and people in tatters," he wrote during his train ride. But Miami was glorious, especially because of a "bit of Titian-haired monkey-doodle" named Walda, "who thinks I'm just grand [. . .] If she keeps thinking that for so long as I live—nothing else will matter, matter, matter, matter, matter!!"

It was to be a week's vacation—quiet time with Walda and June, who was still depressed and uncommunicative and now physically debilitated by her ordeal. But there seemed always to be a force field of action around Winchell that prevented him from resting. He had barely arrived when a demented young Italian bricklayer named Giuseppe Zangara attempted to assassinate the President-elect, Franklin D. Roosevelt, at an American Legionnaires' nighttime rally in Miami. Zangara's shots missed Roosevelt but struck Chicago Mayor Anton Cermak, also on the podium. While being disarmed, Zangara shot several bystanders. Cermak languished in a Miami hospital for three weeks before dying of his wounds.

Walter was leaving the Western Union office that evening after filing his column when a breathless messenger boy related the news of the attack. Stranding June and Walda, Walter raced to the Florida East Coast Railroad siding a block away, where the President-elect's railroad car sat, enveloped now in chaos and confusion. Rumors were circulating that the assassin had already been apprehended. "Where would they put a man in this town if they arrested him?" Walter quickly asked a bystander. The man speculated they might put him in the county jail and indicated the courthouse building just a short distance away.

Now Walter played the reporter—a role he coveted. He dashed to the courthouse and bribed the elevator operator to take him to the eighteenth floor, where the cells were. But the operator was helpless to let him out there since, for security reasons, the elevator door on that floor opened only from the outside. Banging on the bars and yelling, Walter attracted the attention of the sheriff and "told him that I'd print his name all over the world if he would let me in on what was happening." With that inducement, Sheriff Hardie agreed to let him observe the first interrogation. For twenty minutes Winchell had the naked, deranged Giuseppe Zangara virtually to himself.

"I did it because I don't like rich men or presidents," Zangara said in barely decipherable English, giving every indication, acccording to Walter, "of being crazy." "I no shoot working man. I once tried to kill the king of Italy but they wouldn't let me." The next week on his broadcast, Walter attributed Zangara's motives to a "terrible burning pain in his stomach." "[H]e thought that if he killed an important man the police would kill him and that his own pain and torture would be ended for all time . . . Nobody is sorrier, I suspect, than the assassin Zangara that the judge could only give him 80 years."

His scoop in hand, Walter was ecstatic. "[O]h, the thrill of it—the excitement and the nerve-wracking tension that went with flashing the news to my paper in New York," Walter said. "Talk about being lucky! . . . I was blessed with the breaks again . . ." To his fellow journalists he gloated. "Oh, I know I didn't help you get into that elevator leading to the 26th floor* of the jail to see Zangara, and thought of myself first, but my bad manners bested me that time, Kid . . . I won't do it—until the next time, honest. . . ."

In truth, though, Walter's exclusive hadn't made anywhere near the splash he had hoped. Flushed with having beaten the real journalists whose respect he so longed for, he filed his interview at Western Union and then left before the copy had been sent. Steve Hannagan, the Miami Beach press agent who had first coaxed Winchell to the area, was in the telegraph office rooting around the pile of telegraph transmissions when he discovered Walter's story. Apparently to ingratiate himself with the press, Hannagan decided to wire its exclusive quotes to other New York papers. They arrived just minutes after the *Mirror* had received them, making it seem, in the end, as if Winchell hadn't really beaten his fellow journalists to the story.

Four days later he was on his way back to New York and the grind. If he hadn't received the respect he sought for his Zangara scoop, the Mi-

---

*Walter never got the floor quite straight. In one article it was the eighteenth floor, in another the twenty-eighth, here the twenty-sixth.

ABOVE RIGHT: Walter as a small child, outfitted in finery despite his family's poverty—a sign of their affectations. *Rose Bigman collection*

ABOVE: Walter at roughly the time he was appearing in the Imperial Trio, when his chiseled features and china-blue eyes made him the heartthrob of 116th Street. *Rose Bigman collection*

RIGHT: Jenny Bakst Winchel, Walter's mother. An attractive, vivacious woman, she periodically took revenge on her hapless, philandering husband by taking off with the children. The family retained no photographs of Jacob Winchel, her husband and Walter's father. *Pat Rose collection*

Walter, fourth from left, with Gus Edwards's *School Days* company, where he spent his adolescence. Walter's vaudeville mentor, Roy Mack, is second from the right. Nellie Cliff, Walter's love before World War I intervened, is third from the right with the bow and ringlets. *Rose Bigman collection*

Twenty-year-old Walter and seventeen-year-old Rita Greene gazing moonily at each other in June 1917 as they return to New York from Florida aboard the S. S. *Lenape*. *Pat Rose collection*

LEFT: The wedding photo, August 11, 1919, exactly one week after Winchell & Greene scored their unexpected triumph at McVicker's Theater in Chicago. RIGHT: Mamie Hoskins Magee (left) and her beautiful daughter Elizabeth June, two free vaudeville spirits. As June Aster, Elizabeth captivated Walter. *Courtesy of Sarah Fried*

Walter (left) as a *Daily Graphic* columnist, with two of his guides to Broadway: Texas Guinan, the brassy hostess at the hottest speakeasy, and Mark Hellinger, himself a columnist at the *Daily News*. *Author's collection*

LEFT: Editor Emile Gauvreau, Walter's nemesis, first at the *Graphic* and then at the *Mirror*. Tortured by his own compromises with the world of tabloids, Gauvreau seemed to displace his self-loathing onto Winchell. *Wide World Photos* RIGHT: A characteristic pose: Walter at his *Mirror* desk in 1931 or early 1932, chain-smoking, talking on the phone and rapping out a column to fill the gossip maw. *Courtesy of Hal Layer*

Winchell the national phenomenon. His gossip column had become the number-one attraction at William Randolph Hearst's *Mirror*. *Rose Bigman collection*

His role as host of "The Lucky Strike Dance Hour" made him a radio star. By spring 1932, over 45,000 Lucky Strike billboards bore his image and his trademark phrase "O.K.-America!" *Courtesy of Hal Layer*

And his fame made him a headliner, finally, at the Palace Theater in New York, where only the best acts played. *Rose Bigman collection*

His terror of failure made him lonely. *Rose Bigman collection*

Walter with Assistant District Attorney George Carney in February 1932, outside the grand jury room where indictments in the death of gangster Vincent Coll were being deliberated. By predicting the assassination in his column the morning of the killing, Walter had placed himself in jeopardy with the mob. *Harry Ransom Humanities Research Center, the University of Texas at Austin*

A rare respite from the grind with June, Walda (left) and Gloria (right), outside the Roney-Plaza in Miami Beach. In less than two years, Gloria would be dead. Walter called it "the only tragedy in my life." *Courtesy of Hal Layer*

Walter with Jimmy Cagney in Hollywood, where he recovered from Gloria's death. The crisp urban style that Cagney and others purveyed was so much like Winchell's that critic George Jean Nathan cited Winchell as an influence on performance. *Museum of Modern Art Film Stills Archive*

The secret sharers: Walter Winchell (testing the finger-printing pad) and J. Edgar Hoover, director of the Federal Bureau of Investigation. Winchell provided Hoover with support, Hoover provided Winchell with information and favors. *Wide World Photos*

The Flemington, N.J., courtroom where Bruno Hauptmann was tried in 1935 for the kidnapping and murder of aviator Charles Lindbergh's infant son. Pressing for Hauptmann's conviction while covering the trial, Winchell (arrow) managed to thrust himself into the center of the event and helped convert it into one of the first media festivals. *Courtesy of Hal Layer*

ami trip had at least yielded one accolade that would always be a balm: Damon Runyon, also in Miami at the time, had dedicated a column to him. Calling him "The Grey Ghost of Broadway" for his prematurely silver-streaked hair, and "the most publicized newspaper man of our times," Runyon joked that Winchell had hit Miami Beach and then "ricocheted in a northerly direction again before Old Sol could get a good aim at him." Still, Runyon personally vouched for Winchell's having been there. "He was walking around swathed in a blue dressing gown, saying, 'I must get some of this sun.' The chances are he would have gotten some of the sun, at that, if he hadn't been halted at every cabana along the Roney line for a chat."

Runyon seemed impressed that Walter had come all this way at what proved great expense (he had paid $1,500 so his broadcast could emanate from Miami) just to see his family for a few days, and he lamented the passing of Gloria, "a flower of a girl." But Runyon reserved his greatest admiration for Walter's total absorption in his work. "He eats, sleeps and breathes 'shop,' which is his column," lauded Runyon. "He has the joy of accomplishment. He is never blasé about his business. . . . The newspaper game is fun to him. An exclusive piece of news is manna from the heavens. He will always be young in it. . . ."

Runyon, whose own family was anathema to him, didn't detect the desperation in Winchell's absorption or the oddity of Walter's racing back to New York while his wife and daughter, obviously anguished and needy, remained in Florida. The first week of March, with June still withdrawn and suicidal, she and Walda left for California, hoping to find some kind of surcease. But there was no peace there either. An earthquake damaged the Ambassador Hotel where they were staying, forcing them to move in with Walter's cousin Lola and her husband until the hotel was repaired. The quake, said Walter, had "tattered" June's nerves. Afterward on the phone, she described it to him "like the world was coming to an end— the way it did at Christmas."

Walter, in the meantime, joined Ben Bernie for two weeks of personal appearances at the Paramount theaters in Manhattan and Brooklyn, where he did a mock broadcast, sparred with Bernie and introduced celebrities from the audience. (Walter would always claim that Ed Sullivan had stolen this feature from him for Sullivan's popular television show.) Despite heavy sleet, the show, advertised as "Broadway's Biggest Hit," did standing-room-only business and failed to break Mae West's house record in Brooklyn only because Winchell and Bernie did five shows a day while West did six. The week after closing, Walter filmed another short for Universal, *Beauty on Broadway*, costarring chorus girls from Nils T. Grandlund's Paradise Club. His only complaint was that the studio de-

manded he blacken his graying hair to preserve his image. On his broadcast that same week, he sent birthday greetings to Walda, "six years
young."

Estranged and unhappy, the shadow of Gloria's death still adumbrating
her life, June returned east in April for a physical exam and rest at the
Pocono Hay-ven resort in Pennsylvania, then headed back to California.
By the end of May, Walter was complaining about the unbearable New
York heat—"The struggle that goes with gasping for a breeze in the hotels isn't worth the bother"—and pointing toward a reunion with his family in California. " 'Why, then?' a woman recently queried, 'do you have
them so faraway from you for so long?' " Walter wrote as he headed toward his family. "But she wouldn't understand . . . She wouldn't understand how frightened a man and woman can be—in New York . . . Where
the Sun is the name of a newspaper . . . Where the trees are only in parks
or in speakeasy backyards—and where one frail flower—didn't stand a
chance."

Though his thoughts inevitably kept drifting to Gloria, his trip west
was a satisfying one. In Chicago he stopped to visit the Century of Progress world's fair, met Hearst columnist and resident philosopher Arthur
Brisbane ("Devoured every word he said"), laid over for his broadcast and
received a studio visit from Will Rogers, was feted by Ben Bernie at the
College Inn and visited with Texas Guinan, who was appearing in a revue
at the fair, until 5:30 in the morning.

A few days later he arrived in Los Angeles, thrilled to be reunited with
his family and even more awestruck by Hollywood's seeming imperviousness to the Depression than he had been the year before. But Hollywood's style was not quite Winchell's style. For all the oblivious glamour
at the Colony and Coconut Grove, Walter also saw "armies" of "men
and women here who are in despair" and who "must become weary of
being weary in life and the struggle. . . ." Only at Bob Perry's café on
Hollywood Boulevard did he really feel in his element. "Fight promoters,
fighters, wrestlers, screen stars, discarded wives of famous men and other
Broadwayish folk people in the place—and for the first time last night—I
felt at home in this city of make-believe."

Like his Miami trip in February, this excursion to California was intended to be a family respite. "Experiencing what it was like for the first
time to keep normal hours—was a novelty," he later reflected. Again he
was inundated by offers for movies and personal appearances; one theater
in Los Angeles and another in San Francisco offered him $5,000 per
week *and* 50 percent of their profits. Walter turned them all down. "I
didn't come out here looking for vaudeville jobs," he told the Hollywood
Herald. "Five grand a week is serious with anybody who hasn't checked

his brains with his derby; but I'm here on vacation, to see my wife and baby for the first time in three months."

For August he was finally to receive a reprieve from the column and get a real vacation, but Kobler objected to the guest columns Walter had submitted late that June and suggested that Walter now either write the columns in advance or hire another writer at a "very nominal" fee (out of Walter's salary) to fill in. Obviously fearful that he might lose his vacation after all—he had had only one week off since Gloria's death—Walter took the extraordinary step of contacting Hearst. "The important thing is for you to go ahead and get your holiday," Hearst wired back soothingly. But at the same time he warned Walter not to do a movie with Twentieth Century Pictures' head Darryl Zanuck, as Hearst had heard Walter was planning, since the columnist was constantly breaking down as it was.

Hearst's warning had, in fact, come too late. Shortly after arriving in Hollywood, Walter had visited Harry Brand, an old friend from the LaHiff days and now chief publicist at Twentieth Century Pictures. Always prowling for new sources of income, Walter told Brand that he had an idea for a movie. Brand advised him to tell the story directly to studio head Zanuck, who had lately been the chief of production at Warner Brothers and was vigorously searching for stories at his upstart company. "It probably took a half hour or so," Walter later told an interviewer of his meeting with Zanuck. The deal was signed on June 23 with Walter getting $5,000 for his "outline" and the promise of another $25,000 upon acceptance of a script, to be written by a studio scenarist.

In the meantime, Hollywood was having as much trouble adjusting to Walter Winchell as Walter Winchell was having adjusting to Hollywood. Should it be respectful of his power or fearful of it? Should he be embraced as a friend, as he had been by so many the year before, or rebuffed as an enemy? Was he really one of them or was he a smart-alecky New Yorker having sport with them? That June some members of a Los Angeles organization of screenwriters and journalists called the Writers' Club invited Walter to a luncheon. As *Variety* reported it, other members then demanded—with temporary success—that the invitation be rescinded since he was not a "legitimate newspaper man, but simply a chatterer, etc." Then the manager of the club, writing on behalf of its president, screenwriter Rupert Hughes, apologized and asked Walter to be guest of honor at a dinner the following month. *Variety*, in particularly vicious fettle, said the invitation had been withdrawn because Winchell had "gone on a wide open tipping off spree," meaning that he was blowing the cover of philandering husbands and wives. "It can't even be admitted that the Kid Marvel is dumb enough to do that. Mrs. Winchell's egotistical rubberneck knows when he's tipping off and why." But he was so eager to receive tribute from the Los Angeles writers, said *Variety*, that he "managed to blackjack" the Writers' Club into throwing him a dinner anyway.

The dinner itself, on July 15, indicated just how conflicted Hollywood was over Winchell. The first speakers from the gathering of six hundred roasted him humorously. But then Eddie Cantor took the podium and turned serious. He claimed that Winchell was no longer a "dirt digger." Over the last year Winchell had changed, had become "constructive" instead of "destructive," and Cantor saluted him for it. More and more, Cantor said, Winchell was "using the column to get fair play for the underdog" rather than what he called "turnabout-face." "I was hated until I crusaded" was how Walter summarized these remarks, but he burned over the idea that he had gone soft, and he resented Cantor for having turned his gala affair into a criticism session. Will Rogers then rose and promised to "tell the truth." "I didn't come here to honor Mr. Winchell any more than they did," Rogers joked, but not without a tincture of seriousness. "I come here for the same reason that all the rest of you did. . . . *I was afraid not to come.*"

By this time there was a new source of fear from Winchell. Word of Walter's scenario for *Broadway Through a Keyhole* had been spreading, and one Hollywood luminary was appalled. The script concerned a mobster who has romantic designs on a virtuous young woman and sends her to Florida for her own protection during a gang war. In Florida she falls in love with a handsome crooner. When the gangster discovers what has happened, he is hurt and angry and threatens the crooner, then, realizing he cannot win the girl's heart, reluctantly surrenders his love. But when the girl is kidnapped by a rival gang, the mobster rushes to rescue her. The story ends with the girl back with her crooner and the mobster, wearing a crown of nobility, wounded and alone in a dark hospital room.

It may have sounded like a routine potboiler, except for one thing: It had been inspired by actual events. Back in 1928 Ruby Keeler, a pretty teenage dancer at Texas Guinan's Salon Royal, was being romanced by a bootlegger named Johnny "Irish" Costello. Costello was lovestruck, and under his patronage Keeler had become a nightclub and theater headliner. Then Al Jolson, the legendary entertainer, saw her in Chicago in a production of *Sidewalks of New York* and fell as hard as Costello had. When she arrived in Los Angeles for an appearance at Grauman's Theater, Jolson was at the station to greet her, and over the next three weeks he laid siege to her heart with honeyed words and expensive gifts, including a lynx fur.

Confused and frightened, Keeler, only nineteen, wired Costello for money and sped back to New York. Almost immediately, the Warner brothers began pressing her to return to California for more personal appearances. Costello let her go, with the assurance that Jolson was a continent away in Florida at the time. Costello didn't know that the Warners had invited Keeler largely at Jolson's instigation, and he was there again when she returned. Again panicky, she hurried back to New York. Costello greeted her at the train station with a diamond engagement ring. Walter remembered her flashing the diamond at him at Guinan's Salon Royal.

Confident that Jolson was vanquished, Costello now let Keeler fulfill an engagement in Washington. But Jolson was nothing if not persistent. By the end of her run she was phoning her agent, Billy Grady, and telling him that she had finally fallen in love with the singer and asking Grady to please tell Costello. "This nice man lowered his head without a word," Grady later wrote of Costello's reaction, "and for several minutes stared at his clenched fists. The knuckles were white from pressure. That good-looking Irish face was portraying inner agony. A lapse; he looked at me, banged his fists together, and abruptly left the table without a word." By one account, he wept outside Dinty Moore's.

Just before Jolson and Keeler were to wed and sail to Europe for their honeymoon, Costello phoned Winchell. He was upset, he said, by reports that Jolson was still terrified for his life, and he wanted to set the record straight. After hearing the talk about Jolson and Keeler, he said, he had arranged a meeting with Jolson at the singer's Ritz Towers apartment, fully expecting Jolson to deny the rumors. Jolson had instead confirmed them. "I shook hands with him," Costello told Walter, "and told him that he was getting the sweetest girl of them all and that I would step aside." Later he visited Keeler and professed his love one last time. Could she do the same? "She hesitated, bit her lip, and was about to cry, so I said: 'I understand, Ruby. It is okay with me.'"

Jolson and Keeler were married on September 21, 1928. Now, five years later, Keeler had read an item about Walter's movie in Louella Parsons's column and panicked, realizing the film was about her. "She couldn't sleep," said Jolson. "She became hysterical." The next evening, July 21, Jolson and Keeler were attending the prizefights at Hollywood Legion Stadium when Walter and June came down the aisle. By one account, Jolson got up and exchanged words with Walter. By Walter's own account, at least his first account, Jolson got up and, without saying a thing, socked him in the back of the neck, then decked him with a second blow. (Later Walter claimed he was sucker-punched by a "hitman" hired by an aggrieved studio.) Pandemonium followed. June took off her shoe and tried striking Jolson on the head but hit Warner Brothers executive

Hal Wallis instead. Wallis and others tried to pull Jolson off the stricken Winchell.

The packed house broke into cheers. Walter might have been the champion back east, he might even have been the champion among ordinary readers and listeners, but among the celebrated in Hollywood he had emerged as a threat. Later, when Jolson left, the crowd gave him another ovation. He had smote the man who smote the stars. At Walter's own paper Kobler cheerfully radiogrammed the news to Gauvreau, then on an ocean liner bound for Europe: "I hope this will make you feel better."

But if Hollywood's sympathies lay with Jolson, Winchell once again seemed to get the last laugh. Three days after the scuffle, Walter reported that *Broadway Through a Keyhole* had drawn more than $500,000 worth of advance bookings, and he issued a new challenge to Jolson for a rematch "any time, any where, with any thing," with the proceeds going to charity. Jolson declined. More, the fight contributed to Walter's image as a scrapper. "How many fights are you in now?" Ruth Cambridge asked in the column. "I can't remember—" he answered, "it's a lot of fun—making people mad." Three weeks later, seemingly more for publicity and image than for justice, he filed a $500,000 lawsuit against Jolson.*

Within a week after the Jolson bout, Winchell was headed back to New York to resume the column and broadcast. "To the gentlemen and gentlewomen of the movie colony," he wrote in the column only somewhat tongue-in-cheek, "I am indeed indebted for some jolly times...." And he told the Los Angeles *Examiner* that he would move to Hollywood as soon as the tax laws were relaxed. He would gladly leave New York, "where I will be bothered again, by the oppressive heat and humidity." "And then will come the treacherous winds in the Winter—" he wrote, obviously still thinking of Gloria's pneumonia, "which makes me so afraid ... Carrying with them epidemics of dreaded plagues—which man cannot combat successfully...."

---

*As time passed, Jolson would be contrite, admitting that Walter had offered to show him the original scenario but that Jolson hadn't been interested. But the two weren't reconciled until years later, when a mutual friend gave Walter a salve for hemorrhoids that Jolson had used with success.

II

Unable to endure the ghosts at their old apartment in the Park Central, the Winchells returned home at summer's end to capacious new quarters in the Majestic Apartments at West 72nd Street overlooking Central Park. The apartment, covering the entire twenty-ninth floor of the South Tower, contained ten rooms, decorated, said one visitor, in a manner that was "elaborate yet tasteful." There, as fall came, June continued her mourning. Walda attended first grade at the Ethical Culture School. And Walter resumed his scavenging for gossip and money to escape the pain.

The immediate lure, the one which offered the easiest money, was the movies. On September 18 Zanuck screened *Broadway Through a Keyhole* and was ecstatic. "[T]he best picture I've been associated with in the past two years," he wired Walter. "Makes Forty Second Street, Golddiggers [of 1933] look like a trailer and I mean it sincerely." Now Zanuck quickly began contemplating a sequel: *Hollywood Thru a Keyhole*. "I want you to get to work immediately, undercover, on a story to fit the title," he wrote Walter the day of the preview. The next day Zanuck, wasting no time, emerged from a story conference with an idea and wired Walter asking if he would lend his name and how much money he would want to do so. Two weeks later, apparently angling for more money, Walter wrote Zanuck suggesting a story of his own. Now Zanuck was the one who was balking. He said he would have to read it to make certain Walter's story would be a "worthy successor" to *Broadway Through a Keyhole*, but Zanuck realized that "Winchell" was a brand name, and he seemed far more interested in obtaining the label than the contents.

Two days later Walter wasn't so sure about his association with Zanuck, money or not. He had seen a trailer for *Keyhole*, and what he saw made him "sick to my stomach a little." It looked tawdry. He complained to Zanuck that "I left the cheapest newspaper in the world five years ago. It was the lowest of the low in newspapers. Now, suddenly, in 1933, I find myself surrounded by the same type of person who on the Graphic created such sloppy announcements as 'Are they real—or are they fiction?' 'Who are they—do you know?,' " referring obviously to publicity suggesting in so many words that the movie was based on Jolson and Keeler. "I do not see why, Darryl, the exploitation on 'Keyhole' cannot be done in a dignified manner," Walter wrote, trying to protect his image as a respectable gossip and warning that "to even hint that the picture concerns living people" would invite a lawsuit.

While the new project languished, *Broadway Through a Keyhole* opened in New York on November 2 with a traffic-stopping gala premiere. A sound truck festooned with a banner patrolled the streets blaring the song "Broadway Through a Keyhole" and disgorging specially printed tabloids about the movie. Gimbel's and Macy's department stores featured window displays. Five thousand posters were tacked up at newsstands. And a national radio hookup brought the festivities to the country while street amplification of the broadcast tied up traffic for more than an hour.

Though Winchell's participation in the movie had been minimal—Gene Towne and Graham Baker were credited with the screenplay, and Winchell's voice in the picture was his only remaining imprint—almost every reviewer treated *Keyhole* as if it were his creative product. "Walter Winchell, the author of this story, has discovered a way of righting matters so far as true love is concerned, and it is done in a vigorous dramatic fashion," wrote *The New York Times'* Mordaunt Hall. Rose Pelswick in Hearst's *Evening Journal* awarded "[o]rchids, and plenty of them, to Walter Winchell for the story of 'Bway Through a Keyhole.' A smart, colorful and exciting piece about the Main Stem that he knows so well. . . ." Richard Watts, Jr., of the *Herald Tribune* used the occasion to extol Walter as "Broadway's best pal and severest critic," a "distinguished and vigorous chronicler of the vital trivia of this bewildered metropolitan epoch," and an "incisive and dramatic observer of these critical days of perishing bourgeois gayety."

But then Watts went on to say what the other critics had seemed to tiptoe around for fear of offending Winchell: that the movie wasn't particularly good. It "reveals too few signs of its author's shrewdness, knowledge and dramatic instinct. It is a pleasant enough gangster melodrama, but only in a few scenes does [*sic*] the necessary humor, power and knowledge merge. For the rest, it might just as well have been written by any of the studio staff men"—as, of course, it had been.

Walter agreed completely. Greedily as he had taken the studio's money, the movie embarrassed him. As the trailer had forewarned him, it wasn't first-class, wasn't worthy of being associated with the name of Walter Winchell. Starring Constance Cummings as the girl, Paul Kelly as the gangster and Russ Columbo as the singer, with bit parts for Blossom Seeley, Gregory Ratoff and, at Walter's suggestion, Texas Guinan, it had a small-time cast. "I'd encourage newcomers, of course," Walter griped in his column, "but I wouldn't break in seven 'names' who never had big roles or movie experience before—as was done in 'Broadway Thru a Keyhole.' And the next time I sell a picture, if ever, I won't take coin for merely suggesting the theme. Nor would I permit a company to rush a picture of mine just because it wanted to cash in on some front-page publicity."

Three days after the picture opened, Walter suffered another collapse or begged off for another vacation—it is unclear which—and headed back to Florida. On November 5, 1933, the same day as Walter's breakdown, came the sad news from the West Coast that Texas Guinan was dead. She had suffered the fate that so terrified Walter himself. She died an anachronism, hounded from New York by Prohibition agents before the crash and rendered a superfluous figure after it. In September 1931 she had taken her girls to France with the intention of opening a club there, but authorities refused to admit her. She returned to America touring in a new revue she called *Too Hot for Paris*. That too failed when local authorities kept shuttering it for indecency. Guinan had become the scapegoat of the twenties—a hostess without a party.

Still, some vagrant nostalgia lingered. When Twentieth Century offered her the supporting role in *Keyhole*, essentially playing herself, she headed out to California, stopping along the way to make vaudeville appearances. Americans seemed to sense this was a farewell tour of the lost spirit of the last decade, and she was greeted by surprisingly large crowds: 102,000 patrons in a week at the Chicago Theater, 105,728 at the Fox in Detroit, a house record.

In the end, the movie disappointed her as it had Walter; the role, she felt, was so insultingly small that she said she played the "keyhole." But out in California, Texas had an inspiration. Attracted by the peculiar combination of show business and piety—a combination within Texas herself—she got the idea to make a film based on the popular Los Angeles evangelist Aimee Semple McPherson. Since McPherson was touring in New York at the time, Texas received permission to appear in McPherson's temple and wound up enjoying it so much, that she dropped the idea of the movie. Instead, the very image of twenties indulgence decided to become an evangelist herself. Besides, she reasoned, the money was good.

She debuted at a small church in Tacoma which she had urged her manager to book, but as she began to preach, she stumbled, groping for words beyond her slang, then broke down. "I'm sorry—I—I never cry," she told the congregants, "but I have never talked to—to people like you before." From Tacoma she limped north into Canada. Since her appearance at the Chicago world's fair earlier that year, she had been suffering from severe stomach and bowel pains. In Vancouver she fell ill with what was described as ulcerated colitis, was hospitalized for a week and then was rushed into surgery for what was believed to be a perforated bowel. She never recovered. As she lay on her deathbed, she joked about getting the toilet concession at Versailles, though she added it wouldn't be worth anything since there was no indoor plumbing. She died two months shy of her fiftieth birthday. Walter, recuperating in Florida at the time of her death, wrote upon his return: "We learned Broadway from her. She taught us the way of the Street."

THEY WERE ALL passing—all the protagonists of the twenties Broadway that Walter had helped create—as if the new decade had to expunge the symbols of the old one. Earlier that year, on New Year's Day, Larry Fay, Texas's flamboyant partner and onetime head of the milk rackets in New York, was gunned down at his Casa Blanca Club by a disgruntled employee protesting a pay cut. (Mrs. Fay heard the news while listening to Walter's broadcast.)

And just six weeks before Guinan's death, Sime Silverman, the founder of *Variety*, died of a hemorrhage in Los Angeles. Like Guinan, Silverman had fallen on hard times. At the time of his death he was sick and broke and tired, but despite his own troubles and despite the fact that *Variety* was warring with Walter, Silverman was most solicitous of Walda and June when they were regrouping in California that spring and summer, even buying Walda diamond and pearl necklaces. "Why do you give his children costly gifts and take me to dinner, and then beat his brains out in your paper?" June asked Silverman in the coffee shop of the Ambassador Hotel one day. "Sime looked at June and said: 'You don't understand. Walter is a famous man and that makes him news, and anything he does or says is of interest to others.' "

Perhaps the most symbolic of the Depression's casualties was New York Mayor Jimmy Walker. Walker had taken such pride in his wild, errant ways that after the crash, when reformers began scrutinizing his administration, he opined, "Life is a circus and there must be a clown in every circus, and we'll say, 'New York had its clown.' " Clowning now, however, was little tolerated. After months of investigations of kickbacks and bribes, Walker was forced from office in September 1932. As if his city's fate were bound to his own, he rapidly spiraled downward. Walter reported that he was penniless since a partner had absconded with his money; that his wife, having finally granted him a divorce, was now remarrying; that his book couldn't get serialization; that his health was failing.

And as with the personalities of the era, so too with many of its institutions. The scandal sheet *Broadway Brevities* had miraculously risen again after Stephen Clow's imprisonment, but what the courts couldn't accomplish, the Depression did. Even the venerable society gossip tabloids *Town Topics* and *The Tatler* couldn't survive. In 1932 an investigation by New York State's attorney general revealed that salesmen acting for the sheets had pressured prospective investors into buying stock by threatening to disclose "uncomplimentary" information the magazines had collected on cards. As part of a settlement, the attorney general's office forced *Town Topics* to burn all five hundred of its cards in the furnace of the State Office Building—an event which *The New York Times* described as "ceremonious." Both magazines expired soon thereafter.

Another victim of the times was Walter's alma mater, the *Graphic*. Even before Walter's departure, it had been losing money in gushes: $7.5 million by Bernarr Macfadden's own estimate, while another put the total at $11 million. Still, Macfadden kept flogging the paper, even, in desperation, attempting to upgrade it by prohibiting its famous composographs, its photos of scantily clad women and its sex scandals unless they could be corroborated by a court record. Stanley Walker described this rehabilitation as an effort to emerge from "the red light district of journalism—but cautiously and gradually, so that no one would be aware of the transformation until it has become fact." Walker added, "It was no use."

On July 2, 1932, Macfadden filed a bankruptcy petition for the *Graphic*, citing $760,528 in debts and only $165,000 in assets. On July 7, the paper ceased publication. "Gauvreau tried to make it sensational," analyzed one of its employees, "Winchell tried to make it amusing, [editor Lou] Weitzenkorn tried to make it semirespectable, but it remained one thing over all: Macfadden." The *Christian Century* magazine seemed to speak for many when it reported, "Out of the prevalent business gloom comes at least one ray of sunshine—Mr. Macfadden's New York tabloid newspaper, the *Evening Graphic*, has suspended publication!"

ONE SOCIAL WORLD was gone, but in the four years since the crash a new social world had been aborning. Its lineaments may have been less readily perceptible at first than those of the dying Jazz Age, but it would prove every bit as powerful an imaginative landscape, and Winchell would prove every bit as instrumental in promulgating it.

It was called "café society." Exactly where and when it originated would always be in some dispute. One observer dated it from the late 1890s, when a former champagne agent named Henry Lehr induced Mrs. Astor, a regent even among New York's so-called Four Hundred social titans, to attend a dinner at Sherry's restaurant. Until then high society's denizens had dined and entertained exclusively in their homes, and the next morning a society reporter expressed his shock: "I never dreamt it would be given me to gaze on the face of an Astor in a public dining room."

The more generally accepted version was that of Maury Paul, who wrote the society column for Hearst's *American* under the nom de plume Cholly Knickerbocker. As Paul told it, he was sitting in the Ritz on a brisk February night in 1919 and observing the socialites when he mused to himself, "This place! Society isn't staying home and entertaining anymore. Society is going out to dinner, out to night life, and letting down the barriers." The next morning Paul dubbed this phenomenon "café society," and the name stuck.

Exactly what café society was was not easy to determine and became even more difficult as time went on. It wasn't just that high society had gone public. Café society included people whom the Old Guard of high society would never have countenanced privately or publicly. Rather, it seemed to have been born during Prohibition from a combination of Winchell's showy Broadway crowd and a restless group of young socialites who were, in one observer's words, "vaulting the barriers of Newport and Fifth Avenue in search of adventure beyond," with the speakeasies as the catalysts. Certainly the Broadway-society axis constituted an unmistakable new social formation; and in the thirties, when people talked about "café society," this incongruous mix is what they meant.

And they meant a certain set of values that the group seemed to represent. It had traditionally been the function of society to set an example for Americans; not only power but decorum had emanated from the Old Guard. But what was one to make of this new mélange of showfolk and socialites mixing at nightclubs? What were they teaching the unfortunates of this country during the Depression? "We must dispel the idea that we are a frivolous, heartless, Godless coterie, living in a maze of costly dinner parties, wild orgies, etc.," Maury Paul declared. He fully sympathized with those of the Old Guard who were threatening to abandon America for Europe now that high society was being corrupted by café society. "Mrs. Goelet is not a snob," he wrote, referring to one of the Four Hundred. "She is simply of the old school, and will never understand why a Frelinghuysen will hobnob with a songwriter who hailed originally from the Lower East Side [he was speaking of Irving Berlin]."

Café society may have been an odd and ungainly organism with seemingly disparate parts, but if its precise definition was inexact, the engine that drove it was not. The Old Guard had maintained its power partly through the mystification of its own isolation and privacy; one was powerful enough, secure enough, not to need or want attention, unless it was that of one's social equals. Café society was predicated on something else entirely. Here power was really a function not of wealth or breeding or talent or connections but of publicity. "Publi-ciety" Cleveland Amory called it, where the object was to be seen and known, where the object was to be famous.

The ones who could bestow fame, particularly upon individuals who hadn't *done* anything to deserve it, were the press, and of the press, most especially the columnists, and of the columnists, most especially those who were widely syndicated. In a very real sense, then, social authority in the early thirties had been turned on its head; it now derived from the media, or as Walter put it, "Social position is now more a matter of press than prestige." And since the king of the media in the thirties was Walter Winchell, café society was in many ways a function of him. A mention in his column or on his broadcast meant that one was among the exalted. It meant that one's name was part of the general fund of knowledge. It meant that one's exploits, even if they were only the exploits of dining, rated acknowledgment. It meant that one's life was validated, albeit validated by fame rather than accomplishment.

On its face it seemed absurd that a nation racked by unemployment should care about a band of swells whose deepest concern was whether they rated a column mention. (Walter thought it ridiculous too and constantly scolded the idle rich while continuing, hypocritically, to feed their publicity habit.) Yet people did care, and they read about café society as if it were an exciting new social drama to replace the now shuttered bawdy farce of twenties Broadway. If Broadway had been an imaginative landscape coruscating with images of hot freedom, café society was an imaginative world shimmering with glamour, just as so many Depression-era movies did. For most Americans, "café society" immediately triggered images of women in smart gowns and men in satin-collared tuxedos, of tiered nightclubs undulating in the music of swell bands, of cocktails and cigarettes, of cool talk and enervated elegance, all of which made café society one of those repositories of dreams at a time when reality seemed treacherous.

More, with so many of the great personalities of the twenties gone, the café socialites replenished the stock of cultural stars the way young talent might replenish a depleted stock of movie stars at a film studio. According to critic Richard Schickel, these, in turn, provided, "as players in any good sleazy melodrama must, occasions for envy and moralizing in roughly equal measure." As Schickel saw it, that was also one of the dividends that high society got from mixing with show business; it was the writers and the actors in café society who went out to Hollywood and memorialized the socialites in bright, crackling comedies that made high society seem the very apogee of intelligence and sophistication.

But as Schickel also understood, all of this was exciting to the general public only insofar as café society represented a secret world to which ordinary Americans had access exclusively through Winchell's column and through other dispatches from the tabernacle. "It [café society] was a fiction that purported to give outsiders an insider's view of the previously closed world of wealth—with titillating hints of scandal part of the bargain struck between the suppliers of this entertainment and their avid audiences," Schickel wrote. These golden, chosen few would retreat to their clubs, dress, dine, drink, chat, and *live* beautifully, establish their names and then donate their sagas of romance to the public. And the public, far away and trapped in its own travails, would feel that it had, if only briefly, penetrated the very deepest chamber of American society. That was the transaction Winchell brokered.

ONE NECESSARY ingredient of café society was the café. ("The idea of Café Society was all right," grumped Frank Crowninshield, former editor of *Vanity Fair*, "all but the café. What actually ruined the whole goddam thing was alcohol and noise.") In the early thirties there were three primary locales, the Big Three, as they were then known. One was the Colony at 61st Street and Madison Avenue. Really more a way station from high society to full-fledged café society than a gathering place for the café socialites, the Colony was an opulently appointed restaurant where, Walter noted, "frequenters usually attire themselves in their ermines and tall millinery and the cuisine is grand." The food, which was "peddled," Walter said, "at so much a karat," was considered the finest in New York, but of equal appeal to the elite was the Colony's exclusivity. At the Colony, Maury Paul reported as early as 1925, "social grandees feel safe from the prying eyes of those who would exploit them."

Exploitation, by oneself and others, was more probable at the El Morocco. Its owner was an Italian immigrant named John Perona who had worked his way across the ocean from England to South America on a steamer. (A romantic dalliance in Southampton had prevented him from keeping his original assignment on the *Titanic*.) Taunted by the crew, Perona jumped ship in Buenos Aires and became a boxer. It was there he met the Argentine heavyweight contender Luis Firpo. Eventually Perona migrated to New York, got a job as a busboy at the Knickerbocker Grill and opened a small restaurant of his own on Broadway. When Firpo mentioned the place to reporters after his championship bout with Jack Dempsey, patrons flocked to it. With this cachet, Perona ran several speakeasies before opening the El Morocco at 154 East 54th Street in 1931. Among café socialites it became an instant favorite.

The café Walter was to choose for his own listening post, however, was the Stork Club. Like John Perona, Sherman Billingsley, the Stork's owner, had roots about as far from café society as one could get. He had been born in 1900, the son of a police chief, in a white clapboard farmhouse in Enid, Oklahoma. When he was twelve, the family moved to Anadarko, and Sherman quit school to work for his brothers Ora and Logan, selling bootleg liquor at their drugstore; on one occasion the governor of Oklahoma led a contingent of ministers into the store while young Sherman was serving drinks, and Sherman, to destroy the evidence, flung a beer bottle at the whiskey jug, touching off a melee in which a bullet grazed him.

When the Billingsleys moved to Oklahoma City, Ora and Sherman struck out on their own, floating through the West. In Seattle in 1916 Sherman was arrested for violating the local liquor ordinance. A few more aimless years later, the brothers found themselves in Detroit, running three drugstores and bootleg liquor from Canada. In January 1919 they were convicted in federal court of rum-running, fined $5,000 and sentenced to fifteen months at Leavenworth prison. Sherman served three months and twenty days. He came to New York, nineteen years old, with a $5,000 stake from his brother Logan and bought a drugstore in the Morris Heights section of the Bronx, where his best-selling curative once again was uncut whiskey for medicinal purposes. In a few years his single store had multiplied into a chain, and he invested the profits in real estate.

Then two Oklahoma friends asked him to help them find a location for a speakeasy they wanted to open. Drawing on his real estate experience, he suggested a spot on 58th Street near the New York Athletic Club. The Oklahomans thought of calling it the Red Pepper or the Green Onion, but, as Billingsley later told it, "somebody left a toy bird and somebody else put it behind the bar. It looked like a stork and soon the regulars were referring to it as the Stork Club." The club lost money, the Oklahomans and their wives got homesick and Billingsley and a new partner—some said it was New York gang leader Frank Costello—bought them out in 1927. That was how druggist Sherman Billingsley became a restaurateur.

The Stork wasn't an instant success under Billingsley either, but as an old acquaintance said, "Sherman had the instincts of a shithouse rat. He knew how to prevail." In one story that Billingsley would tell about those first months, he was biding time, counting passing cabs, when he happened to talk to the men's room attendant. The attendant said he had once worked in a club where the owner showed up only to pick up the day's take from the headwaiter. But the headwaiter had made friends among the patrons and eventually opened his own place. Now, said the attendant, the former owner works for his former headwaiter. Whether the story was true or not, Billingsley certainly saw its moral. "I went to work on every customer who came in," Billingsley recalled. "Oh, how I went to work on him. Found out his favorite drink, his favorite cigar . . . his friends, his relatives, everything about everybody. Everybody was my buddy."

Meanwhile, he began advertising in college newspapers and paying the bills in chits redeemable for food and drink at the Stork. That drew the young editors. "They were all good kids," Billingsley said, "many of them rich and social, and they began talking about the place. Their parents began to come in to see what kind of a joint their kids were hanging out in. That way I hooked the parents and kept the kids."

The Broadway crowd with its own regular haunts was slower to come. Billingsley made some headway when singer Helen Morgan decided to hold a party at the Stork before it had become chic to do so. But the Stork's own "blessed event," Billingsley would always say, didn't arrive until 1930 with the appearance of Winchell.

At the time Walter was a moveable feast, flitting from one nightspot to another. It was Texas Guinan who told Walter that "there was a nice fellow, a country boy from Oklahoma, running a speakeasy and things weren't going right," and Guinan who asked Walter to give him a plug in the column. Guinan even made the introductions. Billingsley, apple-cheeked, unaffected and, for a host, surprisingly diffident—it took an effort for him to be as affable as the club demanded—was obliging, and Walter liked him. Buried deep in the column that September, Walter wrote, "The Stork Club perhaps is New York's New Yorkiest place on W. 58th," and went on to report a line on the menu warning, "No ladies without male escorts permitted after 6:00 p.m." "The proprietor should be given two lusty cheers if for nothing else than keeping wives from suddenly startling husbands who have weak hearts," Walter quipped. A few weeks later on his Wise Shoes radio program, he broadened the plug. Now, he said, "The New Yorkiest spot in New York is the Stork Club on West 58th Street which entices the well knowns from all divisions nightly."

To Walter this may have been just another favor granted. To Billingsley the words would become immortal. Suddenly the Stork Club, now officially designated the quintessence of New York by the city's quintessential columnist, became the hottest rendezvous in the city. Comfortable with Billingsley, Walter began hanging out there as he had at Guinan's clubs in the late twenties. "He needed a capitol to have people come to him, instead of him going to sources" was how one press agent described it. By settling there, Walter attracted other newsmen and columnists, not to mention celebrities. "They kept coming in and they really tided me over until things got better," Billingsley remembered.

Even then the Stork was not without its difficulties. A successful club was always a target for mobsters horning in on the profits. Billingsley had apparently severed his ties with Costello—if such ties had ever existed—but into the breach "waltzed" Dutch Schultz, Bo Weinberg and Julius Martin, as Billingsley recalled it, demanding a half-interest. "I laughed and they countered with a guarantee of union troubles." Vincent Coll was even less willing to negotiate. Coll kidnapped Billingsley and held him captive for three days in a Bronx garage, beating him repeatedly until a $25,000 ransom was delivered.

What the mob didn't threaten, Prohibition agents did. On December 22, 1931, agents raided the Stork, and Billingsley filed suit for an injunction. In January a federal judge not only denied Billingsley's request, but ruled that agents could seize all furnishings and equipment used in connection with the sale of liquor. Within a week of the ruling, a crew of agents dressed in work clothes loaded all the club's furnishings, including a seven-hundred-pound safe, onto two trucks. "I do not believe that there will be many who will venture in the future into expensive enterprises which have for their objects the breaking of the prohibition law," declared an official.

Of course, he was wrong. Having weathered these threats, Billingsley moved the club to new quarters at 51 1/2 East 51st Street and then into a vacant furniture store at 3 East 53rd just off Fifth Avenue, where he introduced the first champagne cocktail, the first contour bar and, for a speakeasy, the first canopy over the doorway. The aim was an aura of convivial elegance. The one homely touch was Jack Spooner, who had been the headwaiter at Billy LaHiff's when Winchell and Runyon hung out there and who now became the captain at the Stork.

Billingsley admitted that the new club was different from the prior ones, not only in decor but in ambition. Moving to 53rd Street had inspired a "metamorphosis in thinking," he said. Though he was unsophisticated himself—his daughter said he would walk down Fifth Avenue casually munching an apple—Billingsley had always liked the socialites best. He appreciated their civility, the class which they bestowed upon his club and by extension upon its proprietor. Now he wanted only the "right people." "I decided that my clientele would be strictly carriage trade or nothing," he later wrote. "Believe it or not this passion for perfect behavior on the part of the patrons has paid off and soon the glitter circuit was channeling their [*sic*] activities in our direction by the carload."

It seemed anomalous. Within the arid desert of the Depression, café society sat as a gaudy oasis. At the better clubs a ten-pack of Camel cigarettes cost $1, a rag doll $6, a four-rose boutonniere $4.50, a paper gardenia $1, a pitcher of water $2, a pint of whiskey $10, and another $20 went for the cover charge. Nor did Prohibition seem to dampen spirits. By the fall of 1933, even before it had been officially lifted, it had, according to Walter, already ended in New York, where the "ropes are up at the better cabarets—and the crowd bruise one another attempting to crash the gate. . . ."

By April, with Prohibition legally over, Walter had taken up the cause of rolling back the 4 a.m. nightclub curfew, which had been instituted to curb the speakeasies. In May the Board of Estimate in New York agreed—largely, grateful club owners concurred, because of Winchell's efforts. The night of the rollback Billy Rose, owner of the Casino de Paree, hosted a celebration formally in Walter's honor but also in honor of the onset of flush times. When Walter took the stage, he told the assorted celebrities how much this meant to him and how much he wished Texas Guinan had lived to enjoy the occasion with them.

If all seemed well again in café society, the Depression in its own curious way did invade even the tony precincts of the Stork. To keep his patrons from straying to other clubs, Billingsley got the idea of staging a café society version of the bank night giveaways that movie theaters were holding to lure customers. What he understood, said one observer, was that no matter how wealthy their parents were, the young debs and society swains loved getting something for nothing. So Billingsley would raffle off a car ("There is only one catch," reported Walter. "The winner has to be in the Stork Club when his or her number is called.") Or he would hold a drawing for money. Or he would stuff bills and gift certificates into balloons, inflate them and then release them from the ceiling. And as the cascade of balloons drifted down, the young café socialites began their mad scramble, "like starved men and women battling for crusts of bread," remembered one onlooker, falling over one another, elbowing competitors aside, pushing, grabbing, shoving, pouncing to get the balloons and the prizes inside—fighting for balloons while outside the Stork, most Americans lived in dread of what the weeks and months ahead might hold.

III

For most New Yorkers the fourth year of the Depression was bitter and desperate. The day Franklin Roosevelt assumed the presidency in March 1933 fifteen million people, one-third of the American workforce, were unemployed, but the figure was much higher in the cities, where the Depression struck hardest. New York was pocked by Hoovervilles— shantytowns of the homeless constructed out of cardboard boxes, egg crates, tar paper and corrugated tin. The Great Lawn at Central Park had become a vast squatters' village that even the police had taken to calling Hoover Valley. Joseph Mitchell, then a young reporter assigned to find stories of human suffering on his editor's belief that the "man on the street is so gloomy nowadays that a story about somebody else's bad luck cheers him up," found a city of people who were "utterly spiritless." "Poverty and riches side by side and neither knows but what tomorrow they may change places," Hearst columnist Adela Rogers St. Johns wrote that fall.

"Well, now, isn't that fun and gay?" Walter complained, finding the city listless despite a mayoral campaign. "True, the city is in a mood—but hardly a merry one, and I long for diversion, the sort we had night after night before most of us had to be concerned with problems of State and Nation. . . ." Beneath his complaint lay fear. He had lost nothing in the stock market crash because none of his money was invested, but when Roosevelt declared a bank holiday the week of his inauguration to forestall possible runs, it drove home again the precariousness of Walter's success. Caught without cash and without the scrip that was to be issued while the banks fortified themselves, "I was in the same predicament as Mr. and Mrs. New York. . . . To the café cigarette peddlers I said that I would settle the various 15 items—in time . . . I made drastic cuts in tips, and the night club attachés, who once received a dollar for their attention—and who are now rewarded with two-bits—made no sour faces. . . . They understood it seemed." Out in California, June and Walda had less than a dollar between them, awaiting Walter's next check. He had asked three "pals" who had stockpiled some cash and to whom he had lent money in the past if they might advance him a small loan. "But when I practically begged them all to give me some cabfare and barber fees, on account, the excuses they offered made me ill! . . . What made me sicker was the realization that if I *really* needed it, I *couldn't* get it! . . . And from people who got it from me when I was the kid with the 'G!' "

It was scarcely a week after Roosevelt's inauguration, as Walter remembered it, that he received a call at the Stork Club from a man identifying himself as Joe Kenenan of the Justice Department. Kenenan told him that he was wanted at the White House at nine o'clock the next morning. Walter was skeptical, but Kenenan said he could verify the order by calling the FBI or Secret Service and asking for him. When Walter did, Kenenan came on, gave him travel instructions and advised him that the visit was to be secret.

Walter had never been politically inclined. He was impartial throughout most of the 1932 election, only afterward printing a quip from writer Milt Josefsberg: "He said some people voted Republican but most people voted sensibly." At that, Walter said he could sympathize with former president Hoover: "He's a human being, and his heart must have cracked when he saw the returns come in as they did."

But now the new President wanted to see him, wanted to see gossip columnist Walter Winchell. Why had he been sent for? Walter wondered on the 3:20 a.m. train down to Washington. In his autobiography, he speculated that Roosevelt wanted to thank him for his support, but since the support was perfunctory, much more like well-wishing, that hardly seems likely. What is much more likely is that someone in the new administration decided that Winchell with his enormous following might be a valuable ally if one could recruit and politicize him.

Walter's was to be the only account of the meeting. As he told it years later in his autobiography, the President greeted him warmly, asked how his fan mail was holding up and said that whenever Walter had anything he thought the President should know, he should tell him personally.* "That's an order!" Roosevelt snapped. After roughly ten minutes the President hastened Walter out by saying he had the secretary of state and others on his appointment list.

However brief the meeting, it had its intended effect on the outcast from Harlem. Walter suddenly became a rabid Roosevelt enthusiast. In his appearance at the Paramount Theater the week of March 17, Walter called the new President "the one man who certainly did more for his country than any other citizen or United Statesman. . . . Better times are almost here again—because of President Roosevelt!" Two days later on his broadcast, he called Roosevelt "the Nation's new hero" and praised him for wanting to "bring about a more equal distribution of income." He signed off as "Walter Winchell who wants to shout to the world what he thinks of America's new leader, who is certainly facing every issue squarely."

"Winchell developed a blind adoration for FDR," Walter's friend Ernest Cuneo later wrote. "He idolized Roosevelt," his secretary agreed. Of course, it was no secret that Roosevelt had the ability to charm. Even a self-professed curmudgeon like the columnist Westbrook Pegler admitted, "For the first time in my life in this business I might find myself squabbling for a chance to carry the champion's water-bucket." And Walter, who thrived on acknowledgment, was a far easier mark than Pegler. But timing had something to do with Walter's infatuation too. Assuming office as he did so soon after Gloria's death, Franklin Roosevelt filled a void for Winchell—a void that Walter had been trying futilely to fill through work. Roosevelt provided a new attachment, a cause, an outlet for Walter's grief, a way of connecting his own depression to his nation's.

And as his support for the President revived Walter emotionally, it also began sharpening his awareness, actually bringing him a whole new

---

*It is entirely possible that Walter confused dates or, at least, had confused meetings. In this version Walter says that FDR thanked him for funneling information to the FBI and naval intelligence about suspected subversives. Since FDR had been in office only a few days and since Walter had made little mention of subversive activities in his column as yet and since the bureau's own file on Walter contains no information prior to 1934, it seems unlikely that the President would be praising Walter for his assistance.

awareness. In April his newfound civic spirit moved him to suggest that people forgo one meal each day and donate whatever they saved to a fund to feed the hungry. He pushed the campaign in his column before finally conceding, somewhat disingenuously, that a "tiny column like mine isn't strong enough to make it the success it has to be."

He had far greater success with another project also inspired by his devotion to the President. A Los Angeles listener had written Walter suggesting that a President's Day be declared for Americans to go to church to pray for their new leader and express their gratitude. Walter supported the proposal on his April 2 broadcast, designating the Sunday following Easter, and he elaborated in his column the next day. Within a week Hearst promised to put his papers behind the campaign, and soon hundreds of municipalities, from Monroe, Louisiana, to Mishawaka, Indiana, passed resolutions declaring April 30 President's Day.

For Walter, however, President's Day still seemed an insufficient expression of his devotion. Nearly every column and broadcast now dispensed tributes to the President. In one column, titled "If I Had an Aladdin's Lamp," Walter wrote: "I'd fix matters so that F.D.R. never even caught a cold." And he not only praised the President but made certain that Roosevelt knew of his adulation. "Busy as you are, sir, I realize you haven't time to tune in on your New York correspondent—me," Walter wrote him. "However, I want you to know—how often I have mentioned you in an affectionate way on the radio and in my newspaper column, which is syndicated throughout the country." This was just one of many such letters.

By taking up politics, Walter had also found a vehicle to transform himself from a quintessential figure of the twenties, the Broadway wise guy, to a quintessential figure of the thirties, a journalistic populist whose voice would join other voices of protest. There had long been a populist component in his gossip. Despite the left-wing playwright Mike Gold's contention in 1930 that Winchell "never picks on anyone with influence," Walter was proud of his fearlessness, even if it was usually expressed in digs rather than bombs. But whatever Walter's populism prior to Roosevelt, it had always been generalized and fuzzy. He would razz the rich. Or he would devote a column to the miseries of some unfortunate and ask readers to donate money. Or he would award "orchids" to do-gooders and give "scallions" to the socially irresponsible. Now, with a new seriousness of purpose, he became what one paper called a "people's champion" who "picks out the happenings of the world, selfish, heartless, moronic and so on, which arouses *our* spleen, and then proceeds to lash them with savage oratory. . . ."

What he did now, with the President's blessing, was make himself an avenging angel for the dispossessed. With an eye for the scathing anecdote, he could be especially rough on petty bureaucrats. He excoriated a local relief administrator who told a farmer he had to kill the family dog before he could get aid. "It makes me considerably ill," Walter said on his broadcast. He attacked a New York magistrate who sentenced a mother to a day in jail because she let her two-year-old dig with a spade in Central Park. "I'll bet that made Dillinger laugh right out loud. . . . Children, in New York parks, it appears, commit a crime when they damage the grass. . . . But with my own eyes the other day—I saw a police car speed all over the lawn there to chase away other kids who were playing . . . and this is 1934 and we're supposed to be human beings." At Thanksgiving he told of a destitute father who shot a duck for his family and was sentenced to thirty days because he had no hunting license.

Hundreds of ordinary Americans now phoned or wrote Walter asking if he would air their grievances or solve their problems. He was "the man you instinctively turn to in times of distress," reported one columnist, citing an ex-model who had tried to reach Walter before she leaped to her death in Greenwich Village. "How many columnists, and in fact, how many writers of any type in this sorry old world have succeeded in winning the attention of a great multitude of readers day after day and then used that power to help the underdog, and without hesitation or fear?" asked *Plain Talk* magazine in commendation of Walter's new efforts.

It was, of course, one thing to sound grievances and another to get action. Often, as in his anecdotes of bureaucratic cold-heartedness, Walter shamed public officials into restitution. But just as often, out of the public glare, he pressed agencies to assist those who had contacted him as their last hope, asking New York Mayor Fiorello La Guardia to assist a newsstand owner who had wanted a paper delivery service but had been thwarted by the papers themselves, or forwarding to the President a letter from a reader who had been unable to secure a bank loan.

In years to come, critics would impugn Winchell's motives. They would say that his sudden political conversion in 1933 was engineered to advance his career when his old japery had been exhausted. They would say his populism was really irresponsible demagoguery. But writer Jim Tully was right that Walter had learned "early the patter of life from those who faced the economic bullets" and then "became their spokesman." Gloria's death and Roosevelt's ascension had merely given shape to Walter's impulses.

THERE WAS another factor in his politicization that winter: Adolf Hitler. In February 1933, less than a month after Hitler had assumed the chancellorship of Germany, Walter wrote in his column, "Too bad that a man like Hitler can rise so high in politics, who hates so intensely. . . . His hatred of the Israelites is contemptible—and when an assassin shoots him down some day a lot of locals won't be sorry. . . ." In the same column he told a story about Albert Einstein presenting an address on the theory of relativity at Hitler's insistence and Hitler then cracking an anti-Semitic joke. "It's a good thing you're an anti-Semite," Winchell had Einstein telling Hitler. "Why do you say that?" Hitler asked. "Because if you weren't that," answered Einstein, "—you'd be nothing!"

With his proper English surname, Winchell was not often thought to be a Jew, but he never denied it or forgot it. As a boy, "when my nose was even more upstartishly Gentile," he passed a group of children who jeered him and called him a kike—the meaning of which, he made it a point to discover, was one who pries. He certainly wasn't a religious Jew; he hadn't set foot in a synagogue since his confirmation. Nor did the Jewish community particularly rush to claim him. Back in the twenties, when he got into a feud with someone who had made an anti-Semitic slur, a prominent Jew had sent him a letter chastising him. "It is not good for Jews like you to disgrace us with a defense," the man wrote. "It would be more to the honor of the Jews if you didn't make others look ridiculous: you are not what is known as a Jew." Walter felt "painfully ashamed."

He called himself an "intuitive" Jew, but his Judaism ran deep. "If there was one consistent thread in his crazy-quilt life, it was his Jewishness," ghostwriter Herman Klurfeld said, citing especially his "radar-like sensitivity to any form of anti-Semitism." He was always fighting these battles; he had even fought NBC to approve a young Jewish announcer named Ben Grauer for his "Jergens Program" when the appointment seemed stalled by Grauer's religion. "He considered himself a Jew," agreed Arnold Forster, a Jewish activist and Winchell confederate. "He thought as a Jew. . . . He was self-conscious about his Jewishness." And like Klurfeld, Forster believed Walter was never more Jewish than when Jews were under fire. He suffered a vulnerability about being Jewish, a sense that "underneath, they're all anti-Semitic." To him, it was always the latent motive of his enemies: They had to destroy the powerful Jew.

Acting out of his sense of revenge and his fear of anti-Semitism, Walter took on Hitler in 1933, far earlier and with far more prescience than all but a few political pundits. "The best way to fight a person like Hitler is to ridicule him, of course," Walter wrote that February, as if Hitler were another of his Broadway targets. His first point of attack was the chancellor's alleged homosexuality. (The irony of fighting anti-Semitism by promoting homophobia was entirely lost on Winchell.) "I cannot refrain from flaunting the fact that he is a homo-sexualist, or as we Broadway vulgarians say—an out and out fairy. . . ." He concluded one column, "I believe that a man's private life and preferences are his own, but Hitler is so dangerous and such a faker, that any weapon can be used with justification." The jokes continued unabated.

Within months Walter was being called, justifiably, "the most rabid anti-Hitlerite in America." "A recent issue of a Berlin gazette front pages a likeness of me, the caption of which reads 'A New Hater for the New Germany,' " Walter crowed that fall. In the Jewish community his attacks had now made him a hero. An article he had written in August 1934 for the *Jewish World* circulated widely and was even reprinted in the *Palestine Post*. Titled "Down with the Jews," it described what would have happened to the world if the Jewish contributions to art, medicine, science and sport had been expunged. "Let us out-Hitler Hitler," he wrote. "Let us not be satisfied with any half-way measures. Let us not only get rid of the Jews, but wipe from the pages of history all that he [*sic*] has done. If we don't do that he may continue to do some of the pernicious things that he has done in the past. . . . We [gentiles] can afford to throw stones because we have no personal or racial faults." That year the B'nai B'rith named him one of five honorees for its Hall of Fame of American Jewry, declaring that no one "has contributed as much as this gentleman gossip and columnist toward laughing Nazism off the map. . . ."

But Walter's guns were not trained only on Adolf Hitler. Sometime late in 1933, a friend had sent him a mimeographed newsletter from the Silver Shirts of America. Headed by a gaunt, goateed North Carolina reactionary named William Dudley Pelley, who looked like a Confederate general, the Silver Shirts believed themselves to be the last defense between "The Juden Horde" of Jewish bankers and the Roosevelt administration, on the one side, and white, gentile America, on the other. Hitler at least was an ocean away. Right here in America were Hitler's minions, as Winchell saw them, trying to import the Nazi revolution. He was determined to stop them.

Walter forwarded the newsletter to Roosevelt's press secretary Steve Early and began a new campaign to identify Nazi sympathizers here. (One of them, he discovered, was listed as general director of President Roosevelt's Birthday Ball, which raised money for the March of Dimes charity; he immediately fired off a memo to Early with the information.) Throughout the winter and spring of 1934, he was regularly reporting the activities of pro-Nazi groups, prompting Nazis in Milwaukee to launch a smear campaign against him. "Knock Winchell down whenever you can—say anything about him—he's a menace to our cause!" he quoted them as saying. To which he answered, "You bet I am! . . . And to any cause like it, too."

Walter's campaign against the American Nazis that year brought him into the orbit of another government figure who was to play nearly as important a role in his life as his beloved President. "When I was in New York last week, Mr. Frank Fay, the special agent in charge of the New York office of this division, told me of the assistance which you have been to him and of the interest which you have taken in our work," the director of the Federal Bureau of Investigation, J. Edgar Hoover, wrote Winchell in April 1934. "I wanted to write you a personal note and let you know how deeply appreciative I am, not only officially, but personally. . . . [I]t is particularly gratifying to receive the understanding cooperation of one who can so thoroughly appreciate our problem."

And, Hoover might have added, one who could so thoroughly publicize the Bureau. For all his associations with gangsters—he still visited Owney Madden in Sing Sing—Walter had been supportive of the FBI, cheering on its agents and regularly condemning bandits like John Dillinger, Pretty Boy Floyd and Bonnie and Clyde when others were openly wondering why it was taking the Bureau so long to bring these lawbreakers to justice. When, under a presidential directive, Hoover began conducting a limited investigation of domestic Nazi groups, Walter had another reason to laud the Bureau, and he apparently cooperated not only by publicizing the FBI but by funneling intelligence to its New York office. That was what brought him into the FBI circle and presumably what elicited Hoover's letter.

Walter's zealousness in hunting Nazis moved him to apply for a commission in naval intelligence in March 1934, apparently so that he would have official authorization in his efforts. The day after he received the letter from Hoover, Walter wrote back asking for the director's assistance. "I am told that there are hundreds of applications ahead of mine and with vacancies so few, I fear I may be forgotten. . . . Would you please do what you can with the commandant of the third naval district regarding this application?" Hoover wrote an effusive recommendation, and the Faustian bargain seems to have been struck.

A week later, when Walter, June and Walda left for a tour of personal appearances beginning at the Palace Theater in Chicago, it became apparent that he had actually made two Faustian bargains: the new one with Hoover and an old one with the mob. Walter had learned that it was the custom for the Chicago mobsters to shake down performers, and he was especially aggrieved by the idea of paying a percentage of his take for this so-called protection. As Curley Harris told it, Walter contacted Charles "Lucky" Luciano, the head of the New York rackets, for relief. Meanwhile, Walter's new friend J. Edgar Hoover decided that Walter might need *his* protection and assigned two agents to ride with him on the

Twentieth Century en route to Chicago.* At Englewood, on the Chicago outskirts, where the westbound trains stopped before chugging into La Salle Street Station, Walter was having breakfast with the agents when two or three Chicago policemen boarded, also under instructions to protect Walter. Walter told the FBI men that he didn't need them, but they were there under orders and refused to move. So now, guarded by both the police and the FBI, Walter arrived at La Salle Street, where he was greeted by the Fiaschetti brothers, cousins of Al Capone's, who had been enlisted by Lucky Luciano to provide *their* protection for Winchell.

The three groups eyed one another warily—"Get rid of those fags," the Fiaschettis told Winchell when they saw the law officers—then began pushing one another until Walter managed to restore civility. "The three factions all went together," recalled Curley Harris. "And they stayed with him all the time he was there: the cops, the FBI and the underworld." His last night they threw a party for him. As Walter later described it to Harris, the groups sat sullenly at different tables, glowering and tossing insults. "Walter said you never saw such a mess in your life."

This farce aside, the Chicago appearance was a resounding success. "The crowd sounded twelve on the gong of spontaneous approval," trilled Ashton Stevens of the Chicago *American*, one of the critics who had covered Walter back in his vaudeville days. "Nobody can do a Winchell as well as Mr. Winchell can. . . . He is as vivid as a nerve, and he is all nerves." Lloyd Lewis of the Chicago *Daily News* concurred, marveling at how a young man with no more than a hat tilted back on his head and his necktie loosened could generate such energy. "With no action save his voice and the occasional cracking of a telegraph key, he makes something vivid happen on the stage," Lewis wrote. "His own demonic energy crackles. . . ."

The next week he moved on to Detroit while June and Walda continued toward California. COME OUT VERY SOON, Walda wired him from Los Angeles. COME HERE AFTER DETROIT AND BROADCAST FROM HERE [.] WE MISS YOU TOO MUCH AND YOU CAN AFFORD THE WIRE CHARGES. After another triumph in Detroit and another $7,000 for his week's engagement, Walter returned to New York briefly, then left on May 29 to join his family in California for the summer. But he was concerned. "He has been very active in the anti-Nazi movement," Hoover wrote his special agent in Los Angeles, "and feels that there may be some efforts to cause him harm or embarrassment in Los Angeles by reason of his activities along these lines." Hoover also said that Winchell had "considerable informa-

---

*This is Harris's recollection. FBI documents indicate that Melvin Purvis, the special agent in charge of Chicago, assigned the agents when Walter arrived.

tion" which he might like to pass on to the bureau, and the director asked that an agent contact him immediately upon his arrival.

As it turned out, Walter's fears of Nazis seemed ungrounded, and his vacation proceeded uneventfully. He rented a bungalow for the summer at the Ambassador Hotel, fended off new movie offers, partook of Hollywood nightlife and, insofar as he was able, generally relaxed. But Hoover's offer of protection was nevertheless appreciated, as the director no doubt knew it would be. "I had quite a conversation with Mr. Winchell about things in general," reported Los Angeles FBI agent B. E. Sackett to Hoover, "and I am sure you will be pleased to hear that he expressed great satisfaction with, and was very enthusiastic about, the treatment accorded him by the personnel of the New York, Detroit and Chicago Division offices." That very day, Sackett said, Walter had even visited the FBI offices to give them information about Nazi activities.

On August 9 the Winchells returned to New York, Walter to some bad news. The commandant of the Third Naval District in New York had rejected his application to join naval intelligence. "Naturally, I am low with disappointment," he immediately wrote Hoover. "Because your last letter was so encouraging to me—I decided to tell you about it. With the hope that when you find a spare few minutes—you can help put me through into a service I am anxious to be." Hoover certainly got the message, and he promptly pressured the commandant to reconsider.

Meanwhile, Walter decided to go to Washington, in part to report to the President on Nazi activities and in part to press his case. In Washington Walter's fervid support of President Roosevelt and his increasing politicization had hardly gone unappreciated, especially since so many of the establishment columnists were hostile to the New Deal. Winchell was greeted like a conquering hero. When the spotlight fell on him in a club at the Shoreham Terrace hotel, he was mobbed by autograph seekers, and when he was introduced at Loew's Fox Theater, the "ovation accorded him as he left the rostrum, blowing kisses to the top galleries, almost blew the sides of the building out," the Washington *Post* reported.

It was on this same trip that Walter finally met J. Edgar Hoover. The FBI director had heard about Walter's reception at the Shoreham and promptly invited him and Curley Harris, who had accompanied Walter on the drive down, to FBI headquarters, where he showed them mementos from the recently slain Dillinger. (Hoover kept Dillinger's death mask in his outer office.) That week Hoover also put Walter's name on the FBI's special correspondents list, which meant that he was to receive all FBI releases. It was the highest privilege Hoover afforded a journalist.

Since Hoover never wanted to be seen as having cultivated supporters in the media, his own account of his first meeting with Winchell was entirely different. As Hoover told it, he was in New York working out the final arrangements for the arrest of Bruno Hauptmann for the kidnapping and murder of the infant son of aviator Charles Lindbergh. Walter had been trying to cooperate with the bureau to catch the murderer by publicizing the circulation of bills which the FBI had linked to the ransom. "Someone brought me a note saying Winchell wanted to see me outside the conference room," Hoover recalled.

I was just "country" enough to want to see what he looked like.

I came out of the room, and Winchell came out of a crowd of some 200 reporters. In his usual staccato manner, he asked if I had received the letter he wrote me the day before in which he gave me information on where the kidnap ransom money had been found and other details of the case. I suspected he was trying to pull a fast one on me—trying to trick me into giving him a "scoop" on the story we were about to break. I told him I had seen no letter. I was pretty annoyed at Winchell.

But when Hoover returned to his hotel room that night and phoned his office, he discovered that Walter *had* sent him the letter and the details were exactly as Walter had said.

"I felt like a cad," Hoover admitted, and called Winchell the next day to apologize and ask why he didn't print the story since he had it. "He told me he was the father of two children* and deathly afraid of kidnappers. He said he had not wanted to do anything that might hurt the case or hamper the investigation." (All Walter had written at the time was that "federal men are convinced that they will break the most interesting crime on record—the Lindbergh snatch.") Hoover was grateful. "That was the beginning of my friendship with him," he remembered.

In truth, the friendship had been cemented three weeks earlier during Walter's Washington trip, when Hoover began pressing again for Walter's much-desired naval commission. After having waited nearly five months only to learn that his application was being denied, Walter had waited less than a month since his return from California and his letter of disappointment to Hoover, when he learned that he was now likely to be commissioned after all. He knew whom to thank. Hoover had done it. "It was through him," he told an FBI agent, "that my application for lieutenancy in the naval intelligence was not stalled."

---

*In fact, he was the father of only one at the time of Hauptmann's arrest on September 21, 1934.

Walter was overjoyed, and the withholding of the Hauptmann story was really a form of payback. But there were others. Walter applauded Hoover and the bureau at every opportunity—both publicly, in the column and broadcast, and privately. "Winchell was probably the first nationally known radio commentator developed by the FBI," onetime Assistant Director William Sullivan wrote years later in recognition of the consequences of having the media manipulated by Hoover. "We sent Winchell information regularly. He was our mouthpiece." One Hoover biographer said that Walter "did more than any other man to perpetuate the myths of J. Edgar Hoover and his G-men."

As early as 1935, rumors were swirling around New York that Winchell was so tight with Hoover that the columnist was getting information from the bureau before official press briefings.* When an agent visited General Hugh Johnson, the head of the National Recovery Administration, Johnson's son, an NRA aide, exploded that Winchell had already announced there would be an investigation of Communists in the NRA before the NRA had made the announcement, and claimed that it was a "well known fact Walter Winchell has 'an in' in Washington." Hoover seemed untroubled. He defended Walter from a similar charge of having leaked information by scrawling on a report, "He never knew the names & didn't mentioned [*sic*] as I heard the broadcast."

The director seemed no more annoyed by another charge that had gained credence from his relationship with Winchell: that he liked to party. Hoover had, in fact, taken up Walter's invitation to come to New York and visit the Stork Club with his deputy and close friend Clyde Tolson. Soon he was making regular trips. In preparing an article on Hoover, *Time* magazine quoted Walter to the effect that the director very much enjoyed this nightclubbing. It seemed an innocuous remark, but Walter had gotten wind of it before publication and, anticipating that Hoover might be angered by this image, wrote him pleading innocence in the matter. "I, of course, knew that you had never made any such

---

*Most likely one of those stories critics had in mind was the capture of Pretty Boy Floyd in October 1934, the month after the Hauptmann arrest. As Walter told it, he was going on the air but didn't have a big opening item, so he phoned Hoover. "Did any of your boys nab a burglar or maybe a gangster today?" he asked. "Hoover replied casually, 'We caught Pretty Boy Floyd.' And I was flabbergasted." When Walter asked if anyone else had gotten the story, Hoover told him that no one had, and when Walter asked why, Hoover replied, "Well, Walter, you're the only one who has asked me today for any news." Years later, apparently to prove that it and not the local authorities was responsible for Floyd's death, the bureau decided to investigate Walter's scoop and discovered that Floyd wasn't dead when Walter said he was: that he had only been wounded by local police until the FBI finished him off the next day.

statement as attributed to you," Hoover wrote back reassuringly. "As a matter of fact, I do get some real relaxation and enjoyment in attending some of the night clubs, particularly when you have been with me, and I am looking forward to many evenings in the future when we can get together and have some real fun and settle the momentous questions of the nation." The next month, his mind put at ease, Walter was again bragging in the column of having escorted Hoover and Tolson around the town.

The affinity between Hoover and Winchell, however, was grounded in something more than the utility of each to the other. Though Hoover had grown up in Washington under the domination of his deeply religious, deeply conservative mother and Winchell had grown up in Harlem and then on the vaudeville circuit under the domination of no one, they were both poor boys who resented the rich and the privileged, and they guarded their status as outsiders, never seeking to invade the social establishment except as visitors. Never having had any resources but their own, they were both indefatigable, with an abiding faith in their energy and rightness. They were both distrustful, by nature, with a deeply ingrained conspiratorial view of the world. They were both political primitives who translated their personal distrust into professional paranoia.

Perhaps the greatest affinity between them was that they both traded in secrets: Hoover with his thick investigative files, Winchell with his gossip. Their lives were predicated on the clandestine, and perhaps no two men so fully appreciated the value of secrets—of finding them, deploying them, protecting oneself from them. No two men so *believed* in secrets. If the world was a dangerous place where conspiracies lurked under a deceptive crust of civility, Hoover and Winchell would pierce the crust, loose the secrets, reveal the inherent dishonesty and menace beneath. Together they would save the world from itself.

IV

As Emile Gauvreau remembered it, Arthur Kobler seemed distracted that fall of 1934, though Gauvreau had no hint of why. Then, one evening in October, Kobler entered Gauvreau's office and sank into an old Queen Anne chair. "There was an expression of agony in his face which made me stop my work," Gauvreau later wrote. "He was fifty-eight but he might have been taken for a man of three score and ten. 'I've lost the paper,' he said."

Kobler had apparently bought the paper with a $1.3 million note owed to Hearst, which made Kobler the titular head of the *Mirror* and Hearst its real power. So long as the economy boomed, Kobler had no problem meeting his obligations. But the crash had wiped out his fortune, forcing him into a settlement with his creditors that was achieved, so Gauvreau said, only because he let the *Mirror* endorse Roosevelt in 1932 and reaped some political favors for doing so. Now, with the favors exhausted, Hearst had called in the note, and Kobler was gone.

Walter certainly wasn't unhappy about this turn of events. He detested Kobler, whom he called "Mickey Mouse," and he had been making noises again about leaving the *Mirror*, this time to write movies in Hollywood. The new editor in chief Hearst appointed that November was seventy-year-old Arthur Brisbane, one of the publisher's closest associates and already a journalist of legendary proportions. Brisbane looked like a sage, with a huge head, towering forehead (he was nicknamed Double-Dome or Big George) and wrinkled brow that seemed to squinch his features toward his receding chin. He had been born in 1864, the son of a crusading utopian socialist who had known Karl Marx, studied with Hegel and Charles Fourier, and helped establish the Brook Farm colony. The son had started out as an idealist too, becoming a brilliant foreign correspondent for the New York *Sun* and then its managing editor. But eventually the lure of money proved too great to resist. He joined Pulitzer's sensationalist *World*, and when that began softening its tone under the lash of outraged moralists, he left for Hearst's *Evening Journal* as the new managing editor, his salary pegged to circulation. He loved money. "I am paid for doing badly what he did well," he said of his father. "I am paid the largest salary of any editor in the world." Investing his money wisely with Hearst's advice, primarily in real estate, he became an extremely wealthy man, almost certainly America's wealthiest journalist.

Most Americans knew him not as an editor but as the author of a popular daily column, "Today," which appeared on the front page of many Hearst papers and in which he expatiated on subjects as diverse as Nero, whom he considered the greatest man who ever lived, the possibility of a human's besting a gorilla in a boxing match and the superiority of people with blue eyes. ("It annoys many when I talk about blue eyes but any man who ever amounted to a damn in history had them, or gray eyes, even men from dark races, like Napoleon from Corsica, Caesar from Rome.") He dictated these columns by the dozens onto wax cylinders, talking constantly, even as he bustled about, his arms loaded with papers and briefcases. "No matter how vulgarly commercial the topic," wrote King Features syndicate head Moses Koenigsberg of Brisbane, "a classic essay was forthcoming."

Walter, who had just recently re-upped at the *Mirror*, immediately expressed his enthusiasm for the journalistic solon. "Since you came here a few days ago," he gushed like a cub reporter in a note to Brisbane, "it has made me want to work! For it is the first time in ten years that I have felt free. And those ten years it has not been pleasant working for an editor who dislikes me and with whom I have had no contact—at all. . . . I know your being my boss will renew ambition." Gauvreau noticed that Walter "emerged from his rabbit warren, now somewhere in the bowels of the building," and began tagging after Brisbane, toadying up to him as he customarily did with a new boss.

For his part, Brisbane, a man even more full of himself than was Walter, was fascinated by the columnist but not necessarily impressed. "I don't understand a word of his jargon," he told Gauvreau. "I'm always worried for fear he will land us into a pile of trouble. He annoys me." He complained that Walter had even barged into his office once and pulled out a handful of clippings about himself. "Does he think we're working for him?" And yet, with a voluptuary's delight in money, he was intrigued by Walter's enormous salary. Twice, Gauvreau said, Brisbane had asked him to recount the tale of Walter's early days on the *Graphic* when the young columnist was drawing only $100 a week. "That money came fast to him," Brisbane said, shaking his head. "Maybe too fast."

At the *Mirror*, Brisbane had a simple mandate: Build circulation. His first impulse was to refine the paper—not so that its readers wouldn't recognize it, but just enough to make it more competitive for advertising and perhaps draw readers from the *News*. He instructed Gauvreau to "print photographs of as FEW prostitutes as possible unless they commit an interesting murder, or otherwise force themselves into the news, as they are bound to do."

While Brisbane tried to pump circulation, Walter was compliant. After months of arguing with Kobler over the Sunday column, he now agreed to write it, provided he received additional pay. (When Brisbane was dilatory, Walter snapped, "Four weeks or so have passed but nothing has happened to my paycheck." Brisbane finally ordered him to be paid one-sixth his regular salary.) As Gauvreau analyzed it, however, the capitulation was less the result of Walter's deference to his new boss than his fear of surrendering the Sunday audience of 1.3 million readers to Paul Yawitz, who had been writing the Sunday column.

It was in one of his first Sunday columns that December that Walter broke what he called "the biggest scoop in his career!" In bold face capital letters in the middle of the column he wrote: FLASH! SCOOP!! EXCLUSIVE!!! THE WALTER WINCHELLS ANTICIPATE A BUNDLE FROM HEAVEN IN THE SUMMER! In his Monday column the next day, he repeated the news for those who might have missed it: "Sometime next Summer the Winchells will be 4 again."

No longer having Kobler to squabble with and no longer on speaking terms with Gauvreau, and in an obviously expansive mood that Christmas over June's news, Walter picked a fight with Ed Sullivan, almost, it seemed, to prove that he wasn't going soft. (Walter's own explanation a few weeks later was fear: "[W]hen I imagine people are not mentioning me during dinner or supper [. . .] I get a little worried . . . I fear my time has come . . .") In his December 13 column Sullivan had written an open letter to heiress Barbara Hutton, the Princess Mdivani by marriage. As Sullivan later told it, he had seen Hutton around town and had been impressed by her decency. "I got the idea that maybe she could help make a better Christmas for some people . . . sort of like a Fairy godmother." His open letter urged her to be a "regular guy" to compensate for the spendthrift ways of her foreign-born husband—Prince Mdivani was really faux royalty from Russian Georgia and a notorious playboy—and donate $5,000 to charity.

No sooner had the column run than Hutton phoned Walter, yelling blackmail and asking for his help. However he felt about Hutton, Walter saw an opening against his old rival and took it. In his column Walter excoriated Sullivan for trying to extort money from Hutton and commended her for her considerable charitableness. "We endorse anybody who helps the poor," Walter wrote, "but that's beside the argument [. . .] The open-letter-sender took pains to point out that her husband wasn't popular with the gang chiefs 'who would like to meet him on some waterfront.' A remark, incidentally, that some of the 'boys' resented." "[W]e subscribe to the sentiment of many who considered the article in the ugliest taste," he concluded, "and we pledge them all, that every time anybody uses (or abuses) a newspaper in that manner, we'll fight it and protest against it at the top of our lungs and typewriter . . . That means YOU!"

Hutton wound up giving Sullivan $5,000 for charity, but Sullivan was livid at Walter. If there had been any chance at rapprochement before the Hutton incident, there was no possibility after it. Ed Sullivan and Walter Winchell were now at war, and Walter seemed as happy as he had been since Gloria's death.

At the *Mirror*, however, Walter's brief honeymoon with Brisbane was coming to an end. The week after the Sullivan episode Brisbane scolded Walter for seeming to plug businesses and advertisers in his column—the same dispute Walter had had with Kobler—though Brisbane couched his objections in more conciliatory language than had his predecessor. In January, Brisbane struck a more sensitive nerve. Walter had been devoting virtually all his columns to the trial of Bruno Hauptmann, but the syndicate was complaining to Brisbane that it couldn't "dispose" of the

Sunday column "unless it is a *Broadway* column. That is what the out of town papers want." "I am very anxious to build that up," Brisbane wrote him. A short time later Walter signed a contract with the G & W liquor company to serve as a spokesperson in its ads. Again, Brisbane was chillingly concise—"I learned from our attorneys that your contract forbids any work of this kind"—and Walter was forced to withdraw under threat of an injunction.

In February, Brisbane hired Walter's friend, Texas-born Stanley Walker from the *Herald Tribune*, to become editor at the *Mirror* in an uneasy arrangement with Gauvreau, and told Walter that Walker from now on was to advise "what is and what is not the right kind of copy for editorial columns." Brisbane, it would seem, expected the new editor to domesticate Walter. But things did not turn out that way. Walker liked Walter; he called the column "simply marvelous!" Instead of domesticating the columnist, Walker freed him to bedevil Brisbane as he had Kobler before him. Walter even began poking fun at *Mirror* advertisers. The salesmen at the I. Miller Shoe Company, he wrote, coined the phrase "The Shoe Must Go On."

Watching bemusedly from the sidelines, Gauvreau and the other editors could barely stifle their laughter at each new Winchell gibe, but Brisbane was apoplectic. "Who in hell does he think he is?" he boiled. "I'll fix his wagon for him! I'll send him to cover an execution! I understand his stomach can't stand it!" "You have neither ethics, scruples, decency or [*sic*] conscience," he reportedly chastised Walter on another occasion. "Let others have those things," Walter answered. "I've got the readers."

He had, and that made him nearly unassailable at the struggling *Mirror*. A survey by the New York University Department of Marketing conducted throughout 1934 found that Walter's column was not only the most popular feature in the *Mirror* but the most popular in *all* the city's papers. The *Mirror* had more direct evidence. Sunday circulation had increased by 167,066 copies since he had begun writing his Sunday column. "The *Mirror* is a mess of newsprint built around page 10," went a popular saying, referring to the page on which Walter's column now appeared.

So in the end, Brisbane did nothing but splutter, just like the other Hearst executives who silently begrudged Winchell his power, his salary, his flouting of journalistic tradition. "There was something about Winchell that people feared," Gauvreau said of the apprehension with which the Hearst establishment treated the columnist. "By implication, without even the use of a name, he could make the gullible quake and writhe and even suffer." He would say, "I let him have it today," or "He had it coming to him," and his putative enemies would be reminded of their own vulnerability—of some small misstep or indiscretion through which they could be mortally wounded. His friendship with Hoover only intensified the sense of terror. Brisbane was one of Hearst's mightiest, but not even he could contend with Walter's power, so large it was, so ineffable, so uncontrollable and potentially so destructive.

THAT JANUARY, two months after Brisbane's ascension to publisher at the *Mirror*, both he and Winchell were preoccupied with what promised to be the story of the decade: the trial of Bruno Hauptmann for the kidnapping and murder of the Lindbergh baby. Just as the nation had been galvanized in euphoria by Lindbergh's transatlantic flight in 1927, so had it been galvanized in grief in 1932, when the child's body was found near the Lindberghs' Hopewell, New Jersey, estate. For more than two years investigators and journalists studied every false lead, sifted for every tiny shard of evidence, examined motive and execution and reaction to bring closure to the case and relief to the country. No other story had so riveted Americans' attention, possibly because none spoke as poignantly to the sense of national vulnerability.

Walter's own interest was no doubt fueled by his loss of Gloria less than a year after the crime, and he became one of the most assiduous reporters on the progress of the investigation. His primary source was a psychiatrist whom the police had consulted in devising a profile of the murderer and whom Walter had flattered by calling "eminent" in his column. With Walter's own physician as the go-between, Dr. Dudley D. Schoenfeld fed information to the column and permitted Walter, in his own mind at least, to separate rumor from fact. By September 1934 Walter knew the police were closing in on a suspect. A police briefing on September 10 disclosed that officers had recovered several gold notes from the Lindbergh ransom, but reporters agreed to withhold the story until an arrest had been made. A few days later, on his September 16 broadcast, Walter called bank tellers "yaps" for not scrutinizing bills that might be from the ransom money. He repeated the charge in his column that day.

Meanwhile, the day before the broadcast, a Harlem gas station attendant named Walter Lyle had become suspicious over a bill he had received, a $10 gold note, and had brought it to the attention of a bank teller named Walter Strum. (Lyle had also taken the precaution of getting the license number of the car of the man who had given him the bill.) Strum had heard Walter's broadcast and was incensed. He spent the night tossing and turning and cursing Winchell. He wanted to "show that wise guy from Broadway" that tellers were not the "yaps" he said they were.

Strum was not the only one who was incensed. So were the police, who now feared that their investigation might be jeopardized. Gauvreau said that police officials hammered him all evening over printing the information. According to Gauvreau, Joe Connolly, the head of King Features, which syndicated Winchell's column, even told him "it would soon have to be decided whether Winchell's actions were beyond the control of the Mirror itself." But while the police were wondering whether their work had been for naught, Strum verified that Walter Lyle's bill was indeed part of the ransom, and Lyle gave police the license number he had jotted down. Bruno Hauptmann, an itinerant carpenter from Germany, was arrested seventy-two hours after the broadcast. Walter said he had had all the information before it was publicly released, including Hauptmann's arrest, but had withheld it from publication, instead passing what he knew to the FBI in the note he had sent to Hoover.

On his next broadcast Walter naturally claimed partial credit for Hauptmann's apprehension. "I am happy—that an arrest followed immediately after the warning [to be on the lookout for gold notes]—considering that the clue that trapped the Lindbergh crime suspect—was his passing of gold certificates." (Gauvreau said that Walter had raced down to the courthouse to convince Lyle to say that he had turned in the bill only after listening to the broadcast. But Lyle hadn't, and Walter scratched a reference to him from the script.) The question would long remain whether Walter had impeded the investigation or helped it. In his own defense, he always adduced a letter from Hoover written at the time thanking Walter for his assistance. In 1936, after an appearance before the convention of the Newspaper Editors of America, Hoover wrote Walter another letter, once again expressing his appreciation. "I pointed out without, of course, mentioning names specifically," Hoover said, "how a well-known columnist had refrained from printing a truly national and international scoop on the Lindbergh case for twenty-four hours in order not to harm the investigation. . . . Of course you know who that person is. I thought that the editors should know that there was at least one columnist who put patriotism and the safety of society above any mercenary attitude in his profession." Walter had the letter framed and placed on his office wall.

In December, Brisbane notified Walter that he was to be one of the Mirror's three-man delegation to the Hauptmann trial in Flemington, New Jersey. Brisbane himself would provide perspective, Damon Runyon the actual reportage and Walter human interest. Almost immediately, however, Brisbane accused Walter of having taken all the tickets assigned the Mirror. Walter protested that he had gotten his tickets not from the sheriff, as had other reporters, but directly from New Jersey Governor Harold Hoffman and that he had secured tickets for himself, Brisbane and Dr. Schoenfeld, "who has edited and practically prepared my numerous Hauptmann case col'ms." "Without him by my side at the trial," Walter added, "I couldn't get what I intend to get—inside stuff." Since the *Mirror* reporters were to be headquartered in Trenton, miles from Flemington, Walter also requested a police escort, but Brisbane demurred.

Battles for tickets, concerns for a police escort, human interest coverage—all these things were harbingers of the kind of trial Hauptmann would get. The Hall-Mills and Snyder-Gray trials of the twenties, with their battalions of reporters, were hardly decorous affairs, but nothing had quite prepared the American public for the spectacle in Flemington, where radio and newsreels were added to the mix and where the crime involved one of the country's most revered figures. The enterprising sheriff sold tickets: $10 for the main floor, $5 for the balcony. Sightseers arrived by the busloads on Sunday to tour the empty courtroom. (Walter's seat was marked by a sign.) Witnesses were given vaudeville offers. Celebrities regularly attended the trial, sometimes doing crossword puzzles or knitting in boredom, prompting Cholly Knickerbocker to gasp, "What a sorry spectacle New York society has made of itself these last few weeks."

Between 100 and 130 photographers descended on Flemington, and between 300 to 350 reporters, including most of America's journalistic elite. "If all the famous writers covering the trial were placed side by side," Walter wrote, "they'd probably all talk about themselves." One of them, Hearst star reporter Adela Rogers St. Johns, admitted that the trial was an occasion to perform and that she had worked out a wardrobe with designer Hattie Carnegie as part of her expense account. "They had to be things Papa would have approved," St. Johns later wrote; "still they had to be noticeable." Among the most noticeable of the reporters was Walter, who usually sat seven feet from Hauptmann, near the balustrade, in his trademark blue or gray suit and gray fedora and wearing dark glasses, which made him instantly recognizable in the crowd.

The trial began on January 3, 1935, with the selection of the jury, and Walter was immediately thrust into the proceedings. Hauptmann's defense counsel asked one prospective juror if he had ever read Walter Winchell's column. "I wouldn't let a man like that influence me," the juror answered, then continued, "I don't read his column, but I listen to him on the radio." The spectators, reported Walter, "broke into laughter" until Judge Thomas Whitaker Trenchard silenced them. The same question was asked of each juror, allowing Walter to brag that "of all the comments written and said about the Lindbergh case, The Mirror columnist's comments are apparently considered the most damaging and incriminatory."

There was never the least doubt in Walter's mind that the dark, lank German carpenter had committed the crime, though efforts by NBC's legal department to prevent Walter from convicting Hauptmann on radio before a jury had, went for naught. He simply ignored the department's instructions. Walter had already trucked out the evidence in his column and on the broadcast, declaring each new item a scoop: the bank notes from the ransom in Hauptmann's possession, a wooden rung from the kidnapper's ladder that matched a missing plank in Hauptmann's attic, the similarity in speech inflections between the kidnapper and Hauptmann that an intermediary named Condon noticed, the rare postage stamp on a ransom note which had been purchased at a drugstore in Hauptmann's neighborhood.*

That first week the Lindberghs testified, but Walter kept watching Hauptmann, speculating that he had committed the crime to prove that he was as good as Lindbergh. "I, too, am world famous," Walter projected Hauptmann as saying to himself. "Why look! I even have Lindbergh, the most famous man in the world, sharing the same spotlight!" The next day Hauptmann allegedly asked Runyon, sitting behind him, to point out Winchell to him. "He should not be allowed here," the defendant grumbled in his thick accent; "he is not a nice man." "We are never cordial to suspected murderers," riposted Walter in the column.

He devoted his entire broadcast that night to the trial. "I have heard it said of me, and I have read it, too—that I am partial and biased," he announced. "As a matter of record, ladies and gentlemen, when I have encountered important information about the case I have turned it over to both sides—the State and the defense. . . ." But he then proceeded to promise new evidence that "will lift the beard from your face, or the lashes from your eyes." The new bombshell was that the misspelling of the word "signature" on the ransom note matched exactly Hauptmann's misspelling of it when he was asked to write the word by police. As far as Walter was concerned, that made the trial a formality. "I think your theories and deductions have converted many," Brisbane wrote him three days after the broadcast, "or rather convinced them including myself."

For the time being, gossip had drifted away. "I can't get into the mood

---

*Even away in Flemington, Walter could not avoid feuds. One night at Dinty Moore's restaurant in Manhattan, George Jessel, Walter's boyhood friend, said that Winchell seemed to know more about the Lindbergh case than anyone else, and a fellow diner quipped, "Maybe he did it." The story got back to Walter, who now wrote, referring to a mysterious character in the case named Isadore Fish thought by some to be the real mastermind behind the kidnapping: "Could Isadore Fish be George Jessel?" Jessel was booed at his next engagement in Cleveland and for years afterward refused to speak to Winchell.

of writing trivia about people, except those at the trial," Walter said as the proceedings moved into their second week. "At any rate, nothing else interests me, and it's my column, so what are you going to do about it . . ." For Walter the trial was a challenge to prove that he was what he had always claimed to be—a reporter. To prove it, Walter admitted he was driving himself to illness. "You can't eat regularly if at all [. . .] for someone near you is certain to bring up an 'angle' you haven't figured before and you can't wait to jot it down for the wires." After staying up twenty-seven straight hours to put himself on a regular sleep schedule, he found himself rising early, unable to go back to sleep—"from thinking, thinking and thinking of this and that about the case. . . ."

Folded within the challenge to be regarded by his peers as a newspaperman was the challenge to prove that his so-called scoops were in fact accurate: to prove that Hauptmann was indeed the murderer as Walter said he was. Only then would Winchell get the respect he felt was due him. "Every time we ventured a prediction or a bit of advance information on the Hauptmann case, we were rebuffed and rebuked or challenged by opposition newspaper reporters, editors or readers," Walter wrote with the wounded tone of a wronged man. That was why he stayed in Flemington, he said, "not so much to see the trial as to be there to check off the confirmations of advance tips printed here—to column about them chiefly for those who sniffed at them." And so it wasn't only Bruno Hauptmann who was on trial in Flemington. Far more important for Walter Winchell, *he* was on trial.

"The big idea is to keep your eyes on Bruno, your ears on the witnesses and lawyers and your mind on how the soandso are you going to fill the column for tonight's paper?" Walter wrote. Much of the time he sat next to Mrs. Hauptmann, placing himself in the middle of the fray. Watching her as the prosecution questioned handwriting experts who connected Hauptmann to the ransom note, he was amazed by her "dead pan," exactly like her husband's. "You can't tell what might be in their minds by merely looking at their faces," he wrote, though he had also concluded that if Hauptmann were innocent, he "could not sit there so patiently and 'take it' without causing a scene." (During one handwriting expert's testimony Walter sneaked a look at a note Hauptmann had passed to his wife: "Make sure about my insurance.") As a neighbor was testifying against Hauptmann, Mrs. Hauptmann whispered to Walter, "I could choke her," while Bruno tried to catch her attention to warn her not to speak to Winchell.

By the time Hauptmann took the stand on January 25, the outcome seemed in little doubt. "That spellbinding 40 minutes late Friday afternoon will never be forgotten by those of us who were there," Walter said on his broadcast. The entire courtroom was kept on edge by "the fury and fire of the prosecutor . . . Mr. Wilentz, it seemed to some of us, was representing civilization . . . And he was confronting the defendant with facts—hard, stubborn facts—which lies, lies, lies cannot drown out."

As expected, Hauptmann was found guilty, the verdict igniting pandemonium in the courtroom as reporters bolted to the phones to file their stories. By one account, the verdict had no sooner been rendered than Walter jumped to his feet, yelling, "I said that in October. I predicted he'd be guilty. Oh, that's another big one for me! Come on, fellas, put it in your stories. I was the first one to call it." Robert Musel, covering the trial for the United Press, was appalled. "How do they let a fucking child like this in the room?" he fumed.

And so was rendered the "other" verdict: the verdict on Walter Winchell as a reporter. He had stayed in Flemington throughout the trial, nearly two months away from his pregnant wife and Walda, even sending for his dentist rather than return to the city when a tooth cracked. He had written, by one estimate, seventy thousand words since Hauptmann's arrest. He had come down with a severe case of lumbago from the hard benches. He had sat in the courtroom, chewing orange and lime drops, desperate for a cigarette but not allowing himself to miss a minute of the proceedings. He had furiously scribbled notes, passing them to Mrs. Hauptmann, who passed them down the row to a messenger who spirited them to the paper. He had repeatedly crowed over his scoops, at one point even running a tally of each story he had broken. He had done all these things to demonstrate that he was more than a gossip. And he had loved every minute of it. "Never thought I'd ever get to the point where I didn't care a hoot about being on or seeing Broadway," he wrote halfway through the trial. "Don't give my regards to anybody!"

He was also among those who most vehemently decried the whole circus atmosphere surrounding the trial, complaining of the "moron" seated near him "who giggles or tee-hees every time there is a tense and dramatic moment at the trial" and wishing the person would "just go out some place and die." And yet there were many who believed that Winchell was one of the main contributors to that circus atmosphere. On the same day he cheered the end of what he called the "Flemington Follies," he had written, "Smasho! Flash! Crash!!! Verna Snyder, juror no. 3, who tips the Toledos at 261, is said to have fallen out of bed in her Union Hotel boudoir night before last. First rumors were that there had been an earthquake." It was Walter, in his dark glasses, who was constantly forcing himself into the trial as a protagonist. It was Walter who thrilled when Dr. John "Jafsie" Condon, the onetime intermediary between the kidnapper and the Lindberghs, had threatened to "punch Winchell in the eye," and Walter who leaped up to shake Condon's hand as the man left the witness stand. It was Walter who, when a movie cashier testified that the Hauptmanns had spent some of the ransom money at her theater, where Walter's *Broadway Through a Keyhole* was then playing, held up a sign to Hauptmann asking, "Bruno—was my picture good or lousy or good and lousy?" (Hauptmann whispered that he hadn't seen it.)

"He sits in the front row every day at the trial," one paper said, "and leans so far forward you think any moment he is going to fall flat on his face, which isn't a bad idea." *Variety* reported that he had "annoyed the self-exiles from Broadway with his prattling about the Hauptmann trial. For a time all of us thought he was on trial, not Hauptmann. Too bad it wasn't so." (To Walter's credit, he reprinted these criticisms in his column.) "What do you think Hauptmann would rather do," Runyon was said to have asked Bob Musel, "sit where he is or spend the rest of his life listening to Winchell talk?" "He'd jump in the electric chair," said Musel.

As the first trial to be covered by the full panoply of national media, Hauptmann's prosecution was a milestone in the culture. Thereafter, the media would be as much participants in an event as reporters of it, shaping and sensationalizing on a new scale and turning events into occasions, national festivals. "The same thing would happen again, in any part of America, if a similar trial were held next year," Stanley Walker wrote shortly after. "Walter Winchell would bounce about, giving tips and suggestions to the prosecution if his sympathies lay that way, as they did in the Hauptmann case. If convenient, Arthur Brisbane would drop in to size up the situation. Damon Runyon would be there, and Adela Rogers St. Johns with her heavenly prose. Illustrators would be there, some merely for the fun of it, and there would be the usual aggregation of well-dressed women with nothing better to do." And to the extent that this state of affairs seemed to threaten "this civilization," as Walter said some critics believed, he would be judged guilty of having helped make it so, of having helped turn tragedy into entertainment.

V

In large measure it was radio that enabled him to do so. "You had to be around at nine o'clock eastern time* on Sunday night to realize the compelling power of Walter Winchell and the 'Jergens Journal,'" film

---

*The program originated at 9:30 P.M. until October 1, 1939, when it switched to 9:00. Walter broadcast again, at 11:00 ET, for the West Coast.

producer David Brown, then a journalist, recalled, using the program's new name. "He just punched through the air. And we all listened because you never knew what he was going to say." Another listener remembered "strolling one Sabbath evening for 6 blocks through a residential section of Birmingham [Alabama] and never losing a word of WW's broadcast as his voice came through a succession of open windows." His radio ratings, which steadily grew from 11.5 percent of all listeners in his first season on the "Jergens Journal" to 11.6 percent in 1933–34 to 13.8 percent in 1934–35 to 19.2 percent in 1935–36, consistently ranked him among the highest-rated commentators on the air, though in large urban areas the figures were undoubtedly much higher.

In May 1934 General Motors, recognizing his impact, offered him a raise of $1,000 per week to work under its sponsorship. His option with Jergens foreclosed him from taking the offer, but that same month he signed a new contract with the Jergens company calling for $2,000 per broadcast for thirty-nine weeks. Less than a year later his salary rose once again, this time to $2,500 per broadcast. More important, in November, shortly after the Fleetwood Beach Club judgment and his brief dispute with the *Mirror* over its refusal to indemnify him, Walter got Jergens to agree to indemnify him against any damages awarded for libel, slander, invasion of privacy or infringement of copyrights. He also secured himself a sabbatical from the program each summer from June through August. The new contract, Walter announced, made him the "only individual on radio who has held the same job, without a partner or an orchestra—for 5 years—And so my thanks to Mr. Jergens, and to you—Mr. and Mrs. America—for making it all possible."

The broadcast with its insistent rhythm and the distinctive high report of Walter's voice not only burned Walter Winchell into the American consciousness but facilitated his transformation—the transformation that had accelerated in Flemington—from a show business gossip to a gossip-cum-newsman. It was harder to make the change in the newspaper, where Walter was segregated from the hard news, placed in the exile of the entertainment pages, which he could escape only for events like the Hauptmann trial, and even then his contributions were considered less reportage than entertainment.

Radio, newer and without any tradition of its own, made no such distinction between entertainment and news. For one thing, owing to a dispute between news agencies and the young medium, there was very little news on the radio to begin with. Fearing competition from radio, newspaper editors in April 1933 had coerced the Associated Press into withholding its news service from the networks. "If radio companies want news," declaimed Hearst, "let them get their own news." The networks were now forced to do precisely that, though their news departments were often no more than a staff member manning a phone.

The dispute had arisen shortly after Roosevelt's inauguration, at the very time when Walter's own news consciousness was being raised and announcer Ben Grauer was introducing him on the show as "the most versatile reporter in America . . . Walter Winchell covers Broadway and Hollywood, politics and society . . . and his news of today makes the headlines of tomorrow." Stuck for copy while the AP and NBC bickered, Walter enlisted the help of a young Toronto-born journalist named Art Arthur. Arthur began combing newspapers, particularly foreign papers, for hints of upcoming political developments. Using Arthur's tips, Walter often scooped the news agencies; he even predicted the abdication of Britain's King Edward VIII when Arthur sighted an item in an English paper from a royal insider who said that Edward's brother George was well trained for kingly duties.

In March 1934 the newspaper editors and broadcast executives agreed to form the Press-Radio Bureau, which gave the networks access to the wire services so long as the use was limited to two five-minute broadcasts each day, one after 9:30 A.M. and the other after 9 P.M., so as not to interfere with the morning and evening newspapers. But Walter's program fell outside this proposition anyway. Neither news nor entertainment, it was an odd weave of both; "infotainment" another generation would call it.

He seemed to arrange it like a vaudeville bill. It begain with a "flash," usually a dramatic news story. ("Get me a good murder or a train wreck so I can get off to a good start," he later told ghostwriter Herman Klurfeld.) He followed with about a half dozen more items, blending gossip with hard news and opinion. These were followed by "By Way of the High Seas," roughly a half dozen international stories, usually of a political nature. (An electronic beep rather than the telegraphic clack introduced these pieces.) Then came "Dots and Dashes and Lots of Flashes from Border to Border and Coast to Coast"—a series of brief gossip items, mostly marriages, divorces, births and illnesses. "Oddities in the News" came next: four or five offbeat stories that would have been regarded as filler in a newspaper or magazine, though it was in this segment that he often took his pokes at what he thought were bureaucratic idiocies. Then he would snap, "I'll be back in a flash with a flash." After a commercial for Jergens Lotion, Walter reported more small items, some gossip, some not, and answered listeners' mail. He always ended with what insiders called the "lasty"—a sentimental or humorous one-liner. "Get your audience, keep them interested, sell them an idea in the middle, finish with a great line, and get off for the bows" was how he described the process to an associate.

The pace was furious. Grauer said that Walter entered the small studio on the second floor of Radio City "like a comet." Awaiting the signal that the program was to begin, Walter puffed nervously at a cigarette, then removed his jacket, loosened his collar, unzipped his fly to relieve pressure, pushed his fedora back on his head and took his place at the mike. At the opening, as he jiggled his telegraph bug with one hand, he drank a glass of water with the other and his foot beat time. "[I]t is as though the whole broadcast were set to a metronomic rapid tempo, as indeed it is," remarked a journalist watching the show.

He barked the news, racing so quickly that a listener was hard pressed to keep up but was also loath to miss a single word. Grauer said his "voice was not loud," but there was an "adrenaline high at all times." "Considering the important issues you discuss, don't you think your over-emotional manner might irritate some people?" a friend once rebuked him. "Winchell stared at me in amazed silence. 'Okay, so they're irritated,' he said. 'But you and all the other critics are wrong, because you fail to realize that this manner of talking is my trademark. And once a guy's got a trademark, he's set for life.'"

Every week seemed to bring a new shipwreck, train crash or airplane accident, a new kidnapping, murder or police dragnet. And Walter not merely reported these, not even merely dramatized them, but frequently inserted himself directly into the action as he had in the Hauptmann trial. If a ship was sinking, Walter issued a call for help. If a child had been kidnapped, Walter appealed to the kidnappers. If someone had been murdered, Walter often suggested he had evidence about the crime. ("Attention[,] Commissioner Valentine," he once announced after describing a triple murder. "Please phone—I have an alleged clue!") If a suspect wanted to turn himself in, Walter offered his good offices for the surrender. "Benny[,] waited for you for two hours at the corner of 28th Street and Fifth Avenue last night from 7:20 to 9:30," he reported. "Benny[,] did not tell the police anything. Don't believe everything you read."

This was the world according to Walter Winchell, the world that he purveyed to his listeners in the thirties and that formed such an indelible part of the imagery of the decade. And if his effulgence of gossip conveyed a prurient farrago of celebrities, his presentation of news conveyed a world of disaster and violence, a world seemingly poised on the edge, a world that reified the imminent sense of peril that his listeners felt about their own lives and a world in which Winchell seemed always to be either at the center of every event or above events, an oracle prophesying the future and then sharing his knowledge.

Of course, there was still gossip interlarded with the news. There was still humor, still the verbal jousting with Ben Bernie. There was still the cynicism over meanness and ingratitude—stories about a daughter who was arrested by her father, a "so-called human being," for taking flowers from his garden to place on her mother's grave or about a schoolteacher who was fired for giving students free meals even if they didn't have relief tickets to pay for them. And there were the oddities about a cross-eyed man whose eyes were uncrossed when he was hit by a truck or about a robbery victim who got the better of the exchange when the bandit left behind a new overcoat during the getaway or about a jury that convicted a man of grand larceny and then wound up leaving behind a hotel bill for items its members stole.

There were still all these elements, but it was the commingling of them with the news that now made the program the strange, unique, virtually surrealistic concoction it was. The death of ten thousand people in Ethiopia was followed immediately by a Hollywood divorce or romance, and that followed by some coincidence that rated inclusion as an oddity. Dozens of these items raced past listeners each program, not only abutting one another but most given the same urgency and drama. Nothing was differentiated.

Journalistic traditionalists, who had earlier decried his gossip, now despaired over what his acceptance as a news commentator said about America's changing media culture. Though no one could ever know for certain, what it may have said was that many Americans in the Depression had become distrustful of traditional authority and even traditional modes of understanding, both of which Winchell's broadcast directly challenged. What it may have said was that many Americans found Winchell's bald histrionics more open, honest and forthright than more reasonable and conservative sources of information and that his implied promise to tell his audience what was going to happen before it had happened took them into the sacred aerie of secrecy and power from which they had always been barred. And it may have said that many Americans found Winchell's bizarre blend of the most serious news and the most trivial gossip a far more accurate objective correlative for the modern world in which his listeners lived than the hierarchical facts in respectable newspapers, just as his unrelenting gossip had been an objective correlative for the twenties.

And it may have said simply that Americans were having fun listening to Winchell—a conclusion that traditionalists might have found the most depressing of all. It was one thing to gossip; everyone understood that was a distraction. But by applying the techniques of show business to news, as radio permitted him to do, Winchell blurred the distinction between the two. The question was whether hard news could survive once it had been exposed to show business, whether it might not be tainted beyond recognition as it was at the Hauptmann trial. That was what the traditionalists feared and what Winchell as newsman threatened.

VI

The baby arrived on July 26, 1935, shortly after three o'clock in the afteroon at the Park West Hospital. Walter had joked that if the child was a boy, they would name him Reid and if a girl Sue. (Ben Bernie had suggested Lynch.) The child was actually named Walter, Jr. Walter was on vacation from the paper at the time of the birth and missed the scoop, but he returned to work four days later absolutely ecstatic. What had been the most interesting thing he saw during his month's vacation? Arthur Brisbane asked in an editorial welcoming him back. "THE SPELL-BINDING MAGIC OF NATURE AS OUR SON WAS BEING BORN," Walter answered.

It was "the most enjoyable [thrill] I've known," he told a reporter after taking Walter, Jr., home. Though he opened his first column after his vacation with an item on actress Mae Murray's green sandals and matching green toenails, by the second paragraph he was rhapsodizing over his new son. "Portrait of a Bundle from Heaven," he wrote.

His tiny ears are up against his well-shaped head ... Dark blue eyes ... Black hair ... Exceptionally good chest expansion (according to his nurses) ... He keeps his little hands open (denoting strength) ... He rolls both of his huge eyes at the same time ... There isn't a blemish on his sturdy little body [...] He tastes like honey ... And smells like gardenias.

Two days later he filled the column with notes from well-wishers. Hoover wrote: "So you also get your man!" Sports columnist Jimmy Cannon asked Walter to tell the baby that "his mom is the First Lady of Broadway and his dad a great friend who stands up in the pinches," and then joshed that this "should be worth more than a million dollars can buy him. But if he is a true Winchell he'll take the cash."

The euphoria was genuine. Four again. The Winchells were four again. A piece had been put back in place. Now they were whole. Now the happiness would return.

But it was a chimera. If anything, Walt Jr.'s birth underscored how much had changed since, and partly because of, Gloria's death. Walda, like June, had never fully recovered. She was a troubled child who had even withdrawn from first grade after an argument with a teacher somehow triggered an "aversion to men," as her school transcript put it. Now eight, she reacted badly to the baby's birth. She began having night terrors and nightmares. She would see monsters emerging from her closet and drawing closer until she felt she would be smothered, and she would awaken in a state of such "wild terror," as a psychiatrist later described it, that she was afraid to go to sleep. June, though only thirty-two, was fragile and high-strung, smoking almost as much as Walter. And Walter, painfully aware of how he had neglected his family, again talked about scaling back and eventually retiring to California, although almost everything he had done since Gloria's death belied his words.

He was still plagued by insecurity. Now that he was among the most famous men in America, there was more to lose, more work to do just to stay in place. It was the one thing everyone commented upon, his obsession with his work, and it had only intensified since Gloria's death. "It grabbed Winchell from the time he opened his eyes in mid-afternoon till he closed them in the mists of dawn," his friend Ernie Cuneo wrote. Winchell "lives his column," fellow columnist Dorothy Kilgallen observed. "He never forgets his job. When he dines with you, he whips out a black pencil and copy paper (folded three ways, reporter fashion) and takes southpaw notes on what you say." To his associate Herman Klurfeld, Walter himself admitted, "The truth is that any time spent without any value to the column is a waste of time. A bore."

June had been forbearing, but inevitably she had come to resent Walter's single-mindedness, and she seldom accompanied him on his rounds. "It has long been her contention that the whoopee places offered little and she could never quite understand their lure for others," he once wrote. Even at home she found no pocket of calm from the column. "Don't put me in the paper—don't make me say things I didn't say," Walter had her say in a column in the form of a domestic dialogue. "People will think I'm silly or something. Walda, come here. Be careful what you say in front of Daddy—he'll put it in the paper." Walter replied that everything he had her say was true and that anyway "it's a good idea for a column [. . .] intimate, personal, inside stuff about us . . ." In another of these "Mr. and Mrs. Columnist at Home" columns, Walter told June he was going to print their conversation, and June protested, "Don't you dare. I've told you. I don't like being made a character. And I'm not kidding. I'll divorce you if you do!"

Most of all, June had come to disapprove of Walter's lifestyle, disapprove of most of his Broadway acquaintances and his gangland associates. Part of her disapproval, though, was really anxiety over her husband's safety. Early in 1934 he got himself an all-wave radio and tuned to the police band. Later that year he bought a convertible roadster—

"the best investment I ever made" he called it. Now, every night, after the clubs closed, he cruised the streets with two or three other reporters, tracking police calls from three until six in the morning, racing to the crime scenes as soon as he heard a "Signal 30," which meant a crime was in progress. Walter was as excited as a child as he sailed through the streets on his way to a robbery or murder. If he was especially lucky, he would arrive at the same time as the police. Once he and an officer found a murder suspect feigning sleep in an unlocked apartment; the policeman arrested the man because his shoes were still warm.

"She worried that he was going to be murdered or hit or wind up in the hospital," said his friend Arnold Forster of June. By this time Walter was receiving numerous threats on his life, some from crackpots, others from Nazi sympathizers. (One mentally unbalanced woman wrote him a letter every day for years, accusing him of ridiculing her in the column. "Even if we discussed a statue, we were talking about her," said his secretary.) During the Hauptmann trial a court messenger had handed him a series of unsigned cartoons: The first was a swastika, the second a skull and crossbones, and the third a columnist hanging from a tree.

But Walter managed to avoid any physical confrontations with the fascists until December 18, 1935. At 8:30 that night he was leaving the Dawn Patrol barbershop on Seventh Avenue between 52nd and 53rd streets when two young men jumped him. One struck him in the back; the other punched him in the face. Walter crumpled to the sidewalk. (Later there was a question over whether he chased them.) His nose bleeding, Walter staggered back into the barbershop, where the manager sat him on a chair and ordered the blood wiped from his face. While the manager and two customers left to see if they could find the assailants, a tooth of Walter's fell to the floor. The attackers were Nazis, he was certain.

The next day, predictably, the incident landed in the papers, overshadowing a major labor address, the first in New York City in two years, by John L. Lewis of the United Mine Workers. "I am quite ready to admit that if Walter Winchell is punched, that is news; although I would not put it in the list of either epochal or strange incidents," Heywood Broun opined the next week in *The Nation*. In the meantime, the police provided Walter a bodyguard, and Lucky Luciano vowed to "even things up for you" if Walter could find out who had done it. Walter said he would handle it himself, but Luciano had already assigned a bodyguard of his own, a hulk named Pete Boretti, who now accompanied Walter everywhere. Just in case, Walter also started carrying a gun—a snub-nosed .38 that he wore under his coat and brandished to impress spectators.

The gun, the police calls, the snap-brim fedora he always wore, the constant public feuding, the bold taunts to Nazis, even the populism, were now part of a pattern that had firmly established a new Walter Winchell in the public consciousness to replace the twenties model. He was no longer just an imp. He was an avenger who strutted through the culture and blasted over the airwaves, meeting injustice and righting wrongs.

But whether Winchell realized it or not, the new model was no less a role than the old one, and if he didn't realize it, at least some of his public did. In October 1935 Walter had reprinted a letter from a fan who signed himself "Prince Charming." The fan said he had waited outside the Stork Club one evening to see his hero, but Walter had given him the brush-off. "Now I have heard it said that you will print two sides to every story you get—that you are a Lilliputian of a knight fighting the crusades of the little people—the waiters, the cab drivers, the cigarette girls, the honky-tonk acts, the abused, the Broadway halt and the Broadway blind. Occasionally, you scream of treason, of larceny, of treachery in high places—in a shrill and honest voice."

"Prince Charming" said he hadn't really been disappointed when Walter brushed past him. "Maybe, it is just as well you didn't stop the other night when I plucked at your sleeve," he wrote. "It might have spoiled the illusion. My friend is not a guy named Winchell. My friend is a guy with ten fingers on a typewriter—that is my friend—and a voice noisy with news and excitement coming out of a black box. That is what I like. . . ."

CHAPTER 5

Stardom

WALTER WINCHELL HAD CHANGED remarkably in the fifteen years since he arrived back in New York late in 1920 as a naive but aggressive young vaudevillian trying to make his name in the world. He was still handsome, still with fine features and penetrating blue eyes that locked so intently on a listener that they often unnerved those who met him. He still talked like a "magpie," in Ben Grauer's words, and he still sent off waves of electricity that could set a whole room buzzing. He was still fearful and insecure, still always worrying about money. He was still much more outwardly than inwardly directed, still campaigning for himself every chance he got, still at turns sycophantic and resentful.

But he had changed. Physically he was trim, but his five-foot-seven-inch body was no longer lithe. His hair was rapidly turning gray, his hairline receding. He looked older than his thirty-nine years, even if his aging had imparted a certain distinction—something no one could have imagined thinking back on the ambitious, glad-handing young Winchell. The larger change one detected, however, was in his temperament. Though quick-witted and often funny, he had become much more self-conscious about his growing status as a political commentator and much more concerned about preserving his image as an American institution. There was a sobriety one seldom found in the younger Winchell, a sense that he could no longer stand on the sidelines heckling, that to be taken seriously he had to grapple with weightier issues.

Yet at the same time that he was completing his transformation from imp to institution, he realized that he still couldn't rest. He had to move or someone would catch up to him, even surpass him. That, he knew as well as anyone, was how celebrity worked; there was always something new coming along, something hot. So one always had to reinvent oneself. It was out of this impulse that he had first ventured into radio when he felt he had reached a ceiling with the column. Now that he was preeminent in both radio and print, he needed to master another medium to stay ahead of the pack. And this time he looked to Hollywood. This time he was going to become a movie star.

As preposterous as this might have sounded for any other journalist, it was far more than a pipe dream for Winchell. His film shorts aside, he had been courted by Hollywood for starring roles since his first trip there, but he had always rebuffed the studios by asking for a prohibitively high salary. By 1935 Walter was listening more attentively, not only because he wanted something to rejuvenate him but because he thought he had found a way to reduce the risk of failing while he tried: Ben Bernie.

Over the years Walter and Bernie had had their real-life disputes—when Bernie wrote for permission to mention Walter's name in a trailer for a film he was doing at Paramount, Walter refused and warned, "[I]f you persist then I'm washed up with you forever"—but their radio feud had continued unabated since those few weeks back in 1933 when the sponsors temporarily ordered them to desist, and Bernie spent part of 1935 in Hollywood prospecting for movie projects for the two of them. By the fall Walter, obviously over his anger about *Broadway Through a Keyhole*, was also pressing Darryl Zanuck at Twentieth Century-Fox to come up with a vehicle for Bernie and Winchell. "Reliance films have been writing me for weeks for an interview, claiming they have three scripts for me," Walter said. "Thalberg [of MGM] and Harry Cohn of Columbia are also interested but I think you are top man and our alleged prestige would be safer with you."

Zanuck had promised Walter that he would find the "proper and correct vehicle for you and Bernie," but it wasn't until September 1936 that he found it. Zanuck was clearly excited. He dispatched Fox Vice-President Joe Moskowitz to New York with a temporary story treatment and instructions to contact Walter the minute Moskowitz arrived. Less than three weeks later, with Moskowitz trailing Walter on his rounds and by one account pleading with him to agree so that Moskowitz could return to California, Walter signed for his first starring film role. The salary was to be $75,000. "I hope I haven't been swindled!" Walter wrote Zanuck three days later. Walter also asked that he not be forced to come to Hollywood much before actual production began, since his syndicate had complained of too much Hollywood gossip and not enough New York. Zanuck cheerfully agreed. "I will not send for you until I actually need you and you will receive script far in advance so you will have plenty of time to build up your own dialogue and cut down Bernie's," Zanuck joked. To Fox publicist Harry Brand, Walter made one more request: that he be given a bungalow on the lot to race to between takes so he could "get another couple of paragraphs done."

Walter departed New York on December 14, 1936, from Penn Station and arrived in Los Angeles three days later. Though Eddie Cantor, who was to costar, had begged off the picture—Walter later said because Cantor thought it would fail—Walter arrived in high spirits. The story, adapted by Curtis Kenyon from Dorothea Brande's novel *Wake Up and Live*, was a farce about a timid page at a radio station who has a lovely singing voice but gets "mike fright." The beautiful hostess of an inspirational radio program (Alice Faye) encourages him to conquer his fear by practicing in front of the microphone. One day while he is singing to himself, his voice is accidentally broadcast on Ben Bernie's program. The public response is overwhelming, but the page is unaware that he is the object of its affection, and so is Bernie. Inundated by calls and telegrams demanding the singer's name, Bernie decides to call him "The Phantom Troubadour." Suspicious, Winchell demands that Bernie produce the troubadour. When Bernie tries, hiring a stand-in, Winchell reveals the hoax and humiliates his rival. Meanwhile, an unscrupulous agent, who has discovered the truth, kidnaps the page. By the end the page has been freed and, with the help of the hostess, sings publicly at a nightclub while Bernie and Winchell declare a truce. All this was to be punctuated with songs by Mack Gordon and Harry Revel. But as Zanuck had told Walter, "The beautiful part about this story is that neither you nor Bernie have to carry the plot, the plot is carried for you and yet you are an integral part of it without being dragged in. . . ."

"I have just seen the final script on 'Wake Up and Live,' " Walter wrote *Variety* editor Abel Green enthusiastically the first week of 1937, "and really think it is one of the swiftest paced I have ever read or seen. . . . I am playing a semi-menace with the usual windup. 'Why Walter we didn't know you were using it for That reason!' " Walter's confidence, however, rapidly ebbed the closer he got to production, and his mood was souring. "From the office–dressing room windows," he wrote, "it [Hollywood] looks like the front of the Palace used to look . . . The same agents, actors, hangers-on, lobbygows, phonies, front-putter-uppers . . . Strange, too, seeing so many falsefaces. . . ." He admitted he was overtaken by nerves and began suffering a severe case of lumbago. The night before his screen test he had slept only three and a half hours, which "certainly isn't enough to make a guy feel like doing anything but committing a murder."

Zanuck tried to bolster his spirits. After seeing Walter's test, the studio head declared himself "very happy." "Your personality is swell on screen and you have the best pair of eyes I've seen on an actor in a long while," he gushed to Walter. "This is no bull, I mean it. The way they have darkened down your hair looks good. If you know your dialogue and do not let Bernie step back on you, I'm afraid you are going to be a bit of all right." Walter had also objected to several of his lines, and Zanuck readily agreed to change all but one. He had even given Walter the star dressing room.

But for all Zanuck's attempts at accommodating him, Walter was not reassured. One rumor had him fainting on the set his first day. Walter vehemently denied it, saying that he had been on the set for only two minutes that day—just long enough for Patsy Kelly, who was playing his secretary, to nudge him after a crack by Bernie, run a finger across her throat and say, "Hmmm, your pal!" Nevertheless, the film's director, Sidney Lanfield, who had known Walter from the NVA days, said he was always having to shoot around his star in the morning because Walter was too jittery to sleep and usually arrived late. And when he did arrive on the set, he was still so nervous and uncertain that Lanfield usually had him perform the first take to an empty camera until the actor calmed down. Bernie told an interviewer that the technicians on the picture had been bothered for ten days by a strange noise that kept drowning out the dialogue. "We found out it was Winchell's knees rattling madly against each other!"

He finished shooting in late February with high praise in the column for Lanfield, who "finally got what the authors intended, we think, after perspiring blood and dying a little every day . . . It seemed a dirty trick to play on a man—handing him two 'actors' such as Bernie and us." Lanfield was so moved by this little tribute that he wired Walter his thanks rather than phone him, for fear he would lose his composure: TO THINK THAT IT TOOK THE TOUGHEST GUY FROM THE TOUGHEST CITY TO COME OUT HERE AND SOFTEN UP A LOT OF CALLOUSED FARMERS STOP WE ALL LOVE YOU AND WE'LL MISS YOU LIKE HOLY HELL YOU LOUSE.

Walter lingered for several weeks, adjusting his sleep schedule and hitting the clubs again. By the time he returned to Broadway, Zanuck's publicity machine was already cranking up for *Wake Up and Live*. "Prepare yourself for the kick of your life," Zanuck told a journalist even before the picture was cut. "When you see 'Wake Up and Live' you are going to see a new screen actor the like of whom has never been on the screen. Forget that he is Winchell, look at him under the name of Joe Doakes, if you wish, but look at him and you will agree with me he is one of the greatest picture possibilities that has come to the screen in many a day."

At Grauman's Chinese Theater in Hollywood on April 4, two weeks after Walter's return to New York, *Wake Up and Live* received its first press screening. "It is sheer entertainment, fast stepping, sparkling, without a foot of waste material or a dull moment," rhapsodized *Daily Variety*. "Dust off all your SRO signs," joined the Hollywood *Reporter*. " 'Wake Up and Live' will make the box offices of the nation do exactly that. It is headed for record-breaking business." I HAVE TO ADMIT PREVIEW GREAT, Lanfield wired Walter that night. ALL NOTICES RAVES[.] DOUGLAS FAIRBANKS[,] ZANUCK [,] [ADOLPHE] MENJOU AND HUNDREDS OF OTHERS SAY BEST MUSICAL THEY HAVE EVER SEEN.

Walter seemed to have won his gamble and should have been ecstatic. But the day after the preview he was rushing back to Hollywood to confront a new crisis. While he had been in New York, his family had fallen ill. To those to whom he mentioned the crisis, he didn't specify what was wrong, but by way of explaining his sudden trip west, he wrote Hearst, "My wife is pretty sick," and he informed columnist Leonard Lyons that June was going to be operated on the following Monday. "She's a pretty sick girl and so I belong here with them," Walter said, adding that he had already told his radio bosses that his family must come first and that they had graciously agreed.

The nature of the operation or the degree of its seriousness Walter again did not divulge in his letters, but whatever June was undergoing was complicated by another development. The very day that she went into the hospital, Walter tersely ended his column: "The W.W.s anticipate a blessed event in the Winter." June had now lost the baby and possibly the ability to have any others. "The Walter Winchells aren't that happy," he wrote in the column a week after the operation. "Mrs. Winchell was suddenly rushed to a surgeon's stiletto but is on the mend." Privately, he wired his secretary: WE WOULD RATHER HAVE BABIES THAN MONEY.

As June convalesced, Walter remained in California, missing, as it turned out, the New York premiere of *Wake Up and Live* at the Roxy later that month. The critics there had been as enthusiastic as the ones in Hollywood, but they reserved their loftiest encomiums for Walter. Regina Crewe in the New York *American* said that "the Winchellian personality dominates the screen when Walter is in camera range. The qualities that have won him fame in two media are apparent in the third. His acting has the fine virtue of appearing natural." (She added that he was turning down offers of $15,000 now for personal appearances and that his fan mail equaled that of Fox's biggest star, Shirley Temple.) Frank Nugent in

The New York Times called *Wake Up* a "blessed event at the Roxy." "He runs through 'Wake Up and Live' with the assurance of an ex-vaudeville hoofer and the high tension we always have associated with Broadway's Pepys," Nugent wrote. Producer Billy Rose, then in Fort Worth, Texas, for the state centennial fair, saw the picture the same night as its New York opening and sent Walter a glowing telegram offering to back a revival of *The Front Page* starring Walter. He even promised to donate the profits to any charity Walter designated.

Louella Parsons, Hearst's Hollywood gossip, was so impressed that she devoted an entire column to an interview with Walter—a rare beneficence. No longer hedging about his future in pictures—after returning from California he had said that "wild horses couldn't drag another picture out of him"—he openly discussed with her his jitters while the film was being made and said he thought his second movie would be less nerve-racking.

Audiences swarmed to the picture. On opening day more than 6,000 patrons attended a midnight screening at the Roxy, helping set a one-day attendance record of 38,825. More than 1,500 people were in line at ten o'clock the next morning. It broke house records at the theater on Saturday and Sunday by more than $2,000 each day and broke another the following Tuesday despite a continuous rain.

As years passed, however, the luster of *Wake Up and Live* would diminish until the film virtually vanished, as most of Walter's work would. Certainly no one any longer would be calling it one of Hollywood's greatest musicals. Once past the flush of initial excitement and Winchell's power of intimidation, the picture receded as forgettable froth with some tuneful songs, none of which became a standard, and some winning performances by veteran character actors Patsy Kelly, Ned Sparks, Walter Catlett and Jack Haley as the Phantom Troubadour—the same Haley of Haley & Craft who had provided Walter jokes back in vaudeville.

Despite its impermanence, *Wake Up and Live* may have had one effect: Some observers thought that Walter's performance had a lasting influence on screen acting. "Walter Winchell is so positive an acting personality that professional actors imitate him," drama critic George Jean Nathan wrote after seeing the film, citing twenty-seven plays and forty-three movies over the last few years in which actors patterned themselves after Winchell. To the extent that he symbolized the city in the thirties, Walter did seem to define an urban style for actors. Something in his clipped, nasal voice, something in the fast, kinetic, herky-jerky way he moved, something in his snap-brim fedora and the double-breasted blue suits he wore, something in his wisecracking and his slang, something in his bantam size and sharp features, provided a model of tough-guy urban

America, and there would be a little of Walter Winchell in James Cagney, George Raft, John Garfield, Edward G. Robinson, even Humphrey Bogart, all of whom rose to prominence after he had become a national figure.

Whether he could actually have become a successful movie star is a moot point. Though he waffled, he really seemed to have no desire to do any more pictures. In any case a friend had warned him to take his time before making another film. "I think you're a chump to hurry back before the cameras," the friend wrote. "You're in a spot where audiences want more of you, but if you oblige too fast, I'm afraid you might weaken the grand value you have won. You're not a hungry actor who must work to be remembered." "This is very difficult for me to tell you," Walter wrote Zanuck, taking the friend's advice to heart, "but I would be happier if you wouldn't take up my option."

"Whoever wrote you that letter that you quoted in your letter to me should have his head examined," Zanuck indignantly wrote back the same day. "I think your attitude, as expressed in the letter—if you are sincere about it—is certainly a slap in the face at me and ungrateful to say the least." Zanuck promised not to "mince words" with Walter. "In the first place, you asked me to find a picture for you when you were out here last year. I did not ask you. I found a picture and paid the price that you wanted without quibbling. I designed the picture and spent over $850,000 to find out whether I was right or wrong. No one took a gamble except Twentieth Century-Fox and Darryl Zanuck." He said that the studio had extended Walter every consideration, and he ended, "I am surprised at you, Walter." Two months later Joe Moskowitz sent Walter an agreement, exercising the option and ordering Walter to California on September 23 to begin a movie to be called *Love and Hisses*, once again costarring Ben Bernie. Now he was enslaved not only to the column but to Hollywood as well.

Actually he had been in New York only once—a week in mid-July—since June's surgery, and in all likelihood it was only the operation and her convalescence that saved him from the *Mirror's* usual dunning that he return to New York and write a Broadway, not a Hollywood, column. In late June, he made an appearance on Cecil B. De Mille's "Lux Theater" playing reporter Hildy Johnson to James Gleason's editor Walter Burns in a radio adaptation of *The Front Page*. As Johnson, a reporter whose soul belongs to journalism but who struggles futilely to extricate himself from it and live normally, Walter was clearly playing a role wrenched from his own life, and he was brilliant at it. When Hildy's fiancée scolds him for being on the job every time she calls for his presence, it could have been June talking to Walter, and when Burns, after being excoriated by the fiancée, admits, "I'm a bum," Hildy chimes in, "I'm a newspaper-man!," again sounding one of Walter's own defenses. There are not many Hildy Johnsons left, not many journalistic "swashbucklers," Walter told De Mille in an on-air interview after the play, but Walter left little doubt that he considered himself one of that dying breed whose chief dedication was to the paper, and he promised that he would be back on Broadway as soon as he finished his film obligation, probably in October.

But as the starting date for *Love and Hisses* approached, Walter was clearly growing apprehensive again—this time less over his acting than over his workload. He couldn't help remembering how difficult it had been to balance the film, the broadcast and the column during *Wake Up and Live*, and in mid-September Walter advised Jergens that his health would prevent him from doing the broadcast for the next eight weeks. Always protecting himself, however, he asked Jergens not to replace him with another commentator but to do another kind of program entirely. Jergens granted the leave but not the request for a different program. OUR INTEREST REQUIRES US TO PROTECT THE GREAT INVESTMENT MADE IN DEVELOPING THIS PERIOD AS A NEWS SPOT, Robert V. Beucus of Jergens wired him. He got the same consideration from the *Mirror*, with Louis Sobol taking over the column for syndication in his absence.

Now Walter was forced to deny rumors that he was going to let his contract lapse and finally scale back, as he had been promising June for years. He insisted that he was simply going to recharge. "The odds are a good ten to one that if I had not received this leave I would have been a very sick fellow," he wrote a friend. A press release from Fox reported that Walter was suffering from "nervous exhaustion" and that aside from the suspension of his broadcast and column, precautions were being taken on the set to ensure his well-being. A physician was to be present at all times, and the start of shooting had been pushed back from 9:00 a.m. to 11:00 a.m. to accommodate Walter's sleep. But none of these things seemed much to appease him. If he had been nervous and sick with anticipation during his first film, he was ill-tempered and bored during the second, knowing he had already proved himself, and tired of the whole thing. "All I know is that I sit around fifty minutes out of every hour waiting to do a scene that is seldom over four or five lines," he wrote Abel Green. "My God, how they waste time out here! . . . I need more action than that, Abel, or I fall asleep."

THE DAY after he wrote Green, Walter received a letter from a ghost of his youth. It had been years since he had had any contact with Rita Greene. He had expunged her like so much of his past, readily agreeing to an increase in her stipend fourteen months after their divorce and then, less readily, to another in 1931, but neither seeing her nor writing her in the six years since. (Evidently Walter had been so angry over her second request that he instructed his secretary not to put her calls through.) Those years had not been kind to Rita. After the divorce she had continued in vaudeville, but she was exhausted and frequently ill with a thyroid condition, and she finally quit on her doctor's advice. Eventually she enrolled in business school, and on August 11, 1930, her eleventh wedding anniversary, she set out for an employment office and wound up landing a job in the New York branch of Pathé Pictures where, out of consideration for Walter, she dropped the name Winchell.

It was never easy. With one sister married and gone and another unmarried and working only fitfully, Rita became the main provider for her family, living in an airy house on Staten Island. Her life revolved around her job, first at Pathé and later as a legal secretary, around her obligations to her family and around the local church. She and her family huddled in front of the radio each week to listen to Walter's broadcast, but he was never mentioned in the household in any context other than as a reporter and gossip.

Then she got the news, the news of which she wrote Walter that October while he was filming *Love and Hisses.* "Sometime back I found out I had a tumor in my breast," went the letter. "I have been taking treatments for this tumor in the hope that it would dissolve, but I am now of the belief that it must come out." The operation, which doctors advised she have immediately, would cost roughly $500, and she was now asking Walter if he might see his way to giving her $300 toward it. The response, whether Walter authorized it or not, was unspeakably cold. His secretary in California wrote: "[W]e are doing our best to simplify his routine as much as possible for him. . . . I have been given strict orders not to bother him with any mail at the present time. . . . I'm sure you understand."

Of course, all Rita understood was that she had cancer, that Walter had promised years ago he would help her if she needed it and that now she needed what amounted to a pittance, though Walter, always suspicious, probably believed the tumor was a ruse to pry more money from him. Rita angrily wired back that if Walter was too busy to answer his mail, could his secretary please see to it that his *wife* got the request? Within a few days Rita got her money and soon after had a radical mastectomy that saved her life. But she could never forgive Walter his insensitivity, and she bridled at the injustice of her supporting a family on her wage of less than $20 a week and Walter's stipend of $75 while he boasted of making thousands of dollars a week. At any rate, she believed that by getting her to agree to forgo alimony, Walter had conned her into accepting less than what she was entitled to.

After the operation Rita attempted to contact Walter for redress. Again and again she found he was "too busy, or in other words can't be bothered." "My hours are never regular," he wrote her after a year of her trying to arrange a meeting. "I sleep when I can and get up when I can. . . . I just can't make dates." It was, Rita said, after another year of these rebuffs that she devised a new plan. She would write a book about her life with him. She would reveal the secrets he had worked so desperately to conceal. "I am not getting any younger," Rita wrote in her manuscript by way of explanation. "I am getting older, my health is nothing to write about, and I have come to the time when I must have some security. . . . [A]s everyone has written about Winchell, and it appears that he is such good copy, I have tried my hand at it, and perhaps it will give a few people a laugh when they read why Winchell's life is more interesting than the others."

Rita wrote her manuscript, leaving little doubt that she intended it less as a literary effort than as a means to coerce Walter into increasing her stipend. But then she locked it away in a trunk with an old photo album, clippings, letters and other mementos of her life with Walter. For in the end, no matter how desperate her plight and no matter how cold-hearted Walter's treatment of her, she loved him. Rita Greene never stopped loving Walter Winchell.

WITH *Love and Hisses* completed, Walter returned to New York in November and resumed the broadcast on November 14, after his eight-week hiatus, vowing yet again that his days as a movie star were through. In all, he had spent eight and a half months in Hollywood that year, the longest stretch of time he had been away from New York since his last vaudeville tour in 1920, and he had become increasingly disenchanted with it, increasingly restless over its pace and its social life. "There's nothing for me to do in California," he told *Time* magazine. "I can't go to people's homes and then write about them." He was especially struck by Walda's reluctance to tell him anything about her friend Shirley Temple. "You would just put something in the paper about her," she said.

In California, *Love and Hisses* was being previewed. Based on an original story by Walter's friend Art Arthur, who had been the Broadway columnist for the Brooklyn *Eagle* before heading to Hollywood to write pictures, *Love and Hisses* was in the vein of *Wake Up and Live* but even slighter. The plot is triggered when Bernie asks Walter if he will promote a new find of Bernie's, a pretty French singer who, Bernie claims, has entertained the crowned heads of Europe. Discovering otherwise, Walter blasts her on the air instead. The next day a worried French aristocrat arrives at Walter's office, asking the columnist's assistance in finding his daughter, who has run away to Broadway. Walter promptly finds her at a casting call at Bernie's club and is wowed by her voice. What Walter doesn't know is that this has all been part of an elaborate deception by Bernie to make Walter eat crow, since the girl (Simone Simon), whom Walter now promises to publicize, is the same one he has criticized. But before Bernie can make a fool of him, Walter discovers the plot and springs a practical joke of his own on Bernie. He has some gangsters kidnap Bernie and threaten to kill him unless Walter hands over $50,000 in ransom money. At film's end, Bernie, blindfolded, is pleading for his life, not realizing he is onstage at his club before a full house. With Walter now having regained the upper hand, the French girl sings to an appreciative audience. "I'm the guy who brought her over," says Bernie. "But I'm the guy who *put* her over," replies Winchell.

Sidney Lanfield, who directed *Love and Hisses*, wrote Walter that "the consensus out here is that it is much better than 'Wake Up and Live,' " and he added that he had received "fifty rave wires from people who said the audience screamed from beginning to end." When the picture opened early in January, however, the consensus was anything but the one Lanfield had described. Frank Nugent in *The New York Times* was kindest, saying, "As sham battles go, this one is not quite up to the standard of their [Winchell and Bernie's] previous engagement, but it still must be reckoned a lively, well-scored, amusing show. . . ." More typically, *Newsweek* called it "uninspired entertainment," which "misses by a considerable margin" the success of *Wake Up and Live*, but the magazine spared Winchell and Bernie responsibility. Howard Barnes in the New York *Herald Tribune* found a cruelty in the banter between Walter and Bernie that the critics had surprisingly overlooked in the first picture. "Their continual heckling of each other has already lost its freshness."

Lest the film be perceived a failure and a blow to Walter's seeming indestructibility, he was at some pains in the following weeks to tell listeners that *Love and Hisses* was actually outperforming *Wake Up and Live* at the box office. At the same time he was now insisting that he would have continued making movies if the tax bite hadn't been so deep and left him so little return. Yet whatever gloss he put on it, *Love and Hisses* had been a disappointment after *Wake Up and Live*, and the willingness of critics to say so could be laid partly to Walter's long sabbatical without his column and broadcast. Defenseless, he was fair game.

II

"The Column." It was always "The Column," as if it were something holy and inviolable, as if the others were pretenders, which, in a sense, they were. Everyone read "The Column." "I have never been able to get far enough into the North woods not to find some trapper there who would quote Winchell's latest observation," Alexander Woollcott wrote as early as 1933, and he recalled a "painful" scene in Hatchard's bookshop in Piccadilly where a lord was in a dither because his orders to have Winchell's Monday column rushed to him as soon as it arrived had been disobeyed.

But however popular it was elsewhere and however much civilians enjoyed it, it was in New York and especially among show people and café socialites that "The Column" was devoured with the avidity of a child racing to the tree on Christmas morning to see what gifts had been left. By eight o'clock each evening, press agents and other show business personalities were queuing up at the newsstand, waiting for the early or "green" edition of the *Mirror*. "Before anything you turned to page ten," a press agent recalled, referring to the page on which "The Column" was found. "A press agent would grab the *Mirror*, run through it like a dose of salts and run to the telephone and say, 'Pete, you're in Winchell today!' "

And the interest went beyond ego gratification or professional advancement. "The Column" was so sacrosanct and café society's faith in publicity so devout that Winchell's items had an oracular authority. "If Winchell says so, it's gotta be true," Lucille Ball said about a report of Walter's that she was expecting a child. (She was.) Others learned of unhappy spouses and impending divorces or soured romances. David Brown was shocked to read in Winchell that his wife was divorcing him, then heard from her lawyer the next morning.

Walter himself seemed to regard "The Column" with a kind of reverence, too, as if he were merely its custodian and not its creator. "Other columnists have jocular moments when they suggest to a very limited group of intimate friends, that perhaps there are more important matters on earth than their daily essay," wrote one press analyst. "When Winchell says something about 'The Column' it is as if he were discussing an immutable force which he had miraculously unleashed but scarcely understood."

For Walter, everything had to be seen through the scrim of "The Column"; life was reduced to column fodder. As Emile Gauvreau put it in one of his novels, "The interests of others concerned him only in so far as he could make capital out of them." Once Walter was strolling down the beach in Miami while composer Richard Rodgers was discoursing to some friends on an investment he had made. Seeing Walter, Rodgers offered a brief summary, but Walter stopped him after a moment. "Never mind, never mind," he said, holding up his palm. "It's no good for the column."

In one sense his reverence for "The Column" enslaved him to it; in another sense it liberated him from responsibility for it. Walter's "wrongoes" on both the broadcast and in "The Column" were numerous, as might be expected from a column that could contain well over fifty items each day. He repeatedly reported that Judge Joseph Force Crater, a New York jurist who had suddenly disappeared, was still alive. A week after reporting that Douglas Fairbanks, Jr., had given an engagement ring to Vera Zorina, he announced that Zorina had married George Balanchine two weeks earlier, without ever referring to his own blooper. He spent months and even years tracking the romances of Katharine Hepburn, once publishing an "unconfirmed report" that she had married agent Leland Hayward after both had obtained Mexican divorces. Boarding a train in Newark for New York upon her return from the Yucatán, Hepburn instructed her traveling companion to hand a reporter a Mexican peso. "You give that to Mr. Winchell," snapped Hepburn. "It's worth 30 cents. That's what I think of Mr. Winchell."

Walter conveniently managed to ignore most of his mistakes or attributed them to erroneous "reports," as if he hadn't been the one circulating them; when he did correct errors, he did so circuitously by assailing sources. *He* never made errors, never retracted, not necessarily because he was infallible but because "The Column" had to be infallible. That might not have pacified anyone stung by Walter's "wrongoes," but readers and listeners never remembered the mistakes anyway, and his credibility never suffered. They seemed to realize that accuracy was beside the point. The point was creating a sense of omniscience. And for this, Winchell understood, seeming to predict events was just as good as actually predicting them.

WITH "THE Column," the broadcast, the personal appearances and movies, Winchell in the mid-thirties had become his own cottage industry, and though he liked to give the impression that he managed all these activities with a minimum of help—as was somewhat true—he still, of necessity, had gathered around him a small coterie to feed the maws. Ruth Cambridge continued to run the office in her relaxed fashion. Vivacious and carefree, Ruth had met dancer Buddy Ebsen the summer Walter was away in California with June after Gloria's death. Three weeks later they eloped. "Now I know why you've been sending my mail to Chicago (where Buddy was) instead of to California where I am!" Walter quipped in the column.

Ruth enjoyed the tumult at the Winchell vortex. Even after she married, she stayed with Walter, running the office single-handedly except for an occasional temp, until May 1935, when she left for Hollywood, where her husband had landed a film contract. Her replacement couldn't have been more different from Ruth. She was a petite, dark, chain-smoking young woman, nervous and birdlike, named Rose Bigman, who was conscientious where Ruth was convivial and who had a manner and voice almost as sharp as her boss's.

Rose's father had died when she was two, her mother when she was seven. She and her older sister spent their childhood unhappily bouncing from one aunt to another until the girls were old enough to work. Rose had worked as a secretary at a real estate firm for several years until "economic conditions made it necessary to dispense with my services," as she wrote in her letter of introduction, then as the secretary to the man in charge of the New York office of Westinghouse radio stations until these were sold to NBC, and then as secretary to an executive at the Columbia Phonograph Company until her division was closed down. A son of one of her bosses was dating Ruth Cambridge at the time and recommended Rose for a temporary position to help with an overflow of mail. She pounced on the opportunity—for years she had carried a clipping of a lovelorn poem from Winchell's column—and arrived for her interview in a large borrowed coat so she would look older than her years. Ruth hired her at $5 a week, and she began work on December 4, 1932, the day Walter debuted his Jergens program.

Though the job was supposed to last only a few weeks, Rose wound up staying nearly a year before Walter decided that the office work no longer warranted two secretaries. Fortunately Bernard Sobel, the *Mirror*'s drama critic now that Walter had surrendered the job, decided to hire her. But Rose never lost her bond to Winchell—even though she hadn't seen him during her first six months on the job—and Sobel was careful not to disparage him in front of her. When Ruth left for Hollywood, as Rose later told it, "Winchell yelled up to Bernie, 'Send Rose down to me!' " From that day, for the next thirty-five years, Rose Bigman was Winchell's gatekeeper, carving out her own small legend among the Broadway cognoscenti.

By his own admission, he was a tyrannical boss. "Nobody's Girl Friday, I am sure[,] has taken so much from a boss who can blow his top faster than I—before orange juice," he wrote in his autobiography, describing a typical phone call. " 'Fercrisssakes! You let me run the leading item when two of the opposition rags had it the day before! I thawt you read all of them. I can't read every paper every day. I don't mind getting it second. I just don't like getting it third!' (Bang! Hanging up.)" Rose called him the "bantam rooster" when he flared up this way. "We'd have these big fights," she recalled. "But when he'd call again, we never mentioned it. Everything was like a new day."

Even so, she was terrified of leaving the office for fear he would phone. "I never went out to lunch. I would practically die before I would have to go to the ladies' room or anything . . . because I never knew from one day to the next what time he would call. It could be ten o'clock in the morning or six o'clock at night. But I'd have to sit there all day to wait for him, you see." If she did happen to miss his call, he would bark, "Where the hell were you?" She worked seven days a week, including holidays, recovering only when he took his four-week summer vacation.

"Don't let the Boss frighten you—talk back to him when he starts shouting," Ruth counseled from California. But Rose was nowhere near as assertive as Ruth, and she fretted over every little mishap. "You have found out what a worrier I am," she wrote Walter shortly after assuming her duties. "I worry about the column every minute of the day and when I get up in the morning my first thought is 'Did WW leave me any notes? Did I do all right yesterday and other silly things like that?'

"What I'm trying to say is please have a little patience with me. . . ."

At the bottom of the note, Walter typed: "Stop worrying. You're doing bigtime work and I appreciate it. I'm just a nervous guy, get used to me. Love and kisses, Walter." And he gave her a $50 raise.

The routine was killing. Rose arrived at the office at 10:30 each morning and seldom left before 7:30 or 8 o'clock. Each day brought hundreds of packets from press agents. Rose read them and began sorting them by column heading: "Man About Town," "Things I Never Knew till Now," "New York Heartbeat," "Notes from a Girl Friday." The best material she sent to Walter's apartment in what she called the "nightly envelope." Then he composed the column, either at home or in the office late at night after Rose had left, and sent back the rejected items circled in red with comments scrawled in the margins. He also enclosed drafts of letters he wanted typed.

A messenger brought the finished column down from Walter's apartment to the *Mirror* offices on 45th Street. "He'd make so many changes," Rose said. "He crossed out things. He x'd them out. Nobody could read it but me." Frequently he phoned with last-minute emendations. So Rose would retype the column and send a copy to the composing room and another to the Hearst lawyer, who vetted it for libel and sent it on to the editor for another review. It was Walter's expectation that Rose would protect the column from these censors. At first it was "awful," in Rose's word. "I'd be so scared and I'd sit and wait for him [the editor] to call and I'd say, 'What am I going to take out? What am I going to take out?'" But after a while she learned to "fight like mad."

Her most important assignment, however, was not shepherding the column to print or even protecting it against Hearst. Her most important assignment was controlling access to Walter. She learned early that he was never to be disturbed. Ruth was on one of her long lunch breaks one day as a meeting between Walter and some Paramount Picture executives was rapidly approaching. Rose felt a wave of panic. Should she disturb Walter at home to remind him of his appointment or should she let him miss it? She decided she really had no choice but to phone him. Walter was furious at being awakened. He gave her such a dressing-down that she decided thenceforth she "wouldn't call him even if the building was burning." Not even Hearst himself got through. "I'm sorry. Mr. Winchell is sleeping," she told Hearst when he phoned once and demanded that Walter be alerted immediately. "This is William Randolph Hearst," he insisted. Still, Rose refused. Later Walter sent Hearst a note saying that he had been unavailable because he had fallen out of the window.

"Everyone thought I was a battleax until they met me," Rose admitted. When they did meet her, they discovered an unprepossessing young woman—everyone assumed from her phone manner that she was much older—who fully realized that while she was to run interference for Walter, she had also to mediate between Walter and the press agents who serviced the column. When Walter was about to blacklist a press agent from the column for some offense, real or imagined, it was Rose who said, "C'mon, Boss. Wait a minute. Don't put him on the list. He really didn't mean it." In this way, onetime press agent Ernest Lehman believed, she "kept Walter from going to extremes." On the other hand, it was also Rose who, after Walter had erroneously printed that the Lehmans were "writing their own unhappy ending"—he had confused Ernest with another Lehman—begged Lehman not to demand a retraction. "Please don't ask him to retract," she importuned. "Just forget it."

Rose answered the phones, opened the mail, wrote the letters, retyped the column and broadcast, even changed the ribbon on Walter's typewriter. Yet there was still the enormous job of feeding the maws, and these duties fell to hundreds, if not thousands, of contributors, none of whom expected or received monetary compensation; the mention was compensation enough.

One of the most faithful of these contributors, a thin, painfully shy clerk for the Brooklyn Edison electric company named Philip Stack, began mailing poems to the column under the pseudonym "Don Wahn" in 1929. His verses were both melancholy and cynical, about lost romance and jaded lives, but Walter loved them—they may have reminded him of his own *Vaudeville News* doggerel—and they became a regular feature, running just under Walter's by-line and making "Don Wahn" possibly the best-known poet in New York. Still, Stack was never paid. "I think that contributors to columns like you ought to be paid for their work—by book publishers, I mean," Walter wrote in the introduction to a collection of Stack's poems. "For you never heard of a columnist paying for his contribs—and you never will. Never give a sucker an even break, Barnum is supposed to have said.

"But as that Guinan Gal taught me: 'Never even give a sucker (a contributor) ANYTHING!' "

For Walter it had always been part of the Winchell myth as well as a point of honor that he composed the column virtually by himself and that he never paid for items. But both claims were fallacies. In the early thirties he asked his old roommate Curley Harris to collect items for him at $50 a week. Harris agreed. "Sometimes I'd pick up the column, a third of it would be mine. Sometimes more," Harris recalled. So he asked Walter to revise the arrangement up to $100 a week. Money-conscious as he was, Walter acquiesced. But Harris was soon dissatisfied again. "Eventually I thought the hundred wasn't enough," Harris remembered. "He was making a lot of money. He went up pretty fast, you know. . . . So we finally made an arrangement that he would pay me I think it was $10 or $20 for things on the radio and $10 or something for things in the column. Five items would be $50. So we worked that way for a long time." Others worked on the same basis—author Jim Bishop, then a copyboy, made $5 for each "Oddity in the News" Walter used—but always secretly, lest anyone discover that Walter was not the one-man band he made himself out to be.

Regardless of the number of contributors, it fell to Walter to distill and shape the contributions into columns, and no one ever denied that his sensibility governed. One friend recalled watching Walter intently sitting on the bed in his apartment, brandishing scissors, clipping away at press agents' sheets and then connecting strips with Scotch tape, papers strewn everywhere. "It looked like a kindergarten class," observed the friend. "But he knew what was important. *He knew* that." "He could take any guy's twelve lines and reduce it to six lines and make it far more readable, far more pointed, and it hadn't lost a thing that the original writer put in it," remembered Arnold Forster, the Anti-Defamation League attorney who often contributed political material to the column. Just how good an editor he was may have been most apparent when he was on vacation. "The press agents would send the same material that they sent to Winchell when Winchell was around," remembered one associate, "but none of the other columns ever improved. . . . None of them ever had his style. . . . When he came back, it became Winchell again."

Early in 1937, when he was in Hollywood making *Wake Up and Live* and unable to devote as much time as usual to his column, Walter realized that his ad hoc system would no longer be sufficient. He needed someone who could compose portions of the column and the broadcast for him, someone who was young and hungry and discreet, someone who could be trusted. And he already had a candidate in mind: a tousle-haired, bespectacled twenty-year-old gag writer named Herman Klurfeld.

Like Walter, the Bronx-born Klurfeld was the elder son of Russian Jewish immigrants—his father a house painter, his mother a housewife. He spent his youth in Jewish enclaves around the Bronx, speaking Yiddish until he was taught English in the first grade. During his senior year of high school, he was stricken by a lung abscess and was bedridden for two months, passing the time listening to radio comedians and then penning his own gags, which he never mailed. When he graduated, he planned to become an accountant, but with his father frequently out of work and the family in desperate need of money, he took a job pushing handcarts in the garment district. At night he still wrote gags, scribbling them on index cards. Finally a friend convinced him to send a few of his choicest jokes to Leonard Lyons, the new Broadway columnist at the New York *Post*. Klurfeld sent six. Lyons published one: "Girls used to dress like Mother Hubbard. Now they dress like a cupboard." Klurfeld was ecstatic. "To see my name in a Broadway column in the New York *Post* for a kid who lived in the Bronx tenement area—this was startling for me and all of my friends," he remembered.

He kept submitting, and Lyons kept publishing. "Herman Klurfeld at the Stork says . . ." Finally, after six months, Lyons wrote him asking if he would like to become a PR man. Klurfeld hadn't the slightest idea what a PR man was, but he went to Lyons's office, dressed in the same tattered sweater he wore to his job in the garment district. Lyons explained that a press agent named Dave Green had noticed Klurfeld's contributions and wanted to see him. Klurfeld was so dumbstruck by Green's sumptuous office in the RKO Building and by the celebrity photos decorating the walls that he immediately accepted an offer of $10 per week, even though it was $2 less than he was earning in the garment district. When he raced home and told his parents that he was going to work as a gag writer, they were stunned. "But I loved it. I couldn't wait."

Klurfeld was raw and untutored—Green had to buy him a suit so he wouldn't embarrass the office—and he landed so few gags in the columns in those first months that Green kept cutting back his salary. But when Walter returned from his annual vacation at summer's end and received several months' worth of gags that Green's office had stockpiled for him, he made a point of phoning Green to tell him how much he liked the young man's work and told Green to send him over to the office. When he arrived, as Klurfeld remembered it, Walter was in his fedora pecking away, two-fingered, at the typewriter. The office "didn't look at all the way I had imagined. Dingy, narrow, cluttered, it was sparsely furnished with several hard chairs, a row of files, a long table and two desks." He was struck immediately by Walter's handsomeness, especially his mesmerizing blue eyes. On either side of the columnist sat two burly men, who Klurfeld later learned were bodyguards: one from the FBI, the other from the mob. Glancing up, Walter pushed himself away from the typewriter. "You have a way with words, kid," he told Klurfeld. And Klurfeld "glowed, simply awed to be in his presence."

For the next hour Walter expatiated about everything from the Stork Club to "The Column" to the movies Zanuck wanted him to make. But he also questioned Klurfeld about his family, his background, and his aspirations, and he seemed especially to approve that Klurfeld's family was so much like his own. Afterward, ducking into a cab, Walter promised they would be seeing more of each other. Two weeks later Walter asked Green to send Klurfeld to the Stork Club. They ate in a private room, only three or four tables, where Walter introduced him to Tallulah Bankhead ("Go fuck yourself" were her first words) and gangster Bugsy Siegel. Again, Klurfeld was dazzled. When, on another occasion, Klurfeld expressed his admiration for the playwright Clifford Odets and cited him as an inspiration, Walter arranged for Odets to join them at Lindy's for breakfast.

If Walter was trying to seduce the young man into the orbit of W.W., he succeeded masterfully. After the Stork, Klurfeld started dropping by the office several times a week in the early evening, before heading off to night school, where he had enrolled in accounting courses. ("Accountant?" Walter had asked him incredulously when he heard. "Accountants don't have fun.") A short time later Walter left for Hollywood. Shortly after that Klurfeld submitted to the column a paragraph he called "The Headliners," which was a series of quotes from famous individuals, followed by a wisecrack. Walter phoned him, which wasn't unusual by now, but this time "he seemed to be very excited," as Klurfeld remembered it. "He said, 'Kid, I loved those "Headliner" things. From now on I don't want you to contribute to any other columnists. I want you to go to work for me. How much are you making?'" $25 a week, Klurfeld told him. "I'll double it," said Walter. It was understood that no one but Dave

Green and Rose were to know about the arrangement. Klurfeld was to work at home. Rose even cashed his checks lest anyone wonder why Winchell would be giving a weekly stipend to Herman Klurfeld.

As Herman quickly discovered, working for Walter Winchell was never merely a job; it was a way of life. "I would write the Sunday column, which we started calling 'The New York Scene' and then 'Notes from an Innocent Bystander,' " he recalled. "I would write ninety-nine percent of that column, which was what the critics said about the [Broadway] shows. We boiled it down, you know.... I did very little [on Monday] except punch up the Monday 'Man About Town' column—the gossip stuff. I would just punch it up with little phrases to make it more readable. The Wednesday column—the 'New York Heartbeart'—that was for press agents. That was a payoff for press agents. That he mostly did on his own." Of the seven columns that Walter submitted each week, then, Klurfeld said he wrote the better part of three, though Walter edited them all. "Some weeks I did four. Some weeks I did two."

On Thursdays, while he was drafting the Sunday column, Klurfeld also began wrestling with his main contribution to the broadcast in those early days—the lasty. Because of Walter's adamance that listeners remembered most what they heard last, his sign-off—"With lotions of love, this is your correspondent Walter Winchell who ..."—was given assiduous attention. "How about a hundred [submissions]?" Klurfeld said of the number of lasties he wrote each week before Walter was satisfied. "And sometimes he didn't like anything I gave him of the hundred. And very often I'd give him one and he said, 'That's it.' " But even then Klurfeld couldn't trust that his mission was complete; he was on twenty-four-hour retainer. "I'd say, 'I'm going to have a Sunday off. Terrific!' Well, Sunday morning I get a call from Rose: He changed his mind. He needs a new lasty.... And there went my whole Sunday. I sat at that goddamned typewriter and turned them out until he got one he liked. Some days he didn't like it and used the one he had on Friday anyhow.... I worked harder on that goddamned one line than I did in writing four columns."

For both Klurfeld and Rose, the demands were ceaseless, the work was grueling and slavish, the pay good but not great, and Walter seemingly ungrateful. So why did they subject themselves to it for as long as they did? They often asked themselves this question as the years passed. One answer was action. Working for Winchell, even surreptitiously as Klurfeld did, put one at the center of action and connected one, if only vicariously, to power. "Psychologically I got the joy of working for a man who was to me almost godlike, who could change the world, change people's lives," Klurfeld reflected years later. "He was the king of the world and I was one of the assistant kings."

Rose too enjoyed being at the eye of the storm, swept up in the turbulence. It gave her life momentum and meaning. It also gave her deference and perks, like show tickets and free meals at fine restaurants. And when Walter was inundated with Christmas presents, all of which he felt ethically obliged to return, Rose convinced him to let *her* keep them.

But there was another force that bound both Herman Klurfeld and Rose Bigman to Winchell: the force of family. Like Nellie Cliff, Rita Greene, June Magee and Ruth Cambridge before them—like Broadway in the twenties and America in the thirties—Klurfeld and Bigman were young and adrift and looking for a community that would have them. Walter provided it. "He was sort of a father image to me," Rose said. "I think that's why I took the yelling and everything. I didn't have a father, so I took it from him."

Klurfeld also described his relationship to Walter as one of a father to a son. Walter was the one he wanted to please. "If I've made any kind of headway, I'm grateful to you," Klurfeld wrote Winchell shortly after going to work for him. "You've been a sort of guide and teacher for me. You made me do a lot of things I never dreamed I was capable of performing." A year later he wrote again: "I want to thank you for being so nice to me. I hope that someday I'll be able to afford to contribute material without getting anything for it, simply because I don't consider that work. And the pleasure I get[,] the things I learn from you are worth more to me than anything else. That may sound Pollyannish, but it's the way I really feel."

Sometimes Herman even allowed himself to imagine that he was being groomed for the day when Walter would fulfill his longtime promise to June and retire. To Rose, Walter was less paternal and more abusive, and she thought he regarded her only as a "necessity," but he also referred to her only half-jokingly as his "other wife," and in any case, what she mistook for lack of intimacy was simply the way Walter dealt with people, warily, never letting down his guard. He trusted Herman and Rose about as much as he would ever trust anyone besides June. Everyone else wanted something. Herman and Rose wanted only to bask in the reflected glory of Walter Winchell.

III

It wasn't only Winchell, Bigman and Klurfeld who were indentured to "The Column." So were the press agents. "We regarded that column as number one, and we broke our backs to get in there," remembered one. At one agency the going rate for landing a joke in Winchell's column was $75; for landing an "orchid," Walter's method of bestowing praise, $150;

and a single mention would hold a client for weeks. That was why the press agents got what they called "seven o'clock stomach" waiting for the first edition of the *Mirror* to hit the newsstands. One press agent recalled rushing his pregnant wife to the hospital to have their baby, then picking up the *Mirror* while he waited for the delivery. When his wife emerged, she beamed and said, "It's a little girl!" and asked if he was happy. The press agent said, "Happy? I got five items in Winchell."

There were, in the late thirties, hundreds of these press agents—some of them joke and pun writers, others news gatherers, still others outright promoters and ballyhoo artists. "In those days being a press agent was like a girl being a model," said one veteran publicist. "When a guy was arrested and they asked him what he did, he'd say 'publicity.' Everybody was in publicity." Press agents had first materialized around the turn of the century to exploit free publicity in the expanding press. Though a bill was introduced in Congress in 1913 seeking to outlaw press agentry and though the New York legislature passed a law in 1920 restricting publicists' activities after one of them had faked the suicide of an actress to promote her new film, press agentry remained a growth industry not only among the august public relations counselors who ministered to corporate clients but among the low-rent hustlers who promoted bandleaders, stripteasers, banjo players and restaurants. It was the rise of the mass media and the concurrent rise of the idea of celebrity that did it. Even the most minor performer realized that publicity, not necessarily talent, was the way to fame, fame the way to success, and a press agent was the first step along the way.

Virtually all these press agents sent material to Winchell—scores of items, pages of items, thick packets of items—every day. Rose Bigman said admiringly that she didn't know how they did it. But the fact was that they had little choice. "You *had* to service Winchell every single day—'Sounds of the Night,' or funny stories or observations," said Coleman Jacoby, later a comedy writer. Jacoby submitted five pages of jokes to Winchell each day. Press agent Eddie Jaffe submitted as many as ten pages, others even more. "I realized that competing to get into Winchell's column was like a third university for me because you were competing against four hundred other minds every day," said press agent Gary Stevens. Searching for an advantage, Jaffe printed up stationery: "Exclusive to Walter Winchell." Emmett Davis sent his items on pumpkin-colored paper until Winchell scribbled back, "I've had enough of yellow journalism. USE WHITE PAPER!"

Even greater ingenuity was applied to the items themselves. A press agent named Milton Berger once financed a divorce so that the aggrieved husband could sue Berger's client, muscleman Charles Atlas, for alienation of affections. Another time, representing a toupee firm, he planted the story of a man who fell asleep in his barber's chair during a shave and wound up getting his toupee cut. When Marlene Dietrich's press agent was having difficulty keeping her name in the papers, he called on Eddie Jaffe for help. Jaffe, who knew you could always get clippings in the sports department, concocted the "Marlene Dietrich Award" for the racehorse with the best legs, then found a racetrack willing to present it. Another legendary press agent, Jack Tirman, was representing the Kit Kat Club, where "if you didn't get in the papers," the owner "beat you up. He didn't fire you." To keep the Kit Kat in the columns, Tirman began inventing nonexistent acts. One of these, a dance team, wound up getting orchids in Winchell's column as well as a review in the *Post*. When Walter discovered the ruse, he was furious, but Tirman deflected the anger by telling Walter that *if* the dance team had actually existed, Tirman *would* have come to Walter first.

"We and the other press agents fought with each other to see who was in Winchell's favor," remembered Ernest Lehman. Those who weren't in favor had to devise methods to land their client's plugs anyway. This often resulted in elaborate deceptions by which the outcasts routed items through the favored press agents. This way the out-of-favor press agents got the mentions they wanted, and the favored ones were rewarded with mentions for *their* clients because Walter believed they had given him "free" items—that is, items about people and places they didn't represent. The rule of thumb was that Walter would give a press agent one plug for every five "free" items the agent delivered.

There was always more anxiety than honor, more pressure than respite, for the press agents. "We lived in a dangerous world," Lehman said. Clients were seldom satisfied; they always wanted more. Press agents loved to tell the story about dance king Arthur Murray, a dour, laconic man whose press agents got him in the columns by making him the vehicle for their snappy one-liners. Then came a fallow period when Murray wasn't in the papers. So he called his press agent, Art Franklin, and complained, "What happened, Art? Did I lose my sense of humor?"

Even when clients were reasonably satisfied—and the turnover was great in the best of times—press agents found themselves in a daily pincers between competing columnists. That was because columnists seldom returned items, and press agents were forced to guess how much time to let pass before submitting the same items to another columnist, the damage of having the same item run in two columns being incalculable. Of course, Walter received all material first, and press agents appreciated that he alone among columnists always returned unused items promptly, usually no later than a week after submission, frequently with the reason for rejection. Press agents in good standing also appreciated that Walter occasionally sent along a scurrilous item he had received about one of their clients, placing a question mark beside it to show that he wasn't using it.

Still, he inspired terror. Once, at a time when Walter was especially enamored of the rhumba, he was watching a couple on the dance floor and remarked how much he was enjoying them to press agent Sid Garfield, who quickly chimed in, "Look, Walter, I'm enjoying them too." Another time, when a few disgruntled press agents began griping about Winchell, Jack Tirman looked skyward and blurted, "I'm not listening, Walter." Another press agent remembered instinctively checking his car's rearview mirror when a passenger criticized Winchell, fully expecting to find Walter tailing him.

The greatest fear was of winding up on what Walter called the "Drop Dead List." Any one of a number of petty offenses could land a contributor on the DDL, a Coventry that could last months or even years and that would undoubtedly cost the transgressor clients and money and possibly his job. One common offense was giving Walter an item that had run in another column, something that happened occasionally when a press agent or contributor mistakenly thought he had already rejected an item. Another was giving him an erroneous item—a "wrongo." "Sometimes people give you a wrong steer," Walter frankly told an interviewer in 1937. "When I find that a contributor has done that, I never use his stuff again. I don't know why. It's like finding that a girl has been unfaithful." (This was also the main reason why he seldom confirmed items with the subjects, despite claims that he did; contributors knew they gave him false information at peril of being put on the Drop Dead List.)

Like veterans telling war yarns, every press agent had his favorite story about landing on the DDL or narrowing escaping it. Marty Ragaway earned a place on the DDL when, on meeting Walter, he casually mentioned that he had been sending gags to the column since he was in high school. "Well, how dare you do that to me?" Walter fumed. "How dare you send me copy and let me use a kid in high school's material?" Ben Cohn, under pressure from Walter to supply "novelettes," invented one about a showgirl who was about to jump from her hotel room window because she could not pay the bill. Then she got a call to report to rehearsal, but as she walked through the lobby, the house detective stopped her and told her to forget the rehearsal. He had called the producer and said she couldn't do it.

The story had immediate impact. Producer Billy Rose offered her a job. Radio columnist Nick Kenny wrote a poem to her. The Chez Paree took up a collection. Now Walter wanted to meet her. "My world shattered," Cohn said. So Cohn typed a letter, had the receptionist rewrite it in her hand, put it in an envelope, pricked the envelope with two pins and brought it to Walter. When Walter demanded to see the girl, Cohn said he had let her have his room, then returned to find his money gone, his bridgework missing and the note pinned to his pillow, saying that she had been through so much and was now taking a few things of his. "And so you were only stuck for a story," Girl Friday wrote in the column. "Ben Cohn was stuck for $32 and his bridgework." But he escaped the DDL.

Cohn was among the lucky ones. Gary Stevens was representing a singer named Patricia Gilmore, who was conducting a discreet romance with bandleader Enric Madriguera. The Associated Press had reported that the two had wed, but Gilmore, whose Irish Catholic parents disapproved of the relationship, phoned Stevens to dispute it, and Stevens in turn sent on a denial to Walter, who published it along with a dig at the AP. The AP retaliated by publishing a photostat of the marriage certificate. When Stevens confronted Gilmore, she confessed that they had gotten married but wanted to keep it secret.

Now came the storm. Rose phoned Stevens immediately to ask how he could have made such an error. The next day Walter himself phoned, spewing expletives and demanding that Stevens meet him at the Stork Club that afternoon. When Stevens arrived at the club, it was empty except for the waiters and Walter, who was eating. Walter ordered him to sit and began lecturing him, almost paternally at first as Stevens remembered it, about the responsibility to check facts. Then he turned angry. "You're on my shit list for one year," Walter said, and quickly dismissed him.

Every day Stevens sent contributions to Winchell, and three days later they would come back, untouched and unclipped and always with the same note: "Don't send these to anyone else." (Stevens circumvented the ban by rewriting items and submitting them to Dorothy Kilgallen at the *Journal* and to Sullivan and then trading items with other press agents.) Months after the imposition of the ban, Walter was dancing at the Stork with a girl whom Stevens was dating at the time. "Tell your friend to call me," Walter said to the girl. Stevens did, and Walter, as if compensating, published seven or eight of Stevens's items in the first few weeks. Bringing up the incident years later, Walter laughed, punched Stevens playfully on the shoulder and said, "I was wrong and you were wrong."

Usually contributors pleaded with Walter to reinstate them. "I am sorry that you think I deliberately tried to palm off someone else's gag on you as my own, and that as a result you feel toward me as you do," comedian Henny Youngman once wrote him abjectly. "Certainly I respect you too much to try to pull anything as raw as slipping you a gag from another column," and he promised that he would henceforth be "doubly careful in checking on any material submitted to me. . . . I cannot risk incurring your displeasure for a mere line." Eventually all but a few were reinstated. The only capital crime for which there was no reprieve was boasting that one could get an item into the column. Walter made it clear that no one had that ability; anyone who believed he did would be making Walter out to be a dupe.

He was most lenient with young press agents. A new publicist at Warner Bros. named Robert William was assigned to provide Winchell with material, and William's boss invited him to dine with Walter at the Stork. Beforehand, however, the two stopped at the Astor Hotel for drinks. William, a novice drinker, downed a scotch and soda "like a malted" and within five minutes was in "the most advanced state of euphoria you could imagine." By the time he arrived at the Stork, he was goggle-eyed, and while he managed to keep himself composed during dinner, after dinner he was "stricken with the greatest case of narcolepsy." William's boss was irritated, but Walter was understanding. "When I was your age I went to sleep right under the table," he said. William believed "he saved my job."

Otherwise Walter was largely contemptuous of press agents. He hated their sycophancy, their mewling, their obvious insincerity, their desperation, which may have reminded him of his own. "The press agents were all over him," recalled David Brown. He walked around "like a shark with little fish around him" was press agent Maurice Zolotow's description. Above all, he hated his dependence upon them.

For the press agents the feeling was mutual. Most of them deeply resented the power Walter held over them, the peremptory banishments, the constant demands, the need to toady and bootlick. Their resentment toward Winchell may have been exceeded only by one other hatred: their own profound self-loathing. On the face of it, press agents were a strange, colorful breed who prided themselves on being characters in the Damon Runyon mold. But just beneath the surface of the image, one found an unsavory and largely forlorn group of men. Some were lapsed journalists in mid-career who were frantically searching for a way to make money. Some were fresh high school kids who liked to wisecrack and hoped they might become humorists or even columnists. Others were orphans and vagabonds who had drifted into publicity because they didn't know how to do anything else. "A lot of these guys couldn't write their own names," Ernest Lehman said.

They spent their evenings, as Walter did, hanging out at clubs and restaurants, hunting for clients, picking up gossip, trading stories, cadging drinks, pressing items on columnists. They lived with a sense of their own corruptibility, often having to bribe their way into columns. At Walter's own *Mirror*, for example, $25 could buy a picture on the center "split page." For $2, radio columnist Nick Kenny would mention a birthday. Kenny's secretary, who happened to be his niece, would demand tickets to radio programs. His brother, who was married to a radio actress, would demand that press agents help her get jobs. A cartoonist for the column named Bill Steinke ("Jolly Bill" he was called) demanded $10, he said, to make a plate. And Kenny himself was a songwriter who plugged those clients who helped get his songs on the radio.

The whole process was grubby and humiliating, and it was no different at many of the other papers. The submissiveness hurt, and the agony of knowing that you were chasing trivia, leaving nothing. Stanley Walker in a scathing dissection of the press agents in *Harper's* magazine wrote of hearing them "cry softly into the beer, ale, Scotch, and rye along Broadway for years and curse their own strange calling. . . . They do become ashamed of themselves at times, though the majority, if they keep at it long enough, manage to smother their consciences."

They tried, some of them, to boost their status by calling themselves "public relations men" or "press representatives," but the terminology of their trade betrayed them. Press agents talked of "servicing" a column and of "scoring" when one had a successful plant in a column. The metaphors were sexual because the press agents saw themselves as procurers with a stable of clients they had to sell and columnists they had to sell them to. And what added insult to the insult was that clients frequently failed to pay; by Eddie Jaffe's estimate, 50 percent of his clients welched.

Yet however shabby the system, however meager the influence of any one individual, save Winchell, they were all locked in an immense cycle of promotion and dissemination and creation which for better or worse helped define the country. "Publicity is the nervous system of the world," wrote Harry Reichenbach, who was one of its earliest and best practitioners. "Through the network of press, radio, film and lights, a thought can be flashed around the world the instant it is conceived. And through this same highly sensitive, swift and efficient mechanism it is possible for fifty people in a metropolis like New York to dictate the customs, trends, thoughts, fads and opinions of an entire nation of a hundred and twenty million people."

Most of the press agents themselves were so absorbed in the details they were myopic to the rest; they never saw the system whole this way or gave a moment's thought to its effect. But a few did. A few knew. "I always believed that a great deal of our news was shaped by a rather small group of press agents," observed Ernest Lehman. "If I ever saw a feature story in a New York newspaper I knew that that was not the result of some editorial board saying, 'Let's do a feature on so-and-so,' or that the feature writer said, 'I've got a great idea. I'd like to do a feature on so-and-so.' I felt it always started with a press agent calling someone and saying, 'Look, I've got a story for you. Here it is.' "

That is the way the system operated. That is the way the world worked in an age of gossip and celebrity. And the press agents, for all their abasement, were the ants that moved the mountain. For without them, there was no celebrity, no gossip, no mass culture really. And, as he knew only too well, no Walter Winchell either.

IV

He never called them rivals. To Winchell his fellow columnists were always "imitators," riding on the coattails of his popularity. He loved to read their columns aloud in front of an appreciative audience and provide a running commentary. When he saw items and jokes he had rejected appearing in other columns, he would crack, "I see my rejects are ending up in the garbage pails." But this was more than public entertainment. David Brown, then an obscure young journalist writing a column for *Pic* magazine,was shocked to receive tear sheets of his pieces with comments and criticisms from Walter even though Brown had never met him.

"[M]y impression of the Broadway columnists[,] judging from their output, was that they were, by and large, a rather venomous lot, forever clawing at each other," wrote one, recalling his feeling as he was about to join their ranks. By the late thirties there were many more of them clawing, nearly all of them marginalized Americans—Jews, Catholics, women, homosexuals—venting national frustrations through their own. The *Daily News* had both Ed Sullivan and Sidney Skolsky. When Skolsky was fired for insubordination, he was replaced by a aristocratic-looking Georgian named Danton Walker, who had once served as assistant to Alexander Woollcott and then to Harold Ross of *The New Yorker* before joining the *News* as an assistant to the financial editor. Genial Louis Sobol still covered Broadway for the *Journal*, but when O. O. McIntyre died suddenly, early in 1938, Sobol, who had never really had the stomach for the sort of bare-knuckles journalism that Walter loved, took over as the *Journal*'s resident nostalgist. He, in turn, was replaced on the Broadway beat by Dorothy Kilgallen, the twenty-five-year-old daughter of veteran Hearst reporter Jimmy Kilgallen, and a valued reporter in her own right. Lee Mortimer, who had once written the Sunday column in the *Mirror* while Walter sulked, now had his own column. Hal Conrad wrote Broadway gossip for the Brooklyn *Eagle*, and within a few years producer Billy Rose was to launch a syndicated Broadway column.

"Did you know L. Lyons is now a columnist?" Girl Friday asked in May 1934. Leonard Lyons, who had landed on the *Post* that month, was one of the few with whom Walter didn't quarrel. He had been born in 1906 Leonard Sucher, youngest of seven children of an impoverished garment worker from Romania who died in a sweatshop when Leonard was eight years old. To support the family, his mother set up a candy stand at Ridge and Rivington streets on New York's Lower East Side while Leonard, a bright student, sailed through P.S. 160, skipping four grades. He worked his way through high school, making keys at the Segal Lock Company and during summers running errands at the Palisades Park Commission, where one of his brothers was head bookkeeper. After high school he took accounting courses at City College, then went to St. John's Law School, where he graduated second in his class. He joined a law firm and left two years later to start his own practice.

Soon, however, he realized that the law exerted a weaker claim on him than journalism. One reason why, evidently, was his fiancée, Sylvia Schonberger, whom he had met at a party during his senior year of law school and whom he had instantly resolved to marry. Sylvia, moved by the beautiful letters he had written her, was convinced Leonard could be a writer. In June 1930 he landed a column in an English-language insert in the Yiddish *Jewish Daily Forward* at $15 per week. It was the editor there who renamed him Leonard Lyons.

Six months later the section folded. Lyons was now contributing items to the Broadway columns, including Walter's, but he hadn't lost hope of getting another column of his own. "It was the mad dream—the terrific longshot," he later said. Early in 1934 New York *Post* publisher David Stern put out a call for a Broadway columnist. Lyons submitted his clippings and won the job from among five hundred applicants. (Walter claimed to have recommended him.) He was sitting at a nightclub one night that May batting around possible names for the column when Walter said, "Here's a natural for you. The Lyons' Den." Lyons liked it and joked that Walter had won the name-the-column contest, the prize being a night on Broadway.

"Why would a lawyer become a columnist?" his son Warren reflected many years later of his seemingly modest and unambitious father. "I asked him this many times. His answer was, 'I don't know.' That's what he said to me. 'I don't know.'" There was always a lingering suspicion both within the Lyons family and without that Lyons hadn't really wanted to be a columnist, that his wife, Sylvia, was the driving force behind his career and the one who stoked his ambition. Lyons would admit only that he liked the excitement of being a columnist, and there certainly were perks. But he may have been unwilling or even unable to admit the deeper attraction that a Broadway column held for a poor boy from the Lower East Side who devoutly wanted to be accepted, and for his wife as well: a Broadway column allowed them to circulate among the famous.

Walter hated having to mix with celebrities; he thought of them as unavoidable nuisances. "I just don't like celebrities," he told an interviewer. "I'm like the violinist in the story who played with the orchestra for forty years, and when the conductor asked him why he made such faces he replied, 'Because I hate music.' " Lyons, on the other hand, loved to mingle with them, and in his column he told tales *about* the famous rather than *on* them, lest he offend. "My father never printed gossip," said Warren Lyons. "If you look through his columns, you'll never find a blind item. . . . You'll never find anything 'who was going out with whom.' . . . He prided himself on not printing gossip." Lyons printed anecdotes instead, which is the main reason Walter was so magnanimous toward him. "You are the first column to come along who [*sic*] doesn't copy me," Walter wrote Lyons his first week on the job.

Lyons cultivated a different image, too, from the pugnacious one that Walter had perfected and that the others copied. He avoided the crossfire that was a staple of the columns, and one of the few times he did attack was to scold Louis Sobol for hosting vaudeville shows because he thought that using celebrities and then writing about them was unethical. Lyons was "a real gentleman," said press agent Robert William. "Pleasant," Eddie Jaffe called him. "Made a real *effort* to be pleasant." *The New Yorker* closed its profile of him by saying, "Everyone is Lyons' friend." And one of those friends, the playwright William Saroyan, observed, "There is not a great deal of desperation in him—if there is any at all."

But anyone watching the tiny man with the prominent nose flitting restlessly from nightclub to nightclub and from table to table, scribbling notes—he was famous for mangling stories to the point of nonsense— knew there was quite a bit of desperation in him, whether his own or Sylvia's. "Driven, dedicated," were words used to describe him. "The hardest-working newspaperman I ever met," said one Broadwayite. "Lyons never drinks, not even coffee," wrote Westbrook Pegler admiringly, "and he tells how when he gets home at 6 A.M. and says 'Good night' the elevator man thinks he is drunk and how his baby is just waking up when he gets in and just being put down when he starts back to work at four in the afternoon—the gay life of a Broadway bon vivant."

Of course, it wasn't gay. It was long and arduous, and by the late thirties even members of the fraternity were questioning whether a Broadway column was worth the effort. In the twenties and early thirties Broadway, pulsating with uninhibited energy, was undeniably the center of the celebrity universe, and the Broadway columnist at the center of the center. But the evolution of café society couldn't conceal that the center was gradually shifting westward to Hollywood, where the movie stars dwelt. More and more, that seemed to be the place for a gossipmonger.

Partly in recognition of the changing order, the *Daily News* had dispatched one of its Broadway columnists, Sidney Skolsky, to California for what was supposed to be a year's tour of duty. Four years later, Skolsky was still in Hollywood. But then Ed Sullivan, jealous of what Walter had accomplished in the movies, convinced *News* editor Frank Hause to recall Skolsky at long last and send Sullivan instead. "I pleaded with him by wire and phone to return," Hause later wrote Walter of the efforts to bring Skolsky back, "but no dice. I guess the competition on the Broadway beat was too much for the Little Mouse, and he liked the easier tempo and climate of Hollywood." Skolsky saw it differently. He fired back a letter of resignation, saying that "Broadway columns are as passé as Broadway" and closing with a slight variation on the tag line of his column: "They got me wrong. I love Hollywood." Skolsky then switched to the *Mirror*, Sullivan left for California and Danton Walker took Sullivan's place on Broadway.

Wisely Walker began by soliciting advice from Walter on how to conduct his column. "Well, how shall I start?" Walter wrote back.

I think it's important for anyone on a newspaper, particularly one who is doing a column, to "build his fences." The politicians do this a great deal, and it is a wise thing. Of course I mean make as many friends as you can. You never know from where the next line or paragraph is coming. One of your best stories may come from a fellow whose face you never liked, but whom you were nice to—and he appreciated your being civil to him, which is why he gave you the break.

And he issued a warning about press agents: "Try your best to avoid the shyster press agent. There are many of them on our beat, and they think nothing of using one's column to spoil it if it will help them gain something." As for finding the right voice, "Try to be yourself as often as you can. I mean in style." He closed with an ethical consideration: "Never permit anyone to give you a gratuity because if you do, Danton, you will be putting yourself where they want you—in a spot."

Meanwhile, out in Hollywood, Sullivan was exploiting the film industry even more aggressively than Walter had. In short order, he sold three story ideas and appeared in the film of one of them, *Big Town Czar.* (*The New York Times'* Frank Nugent wrote, "[T]he only word for Ed Sullivan's portrayal of Ed Sullivan is 'unconvincing.' ") But as with Skolsky, Sullivan was eventually recalled to New York, and as Skolsky had, Sullivan refused the order. Frank Hause was visiting Sullivan at the time the wire arrived from *News* publisher Joseph Medill Patterson. "I pointed out to the great Port Chester athlete the advantages of the Broadway beat and the News growth and prestige," Hause remembered, "and then dictated a wire to JMP, in which Sullivan stated, 'I acted hastilly [*sic*]. Please ignore earlier telegram. Am returning New York.' He did return, and Patterson, flattered, made Sullivan the fair-haired boy."

Skolsky, in the meantime, was finding Hollywood less hospitable than he had at first thought. Working on the *Mirror* had brought him into direct competition with Hearst's veteran Hollywood columnist, Louella Parsons. Skolsky had been on the paper only a short time when Parsons published a front-page story announcing that Greta Garbo and conductor Leopold Stokowski were to be married. In the very same paper, Skolsky's column reported that the rumors were false. Infuriated, Parsons labeled Skolsky a Communist, and Hearst refused to hear his defense: He would be fired as soon as his contract expired. Three months later he spotted Parsons at Chasen's restaurant with her niece—a movie publicist named Margaret Ettinger—and the journalist Alva Johnston. Johnston and Ettinger waved him over. As Skolsky told it, he spent the next fifteen minutes pleasantly conversing, never addressing a word to Parsons, until she finally chirped, "If I'd known you were so nice, I wouldn't have told Mr. Hearst you were a Communist." Skolsky was so angry he bit her. All told, he was out of work for eight months.

Skolsky should have known better than to take on Louella Parsons. There were others purveying gossip in Hollywood in the mid-thirties, notably a onetime actor and movie publicist named Jimmy Fidler who had a fifteen-minute radio show, but Parsons was the undisputed queen, the Walter Winchell of the West. "I've always claimed a story wasn't a story unless I got it first," she wrote. She had set her sights on being a reporter from the time she was a young girl in Dixon, Illinois. In 1896, at fifteen, she got a job moonlighting as church, social and sewing circle reporter for the Dixon *Star* while she taught school. At twenty-four she married John Parsons, a wealthy real estate agent eight years her senior, who moved her to Iowa, installed her in a boarding house, gave her a daughter and then abandoned her. At twenty-nine, she moved to Chicago, where she wrote articles for the Chicago *Tribune* by day and dreamed up screenplays at night. In the meantime, she married again, this time to an impoverished but attractive sea captain. Eventually she was hired by the Chicago *Record-Herald* to write film reviews and features, but when the *Herald* was folded into Hearst's *American*, Parsons left for New York and landed the job as motion-picture editor on the *Morning Telegraph*, whose current editor had left for the war. Five years later she assumed the same duties on Hearst's New York *American*.

The dominatrix of the relatively small but rapidly growing field of movie news, Parsons worked tirelessly not only building her column but cultivating contacts. Chief among them was William Randolph Hearst's paramour, the actress Marion Davies. It was Davies who invited Parsons to join her on an excursion to Hollywood in May 1925. Parsons was captivated. Feted by the Hollywood community, which respected both the power of her column and her relationship to Davies, the plain, plump, unsophisticated woman from rural Illinois had found her spiritual home. She returned to New York at summer's end, but a bout of tuberculosis sent her back to California for convalescence that fall. When she recovered, Hearst insisted she remain in Hollywood as motion-picture editor of his Universal News Service. It was the syndication of her column in the Hearst papers that cemented her status as the most important of the Hollywood journalists.

In New York the premier gossips were the ones, like Walter, whose tongues were the sharpest and whose scruples the lowest. Power there was a function of one's insolence. In Hollywood, a one-industry town as far as gossip was concerned, things were entirely different.* Parsons was part of Hollywood's social order, not antagonistic to it. Her power derived from her relationship with the studio establishment, and her column was largely a compendium of trade news, interviews and other information which the studios wanted to have disseminated. As a result, stars and other employees feared her not because her column could harm them with the public (though it could) but because her coziness with the men who ran the studios could destroy them with their employers. Even so, she was ordinarily quite benign, despite her despotic reputation. "The only time she would get burned up with a star was if they [*sic*] had a big scoop and didn't give it to her," recalled her longtime assistant Dorothy Manners. "She'd ask if they'd lost their minds."

"She was always in the swim," said Manners. She began working the phones at nine each morning, tramping to her desk in her office, which adjoined her bedroom, sometimes still in her robe. The phones rang con-

---

*Always toothless, Hollywood gossip became even more so in the mid-thirties, when the studio chiefs issued an informal edict compelling writers to submit their stories to the studios for approval. Newspapers and magazines complied on threat of losing movie advertising.

stantly, and each of her two secretaries had two. As the secretaries fed her information from the studios and from her legman, Neil Rau, Parsons composed the column, then read it to her staff for suggestions. (When a messenger glanced at the column one day and said he didn't understand something, Parsons began reading the column to him too.) By one o'clock in the afternoon the column was filed, and Parsons began her rounds of the studios. By late afternoon she had returned to the office for her hairdresser, and then it was off to Romanoff's or Chasen's or a party.

Once a month she hosted a large gathering of her own, putting up a tent in the yard of her Beverly Hills mansion and inviting as many as two hundred guests. (Later she bought a farm outside Los Angeles, built an oversized porch, outfitted it with bunk beds and entertained on weekends there.) She lived regally with a maid, a cook and a chauffeur, and she expected from the community the deference due a sovereign. Unsurprisingly, everyone paid tribute. Warner Bros. publicist Robert William remembered Parsons's coming to the studio lot at Christmastime to collect her bounty. He filled her station wagon with presents. "And she took it as a kind of princess [from her] devoted crowd," he said.

The princess treated Walter like visiting royalty—at first, no doubt, because they were both members of the Hearst family and thus technically noncompetitive, and later because she had a fifteen-minute radio program that followed Walter's and she realized she inherited part of his massive audience. If she ever said an ill word of Walter, no one could recall it, and she even offered to send him hot stories. "Sometimes things break out here that you could have on the air before they are printed in New York," she told him.

Her spite, all of it, was reserved for Hedda Hopper, a former actress who, in 1937, had the temerity to begin a Hollywood gossip column of her own. Parsons "hated her guts," said Dorothy Manners. Hopper, born Elda Furry, was one of nine children of a butcher in Hollidaysburg, Pennsylvania, in Quaker country just outside Altoona. Her childhood dripped with bitterness and resentment; her seminal experience was nursing her wealthy grandfather back to health after his eyesight had failed and being rewarded for her months of effort with a silver dollar. Bored with school and angry at the favoritism shown her brothers, she ran off to New York to become an actress and met De Wolf Hopper, an aging, physically imposing thespian with the voice of a church organ.

De Wolf Hopper, already four times married, doted on pretty Elda. "To him I was a new audience. I was as fresh as an unhatched egg. He enjoyed the attention he got from his raw recruit, went all out to give a continuous performance." When she landed roles in two shows and toured the country, he wrote her ardently at every stop, and when she returned to New York, he met her at the station and immediately drove her to New Jersey to marry him. De Wolf was so much older than Elda's own father and such a notorious philanderer to boot that a friend of hers wept uncontrollably at news of the marriage. Meanwhile, he had such a difficult time distinguishing his new wife's name from those of his previous wives that Elda consulted a numerologist who, after much deliberation, dubbed her Hedda. Hedda said she hated it, but "I never heard him call me Ella, Ida, Edna, or Nellie again."

Thin and delicate where Parsons was round and thick, pretty where Parsons was snaggle-toothed and jowly, Hedda found work in movies and on the stage through the twenties and early thirties, but by the time she turned fifty in 1935, she was divorced and jobless with a child to support. Eleanor "Cissy" Patterson, an old friend and the publisher of the Washington *Herald,* suggested she write a weekly "letter from Hollywood," and Hedda eagerly seized the chance. She lost the column in an economy move, but in 1937, on the recommendation of a publicist at MGM who claimed that Hopper seemed to have the best intelligence network in the film community, the Esquire Feature Syndicate signed her for a new Hollywood column. When the Los Angeles *Times* picked it up early in 1938, Parsons for the first time had real competition.

There were those who believed that Hedda Hopper had been energetically, if secretly, promoted by the studios as a way of balancing Parsons's power and keeping her in check. If so, Hopper eventually proved less compliant than Parsons and drove her into being less manageable too. Together the two guarded their domains, terrorizing stars, demanding scoops, punishing those who wouldn't provide them and creating a terrible dilemma for the unfortunates who wanted to stay in the good graces of both. "[H]alf the movie colony has gone schizophrenic handling those two old bags," Errol Flynn allegedly complained once. "You've got to please one without alienating the other!"

But however much they loathed each other, Louella Parsons and Hedda Hopper were really very much alike. They were both conservative, prudish, narrow-minded small-town women in an essentially conservative and prudish community, and they used their gossip as a club to keep celebrities in line rather than as a needle to make celebrities scream. This was also one reason why Parsons and Hopper never had anywhere near the impact that Winchell had, even though their names became almost as well known as his. Winchell took on the world. As members of the establishment, Parsons and Hopper, like two biddy schoolmistresses, always fought to conserve the old order until the world passed them by.

V

One night in 1936 or 1937, after one of his broadcasts, Walter was being served at his customary table in the Stork Club when he announced to his tablemates that he was now, according to his accountant, a millionaire. In all likelihood, as Walter liked to boast, no working journalist made more money. His new contract with Jergens, signed in June 1937, raised his salary from $2,500 to $4,000 per broadcast with another $1,000 added per broadcast when the option was exercised in May 1938. One publication estimated his 1937 earnings at roughly $300,000 and "maybe a lot more." His actual earnings that year, at least as he reported them to the Internal Revenue Service, were $362,145, including his Fox income, but even without Fox, he earned $302,473 in 1938 and $358,467 in 1939.

Taxes were his new bugaboo. He complained in *The New York Times* that he paid $83,000 in taxes in 1936 while financier Andrew Mellon escaped unscathed with refunds. The next year Fox Movietone asked him to narrate the domestic portion of its newsreels with Lowell Thomas narrating the international portion. It set a fee of $500. "I was on the verge of doing it," Walter wrote *Variety's* Abel Green, "when my tax accountant told me that out of the $25,000 I would be allowed to keep about $6400, so the hell with it." But even Walter saw the irony. "It's a far cry, isn't it, Abel, from the days of hustling around trying to sell ads for 'Vaudeville News' to get enough money to pay Billy LaHiff the rent to turning down $25,000 because I would only get $6400 out of it."

There were, of course, other measures of Winchell's success than the money he earned. On July 11, 1938, he made the cover of *Time* magazine. It had been, said *Time*, Walter's best year. "He had never before been so fully seen, heard, read or paid. And having progressed from a scandal to a national institution, the Winchell story had become more fabulous than any that even he had ever told."

As the center of so much attention, it was hard for Walter not to be full of himself, and he didn't resist the temptation now. He talked incessantly and always about himself. Ben Bernie joked that Walter "seems disconsolate. It seems the letter 'I' on his typewriter has become disabled!!!" And Bernie added that "[e]very time Winchell stops reading his own column, it disrupts one of the great romances of all time." One night at the Stork, Oscar Levant approached Walter and Al Jolson, another noted egotist, and asked, "May a simple egomaniac join you?" Walter's own excuses for his being such a "conceited lugg," he wrote in the column, were that he crowed "[t]o annoy people who don't like us" and "[b]ecause we are madly in love with ourself. . . ."

"Winchell is a great bore and vanity of all vanities," Clifford Odets told his diary after he had sat in the Stork and listened to Walter's out-pourings. Running into him on the street a week later, Odets said Walter "spoke broadly and grandly of his money, of the problems concerning it, how he is worried about another run on the banks." And Odets wondered as he listened, "how a human being could have so little sense of other human beings." After one half-hour talkfest with Walter, George Jean Nathan was asked what it was he had said. "He said in several thousand words how wonderful it was to be Winchell."

To BE Walter Winchell, yes. But to be the man *playing* Walter Winchell was something else. Though clearly one of the most famous personalities in America, he was nevertheless a man apart and alone rattling around within his persona. His life resembled the column he wrote; as the column was assembled from scraps with Walter as the unifying force, so his life was assembled from superficial acquaintanceships. Klurfeld remarked on how "compartmentalized" Walter's life was, how consciously he kept any one of his friends or subordinates from knowing any of the others, almost as if he feared their knowing too much or feared that they might conspire against him.

In truth, there were very few real friends and no socializing save the professional socializing he did at the Stork, and what passed for friendship was always provisional and easily withdrawn. When Leonard Lyons mentioned in his column that Jack Haley's voice in *Wake Up and Live* had been dubbed by a singer named Buddy Clark of the "Lucky Strike Hit Parade," Walter saw it as perfidy and wired Rose with a disquisition on friendship. TELL LYONS I DIDN'T THINK OR SUSPECT IT WAS NECESSARY TO BE AFRAID THAT SO CLOSE A FRIEND AS HE WOULD DO ANYTHING IN ANY WAY THAT MIGHT RETARD OR HURT OR MAR THE FIRST MOVING PICTURE I WAS IN. TELL LYONS I'M ACCUSTOMED TO THIS STOP MY ENEMIES NEVER HURT ME STOP ASK HIM PLEASE I'M VERY CURIOUS TO FIND OUT DID HE THINK HE WAS SCOOPING ME ON SOMETHING I DID NOT KNOW? THAT IS THE IMPRESSION HE PROBABLY GAVE TO A FEW PEOPLE IN LINDY'S OR MAYBE IT WAS A FEW HUNDRED PEOPLE STOP. And Walter insisted that Rose read the telegram to Lyons. "I'm tired of my intimates annoying me and I am tired of having to worry about reminding them to do something or not do something."

Lyons seethed, writing and then tearing up three letters before finally calming himself enough to send one. As for the charge that Walter's friends were his real worry, Lyons sneered: "Mister, I'm almost tempted to believe that you're getting to believe those stale platitudes you stick into your column about pat on the back room for the knife junk. . . . It's funny, but where I come from, we never philosophized about friendship. We either believed or didn't. . . . If I were a real pal of Winchell's, I'd show it just like his other real pals do—by becoming a parasitic sycophant, taking dough from stars to get their names into Winchell's column, and bleeding a living out of them." He closed: "Of all the people you know and have known, I am the only one who has never asked for money, a job, or favor. Mull over that."

But Walter *did* believe, had always believed, the platitudes in his column about the unreliability of friends, and for precisely the reason Lyons stated. He knew that his life was really a series of transactions, of giving and taking. Everyone wanted something: everyone. That was the only reason people were nice to him; if he lost the column and broadcast, he knew he would lose their friendship.

And it was scarcely different with his own family. His father appeared largely to collect his allowance and some old suits Walter handed down. His brother, Algernon, had come to suspect that his wife, a would-be singer, had married him only to get to Walter. Desperate for Walter to help her, he waited for his brother one evening and then slid into the cab with him and spent the ride pleading. When the cab stopped, as Algernon bitterly recounted it to the family, Walter groused, "Oh, for goodness sakes! What are you bothering me with this for?" "I understand you're worth over a million dollars," one of Walter's companions remembers another relative shouting as Walter left the studio. And Walter shot back, "That's true, and I'm going to keep it."

Against all the parasites and traitors, there was only June. Walter trusted her, relied upon her taste and judgment, loved her. Each evening he phoned her three or four times to report his latest adventure, never considering that he might be waking her. And June, while not uncomplaining about Walter, clearly loved and admired him as much now as in the beginning. Yet it was love largely in the abstract. He was gone most of the time, including weekends when he prepared for the broadcast, and when he was home, he was either sleeping or composing the column. To reporters who wondered why June eschewed public places, Walter answered revealingly, "Mrs. Winchell is seen in them whenever I can get up the time to take her out."

The physical distance between them grew even greater after October 1938, when Walter bought a twelve-acre estate in Greenburgh, a lush, tree-lined community in Westchester County, separated from the posher community of Scarsdale by the Bronx River Parkway. In the eighteenth century the property had been part of a huge estate called Phillipsburg Manor. By the turn of the twentieth century it had become a farm. During the Depression it had evidently fallen on hard times or had been foreclosed. Walter bought it from the town for the paltry sum of $2,200 and called it "Twelve Acres."

The name fitted what it was: a secluded, pastoral estate surrounded by shaggy forest. The stick of the Popsicle-shaped plot rested on Fort Hill Road, a quiet lane along a bluff set well back from the main street below. A driveway curved gently from the gate to the mansion. Tall trees shaded the way. At the end of the driveway sat a spacious three-story white clap-board colonial house with green shutters—an oversized monument to Rockwellian domesticity. A canopy supported by two stout columns sheltered the doorway, and above the entrance was carved a sun, its rays extending in radiating warmth. Three tall stone chimneys rose out of a roof of long sloping shingles, and a large deck jutted from the third-story in the rear. Out front was a greensward with an elm and a half-buried boulder. Out back another lawn sloped to the woods. On the right, among the trees, was a swimming pool, on the left a carriage house.

Inside, the house was comfortable, if modest. On the ground floor were a den, a garden room and a large, sparsely furnished living room, though Walter and June never entertained. On the third floor, to dissuade kidnappers, were the children's rooms. On the second floor, at the head of the stairs to the left, were June's room and, to the right, Walter's. June had it decorated especially for him with an enormous custom-made bed, which his daughter-in-law described as "two mattresses and a board across."

Walter's room commanded a view of the property, looking to the right over the apple trees to the swimming pool and the woods and swamp beyond and to the left down toward the gate. "When you were in that room you were looking down on everything," his daughter-in-law remembered, summoning the "serenity that I felt there and the simplicity. There was nothing fancy. No luxuries." And she remembered that Walter always had the shades drawn. In effect, it was his cocoon, separate from the rest of the world, separate even from June.

June admitted in a rare interview that she had bought the house with "considerable misgivings." She wanted to raise the children outside the city, but she realized that Walter was an urban creature who abhorred the country. After a long deliberation June said he answered "the way he always does when the question of spending huge sums of money comes up: 'I don't care, darling,' he said. 'It's all yours. Do what you want with it.' " Even so, for weeks after the move, Walter remained in the city, unable to transform himself into a country gentleman.

Soon, though, he began commuting, driving up to Twelve Acres at dawn to sleep, then driving back into the city in the afternoon for the column and his rounds. It was an effort, physically and emotionally, and in the end he couldn't keep it up. Twelve Acres was never really his home. "I bought a farm for June and the kids," he tellingly wrote his friend Art Arthur. To Klurfeld he complained jokingly about noisy birds, as he had on an earlier foray into the country. And there was, despite an electrified fence he had built around the property, always the problem of trespassers who wanted a look at him.

Not long after the move, he took an apartment in the St. Moritz Hotel at Central Park South and Sixth Avenue in Manhattan and gradually reduced his commutes from nightly to two or three times a week. But it was more the lure of Manhattan than the disturbances of Greenburgh that determined his residency. "For him the roses grow and fade on the streets of New York," wrote Jim Tully. "The buzz of voices—'There's Walter Winchell'—is part of his life."

June had long since made the adjustment to her husband's absences and incorporated them into their relationship. The ones who suffered were Walda and Walt, Jr., whom everyone called Boy. One friend of Walda's got the impression that Walter was "sort of a visitor when she was a child." It was no different with Walt, Jr. His wife, Eva, said her husband always remembered asking his father to take him to a ballgame and Walter, Sr., snapping at June, "Why do I want to go with a little kid to the ballgame?"

Even if there hadn't been the absences and the neglect, Walter's schedule, with his three-month winter vacations in Miami and his two-month summer vacations in California, would have still wreaked havoc on the children, especially with their schooling. Walda was never able to accommodate herself, became a lackadaisical student and was finally sent away to boarding school. Walt, Jr., begged his parents not to send him away to school, but when he was six, they packed him off to a military academy in Pennsylvania where the Hearst boys went. Later he ran away from school and returned home only when Walda had mediated. After that he attended the local school in Greenburgh, where a librarian remembered his bringing in a birthday cake. "Is it your birthday today?" she asked. Walt said no, it was his father's birthday, and his father wanted everyone to have a piece of cake.

And so June and the children holed up at the fortress in the woods of Greenburgh. And Walter holed up at his penthouse apartment in the St. Moritz, basically alone except for his nightly rounds. Herman Klurfeld thought he might even have preferred it that way, that he was basically shy. Occasionally, on Thursday nights, when Klurfeld delivered his broadcast material, Walter would invite him up to the apartment. These were among the rare times when Walter seemed absolutely relaxed. Sometimes they took naps, Walter in one room, Klurfeld in another.

Sometimes Walter even prepared dinner, a pot roast with canned fruit cocktail. And in these lonely but serene moments, the power and the wariness and the cynicism all disappeared, and with them "Walter Winchell."

WE LOVE YOU AND ALREADY MISS YOU. BOY HAS ASKED FOR YOU MANY TIMES, June wired Walter as she headed back to New York on New Year's Eve 1938 while Walter remained in Miami. NINETEEN-THIRTY-EIGHT HAS BEEN A VERY GOOD YEAR FOR US DARLING AND MY HOPE IS THAT THIRTY-NINE WILL BRING AS MUCH HAPPINESS FOR ALL OF US. For Americans generally, 1938 had held out promise. It was the first year since the crash that hinted at recovery, and Walter cheerfully reported at Easter that the "biggest bankers of New York and elsewhere in these United States are most optimistic about the immediate future," citing the recent stability in Europe with the winding down of the Spanish Civil War, the truce between Britain and Italy, the rightward drift of France and internal distractions within the Soviet Union that seemed to foreclose external adventurism.

One of the most conspicuous beneficiaries of the small economic uptick seemed to be café society. Though it had hummed obliviously throughout the lean years, in 1938 it seemed to reach an apotheosis. Debutantes like Cobina Wright and Brenda Frazier were suddenly household names, their faces adorning magazine covers as their exploits filled the columns. The clubs seemed brighter, gayer, louder, the sense of privilege more palpable than before. A Cleveland reporter making his first visit to the Stork found it "as soothing as a nightmare, and as quiet as the monkey house when the bananas are being served.... The moment you've hocked your hat in the mirrored outer lobby, you step into a blaze of flash bulbs and movie flood lamps."

Part of the revivification of the nightclubs was the socialites' growing reliance on the clubs as status became a function of being seen in the right places at the right time by the right people in order to get more publicity. "Not to be able to get a table at El Morocco was a terrible blow to people's egos," said Jerome Zerbe, who was El Morocco's resident photographer and an arbiter of society in his own right. "Grown men would break down with frustration at failing to catch the eye of Carino, the maître d'." At the Stork a "debutante disbarred from the inner sanctum will move heaven and earth to be reinstated," reported *The New York Times*. "[P]eople must come to the Stork if they would consider themselves bona fide participants in the absurd drama of Gotham night life," said an article in *Pic* magazine. "The Stork is more than an institution. It is a religion."

To the uninitiated, the outsiders, it may have seemed like a single constellation of wealth and glamour, but neither John Perona, who presided over El Morocco, nor Sherman Billingsley who presided over the Stork Club, appreciated his establishment's being lumped with the other, and habitués of each assiduously enumerated the differences. The Stork was larger, seating one thousand, while El Morocco seated fewer than half that number in its distinctive zebra-striped banquettes. The Stork was open for lunch, El Morocco only for dinner. The Stork had a gold chain restraining would-be customers, El Morocco a velvet rope. At the Stork Billingsley gave gifts to favored patrons; at El Morocco Perona said gifts would "embarrass the customers." The Stork was noisy with what one patron described as "elegant din," El Morocco subdued. The Stork attracted the young socialites and rising young entertainers, El Morocco the remnants of the Old Guard of society and established stars. Ernest Cuneo, a Stork partisan, called it the "racetrack and the showplace of the Meritocracy" and El Morocco "the base of the idle, untalented rich," while Jerome Zerbe, a partisan of El Morocco, crystallized the difference as "one had class and the other didn't."

But the biggest difference between them may have been that while El Morocco was home to Cholly Knickerbocker, the high priest of high society, and to New York *Herald* café columnist Lucius Beebe, widely regarded as the best-dressed man in New York and the very image of urbanity, the Stork, as everyone knew, had Walter Winchell. And not only was this a symbolic difference, but it helped explain the difference in ambience. Walter generated the buzz at the Stork and attracted the celebrities eager for his benediction. "Is Walter there?" George Jessel asked Klurfeld as they were about to enter the Stork one evening. When Klurfeld said he wasn't, Jessel shrugged, "Well, I'm not going in."

YOU AND YOU ALONE ARE THE STORK'S SANTA, Billingsley wired Walter one Christmas. THE THRILL THAT LITTLE KIDS GET ONCE A YEAR FROM SANTA'S LEGENDARY APPEARANCE DOWN THE CHIMNEY IS MINE EVERY TIME YOU PUT IN AN APPEARANCE AT THE CLUB AND FREQUENTLY WHEN YOU GLORIFY THE PLACE IN YOUR COLUMN STOP I KNOW OF NO WAY TO EFFECTIVELY SHOW MY APPRECIATION STOP YOUR PERSONALITY IS SO GREAT YOUR POWER SO POTENT AND YOUR EARTHLY POSSESSIONS ARE SO COMPLETE THAT I CANNOT ATTEMPT TO ADD TO THEM BY ANY MERE GIFT.

Nevertheless, Billingsley did shower Walter with gifts, favors and attention. Walter never picked up a tab at the club. Headwaiter Jack Spooner personally supervised the preparation of his meals, and one of his favorite entrées was memorialized on the menu as "Chicken A La Walter Winchell." When Walter complained that the noise in the room was too loud, Billingsley built a glass partition between Walter and the band. When Walter wanted a place to shave, Billingsley installed a private barbershop on the second floor. He screened petitioners for Walter, took calls for Walter, handled mail for Walter, gave Stork Club neckties by the caseload to Walter and sent Walter gift certificates for $350 suits at Knize's, an expensive clothier on 56th Street.

They were an odd pair, Winchell and Billingsley, these two arbiters of the elites. Walter was loud, logorrheic, gregarious, defiant, egocentric, stingy, democratic but commanding. Billingsley was subdued, laconic, diffident, submissive, self-effacing, generous, snobbish but servile. Walter was the cynosure of the Stork. Billingsley hovered on the sidelines, quietly circulating among the patrons and smoothly orchestrating the operation through a series of nearly imperceptible hand signals: playing with his tie to indicate that a complimentary bottle of wine should be brought to the table; toying with his pocket handkerchief to indicate that there would be no bill; running his hand through his hair to indicate that he wanted to be relieved from having to talk to the bores at that table. One reporter compared watching him to watching Admiral David Farragut on the bridge, "the orders quickly and quietly issued, the ship held steady on its course through the night."

Billingsley's quiet management of the Stork, like Walter's noisy commandeering of it, revealed the essential man. To many, he was an enigma and a contradiction. The city's most famous host, he was secretly resentful of having to drink and chat with his guests. "The world is full of drinkers who will come and spend money in your joint if they can have a slice of your ass," he told a friend. He told another, "What counts most to the people who come in here is how other people feel about 'em. They already have the money. With most of 'em now, it's just a question of how much and how often they get their asses kissed—when you get down to the bare-ass facts!" Though an Oklahoma farmboy and ex-convict, he succeeded ironically, according to another patron, "by selling the assumption that everyone was not equal." Once he even put out a casting call requiring that the applicants be listed in the *Social Register.* "If they get tossed out of the Social Register, they get tossed out of the Stork Club too."

If any of the café socialites saw the irony of their being judged by an uneducated former prizefighter (Perona of El Morocco) or a bootlegging ex-convict (Billingsley at the Stork) or a onetime second-rate vaudevillian, they certainly didn't voice it. And in a sense these roughhewn outsiders may have been the most apt monitors of cafe society. Like Damon Runyon, who fantasized about New York as only a non-native could, Billingsley fantasized about café society as only a poor boy could, and he held it to stricter rules of conduct and higher standards of glamour than any to which it would ever have held itself. He barred Jackie Gleason for boisterousness, Humphrey Bogart for fighting, Milton Berle for shouting greetings to celebrities whether he knew them personally or not and later Frank Sinatra for the associates he brought with him. When he thought a young press agent was table-hopping, Billingsley barred him too until Walter came to the man's defense by pointing out the hypocrisy of admitting rich press agents but not poor ones.

For both proprietor and patron, it was a world in which appearances counted for everything. "A Storker must be at least five feet five inches tall," advised an article in the liberal newspaper *PM* on how a commoner might become a Stork Clubber. "It is preferable to have blonde hair held with a little bow (this year) or covered with a large brimmed hat, turned up in front. Most Storkers wear black. They all wear very short tight dresses and very high heels. In winter they wear fox coats. They don't wear much jewelry because they know it would detract from their faces and figures." There was even an appropriate expression for the Stork: impassive with glazed eyes staring straight ahead.

While all this may have been the fulfillment of a fantasy for Billingsley, a perfect world of his own devising, it was no less a fantasy for Winchell, albeit of a different sort. At the Stork Walter wasn't fashioning a world of celebrity; he was mastering it. He entered the club "like a conquering Caesar entering Rome," wrote one who observed it. He went past the long bar near the entrance and then down a short hallway, but rather than enter the main room beyond, where what he called the "civilians" dined, he turned left into a much smaller room, where a captain barred the way to all but the exalted few.

This was the sanctum sanctorum of the Stork Club: the Cub Room. A patron called it a "Kremlin for those with blue noses, white ermines, striped trousers, and checkered lives." It was a small rectangular room, its undulating walls hugged by banquettes with tables sparingly placed down the center. The decor changed frequently. One period there was a leaf-and-vine pattern on the upholstery, another period it was unpatterned; one period the banquettes were leather, another period velvet; one period the walls were covered by illustrations of beautiful women in the James Montgomery Flagg style, another period by mirrors; one period the dominant color was burgundy, another black. The only constants seemed to be the squat black decanters and black ashtrays, both emblazoned with the Stork Club logo of a monocled, top-hatted bird—Billingsley placed these strategically on each table so that photos in the club always publicized it the way the zebra-stipped upholstery always publicized the rival El Morocco—and Walter Winchell.

Walter usually sat at Table 50, just to the left of the entrance. "You'd go into the Cub Room," remembered David Brown. "As you walked in, you would turn right, and to your immediate left would be Walter Winchell at a table that could easily accommodate six.... If he deigned to wave or something, you'd go over to shake his hand. If he ignored you, you wouldn't go near him because he'd be very rude." For most celebrities—and the celebrities included not only entertainers and social-ites but artists and political figures and athletes and business magnates and even royals—a visit to Table 50 and an audience with Winchell were obligatory. For if the Stork Club was the grand palace of café society and the Cub Room the sanctum sanctorum of the Stork, Table 50 was its throne and hence the seat of café society itself.

Sometimes Winchell sat with his back to the entrance, knowing who entered by seignorially watching a mirror above the banquettes. As al-ways, he talked—talked without stopping—expecting his auditors to sit attentively and fixing them with a deadly stare, demanding to know where they were going, should they get up during one of his monologues. (He called it his "superior look.") "He talked through you," said Ethel Merman. He talked about his adventures, accomplishments, illustrious acquaintances, predictions. He talked because he knew people had to lis-ten. And the celebrities listened not only because no one wanted to of-fend him but because they were relieved at not having to say anything themselves. "[T]here was always the danger," wrote Merman, "that he would misconstrue or even distort the meaning in some embarrassing way."

When he wasn't holding court, he was eating; he loved the food at the Stork. When he wasn't eating or holding court, he was on the phone; he fielded as many as fifty calls in an evening. When he wasn't talking, eat-ing or taking calls, he might venture out onto the dance floor in the main room. "In his prime, I saw him do a double rhumba samba with June Havoc one night at the Stork which cleared the floor," wrote Ernest Cuneo. "They were great, like a pair of flamenco dancers with winged feet, and they brought down the house." Whatever he did, he left no doubt that *he* was the sovereign here: an outsider lording it over the in-siders. That was the symbolism of Table 50, and everyone who read his column knew it.

Yet far from resenting him, many of the Clubbers, particularly the so-cialites whose lives consisted of little more than nightclubbing, found in Winchell's column the only validation they were ever to get. Remem-bered one Clubber thirty years later:

In the pre-war days around the Stork Winchell was the most exciting man in the world to us. When I first began dating the man I later married, Winchell said we were "closerthanthis." When we married he called it "a slight case of merger," and when I became pregnant he said we were "infanticipating." When the baby arrived, he noted that we had joined "the mom and population."

When the marriage soured, WW told the world we had "the Mister and Miseries" which quickly developed into "the apartache" which led to our "sharing separate teepees." It was only a matter of time until we "Renovated" and disappeared from the column as though we had never existed.

Strange as it sounds now, we got a tremendous kick out of it at the time. It made us feel very important to rate a mention in Winchell and our friends envied us. I still have those columns someplace, probably stacked away with my daughter's baby shoes, our wedding license and my divorce decree. It all seems like something that happened in another country.

VI

Café society may have found meaning in Winchell's notices, but Walter's command over the socialites and celebrities was also an expression of his contempt for them.

Easily bored, he was now increasingly uninterested in celebrity chitchat. "My interests are growing," he told one interviewer in 1938. "I don't care who phffts on Broadway, but if Hitler and Mussolini phfft, that's news." Another acquaintance remembered Walter's banging his fist on the table at Lindy's one night and declaring, "Lots of important things are happening today. I'm going to talk about them." It was shortly after that announcement in 1938 that he added a new editorial segment to his broadcast; it was to be the single longest portion of the program and the one that decisively tilted it away from gossip toward news and commentary.

In doing so, he was riding a journalistic wave. Editorial pages had been steadily declining in influence over the decade, many of them discredited in readers' eyes by fierce opposition to Roosevelt. In their place had sprung a host of syndicated political columnists who provided new guideposts for readers in a complicated world. "I have said in all seriousness that a widely syndicated writer has far more political power than any Senator," observed Heywood Broun in an article in *The New Republic* in 1938. "As things stand, America is very largely governed by a little writing oligarchy that is higher than the upper House." And whatever power a widely syndicated columnist might have wielded, how much more power · accrued to a political pundit like Winchell whose audience was decisively larger than that of any other commentator.

A survey conducted for *Fortune* magazine in 1939 showed that the readership of syndicated columns had increased 5 percent over 1937 and that of the 35.8 percent of the respondents who read columns regularly, Walter's was by far the favorite. He led in all parts of the country and with all professions but retirees, executives and farmers. He also led in all but the top two income groups. Moreover, his column was being syndicated to papers with an aggregate daily circulation of nearly 9 million and an aggregate Sunday circulation of just under 6.5 million. And this didn't factor in the broadcast, which Walter claimed had an estimated audience of 25 million at the time.

With these millions came influence. Washington columnist Drew Pearson wrote that Walter had "emerged as such an expert on national affairs that Washington officialdom watches his columns constantly. He has become one of the most powerful liberal forces of the country." What Pearson didn't say was that Walter was increasingly becoming a part of Washington officialdom as well as a commentator on it—a willing instrument of administration policy that could both flog the President's positions and thrash his enemies in a way that would have been unseemly for the policymakers themselves.

Like the movie studios, each of which had a publicist assigned to serve him, the White House established liaisons who would feed Walter inside information, discuss policy and suggest approaches to issues. "What Winchell did for FDR," Cuneo later wrote, "was translate his official acts into the American language, to take government jargon and make it understandable in terms of the American argot." Cuneo cited the case of eighty Arkansas families who were washed out in a flash flood. One government department furnished routine disaster aid. "Winchell accurately and dramatically translated it: 'The White House, Washington. The President ordered the full resources of the United States government placed at the disposal of eighty stricken families washed out in Arkansas. Food and medicine are already on the roads. Hold on [,] Arkansas! Your President is with you.' "

Close observers might have even noticed a change in the personal relationship between Winchell and Roosevelt from Walter's first visit to the White House in 1933, when he was quickly hustled out of the office, to his visit on May 10, 1938, after he had virtually become part of the Roosevelt team. The one-day trip—ostensibly for Walter to judge a local beauty contest after he had reported a comment by a recent visitor that Washington had no beautiful women—was treated like a grand event by the press and politicians. The Washington *Times* assigned eight writers to record Walter's activities on its front page, and Drew Pearson, Democratic Party Chairman James Farley, Senator Gerald Nye and J. Edgar Hoover, among others, attended a luncheon in his honor. Then, at four o'clock that afternoon, he and Walda visited the President. The meeting, arranged by Earl Godwin, the president of the White House Correspondents Association, was scheduled to last five minutes following the President's press conference. It wound up lasting nearly forty-five minutes while others waited impatiently outside. Roosevelt's secretary "bounced in three times," according to *Newsweek*, "only to find that Roosevelt, not Winchell, was prolonging the conversation."

What disturbed some members of the more traditional press, however, was that Winchell was no more qualified to pontificate on political matters than he had been to report the news. Unlike Walter Lippmann, Dorothy Thompson, Boake Carter, David Lawrence and other sage political analysts, Walter was seen as simply a firebrand who had no cogent political philosophy save blind support of the President and J. Edgar Hoover. When it came to political abstractions, he delivered windy generalizations and empty patriotic bromides. He signed off one broadcast as "Walter Winchell . . . who is sure that America would be a better place to live in if all the people who didn't like it—would leave it—to the rest of us—who love it!" "I am not a communist nor am I a Fash-ist [*sic*]," he declared on another broadcast. "I am an American." "There is no room for any ism—except patriotism" was a frequently expressed sentiment.

While deeper political thinkers may have been dismayed by Winchell's simpleminded populist rhetoric, his combination of New Deal liberalism and flag-waving chauvinism clearly struck a chord with the public. He was never an Olympian, like so many of the other political analysts, standing coolly above the battle. He gained credibility because he always seemed to be in the middle of the battle and because, as he liked to say, "I took them all on." "Walter Winchell is the only prominent newspaper and radio commentator whose viewpoint is consistently that of the masses of Americans," praised *International Teamster,* the organ of the Teamsters' union. "The huge combinations of wealth and monopoly have silenced most of those who would speak for us. They have not silenced Winchell. Winchell speaks for the things most of us believe in. May he continue his crusade against his enemies, who are also our enemies."

By the late thirties, one of those enemies certainly seemed to be Winchell's own publisher, William Randolph Hearst. Though Hearst had been a progressive early in his career, his politics since had ridden a roller coaster. He reluctantly supported Herbert Hoover for the presidency in 1928, then broke with him in 1931, when Hoover refused to initiate a public works program to end the Depression. The next year he threw his support behind Roosevelt, helped Walter promote President's Day after the inauguration and on the first anniversary of the inauguration editorialized, "I personally think Mr. Roosevelt is a very great President and a very sincere patriot."

But over the next year, after a general strike in San Francisco in July 1934, Hearst suddenly became fixated on what he saw as a Communist threat to the country and began to believe that Roosevelt was encouraging it. "I think we will have to settle down to a consistent policy of opposition to this administration," he wrote one of his executives in April 1935. "There is little difference between the President's policy and the policy of Huey Long," the demagogic senator from Louisiana. His enmity toward Roosevelt only increased when the President pushed a "wealth tax" through Congress which Hearst described as "essentially Communism." By 1936 not only was Hearst attacking Roosevelt and supporting Republican presidential candidate Alf Landon, but in liberal and administration circles he was considered a dangerous fascist.

So long as Winchell wrote gossip, none of this mattered. Hearst didn't particularly like Walter, but he understood his value to the papers. "Winchell seems to satisfy the whims of the younger degeneration," he told Gauvreau. "It is typical of the times." He had even come to Walter's defense after the Jolson fisticuffs, when, Walter claimed, "my column was almost stopped temporarily," and again when a department store executive threatened to "have me put in a soup line" over something Walter had written about the man's marriage. As for Walter's attitude toward Hearst, he curried favor by promoting Hearst's mistress, Marion Davies, and Hearst's wife's favorite charity, the Milk Fund, often called him "Daddy," and didn't seem to hesitate to seek redress when he was annoyed by Hearst's minions.

Thanks to Hearst, Walter had, in fact, outlasted his antagonists at the *Mirror*. Gauvreau was summarily dismissed by Hearst when the editor took a trip to the Soviet Union and wrote a cautionary book that reviewers regarded as a satire of Hearst and that Hearst himself regarded as far too lenient toward the Communists he despised. (Hearst told Walter, however, that Gauvreau was fired "largely because of the way he treated you.") Brisbane didn't fare much better. The self-styled great man had come to the *Mirror* with a disdain for much of its content, including Winchell's column, and had brought an "icy atmosphere," according to one columnist who was asked why he couldn't write a comic strip instead. It didn't take long, however, for desperation to set in and for Brisbane to try to outscandalize the opposition in an effort to build circulation. "Under Brisbane's generalship," sniped Gauvreau, "the handling of legitimate news had become a farce."

But these efforts to boost readership failed, partly because Brisbane never fully grasped the connection between so-called trash, which he happily purveyed, and the subversive cosmology of the tabloid, which he feared. It was one thing for him to turn the paper into a receptacle of harmless effluvium, such as whether a prizefighter could defeat a gorilla, and quite another for him to challenge the prevailing social order, as Walter did. Brisbane never had much sympathy for the latter. When he began attacking Roosevelt for "soaking the rich," he revealed his true colors and betrayed his largely working-class readership. In the end the *Mirror*'s circulation remained far behind that of the *Daily News*, and Hearst bristled: "You are now getting out the worst newspaper in the United States." Brisbane raced to San Simeon, Hearst's palatial California estate, to plead his case. As the story went, when he got to the gate-keeper, Brisbane was told he was not expected. Thus ended Arthur Brisbane's stewardship of the *Mirror*.

Throughout Brisbane's tenure, even after Gauvreau's dimissal, Walter had wrestled with whether he should stay at the *Mirror* or sign on with another paper. On March 18, 1937, the day he returned from California after making *Wake Up and Live*, he wrote Hearst a long letter complaining that while he wanted to cover stories wherever they broke and had even been given instructions from Brisbane to do so, he was charged for expenses for any story he filed outside New York. He was especially unhappy at having to leave a taxi strike in Chicago that subsequently erupted into rioting. "I certainly think I should pay them [expenses] when I go away to make a moving picture and make all that money, but I am discouraged about taking Mr. Brisbane's counsel. Suppose another Hauptmann thing breaks somewhere? Shall I go? And who will pay the cost of that?"

Hearst responded paternally. "You have to be a little patient with folks," he advised Walter. "I would hate to be punished for every time I made a damned fool of Myself." He promised to "take care of the expense matter" and added, "Your 'future' is assured with us as long as you want it to be." The next week, just before Walter headed back to Hollywood to tend to June, Hearst revised his contract, underwriting his expenses and stipulating that if two individuals (probably Gauvreau and Kobler) "are employed by the Corporation in any capacity superior to the capacity of Winchell, and if in the opinion of Winchell, either of said parties harasses or annoys Winchell in any respect, Winchell shall have the right, at his option to terminate this agreement by giving two weeks' written notice. . . ."

Even with these new stipulations, by the late summer of 1937, his contract expiring, Walter was again agonizing over whether to re-up with Hearst. He was tired: of the constant bickering, of turning out seven columns a week, of having to justify himself. Ward Greene, the managing editor of Hearst's King Features syndicate, had gone to California early in September to discuss a renewal, but Walter hesitated, the sticking point reportedly being that he wanted to cut back to six columns a week. Two weeks later he succumbed, signing on for a $10,000-a-year increase and winning the reduction to six columns. The new contract was directly with the *Mirror* rather than with King Features, but as Walter explained it to Abel Green, "They are all the same family."

The hang-up, Walter told friends, had had less to do with specific clauses than with the fact that "I just dreaded signing any more contracts, not being sure what my plans were." A short time later he was fretting again over having signed it. "I told you I never should have signed that contract with the paper when I was out there," he wrote Art Arthur. "Remember how I stalled for months?" He had received another offer from a man "more eager to have me join him than ever," but his new contract with Hearst included a two-year option, so Walter was stuck.

The problems now, however, were political. Walter's plunge into political commentary coupled with his increasingly close association with Roosevelt irritated Hearst. Walter had written a letter to Jergens trying to allay fears that politics would harm the broadcast. "Controversy, as you know, brings circulation," he began.

> In radio it brings us more listeners. There will always be people who don't agree with us, no matter what we discuss. Today it appears to be European politics and domestic politics. Not long ago, during the Hauptmann case we had people opposed to us because we were frank about the trial. It seems I have always been in the middle of some controversy. I thrive on it. It seems only yesterday that my critics condemned me because I mentioned that people were getting divorced or having babies. Now it is usually someone who thinks I have insulted Franco, Hitler, Mussolini, Roosevelt, Landon or someone else.

Though a Republican, Jergens was tolerant. Hearst was not. "I must ask all columnists to keep off these highly controversial subjects," he wired Winchell after Walter had invited Lillian Hellman to write a guest column on the Spanish Civil War.

> You are engaged to do a Broadway gossip column. . . .
> [A]ny political columns, written in my papers will be American in spirit. Not alien. They will be democratic in character, not communist or fascist.

Furthermore, Walter, you are not a little boy, although you are acting like one.

As a matter of fact, you are old enough to know better.

But Walter did not desist. He was no longer merely a gossip columnist, and he wouldn't allow himself to be forced back into that hole. Meanwhile, the Hearsts steamed. At "21," a former speakeasy that had become a gathering place for the rich and powerful, early in March William Randolph Hearst, Jr., had cornered Walter and reprimanded him for mentioning the *March of Time* newsreels that Hearst, Sr., detested. Junior said he was going to draft a memo ordering Walter to eliminate the references. Walter told him not to bother. "I'm fed up with all the things I mustn't put in the column!" he sneered, then walked away while another Hearst executive begged him to stay.

"We may as well face it," Junior wrote his father a few days after the incident. "We no longer have a first-rate Broadway columnist in Winchell. His main interests apparently lie in international, social, and religious problems. He is, so I am told, getting increasingly hard to handle, and continually threatening to quit." A few weeks later Hearst, Sr., wrote back, "I agree with you entirely about Winchell. In fact, the next time he wants to quit, please let me know so you can accept the resignation."

On March 28, two weeks after Hitler's annexation of Austria, Walter's column contained three long paragraphs blasting foreign dictators. The same day Hearst drafted a memo to "Editors of All Hearst Newspapers Using Winchell." "Please edit Winchell very carefully and leave out any dangerous or disagreeable paragraphs," it said. "Indeed, leave out the whole column without hesitation, as I think he has gotten so careless that he is no longer of any particular value."

The same day, Walter wrote Joseph Medill Patterson, the publisher of the *Daily News*, on the pretext of asking for information about a new Broadway column the paper was said to be considering, but Walter included a status report. "I expect to be fired any day by Mr. Hearst for mentioning the Daily News by name," he said, knowing full well that the tension with Hearst had nothing to do with the *Daily News*. Within days, rumors were circulating that Walter had met with Patterson and would be leaving the *Mirror*. Walter himself said only that he had paused to say hello to Patterson during lunch one day, but he made a point of sending Patterson a telegram two days after his first letter, this time congratulating the publisher for an editorial supporting asylum for oppressed people.

Meanwhile, Walter's position with Hearst hardened. "My opinions are not for sale," he told his radio listeners on April 3. "I mean that I do not repeat, echo or parrot the opinions of my employers." Four days later he confronted Hearst directly about the memo. "You say that the Winchell column has become dangerous and careless and that all of your editors can omit it without the slightest hesitation," Walter snarled, saying that his editors had been instructed to tell him that the edict was issued after he had run an item about how the "Amos 'n' Andy" radio program had boosted sales for its sponsor and Hearst thought the item a dig at newspaper advertising. Walter knew this was idiotic. As for the column's danger, he said he trusted that Hearst knew the column was examined by five of his top editors with "magnifying glasses" before it was published.

Now rumors of the Hearst-Winchell feud were circulating everywhere. *Newsweek* reported that Hearst was going to retire Walter to an executive position until his contract expired but that Walter's contract stipulated he be published regularly in a New York paper. *Variety* wrote that Walter's contract wasn't up until 1939 but that he was already negotiating with the Chicago *Tribune*–New York *Daily News* syndicate. *Ken* magazine ran the Hearst memo that May with criticism of Hearst, and in September the *Mirror* even ran an editorial with a simile implicitly criticizing Walter: "[H]e had as much trouble explaining how those things happened as Mr. Winchell would have in explaining why he soared above Broadway into international problems."

It was now open warfare, but neither combatant wanted to drop the bomb. Walter was a very valuable franchise for Hearst, however much he may have antagonized Hearst personally. Without Winchell there was virtually no chance of ever catching the *Daily News*, and syndication only increased his value. Walter could always have gotten another job, yet he too was seized by fear. "What if I lose my column?" he wrote in a note to himself at the time. "Then I'm no different than the loudmouth in the bar. The man who sells papers on the corner may have a more secure future." So Hearst kept Winchell even while he continued to clip his wings, and Walter stayed even while he chafed and complained—two men locked in an uneasy embrace of commerce and power.

VII

When the manhunt for Louis "Lepke" Buchalter began, J. Edgar Hoover called him "the most dangerous criminal in the United States," and New York Special Prosecutor Thomas Dewey said he was "the worst industrial racketeer in America." Buchalter was said to have been responsible for seventy killings and to have extorted between five and ten million dollars each year for a decade from labor and industry. At forty-two, the same age as Walter, he hardly looked like a killer. He was short, basset-eyed, dimpled, modest and temperate in his tastes, if not his actions; in gang circles he was known as the Judge. He had been born in New York, then abandoned at age thirteen with his older sister when his widowed mother moved west. He spent his adolescence in reformatories and in prison for burglaries, then became a strikebreaker and finally crossed the line to join the unions. In time he controlled them, once demonstrating his power by murdering a recalcitrant union leader in front of thirteen witnesses during an arbitration hearing. His nickname, Lepke, meant "butcher" in Yiddish.

Angling for the Republican presidential nomination, Dewey was determined to jail Buchalter and placed a $25,000 bounty on his head. Not to be outdone, United States Attorney General Frank Murphy offered another $25,000. Twenty New York detectives were assigned to the case. In midsummer 1937, with the pressure on him mounting, Lepke went underground, growing a mustache as a disguise and directing his rackets from a Coney Island dance hall, then a Flatbush apartment, and finally a basement flat in an Italian section of Brooklyn, where he posed as the invalid husband of a Mrs. Walker.

For twenty-one months he eluded both local and federal authorities, but by the summer of 1939 his own associates were urging him to turn himself in. By one account, Hoover had threatened mob heads Joey Adonis and Frank Costello that unless Lepke surrendered, the FBI would arrest every suspected Italian gangster in the country. Others close to the investigation claimed that Dewey had so disrupted the mob that mob leaders had no choice but to ask Lepke to surrender. Now the question was how.

On August 5, 1939, Walter received a phone call, presumably at the Stork.* "Don't ask me who I am," said the caller. "I have something important to tell you. Lepke wants to come in. If he could find someone he can trust, he will give himself up to that person. The talk around town is that Lepke would be shot while supposedly escaping." Walter asked, "Does he trust me?" The contact said he would find out. As Walter later told it, when he was contacted next and informed he was trusted, he offered to phone Hoover to get assurance that Lepke's constitutional rights would be protected. According to Ernie Cuneo, Walter phoned him immediately at Normandy Farms, where Cuneo was dining with a pretty girl, and asked if Lepke was wanted by the federal authorities. Cuneo phoned Attorney General Murphy, who then phoned Hoover out in

*In his autobiography, he recounts the same conversation, only this time he places it on Broadway near Lindy's and in the mouth of a man "on the fringe of gangdom."

Iowa, where he was attending the funeral of the father of his deputy, Clyde Tolson. Hoover became "excited" at the prospect of getting Lepke, who, he said, was indeed wanted on a federal drug charge.

For Hoover, the opportunity to capture Lepke was largely an opportunity to best Dewey, whom he hated. (Dewey had a much better claim on the criminal: potential murder charges.) Hoover and Tolson rushed to New York after the funeral. In the meantime, Walter received a midnight call asking him to broadcast that Hoover would guarantee Lepke's safety. The two FBI officials were sitting next to Walter during his program the next evening, August 6. "Your reporter is reliably informed—that 'Lepke,' the fugitive, is on the verge of surrender, perhaps this week," Walter reported in unusually slow tempo. "If Lepke can find someone he can trust (I am told) he will come in . . . I am authorized to state by the G-Men—that Lepke is assured of safe delivery . . . He may contact me (at the N.Y. Daily *Mirror*)—or John Edgar Hoover (in charge of the search for several years) in Washington at National 7117 . . . No part of the $35,999 reward to be claimed by me."

Now began a long series of feints and dodges. Each night for the next three weeks Walter received a call at the Stork from mysterious go-betweens suggesting a "meet" but telling him to await further instructions. Finally, late one night, a caller asked if Walter had his car with the "four lamps," meaning his car with fog lights. Walter explained that he had left the car with his wife in Greenburgh, but the caller advised he go get it—"That's the one we recognize," he said—then drive through the Holland Tunnel, make an immediate left and then a right at the second light. Billingsley drove Walter out to Twelve Acres to get the car. June, who happened to be awake reading a book when Walter unexpectedly arrived, was terrified that something might happen to him. Later she told him she had grabbed a box of thumbtacks from the kitchen and spilled them under the wheels of the car, hoping for a blowout.

Walter reached the designated spot, a deserted swampland, at 3:30 A.M. For fifteen minutes he drove slowly, trolling for his contact, then suddenly got spooked, thinking that this might be a setup by the Nazis, and sped back to Manhattan. It had apparently been a test to see if Walter had been tailed. The next night he got another call at the Stork from still another caller, this one directing him to an assignation at a bar and grill a half mile from the George Washington Bridge in upper Manhattan. At the bar Walter was greeted by a man who escorted him to an automobile. "Ask your friend the G-man what the possible sentence will be if the Lep comes in," the man said. Back at the Waldorf-Astoria Hotel, where the FBI chief stayed when in New York, Hoover informed Walter that Lepke could expect a sentence of between twelve and fifteen years on the narcotics charge. (Dewey was threatening the death penalty.) Hoping to expedite matters, Walter told the next caller that he had to relay Hoover's answer in person. An hour later he received a call instructing him to drive along Fifth Avenue to Central Park and enter at 60th Street. At a red light at 72nd Street, a car pulled up with two men inside, one of whom ordered him to drive to 72nd Street and Madison Avenue. Again Walter did as he was told. At the designated corner he rendezvoused with the car. One of the men got out and slid into Walter's auto. Walter reported Hoover's assessment. The man told Walter to wait while he conferred with a friend, whom Walter recognized as a chief in Murder, Inc. Then the man told Walter to be at a specific pay phone in an hour to receive an important call.

By this time Lepke was a headline story. On August 14 five of his cohorts were indicted by Dewey for harboring the fugitive. Two days later Dewey's agents claimed to have discovered a cache of documents in New Paltz, New York, that "tell the whole story of Louis Buchalter's crime empire." The next day Lepke's longtime confederate Abner "Longy" Zwillman refused to testify before a grand jury convened to consider Lepke's crimes. Another story the same day accused Lepke of masterminding a Long Island robbery. Dewey even sent three of his men to stake out the Stork Club because he had heard that Lepke owned the place and frequented it every night in disguise.

When Walter returned to the Stork after his Central Park meeting to tell Hoover the news, he found himself in a row instead. Hoover was furious at the weeks of unproductive skulduggery. "I am fed up with you and your friends!" Hoover shouted at Walter in front of hundreds at the Stork. "They can make a fool out of you, but they are not going to make a fool out of me and my men!" Walter remonstrated, "These aren't my friends, John." "They are your friends! They are your friends!" Hoover roared back. "And don't call me John! I'm beginning to think you're the champ bullshitter in town! You can tell your friends that if Lepke isn't in within forty-eight hours, I will order my agents to shoot him on sight!" As a final indignity, Hoover suggested that Walter might have concocted everything to boost his radio ratings.

Walter admitted he was "on the verge of tears." He had been publicly humiliated by one of the few men for whom he had respect. He was certain that the charge of fakery would end his career. He was so distraught at the dressing-down that he said he even contemplated suicide, a measure of how much Hoover's approval meant to him and how much Walter's life depended upon his career. As Walter hurried out of the Stork, Clyde Tolson grabbed his arm and advised he do as Hoover said. But Walter snapped that he was finished acting as a "goat-between" and added sarcastically, "He said if the Lep wasn't in within forty-eight hours, he'd order him shot. You people haven't been able to find him for two years. How you gonna find him in forty-eight hours?" Then he broke free.

Back at the pay phone Walter took the expected call and told the caller that Hoover was "fed up." "If Lepke doesn't surrender by 4 P.M. tomorrow, Hoover says no consideration of any kind will be given him." "He's coming in," the caller said, "but you simply have to wait until he can arrange things." Once again, Walter was told to expect another call the following day at 6:00 P.M. "How soon can you get away?" the caller asked when he phoned. Walter left immediately for Proctor's Theater in Yonkers as ordered. On the way a car pulled up alongside his, and a man with a handkerchief over his face slid in beside Walter. He told him to be in a drugstore at the corner of 19th Street and Eighth Avenue at nine o'clock that evening. Walter's first impulse was to think that "[m]y reputation as a newsman with Hoover would be restored. I got so nervous I shook from head to toe."

At 8:55 Walter was sitting in the crowded drugstore sipping a Coca-Cola when a stranger motioned him outside. Hoover should be at 28th Street and Fifth Avenue between 10:10 and 10:20, the man said. "John, this is the champ bullshitter," Walter greeted Hoover on the drugstore phone when he passed on the information. Back outside, Walter and the man got into Walter's car. "Whatzzamatta, you nervous?" the man asked when Walter wasn't able to put the key in the ignition, and then took the keys to drive.

They spent the next hour cruising the streets, killing time, nervously waiting for the rendezvous. It was a humid night, and Walter was drenched in perspiration. At 10:15, the man stopped at Madison Square at the southeast corner of 24th Street, got out of the car, kissed a small gold star of David and asked that Walter give it to Lepke. Couldn't Lepke be driven directly to Hoover now without Walter's having to meet him? Walter wanted to know. "Lepke won't do that," said the man. "He doesn't want to take the risk of somebody shooting him for the fifty-thousand-dollar reward before he gets to Mr. Hoover." Walter insisted he didn't want to be around if there was any shooting. "Oh, nobody will take a shot at the car if you're in it," the man answered. "And if anybody did hit you it would raise a hell of a stink."

As he waited alone on the dark corner for what seemed an eternity, Walter fiddled with his police radio. He was startled when Lepke suddenly materialized, introduced himself and got into Walter's car. Walter drove slowly toward 28th Street and Fifth Avenue, where Hoover was waiting in his automobile. Walter was so jumpy that when Lepke tossed out the window some plastic sunglasses he had been wearing and they clattered into the street, Walter thought it was a gunshot. Walter's other fear was that someone might have tipped off the local police. If they were intercepted, Hoover would lose his collar and Walter would lose his exclusive, the kudos for bringing Lepke in and the substantial debt Hoover would owe him.

Minutes later—10:17, as Walter reported it—they pulled up behind Hoover. Walter gently took Lepke's arm and escorted him to Hoover's car, where he made introductions. "Glad to meet you," Lepke told Hoover. "Let's go." On the ride to the Federal Building at Foley Square in lower Manhattan, Lepke complained about his celebrity. "Lepke, Lepke, Lepke! Everything is Lepke. All of a sudden I'm a big shot!" At 14th Street, Walter leaped out of the car to phone in the story before the reporters downtown got it. When he phoned June, she was unimpressed, wanting to know why he was chasing gangsters when Walt, Jr., had injured himself that day.

It was finally over: the weeks of intrigue, the weeks of terror that Walter might lose his exclusive as well as his privileged relationship with Hoover. (Since the first contact in early August Walter said he had lost six pounds and one and a half inches from his waistline.) The day after the capture Hoover wrote him a letter of commendation. "Without your unselfish and indefatigable assistance I know that Buchalter would not have surrendered," Hoover said, "and therefore in rendering this aid you have performed a most patriotic service, not only to your Government, but to the American people." Walter refused the reward money, calling it his gift to the government. When one of the film studios asked if he was interested in writing the story for the screen, Walter cited the reward money he had forgone and asked, "How much do you imagine I'd want to write the picture?"

The story of Lepke's capture would always be a favorite in Winchell's repertoire: his own real-life movie. He told it endlessly, in great detail and with elaborate embellishments. Longtime acquaintances could practically recite it verbatim. But there would always be some question over how much credit Walter was really due, not to mention how much bravery was really required. One report claimed the whole thing had been prearranged by Hoover and Winchell. Others said that Frank Costello had made the arrangements, that Walter's role was nominal. An equally credible account attributed most of the spadework to a prominent press agent and friend of Walter's named Irving Hoffman, most likely the man "on the fringe of gangdom" to whom Walter had referred. Hoffman, who was really much more than that, never sought credit. He handed the matter over to Walter the way Walter handed it to Hoover—as a transaction.

"Irving Hoffman did the entire thing," said attorney Arnold Forster, a friend of both Walter and Hoffman. "He took Walter with him. . . . But when you read about it in the paper or heard about it on the air, Irving Hoffman was nowhere to be noted."

Lepke was tried in December, convicted of the federal drug charges and sentenced to fourteen years in prison. He was enraged. Walter, he said, had assured him that he would not receive a sentence over ten years and said that Hoover had gotten these assurances from the attorney general and the President. Now Walter had "double-crossed" him. For his part, Walter was at pains to assure Hoover that he had made no promises to Lepke; he had said only that in Hoover's personal opinion Lepke wasn't likely to receive more than twelve or fifteen years, but that sentencing was at the discretion of the judge. He reiterated the same thing to Judge John C. Knox, who presided at Lepke's trial. Nevertheless, Walter was "very much worried and concerned," according to an FBI report, "as he believes the gang will now start a war of bumping certain individuals off and that Winchell will be one of the first victims." Nor did Walter believe FBI protection would be of much value, since he "could not carry on certain phases of his work in the presence of G-Men."

Though Walter's fear may have been more justifiable here than his fear during the capture itself, no harm came to him. Lepke eventually was remanded to New York State custody to stand trial on the state racketeering charges, and then stood trial for murder. He was convicted and on March 4, 1944, was executed in the electric chair. As for Walter's exclusive on the capture, which had started the whole process of Lepke's demise, it turned out, like the Zangara exclusive, to be less world-shaking than Walter had imagined. When he jumped out of Hoover's car at the 14th Street phone booth to relate the events of the evening to his editor at the *Mirror*, the editor "groaned" at the injustice of having such a scoop at such an inopportune time. Though LEPKE SURRENDERS was bannered across the top of the paper on August 25, the front page of the *Mirror* was dominated by a photograph of Hitler, Göring and Ribbentrop and stories of impending hostilities in Europe. Winchell had captured Lepke one week before Hitler captured Poland.

CHAPTER 6

At War

Long before Adolf Hitler invaded Poland, Walter Winchell had been closely monitoring the prospects for war in Europe. As early as 1935 he was quoting administration sources that "war is not expected for another three years" and predicting that the "United States will remain neutral, no matter what happens." Almost exactly one year later he reported that Wall Street bettors were wagering there would be war within sixty days. There wasn't, of course, but tensions continued to mount steadily throughout 1936 and 1937. In March 1938 Hitler annexed Austria, and a few weeks after that Walter was reporting that "it will be up to Russia to keep peace in Europe" by threatening to come to the aid of the beleaguered Czechs and Slovaks, who were next on Hitler's wish list.

Throughout the summer, the world's attention focused on the fate of Czechoslovakia. In late July, Walter predicted that Hitler would invade Czechoslovakia within two weeks. (He led off the broadcast with an announcement of actress Dorothy Lamour's emergency appendectomy.) August 15 passed without the anticipated invasion, but tensions did not subside. Now, remembered one observer, came "the most dramatic and hysterical period of American broadcasting." Throughout September "crisis followed crisis: emergency orders, mobilizations, fervent prayers, soaring hopes and bitter despondency."

Three times that month, British Prime Minister Neville Chamberlain flew to Germany to dissuade Hitler from starting hostilities, even if it meant that Czechoslovakia would have to cede the Sudetenland to the Germans. "It is said that Premier Chamberlain flew to Hitler because he had courage," Walter wrote unsympathetically. "Many of us think he hastened there because he is scared stiff of having a bomb fall on his loved ones in England ... He apparently doesn't care what becomes of some Czech's loved ones—so he offers Hitler any part of the Sudeten area!" By month's end Chamberlain and Hitler had concluded the Munich Pact, which supposedly bought peace by appeasing Germany's territorial ambitions. "Trying to make peace with Hitler is like trying to reduce by overeating," Walter wrote shortly before the agreement. After it he wrote, "Those European nations have given us a new definition of Justice: Giving a criminal what he desires—instead of what he deserves."

That fall the march toward war continued, the sense of crisis ever intensifying. In December Walter quoted administration sources that Germany and Japan would start "squeezing the Russian bear into submission in the Spring," though by the spring he had reversed field and was predicting that "Stalin and Hitler will soon reveal a secret agreement." In March he reported massive troop movements on both sides. He warned in May of the imminent German takeover of Gdansk and in June of the massing of German troops on the Polish border. In August he reported the Nazi-Soviet Nonaggression Pact that he had earlier prophesied. "Just as many of us suspected right along, the Nazis have nothing against the Communists—and vice versa." The next week he editorialized that the "most fateful hour—of the most fateful week of history is at hand [. . .] For a long time—only a few believed—that the dictators intended to divide and rule. Now we *know*—they intend to separate and slaughter." A few days later Hitler invaded Poland.

Walter's first response to the invasion was to cable immediately Chamberlain and the U.S. ambassador to England Joseph P. Kennedy. MAY I RESPECTFULLY OFFER THE SUGGESTION, THAT IF BRITAIN DECLARES WAR THE DECLARATION MIGHT BE WORDED NOT AS "WAR AGAINST GERMANY" BUT AS WAR AGAINST HITLER PERSONALLY AND HIS PERSONAL REGIME, STRESSING THE FACT THAT HITLER DOES NOT REALLY REPRESENT THE TRUE WILL OF THE VAST CIVILIAN POPULATION OF GERMANY STOP SUCH DECLARATION MIGHT HAVE THE ASTONISHING EFFECT OF BRINGING THE GERMAN PEOPLE TO THEIR SENSES ESPECIALLY IF SUCH KIND OF DECLARATION COULD BE MADE KNOWN TO THE GERMAN PEOPLE.

Ernest Cuneo, sitting with Walter at the Stork when he announced his intention to send the wires, thought it took enormous gall for him to believe that Chamberlain or Kennedy would want advice from a gossip columnist. Cuneo was astonished, then, when Kennedy responded that night with a long telegram of his own. HE WAS GRATEFUL FOR YOUR SUGGES-

TION, wrote Kennedy of Chamberlain, AND SAID THAT WHILE FOR CON-
STITUTIONAL REASONS IT WOULD SCARCELY HAVE BEEN POSSIBLE TO MAKE
BRITISH ACTUAL OFFICIAL DECLARATION IN THE FORM SUGGESTED BY
YOU, YOU WILL PROBABLY HAVE SEEN IN THE PRIME MINISTER'S SPEECH
IN THE HOUSE AND IN OTHER STATEMENTS MADE ON BEHALF OF THE
GOVERNMENT THE LINE SUGGESTED BY YOU. "What absolutely enraged
me," Cuneo later remarked, claiming that Chamberlain had sent a wire as
well, "was that Winchell didn't think there was anything remarkable
about their instant and complimentary telegrams."

What Cuneo apparently didn't realize is that Walter saw himself now
as a statesman. For months he had been urging the democracies in Europe to stand up to Hitler, but he had been equally adamant that the United States not get engaged in the conflict. "I honestly think that the
best way for Americans to keep from getting into another European war,"
he broadcast just before the Czechoslovakian crisis, "is to remember what
they got out of the last one." Europe was "morally bankrupt," he broadcast three weeks later, when Chamberlain was appeasing Hitler. "The so-
called Peace Conferences of Europe have done nothing but emphasize
the deepest differences and the blood-feuds between [*sic*] all European
nations. In fact, the only thing they have in common is the overwhelming
desire to use American money and American soldiers—for their own selfish and short-sighted purposes." "[T]he future of American youth is on
top of American soil," he reported again in April as the tides of war were
rising, "not underneath American dirt!" A week after the outbreak of
the war, he began a new feature on his broadcast debunking both Allied
and German propaganda with the hope, he said, "that it will help keep
the United States out of their war."

To many Allied supporters, he sounded like an isolationist. Yet at the
same time that he was advising caution in dealing with Europe and warning Americans to "stop being kibitzers" when it came to the European
conflict, he was also cautioning them to realize their responsibilities.
"The total isolation idea," playwright and presidential speechwriter Robert Sherwood wrote him approvingly after Walter's condemnation of
Munich, "the notion that we can sit tight behind our oceans and let the
rest of the world stew in its own juice—that, to me, is the supreme expression of the horse and buggy point of view."

Walter seemed to agree. He advocated activism; he just didn't want involvement. As early as the spring of 1938 he was pressing for a buildup
in American arms. "The reason the United States needs a bigger army
and navy," he wrote in his column, "is not to start a fight—but to be able
to finish one." After Munich he was saying that the surest guarantee of
peace was a larger army and navy. "Not to be used as tools of Aggres-

sion . . . Not to be used as a means of Oppression—but simply as the necessary barriers—behind which free men can live!" The outbreak of war
had only amplified Walter's drumbeat for a strengthened military. "A
tough-guy world calls for a hard-boiled statement, and here it is," he announced in March 1940. "Any country believing in a Bill of Rights—
needs heavy artillery. Any nation with a free constitution needs plenty of
pursuit ships and bombers." And he added, "We must stop kidding ourselves, ladies and gentlemen, that Americans can lick anybody. Maybe we
can't."

None of this might have counted for much if Winchell hadn't become
so influential a molder of public opinion. Walter Lippmann may have had
the ears of the policymakers. Walter Winchell had the ears of tens of millions of ordinary Americans. But what exactly was he advocating they do?
A government official returning from Canada found Walter damned
there by certain notables for "doing more than anyone to keep the U.S.
out of war," while editor Burton Rascoe scolded Walter a few months
later for seeming to promote America's entry into the war. To those who
wondered how he reconciled his isolationism with his stand on preparedness, he answered, "I am opposed to another American Expeditionary
Force on foreign soil . . . I am *even more opposed*—to any *foreign* expeditionary force—on American soil. . . ."

Part of Walter's hands-off attitude toward Europe was his conviction,
shared by many Americans, that the Allies outnumbered the Germans
and would either win a swift victory or persuade Hitler to sue for peace.
As Britain and Germany braced for the battle over Norway in April 1940,
Walter predicted the confrontation would be decisive and reported "military experts think that the Nazis cannot hold out longer than 3 more
weeks." Two weeks later Norway was occupied, and a week later German
armies marched through Belgium and Denmark. Still, Walter sounded
optimistic about the Allies' chances of stopping the German assault. "The
Allies are going through a period of holding the Germans at any cost and
readjusting their troops and their lines," he broadcast in May, predicting
that the Allies "will not have to wait much longer for their chance to
come." Instead three weeks later the Maginot Line, France's last defense,
fell.

Now, Walter concluded, the "continent of Europe is lost to Hitler,"
leaving himself and his fellow Americans to ponder a new course of
action.

THOUGH READERS and listeners assumed Winchell was privy to inside
information, there was something most of them didn't know that lent

weight to his predictions and positions on the conflict, something that prompted even the Germans to monitor his broadcasts. What his audience didn't know was that in shaping American attitudes toward the war, Winchell was often speaking for the Roosevelt administration just as he had in areas of domestic policy.

The source of this authority was Ernest Cuneo, the affable, erudite associate counsel of the Democratic National Committee. Weighing nearly three hundred pounds—Walter affectionately called him Fatso—with small, dancing eyes and a huge swath of a smile, Cuneo was a man of Falstaffian proportions both physically and temperamentally. A friend described him as a Renaissance man who was equally comfortable with Greek, Latin, the history of science, world history and English literature. A florid speaker with a booming voice given to orotund expression, he could and did quote Shakespeare at the drop of a hat. But he was hardly a dry pedant. "Ernie looked like what he was," said another friend. His girth testified to his love of the good life, and his spirit was large, generous, and infectious. " 'Champagne for everybody in the house,' " remembered Herman Klurfeld. "That was Ernie."

The son of an Italian immigrant who owned a scrap metal plant, he was born in 1905 in Carlstadt, New Jersey, and attended East Rutherford High School, which he described as a "very small school set in a middle-class Dutch, Huguenot town," though the "backbone of its athletic power came from working-class Wellington, straight Polish." A scholastic football phenom himself, Cuneo enrolled at Penn State University but was bounced from the freshman football team for reasons he never disclosed. (His son believed that a prank probably had misfired.) Having transferred to Columbia University, Cuneo starred as left guard on its football team and won All-American honors while working his way through school writing for the *Daily News* and, as he put it, "recording the strife of working people, criminals both unsung and famous."

More important, at Columbia he fell under the influence of three brilliant liberal professors—Adolf A. Berle, Jr., Drew Pearson, and William O. Douglas—who instilled in him a sense of justice and a spirit of liberalism he was never to lose. He attended Columbia Law School, was thrown out, again for reasons he never disclosed, and was eventually graduated from St. John's Law School. Fresh out of school, he landed a job with New York's new progressive mayor, Fiorello La Guardia, while on the weekends he played professional football for the Stapleton Cardinals on Staten Island.

No one seemed to know exactly what he did for La Guardia, but Cuneo was a born fixer who did a lot and always in good humor. When Roosevelt entered the White House, taking with him Cuneo's mentors

Berle and Douglas, Cuneo joined the administration and served as a trou-
bleshooter for Tommy Corcoran, a young Harvard-educated attorney by
way of the Irish ghetto and a political Machiavellian who served as counsel to the Reconstruction Finance Corporation when he wasn't scheming
on the President's behalf. It was Corcoran who assigned Cuneo the task
of assisting Michigan Governor Frank Murphy and pro-Roosevelt labor
leaders in keeping the lid on labor tensions after the auto strikes in 1937.
When Murphy became attorney general, Cuneo became his self-
described "legman" in the fight for civil rights from the Kentucky coal-
fields to the political back rooms of Louisiana, Kansas City and Jersey
City. It was then, he said, that he began funneling information to
Winchell, though in actuality by the time Murphy was appointed attorney general in January 1939, Cuneo was already an intimate of Walter's.

They had met early in 1938, when the President, a presumed lame
duck, was locked in combat with conservatives of his own party position-
ing themselves to take over when he left office. The President's liberal
supporters were pressing him to name an heir who might serve as a rallying point. Surprisingly, Roosevelt designated Robert Jackson, the solic-
itor general, and maneuvered him toward the Democratic gubernatorial
nomination of New York as a stepping-stone. The attempt failed miserably. Democratic National Chairman James Farley, who coveted the
nomination himself, told Roosevelt that Jackson hadn't a chance of being
nominated governor, much less President.

Cuneo relayed Farley's assessment to Corcoran, who was more or less
in charge of the Jackson effort and told him that if the Roosevelt supporters were to hold on to the party, they needed a candidate with national
recognition. "There was only one person who could give instant recognition to a dark horse candidate," Cuneo advised Corcoran. "Walter
Winchell." Though Cuneo later wrote that Corcoran "bitched a bit"
about recruiting Winchell, complaining that Walter was "notches below
the dignity of the White House"—unlikely, since Corcoran himself had
been using Winchell to push New Deal policies—Cuneo said he won
Corcoran's approval by invoking the Greek proverb "Necessity is above
the gods themselves."

Now Cuneo arranged to meet Walter. Fearing they would be too conspicuous on the columnist's turf at the Stork, Cuneo phoned Leonard
Lyons, a friend, and asked if he would invite Walter to "21." "I opened
with an amenity," Cuneo remembered, telling Walter that he had seen
George Jessel the other night and that Jessel had reminisced about his
days in vaudeville when he and Walter were children. "The hell with
that," Walter snapped. "That son of a bitch started to reminisce when he
was eight years old." What Walter wanted to know is "What's going to
happen tomorrow?"

Cuneo was shrewd enough to realize that if he were to ingratiate himself with Walter, he would have to deliver for "The Column." Scanning the room, he spotted Lord Lothian, the British ambassador to the United States, and introduced Walter in the hope that Lothian might provide some news on British policy. "Lord Lothian, what is Great Britain going to do about Hitler?" Walter asked immediately. "Mr. Winchell, we shall try to fatten the tiger without strengthening him," answered Lothian, one of the champions of appeasement. "I've seen some big tigers and some little tigers," Walter said. "I've never seen a fat one." The next day Walter reported that "Britain will marry Hitler in the fall. The marriage will blow up into a World War."

Cuneo left that night impressed with Walter's quickness of mind. "I came to a conclusion which I never altered: I believe Winchell had an I.Q. of brilliant proportions, nearly the equal of Einstein." But what fascinated and intoxicated him was not Winchell's intelligence; it was his power. "I was under the terrific tension," he wrote years later, "of believing he was carrying the fate of the Nation with him every time he went to the post. He was the only man who could simultaneously elevate FDR back into the White House and meet Goebbels, Hitler's propaganda chief, down in the gutter and stomp him and his lies into the mud."

When Cuneo met Walter at "21," the idea of returning Roosevelt to the White House for a third term hadn't yet been hatched. Instead Cuneo began spending hours with Walter, feeding him inside information and using him to float trial balloons for the liberal Democrats who still hoped to maintain control of their party in the face of a growing conservative revolt being led by Roosevelt's own vice president, John Nance Garner. It was only after Roosevelt had failed in his attempt to purge the party—he had tried targeting conservative foes in the 1938 off-term election—that Corcoran and others realized the President would have to run again himself if the liberals were to succeed. Walter quickly became their stalking-horse, blasting the " 'Draft Roosevelt' trumpet from 'Border to border and coast to coast.' " By doing so, as Cuneo told it, Walter smoked out the conservative opposition and gave Roosevelt's supporters two years to destroy it.

Still, it seemed uncertain whether the President had committed himself to the plan to return to the White House or whether this was a rogue operation of Corcoran's. For months, at Cuneo's behest, Walter seesawed from announcing that Roosevelt would seek a third term ("The President feels the nation needs him in the White House for another four-year term," he broadcast in July 1938) to declaring that he wouldn't. ("The so-called political insiders now believe that F.D.R. will not run for a Third Term," he said in April 1939.) At the same time, presumably at Roosevelt's request, press secretary Steve Early enlisted radio commentator Earl

Godwin to answer Walter's predictions that the President would be running, once getting Godwin to issue two denials in a single day.

As the Democratic convention drew near, Walter's anxiety over the possibility of being wrong about Roosevelt's declaration was growing. What Walter didn't realize was that he was almost single-handedly carrying the fight. "Look, Walter," Cuneo said he wanted to tell him, "you *are* the Third Term campaign." But, Cuneo later wrote of Walter, "for once in his life, he underestimated his own importance; the guy was far more powerful than he knew." In the end, of course, Roosevelt was nominated. "I quoted others as believing he wouldn't run," Walter crowed disingenuously after the convention, "but I kept saying he would."

Walter's relationship with Cuneo was to resemble those he had had with Sime Silverman, Texas Guinan and Mark Hellinger. Coming along at the very moment in the late thirties when Walter was assuming his political mantle, Cuneo guided him through Washington the way those previous mentors had guided him through Broadway nightlife. Cuneo raised Walter's consciousness, framed his opinions, introduced him to government insiders. By the time Walter visited Washington in May 1938 to judge the "Prettiest Girl" contest, he was already referring to Cuneo as a "dear friend of mine" and asking Cuneo to accompany him on his rounds.

Both of them garrulous and expansive, they were boon companions. Though Cuneo lived in Washington, he shuttled regularly to New York, where he was a fixture at Table 50 whiling away the nights with Walter. Still, like virtually all of Walter's relationships, this one was basically a symbiosis: Walter getting a pipeline to the administration, Cuneo getting a bullhorn to the public to promote Roosevelt and liberalism; Walter enjoying the benefits of what he believed was an educated and superior mind, Cuneo enjoying the benefits of raw power; Walter gaining entrée to the world of politics and diplomacy, Cuneo gaining entrée to the world of show business and society.

The only glitch was money. Walter obviously had a great deal of it, while Cuneo, notoriously profligate, never seemed to have enough. The relationship nearly collapsed early in 1940, when Cuneo apparently asked Walter to lend him funds for an investment opportunity and Walter refused. Soon after, however, Walter put Cuneo on a $10,000-per-year retainer for "legal services rendered in connection with column and broadcast," though Cuneo was now not only examining these for possible libel but often writing the political material. In effect, from being Walter's mentor, Cuneo had become his employee—his personal ghostwriter and very own political mole.

With the outbreak of war Cuneo's services became particularly valuable to both Washington and Winchell. In March 1940 Secretary of State Cordell Hull and Assistant Secretary Berle met to discuss the dangers posed by a possible fascist victory in Europe. Hull and Berle worried that America was vulnerable and that something had to be done to awaken the country to the danger. Berle's answer was to get Cuneo to get Walter to deliver on the broadcast a "stiff editorial" supporting a new arms buildup. As Cuneo told it, Berle asked him if Walter might "help prepare the country for war." Cuneo said he answered, "Adolf, the guy thinks he's been doing it since 1930."

Berle and Hull listened to Walter's call to arms on the broadcast that Sunday. An hour after the program Cuneo phoned to tell them that the switchboard had been jammed with favorable calls. "This was interesting," Berle wrote in his diary that evening. "[T]he Secretary had pointed out that it was politically dangerous to tackle this line and he doubted if anyone would have the courage to do it. But the columnist did try it. . . . It seems to me as though our politicians are far more timid than they need to be; maybe Walter Winchell will give them enough of a demonstration so that they can be stimulated to take a strong line. . . ."

Over the next several months Walter not only aggressively pushed for a military buildup and a two-ocean navy but, clearly acting with the administration's blessing, confronted Congress itself, challenging those senators and representatives who opposed the buildup. His two favorite targets were Representative Jacob Thorkelson of Montana, whom he branded the "mouthpiece of the Nazi movement in Congress," and Senator Burton Wheeler, also of Montana, who was leading the Senate battle against preparedness and against American assistance to the Allied forces. Thorkelson was so outraged by Walter's attacks that he demanded and received time from NBC to answer the charges. Swearing that he "firmly believes in the fundamental principles of this Republic as set forth in the Constitution," he went on to say that "the greatest danger which confronts us today comes from those who wield the power of gold money and credit." Lest anyone miss his point, Thorkelson took the floor of the House later that summer to denounce Walter as a "Jewish vilifier" who slanders anyone "who cannot see eye to eye with his own organized minority." Three weeks later Thorkelson was defeated in a primary election.

As for Wheeler, he and Walter jousted for months, Walter calling Wheeler an obstructionist who would prevent America from defending itself, Wheeler calling Walter an "alarmist" who advocated that the country "immediately join the Allies and help them not only in materials, but that we actually get into the war." Because Wheeler was a cunning old verbal pugilist himself, Cuneo called the Wheeler-Winchell brawl "the worst political Pier Sixer I ever witnessed." More, the "savagery of their exchanges was transferred to their followers." Walter had roused such anger at Wheeler that at one point the senator was pelted with eggs while trying to speak in his native Montana. Walter was delighted, but Cuneo warned him that if Wheeler were killed, Walter would be held responsible for his death. So Walter halfheartedly broadcast an editorial denouncing the violence—"I believe Senator Wheeler is wrong in his premises—and wrong in his conclusion. . . . But I am sure of his right to be heard"—then broadcast another the following week defending himself against charges of having caved in to pressure. "I would rather die first," he told his listeners.

In one respect Wheeler was right: Along with his campaign for preparedness, Walter had become increasingly alarmist and even interventionist. "For five years, American isolationists have told us how to isolate America," he broadcast in September 1940, taking no note whatsoever of his own recent isolationist leanings. "The time has come for them all—to tell us how—to isolate—both oceans. America now realizes—that the road to isolation ends where it always ends—with the enemy on our doorstep." A month later, again apparently venting State Department sentiments, he declared that "appeasement has taught America its lesson . . . We know now—that a nation which gives up an inch of its soil gives up *all* of its soul . . . A nation which appeases insult abroad—will suffer outrage at home. . . ."

Walter's sudden pro-interventionism now prompted Wheeler to accuse him of being in the pay of the British. Again, the senator wasn't far off. The British, eager to forge ties to the American intelligence community, had dispatched a Canadian businessman named William Stephenson to the United States in the spring of 1940 to see if he could covertly coordinate efforts with the FBI under an umbrella agency to be called the British Security Coordination office. Rebuffed by J. Edgar Hoover, who felt proscribed from communicating with British intelligence for fear of breaching American neutrality, Stephenson contacted Cuneo—he had probably been routed to him through William Donovan, an intelligence officer who, like Cuneo, was a Columbia University alumnus—and Cuneo brought the request directly to the President. As Cuneo related it, the President told him, "There should be the closest possible marriage between the FBI and British intelligence."

Using a dummy trade commission as a front, Stephenson installed the BSC in an office in Rockefeller Center in New York, and Cuneo became the liaison among British intelligence, the FBI and later the Office of the Coordinator of Information, which was established under William Donovan's command to provide its own intelligence. Stephenson essentially gathered information on enemy activities and routed it to these sister agencies, but that was not all he was doing. He was also running a covert operation the mandate of which, according to an official history of British wartime intelligence, was "to do all that was not being done, and could not be done by overt means to assure sufficient aid for Britain and eventually to bring America into the war." To this end Stephenson planted stories in sympathetic papers to discredit isolationists, harassed America First rallies, even devised a plan to drive the isolationist Hearst press out of business by buying up $10.5 million worth of notes held by a Canadian paper mill against Hearst's account and then demanding payment.

One of the most important components of the plan was Walter Winchell. On the one hand, Cuneo was feeding Walter information at the behest of the White House, which was coming to believe in the inevitability of America's entrance into the war. On the other hand, he was secretly feeding Walter British propaganda and top-level intelligence through Stephenson. The effect, as Wheeler knew too well, was to destroy the opposition to preparedness and soften the public toward intervention. "From then on," Cuneo wrote of the period after the success of Walter's full-scale 1940 preparedness campaign, "State and War surpassed Justice as the source of Winchell's broadsides. This, of course, was pure Clausewitz. Winchell became the firepoint. His rolling barrages could and did clear the way for the President and the preparation of war."

But before Walter could bring America to war, there was first the matter of reelecting Roosevelt to a third term against the Republican candidate, businessman Wendell Willkie. Walter set himself to this task with the same eagerness he had displayed in campaigning for preparedness. Hearst, however, was less enthusiastic. In July 1940 he once again instructed Walter's editor at the *Mirror*, Jack Lait: "If any of our contributors inject politics into their writing, it is to be stricken out. These writers are engaged to write a certain type of column and if they do not want to do that they will have to go where a different kind of column is desired."

Thus prohibited from running his pro-Roosevelt pieces in the *Mirror*, Walter turned to the liberal tabloid *PM*, which former *Time* editor Ralph Ingersoll had launched that June with the determination, in the words of one staffer, "to scrap all the old rules of journalism." Ingersoll seemed most intent on scrapping the political conservatism espoused by most of the New York papers, which was exactly why *PM* welcomed Walter. Early in September *PM* started running a feature from Walter's broadcast called "Politics Makes Strange Bedfellows' Stories." By September 19 he was contributing a daily "special" to the letters to the editor page. On September 20 *PM* ran a full column of Winchell material culled from his broadcast, including a new slogan, "Willkie for the millionaires; Roosevelt for the millions!" Finally, on September 23, Walter began writing a regular column on politics under the pen name Paul Revere II with all the items Hearst would not let him run. He ended only when Klurfeld complained about the additional work.

THAT SUMMER, while Walter was stumping for Roosevelt's reelection, Jacob Winschel died. Jacob's wife, Adelina, had found him lifeless in bed at their Washington Heights apartment the morning of August 18. He had been suffering from rectal cancer, and he had never fully recovered from an operation two years earlier. He was seventy years old.

Walter immediately departed Miami, where he was vacationing, to attend the funeral, but it was more an act of obligation than affection. He and his father had never been close, even less so when Jacob became his son's petitioner. Whatever filial devotion Walter had, he had displaced onto his real father figure: Franklin Roosevelt. Walter's contributions to Roosevelt's reelection as well as his past and potential service in the reenergized campaign for intervention had strengthened an already close relationship. Where he had once been only an infrequent visitor to the White House, he now, in Cuneo's recollection, "saw the president often and always alone" and always emerged from the meetings "like a kid whose scorecard had just been autographed by Babe Ruth. 'Ernie,' he said a thousand times if he said it once, 'the guy gets to you. He just gets to you. He's the greatest.' "

But intimacy for Franklin Roosevelt, like almost everything for Franklin Roosevelt, had a political purpose. The President obviously appreciated that Walter was a peculiar media phenomenon whose influence on the public mind nearly rivaled his own, and where petitioners would ask Walter to intercede with the President, there were now public officials asking the President to intercede with Winchell. Even the President's wife wanted to meet him. "I have a little apartment in New York City with my secretary, to which I invite my friends," Mrs. Roosevelt wrote him. "If you think you could find the time and fortitude enough to climb three long flights of stairs, I should be happy to have you come there for lunch or tea with me sometime when I am in town." But the First Lady admitted she had an ulterior motive, a favor she wanted Walter to grant. He had accused a friend of hers of subversive activity. Mrs. Roosevelt wanted him to print a retraction, a request that only demonstrated once again there were things Walter Winchell could bestow that not even the President of the United States could.

II

As 1940 ended, Allied supporters in America were beating their war drums and few as vigorously as Winchell. "In the war of combat journalism," Cuneo later wrote, "if 1940 was like the start of a rough chariot race, 1941 was its brutal climax. Once having cleared the election barrier, FDR threw off his wraps, strapped on his helmet and went in, went in, that is, as far as he could push American opinion to permit."

Just how far he had to push was difficult to gauge. In a Roper poll shortly after the Nazi invasion of Poland, 38.3 percent of the respondents called the English their "blood brothers," and 61.2 percent believed that if the Allies were defeated, Germany would be a threat to the United States. The fall of Europe had obviously intensified the threat, but as Walter himself had demonstrated, there was still a distance from solidarity with the Allies to active combat, from the Lend-Lease Act, which provided material assistance, to a declaration of war which would provide American soldiers.

By 1941 Walter had traversed the distance. "[S]ome people have wondered about my stand," he broadcast early in February.

Am I for or against the United States entering the war in Europe [?] No sane man likes war. . . . All good people abhor violence, yet all people would use violence to defend their children from kidnapping. All good nations hate force yet every good American would not hesitate to defend his country from attack by international bandits. [. . .]

The so-called war mongers, alarmists and Walter Winchells have this answer—men cannot be free when their country is in chains. Those who try to keep their security by avoiding risk, thereby invite attack.

Three months later, when President Roosevelt, dedicating Woodrow Wilson's birthplace, declared the American people ready to fight for democracy, Walter cited recent pronouncements from Hitler, German foreign Minister Joachim von Ribbentrop and Propaganda Minister Joseph Goebbels that America was too divided to fight. "And there you are, Rip Van Winkles from border to border and coast to coast . . . But don't worry about it happening over here . . . Don't forget we have two lovely oceans—one on each side . . . To drown in." Three days later, Senator Wheeler took the air on the Mutual network, amid the swelling chorus of interventionism, to accuse Walter and others of "blitzkrieging the American people into this war" and to ask Americans to use the "same machinery that your interventionist foes are using in this hour" to resist involvement.

To Walter isolationism had now become unconscionable, a form of treason. He was determined to prove that the isolationists were not, as they claimed, patriotic Americans who happened to hold a different point of view from his own; they were Nazi collaborators, anti-Semites, and racists who cared far less about saving American lives than about ensuring Hitler's victory. In 1940 Walter inaugurated a new feature in his column, "The Winchell Column vs. The Fifth Column," thrashing Nazi sympathizers, and early in 1941 he replaced the "oddities" portion of his broadcast with a report of Nazi activities in this country called "The Walter Winchell Quiz to End All Quizzes . . . And All Quislings!," an allusion to the Norwegian leader who collaborated in the Nazi occupation of his country. A few months later he changed the feature's name to "Some Americans Most Americans Can Do Without."

Every week brought new charges from Walter linking the radical right to Nazi Germany, but Walter's prime source was not, as most assumed, the FBI; in fact, he was one of *its* prime sources, channeling hundreds of documents about Nazi groups to the bureau both before and during the war. Rather Walter's most important source was Arnold Forster, the young basso-voiced attorney who, at the time he met Walter early in 1941, was New York counsel for the Anti-Defamation League (ADL) of the B'nai B'rith.

Forster, né Arnold Fastenberg, had grown up in the twenties in the Hunts Point section of the Bronx, the son of a struggling clothing manufacturer. With his aquiline nose, his dark eyes, and that deep, mellifluous voice, Forster was a dramatic presence, and he had appeared with Julius Garfinkel (later John Garfield) in several local theatrical productions until the Depression forced him to forsake acting and pushed him instead to St. John's Law School. After a confrontation with a group of anti-Semitic thugs in 1937, the head of the Brandt Theater chain approached Forster, now an attorney, to do something about growing anti-Semitism. Forster formed a group called the Junior Guild that monitored anti-Semitic gatherings and complained to police officials about incitement to riot, disorderly conduct and breach of the peace. From the Guild he was recruited by the ADL.

At the ADL Forster was assigned to investigate a rumor that auto magnate Henry Ford might be financing a new anti-Semitic publication. When confronted with the rumor, Ford, a longtime anti-Semite, nevertheless expressed shock and contrition and even issued an apology for being linked with anti-Semitic literature. ADL chief Richard Gutstadt thought it might be advantageous to have the apology leaked to the press.

A lawyer on Forster's staff happened to be a friend of a press agent named Ed Weiner, who was a friend of Walter's. Weiner invited Forster to bring the letter to the studio before one of Walter's broadcasts. Walter read it on the air that night and later told Weiner, "Tell that Forster guy that when he has anything of value of this kind, call me."

When it came to the radical right, Forster had one of the best intelligence-gathering operations in the country, with spies everywhere. He had even infiltrated the inner circle of Mississippi Senator William Bilbo, a vicious white supremacist and isolationist. "I was soon receiving a continuous flow of reports about the conduct of the senator against Jews, blacks, the Administration, the 'internationalists' and other 'dangerous elements,'" wrote Forster, "reports that I would rewrite into column items for Winchell's broadcasts." It drove Bilbo crazy to see in the column or hear on the broadcast everything he said privately.

Within a year Forster was devoting between ten and fifteen hours to Walter each week and had joined Cuneo in the columnist's inner circle. "I would get a call from Rose: Meet the Boss," Forster recalled. "I'd meet him at the barbershop. I'd go to his house. I'd meet him at the [Stork] Club." Usually Walter wanted a rumor about a Nazi sympathizer checked or a story investigated. "We got mountains of stuff" on American fascists, remembered Klurfeld, most of it from Forster, which Klurfeld then boiled down into a few paragraphs for the column. Occasionally Forster himself drafted whole columns for Walter, and every Sunday he appeared at the studio along with Cuneo, Klurfeld and a handful of others to lend his expertise to the broadcast and vet the antifascist portions of the script, which kept growing larger and larger.

Walter was almost as unsparing on the domestic Communists as he was on the fascists and isolationists. "We are less in danger today from Hitler's army in Paris," he reported in June 1940 shortly after the fall of France, "than we are from Staleen's [*sic*] agents in America . . . Hitler has stormed the French Forts—but Staleen is assaulting American factories." That same month he accused the Communists of infiltrating the National Maritime Union. "These communists have mercury and emory dust for sabotage purposes," he said. Three weeks later the union slapped Walter with a million-dollar libel suit.* Walter complained that if they had

---

*Nearly six years later, in April 1946, the suit was finally settled when Hearst offered $10,000. Walter said he begged the publisher not to settle and offered to meet union representatives "in any well lighted courtroom or any dark alley for a complete showdown." A few years later he told an interviewer, "I wanted that case to go to trial. I would have declared in front of the jury, The Government of the United States ordered me to write that story," apparently referring to White House orders to discredit the union.

waited until Sunday to announce the suit, he could have used it for his broadcast.

"He shouts a few bits of choice gossip, then launches into the meat of his program," analyzed the Communist *Daily Worker* in a negative two-part series on Walter in March 1941. "Usually he strikes out at Hitler or the Nazis. Then he turns to his other pet topics—the Communists and his own personal patriotism. Toward the Communists he is venomous. He names names, demands prosecutions, deportations, acts as a finger man for the red-baiters." And why was this so-called liberal so hostile to the Communists? Fear, answered the *Daily Worker*. "When first he tried his hand against the Nazis, he stood in the line of fire of those red-baiters who were then declaring that all Jews who spoke out against fascism were Communists. The easy way to prove he was not a Red was plain— Winchell decided to attack the Reds; it was a popular pastime. . . . Cowardice has done this."

Just as the native fascists inundated Walter with anti-Semitic letters and threats to boycott Jergens products, so the Communists waged a campaign of harassment. "This pro-fascist is still the big threat he has always been to our party," the Communist Political Association of New York County announced in an open letter to its members. Other leftist groups planned campaigns to discredit him. And at one clandestine Communist meeting in Chicago an attendee allegedly warned, "Walter Winchell must be stopped—one way—or another."

To all this Walter displayed less fear than enthusiasm. He loved the action, loved being the center of attention, and he behaved as if these disputes were no different from his squabbles with his newspaper rivals. "I have never been in so many brawls at the same time as now," he said in May 1941, when NBC eliminated one of his attacks on Senator Wheeler and the *Mirror* yanked another political tirade of his. "The Bund, the Commys, this Senator, that one. This group, that clique, and so forth. With all of them hitting from all sides, however, I'm not dizzy. Just busy." Still, some readers wanted to know why certain attacks had gone unanswered. "I will, in time," he cracked, "but I really shouldn't answer them . . . It might make them as big as me."

FOR BROADWAYITES who longed for his old racy material, Winchell's preoccupation with politics was a disappointment. "If you picked up a column and he didn't have [show business] news or he didn't have gossip or things like that," remembered a press agent, "among our peers, you'd say, 'What's Winchell got tonight?' 'Ah, forget about it. He's got an essay.' " But among the general population, eager for inside information on world events, Walter's politics had only increased his popularity. "A year and a half ago we eschewed politics, war, national news—and emphasized Broadway and Hollywood trivia," he wrote in November 1940. "Our reward was appearing in 100 newspapers. Our Sunday night 'Crossley' was 9.4—sometimes 9.6 . . . The latest count reveals 330 odd newspapers and the Crossley (which is radio's barometer) gave us a score of 18.7—the 'high' among news commentators . . . In short, when you ignore what is happening in the world—you have half as many readers and listeners."

He had fully expected that his ratings would fall once the 1940 election was over, but they kept rising instead—to 20.3 in December and then to 25.3 six months later, tying him with comedian Bob Hope for the highest-rated program on radio. "It is the first time in the history of radio measurement when a fifteen-minute once a week broadcast has achieved this prominence," announced a press release from the C. E. Hooper rating agency, adding that "Winchell's progress to the top of that 'First Fifteen' has been so rapid in recent months as to match in newsworthiness many of his own broadcasts."

In part, his growing popularity testified not only to Americans' interest in the war but to what one observer called "the amazing adaptability of the Winchellesque style." As a medium Winchell was a message. "What served to sell Broadway gossip—and still does—serves at least as effectively to sell fervent, quippy patriotics, even straight war news," ran the analysis. "Winchell, apparently, can sell anything he puts his tongue to." Another observer trying to dissect the Winchell appeal attributed it to the suggestiveness of his delivery. "The agitated listener waits breathlessly for astounding exposés."

Certainly Walter gave the impression that he was just as much an insider when it came to world events as he was when it came to celebrity romance—as, in fact, he was—and most Americans had come to realize, if only because of his relationship with Roosevelt, that at least on war matters he now spoke for the administration. (Cuneo called him the "principal *daily* conduit to the people.") But interventionists were also coming to regard him as the symbol of the American spirit: a patriotic exemplar at a time when it was important for Americans to define themselves before going to war. "There is today a 100% American—a man who for the future sake of this country should exist not as an individual but in innumerable numbers," the Mount Airy *Times* in North Carolina editorialized in a sentiment that was typical of the new outpouring of support for him. "He is Walter Winchell, one of the most intelligent men ever to speak into a microphone or write for a newspaper." Lakewood, New Jersey, named a street after him, calling him "the first soldier in our land in the cause of democracy," American Legion posts now sought to honor him and Democratic National Chairman Ed Flynn asked Billingsley to ask Walter if he would consider running for Congress, guaranteeing Walter victory. (Walter said he wouldn't, since he couldn't take orders from the mob.)

Walter loved the image of himself as the standard-bearer for intervention as much as he loved his image as defender of the public weal. It puffed him up, but it increased the pressure too. He was important now, not just famous. He was responsible for democracy itself. Cuneo described him three nights before a broadcast as "cantankerous, testy" like a racehorse pumping adrenaline as it waits for the post. "By Friday night he had to be held in; he had to be 'rated.' " By Saturday night he was "ungovernable." If Cuneo were in Washington and Walter in New York, Miami or Hollywood, they would scream at one another over the phones for hours, then "each limp off, limp, around 3 A.M." On the afternoon of broadcast day, Cuneo said, there would be "calmer exchanges" as Walter "gathered himself, calmed by the imminence of the contest." When they arrived at the studio early in the evening, their desks opposite each other, Cuneo would scrutinize the script for possible libel and suggest changes. This triggered new arguments as Walter defended his copy and stubbornly refused to change it. (What the sensitive Cuneo did not say is that he often left in tears, sobbing outside the studio until Walter fetched him back in.) Even after Cuneo thought he had convinced Walter to comply, Walter often departed from the script, Cuneo thought, "for the pure sadistic joy of forcing me to turn on my supercharger. When he did swerve, he'd pause to sneer through the glass as I leaped into action. Clearer than words, his face indicated, 'You try it for awhile, you bastard.' "

As for the broadcast itself, the routine varied little from the early days. As Cuneo described it, "Exactly at 8:58, Walter would enter the broadcasting studio, open his shirt, loosen his belt, open the waistband of his pants and tap on his sound effects key. . . . It was like Man O'War bursting out of the chute. Walter went to the whip as he broke from the gate." Visiting the broadcast once, comedian Bob Hope noticed that Walter was visibly edgy and asked why. "Gotta go to the bathroom," Walter said. When Hope asked why he didn't go, Walter said, "The show's better if I don't."

Afterward he sagged, visibly wrung. But it took only a minute or two for him to rebound and explode out of the booth and into the control room to listen to the transcription, squatting silently before the speakers, wincing at every mistake. Always he called June for her reaction. "If June was enthusiastic about the broadcast, it had a magical effect on him," recalled Cuneo. "He would blossom into great exuberance. If she merely liked it, he was pleased and happy." But if she didn't, he was "desolate," like a kid "who had just broken a window pane." On those days when it hadn't gone well, he would stalk out of the studio. ("He was his own worst enemy," Rose Bigman recalled. "He didn't think anything was good.") When he was pleased, he might begin answering the phones, startling listeners who expected to get an operator. (Once, when a caller began quarreling with him, he snapped, "You listen too fast," and hung up.) If he felt there were too few calls, he might lament, "No one's listening to me anymore." Good program or bad, every week, unfailingly, he repaired to the Stork, asked Jimmy, the barber, how he thought the broadcast had gone, ate, and awaited his West Coast broadcast three hours later, when he once again became the "Voice of America" and the country's savior.

WITH WINCHELL'S growing stature had come some loud dissenters too—not just the political dissenters but cultural objectors who revived all the old criticisms that Walter had obviously hoped he had put to rest. Early in 1940 Westbrook Pegler, the sportswriter turned syndicated political columnist, leveled four scathing attacks on Walter's journalistic style, which he labeled "gent's room journalism." To Pegler, whose own pen was so venomous that Secretary of the Interior Harold Ickes once said he would no more think of reading him than he would of handling raw sewage, Walter was still the bane of ethics—a sloppy reporter, a key-hole voyeur, Hoover's chief logroller and a deadbeat who gave mentions to clubs in return for favors.

It was an oddly timed attack since Walter was just then enjoying favor less for his gossip than for his political pronouncements, but Pegler had turned on Walter's idol, Franklin Roosevelt, and he seemed to begrudge Walter the respectability the association with FDR had bestowed. Walter tried to answer in kind and realized he couldn't. "Maybe now that I've turned 43 I have acquired some wisdom," he wrote in the column. "I wish I could get my dander up instead . . . I remember the time not so long ago that I got my best exercise and recreation throwing typewriters at punks who threw them at me." Even so, he proceeded to attack Pegler's veracity and recounted a big favor he had done for him when a friend of Pegler's was threatened with blackmail. "A louse in the blouse of journalism," Walter called him now, brushing off the whole skirmish.

There were, however, misgivings about Winchell from a far more serious and personally hurtful corner: the intellectual elites. Once they had admired him as an urban novelty. Now that he had become a power in his own right, now that he was invading their territory, their attitude had changed, even among those who agreed with him politically. He "offended the refinements of intellectuals," said public relations man Edward Bernays. He represented a kind of emotionalism and rabble-rousing that they found both unacceptable and threatening. When Franklin P. Adams was asked on the "Information Please" radio quiz to name three hoofers who later took up serious work and FPA replied Cohan and Winchell, the moderator, Clifton Fadiman, quickly interrupted, "Would you call Winchell's work serious?" Adams said, "Well—no."

But all this cultural snobbishness remained no more than inchoate grumbling until *The New Yorker*, then the house organ of smart New York, decided to profile Winchell. The idea had originated sometime in 1937 with St. Clair McKelway, a veteran newspaperman and a *New Yorker* stalwart. Though Walter welcomed it—"If the New Yorker does do one [a profile] on me don't pull any punches. I wouldn't if I were doing one on you fellows," he wrote McKelway then—editor Harold Ross had balked, fearing that the piece might have too much high dudgeon in it. Two years later, when Walter had begun enjoying the status of political commentator, Ross relented, saying that someone had to take on Winchell and *The New Yorker* might as well be the one.

It was more than two and a half years after their first correspondence on the profile that McKelway wrote Walter to say that he was finishing a piece on Clifton Fadiman and would soon start one on Walter. "It will take a long time," he said. "I plan to write at least three parts and possibly even four." It was a full seven months later—and six parts instead of four—in May 1940 that the profile was finally finished. McKelway offered to let Walter read the proofs, and Walter assured McKelway that he wasn't going to "beat you to the punch" if he found inaccuracies. "I might, however, if you think I should, try to correct in my column, any false impressions—after the article appears. Mainly, of course, so that future historians would not be misled."

Three weeks later McKelway reneged on his offer. "It just seems a more politic thing to do," he wrote Walter, claiming that he had made "strenuous efforts to check every fact in it" so that Walter would very likely not be bothered by anything in it. (Walter noted to Rose after the first installment, "I counted 32 of them," meaning inaccuracies.) But then McKelway revealed his real motive behind the series. "I am against gossip writing as a part of journalism, and the piece therefore attacks much of what you have done as a journalist; on the other hand, I am told you are concerned about what I have said about your private life and I don't mind reassuring you on this point." Public figures are entitled to privacy, he said, "and you have been given the benefit of this belief, although God would probably say that you don't deserve it."

It was to be the longest profile in the history of *The New Yorker*—a series of blasts intended to discredit Winchell. McKelway attacked Walter's credibility, finding that of 239 separate items in Walter's five April "Monday" columns, 108 were unverifiable, and of the 131 verifiable items, 54 or 41.2 percent were completely inaccurate, though McKelway's own criterion for accuracy was the testimony of the subject. He portrayed Walter as self-important, untrustworthy, thin-skinned and hypocritical, and he downplayed the achievements on which Walter prided himself, like the capture of Lepke or his Hauptmann scoops. He even denigrated Walter's prose style—the very style which *The New Yorker* had once extolled.

McKelway found Walter's politicization equally appalling. He thought it outrageous that Walter pontificated on political issues, that he hobnobbed with the President, cabled advice to the British prime minister, acted as if he were the last defense in preserving democracy from danger. "Here's a problem," McKelway quoted a *Mirror* reader as having said. "Pretty soon now important people are going to want to use the words liberty, freedom, democracy, and so forth when we go to war and they are going to find that Winchell has spoiled them."

But the real grievance against Winchell was none of these things. The real grievance was the control he exercised over his social and intellectual superiors and what that control portended for the elites. McKelway devoted a long section of the profile to the anxiety Walter provoked in a prominent man about to change his job. Though Walter hadn't any contact with him, the man fretted endlessly over how Walter might handle the announcement and whether Walter might suggest he was fired. For McKelway, this was just too much. Winchell had disrupted the social order. Good people now felt constrained to toady to him in order to protect themselves. "When statesmen, novelists, artists, composers, professional men, book publishers, and entertainers go beyond mere toleration of gossip-writers and actually co-operate with them, as they do every day," wrote McKelway, "they suffer inevitably from a loss of human dignity, as does the girl who shows Winchell how she can wiggle a muscle in her chest. This is a social evil."

Even so, McKelway seemed confident that the social order would survive, and lest he appear a cultural royalist himself, he saved his final hand-wringings for journalism. Walter had almost single-handedly destroyed journalistic respectability. "Winchell has no taste and he has no sincere respect for accuracy," McKelway complained, though these are the very properties, he said, on which the power of the media rests. Popularity doesn't mean influence, he insisted, as if trying to convince himself it were so. People can make the distinction between what entertains them and what informs them, even if journalists themselves were having difficulty doing so. The "people cannot be hoodwinked into thinking that men who tell them spicy tales are men of any consequence intellectually or ethically," he wrote. But if all that were so, there wouldn't have been any need to savage Winchell in the first place. For all his alleged confidence in the people, by doing the series, McKelway was admitting that Walter *was* threatening the cultural elites and *was* demonstrating that being a "respectable" gossip was not at all an oxymoron anymore. McKelway was admitting, in short, that there had been a changing of the guard, symbolized by Winchell.

For his part, Walter felt ambushed. He had read the first installments about his early career with little reaction, a spy reported back to McKelway. Then his ire grew steadily with successive installments until, by the fifth, he was boiling. He knew the political reactionaries hated him, and he knew he ruffled the journalistic traditionalists, but he hadn't expected an assault from what should have been a friendly precinct, a liberal precinct; he hadn't expected it because he himself didn't fully understand the cultural ramifications of his power.

But he did understand revenge. In one column he announced that McKelway was being sued for libel by a subject (not Walter) who accused the journalist of "numerous misstatements and dozens of inaccuracies—haw!" The next day he printed an item about one fellow calling Ross a "so-and-so" and another defending him as a friend. "Well, can't he be both?" ripostes the attacker. And a month later he lit out against McKelway's grandfather, once the editor of the Brooklyn *Eagle*, who had long ago launched a campaign against houses of ill repute near the Navy Yard. The police conducted a raid. "One of the prisoners was a certain profile writer's grandpater!"

Meanwhile, Harold Ross received word that he was no longer welcome at the Stork Club. (Walter, claiming innocence, said Ross was barred because he had implied in the profile that Billingsley was having an affair.) When Ross remonstrated with Billingsley that McKelway had "encountered slime in his job and when you handle slime, it nearly always splatters all around," Billingsley said he sympathized with McKelway's "attempt to cut a line through the maze of legend and truth and misinformation" about Walter but insisted that "Winchell and I are friends, have almost daily contact, and I wouldn't want him to think I might say behind his back anything I wouldn't say to his face."

Moving from his attacks on McKelway to attacks on Ross, Walter kept jabbing in the column until Ross finally importuned him, "[F]or godsake let up on me." At the same time, through Woollcott and others, Walter collected a column's worth of items on Ross, though the *Mirror* and King Features refused to run it. Barred from dropping one large bomb on his enemy, Walter had to be satisfied with continuing to fire round after round at him. The Harold Rosses "should hire a hall according to their neighbors, who are banging on the ceiling with the broom," he wrote in April 1941. Shortly after America's entrance into the war, he called Ross, then suffering from nervous exhaustion, "Cafe Society's first war victim" on the broadcast and repeated it two days later in the column. Six months of digs later Jack Lait, his editor at the *Mirror*, ordered him to desist, but Walter was feeling mutinous. "Here is a man who in an interview says, 'I believe in being malicious,' and lets me have it. You know, Jack, that I will send it back to him no matter where I work and no matter what medium I use."

But by this time Harold Ross and the rest of the cultural elite were distractions from Winchell's real business. The real business was war.

III

"Good evening, Mr. and Mrs. America," Walter barked the evening of December 7, 1941. "The American population is electrified tonight with the knowledge that every quarter of the globe will be at war tomorrow night. President Roosevelt will ask a war declaration and the United States Government will immediately assume Constitutional wartime powers in every department. [. . .] This will mobilize the efforts of the whole American people. [. . .] The National Emergency is no longer a phrase." But Walter still directed attention to the internal threat. "Persons who arouse suspicion by their conduct, speech, or deed are inviting microscopic examination, perhaps prison. Nothing matters any more now except national security."

Now that war had come, his course of action was clear. Way back in March 1935 he had had June ask him in a column whether there might be war. "I dunno," he answered. "If we have to get in it—I'll have to go the first day. Can't you see the hecklers sending me letters saying: 'How about you?' I'm in a spot—all I hope is that I get my commission. Can you imagine me being under some bird I've taken a rap at?"

Even though he was forty-four, Walter was a lieutenant commander in the naval reserve and had been angling throughout the spring and summer before Pearl Harbor for active duty. In June, at the request of his superiors, he had asked to defer his inactive status so that he could take five weeks of training during his vacation. He concluded his training with a "breathless week at sea" on the shakedown cruise of the USS *North Carolina* and broadcast an offer that week to his commander in chief: "I am considered available for call at any time, sir."

At the same time Walter was pondering his future as a newspaperman. His contract was due to expire in November, and Hearst had assigned King Features' head Joe Connolly to renegotiate despite, Walter said, "the rumors of a few years ago that I wasn't going to be renewed." But Walter was uncertain, partly because of the prospect of war. "I don't see why I should sign my name again to a piece of paper," he wrote Mark Hellinger, "and while I haven't discussed this with Connally or anyone, I really don't know what to do at this writing." Joseph Medill Patterson had come courting once again, as had Mrs. Ogden Reid, the publisher of the *Herald Tribune*. United Features had made him a "proposition," but Walter admitted "there is something missing. No proposition is interesting anymore." He closed with a story about his scolding fifteen-year-old Walda one day and Walda retorting "in a sort of pitying way" that he just didn't understand. "I felt my age," he told his old friend.

After all this vacillation, he re-signed with Hearst in November for one year, confessing again that he didn't want to sign at all "because I knew things were going to pop." When they popped on December 7, Walter, for one of the few times in his life, forgot about "The Column." The next day, with little fanfare, he applied for active duty to Admiral Arthur J. Hepburn, the director of the Office of Public Relations for the Navy. Nine days later came Hepburn's reply, rejecting Walter's request. "While we all appreciate your desire to get into active harness," Hepburn wrote him, "there is really no place in Public Relations open at present which is commensurate with your rank, experience and special talents. We all feel that you are doing better work for the Navy in your present broadcasting activities than you would do in some active station of minor importance."

It was a great disappointment to Walter. He wanted to serve, not just to silence his enemies but because he regarded himself a patriot, and it irked him, as he frequently said in his column and broadcast, that old men sent young men to die. He tried to content himself by raising money for the Navy Relief Fund on what he called "volunteer active duty," but it was not enough to satisfy him. He needed to be in the fray, and if he couldn't do it in active service, if he couldn't do it overseas, he would find enemies here to lacerate. America at war, Winchell at war—that was to be his guiding precept for the next four years.

But his first fight had nothing whatever to do with Nazis. After a broadcast Walter was sitting in Lindy's with Leonard Lyons and a few others at four-thirty in the morning of January 21, when, as he told it to a friend a few days later, a stranger approached and said, "How do you do, Mr. Winchell?" Walter returned the greeting, but the man, now standing with three "powerful-looking" friends, "started a barrage of the vilest language I have ever heard," and taunted Walter, "Go on, you grey-haired son of a bitch!" and "What are you running away for—take off your glasses, you yellow bastard." Walter spotted a detective in a nearby booth and asked for his intervention. The detective didn't move, but the heckler now jumped on a seat and gibed at Walter for requesting assistance. Claiming he feared for his safety, Walter grabbed a ketchup bottle, took dead aim and hurled it at his tormentor. The bottle smashed into the man's face. Stunned, with blood streaming down his cheeks, the man, a forty-four-year-old Manhattan building contractor named William Lippman, was carried to the Polyclinic Hospital, where he took five stitches over his right eye and two more over his left lip. (Later Walter learned that Lippman had been turned away from the Stork on three occasions, had written to Walter to protest and was upset that he had not received the courtesy of a reply.)

The next day Danton Walker, the *Daily News* Broadway columnist, leaped on the irony of Walter's hurling ketchup bottles while our soldiers were fighting overseas. "Now that Lieut. Commander Winchell has won his first engagement in the Battle of Broadway, with ketchup bottles at six paces, the air is bristling with inquiries," Walker wrote. "Will the Navy be requested to strike off a bronze plaque to commemorate the event, the boys ask, and will the new slogan be 'Remember Lindy's!' in lieu of 'Remember Pearl Harbor?' . . . Will the Cub Room be converted into a bomb proof shelter, or will Sherman Billingsley declare the Stork Club an 'open' bistro when the bombings begin?"

Walter immediately met the attack with juvenile ones of his own on Walker's masculinity, printing a letter saying that Walker, a homosexual, had started out as a female impersonator and reprinting another item from Frank Farrell's column saying that Walker's contribution to the war cause was learning how to fry doughnuts so he could enlist in the Salvation Army "because the lasses' uniforms are so pretty!"

At the same time Walter suspected that the real instigator behind the Walker digs was the sister of Walker's publisher and the publisher of Walter's Washington outlet, Cissy Patterson of the Washington *Times-Herald*. Cissy Patterson, the granddaughter of Joseph Medill, who had owned the Chicago *Tribune*, and the sister of Joseph Medill Patterson, was a woman of strong temperament and peculiar inclination. Tall, attractive and flighty, she had married a dissipated Austrian count who abandoned her and the daughter they had, then later kidnapped the girl for ransom. After her divorce Cissy was courted by a series of lovers, ranging from a topflight polo player to editor Walter Howey to diplomat William Bullitt to attorney Elmer Schlesinger, whom she made her second husband. When Schlesinger died suddenly in 1929, Cissy decided that she wanted to buy a newspaper and tried persuading her friend William Randolph Hearst to sell her his Washington *Herald*. Hearst refused an outright sale but offered to appoint her editor with one-third of the profits as her compensation. By 1937 she had bought not only the *Herald* from Hearst but the Washington *Times* as well.

Walter had met her when she came to New York and "romanced" him into taking her on police calls. The tension between them began sometime later, in May 1941, at a party honoring the British ambassador and hosted by Evalyn Walsh McLean, a friend of Cissy's. "It was the first party I had gone to since I got my long pants and some sense, but it was all veddy lifted-pinky and ho-ho rather than ho-hum," he quipped in the column, making it seem far more decorous than it obviously was. Sitting at a table with Senator Alben Barkley, Mrs. McLean and Cissy, Walter found himself under attack from the publisher. At the time he said that she scolded him for letting "imitators steal your act—while you've been neglecting it to mould opinion." In his autobiography he described a more heated exchange. He said Patterson lashed out, "Why the hell don't you quit looking under the bed for Nazis?" and called his column a "bore." As Walter told it, he then said, "Mrs. Patterson, why don't you get another boy?" At that she rose and raced off to the kitchen for a "good cry," or so said his hostess, who begged him to apologize. He wouldn't.

Now began hostilities between two extremely headstrong, intemperate individuals. Ernie Cuneo, a friend of Cissy's, said she "couldn't live without a violent hate." She told him that she frequently woke up at night screaming. That hate she concentrated on Walter. Partly, of course, it was because he had insulted her. And partly it was because she was vigorously opposed to American involvement in the war. But J. Edgar Hoover, writing to Walter that January, adduced another reason. "You had some items about Joe Kennedy's son carrying on an affair with a certain Washington newspaperwoman," Hoover said. "Mrs. Patterson assumed you meant Inga Arvad.* She apparently has a very strong feeling for this Arvad woman."

Whatever the reason, Cissy Patterson began attacking Winchell with the same sort of vitriol he used. Walter, she said in print, suffered from

---

*Arvad was a beautiful, Danish-born journalist then writing a column for Patterson's *Times-Herald*. Though she was married, she was carrying on an affair with John F. Kennedy—a relationship complicated by the fact that she had been accused of being a Nazi agent. In his January 12, 1942, column, Walter ran an item: "One of Ex-Ambassador Kennedy's eligible sons is the target of a Washington gal columnist's affections. So much so she has consulted her barrister about divorcing her exploring groom. Pa Kennedy no like."

"a chronic state of wild excitement, venom, and perpetual motion of the jaw." He was a "popgun patriot," a "grimy clown," "one of those whispery, furtive characters who used to pop up from nowhere to ask if we'd care to buy some spicy French postcards." One headline called him a "Cockroach." But these were less worrisome to him than Cissy's main line of attack: She began editing anti-isolationist and anti-Nazi items from his column, frequently killing the column entirely.

"What is being done, please, to get me out of the Washington Herald at once?" he demanded of Joe Connolly. "You don't know what I know, but Danton Walker's raps in his column are merely minor bits of needling in a huge campaign by Cissy Patterson to get her brother and cousins [Robert McCormick, publisher of the Chicago *Tribune*] in a total war against me." He had been told that Cissy was inveighing against him the other night at Drew Pearson's house. "How I hate that man," she was quoted as saying about Walter. "Never have I hated anyone so. I only hope and pray every night that he is detached from shore duty and put on a destroyer which is sunk." That prompted Walter to opine that she showed the "same consideration for any destroyer's one-hundred and twenty Americans that she and her relatives have shown in their editorials." He warned Connolly that unless they got the column away from Patterson soon, Walter would embarrass them all by getting out the story of her vendetta on his broadcast and in other papers.

By the end of January the column was running only three times a week in the *Times-Herald*, and by the end of February, after one last appeal to Connolly, Walter decided to sue Patterson for breach of contract to get his column out of her paper. "First time a reporter fired his publisher," Walter announced.

But the course of a lawsuit was too long for the impatient columnist. Early in March he announced that he would not re-sign with Hearst when his contract expired in November unless Hearst dropped the *Times-Herald*. He reasoned that if he weren't writing for the *Mirror*, there would be no column for the *Times-Herald* to cut, even though the *Times-Herald*'s option on Walter's column had three more years to run. That same week he took out an ad in the Washington *News* attacking Patterson and complaining of omissions in the Washington syndication of his column. "The omissions are usually about certain so-called Americans, pro-Nazis and pro-Japs," went the ad, while suggesting that readers buy the New York *Mirror* to see his "drivel" as written.

Still unable to win his release, Walter decided to escalate. "I think we have been too kind to Cissie [*sic*]," he told Herman Klurfeld. "No more jabs. Let's try to retaliate with a knockout blow." When Cuneo warned him that a gentleman wouldn't attack Patterson as Walter had done, Walter said, "I'm not a gentleman, and the bastard doesn't live who dares call me that to my face." Klurfeld's torpedo was fired on Walter's March 15 broadcast. Citing an editorial on American foreign policy—"from the Washington newspaper—which buys, but suppresses—and hand-cuffs—my daily articles"—that had been placed in the *Congressional Record* back in May 1940 by Senator Ernest Lundeen, who "worked with the convicted Nazi agent [George Sylvester] Viereck," Walter mused on "how the pieces of the jigsaw puzzle fit together," leaving the unmistak-able impression that the *Times-Herald* was somehow in league with the Nazis. The next week Cissy Patterson filed a $200,000 defamation suit.

At the same time that he was embroiled in his feud with Patterson, Walter was taking the fire of the congressional isolationists, who, now that America was officially at war, should have found themselves chas-tened but were surprisingly unbowed and contentious. They refused to close ranks around the President just because he had managed to trick the American people into going to war. All the war did, in their minds, was verify Roosevelt's villainy. *He* was the real enemy.

Of course, it wasn't just about war. For years conservative extremists had hated Franklin Roosevelt, hated him with a searing, white-hot inten-sity. His political appeals to the masses and his charges of economic roy-alism; his social programs, which they perceived as a left-wing Trojan Horse; his bright young advisers, many of them Jewish; his faith in gov-ernment action and his belief in America's international responsibility—all these things had driven conservatives to rage. More, they hated him personally. They hated his ebullience as he destroyed their country. They hated his confidence, his control, the high lilt of his voice. Some of them even hated his disability, calling him syphilitic. They hated his wife. They hated his children. They hated his cigarette holder, his cape, his little dog Fala. But above all, they hated the fact that he was seemingly impervious to their hate. No matter what they said—and they had the better part of the media establishment on their side—no matter how vehemently they demonstrated the error of his ways and, now, no matter how they railed against his sending Americans to die, Roosevelt not only survived, he flourished.

But if the President was impervious to their assaults, his most vocal supporter, Walter Winchell, was not. Winchell did not have an office be-hind which to hide. Winchell could be punished.

Shortly after Pearl Harbor the conservatives began an attack on his military service. Much to his own chagrin he was still doing only volun-teer work for the Navy, though he took this work seriously. Five days a week he hopped the subway to the Third Naval District headquarters at 90 Church Street in downtown Manhattan, where he wrote speeches and press releases and organized a gala scheduled for March 10 at Madison Square Garden to raise money for the Navy Relief Society. "He talks navy, navy, navy," wrote an interviewer at the time. "He is terrified these days lest he do something to cause him to lose his commission or to bring disgrace upon the navy."

Walter was taking no pay and had no official position in the service, but the congressional isolationists thought it scandalous that the Navy should be giving *any* sort of imprimatur to Winchell. On March 2 Representative Clare Hoffman, a Republican from Michigan, took the floor of the House to ask Naval Affairs Committee Chairman Carl Vinson why Winchell was permitted to broadcast in uniform. "Now, I may be wrong about that," Hoffman admitted (and he was), "and I wish the gentleman would give us information on his record tomorrow." Vinson replied that he had already asked the Navy Department either to call Walter to active duty or to disenroll him from the reserves.

This was news to Walter. Upon hearing it, he said he would head for Washington immediately to request active duty from President Roosevelt. "My thought would be that in view of his past experience and operations," Hoffman told the House the next day, "there might be in the Navy some division corresponding to the scavenger department. . . . He is fully qualified for that." The Navy defended Walter, saying that he had raised considerable sums for Navy Relief and was responsible for an increase in recruiting, but even Walter wanted more. "How about some active duty and stop wasting the taxpayers' money?" he begged in his column that day.

The next day he reprinted editorials in his support. "He is being sniped at, attacked and maligned as a result of having volunteered to do his bit in the war effort," he quoted the Montreal *Gazette*. Damon Runyon opined in his column that the "sacrifice of Winchell's life might satisfy his pride and gratify some of his enemies, but it would scarcely make up for the gap it would leave in his present field of patriotic endeavor. The Navy does not want influential middle-aged gentlemen at its battle stations, but it does want them behind the lines, especially those who, like Winchell, are willing to work night and day in practical effort for the Navy."

That week, after the President's press conference, Walter stayed to request active duty. Roosevelt understood Walter's frustration. The President's own sons had been under attack, first for having received preferential treatment when the Navy granted Lieutenant Franklin Roosevelt, Jr., a thirty-day leave to undergo an emergency appendectomy and then for not having been assigned to the front lines. Walter offered to set the record straight, but the President refused, and when Walter pressed the issue, Roosevelt opened his drawer, pulled out a letter from one of his sons, and read, "Dear Pop, I only hope one of us gets killed. Maybe then 'they' will stop picking on the rest of the family."

"I had seen and heard FDR laugh at jokes and stories," Walter remember, "but I had never seen a President weep. His eyes filled. He tried to swallow a lump that stuck in his throat." Then he put the letter back in his drawer. Walter asked if he might read it on the air, but the President said no. Just before leaving, Walter again pleaded with the President to be put on active duty. "I know what I want to do, Sir," he said he told the President, "but what do you want me to do?" Though Walter didn't tell anyone, the President apparently wanted him to continue doing what he was already doing.*

Meanwhile, in the two weeks since Clare Hoffman had questioned Carl Vinson about Walter's military status, the issue of his service had become a conservative rallying point: the isolationists' way of discrediting intervention after the fact by discrediting one of the leading interventionists as a "penthouse lieutenant." The passionately isolationist Chicago *Tribune*, Walter believed, was running an anti-Winchell campaign by sending anonymous communications about him to each congressman, and Joseph Kamp, among the most rabid of the American fascists, was now bombarding the Navy and Congress with letters attacking Walter's continued commission, accusing him of being a Communist dupe and, in one letter to Hoffman, asking the old anti-Semitic question, "Is his name Moses Weinstein or Lipschitz?"

By the same token, many others were raising their voices in Walter's defense. When comedian Phil Baker said over the radio, "Instead of chasing storks, he's chasing rats," he got a "terrific hand." Ben Bernie told Walter that after needling him during an appearance, he was bawled out by a woman from the audience. (Walter's good deeds, in fact, ended the long-running Bernie-Winchell feud.) Even in Congress there were representatives taking his side. Representative Luther Patrick declared, "I doubt, with the possible exception of the Chief Executive himself, there is anyone in the United States that will disseminate more proper and nec-

---

*Walter, however, couldn't just let his President take the conservatives' hits. Two years later he discovered that the son of one of the most persistent of the President's sons' critics, Representative William Lambertson of Kansas, had claimed status as a conscientious objector. Walter happily blared the news. The next morning he received a call from the President's secretary Grace Tully asking him to come down to the President's press conference before the other journalists arrived. Walter found the President in his office signing documents, the morning's newspapers headlining the Lambertson affair lying on his desk. The President removed his glasses, tapped the headlines with his cigarette holder and whispered, "Thanks."

essary information for Uncle Sam to his folks over the country than Walter Winchell."

Nevertheless, during all this flurry Walter's military status still had not been resolved. Despite the President's instructions, Walter decided to return to Washington the following week to press his case for active duty with Admiral Randall Jacobs, chief of the Bureau of Navigation. In his March 13 column, "Gal Friday" opened with the bulletin that "Capt. L phoned from Washington to 'report forthwith,' not later than today at 5. Said he had no idea what would happen—but to have your civilian affairs in order." Shortly after the Madison Square Garden Navy Relief benefit, which raised $160,000, Walter raced to Washington again—he had seen June only six hours in twelve days—but the weekend came and went without any change in Walter's status.

In the meantime, the campaign for active duty wasn't the only cause Walter was pressing. He was also taking the attack directly to his critics in Congress again. Early in April he announced that Clare Hoffman was going to be called before a Washington grand jury investigating improprieties. A few months later, after the Justice Department won indictments against twenty-eight Nazi sympathizers for sedition, he raised the ante by accusing certain unnamed congressmen of trying to remove the prosecutor, William Power Maloney. "In nearly every case of alleged subversive activities," Walter wrote in the column, "one or more members of Congress have been directly or indirectly linked!"

In effect, Walter had now publicly accused his congressional critics not only of opposing the President but of collaborating with the enemy. "How much longer is Winchell to be permitted while an officer of the Navy to undermine the faith of our people in their representatives?" Clare Hoffman declaimed in the House. When Walter then went on to say that certain congressmen were demanding that the accused saboteurs be executed because "they might talk too much," Hoffman was nearly apoplectic. "Are you going to let them get away with that?" he stormed on the House floor. "Are you going to let anyone say that, even a lieutenant commander? . . . Next week my boy goes into the Navy. Does he have to associate with such a man as that?" Representative William Lambertson interrupted Hoffman's harangue to ask, "When the gentleman speaks of Walter Winchell, why does he not give his real name?" But Hoffman, to his credit, didn't take the anti-Semitic bait. "He is a disgrace to any name," the congressman answered.

All this invective was tame, however, compared with Cissy Patterson's renewed attacks in the *Times-Herald*. In a long article on July 19, titled "Apology to Winchell, The Popgun Patriot," which was part of a series of articles on interventionists who pushed for war and then stayed home, writer Georgiana X. Preston called him a "twisted, inferiority-ridden soul, perpetually sick with hidden shame over his past and origins" and a "marred vessel that many of us had an unconscious hand in fashioning." Subheadings included "Rode Roughshod over the Decencies," "Potential Feelthy Peecture King," "How Winchell Is Like Hitler," and "He Has a Fox-like Face." It closed; "Winchell is forever boasting that he is the American [whom] Hitler would most like to hang. In what respect does that make him different from anyone else?"

Rather than respond to the ad hominem attack with one of his own, Walter broadcast an editorial that same day denouncing newspaper publishers for sniping at the President while the country was at war. "These publishers refuse to see that in viciously attacking the American President, they are sabotaging the war effort of the American people," Walter announced. "Their reason is not hard to find. Franklin D. Roosevelt is the spokesman for the common man and his family, not for any publisher's privileged money." Like a child seeking approval, Walter sent a copy of the editorial to the President. "[I]t might refresh him a bit," Walter noted to Steve Early.

While obviously enjoying himself immensely with this surrogate form of combat, Walter was nevertheless genuinely concerned about the American fifth column. He believed that the Nazi sympathizers were eroding American will from within, and he also believed that he was the one to sound the klaxon against them. In August he launched a four-part series in *Liberty* magazine called "Americans We Can Do Without" after the radio segment. "The American people have a right to know who the enemy is on the homefront," he wrote in the first installment.

In the first two parts he confined himself to the usual right-wing crackpots: Gerald L. K. Smith, a notable anti-Semite who was then running for the Senate from Michigan; Joseph E. McWilliams, the head of the Christian Mobilizers; George Deatherage, leader of a group called Knights of the White Camellia; General George Van Horn Mosley, who openly approved of the Nazi way of life and wanted it instituted here; and Fritz Kuhn, the chief of the American Nazi Bund. (Walter reported that Kuhn would call his office, disguise his voice and convey libelous material on himself in the hope that Walter would use it, opening the way to a suit.)

In the third part, Walter took on Congress again. "There were not many of you who imagined we would live to see the day when members of the federal legislature would advocate trading with the enemy," he wrote, "or would take it for granted that we drop to our knees in fear just because of Goebbels' threats over the Berlin radio." But that was precisely what Congressmen Hamilton Fish of New York, Lewis D. Thill of

Wisconsin and Walter's old target Jacob Thorkelson of Montana were doing. "Do not forget," Thorkelson had said. "It will require the same medicine to cure the United States that brought about cure in Germany." Walter concluded with an attack on Clare Hoffman, who, he said, had once suggested that President Roosevelt be impeached. "Remember these things when you cast your vote," Walter cautioned.

A few weeks later Walter cheerfully announced that Representative Thorkelson had filed a $2 million libel suit against him for the *Liberty* pieces. Gerald L. K. Smith was contemplating legal action too, but he confided to his attorney that he couldn't afford the $200 necessary to proceed with the case and asked that it be dropped. As far as Walter was concerned, none of these threats mattered very much anyway. For he was finally getting what he and his opponents had both wanted so very badly.

Walter Winchell was at last going to war.

IV

In November 1942 American troops landed in North Africa, and as Walter reported in his column, it "means we're getting down to cases . . . We are getting within shooting distance of the Nazis." Americans, he said, were exhilarated by the news. "There were loud cheers for Midway, and the triumphs in the Solomons were hailed," he wrote, referring to American advances in the Pacific theater. "But it's more inspiring when the senior partners of the Axis are getting the slapping. [. . .] There's something very beautiful about one of those bragging squareheads biting the dust." Again he sent the column to Steve Early and asked Early to give the President "many thanks for HE KNOWS WHAT."

The thanks Walter extended to Roosevelt were for the President's concession at long last to call Walter up for active duty. Four times, according to *Time* magazine, Walter had beseeched Washington to call him up, and each time he had been rebuffed, no doubt because, as he had been told, he was of too much service to the administration in the column and on the air and because his call-up would inevitably mean another contretemps with the conservatives in Congress. After another of the President's press conferences that fall, Walter once again begged for sea duty, and this time the President gave in. "I report December 1st for my tour of duty, sir," Walter wrote like a child heading for camp. "You have made me very happy."

His assignment, which he was careful not to divulge publicly, was to visit Brazil on a fact-finding mission for the State and Navy departments, mainly to find out what the Brazilians thought of Americans. Though

German submarines were patrolling the South Atlantic off the Brazilian coast, there seemed very little danger from the enemy. Walter, however, had never taken an airplane—he had always traveled to California and Miami by train—and he was as terrified at the prospect of flight as he was excited by the duty. The night before departing for Miami, he sent a limousine to Mount Vernon, a New York suburb, to pick up his accountant-lawyer Harry Geist and drive him to Twelve Acres, where Geist redrafted Walter's will.

There were two other matters to settle before he left: the column and the broadcast. It was decided that assorted contributors would take over the column in his absence, but Jergens wanted a single replacement and chose Hollywood gossip Hedda Hopper. Walter was livid. Two weeks after Pearl Harbor, when he was first pleading to be put on active duty, Hopper had written in her column, "Since Walter Winchell got into the navy before the navy knew it, they've sent out an edict that These Three Shall Not pass," citing gossip Jimmy Fidler and actors Errol Flynn and George Brent. "Do you mean that the three you mention cannot enlist in the Navy?" Walter wrote her angrily. "Do you mean, too, that the Navy regrets commissioning me?" And he closed hoping "someday to be able to return the compliment." Now he did. Having the contractual right to approve any substitute, he vetoed her selection. He was replaced instead by three news commentators.

Meanwhile, everyone wanted to know why Walter was taking a leave. "When I got off the train [in Miami] my own paper, the Herald here, had a photographer," he wrote Admiral Hepburn. "For fear they'd print I was here for the usual winter holiday (a story that would be harmful with everyone else at war) I said: 'I'm here for one broadcast and then leave town.' " All that did was pique the curiosity of reporters who knew that Walter usually spent the entire winter in Miami. When he was pressed for more information, Walter cryptically told them, "I'm running an errand for Uncle," believing "that might do it . . . Next thing I knew they printed it was a secret mission, etc." That was the news transmitted through the country.

Walter delivered a final broadcast in Miami, then prepared to ship out for Brazil in the morning. His mood was wistful. At 3:00 A.M. Ernie Cuneo remembered, he and Walter sauntered over to a park. While Cuneo sat on a bench, Walter suddenly broke into his old vaudeville act. He performed the entire thing. "He was terrific," said Cuneo, recalling in particular "a little walking poodle routine with his arms as paws which damn near charmed me off the bench."

On the orders of Vice Admiral Jonas H. Ingram, the commander of the Allied forces in the South Atlantic, Walter began crisscrossing Brazil and talking to officials and ordinary Brazilians alike, though *Time* reported that the first three women he met were chorus girls who had married into Brazilian wealth. In São Paulo he gave brief talks to factory workers. At a new fifty-thousand-watt government-owned radio station, he attacked Nazi broadcasts from Spain which sought to separate Brazil from the United States and warned against fifth columnists. And at a press banquet in his honor in Rio de Janeiro, he endeared himself by raising his cup to that of his Brazilian host and saying, "Never above you—never beneath you—always beside you." (Walter told a friend he had remembered it from an old movie.) It became a widely quoted slogan for Brazilian-American relations.

"How'd you like to go on a killer group?" Vice Admiral Ingram asked Walter when the columnist returned to Recife after his tour, meaning a mission to hunt German submarines. Walter was too frightened to say no. On January 5, 1943, he boarded a PBY naval patrol plane flying reconnaissance over the South Atlantic. "Some men are more fortunate than others. Some men are richer than others. Some men stay in love longer than most," Walter wrote in his column after he returned from duty, "and most men never experience the wallop that goes with being at the bow-gun of a Navy patrol plane (a PBY) a few feet over the submarine-infested South Atlantic." Walter had been asked to sit in the copilot's seat, wearing headphones and sunglasses, and watch the Atlantic "as tame as any Florida lake." Then, about a hundred miles from the plane's destination, the PBY was ordered back. Enemy submarines had been sighted and a new squadron of PBYs was sent for the attack. As they winged back to the field, some crewmen asked Walter if he wanted to slither into the ship's belly and man the gun, and being an officer, he felt he couldn't refuse. "When the damb [*sic*] miniature cannon rat-a-tatted at a 'million miles per hour,' it shook me from skull to toes. I felt that the crew were in stitches."

Three days later Walter returned to Miami, his mission accomplished and he feeling fulfilled. "I daily bless the moment in which I was chosen to carry out the mission confided to me by the naval authorities of my country," he said before leaving Brazil. Reporting to Seventh Naval District Headquarters in Miami, Walter made one last request of the commanding officer there. It was important that he have a record of his moment in combat; it was important that he have official documentation. On January 21 he received a brief dispatch certifying that he had been aboard a PBY during an antisubmarine search and that he had manned a cannon. Walter was thrilled. He called this one of his "most priceless inheritances" and insisted that Rose read it to June over the phone. No matter what his enemies said now, this proved he had done his service. This proved that he had, after a fashion, risked his life for his country.

"YOU CAN be sure that while you were out of sight, you were never out of mind," press agent Ed Weiner wrote Walter a few days after the end of the Brazilian mission. While away, Walter had had Hoover wire him updates on various political happenings, but Weiner was now updating him on the wars raging in the Stork Club and among the tabloids. Ed Sullivan and Danton Walker had been criticizing Walter steadily in his absence with only Leonard Lyons coming to his defense. "There is no doubt that Sullivan had gone over to the Patterson line of thought," Weiner reported. "He most likely realized that Walker had become the fair-haired boy, and so he was undoubtedly trying to climb on the bandwagon with his continued attacks on you. . . ." Weiner urged Walter to return from Miami soon "to let them know their field day is over."

This sort of internecine warfare had, in fact, been about the only excitement at the Stork since America entered the war. Less than two months after Pearl Harbor Walter had described New York generally as forlorn and depressing. He noted "[d]ingy burlesk houses that reek with the fumes of stale tobacco and staler jokes," "[f]rigid winds howling their tales of Winter to a populace that isn't interested." Even on South Street, "once one of the swankiest spots in New York," he now found "almost every alleyway and doorway" draped "with snoring derelicts."

"Booze is getting scarce," Sherman Billingsley complained to Walter in 1943, recounting the sacrifices that the war had exacted from café society. "It's practically impossible to get French champagne and brandy. Better brands of Scotch sell for $100 per case, rye and bourbon for about $75—black market prices, of course." But if the war had disrupted the supply of liquor and slightly dampened the high spirits at the Stork, the club did its very best to remain unaffected. It was still jammed each night; only some of the cast members had changed as socialites marched off to war and their younger brothers took their places. One guest described the Stork during the war as "a sort of rose arbor for gilded youth, a Cheshire Cheese for the solvent intelligentsia, a town pump for Park Avenue clubwomen," as well as "a subject of fond dreams in fortresses and foxholes."

On this last he wasn't wrong. *New Yorker* staff writer E. J. Kahn, Jr., then soldiering in the New Guinea jungles, wrote a dispatch to his magazine after receiving a copy of a new publication called *Stork Club Talk*, a house organ that Billingsley was now distributing. Though, Kahn remembered, he hadn't even been admitted to the Stork the last time he tried—Billingsley had made a "slight negative twist of his head" to indicate to the doorman "that our tentative advance was to be halted"—he joked now, "It was a gay night amid the foxholes, let me tell you, when, by the light of a shaded candle, I pored over the pages." The lead story was headlined MANY BEAUTIFUL GIRLS AND MEN IN UNIFORM CROWD THE STORK CLUB NIGHTLY—NEW ROMANCES ABOUND. Kahn said that the corporal of the guard had hardly read that "flash" before word was spreading through the jungle. " 'Nightly—did you say nightly?' an excited voice would whisper out of the hostile dark. 'Yeah,' would come the tense answer. 'New romances abound.' "

War or not, socialites had to have their assemblies; otherwise they had nothing. In 1941, before America's entrance into the war, the Stork grossed $900,000. In 1943, with the war in full swing, it grossed $1.25 million and was averaging two thousand guests per weeknight, three thousand on weekends.* Breakage and theft alone—mainly of the famous Stork Club ashtrays—amounted to $25,000 per year.

With his rampant populism and his fierce dedication to the war effort, Winchell could hardly mingle with slackers—which was, indeed, one of the charges being leveled at him by his detractors. Walter continued to hang out at the Stork—it was his lifeblood no less than the café socialites'—but he did draw some lines. When the Duke and Duchess of Windsor, whom Walter had castigated for their civility toward Hitler, visited the Stork and asked Billingsley to invite Walter to join them, he pointedly refused. When, on another occasion, he heard that Fritz Kuhn had entered the club, he immediately handed his pistol to Billingsley for fear he might be tempted to use it. And when he heard that Westbrook Pegler had arrived at the Stork with a Nazi official and that Billingsley—in ignorance, he later said, of who Pegler's guest was—had given them a good table and special service, Walter was so furious that he stayed away from the club until Billingsley managed to mollify him. But he was soon back again, talking, commanding, eating, doing the rhumba and telling one disapproving friend who felt this sort of dancing was now beneath Walter's dignity, "I'm getting in trim to take on some of my jittery enemies."

. . .

---

*In 1944 agents of New York Mayor La Guardia discovered that the Stork Club had been padding its sales tax, remitting the proper amount to the city but bilking its customers of some $181,029. Since the Stork placed checks facedown with the total written on the back, a defender said that "only an outlander who should not be at the Stork Club at all would turn the check over to tote up the bill." [*Time*, Aug. 7, 1944, 73.]

HE WAS. No sooner had he returned from Brazil than he ignited a new firestorm in Congress. On his January 31, 1943, broadcast, Walter editorialized, "You bet I'm prejudiced against those in high office who guessed so wrong about Pearl Harbor. They're still guessing wrong. I am not in the least comforted by their confessions of ignorance. What worries me most are all those damned fools who reelected them." Even before this pronouncement, Clare Hoffman had been demanding an investigation of Walter and his relationship to the Justice Department, which, he believed, had been leaking information about the prosecutions of alleged pro-Nazis. Now, three days after the broadcast, he introduced a resolution calling for Walter's court-martial.

Hoffman, at the time a five-term sixty-eight-year-old congressman from western Michigan who spoke with a midwestern twang and looked like Will Rogers, had been born in Pennsylvania and grown up on a 210-acre fruit farm in Constantine, Michigan. He attended Valparaiso University, earned a law degree from Northwestern and began his political career in 1910 as district attorney of Allegan County, where he was known as the "punching lawyer." He had lost none of his combativeness in the House. As a congressman, noted one critic, he "established a world record for dishing it out, by rising in his place each morning, for something like 600 consecutive mornings, each time to deliver a one-minute speech usually devoted to linking Mr. Roosevelt with the Kremlin and the Kremlin with the American labor movement." He had opposed every piece of New Deal legislation, including the Social Security Act and the National Labor Relations Act, and had once introduced legislation making it a federal crime to be a member of the B'nai B'rith Anti-Defamation League.

Above all, Hoffman, of German extraction, was a true believer that America should not have gone to war. For the intervention he partly blamed Winchell. For smearing isolationists he blamed Winchell wholly, but the "damned fools" statement, in which Walter for the first time attacked the voters themselves, finally presented Hoffman with an opportunity for redress. Fulminating against Walter on the House floor even after the gavel fell, Hoffman now offered an amended resolution proposing that Secretary of the Navy Frank Knox be required to answer a series of questions about Walter's service. One of these was to give a reason why Walter shouldn't be tried by a military court for having violated Article 8, Title 34 of the U.S. Code, which forbids military personnel from engaging in "scandalous conduct."

Trying to head off still another squabble over Winchell, House Naval Affairs Committee Chairman Vinson recommended that the resolution be reported adversely to the House. By this time Vinson had submitted his own privileged resolution, this one asking Secretary Knox whether Walter might have violated Section 1534 of Title 10 of the U.S. Code, which states that an officer using "contemptuous or disrespectful words" against Congress shall be dismissed or punished. The Navy was given seven days to respond, but Knox acted immediately, on February 10, 1943, one day after Vinson's resolution—the same day that Hoffman resubmitted his proposal to the committee.

Now the political wheels began turning. Knox answered that he did not consider Walter's statements "scandalous conduct tending to the destruction of good morals." Vinson quickly forestalled further action by Hoffman by submitting Knox's report to the committee and promising to call Knox and others before the committee for public hearings the following week after it had considered the appropriation bill. "I am glad it is to be public," Walter, in Miami, blustered to reporters. "It is about time. My status is no secret. I am on inactive duty, recuperating from a nose and throat ailment as a result of my flight to Brazil." He also bragged that his duty had not cost the taxpayers one penny. "I paid for my own uniforms and my own expenses on assignment. I paid my own way on the Brazil trip. Every Navy paycheck I ever got I signed over to the Navy Relief." He was contrite about only one thing. He admitted that he had erred in calling the voters "damned fools" and he apologized for departing from his prepared script.

The second week in February, as the hearings over Walter's status drew near, Knox summoned him to Washington. Walter arrived in the capital in low spirits. For the last week sympathetic congressmen had been pressuring him to submit his resignation rather than subject the President to another round of fire over what Winchell was doing in the military. Though he always enjoyed a good fight, Walter had decided to protect Roosevelt. The day before his scheduled meeting with Knox, Walter went to the White House, his resignation in hand. "What's that?" the President asked when Walter placed it on the desk. When Walter explained that it was his resignation, the President swept it to the floor without even looking at it. Then he picked up the phone and called Representative Lyndon Johnson, a member of the Naval Affairs Committee and a dependable New Dealer. The President told Johnson that there was a plot against Walter and that Johnson and Senator Warren Magnuson of the Senate Military Affairs Committee were to be at Knox's office the next day to see that Walter wasn't railroaded out of the Navy. ("We can get another Admiral," the President later told his assistant Harry Hopkins, after grousing about the Navy's attitude toward Walter, "but where in hell could we get another Winchell?") Still hoping to spare the President further embarrassment, Walter offered to go on sea duty, but

Roosevelt told him he was needed here to fight the domestic enemies hoping to plant a "knife in the back."

The next morning, February 17, Walter reported to Knox's office. Johnson was there, and Magnuson and Vinson and Admiral Randall Jacobs, chief of naval personnel, and a representative from the judge advocate's office. Before being appointed secretary of the navy, Knox had been a Republican newspaper publisher in Chicago. (He had been the GOP candidate for vice president in 1936.) He had been chosen, presumably, because as a Republican supporter of preparedness he would help deflect criticism of the President, but Cuneo thought him weak, and around Washington he was known as a "hostess." The Winchell affair did nothing to dispel that notion. When Walter arrived and asked Knox what the charges against him were, Knox answered that there *were* no charges. Then why had he been summoned? Walter wanted to know. Knox "hemmed and hawed" about Walter's staying away from controversial subjects before finally suggesting that he was trying to appeal to Walter's sense of fair play. For the President's sake Knox wanted Walter to resign from the naval reserve.

"The silence that fell over that spacious room was deafening," Walter remembered. "Then I blew my cool and told them what I thought of them for cowering before congressional people on Hitler's team." Glancing over at Lyndon Johnson, Walter saw him mouth, "You are talking too much." But Walter couldn't be headed off. Walter told Knox of the President's instructions that he was to remain in the reserve. The meeting lasted an hour and a half. At the end it was decided that Walter would be placed on inactive duty and would not be called into service again, thus ending, they hoped, the congressional eruption. After the meeting Vinson phoned the White House. "Tell the President I will handle the battle from now on," he reported.

Walter crowed as if he had won a victory, and since his object had been to remain in the Navy, in a sense he had. "Those who tried to force me off the air waves have failed," he announced. "I am now free to carry on, no longer strangled by gold braid." Saying that he had offered to resign but that a "high official" had rejected it, he added, "I am to continue fighting the undercover menace." Meanwhile, Clare Hoffman was also declaring victory. Winchell's deactivation would be a "boon to naval morale," he said. "No longer will Navy men wince at the spectacle of a Broadway gossip sporting a lieutenant-commander's stripes while he snoops about night clubs in search of sexy tidbits."

But not all of Walter's enemies were so sanguine. Westbrook Pegler thought his vaunt—that he was now free to fight the undercover menace—"sinister and mysterious." "This would seem to mean that he will be sending reports on individuals, a considerable proportion of them unfounded, to Naval Intelligence and to the FBI with which he has been more or less intimate," Pegler said in his column. And Pegler's concern, like Senator Wheeler's over Walter's ties to British intelligence, wasn't entirely misplaced.

In many respects the war had created an even greater community of interest between Winchell and J. Edgar Hoover. Walter was fighting domestic Nazis, and so was Hoover. Walter was also fighting off the attacks of isolationists and Nazi sympathizers, and so was the beleaguered Hoover. The flow of paper between them was enormous. Walter sent Hoover reams of material on possible subversives, some of it simply gossip, more of it from Forster's ADL files. Hoover in turn funneled information to Walter in long plain white envelopes. Walter's radio producer, Paul Scheffels, remembered Walter beaming as he said, "Look at this. You know who this is from? This is right from the Bible," because if it had come from Hoover, "there was no question of its accuracy or veracity."

While conservatives raged over this unholy alliance, journalists were once again howling that Walter was getting privileged information from Hoover—a charge that Hoover hotly denied and worked ferociously, sometimes ridiculously, to stem. In truth, the source of many of Walter's best Justice Department scoops was not Hoover but Cuneo, whose contacts in the department were impeccable. Hoover's own internal FBI communications confirmed the fact that Walter frequently knew more than Hoover did, and Hoover was soon assigning agents to monitor the broadcast each week and list items the bureau might find of interest. There was even the possibility that he was tapping Walter's phones.

Though Walter remained a faithful Hoover supporter, Cuneo's Justice leaks proved that Walter's agenda was not identical to Hoover's. It galled Hoover to have to get his information from the radio. It exasperated him even more that Walter, in playing up the subversive threat, was also inadvertently playing up the FBI's inadequacy in meeting it. "I am getting fed up with his hysterics," Hoover growled when Walter predicted the Gestapo would target American railroads with explosives.

What exasperated the director most was having to jump to the crack of Walter's whip. "You will note that Mr. Winchell from time to time forwards memoranda on various matters to the Bureau," Hoover wrote his top aides. If the FBI failed to act promptly, it could expect to hear Walter on the radio asking what action had been taken. "I think it is imperative that we give immediate attention to these matters," Hoover warned, "so that the Bureau's record will be entirely clear and we will not be embarrassed by any subsequent follow-up by Mr. Winchell."

. . .

FOR WALTER Winchell the warfare never abated.

That February, with his military status resolved, he found himself fighting still another battle—this time against his own network. On February 9, 1943, the day before Clare Hoffman introduced his resolution questioning Secretary Knox, NBC President Mark Woods announced that he was tightening restrictions on "several commentators [who] have recently departed from their prepared scripts to discuss controversial issues in a biased and inflammatory manner." Though he didn't mention Walter by name, Woods sent the memo to him and to Drew Pearson with an additional proscription against "derogatory or insulting remarks" about any member of Congress or any other officeholder.

It wasn't the first time NBC had censored Walter. The network frequently blue-penciled lines from his script, and shortly after Pearl Harbor, two subordinates of General George Marshall's, had even tried to pressure NBC to remove Walter from the air "when the first opportunity arose" because Marshall believed Walter was revealing sensitive military information. But NBC had obviously kept him on the air, and Walter had vigorously resisted any changes in his script, which was vetted not only by Cuneo but also by two attorneys, Harry Alexander and Mac Powell, who represented the sponsor, and another, Ted Cott, who represented the network. When one of the attorneys would ask him to remove an item, he "would fight like hell," Arnold Forster remembered, "and then not use it" because he knew he would lose his libel protection.

Cuneo described these vetting sessions more colorfully, with Walter storming off to his typewriter after being asked to cut a line and then pounding out a "Declaration of Independence." "He would state his grievance," Cuneo wrote, "adding that NO ONE—NO ONE was to interfere with his copy." He would pass this to the network vice-president, who would pass it to the crew, who would read it and pass it to Cuneo. "I would write some appropriate comment such as 'Balls!' and pass it back" to the vice-president, who "would ponder its great depth and see to it that it got lost." "You had a tough time taking a single line out of a broadcast," Klurfeld concurred, but for all the shouting and fist shaking, Cuneo admitted the arguments usually ended in "riotous laughter."

But the new policy announced by NBC was no laughing matter for Walter or for those defenders of the press who thought it an incursion on free speech. In Miami Walter fumed, "My fangs have been removed and my typewriter fingers rapped with the butt of a gun. The only thing left is the newspapers," though his past disputes with Hearst had been far more hostile than those with Jergens. Hinting that NBC had succumbed to powerful forces in Congress, Walter said that he had asked Mark Woods, "How about using your network to say that I think the time has come when the Blue Network should be taken over by the people?" He insisted that he would remain "as free as the air, not as free as the airwaves."

When he returned to New York, Walter was more restrained, describing his disagreement with Woods as a "frank discussion between businessmen." Matters remained calm for several weeks, but when Lennen & Mitchell, Jergens's ad agency, insisted Walter delete an item on his April 4 broadcast supporting the President's opposition to a bill backed by the farm bloc, he signed off "with lotions of love and oceans of censorship" and raised the issue anew. A similar request to delete an item the next week sent Walter into a tirade. "What you fellows want me to do is to begin looking around for another show," he yelled at the agency's representative. "You boys don't want me. Our ten-year honeymoon is about over," and he asked that Jergens break the contract.

But neither Jergens nor NBC would oblige him. Instead, Walter stewed each week. When NBC censored Walter's flash that Representative Lambertson's son was seeking conscientious objector status, Walter used it as a blind item anyway. "All they can do is put you in the electric chair," he told reporters. Now Woods insisted that Walter submit his editorials by 5:30 Sunday afternoon for approval. Walter complied, and Woods traveled to Washington, where Walter was broadcasting that week, to show Walter the changes the network wanted, but Woods pointedly refused to discuss them.

A showdown was inevitable. One report predicted that Walter would go over Woods's head to NBC's owner, RCA, leaving Woods little choice but to fire him. Walter did, in fact, go over Woods's head, but to a higher authority than RCA. He told the press he had wanted to read an editorial on the air from the Miami *News* that criticized Representative Hoffman for insinuating that Eleanor Roosevelt had trafficked with Communists. Walter insisted that he had wanted to make no editorial comment of his own but that NBC had refused anyway. So Walter sent the clippings in which he discussed the incident to the White House. One, from the New York *Post*, was headlined WINCHELL SAYS NBC WOULDN'T LET HIM DEFEND FIRST LADY. He knew what would happen.

That week the President asked his secretary Edwin Watson to arrange a meeting with RCA head David Sarnoff. The President also ordered Watson to bring in Walter's clippings during the Sarnoff session. Sarnoff met with the President two weeks later. On June 9 Walter wrote the President a note of thanks "for finding the time to do something about the Blue Network and censorship." After Sarnoff's trip to the White

House, Walter said, the RCA head had asked to huddle with him and Woods. While Sarnoff at the meeting professed ignorance about NBC's censorship policy, Woods feebly defended himself for preventing Walter from reading the Miami *News* editorial by claiming he thought it would be an "insult" to the First Lady. Walter snapped, "Oh, please stop kidding me." "It was a real heart-to-heart cards-on-the-table conference," Walter told the President, "and everything now looks rosier on the Blue Network, thanks to you."

The reason Woods had suddenly become censorious and Sarnoff so eager to appease the President, however, had much less to do with Winchell than with media politics. Early in 1941 the President, outraged over the radio-press monopoly, which was almost unanimously opposed to him, asked Federal Communications Commission Chairman James Fly to draw up a policy divorcing newspaper and radio ownership. Instead Fly wrote Roosevelt that the President was looking at the wrong monopoly. "Two men (Sarnoff and Paley) can say half of what people may or may not hear. NBC and Columbia networks control 86 percent of the total night-time radio power in the country." The policy the FCC should be pursuing, then, was breaking up NBC and CBS.

At the time NBC operated two separate networks, the Blue and the Red. Late in 1941 the FCC promulgated what it called "Rules Applicable to Stations Engaged in Chain Broadcasting," which ordered NBC to divest itself of one of them by April 12, 1944. Since the Red was the more powerful of the two, it was assumed that NBC would sell the Blue, and in January 1942 it incorporated the Blue as a separate organization precedent to doing just that.

The last thing NBC wanted while it was fattening the Blue for prospective buyers was any controversy that might drive a buyer away or anything at all that might prompt Congress to take action against it and lessen its value. (There was one story that *Time* publisher Henry Luce decided not to buy the Blue because he didn't want to be responsible for promoting Walter's gossip and politics.) Better yet, NBC was still hoping that Congress might amend the radio law to prevent the divorcement. By the same token, Sarnoff couldn't afford to antagonize Roosevelt, whose FCC would be overseeing the sale, especially after the Supreme Court upheld the constitutionality of the FCC divorcement edict on May 10, all of which made Walter a hot potato.

As it turned out, that October the Blue was purchased by Edward Noble, the owner of the Life Savers candy company and onetime undersecretary of commerce in the Roosevelt administration. Under persistent questioning by Fly at their FCC hearing, Noble and Woods reluctantly agreed to run the network "in accordance with true democratic principles." Walter wrote Noble the week of the purchase to commend him for "your courage in risking all your money and your life to buy the Blue network." For the time being, at least, that restored quiet to the radio front.

There was quiet on another front as well. That May, at the same time that the President was persuading Sarnoff to end NBC's censorship, Cissy Patterson decided to drop her libel suit against Walter. In some ways this was a disappointment to him. At his deposition in July 1942 he insisted that he wanted the case to go to trial, and he had hired famed civil rights lawyer Morris Ernst and a high-powered Washington attorney, John J. Sirica, to defend the action. Ernst wrote Roosevelt that he planned to "examine Cissy down to her undies." The President responded that in that case he couldn't attend the trial because "I have a weak stomach."

The weaker stomach was Cissy Patterson's. In February she had offered to settle her suit for $25,000. Walter refused. Instead he was in court on May 10 for the beginning of the trial. It never came. Patterson's attorneys asked that the case be dismissed on the basis that Walter in his deposition said he had never intended to harm the *Times-Herald*. They added that because the Jergens company was contractually obligated to indemnify Walter for any judgment against him, Patterson wouldn't get her retribution anyway. Since Walter had been deposed nearly a year before, his alleged apology was a flimsy excuse to drop the action, and Patterson's attorneys knew it. They reportedly argued with Walter's counsel in the corridor outside the courtroom, trying to wrest a promise from him that he wouldn't go off claiming victory.

Walter was surprisingly quiet afterward—publicly. Privately he chortled to columnist Earl Wilson over a one-inch ad that had been sneaked into the *Times-Herald* real estate section: "Shit on Eleanor Patterson!" Nor did Cissy lay down her arms. After World War II ended, she wrote an article calling her "liberal" enemies, including Walter, clinically insane. In his autobiography Walter claimed final victory over Cissy by taking his column to the Washington *Post*, where, he said, the publisher's son-in-law Philip Graham credited him with helping boost circulation by ten thousand papers each day. In fact, Walter's column didn't appear in Washington for two years, and when it finally reappeared, it wasn't in the *Post* but in a new eight-page gossip sheet called *U.S. Journal*, making Cissy Patterson one of the few who fought Walter Winchell to a draw.

V

While he had been ricocheting through life, taking on Cissy Patterson, touring Brazil, shuttling back and forth between New York and Washington, attacking isolationists, running his own intelligence network and getting government action for the scores of ordinary people who continued to petition him as their only hope—as well as writing his column and his broadcast—June remained secluded at Greenburgh. Walter always said she preferred it this way. June "didn't want to lead the Broadway life," wrote Art Arthur, a family friend. "She wanted to keep the two worlds separate—Broadway and family."

Yet it was lonely for her. As she poignantly told one interviewer years later, she was still waiting for her husband "to come home." Now, left alone, she decided to do something she had done before she had met Walter when she felt disconnected: She decided to take in children. Though she already had two affection-starved children of her own, she wanted other children, younger children. Walter said she "likes to play with live dolls." So early in 1944, without informing Walter, she phoned a foster care agency and asked to have an infant placed in her home. The child she received was a fourteen-month-old Chinese girl named Jane. "She scooped me on a blessed event!" Walter supposedly told a friend when he found out. A few months later she took in another child, also Chinese, named Jimmy.

Within the severe limits of his abilities and time, Walter gave these children as much attention as he could, taking them on shopping expeditions or meeting them and June at Lindy's for lunch. Outsiders thought the Winchells generous. But Walt, Jr., then only nine, found the whole situation inexplicable. *He* was sent away to boarding school, while his mother tended to her new family. Rose Bigman said that June adopted babies "because she liked babies. But as soon as they weren't infants any longer, she'd give them back."

As it turned out, this was only partly true. June expressed a desire to adopt Jimmy and Jane legally, and though she never did, the children lived with the Winchells for three years. When Walter claimed them as dependents and the IRS requested documentation of their adoption, Walter told his accountant that there were no such papers. "They are wards of the state," he wrote, but added, "We are giving them love[,] affection[,] shelter[,] support until they grow up." By late 1947, long before they grew up, June had them placed in institutions. Even so, friends said that she maintained contact with them and that Walter later put Jimmy through medical school.

But that was *June*'s family, hidden away in Greenburgh. Walter spent far more time with his entourage—far more time, in fact, with a press agent named Ed Weiner. He was Brooklyn-born, tall, good-looking and well-built, an outstanding athlete like Cuneo. He had starred in football at New York University, where he majored in journalism. While in school, he worked as a stringer in *The New York Times* sports department and after graduation had gone on to work for Ivy Lee, a legendary public relations genius who was regarded as one of the founders of the profession. After three years with Lee, he quit to join another legendary PR man, Steve Hannagan, but Weiner had dreams of being a "little king" and opened his own office.

On Broadway, where he was known as the Horse because of his size, Weiner became one of the dozens of hustlers who spent their nights courting clients and planting items. Like most young press agents, he never dared approach Winchell, until one evening when he got an item he thought was so important he knew that Walter would want it for the broadcast. Weiner found him at Lindy's in the middle of a conversation and offered to wait for him by the entrance. Fifteen or twenty minutes later Walter appeared. "I like the way you conduct yourself," he told Weiner. "You didn't barge in and take over as a lot of these guys do— your brothers in the PR business. And I appreciate that very much."

Now, just as Walter had done with Herman Klurfeld, he began inviting Weiner to join him—much to the consternation of the other press agents. Weiner was "lucky," observed one of them. "He was a garrulous fellow and a gregarious fellow but no great talent of any kind." Others thought that Walter liked having the hulking ex-football player around him for the same reason that he liked having the equally large Cuneo around him: because they provided physical security and kept nuisances at bay. Still others called him Winchell's "lapdog" or "hand-holder" or "shadow." Klurfeld called him an "errand boy." "If Winchell wanted a drink, Eddie would go run and get it. If Winchell wanted *anything*, Eddie would go and get it." "Where's your friend Winchell?" a rival once asked Weiner. "You're a little far from his ass. You've got to kiss it every few minutes." Weiner punched the fellow out.

"I would say most of it was jealousy," Weiner commented years later, reflecting on the stories that circulated about his relationship with Walter. He preferred to attribute his closeness to Walter not to subservience but to ability: "I was one of the best news gatherers of the whole bunch." Mike Hall, who worked for Weiner, agreed. "He filled a very important part in Winchell's daily existence," Hall said. He was "very alert and aware of that whole life around them." Walter depended on him. Once, when Weiner failed to show up at the broadcast because he had a golf date, Walter spluttered, "How do you like that bastard, Eddie, not show-ing up tonight? They ought to break every golf club in America."

There was one other reason Weiner gave for Walter's befriending him: "I never asked Walter to do me a favor." This had always been Walter's test of loyalty. The only friends were the ones who didn't want anything or, at least, had the sense not to ask for anything. "That seems very strange," Weiner admitted. But "I would submit my material about my clients the same way any other publicist [did]." Twice a week he dropped off a packet to the St. Moritz—one of news and plugs, the other of gags and vignettes. Walter then handed him that day's mail, which Weiner pored through, marking off the items that he thought were worth Walter's attention. But because Weiner never asked for any special con-sideration, he got it.

He just served. And like Rose's and Herman's, it was a slavish routine—from the St. Moritz to the barbershop where Walter got his daily shave to the Stork to Lindy's to the police calls and back again to the St. Moritz at dawn. Sometimes he even accompanied Walter out to Greenburgh, where Walter whipped him up some scrambled eggs the same way he had made pot roast for Klurfeld. "There were seven days and seven nights that I worked," Weiner said. "I never took a vacation." Another press agent thought Weiner "must have lost five years of his life around Winchell. He would wait out in the cold—wait for him for hours. . . . Just to walk him home."

There was no question why he did it. As a fellow press agent said, "The minute the word is out that you 'got' Winchell—he [Weiner] must have had twenty-five accounts on the strength of this. In order to main-tain it . . . he had to take any shit there was." Still, Weiner deserved some credit. Joe Moore had been a world speed-skating champion before retir-ing and becoming a Broadway bookmaker. Moore wasn't particularly charismatic or clever; Weiner described him as a "complete illiterate." But Weiner recognized that Moore had something far more important for a press agent than intelligence or talent. He was Ed Sullivan's best friend. So Weiner hired Moore with the understanding that his primary responsibility would be submitting material to Sullivan. "That opened up the doors pretty wide," said Weiner, "because I had access to the two ma-jor sources of news at that time."

WEINER WASN'T the only one helping to keep Winchell's loneliness at bay, as congressional investigators discovered when they tapped Walter's phones. There was a girl. Her name was Mary Lou Bentley, and when men spoke of her, even decades later, they spoke with something like reverence. She was tall, five feet nine inches, naturally blond with large, limpid brown eyes, a sensual mouth accentuated with lipstick, long legs and a breathtaking figure. One person described her as looking like a "young Lana Turner," only even more buxom. By consensus she was one of the most beautiful women in New York, more beautiful still because she seemed so fresh and unaffected and wore her sex appeal so casually—"like the little girl next door."

Hers had not been an easy life, and her story was remarkably like that of Rita and June. She had been born on November 21, 1921, in the small, sunbaked town of Weatherford, Texas, just outside Fort Worth, to two struggling vaudevillians. "They were dirt poor," her son remembered her saying. Nell Bentley died when Mary Lou was four, just a few weeks after the birth of Mary Lou's brother, Harry. With their father unable to manage, Mary Lou, her sisters, June and Maxine, and little Harry were trundled off to their maternal grandmother and a young aunt whom the children nicknamed Tee-Tiny. It wasn't a moniker of affection. Tee-Tiny resented the burden placed upon her and took it out on the children with a switch.

June Bentley was the first to leave the abuse. Though not as pretty as Mary Lou, she had a lovely singing voice and set out to make a career as an entertainer. Mary Lou was next to escape. She was only fifteen—though she looked much older—when she headed to Fort Worth to audition for Billy Rose's spectacular at the Dallas–Fort Worth centennial celebration and won a part. (Her childhood friend who joined her, Mary Martin, did not, though Martin later went on to become a Broadway star.) When the centennial fair closed the next year, Billy Rose brought Mary Lou to New York for the chorus line of the new club he was opening, the Casa Mañana.

She was a sixteen-year-old country girl living in the Forest Hotel two to a room, but when the 3800-seat Casa Mañana opened in January 1938, she immediately stood out among the showgirls. "I thought she was beautiful—at the beginning, before she became *the* Mary Lou," remembered press agent Irving Zussman. One millionaire department store magnate showered her with flowers every night. Billy Rose's young press agent, Sydney Spier, romanced her, and so did Eddy Landy in the orchestra. They were "closer than a Princeton haircut," in Walter's description at the time.

And Walter had taken notice too. The week the Casa Mañana opened, he raved, "[Billy] Rose advertises that his latest show has '72 Girls—Mostly from Texas!' . . . He means 'Mostly From Heaven!' " A few days later, apparently having become a frequenter of the new club, Walter wrote about a get-together at 3:00 A.M. where Rose persuaded the bandleader to play some standards. The scene reminded Walter of "that form of narcotic some of us have missed with the passing of Texas Guinan and others." He cited in particular one notorious "torch carrier" who was "telling lies to a pretty blonde named Mary Lou Bently [*sic*] from the Lone Star State" and musing that "there must be a lot of lonesome cowboys in Texas tonight." It was the first time Walter mentioned her name.

As her son remembered her telling it, they met when she was called over to Walter's table or he passed a note to her. Mary Lou was so unschooled she hadn't the slightest idea who he was, but she was "frightened" nonetheless, knowing that whoever he was, she could tell he was important. At the time there wasn't even a hint of romance between them. Walter just liked meeting pretty girls. Mary Lou continued her career, moving later that year to the Paradise, where she headed the chorus, to the Versailles Club and then to the Diamond Horseshoe. In January 1939 *Look* magazine featured her in a group of America's most beautiful women. (Walter, a celebrity judge, selected someone else.) Walter continued to write about her, as he did about other Broadway personalities, calling her now simply "La Bentley" or "The Long-Stemmed Rose."

"It was a very platonic situation for a long time," said her son. But the friendship had also been a kind of courtship. By 1941, if not earlier, Walter and Mary Lou were romantically involved. Along Broadway the legend had it that Sydney Spier had to step aside and died soon after of a broken heart, not only because he had lost her but because he had had no choice *but* to surrender her to Winchell. "That's where a genius turns into a schmuck," Ed Weiner said of Walter's infatuation. "All of these people like her [were] all looking to grab somebody off that would be a good provider and take care of them. . . . These people were pretty good for the taking."

But if the relationship was another of Walter's transactions, it was nowhere near as cold and mercenary as Weiner believed. There had been dozens of showgirls, dozens of brief liaisons over the years, especially after June had retreated to Westchester. His romance with Mary Lou was much more serious and long-term. For Walter, who was then forty-four, the twenty-year-old Mary Lou provided renewal. "It's the first time I've ever really been in love," he was said to have told a friend. She was big, bouncy, beautiful, innocent, free, uncomplicated and fun-loving. Another friend of Walter's, columnist Frank Farrell, remarked, "Five minutes' conversation and you knew all she had to say," but she was also incapable of putting on airs. With Mary Lou, her son said, Walter "could escape the troubles of his life. Because he was hounded by everybody. . . . When they were together, he could forget that world, and they could play with each other."

Walter provided for her and bought her small gifts, but she earned her own living, and if she needed something she couldn't afford and asked him for help, she made it a point of giving him change. In Walter's eyes that proved her honesty. Their only confrontation over material things came when Mary Lou wanted a fur coat. Walter's attitude, according to a friend, was that he didn't give gifts, he gave publicity. He relented only after press agent Eddie Jaffe, who was dating Mary Lou's sister June at the time, submitted an item to the column about the poor chorus girl whose boyfriend was too cheap to replace her cloth coat with a fur. Mary Lou wound up with a full-length beaver coat *and* with a means of getting back at Walter whenever the two got into an argument at the Stork. She would stalk out, dragging the coat behind her and sending him into paroxysms of anger.

Perhaps just as important as the money, Walter was a father figure for a young woman who had lived a life of insecurity and rootlessness. So long as she was attached to him, the whole city was hers. She liked to tell the story of how, very late one night, she and he impulsively decided that they wanted to go to the top of the Empire State Building. So Walter simply called the guards and ordered the building opened. Or there were the times, after midnight, in her hotel room when the bell rang and she opened the door to find room service from the Stork Club. Or there were the nightly occasions when this young country girl found herself in the company of the nation's most celebrated personalities. Or there was just the fact that no one ever dared write anything negative about her. "She was the columnists' favorite," as one press agent put it, "because she was *the* columnist's favorite."

Walter never hid the affair, feeling, perhaps, that Mary Lou was part of his public life—his life as W.W. She accompanied him everywhere, even occasionally to Miami, and if one didn't grasp the situation from her presence, one would soon understand from the way Walter permitted her to treat him. Save June, she was the only woman who could tell Walter to "shut up." And Walter would shrug his shoulders like a chastened schoolboy as if to say, "Cute, huh?"

Everyone knew but one. A close friend of June's was certain that June didn't know about Mary Lou—at least, not then, not at the beginning. (Mary Lou did recount one uncomfortable evening when June unexpectedly appeared at the Diamond Horseshoe.) The other columnists, abiding by Walter's own rule that one never wrote about a romance involving a married man or woman unless the individuals were separated, generally kept the matter to themselves, though a particularly big blowout between Walter and Mary Lou might make a column as a blind item. Only Ed Sullivan, still vengeful when it came to Walter, wanted to blow the whistle on him. Sullivan submitted a column with an item on the romance, but *Daily News* managing editor Dick Clark removed it. That sent Sullivan racing upstairs to scream at Clark to include it. Clark coolly told Sullivan that if he ran the item on Mary Lou, Sullivan could be absolutely certain that Walter would retaliate by running items on Sullivan's affairs. Sullivan conceded the point.

Walter's political enemies, on the other hand, were not so easily dissuaded. Whether or not Walter knew about the taps that House Un-American Activities Committee (HUAC) investigators had placed on his phones—taps that revealed frequent calls from Mary Lou, then in Cape Cod, to Walter during the summer of 1942—he did fear that he might be blackmailed or even that Mary Lou might be kidnapped. At one point he moved her to a new apartment, where he obviously felt she would be safer. At other times he had a bodyguard protect her. In the end, however, not even Pegler, who had obtained the phone logs from HUAC, used them. The affair continued. All was safe for now.

VI

In January 1944, like whipped soldiers making one last-ditch assault on a seemingly impregnable citadel, Winchell's congressional enemies launched a new attack. For them it was a final chance to avoid the political fallout of an Allied victory; a final chance to avoid being discredited as traitors for failing to close ranks around the President; perhaps, most of all, a final chance to muster their forces to defeat Roosevelt in the fall election.

The first volley was lobbed this time by Representative John Rankin of Mississippi, a thin white-haired orator of the old southern stentorian school who took the floor of the House after Walter had run a column denouncing Rankin's ridicule of foreign-sounding names. Rankin, an open racist, nativist and anti-Semite, had received twenty-five copies of the column from Winchell supporters and now railed against Walter, whom he referred to as "Lipschultz," for "stirring up dissension throughout the country." When asked by a colleague the significance of calling him "Lipschultz," Rankin snapped, "I may say I am a little skittish about a man who has his nose manicured, his face lifted, his name changed, and then goes on the radio to smear somebody else." Walter jabbed back, ending a column a few days later, "Very special $64 question for Congressman Rankinsteen: If an American's name is important—what's Uncle Sam's?"

During a House debate the following week over whether to grant soldiers the right to vote—denying soldiers the vote was one of the congressman's pet issues—Rankin had taken the occasion to unburden himself of more anti-Semitic fulminations. A number of House members broke into laughter. Walter was amazed. He couldn't understand a "representative body of elected officials who laugh at vicious comments on a man's race." "Consider the time it is," he wrote. "We are at war with Nazi Germany, whose present rulers came to power on a program of racial persecutions and murders. Now, in the American Congress, these Hitler prejudices get applause and laughter." Walter thought them the "House of Reprehensibles." That same day the House voted down the bill granting servicemen the vote. Later that week Rankin introduced a bill making it illegal for any newspaperman to be indemnified against libel or slander.

Now it became a slugging match. Another swing at Rankin on Walter's broadcast February 20 sent the congressman into new flights of indignation and rhetoric. Calling Walter "that little communistic 'kike,' " he compared him to

the loathsome ghoul at night, that invades the sacred precinct of the tomb, goes down into the grave of a buried child, and with his reeking fingers strips from its lifeless form the jewels and mementoes placed there by trembling hands of a weeping mother.

God pity such a scavenger! God pity the Blue Network, or any other radio system that would permit such salacious broadcasts.

How much longer will the decent people of America have to endure such filth?

Clare Hoffman was weighing in too. On January 4 Hoffman had told the Niles (Michigan) *Star* that the American people must march on Washington to end the war. Walter pounced on the pronouncement as evidence that the congressman was overwhelmed by his job. If that was so, added Walter, then the voters of Michigan ought to keep him at home or the House ought to expel him.

After submitting a new resolution directing the secretary of the navy to answer if Winchell was still officially connected to the Navy, what his duties were and what compensation he was receiving, Hoffman took the House floor on March 16, with information, he said, that would show why Andrew Jergens had permitted Walter to use the airwaves for his smears. Hoffman was referring to a report he had received that a housekeeper of Jergens's had been arrested as part of a German spy ring and that Winchell had used the information to bludgeon Jergens into submission. Meanwhile, Hoffman was moving behind the scenes to have HUAC Chairman Martin Dies subpoena two key Jergens employees and make the matter public. The only problem, announced Walter, was that *he* had already made the whole thing public a full year earlier. "I heard about the matter when I came back from Brazil in January a year ago," he told *PM*, "and called Jergens and told him that we had been announcing these things about others and I thought it proper that we should be the first to announce this. He told me: 'Go right ahead,' and I went right ahead."

While Rankin and Hoffman continued their attacks in the House, there was a far more ominous threat for Walter: a full-scale congressional investigation. One of the prime instigators was General Robert Wood, former chairman of the America First Committee. Wood had given money to a professional reactionary named John Flynn with the mandate to collect enough material to enable Senator Wheeler, Walter's old dueling partner, to conduct a congressional investigation of *Under Cover*, an exposé of America's pro-Nazi network and a book Walter had vigorously promoted throughout 1943. Flynn, however, had concluded that it was a mistake to investigate the book. That would generate criticism from civil libertarians. What Wheeler *should* investigate was what the right wing was now calling the "Smear Bund"—in Flynn's words, the "highly organized and centrally directed smear campaign to destroy the character of everybody opposed to the objectives of the groups which carry it on." Happily, Flynn wrote Wood, "Congress is hot about the whole thing and I believe that something impressive and even devastating can be done about it."

Wheeler, however, was not to be involved as they had planned. His committee wouldn't authorize the investigation of the "Smear Bund." So Flynn turned to another ally: Martin Dies.

Dies was a big, beefy, cigar-smoking Texan with a broad smile, a glad hand, a sharp tongue and an intense hatred of Franklin Roosevelt, whom he regarded as a left-wing radical. As head of HUAC Dies was responsible for investigating subversive activities. With his own profound interest in subversion, Walter had corresponded with Dies for years and early on had even sent him information on right-wing hate groups. But over time Walter came to realize that Dies was far more exercised by Communist subversion than fascist subversion. They had a falling-out, Walter said, after Dies phoned him to ask the propriety of speaking at a rally of the American Fellowship Forum. Walter told him that it was a fascist organization, but Dies spoke there anyway and was photographed between Fritz Kuhn and another Bundist named Kunze.

By Pearl Harbor they were already on a collision course, with Walter wanting to know why the committee seldom acted against the hate groups he so despised and Dies wanting to know why Walter was so consistently leftish in his positions. But open hostilities between them didn't begin until March 1944, when Dies added his voice to that of Rankin and of Hoffman. On March 9, in a one-hour harangue in the House, Dies accused the Congress of Industrial Organization, one of the country's largest labor groups, of being a branch of the Communist party and at the same time warned that John Roy Carlson, the author of *Under Cover*, was engaging in smear tactics to discredit Congress and establish a totalitarian regime in America. Winchell was said to be one of his handmaidens. Four days later Hoffman repeated the charge, adding what had been implicit in Dies's speech: that the CIO, Carlson and Winchell all were conspiring with the President "to convince our people that Franklin D. Roosevelt is the indispensable man."

In an interview a few days later Dies concentrated his fire on Walter. He charged that "fully 60% of the statements" of some radio commentators could be proved to be "utterly false," leaving no doubt of whom he was speaking. Now Dies wanted time on NBC to answer Winchell's charges that HUAC was soft on fascists, and he threatened that he would soon be investigating the commentator and subpoenaing his scripts to show that Winchell was conducting a campaign of "un-American propaganda."* "The whole question will be brought to a showdown in the near future," he warned, "and in my opinion it will develop into a major issue."

Walter said he would welcome a hearing and had, he claimed, rebuffed an overture Dies had made through Drew Pearson that "he would lay off me if I would lay off him." Dismissing the subpoena for his scripts—it "doesn't mean anything"—what he really wanted, he said, was to be subpoenaed himself. I. F. Stone, writing in *PM*, wasn't sure Walter knew what he would be getting himself into. He urged that newspapermen and radio broadcasters form a united front opposing the subpoena of the scripts. For Walter's own personal appearance before the committee, Stone believed, "If Winchell enters that ring, he'll find the referee biting him in the ankle while somebody else kicks him in the gut during the clinches."

The more immediate issue was Dies's request for airtime. Mark Woods and Jergens both were eager to grant the request, hoping that it might defuse the bomb. Walter, far from being opposed to the idea, suggested that Dies could even follow him on the air. Philip Lennen, the head of Jergens's ad agency, Lennen & Mitchell, tendered an offer on March 18, two days after another of Dies's blasts at Walter, this one comparing him

---

*In fact, Dies had been trying to get transcripts of the broadcasts for over a year, but NBC kept stalling, claiming that Walter was always changing the scripts. Dies never got them.

to Hitler propaganda chief Joseph Goebbels and promising that "this drunk-with-power gentleman will be exposed for what he is." Dies immediately accepted Lennen's invitation. The confrontation was set for March 26.

The week leading up to the broadcast was like the week before a heavyweight championship bout. Expectation was thick, and both sides jockeyed for advantage. Winchell wanted to use his March 21 broadcast to slam Dies for attempting to suppress a new antifascist best-seller called *Sabotage*, but Jergens and Lennen & Mitchell deleted the attack on the ground that Dies would soon be a guest and "if you invite a guest to your home you must treat him with fairness." He wanted to run another attack on Dies in his column that same day, but King Features refused to syndicate it on the ground that it only served to promote Walter's debate with Dies on the radio and "newspapers are in competition with radio." (*Mirror* editor Jack Lait was more truthful when he said, "The Winchell columns should not be used to attack the figures in American life who agree with the policy of the *Mirror*.")

In the meantime, Dies, working out of John Flynn's office, was preparing what he called a "bill of particulars" against Walter. Winchell's task was more difficult. With Dies scheduled to speak first, Walter would be expected to respond, though he would have no time, really, to frame a rebuttal. To prepare himself for any contingency, he decided to have three editorials written in advance. Arnold Forster drafted a combative editorial, taking the fight to Dies. Ernie Cuneo took a more philosophical approach, addressing the larger issues of free speech and abuse of congressional power. And Herman Klurfeld wrote a draft that converted Cuneo's high-blown rhetoric into plain "Winchellese."

Traveling with Walda, Walter arrived in Washington from Miami on Tuesday and settled in at the Shoreham Hotel for Sunday's battle. Like the seconds of a fighter, Cuneo, Klurfeld and Forster were there to assist. For Walter, the prospective spoils were great, and so were the risks— political and personal. Even before the war Walter had received threats on his life. Once the war began, he had become more concerned that Bundists or Nazi agents might try to murder him. On broadcast nights he parked his car around the corner from the studio, then had an attendant fetch it in case an enemy had planted a bomb.

He had gotten word of another threat in Washington before the Dies broadcast. The same day as the warning, Forster was felled by a severe migraine headache. Walter took him down to the barber for a head massage, but that only made the headache worse. When they returned to their rooms, Walter suggested they switch—not because Forster was ill but because Walter needed rest and didn't want to be bothered before the broadcast. It was only much later that Forster learned someone had threatened to assassinate Walter in his room. "So you see what friendship meant?" Forster remarked.

Dies took to the air at nine that evening in the studios of station WMAL. He did not intend to "exchange insults with Mr. Winchell," he said at the outset. "While I am interested in replying to the false statements many times repeated on this program, I am more concerned to fix the attention of the American people on one of the most sinister forces this nation has ever faced." This force was out to vilify Dies by suggesting "that I am shielding Nazis." "Actually the facts are *precisely* the reverse," Dies asserted. He had been tireless in his investigation of Nazi, fascist and Japanese agents and had provided hundreds of pages of documents to the Justice Department to aid in the prosecution of subversives. "Now in the presence of these facts why does Mr. Winchell say we are protecting these people?" Because, answered Dies, Winchell is not interested in exposing Nazis so much as he is interested in discrediting anyone who refuses to join the conspiracy against Congress—a conspiracy whose goal is "setting up an all-powerful central executive."

"Mr. Winchell is not in himself important," Dies went on. He is simply being used as a "transmission belt to deliver political propaganda, handing it on, sandwiched in between his collection of divorces, infidelities and other social derelictions." But if Winchell wanted to know the charges against him, here they were:

> It is charged that you, Mr. Winchell, as the Charlie McCarthy of this Smear Bund, are promoting disunity in time of war and doing more to arouse intolerance than anyone. It is charged that you are not so much interested in freedom of speech as license to slander. It is further charged that you have ignored the great truth that those who expect tolerance from others should practice tolerance themselves. It is charged that you seek to prostitute the noble profession of journalism based upon truthful reporting by reporting rumors as facts and gossip as news.

He closed by telling his listeners that America was in the midst of two wars: one of guns, the other of ideologies. (Essentially he meant one against Hitler and one against Roosevelt.) "We must win both of these wars to preserve our freedom. . . ."

Dies finished at 9:15. Now Walter, standing by in another studio, took the microphone. Rather than respond with Forster's fiery draft or Klurfeld's punchy one, he quickly decided to use Cuneo's philosophical one. For Walter the fundamental issue of his feud with Dies was whether any congressional committee should be permitted to conduct an inquisition. Walter had been attacked by Rankin, Hoffman, Dies and others as à vilifier and smear artist. He had been threatened with investigation. But "I am charged with absolutely nothing, and no Congressman has yet elected to challenge me in any open American Court or to lay aside his immunity long enough so that I can challenge him there." Once again he offered to appear before any court so long as the court was open and so long as he was able to cross-examine witnesses. As for the charges he had leveled against Dies and HUAC that they coddled Nazis, "Far from retracting a single statement, I reiterate every one of them."

Dies had all but accused Walter of cooperating with Communists in questioning the patriotism of those opposed to Roosevelt. Walter now demanded that "if any Congressman or Senator has information or evidence that I am guilty of activities against the United States Government, let them run, not walk, to the nearest Federal Grand Jury or United States District Attorney." But, knowing his enemies, Walter said, "If such evidence ever existed, it would have been offered against me long before this."

It was a brilliant performance. He had sounded temperate, reasonable and high-minded. "I thought Walter had made the largest mistake in the world, using Cuneo's beautiful, elegant statement," Forster said to himself when Walter first made his choice. But afterward he felt "Walter was absolutely right and I was absolutely wrong."

Their exchange finally over, the combatants met in a packed reception room. Walter wanted to know where the subpoena was. "All in good time," Dies replied coolly. Then Walter goaded him. "Let's get together and tell some more lies about each other." To which Dies riposted, "I'd have to go some to get even," and bulled his way through the crowd of reporters.

For John Flynn, Dies's address had been designed as only the "opening gun in this little offensive I have in mind." Dies had already agreed privately to launch his investigation of Walter and the Smear Bund and to "turn the whole energies of his committee" to the task. That was the subtext of the speech, Flynn said. To build public support for the investigation, Flynn now outlined a massive publicity campaign which he budgeted at $30,000. Writing Wood in high spirits, he said, "I feel we have in our hands now the greatest chance to strike at these damnable smearers who are trying to destroy everybody opposed to Roosevelt." Wood wholeheartedly agreed. "If you can take the offensive and get these people on the defensive, I think they will soon cave in. After all, they are in the same class as the gangsters and mobsters."

But the Dies broadcast did not suddenly mobilize opinion against Walter Winchell or Franklin Roosevelt. Despite the air of expectancy, the ratings for the "debate" were actually lower than those for a normal Winchell broadcast—a fact that *Variety* attributed to radio's own delinquency in failing to create a regular and familiar forum where controversial issues could be discussed. Among those who did listen, the response seemed to be overwhelmingly pro-Winchell. The NBC switchboard had been clogged afterward with calls supporting Walter, and he received dozens of telegrams, many of them from soldiers, thanking him for the fight. Jack Lait, no great defender of Walter's, thought that Dies "stunk" and that Walter "sounded very sincere and eloquent."

As the little man standing up to government pressure, Walter found even the traditional press rallying to his cause. Commentator Frank Kingdon called the feud a "battle of freedom of speech as decisive as any we have ever had in this country." *The New Republic* praised Walter for calling "attention to persons who in this country were doing the work of Goebbels" and condemned Dies for "trying to embarrass Mr. Winchell by all the methods in his arsenal." Even Walter's longtime critic *Editor & Publisher*, while admitting, "We hold no brief for the type of journalism exemplified by Walter Winchell," believed that "Winchell does not have to be responsible to the Dies committee or to any other Congressional committee for his criticism," and it too demanded that Dies prove his charges against Walter or be silent.

The day after the broadcast, however, Hoffman and Dies were back in the House continuing their campaign against Walter, this time touching off a wild shouting match with Representative Adolph Sabath, the chairman of the House Rules Committee, that was soon joined by visitors in the gallery and ended only when John McCormack, the acting Speaker, gaveled them to order. But Sabath had had enough. In his thirty-eight years in Congress, he remarked on the floor, he had never seen a session devote so much time to one individual. "[I]t would not only be in the interest of the congress but in the interest of the members whom Mr. Winchell has answered that both sides would cease this diatribe."

Walter, though, seemed to be enjoying the whole spectacle as usual. "Don't you envy just a little the excitement I've had lately?" he wrote Joseph Medill Patterson. The Dies feud had yet again made him the center of national attention. Within days he had already prepared a new jab at Dies which questioned the committee's authority once again and ended, "I no longer ask for your subpoena. I now defy it." Andrew Jergens phoned from Miami Beach ordering Walter to delete the attack—the "makers of Jergens Lotion have no wish to turn this program into a forum for political discussion—nor will it permit that to happen," said a press release—but Walter seemed less disturbed by this intrusion than he had been by those in the past. His opinions about Dies were getting wide circulation on the news pages now, and in any case, Dies wasn't the only target.

There was also Clare Hoffman. In a conversation with a newspaper friend back in Michigan, Hoffman had claimed that he was responsible for having stripped Walter of "his Naval uniform, his duties and pay." The friend had published the item, unwittingly stripping Hoffman of his congressional immunity. "This is libelous. Congressman Hoffman knows it is," Walter steamed in a memo to Cuneo. He demanded a retraction. When no retraction was forthcoming, Walter filed a $250,000 libel suit against the congressman in the District Court for the Southern District of New York.

By this time Flynn's campaign against the "Smear Bund" was in full swing. What Walter may not have known is that HUAC, in accordance with Flynn's plan but without formal authorization, was already conducting a full-scale investigation of him and leaking material to its friends, like Pegler, in the press. Because it still hadn't adduced any charges against Walter that would justify an investigation, other than that he had linked various congressmen to hate groups, the committee moved stealthily, collecting not only phone logs but birth certificates, census data, Walter's father's bank records and business statements, obituaries, even his grandfather's naturalization papers.

But the bombshell they were looking for never came, Walter was never called before the committee and the investigation was apparently dropped. The press reaction against Dies had, no doubt, been one factor; by threatening to examine Walter's scripts, Dies had become a pariah. Fear of Walter may have been another factor. Aroused, and he was usually aroused, Walter was no man with whom to tangle, especially when he had the full force of the White House behind him. Within a month of their broadcasts Dies had decided not to stand for reelection. He cited health reasons, but the President's determination to defeat him certainly figured in the decision.

In the meantime, Flynn's campaign continued—the battle taken up now by the Chicago *Tribune*, which flayed Walter in an editorial that May as the "last-ditch weapon by the New Deal administration." But the fire had gone out of the fight. After two years of nonstop attacks the isolationists were exhausted. They had given it their best, but it hadn't been enough. Walter Winchell had outlasted them.

He was a champion. He had defended the American faith. Billy Rose exulted to him, "Little did we think in the days we sat around Guinan's that you would be able to polish off a king in a day." In the wake of the Dies episode the Eversharp pencil company made him a new radio offer at $8,500 per broadcast and $5,000 for each of his six weeks of vacation. Walter let it pass without response, and the offer lapsed, but Eversharp's representatives assured him that if ever he were "anxious to take it up with us, we will enthusiastically cooperate."

Meanwhile, Walter's contract with Hearst was again due for renewal. This had now become an annual ritual: Walter moping and griping before finally agreeing to sign and Hearst promising to honor Walter's column. In an election year Jack Lait and Joe Connolly had been slashing the column, but Walter nevertheless signed with Hearst again, and Hearst responded by issuing an edict to his editors. "All Hearst papers using Walter Winchell column," he wrote.

> Winchell is a good feature and should be treated well.
> There may be some things he says which he should not say and those things we need not print.
> But let us print his good stuff, and feature it.
> Let us make him happy.
> Let us give him credit.
> Let us please the readers who like him.

Among the items that Lait and Connolly had killed that fall was one deriding FDR's opponents for "juggling the same flawed glip glop . . . It didn't stop the people from electing him three times," and, wrote Walter, it wouldn't stop them from voting for the President again. Roosevelt was almost certain to win reelection. What Walter wondered, privately, was whether the President was capable of running.

The morning after he had bested Dies, Walter visited the White House. The President, he told Klurfeld, "looked awful. . . . He sat with his hands on his head as if to hold it up. . . . His voice was so weak, so very weak." Among Roosevelt's intimates and within the councils of the Democratic party, it was well known that the President was ill and frail and that he almost certainly wouldn't survive another term should he decide to run. In May Walter sent Roosevelt a tip sheet he had received saying the President's advisers were unanimous in believing he wouldn't run, though even if he did, Thomas Dewey, the Republican candidate, would probably beat him. Walter also enclosed an item from his column shooting down the rumors: The President, his associates report, "feels better than they do. 'They're worried, he ain't!' "

Roosevelt easily won the Democratic nomination to run against the candidate Walter had described in 1940 as "The Little Man on the Wedding Cake"—slick, robotic, mustachioed Tom Dewey. Two weeks before the election Walter sent the President a long mimeographed report, marked "confidential," on the campaign. Roosevelt had asked Harry Hopkins to read it. As Walter saw it, the President is the "sole" issue and since everyone had made up his mind about the President by now the only problem is getting out the vote. The campaign as managed by Bob Hannegan hadn't any "spark." Compared with the last campaigns, "the atmosphere is a mixture of shock and alarm." The miracle was that big city bosses, labor, the liberal North and conservative South "could meet without bloodshed, much less unite for one man." They were the ones who would carry the day.

Walter was right. The President won handily, and Walter spent an uneventful winter in Miami bracing for war's end and pondering an invitation from the Blue Network to report the cessation of hostilities from Paris and make the first radio broadcast for the Blue from an occupied Berlin. American and Russian armies were advancing, and it seemed only a matter of weeks before Germany would be forced to surrender. But before that happened, Walter was shaken by what may have been, after Gloria's death, the second most cataclysmic event of his life. Before that happened, Franklin Roosevelt died.

CHAPTER 7

Lost

"THE PRESIDENT IS DEAD," Walter Winchell wrote in his column on April 13, 1945, the day after Franklin Roosevelt had been felled by a cerebral hemorrhage.

All that is mortal of Franklin D. Roosevelt will soon pass from the sight of man.

But the things for which he lived, fought and died, will live forever, while there are free men left to draw breath. . . . It can be no accident that Franklin Roosevelt enters the hall of the immortals as the victorious armies of democracy are about to enter Berlin.

His work is done. He has taken us to the borders, the Promised Land of liberty.

There need be no monument for F.D.R., ever. His monument is forever in the hearts of the common people.

The country had lost its leader. Walter had lost his own leader and much more: his friend, his father figure, his benefactor. He had worshiped Franklin Roosevelt. Roosevelt had helped fill the gaping hole left by Gloria's death. He had given Walter purpose. He had provided reliable political bearings for Walter. He had legitimized Walter and elevated him from gossip. He had lent Walter the power of his office when Walter needed protection. Now that he was gone Walter's life would change.

Already, with Roosevelt's death and the impending defeat of the German armies, the world was changing too. A week after the President's passing, Walter, Ed Weiner and Cuneo joined dozens of journalists in San Francisco for the World Security Conference, which was meeting to establish the United Nations and, they hoped, the institution of a new world order. A week after San Francisco the Germans surrendered, and two months later the new President, Harry Truman, was heading to Potsdam for a summit with Churchill and Stalin.

MY DEAR MR. PRESIDENT. YOU ARE OUR LEADER. WE ARE YOURS TO COMMAND, Walter had wired Truman when the new President took office, but within months Walter was pining for the heady, rambunctious days of the New Deal and bristling that his old conservative foes could lay waste to Roosevelt's legacy now that he was no longer there to defend himself. "Victories fought and won years ago were suddenly in doubt," commented TRB in *The New Republic*. "Everything was debatable again." Once again the right declared that the New Deal had been analogous to communism and Roosevelt to Stalin. For twelve years the country had been betrayed. Now they would deliver it from the traitors. In a column that September, shortly after V-J Day, Walter had Truman strolling the White House grounds one foggy midnight when he comes upon the ghost of FDR. "I thought you were, er-er-er . . ." " 'Dead?' says F.D.R. with a sigh. 'Yes, but I have been having quite a tough time of it. Some of my political enemies won't let me rest in peace.' "

With the liberals on the defensive, Walter now fought as much for Roosevelt's personal honor as for the late President's political program. "Americans! Every time you can pray in peace—thank Roosevelt," he began his column that Thanksgiving. "Every time you can speak freely or read a free American newspaper—thank Roosevelt. Every time you gaze at your home which was mercifully saved from bombs—thank Roosevelt. Every time you look at a child that has a warm bed to sleep in and enough food to eat—thank Roosevelt."

In fact, as Walter saw it, there seemed a growing wave of ingratitude. Increasingly Congress was bottling up the new President's efforts to carry out Roosevelt's policies. "Neither the American Congress nor the American people are giving their President a square deal, in my opinion," Walter editorialized on his broadcast late in 1946. "Every program suggested by the President has been turned down." But the denunciations that only a year before had stirred the country no longer worked. There was not the same imperative, the same moral clarity that Roosevelt and the war had brought to the battle against the right. The rules were in flux, the guidelines gone. After the Democrats had ended the Depression and steered the country to victory in war, the Republican campaign slogan that year was "Had enough?"

Nor could Walter expect guidance from President Truman. Many steadfast Roosevelt supporters believed that Truman was reneging on his commitment to the New Deal, and while Walter hadn't publicly challenged the President on these grounds, he was disappointed that Truman seemed always on the defensive where Roosevelt had always been on the offensive. With neither FDR's charisma nor his seeming ideological passion, Truman wasn't able to rally the liberal troops the way Roosevelt had. Instead, dispirited and divided, the liberals had let the conservatives seize the initiative while Truman seemed to lurch from one crisis to another.

It quickly became evident, however, that there was a deeper wedge between Truman and Winchell than politics. There was personality. Truman was the quintessence of nineteenth-century rural midwestern America, Walter of twentieth-century eastern urban America. Truman was self-effacing, Walter self-aggrandizing. Truman was dispassionate, Walter the very model of hot unreason. Truman was a moderator by instinct, Walter a crusader. Truman was a private man thrust into a public role, Walter was a man without any private life at all, a man always onstage. Perhaps the biggest difference between them was that Truman believed in the sanctity of his office, Walter in the sanctity of "The Column." It followed that Truman's man in the Broadway press corps would be the affable, uncharismatic, comparatively modest Leonard Lyons. It was Lyons, insiders said, who had a "pipe line" directly into the Truman White House.

Moreover, Truman was notoriously thin-skinned. When Drew Pearson reported in September 1946 that Democratic National Chairman Bob Hannegan would not be supporting the President in 1948 and Hannegan wrote the President to deny it, Truman responded privately, "Whenever I get my information from Pearson, I hope somebody will have my head examined—I'll need it.

"Articles like that are merely an attempt to upset the 'apple cart' and Pearson and your friend Winchell are the 'sphere heads' for that purpose. If either one of them ever tells the truth, it is by accident and not intentional."

The breach widened considerably when Walter visited Truman in the White House for what was intended as a peace meeting. Though it is unclear precisely what happened there, all versions agree that the President committed a faux pas. "I knew that Truman made a remark," recalled Walter's radio producer, Paul Scheffels. "I don't remember it word for word—but something about that 'damn kike,' and of course you call anybody a 'kike,' and he'd go after you like hammer and tongs. . . . That was the beginning." As Herman Klurfeld recalled it, Truman had called New

York *Post* publisher Dorothy Schiff a "kike." Cuneo remembered it a little differently: Truman had extended an invitation to Walter, who arrived at the White House, where he was warmly greeted by a member of Roosevelt's old Secret Service detail. Walter then had his meeting with the President. When he left, he realized he had forgotten his hat, and on returning to fetch it, he heard Truman say, "I guess we pulled the wool over that SOB's eyes."

Klurfeld met Walter at the Stork Club shortly after Walter returned from Washington, and the first comment Walter made was "He's not a President." "Roosevelt was an awesome giant to him," Arnold Forster said. "He thought Truman was a mediocrity."

Walter, to be sure, wasn't alone in this view. Many Americans felt that Harry S. Truman, the career politician from Missouri, was too small for the responsibilities now thrust upon him. Short, ordinary-looking, prosaic, profane and, as rumor had it, occasionally bibulous, Truman lacked majesty. He lacked the theatricality that Roosevelt had in abundance and that was so important to Walter. Truman would never command events. He would never, in Walter's eyes, create history as Roosevelt had. And he would never court Winchell as Roosevelt had.

Even after the White House debacle, many liberals, realizing how mutually beneficial the Truman-Winchell relationship could be, were eager to patch up the quarrel. But neither man would have any of it. When comedian Joey Adams, who was married to June's sister, Mary, at the time, encouraged Walter to settle his differences with Truman, Walter was incensed that he should be the one to make the overture. "I'm a little busier than he is," he said. "Does he have six columns and a radio show to get out each week?"

But it wasn't only Truman, and it wasn't only politics. In the year since the war ended, Broadway had changed as well. The enforced savings during the war now burst forth in a frenzy of big spending and high living. *The New York Times* estimated that attendance at the city's eleven hundred nightclubs was 2.5 million in 1945, up from half a million in 1939, and estimated the gross receipts of these clubs at between $50 million and $60 million. Early in 1946 the *Times* reported that "[t]he war years brought a new high to after-dark entertainment, and a new and almost feverish habit of going places to a lot of people who used to stay at home at night," and it predicted that the "Fabulous mid-Forties" might take their place beside the "Elegant Eighties" and "Gay Nineties."

Rather than mark the beginning of a new era, the nightclub boom actually turned out to be the last throes of an old one. By 1947 profits had declined precipitously and "snowblindness," caused by too many white tablecloths uncluttered with customers, had set in. More, the character of nightlife changed; the high glamour disappeared. *Life* magazine reported that the " 'career girls' at ringside seemed made up more heavily, their escorts seemed balder." New celebrities appeared in the postwar boom, nudging aside the old alliance of socialites and Hollywood stars that had formed the basis for café society. And the young cohort of café socialites that had included Brenda Frazier and Cobina Wright, among others, dispersed and disappeared.

Others traced the beginning of the decline of café society even earlier, to Frazier's shameless grab for publicity before the war—she was booed at a nightclub after spending $50,000 for her coming-out party—when she seemed to violate the unwritten rule that no one was supposed to *disclose* that the purpose of café society was publicity. But even if the secret hadn't been revealed, café society seemed doomed. "[T]he return to general prosperity during and after the war," wrote Richard Schickel in a postmortem of café society, "redirected our priorities and our fantasies." The idea of an island of glamour in the great dark sea of Depression poverty no longer held the same allure for most Americans once the sea was shining again. "[I]t began to occur to a lot of people," noted Schickel, "that passive, envious mooning over the rich was a waste of time, that if one cared to be up and doing one might become at least a little bit rich oneself."

Sherman Billingsley reacted to the change by renovating and expanding the Stork Club with a new room to be called Sortilege after the perfume Billingsley handed out at the club. But providing a lavish new set for café society could not forestall its demise. The great clubs—the Stork, El Morocco, the Colony—survived. The sense of rarefied elegance, the sense, as one patron put it, of being "at the top of the world," did not.

For Walter personally, perhaps nothing so signified the end of an epoch, not just of café society but of the Broadway era itself, as the demise of one of the men most responsible for creating it: Damon Runyon. For years Runyon, like Walter, had been a chain-smoker. Early in 1944 his throat began feeling raw and his voice became noticeably hoarse. When the pain grew unbearable, he reluctantly visited a physician. The diagnosis was cancer of the larynx—cancer so severe that it took two operations to remove it. He convalesced that summer in Los Angeles, but by the time he returned to New York in the fall the cancer had metastasized to his lymph nodes. He was operated on in October. Voiceless now, he communicated by scribbling notes on a pad.

Runyon had long been a distant figure in Walter's life. "He didn't lend himself too easily to friendship—was too often suspicious of friendly gestures," wrote Louis Sobol, "especially after he became successful and world famous." When his son, Damon, Jr., asked that he contact a Hollywood friend to help Damon's mentally ill daughter, Mary, then in the West, Damon refused. "But I understand he was very close to you," Damon, Jr., protested. Damon "jabbed emphatically" at his typewriter, then rolled out the paper. It said: "No one is close to me. Remember that."

Understandably the cancer had made him even more bitter and morose, but it was only the largest of a torrent of troubles that rained down upon him now. Mary suffered a nervous breakdown. The Internal Revenue Service hounded him for back taxes. And his second wife, Patrice, a onetime Spanish dancer, decided to leave him. This last was a devastating blow. Though the editor and writer Gene Fowler may have accurately identified Runyon's tragedy as "his great longing to reach out and love, and be loved, and his inability to do so," Runyon was absolutely smitten with Patrice. Even after she filed for divorce and remarried, Runyon didn't lose hope. "Ha-ha. She'll come back to me," he scribbled to a friend. But she didn't.

"Damon Runyon, now promoted to the role of 'last man to leave the Stork Club,'" Walter wrote late in 1945 in a line that seemed to summarize Runyon's forlorn existence. Walter certainly understood the feeling, since Runyon in closing the Stork was only "pinch-hitting for Winchell." Both of them restless and lonely that year, Walter and Runyon gradually formed a nocturnal community of two. "He had always scoffed good-naturedly at my habit of prowling New York late at night in my car, listening to police calls on my special radio and chasing excitement where it was happening," Walter wrote years later. "Now, sensing his loneliness, I persuaded him to come along with me. We would meet every night at the Stork Club, where we would sit in the Cub Room with old friends. Then about three in the morning we would go out chasing police calls until dawn. [. . .] Finally after a nightcap of ice-cream sodas, I would drop him by his hotel, where he would write his column and then try to doze off."

There was a deep attachment between them now. When Runyon cracked one night that radio listeners were illiterates and Walter took offense, Runyon quickly sought to make amends, writing Walter that the remark was intended as a "rib." "Any time I make a crack that sounds belittling," he went on, "it is probably in an effort to steam you up and I want you to remember it is always from the tip of the tongue and never from the heart." Another time, when Walter returned to New York after the two of them had been vacationing in Florida, Runyon wrote him longingly from Miami—"I have missed you"—and explained how, "sitting here in a lonesome mood," he had called the Stork "twice paging you for gabbing purposes." (He meant listening to Walter.) And he closed admonishing Walter to "Watch your health. Nothing counts but that, as

I've discovered. Money, and all the rest of it are nothing compared to feeling well."

Back in New York together, they began their nightly forays again, usually driving down to the Battery at Manhattan's southern tip, then working their way back up through midtown and Harlem, where Walter repeatedly pointed out landmarks from his childhood—Runyon knew this recitation by heart—until they finally reached the Bronx. These excursions, publicized as they were in the columns, became obligatory entertainments for visiting celebrities. Darryl Zanuck of Twentieth Century-Fox was so fascinated that he assigned Runyon and Winchell to write a film treatment of their exploits, describing the project as a "sort of Grand Hotel of New York." Runyon himself, usually so jaded, admitted he was having the time of his life. "Let me tell you a secret," he wrote his son when he was spending nights with Walter. "I never liked doing a column until lately. I could always make so much more money with much less effort on fiction. But lately for some reason I have taken a fancy to columning, trying to prove, I think, a theory that people are more interested in people and in things that happen to people than in politics."

They were, Runyon's son observed, a "perfect team"—both desperately lonely, needing to fight the terror of their isolation and loving the stimulation of the city, one unable to speak, the other unable to stop talking. ("I figured out why you like to spend so much time with me," Runyon once joked on his pad. "I'm the only man who can't interrupt you.") Walter saw their relationship as a cherished responsibility, a form of tribute to a writer he admired and envied. "Winchell was nicer to Damon Runyon than he was to anybody in his life," said Ernest Lehman, who briefly worked for Runyon. To those who asked Runyon why he was now spending most of his time with Walter, the answer was simple. "I know of no man who's more entertaining than Walter when he is in the mood," he said, "nor one who has a greater store of experience from which to draw." Cuneo's answer for why these two "old men simply cruised about all night following police alarms," was simpler still: "I think they knew no other life."

As death approached for Runyon late that fall of 1946, there was the awful sense among his compatriots that when he died, he would take the glory days with him—a sense no doubt deepened by the death of another symbol of the age, Mayor Jimmy Walker, in November. So they clung to him as he clung to life. Each day the press agent Irving Hoffman, an accomplished artist, sent Runyon a caricature with a note urging him to get well because his friends loved and needed him. Leo "Lindy" Linderman and his wife took him bowls of crushed strawberries mixed with fresh, rich cream. And Walter and Runyon remained in constant contact. I AM GETTING LONESOME FOR YOU, Runyon wired Walter in Miami that November. BETTER GET OUT OF THAT SQUALOR AND RETURN STOP MY BLACK HAIRED NURSE WITH THE BIG BLUE EYES AND THE BABY STARE JOINS ME IN THIS SENTIMENT.

Finishing his broadcast in Miami on December 8, Walter teletyped Rose in New York complaining about the attorneys vetting his script— "I'm getting a lot old and haven't got the energy to grapple with the men who don't seem to know the law but who seem so frightened of anything that may sound harsh"—and then asked about Runyon. Rose teletyped back that there was some confusion over whether Runyon had lapsed into a coma or not. Walter advised she contact Billingsley, who would know. "Runyon will not be alive in the next 24 hours," Billingsley told Rose after speaking with Runyon's physician and with a mutual friend. "He is delirious and no one can see him and he keeps talking about Winchell."

RUNYON DIED AT 7:06, read a wire from Walter's editor Glenn Neville on December 10, though the Miami *Herald* had already informed Walter just minutes after Runyon died. That night Walter granted an interview to the Associated Press. For once he groped for words. "I don't know what I'm going to do. I sat down to write a piece about him, but couldn't do it. I kept thinking he hated gushing."

"Tell 'em to lay off crying," Walter, acting as Runyon's voice, wrote two days later in his column. "A fellow ought never to cry. When he does he can't see things clearly. And if he sees things clearly he won't cry at all." What Runyon had seen and learned, Walter said, is that "one ounce of understanding was worth a ton of sympathy." He especially tried to understand the "local boys who went bad" as a way of understanding himself. "The world calls them Broadway characters," Walter had Runyon say, "but I knew the disappointment most of them had to swallow did more to hurt them inside themselves than any pushing around anybody else could give them on the outside." In the end it was the intrepidness with which they and Runyon faced the hardships that was their memorial. "Life itself is a risk, Walter—and you measure a man by the way he takes it. . . . "

In his last months Runyon had worried over whether he would be remembered once he had passed away. One August night at the Stork he was poring over *Variety* when he caught a memorial for the late playwright Paul Armstrong that a friend had placed in the obituary section. "When I die if I had one man remember me so faithful despite the many passing years," Runyon scribbled on his pad, "then I'd be happy." "I'll make sure you're never forgotten," Walter said he told him.

Precisely what sort of memorial he would erect to Runyon, he wasn't yet sure, though he was certain of one thing: Whatever memorial there was would be his brainchild. Runyon had mentioned that he would like to see a room at Memorial Hospital for newspapermen who were victims of cancer—a room where all their bills would be paid. With that in mind, Walter took the air for his broadcast on December 15. "There I was with the mike in front of me," he remembered a few years later, "and for the first time in my life the words came hard." What he did was make an impromptu appeal for funds to start a Damon Runyon Memorial Fund that would endow a new wing at Memorial. He had made the first contribution himself with a $5,000 check, and he asked his listeners to send their contributions to him or to their favorite columnist.

He was shocked when he cruised the clubs in Miami after the broadcast and people rushed forward to stuff donations into his pockets. The scene was repeated the next day when he visited Tropical Park racecourse. From across the country contributions flooded his office. A race car inventor offered to donate 5 percent of his profits. A toy company offered the profits on its nursery rhyme toys. Sixteen hundred New York liquor salesmen took up a collection for the fund. A broker for a Stradivarius violin offered $1,000 for a mention of the instrument in the column. Within two months the fund had collected nearly $200,000.

Without intending it, Walter suddenly found himself the head of a new and surprisingly well-endowed charity. Still without a firm plan over how and where to allocate the money, he had incorporation papers drawn up and promised to convene a meeting of Runyon's friends as soon as he returned to New York in February. The group—Walter, Leonard Lyons, Leo "Lindy" Linderman, sportswriter Dan Parker and agent Paul Small—met for the first time on February 28, 1947. The next week the same group elected Parker president, Lyons vice-president, Linderman secretary and Walter treasurer, the position of foremost power in an organization dedicated to fund-raising and one he held until his death.

Now the fund had officers and money, but it was still floundering for an outlet. Somehow the Memorial Hospital wing seemed too small an endeavor. The American Cancer Society readily offered its assistance, obviously hoping to become the fund's main beneficiary, and Walter turned over a check for $250,000 to the ACS that April, but he was not about to turn over authority or surrender the fund's autonomy. He had rapidly come to enjoy his role as one of America's chief cancer fighters, and given his own fear of cancer, he brought a sincere commitment to the battle. At a time when he had lost his White House cachet, the fund also provided new cachet: He was now a philanthropist.

II

Just as cancer was for Winchell not only a disease but an insidious enemy to be defeated, cancer was increasingly becoming a metaphor for the postwar world too. By the middle of 1946 Americans were coming to doubt the Soviet Union's intentions, and many top policymakers feared that the next confrontation would be between the United States and its wartime ally. None of this, however, seemed to rouse Winchell. Even after Stalin had delivered a bellicose speech in February of that year highlighting the incompatibility of communism and capitalism, and just three weeks after Winston Churchill's famous "Iron Curtain" speech, Walter wrote a surprisingly adulatory column about the Soviet dictator. "Americans who have interviewed Stalin usually are impressed by his keen sensayuma," Walter remarked, adding that "Joe is a handy man with the rapier retort." Moreover, "many American and British military leaders say Stalin originated the military strategy which resulted in some of Russia's greatest triumphs over Naziland." His most "dominant trait," Walter said, was his "stern realism." And Walter believed that the best way for America to avert another depression was to begin trading with the Soviets.

Though he had always detested communism, it was, in fact, much harder for him, as it was for many postwar liberals, to summon the same fury toward it that he had shown toward fascism. The fascists were racists, nativists and, perhaps worst of all for Walter, anti-Semites. They spewed a vicious philosophy of hate, and they condoned Hitler's atrocities. The Communists, on the other hand, had opposed nazism, at least after Hitler invaded Russia, and had helped defeat it. Walter hated them for their territorial ambitions, hated them for their agitation in America, but early in 1946 he was clearly seeking some kind of accommodation.

It was much easier for him to apply himself fighting Norwegian opera singer Kirsten Flagstad's attempts to perform in America after her husband had allegedly abetted the Nazis or to campaign, as he did several years later, for the imprisonment of "Tokyo Rose," the Japanese-American woman who broadcast propaganda to American troops during the war.* It was much easier, especially since a national consensus about and against the Russians was only gradually emerging.

---

*Ironically, it was Walter's old adversary Earl Carroll who heard about Tokyo Rose's case while he was visiting Japan and advised her to clear her name through Winchell. Carroll had forwarded a letter from "Rose" to Walter and was intending to plead her case before him personally when he (Carroll) died in a plane crash.

But the very absence of a dire threat created a terrible dilemma for Winchell just as it had for the rest of America. He was accustomed to clanging the alarm bell. It was what he did: waking up America, exposing its enemies, saving his country from peril. It was what had won him recognition and honor both before and during the war. It was, moreover, integral to the way he viewed the world—as a kind of damsel tied to the tracks by nefarious villains. His cosmology didn't allow for doubt or relaxation of vigilance. "He knew black and white," said Arnold Forster. "He didn't know shades."

He, of course, still wore the white hat. The question was, Who wore the black? And it clearly wasn't enough to answer that the black hats were the same old group who had worn them during the war: the isolationists, the appeasers, the reactionaries. There was only one potential antagonist large enough now, only one crusade momentous enough, to make Winchell relevant again.

Though Walter kept temporizing throughout 1946, it was ordained, psychologically, if not politically, that he would eventually take up cause against the Soviet Union, and by the end of the year Stalin had made it much easier for even the most charitably inclined to do so. Stalin had declared that war with capitalism was "inevitable," thereby edging Walter back toward the offensive. "I wish that I could agree unconditionally with Henry Wallace," Walter wrote former Roosevelt speechwriter Robert Sherwood in September after Secretary of Commerce Wallace made a speech calling for peaceful coexistence with the Soviets. "And if I thought his present policy of appeasement would bring peace—I would gladly support it . . . but I cannot see that the further disarming of America—while Russia continues to arm to the teeth will bring anything but quick and terrible disaster to American cities. . . ." Sherwood wrote back, giving Walter the assurance he most needed: that FDR would have stood firm against the Soviets too.

Always taken by simple analogies, Walter now found one that he could apply to the present situation. During the thirties the United States had remained supine while Hitler rearmed Germany and intimidated its neighbors. It was only the urgent calls for military preparedness, many of them issued by Walter himself, that enabled the United States to defeat Germany. Now, in the wake of World War II, when many were calling for America to demobilize rapidly and substantially disarm, there was a new aggressor, already rearming, already intimidating its neighbors. In this view, the late forties were the late thirties all over again. The logical extension of the analogy—and Walter certainly wasn't the only one making it—was that the United States had to prepare itself for war once again. This was the line Walter was now taking.

Not surprisingly, the Soviets declared themselves appalled by the new belligerence toward them and treated demobilization as a ruse. Addressing the General Assembly of the United Nations at Lake Success, New York, on September 26, 1947, Soviet Deputy Foreign Minister Andrei Vishinsky denounced American "warmongers" for more than two and a half hours and demanded a new law that would outlaw warmongering in the press. Of all the American warmongers he singled out two for special reproof: the former American ambassador to the Soviet Union William Bullitt and Walter Winchell.

Winchell was, he said, the "new American Baron Munchausen, famous as is known, for his utterly absurd lies." "According to the logic of this sage," Vishinsky continued, "you cannot dominate anything or anyone with a demobilized army, a laid-up navy and a grounded air force. It is an amazingly stunning argumentation. Winchell finds it irresistible as if an army could not be mobilized as is the case when a war is launched, and as if a navy could not put out and an air force could not take off. But when there is lack of logic, one seeks salvation in cheap lies." Winchell's real motive, Vishinsky declared, was to disguise how much money capitalist profiteers had made from the war and how much more they stood to make from a new arms buildup.

Walter responded that the Soviets had been the ones vowing to wage war against capitalism, but he believed that war could be averted if the Soviets would permit newsmen to gather information without restrictions and disseminate it to the Russian people. Walter volunteered to be in the first wave of Western journalists to visit Russia, *if* the Soviets extended to him the same freedoms that America extended to Soviet journalists. "I would then leave it to my competitors in newspapers and on networks to decide who is the liar." But Walter knew this was a pipe dream. "They don't want the truth made known."

However subdued and temperate his immediate response, Walter was energized, even elated, by Vishinsky's remarks. He was back on center stage, slugging it out with America's new enemies just the way he had with Hitler. He had a cause again, a renewed sense of purpose. "Winchell became downright manic," Klurfeld wrote of him in this period.

Triggered by Vishinsky, Walter now escalated his attacks. "Stalin admits in this book [*Problems of Leninism*]," Walter wrote in a column-long defense against Vishinsky's charges of warmongering, "that the success of his regime in Russia is not sufficient. He states it is just a prelude to similar victories in other countries: 'The Russian Revolution is a prerequisite of World Revolution.'" "I believe that America was never in greater peril," he announced on his October 12 broadcast, sounding very much the way he had in the period before Pearl Harbor. "Except for the armies in the field, the Third World War is already being fought. The government at Moscow has sworn to destroy us [. . .] I tell you again we are losing [the cold war], and unless we wake up, we are going to lose the fighting war."

In the Soviet Union, according to a Reuters dispatch, Walter was now an object of public scorn, with the trade union paper *Trud* mocking him in a cartoon captioned "Radio Liar" and *Izvestia* reporting that Walter had "broken all records for demagogy." But if the Soviets were understandably angry, the American reaction to his anti-Soviet campaign was enthusiastic and overwhelmingly supportive. *Newsweek* reported that he had received more than ten thousand letters, including one from the man he had so often razzed, Thomas Dewey. "[S]ome state department officials felt that Walter Winchell has done more to arouse public opinion on the Russian problem in 60 minutes of broadcasting than the other radio commentators had accomplished in two years," wrote Dickson Hartwell in a profile of Walter that ran in *Collier's* that February. "Even the Russians began to suspect that attacking him was a diplomatic blunder."

Caught up in his own hysteria, Walter was broadcasting new and more heinous charges of Soviet skulduggery each week, including a plan to wage germ warfare against America. Klurfeld remembered Walter's being interviewed in the studio after a broadcast at this time. "With his suspenders dangling, collar open, tie askew, and the inevitable hat perched on his head," Klurfeld wrote, "he talked for almost two hours. During the interview he repeatedly leaped out of his chair, waved his arms, held his head, rubbed his eyes, and stroked the back of his head. He had every symptom of a man on the brink of complete exhaustion." When a reporter finally asked him if he thought the United States ought to drop an atomic bomb on Russia, Walter said he did. Announcer Ben Grauer and Ed Weiner immediately pulled him aside and advised that he moderate the statement, and Walter complied. But when Grauer asked him how he could withstand a two-hour barrage like that, Walter waved him off. "Don't be silly. I loved it. It is the bullshit on which I thrive."

For Walter's conservative foes that is exactly what his anticommunism was. They wanted to know why he was such a Johnny-come-lately to the Soviet threat. To these charges, Walter said, "Nutz!" "Browse through the files and read our opinions on Russia when it invaded Finland," he wrote in December 1947. And he needled the liberal *New York Times* in the same column for publishing James Reston's warnings that Soviet foreign policy was predicated on war when that "gazette's editorial page called us names (last year) when we pioneered similar warnings."

It was, indeed, Walter's old liberal allies who were most perplexed and distressed by his postwar preparedness campaign, not necessarily because they underestimated Soviet adventurism—though many did—but because they thought his dire warnings precluded rational debate. Walter easily disregarded criticisms from obvious radical sources like the *Daily Worker*, which accused him of following J. Edgar Hoover's orders. It was much more difficult, however, to brush off the concerns of legitimate liberals who had long been his allies, especially those who worried about the impact Walter's anti-Soviet campaign would have on domestic tolerance. "You have done such a magnificent job in fighting bigotry in the United States," Walter White, the secretary of the National Association for the Advancement of Colored People, wrote him, "that I was shocked and even terrified to read in your Sunday column that 'The question [of Communist party legality] should be answered not by the ifs and buts of the U.S. Supreme Court, but by the rifle butts of the U.S. Marine Corps.' Do you not realize, Walter, that mob violence today against Communists means almost inevitably mob violence tomorrow against Negroes, Jews, labor, or any other minority?"

What seemed to disturb Walter, though, was not that he was striking a blow at political tolerance and democracy, as White feared he was, but that he was finding himself increasingly in the conservative camp with people he neither liked nor trusted. "What the hell are you doing over there with the Hearsts, Patterson-McCormicks and Gerald L. K. Smiths?" an irate reader wanted to know. "Hypocrisy, thy name is Winchell." Walter sent the letter to Klurfeld with a note: "This guy makes sense! By golly he is so right!"

In his own mind he was still a Roosevelt liberal. When *Time* magazine reported that liberals were no longer as welcome on radio now that Roosevelt was dead, Walter crowed in his column after the new radio ratings had arrived, "One liberal broadcaster (for decades in Hooper's First Fifteen) just hit his tallest score for the year. . . ." At the same time, because he saw himself as a liberal, he was beginning to regard anyone who attacked him from the left as a Red or fellow traveler. He was especially annoyed by Jewish groups that criticized him in the wake of the Vishinsky incident. "Good Heavens[,] you mean its [*sic*] true what they say that commies and Jews are the same?" he wrote Arnold Forster after a speaker at a Jewish Community Center in Portland, Oregon, called him a "warmonger."

III

Having foundered in politics without Roosevelt and on Broadway without Runyon, Walter was foundering with his family too. Early in 1947

there was a rumor that Walter would ask for a divorce. "Truth or consequences," Hedda Hopper wired that January. "Are you seeking freedom?
Yes or no." Those who knew Walter realized it was highly improbable
that he would ever seek a divorce to marry Mary Lou. "There was no
need to divorce June," Arnold Forster said. "He lived his own life. He
satisfied whatever needs he had in his own way. . . . I never heard a word
of any kind that suggested he thought twice about his marriage to her."
As for June, her brother-in-law, film executive Seymour Mayer, insisted
she never considered leaving Walter. "She was madly in love with Walter," Mayer said. "I don't know about him. But she was."

In any case June was discreet. By the late forties she had doubtless
heard about Walter's flagrant affair with Mary Lou, but she ignored the
rumors. Her daughter-in-law said that June didn't so much ignore them
as refuse to believe them. "They created their own reality," she said.
"Whatever they wanted to believe was real." Seymour Mayer, though,
was certain she knew. "Never ask him any questions that might cause a
rift in your family," June once advised her sister, Mary, who had divorced Joey Adams and married Mayer. "I do it with Walter and I'm still
married."

It wasn't just June who was holding on to Walter; he needed her too.
June was his ballast, the "only person who knows me," Walter said. She
was the only one who appreciated his sense of precariousness, the only
one who saw him with his defenses down. And "The Column" needed
her. She read novels, saw movies, listened to records and radio programs
for Walter and delivered her opinions, which then became his opinions.
"She hasn't been wrong yet," Walter once said.

But even if he hadn't had the dependence on June that he did, there
was another reason why he would never have contemplated divorce: June
would have contested it with everything she could muster. She would
never have allowed what happened to Rita to happen to her. "No one was
going to push June aside," Ed Weiner said. The columnist Jack O'Brian
remembered June's saying, "If anyone comes up and tells me this is
Walter's baby, I'll kick him down the stairs." According to one story, she
once pummeled a Communist sympathizer with her handbag when he
applauded at inappropriate places during a film. Another time she spit
in Ed Sullivan's hand when he offered it to her to show that his feud
was with Walter, not Walter's wife.

Walter was intimidated by her. "She owned him" was how O'Brian put
it, remembering how she needled him about his oversized ego over dinner at Dinty Moore's. Rose Bigman remembered how Walter's confidence suddenly evaporated whenever he talked to June on the phone.
"She made a little boy out of him," Rose said. He would stammer and

say, "Yes. Yes. Yes, ma'am." Once Rose had to run out of the room rather than witness the humiliation.

But if Walter accepted her browbeating and June his peccadilloes, it was because they did share the same reality, coauthored the same version of events, as their daughter-in-law had said. If Walda caught her father with Mary Lou, Walter and June simply denied it. If Walda complained of her father's absences and the tensions they had caused, Walter and June were incredulous. And if she cited bitter familial fights, violent charges and countercharges flying between her parents, Walter and June acted as if these all were figments of their daughter's imagination. Indeed, the more the Winchell family flew apart, the more aggressively Walter and June maintained the fiction of domestic harmony, just the way he had invoked the Communist threat when his political sphere was flying apart. Even when it came to their children, it was Walter and June against the world. It would always be Walter and June against the world. In the end that was what kept them together.

WHERE WALDA Winchell was concerned, the fiction had become imperative. In 1947, at twenty, Walda was stunning, "the brightest redhead you ever saw in your life," as one beau described her. She very much favored June. She was petite and slender with high cheekbones and delicate features, and she carried herself with a certain aplomb that was very un-Winchellian. She even spoke like June, theatrically, her speech peppered with "darling's" and trilled "wonderful's." "She looked like a girl from Bryn Mawr," recalled a Stork Club habitué. "A classy girl."

But Bryn Mawr was the furthest thing from her mind. Walda wanted to be an actress. She had quit school at sixteen, joined the American Theater Company, then went out to Hollywood on a six-month contract with Twentieth Century-Fox, presumably arranged by her father, where she took classes on the lot and was groomed as a starlet. She appeared in one film, *Something for the Boys*, before she got bored and returned to New York to attend drama school and try her hand at Broadway.

It was certainly no wonder that she was eager to strike out on her own, even though she was still a teenager. June was a steely and strict parent who lost her temper easily. "I've seen her face[,] how it gets tense and all nerved up," Walda once observed. "Especially when she used to spank my brother and I used to tell her, 'Mother, don't spank him. You should see yourself in the mirror. You look sick.' " When he had the time, Walter was smothering. He was "crazy about her," said his friend Curley Harris, but he also described Walter's attentions as an "almost unnatural affection for her, and they had some terrible falling-outs about it." He was suspicious of people who courted his daughter and did what he could to preempt them. When she was eighteen, he gave her a mink coat. Watching her model it, he told her, "I am so happy that we are able to give it to you, although I knew some day a man would have given it to you."

Using the stage name Tony Eden, which she took from the British Foreign Secretary, Anthony Eden, she made her Broadway debut in January 1945 in a musical produced by Walter's friend Mike Todd called *Up in Central Park*. By March she had taken a small part in another Broadway production, *Dark of the Moon*, eliciting one line from *Variety*: "Tony Eden (Walter Winchell's girl, Walda, and a looker) and Conrad Janis are among the best contributory bits." Later, when the play's female lead fell ill, Walda took over her role. Walter was ecstatic. Ed Weiner remembered how he "jumped around that auditorium getting different angles on her like a kid, he was so concerned about her. He was proud of her."

But Walda chafed under her father's supervision as she had wilted under what she saw as his neglect. "She used to complain about him trying to run her life," recalled Harold Conrad, a friend. Like June in *her* younger days, she was rebellious and unpredictable and, Walter feared, promiscuous. According to Herman Klurfeld, the first person who went to bed with Walda was Walter's old friend and newspaper colleague Frank Farrell. Walter was initially enraged, but Klurfeld said that it didn't create the expected rupture. "I think he felt that if she had to be with someone, it was better with Frank instead of some soldier."

The soldier, in fact, came later. She met him on June 3, 1945, during the run of *Dark of the Moon*. His name was William Lawless, a twenty-nine-year-old interior decorator from Cambridge, Massachusetts, just out of the Army Signal Corps. They were married in West New York, New Jersey, the very next day. Walda later admitted it was an act of rebellion. "I was getting so much fighting from my mother and father," she would say. "I had always been told that I had to be careful what I did because of my father's position. Mr. Cuneo always told me that what I did would be news." She didn't love Lawless; she hardly knew him. But he said he loved her and told her that she might grow to love him. "I wanted love. There was no one to care for me. People I worked with in the show all had families that loved them, or someone that waited for them at home. I had no one to turn to or that needed me. So he was the first man who came along and said he loved me, and that made me feel good." Walter was in Hollywood at the time the couple met and June was "busy," so Walda and Lawless took the ferry to New Jersey and eloped.

By the time they returned to New York that evening, Walda realized that she had made a mistake. Celebrating at the Latin Quarter, she introduced her groom to a friend and then retired with her to the ladies' room. "I don't want to go home with him," she confessed. Later the newlyweds arrived at Walter's apartment at the St. Moritz, where June was staying, to receive her blessing. Making the best of the situation, June explained the responsibilities of marriage and offered to arrange a party for them. But Walda now said she was afraid and frightened of him, that she did not love him, that she never intended to sleep with him and that she never wanted to see him again. "It was then that I thought I better leave her alone for awhile," Lawless later said with deadpan understatement. The marriage was never consummated. On the ferry Walda had started her period, and as she later recalled, "[W]hen it was over I wasn't with him anymore."

In September Lawless filed for divorce in Massachusetts, charging cruel and abusive treatment and asking for alimony. June insisted that Walter arrange an annulment instead, and when the Massachusetts court denied Lawless's petition on the ground that it had no jurisdiction, the case dragged on, with Walda still technically married to William Lawless.

For Walter the marriage had only reinforced his worst presentiments about his daughter. He immediately charged Arnold Forster with investigating what had happened. Forster arranged that they meet in Central Park rather than Walter's St. Moritz penthouse to discuss the report because he was afraid Walter might leap out the window. "After she ran off with that soldier, the relationship changed," Klurfeld remembered. "It was never the same. He couldn't trust her." Klurfeld compared it to Walter's Drop Dead List for the press agents who crossed him. Walda was now on his DDL. But disappointed as he was with Walda, he also assumed some blame himself. "What can you expect?" he sighed to Klurfeld. "Her father is a whore too."

Two months after her abbreviated marriage Walda fell madly in love again. The object of her affection this time was William Cahn, a sometime Broadway producer whose biggest credit would be *Toplitzky of Notre Dame*. Walter, who had once threatened to shoot anyone Walda went out with, strongly disapproved. June refused to meet him. Walda thought both of them intolerant and uncaring, but the Winchells had good reason to distrust Billy Cahn, even if Walda hadn't been impulsive and untrustworthy herself: Cahn had a reputation as a notorious sharpie.

Born William Cohen in Woodridge, New York, in 1909, he was a high school dropout who ostensibly worked as a photographer but always seemed to have some sort of scam going. In August 1937 he served ten days in a Miami jail for vagrancy, and he served another sentence, this one for petty larceny, at Riker's Island in New York in 1940. (An arrest for grand larceny in another case was dismissed.) Five days after Pearl

Harbor he was inducted into the Army, served as a public relations officer at various camps across the South and West, was promoted to sergeant and then busted to private when he went AWOL. In December 1944 he was admitted to Fitzsimmons General Hospital in Denver and was honorably discharged three months later for psychoneurosis: "severe hysteria of an undetermined cause, which incapacitates him."

Back on Broadway after the war, the tall, husky, good-looking Cahn, in his flashy clothes and with his rough, Runyonesque manner, became a character. Cahn's brother was a bookmaker, and that was his milieu—surrounded by the petty crooks and small-timers of the underworld. His friends uniformly described him as a "hustler" and "con artist," his detractors as "oily," though everyone conceded that he had a gambler's bravado. A friend remembered his driving up in a limousine and suggesting they go to Newark to see if they could raise some money shooting craps. "Limousine, and he hasn't got twenty-five dollars to his name!" The same friend remembered another occasion when a bookmaker approached Cahn on the street for some money owed him. Cahn began shouting at the top of his voice, "All you bookmakers are the same," until the man slunk away.

What he really fancied himself was a theater impresario on the order of Mike Todd. In September 1945 Cahn, possibly with Walda's help, had raised enough money to produce a comedy called *Devils Galore*. Its star was Tony Eden as a naive young novelist whom the devil attempts to seduce. Reporting on the production, which was unanimously panned by the reviewers, *The New York Times* called Walda "pretty" but believed "the part is no test of her acting." Howard Barnes in the New York *Herald Tribune* also found her "attractive," but "she is at her best when she ignores the comedy and merely poses prettily." Other reviewers found her "pretty and wide-eyed," "lovely," "appealing" and "refreshing to look at" but spared the adjectives on the performance itself. (Walter's own *Mirror* called her "one of the better ingenues.") Walda's beauty notwithstanding, three days after its opening, the play closed.

The romance, however, continued despite Walter's best efforts to terminate it. "It really broke his heart that she was mixed up with him," said the columnist Jack O'Brian. "I can remember him saying, 'Why that big, greasy-looking, fat son of a bitch?' " He couldn't understand why Walda didn't see through Cahn. Cahn was a phony. He was an ex-convict. (Walda said she believed his story that he was framed for embezzlement by a friend when he tried to repay a debt, leaving a psychiatrist to conclude that "she is either emotionally or intellectually naive and childlike enough to accept it as an adequate explanation of his imprisonment.") He was using Walda the way people tried to use Walter.

Yet, though Cahn was by no means an altar boy, Walter's assessment wasn't entirely correct. On one thing almost everyone who knew both Walda and Cahn agreed: They were truly mad about each other. "Billy Cahn treated her with the greatest respect," said Nat Sobel, a young judge who also dated Walda occasionally. "He really took very, very good care of her." Walda's friend Gertrude Bayne found him a "happy-go-lucky sort" who "was very nice" and very crazy about Walda. They couldn't stay away from each other for long, and Cahn laid the blame squarely on Walter. If Walter had really loved his daughter, the gambler said, he would have met with Cahn and tried to make some arrangement, though Cahn was ambiguous over what sort of arrangement he meant.

Walter *had*, in fact, made arrangements—of the only sort he knew how to make. Already he was stymieing Walda's acting career. "She was very despondent," remembered Nat Sobel of this period. "She had a lot of opportunities and her father had called up the producers in each case and said, 'I don't want my daughter in the theater.' " Now Walda was growing as paranoid as her father. She was certain her family was having her and Cahn followed and that their phones were tapped. The doorman at Cahn's apartment swore he saw Walter loitering nearby. At the St. Moritz, where she had taken a room, she would hear a door slam each time she closed her own door. And she believed that a man across the street on the bench was watching her window. When she confronted her father, he said, "Maybe he *is* watching you."

Meanwhile, Walda and Cahn were doing their best to steer clear of Walter while Cahn desperately tried to raise money for his Broadway productions. "He would run house parties," recalled Ed Weiner, "and the hostess of these parties was Winchell's daughter. He was using the Winchell hype, which seemed awfully important to a lot of people who came in from out of town, so he could talk them into investing in his shows. He was using her as a come-on."

This had been one of Walter's greatest fears all along. While Cahn was using Walda to attract money now, if he were actually to marry Walda, he would not only corrode the legitimacy Walter had worked so hard to get but tap into Walter's financial resources. *That* was Cahn's scheme, he thought. "He's going to end up with all our money—the money I worked so hard for," Walter fretted to Curley Harris. And Walter knew just how profligate his own daughter could be without the additional drain of a penniless husband. Now jobless because of her father, Walda was also being supported by him. She bounced from the St. Moritz to the Essex House to the Savoy Plaza and then to the Madison, running up huge tabs wherever she went and so overspending even her parents' generous allowance that she was forced to sell the mink they had given her.

The possibility of his daughter's marriage to Cahn was also the reason Walter hadn't pressed harder for Walda's divorce from Lawless. The very idea of Cahn as a son-in-law so enraged him that, at least as Walda told it, he once stormed into her hotel room very late one night, brandished his pistol and threatened to kill her rather than let her marry him. But none of this deterred either Walda or Cahn. Ed Weiner once took it upon himself, six o'clock one morning at a Broadway cafeteria, to warn Cahn of what he would suffer if he dared marry Walda. "Now here's where I become your best friend," Weiner told him. "He will stop you or try to destroy you if you persist." Cahn was unconcerned. "He's not going to interfere with me," he told Weiner, who suspected that whether he really loved Walda or not, standing up to the mighty Winchell was too irresistible a challenge for Cahn.

While Walter hounded Cahn unmercifully in the column, June resigned herself to the inevitable. In October 1947, more than two years after Walda had met Cahn, June invited her daughter to lunch at the Stork. She had a secret she wanted to share: She wanted to see a psychiatrist in order to understand her daughter. Walda was perplexed. The Winchells never revealed their problems to anyone; it was Walter's law. Walda thought her mother might be going through menopause, and she even phoned June's physician, Dr. Sophia Kleegman, to determine if this might be the case. Still, Walda encouraged her mother to seek help, and balked only when she suggested that Walda too get psychiatric counseling. June begged her, "Please don't tell anyone what I said."

Whether June had ever intended to see a psychiatrist herself, she clearly intended for her daughter to see one to free her of what June and Walter saw as her inexplicable obsession with Billy Cahn. To love a lowlife like Cahn, they reasoned, Walda must be clinically insane. A few weeks after their conversation at the Stork, Walda checked into French Hospital for an operation to correct a lingering "female problem." While she was there, Dr. Kleegman visited her and advised that if she were to enjoy mental as well as physical health, Walda should see a psychiatrist. The next morning a nurse brought in a set of Rorschach tests, but Walda refused to look at them. Still, Kleegman, obviously under pressure from June, did manage to convince Walda to talk with Dr. Lawrence Kubie, a highly regarded Freudian analyst who had been trained at Harvard and Johns Hopkins and who had a special interest in the problems of children.

In an eight-page letter to Dr. Kleegman, Kubie described Walda as so "childlike" that he wondered "whether she is intellectually retarded," one of those "high-grade mental defectives who keeps up a good front which fools everyone." He dismissed as "paranoid" Walda's characterization of her home as having had a "general atmosphere of suspiciousness and distrust" and her assertion that "all through her life she has constantly been warned by her father never to trust anybody," though anyone who knew Walter would have understood that this was a case of the chickens coming home to roost. Kubie believed that in any case Walda "should not be allowed to remain unprotected in the community," lest she become an "easy victim of anyone who wishes to exploit her," as Cahn was presumably doing. He closed by recommending that she be declared legally incompetent and that shock therapy, even lobotomy, be considered. So that they would be aware of the severity of the problem, he sent a copy of the report to Walter and June, even though he had explicitly told Walda that he would keep her confidence.

Over the next several weeks June pressed Walda to talk further with Dr. Kubie, and he repeatedly phoned, but Walda was wary. Then came the Thanksgiving weekend and what proved to be one of the major dramas for the Winchell family. By Walda's account, shortly before two o'clock on the afternoon of November 26, she was in her apartment at the Gotham Hotel primping for an appointment when her mother phoned, offering to stop by and pay the hotel bill. Though suspicious—Walda had always had to call her mother when bills were due—she told her mother she would leave the door unlocked while she was in the bathroom readying herself. When June arrived, Walda saw immediately that something was amiss. Her mother looked pale and ill. Walda asked her to sit down, but June snapped, "You are crazy," and told her there was someone outside waiting to take her to Doctor's Hospital for treatment. Just then the phone rang, and June grabbed the receiver. It was Cahn. Before June could hang up, Walda shouted, "Bill, come over quickly, they are trying to take me away."

Hearing the commotion, two assistant managers of the hotel appeared, inquired about the situation and then ordered June into the hallway. With her mother at a safe distance, Walda phoned Cahn and then John Sperry, an attorney Cahn had recommended, asking for his help. Cahn and Sperry both arrived a short time later, and while June and Cahn argued, Sperry advised them that unless June had a court order for Walda's commitment, Walda was, as a legally married woman, entitled to leave. By this time Cuneo had arrived to argue the point with Sperry. As he huddled down the hallway with Sperry and June, Walda and Cahn hurried into the elevator and escaped to the Waldorf-Astoria. After drinks Walda asked Cahn to drive her to New Jersey to visit some friends. She spent the night there, sleeping in the bedroom of the friends' young daughter.

On November 28, the day after Thanksgiving, the *Mirror* ran a bulletin reporting the disappearance of Walda Winchell. June confirmed that Walda was "very, very ill, according to several doctors, and needs hospitalization and immediate treatment." Ed Sullivan in the *News* also reported Walda's disappearance but added that "[h]er future husband, Bill Cahn, spirited Toni [*sic*] Eden away at her request," sending Walter into a fury. "I have verbally instructed several news editors on the head of the copy desk thru whom Sullivan's column goes that there is to be NO further reference to this case," Gene McHugh, the *News*' editor, assured Walter. "You and June have had more than your share of tragedy in this life. . . ." Walter sent the letter on to June with a note: "Yes, Sullivan knew all along the man is an ex-cahnvict. He kept playing him up only to needle you (for your insult to him in [Dinty] Moore's) and needling me for making it possible for him to make a living twenty years." He signed it, "Daddy XXX."

Two days after her disappearance Walda reappeared, and the police search was called off. While she was gone, June had filed a petition for a writ of habeas corpus ordering Cahn to produce Walda, and Cuneo and Sperry had arranged for the girl to testify at a hearing on whether she should be remanded into her mother's custody for the purpose of having her confined. Cahn brokered Walda's consent only because Cuneo had personally guaranteed her protection and because the presiding judge was to be Ferdinand Pecora, a distinguished jurist occasionally mentioned as a possible Supreme Court nominee, who Cahn believed was beyond Winchell's reach.

By any measure, the hearing was extraordinary. It took place in Pecora's apartment at the Ansonia Hotel at midnight on November 29. June was present, represented by Cuneo; Cahn and Walda were there, represented by John Sperry. Dr. Kubie and another psychiatrist, a Dr. Feigen, who had examined Walda earlier that evening, were also in attendance. (Walter remained out of town at June's suggestion; he kept his distance from Walt, Jr., too, then apparently in Miami, for fear he "might press me about Sissy and I might fumble and the impact of shock would harm him.") Walda explained to Pecora that she only wanted to be with "the man I am in love with." "Everybody knows we've never been a family," she said of her parents. "There was never any routine. There was never any closeness. There was no love or devotion." Kubie and Feigen both testified, however, that Walda was in need of hospitalization. When Pecora asked her if she would voluntarily submit to treatment, Walda insisted once again that all she wanted was to obtain a divorce and be permitted to marry Cahn. Pecora then invited her to discuss matters with him privately in an outer room.

When they returned two hours later, Pecora still had not obtained her consent. Hoping her mother might convince her, he asked June if she might like to talk to Walda privately, but June, instead of taking her daughter aside, launched a long, disjointed monologue about the expenses she incurred for Walda and her daughter's peculiar distortion of events. Again, Pecora urged Walda to place herself in a rest home for a few days before deciding on treatment. "I will go if you promise me that my mother is never allowed to come near me again as long as I live," Walda replied before turning to June and beseeching her, "Mother[,] what is going on inside of you?" "I really don't know, dear," June answered.

Under incessant prodding from Pecora, Walda at six that morning finally and reluctantly consented to go to the Regent Nursing Home on 61st Street in Manhattan until Sperry and Cuneo could agree on an independent psychiatrist to conduct an examination. In the meantime, neither June nor Cahn was to contact her. But Sperry failed to appear at a meeting to select the psychiatrist, and on December 2, three days after the hearing, Walda, according to a doorman at the Regent, was strapped to a stretcher and spirited away into an ambulance. That same day Pecora granted June custody of her daughter. The next day, said the doorman, a man appeared and handed him a dollar bill with red marks across the front. "It looks like there is blood on the face of this," the doorman observed. The stranger didn't reply. He simply slid into his car beside Dr. Feigen and a third, unidentified man and drove away.

Desperate to find Walda, Cahn apparently threatened that unless the court was reconvened, he would tell Sullivan that Winchell had had his own daughter beaten and put in a straitjacket. But Cahn, having no legal relationship to Walda, had no standing to bring a petition for a writ of habeas corpus. So he contacted the one person outside the Winchell family who did have standing: William Lawless. Because Walter had stalled the divorce, Lawless was still Walda's husband, and on December 19, contending that Walda was being imprisoned against her wishes, he filed his own petition for a writ of habeas corpus against June to have her present her daughter. The judge granted the writ, but June appeared at the Foley Square courthouse the next morning without Walda, claiming that Walda was not in her custody. As June told it, Walda had voluntarily committed herself to an unnamed institution. After hearing two days of testimony, Judge Kenneth O'Brien ordered June to produce Walda so that he could determine for himself whether she had consented to be confined.

Now the invisible hand of Walter Winchell seemed to intervene. When the hearing reconvened on December 26, Justice O'Brien no longer demanded that June produce Walda. Though Lawless's attorney had spoken with the director of the clinic where Walda was being held, the Craig Institute in Beacon, New York, and the director said he had found "nothing psychiatrically wrong with Walda Winchell," Judge O'Brien had spoken with Walda by phone that morning and now suddenly concluded that she was there of her own volition. Lawless's attorney immediately filed an appeal, but three weeks later O'Brien's decision was affirmed. Walter and June had succeeded in having their daughter incarcerated. By having her sanity questioned, they had finally kept her away from Billy Cahn.

But if they had won the battle, they would certainly lose the war. Walda never wanted to see her father again, blaming him for the entire episode. Walter, also searching desperately for someone to blame, chose his mother of all people; her anxieties, he believed, had disoriented Walda. June blamed herself. In truth, though, the blame almost certainly lay with "The Column" and the broadcast and the terrible demands of being W.W. Because of these, Walter had long since ceased being a father and the Winchells had long since ceased being a family. Because of these, the dreams of retiring to his family that Walter had harbored so long ago and had once written about so lovingly had disappeared. All that remained was Walter and June's fiction of happiness.

IV

Yet even "The Column" was no longer immune from the kind of destabilization that had plagued Walter since the war's end. Three months after Walda's abduction Philip Stack, the Don Wahn of Walter's column, took his life by leaping twelve stories from the offices of the Gibson Greeting Card Company, where he worked writing verse. Though his poems may have been second-rate, their sentiments were clearly wrenched from his own life. Once, when Walter hadn't received a contribution for a while and had another contributor copy Stack's style, Stack explained, "I've been very happy recently and just couldn't get in the mood."

Sadly there were fewer happy times than tragic ones. In 1942 Stack's young son died, and two years later his wife died in childbirth. He remarried, and his new wife bore him a son, but Stack never recovered from the grief of having lost his first family, and he suffered a nervous breakdown. After his death the police found a note: "I am incurably ill. I leave everything to my wife." He also left a poem he had submitted to Walter's column. It closed: "This is a world of never-ending strife/ Dreams are a one-way passage out of life!"

Walter had lost one of his favorite contributors. That same month he had a falling-out with another. The provocation had seemed innocent enough. After years of keeping Walter company, Ed Weiner decided to pay tribute to him. He was going to write a book. As Weiner later described his motive, "I felt that this man had made such an important contribution to journalism. And that was the main topic, the main idea in my mind: that this man had initiated a new force in journalism." Weiner believed he was uniquely qualified to tell this story because of his close association with Walter, though he said he also realized that in writing a book about Walter, he would have to curtail that association.

Weiner approached the task with great seriousness. After a full day at work and often a good portion of the night as well, he retreated to his office to peck away at his Winchell biography. On the other hand, Arnold Forster claimed that *he* wrote most of the book. "Ed Weiner was a lovely man," Forster recalled. But "he couldn't write to save his life—except a paragraph. A book was way beyond him." Nevertheless, Forster said, Weiner "was tired of being known as Winchell's bodyguard, and he decided that if he wrote a book and it was a literary accomplishment, people would stop regarding him as a bodyguard." So, as Forster told it, Weiner approached him, asking if Forster might consider writing the book for him and leaving the unmistakable impression that he had Walter's blessing. Forster, in turn, hired a young assistant to research and write a first draft which Forster would then revise. Forster took no money. "This was a labor of love for a guy I respected who was one of the single most important weapons in exposing nazism and anti-Semitism in the United States, no matter what else you thought of him."

But Weiner had not obtained Walter's permission, as he had led Forster to believe. He hadn't even notified Walter that he was contemplating a book. Instead he showed it to June, who, he said, approved. He just assumed that Walter would be equally enthusiastic about being immortalized. Proud of his accomplishment, Weiner took the manuscript to Florida that winter of 1947–48. As Weiner later described Walter's reaction, "He opened it up, and he says, 'What did you do—write my obituary notice?'" Weiner tried to explain that this was only the first of what would almost certainly be a number of biographies and "at least what I've written is honest." "Please don't do it," Walter asked. Weiner, stunned, said he would do whatever Walter asked. "So I just took the book and went back to New York." There were other versions of Walter's reaction. In one he took the pages and began tearing them in two. In another, he took the whole book and threw it out the window, letting the pages waft and scatter on the beach below.

Weiner returned to New York disconsolate. "Ed was kind of in a dither," recalled his assistant Mike Hall. "I just remember how crushed he was, and I felt very sorry for him." Walter did, however, read the manuscript, even after Weiner had submitted it to a publisher, Longmans Green. "I wish to thank you very humbly for returning the book to me with the suggestions you made," Weiner wrote him abjectly that March. "At the same time, I want to apologize for something I did in haste, without being careful. I had taken the manuscript from the publisher's desk after the editing and hurriedly brought it to your home, without reading it first. On its return from you, when I perused the script, the ulcer department set in. I've tried to correct this matter very diligently."

But Weiner must have known that no matter how he revised the manuscript he could never publish the book without Walter's approval, which Walter would never give to him. Walter, always looking to be betrayed, now felt betrayed. Without mentioning Weiner by name, Walter, in his autobiography, said he disapproved because Weiner had gotten the old story of the baby carriage outside LaHiff's all wrong and because "most of his 'book' was crowded with material from my newspaper and radio-TV files, all lifted without my Go-Light." Walter's friend Jack O'Brian believed that he disliked the book because it made him out to be a saint. Later Walter wrote of the book, "It is such a big plug it embarrasses me." In any case Weiner, Walter's nightly companion for years, was now on the permanent Drop Dead List, and though other press agents rushed to fill the gap, there would be no replacement.

Soon even Mary Lou left. Though she had dated other men—"Of course, guys got scared shitless when they found out [she was Winchell's girl]," said Harold Conrad—she and Walter were still in love and saw each other regularly. She provided his home away from home, his family outside the family. "You know what's going to finally kill me?" he told a friend while walking to Mary Lou's apartment one Thanksgiving. "Those two fucking holiday dinners."

She knew, however, that the "party was going to end," as her son put it. Walter would not divorce June no matter how strongly he felt about Mary Lou. And for Mary Lou's part it was becoming increasingly difficult to operate in the public eye as Winchell's paramour was forced to do. They were constantly running into Walda, who was furious over her father's unfaithfulness. (There were those who suspected her relationship to Cahn was her retaliation.) And Mary Lou didn't like being indicted as a home wrecker or a gold digger who was "corrupting an old man," as she later described the situation.

Accounts differ as to who initiated the breakup. By one story, Walter ended the relationship when he learned that Mary Lou was having an affair with a bandleader named Maximilian Bergere and confronted her at the Stork. Another story had Mary Lou, frustrated over Walter's refusing to leave June, exiting their apartment and subletting her own apartment on Park Avenue. One of the other tenants in her new building was an elegant, deep-throated radio announcer named Frank Gallop, later the voice on singer Perry Como's television program. Mary Lou and Gallop became a couple, Gallop teaching Mary Lou the kind of refinements that Walter could never have taught.

But Walter was hardly out of her life. Furious that she had replaced him, he began lingering near her apartment, calling her, sending her notes and gifts, extravagant gifts, and dozens of roses. He also had her followed, and she suspected that her phones were being tapped. "It was chronic jealousy," her son later said. "He wouldn't let go. He didn't want her to see *anybody* else. He'd rather give her money and keep her happy than see anybody with her."

Mary Lou was now terrified of him, afraid he might do something to hurt her. But it was Gallop whom Walter wanted to hurt, not Mary Lou. Gallop said that police trailed him everywhere, obviously at Walter's instruction. Whenever he auditioned for a job, Walter would put in a call to make sure he didn't get it, and Walter blacklisted him with all the advertising agencies that sponsored radio programs.

Exasperated after having been fired from a radio soap opera as a result of Walter's intercession, Gallop once waved Gary Stevens, a press agent and Winchell favorite, over to his table at Toots Shor's saloon. "I've got to have this thing straightened out," he begged Stevens. "I'm being crucified." Gallop offered to pay Stevens whatever he wanted if he would only plead Gallop's case to Walter. Stevens refused, calling it a personal matter. Still, Gallop kept phoning him, frantic to find a go-between to Walter. Stevens couldn't help and couldn't think of anyone who would. No one wanted to brave Walter's wrath.

As Walter had no doubt hoped, the relationship didn't withstand his assaults. Eventually Mary Lou and Gallop parted. It was sometime late in 1949 or early in 1950, when she was appearing at the Diamond Horseshoe, that she met a young Canadian-born Air Force officer named William Purcell. Like so many men, Purcell immediately fell for her. A tall, strapping, flamboyant Irishman who loved to drink and gave bear hugs so fierce he could crack your ribs, Purcell was determined to win Mary Lou. Each day he sent her roses until he broke down her resistance to date him. Even then he called himself "Stage Door Johnny One."

The relationship continued when Purcell was reassigned to Mitchel Air Force Base on Long Island and Mary Lou temporarily worked at the PX there before returning to Manhattan. By this time Mary Lou was nearly thirty and getting too old to be parading in a chorus line. She and Purcell were married on December 31, 1950, at Mary Lou's apartment on 58th Street. Walter had an announcement in his column. Shortly after her wedding Mary Lou moved with her husband to a military base in Maine. She never returned to Broadway, and she never saw Winchell again.

LOST, WALTER retreated further into his persona. More than ever, he became W.W. Felice Early, a café socialite, noted that he "wouldn't dream of saying anything that was not in character with what 'Winchell' is supposed to do. . . . He would never *not* be Winchell." More than ever, his clothes were a uniform. He wore virtually the same outfit every day: a navy blue suit, a button-down pale blue oxford shirt, a navy blue tie, blue socks and Florsheim shoes. (He bought the same pair year after year.) And on his head always the snap-brim gray fedora. Seymour Mayer asked him during one visit at Twelve Acres how he could wear the same suit every single day. "It's not the same," Walter said, and directed him to the closet. "And he opens it up," Mayer recalled, "and he has fifteen blue suits hanging in the closet. And maybe a hundred blue shirts and gray felt hats."

Yet W.W.'s bold facade could not disguise the old insecurities that were resurfacing now, more exaggerated than ever before. He was constantly straightening his pocket handkerchief or fiddling with the knot on his tie. When he sat, his fingers drummed the table. Despite his work for the Runyon Fund, he still chain-smoked. He ate voraciously, nervously, sometimes as often as every two hours—a favorite family story had him raiding the icebox one morning, eating dogfood and then asking June what delicacy he had finished—but he suffered from chronic diarrhea. He needed sedatives to sleep. Once, when he kept flubbing the word "photographers" on the broadcast, June advised that he try to stay calm. "Dead people stay calm," Walter replied.

He was phobic; when a man sneezed in his office, he left and wouldn't return until it was fumigated. He was compulsively neat; his suits were pressed daily, his face professionally shaved daily; and Rose Bigman said he took four showers a day. And he was more fearful—fearful that his phones were being tapped, that his life was increasingly endangered by enemies, and, worse, that his friends were turning on him as he thought Weiner had. "Too many anti-Winchell stories in PM (Worker), Variety, etc. could only come from people *near* me," he griped to an ABC radio official. "Fed up."

Most seriously of all, he was afraid that he was losing favor. When a set of advance Hooper ratings in November 1947, at the very time he was blasting Vishinsky, indicated that Louella Parsons was outdrawing him,

Walter was skeptical but still conceded, "Could be. Maybe I'm slipping and don't know it." (In actuality, his rating turned out to be more than double Parsons's for the season.) Always hypersensitive to criticism, he believed that the press was now targeting him. Even his attempted good deeds seemed to meet with increasing ridicule in the media. When he opened his December 29, 1946, broadcast with an urgent appeal for type AB blood to help a Miami tourist suffering from bleeding ulcers, three hundred people descended on the hospital to help, and one man in Georgia even chartered a plane to Miami. But when it was later reported that Walter had neglected to mention that the donee needed AB Rh-negative blood, a much rarer type, he was promptly skewered.

He received more scorn when he launched a campaign in January 1947 against dialect comedians—"I call them vomics"—who "use jokes offensive to any race or people" and promised "to ridicule them right off the stage." "In the course of telling the State Department what to do, service men what to think and the country how to act," sneered one editorial typical of the outcry against him, Winchell "announced that he had taken on a new chore—the nixing of jokes he doesn't like from stage and radio. . . . [U]p to now mirth provoked by stories of the two Irishmen—or Jews or Germans or negroes or anything—has been unconfined. But no more. Winchell has spoken!" *Life* magazine called his efforts against dialect comedy "outrageous." Walter rejoined that he meant only "offensive" racial and ethnic humor, not all dialect comedy, and then riposted, "Wonder if Life's editorial writer will ever replace the old-fashioned snore?"

Only the closest, most sensitive observers would have detected how deeply these little indignities hurt Walter, how they gnawed at his self-confidence. Others saw the same old self-absorption. "They pay to read me and they pay to listen to me," he snapped at a press agent to whom he was justifying why he talked and never listened. "That's how I got rich. Nobody pays me to listen to them." But to a friend, in a rare moment of introspection, he confessed that he was always promoting himself because "Who else will write about me?" Another time, chided for talking too fast on the air, he said, "If I slowed up, listeners would understand what I'm saying. Then they'd realize how unimportant it is and turn me off."

To these insecurities was added one other, long-standing one: money. Wading in the surf with Walter outside the Roney-Plaza when it still seemed Walter was atop the world, Cuneo, in an expansive mood, once asked him, "Well, King Canute, what more do you need? What more do you really want?" And Walter answered with what Cuneo recalled as "tremendous vehemence": "I want all the news in the world." Then he added, seriously, "And all of its money too." By the late forties it must have seemed to many that Winchell did have all the money in the world. He made just under $500,000 in 1946 and just over that amount in 1947, which, even allowing for his payroll, still made him an extremely wealthy man, certainly among the highest-salaried individuals in the country.

Money was totemic for him and he took an aesthetic, almost tactile delight in it. As in the old days, when he carried his bankbooks to show his acquaintances how much he had, he now invited a friend up to his St. Moritz penthouse, handed him a stack of bankbooks and asked him to tally the amounts. (Four decades later the friend vaguely recalled the total as $7 million.) Klurfeld remembered visiting Walter's penthouse and seeing the bed covered with stacks of one-hundred-dollar bills. "Know how much money that is?" Walter prodded rhetorically. "A million dollars!"

His enormous wealth notwithstanding, his parsimony was still a joke among his acquaintances. "A dime didn't mean anything more to him than his right arm," his longtime accountant Harry Geist once jested. A friend having a shave with Walter remembered being chastised for tipping the barber a dollar. "Listen, you son of a bitch," Walter grumbled. "I give him a dime." Klurfeld remembered another scene after dinner at Walter's apartment when Walter picked up an uneaten slice of bread and placed it in the breadbox. " 'You can never tell,' he remarked solemnly, 'when I'll need that again.' "

"He never had enough," said Klurfeld, "because he always felt he might lose it all." Many times, thinking possibly of Runyon, he would say to Klurfeld that if he lost his voice, he would lose everything. But if it wasn't his voice, it was Hearst and if not Hearst then Jergens and if not Jergens a fickle public. The thread of celebrity, as he knew better than anyone, was thin. Eventually it would snap, and he would fall.

And not even the money he had saved would necessarily cushion the fall since money could always be lost, stolen, squandered, sapped by leeches like Billy Cahn. In two months alone Walda had run up a clothes bill of more than $4,000, and a month after her hospitalization he was presented with a medical bill for $11,530. June wasn't much more responsible than Walda. When she spent $15,000 at a furrier's and Walter's accountant said there wasn't enough in the checking account to cover the amount, Walter circled the warning, wrote, "Oh my god," and lamented to Rose, "[Y]ou see now what I mean by putting up barriers! Once you let them down—you find yourself out nearly 12 G's. I know they must be paid but how about me being informed?????????????" He ordered Rose to confine "my wife's checks (for her signature) to $100 and under[.] NOT A DIME ABOVE THAT!"

It wasn't only that money was unreliable; money was a snare. Money could compromise him. No matter how much he wanted money, he had to make absolutely certain that he never gave the appearance that he could be bought. Even tax deductions were minimized lest an enemy accuse him of trying to evade his obligations. Everyone around him knew. Rose once accepted a gift of stock, then, upon brief reflection, decided to return it. "That was the only thing I could think of that would have been bad for my entire life," she recollected. Similarly, Paul Scheffels down in Miami with Walter for the broadcast, once noted that three out of every four cars there seemed to be Cadillacs. Walter used the item, and the president of General Motors was so pleased he came down to Miami and offered Scheffels a car. Like Rose, Scheffels refused, "because I knew that would be the end."

The only good money was money earned. Early in 1947, for the first time in seventeen years of employment under Hearst, Walter was working without a contract, and he publicly warned the publisher that if he wanted "to keep me interested," they should talk. According to a report in *Variety*, Marshall Field, Midwest department store heir and publisher of the Chicago *Sun* as well as one of the backers of *PM*, had offered Walter $200,000 to leave the *Mirror*—a spokesman for Field denied it—but Walter insisted salary wasn't the issue since taxes gobbled that up anyway. The issue was working out a capital gains arrangement that would enable him to keep what he earned.

If matters were unsettled on the Hearst front, they were becoming equally uncertain with Jergens. When in the spring of 1947 Walter began rapping Republican presidential hopeful Senator Robert Taft for opposing the Marshall Plan of American aid to Europe, Jergens, whose company was based in Taft's hometown of Cincinnati, warned Walter: "Your continuation of these attacks is leading many to believe they are politically inspired and that not only injures your reputation for fairness, but it also retards sales." Walter was clearly angry and scribbled a number of notes in the margins—his usual form of correspondence—then crossed all of them out and sent the note on to Rose, telling her to hold off on a response until Cuneo advised him what to do.

His broadcast had been sponsored by Jergens Lotion since the program's inception in December 1932. Jergens had generally been a supportive boss when the reactionaries were raining abuse on Walter during the war, and Walter, again preferring comfort in a known situation to higher salary in a more uncertain situation, had rejected the Eversharp offer just two years before. Jergens had met the challenge then by assuring Walter, "We're not thinking in terms of five years merely, but in terms of an indefinite relationship over many years."

The next year, Walter said he received an offer of $25,000 per broadcast from Stanley Joseloff of the Biow Advertising Agency acting for an unspecified sponsor. As Walter recounted the conversation to Robert Orr of Jergens, "I looked at him indifferently and he said (my witness is Sherman Billingsley): 'You're the coldest so-and-so off ice I've ever seen.' " "Why do you say that?" Walter asked. "Because of the indifference," said Joseloff. Walter admitted that he thought the offer was "nuts." Joseloff replied, "You may not have heard about it, Winchell, but we pay by the [rating] point!"

Again Walter refused the offer, preferring the long-term security that Jergens promised, but by the spring of 1948 he was entertaining offers, and he was entertaining them seriously. "[T]his is the year (the only year, I believe) that anyone can keep part of his income—because taxes will go up again, I am sure," Walter wrote Orr. "I am $60,000 poorer because I made so much money last year, $60,000 of which I had already saved after many years of hard work, which I had to take out of a box to pay taxes. So I am going to consider the top offer I can arrange for '49." (By Cuneo's estimate, Walter had paid over $3 million in taxes.) Walter said he had already received a new offer from Eversharp, a television offer which would make him part owner of the company, and an offer from a radio manufacturer which guaranteed him $500,000 for thirty-nine weeks and no commercials. Another offer had just been submitted giving him $620,000, including $100,000 for the Runyon Fund, though Walter averred that he wished they would pick up Cuneo's salary instead and let Walter make the charitable contributions. His Jergens salary, by comparison, was $390,000.

Walter had submitted these proposals to Jergens for a response and got none. "Your indifference (in my opinion) is a careless way of fooling around with the Jergens Company's hardest working salesman," he told Orr, and he was clearly wounded. "I repeat, I don't want to leave the Jergens Company, but the first new girl that comes along (and shows me how to make a few bucks for myself instead of for the income tax people) will interest me very much." And he closed bitterly, "None of you in all these years have ever done a thing to keep me from being interested in other offers."

The $620,000 offer that Walter had waved before Jergens had come from Chesterfield cigarettes but was contingent on his moving to CBS. ABC was terrified at the thought of losing Winchell. "I know that before you make any decision, you would sit down with Mark [Woods] and me to discuss it," Robert Kintner, ABC president, nervously wrote Walter. Kintner assured him that ABC would give him "complete editorial freedom" and that any advertising agency with which Walter signed could just as easily put him back on ABC, where he would be more than welcome. By May Jergens was refusing to negotiate further. Moving quickly lest Walter close with CBS, ABC decided to match Chesterfield's offer itself. Walter would get $520,000 for the 1949 season, with ABC finding him a sponsor. Any difference between the $520,000 and other monies that ABC would receive from a sponsor for Walter's services would go to Walter.

WINCHELL QUITTING LOTION *Daily Variety* headlined on June 2. The public line was that Walter was leaving because he refused to do a commercial for a new deodorant Jergens was launching. He said he found talking about the "decaying action of bacteria" distasteful and claimed he would have re-signed "if they had just shoved that commercial over to [Louella] Parsons." But this was a face-saving gesture of Walter's to make it seem as if he had rejected Jergens rather than admit that Jergens had rejected him. In fact, according to an internal memo that a fan of Walter's had found on the floor of an airplane and sent to him, Jergens had decided that Walter was expendable. "His political and controversial programs have been drawing more heated complaints from customers," went the memo. It continued, "His change of program in recent years has lost many women listeners. He gets very few listeners among young people— which is an important market." Instead, Jergens had devised a new format for Louella Parsons "at only one-fifth the cost of Winchell."

Regardless of Jergens's assessment of Walter's value, a scramble had begun to see which company would win the right to sponsor him. Reports had Old Gold cigarettes offering $520,000 and Lever Brothers weighing a bid. But the winner that July was Kaiser-Frazer, a car manufacturer, which offered Walter $650,000 for the first year, to begin on January 1, 1949, with an option for a second at a salary of $702,000. *Variety* said the contract made Walter "the highest paid single in show business history."

At a time when he himself feared he was declining, the question was: Was he worth it? All indications suggested that Winchell was, indeed, still the most valuable property on radio. In March 1948, just a few months before he concluded his new agreement with ABC, *Variety* enthused that as "a show business entity he has been parred only by the now historic America-sets-its-time by Amos 'n' Andy, when they were in the 7 p.m. nightly slot." But, *Variety* went on, "on top of all these time-honored, habit-forming influences, never before in the history of Winchell on the radio has his impact been as vivid as in recent months," referring to his anti-Soviet attacks and his new preparedness campaign. "[W]hat appeared to be alternately a voice in the wilderness, or (to many) a sensation-seeking paean of hate—glibly dismissed as warmongering— suddenly has taken on new values."

Visiting Walter's Miami studio in the heat of the Vishinsky attacks in

November 1947, Alistair Cooke of the British magazine *Listener* thought Walter had not lost a thing. Cooke described him as "some freak of climate—a tornado, say, or an electric storm that is heard whistling and roaring far away, against which everybody braces himself; and then it strikes and does its whirling damage." And Cooke went on to cite Winchell's mythic possibilities, saying that in years hence "he will pass into American folklore, and his memory will mushroom its own legends as easily as Paul Bunyan or John Henry or Johnny Appleseed, who also were actual men, ridiculously smaller and duller than the creatures they struck off from the imagination of the American people."

Media analyst Marshall McLuhan, fastening less on Walter's political commentary than on his gossip, called his "telegraphic rattle" the "voice of the symbolic 'gunman' reporter of the big night spots. The Winchell imitators always miss this breathless tension which establishes his role as the mock executioner. Reputations, marriages, and romances wilt and vanish under his spate of wordy gunfire." Winchell's genius, as McLuhan saw it, was to realize that disaffected citizens who were bored with their own lives would be thrilled by the lives "of a group of invisible yet deliciously wicked society folk," and that their fascination was mixed with envy. The envy, Walter also understood, "called for a heavy note of savagery. This is why Winchell functions both as reporter and executioner on the Broadway beat."

In his last months broadcasting for Jergens, he was scoring his highest ratings ever. "Your rating keeps going higher and higher," ABC News president Tom Velotta happily wrote to him early in November. "As of November 7 it was 27.0. It does my heart good." That made his program the top-rated on all of radio, edging out "Fibber McGee and Molly," "Jack Benny," and "Bob Hope," and up nearly four rating points over a year earlier, when he was already scoring with his attacks on Vishinsky.

Who were these listeners? According to an extensive Hooper rating analysis, he drew a much larger audience, as one might have expected, in urban areas with a population of over fifty thousand than in towns or rural areas where his rating was a comparatively low 9.89 in a January–February 1948 sample. He drew much more heavily in the East (57.4 percent of his audience with 50.1 percent of the nation's radios) than in the Central states (28.5 percent of his audience), the Mountain states (1.5 percent) or the Pacific states (12.6 percent). The distribution of his audience by income was remarkably close to the distribution of radios by income: Of Winchell's audience, 19.4 percent earned from 0 to $2,499 while that income group had 26.8 percent of America's radios; 47.8 percent of his audience earned between $2,500 and $3,999, an income group with 47.2 percent of the nation's radios; and 32.8 percent of his audience earned $4,000 and over, a group with 26.0 percent of the nation's radios. At the same time, surprisingly, he scored highest with professional and managerial workers (33.5 percent of his audience) and with skilled workers (37.6 percent), slightly less well with unskilled workers (21.1 percent) and least well with farmers (7.8 percent). By sex, he had 1.38 male listeners per set compared with 1.08 female. And 72.6 percent of his audience could identify his sponsor.

The demographics, however, may have explained less than the national temper. "I never listen to Winchell, but I just happened to hear him last night," New York *Herald Tribune* radio critic John Crosby, trying to analyze Winchell's skyrocketing ratings, said people often told him. "There's a definite feeling of guilt connected with listening to Walter Winchell." But people listened anyway, Crosby believed, because Walter was an anxiety-monger who brilliantly captured the national mood in times of uncertainty. His Hooper rating, said Crosby, was "an almost infallible index of how nervous we all are. When the country is worried Winchell's Hooper soars; when it relaxes it drops." He was rated number one just after Pearl Harbor, and late in October 1948, when Crosby was writing, he had been riding atop the ratings for months as Americans faced a new possibility of war.

V

World War III. That was the prospect facing the country, and Winchell now took to the idea with an almost gleeful alacrity. "The United States has had a secret history for the past five years," he told his radio audience on March 14, 1948. "This is the truth. During the war we did not receive the cooperation of the Kremlin. On the contrary, they distrusted us completely. They even refused to accept delivery of lend-lease on Russian soil." But the United States wanted to think the best of its ally, so it aided the Russians anyway. Then, after the war, came Secretary of State James Byrnes and Secretary of War Edward Stettinius's "tragic mistake" of "appeasing a Communist dictator." While we disarmed, our officials "ratified" the Russian plunder of Eastern Europe. Walter urged his listeners to demand that their congressmen "vote yes on every defense measure that comes up, without wasting time on ridiculous debate—or you will vote no in November."

It was his loudest call yet for American preparation for full-scale war, prompting liberal critics this time to berate him for what they saw as his reckless alarmism. Walter, however, would later deflect the blame by claiming that he had been acting at the behest of highly placed govern-

ment officials. Shortly before the broadcast Stuart Symington, then secretary of the air force, invited Walter to a dinner at the Georgetown
home of James Forrestal, the secretary of defense and one of the most devout advocates in the Truman administration of resistance to the Soviets.
"We are at peace," Walter said Forrestal told him after dinner. "None of
us in government can say things that must be said. You have a wide audience. Would you consider performing a service for our country? Tell
the people how serious things are with Russia." Forrestal offered to provide Walter any information he needed and even outlined the broadcast
for him. Walter's renewed attacks on the Soviets came a few days later.

On his March 21 broadcast, recognizing the policy of containment of
Communist aspirations, Walter declared that the administration had fixed
a line from Scandinavia through Italy from "which there will be no retreat in the fight against communism." The American people didn't want
war, he asserted. But they would not sit idly by while Russia swallowed
Europe. Two days later he was back at Forrestal's home with a copy of
the editorial and the news that he had received a thousand telegrams
within an hour of its delivery, including one from the Russian intelligence
chief in New York City requesting a transcript. Later Forrestal apparently
presented copies of Walter's editorials to the President; when the Cleveland *Plain Dealer* scolded Walter for his warmongering, Walter replied
that Truman himself had approved. "Mr. W. You can't do enough of
these!" he wrote Walter.

But if Truman approved of Winchell when it came to Soviet-bashing,
Walter was still disapproving of Truman. Taking Walter aside at another
get-together in his Georgetown home, Forrestal made one last effort to
heal the breach in the apparent hope that Walter might nudge administration policy toward a more belligerent stance toward the Soviets.
Would Walter see the President the next morning? Walter accepted.
When they returned to the other guests, Walter told about an item he
had written for his next column asking Mrs. Roosevelt to fly to Oslo,
Norway, and phone Stalin to tell him that the United States was prepared
to fight. Cuneo had seen the item and, fearing it might make Walter a
target of ridicule, ordered Rose to cut it. Walter wanted it restored—he
was afraid that Henry Wallace, then considering a presidential bid as a
peace candidate, might steal the idea—but it was too late. Forrestal suggested Walter float the idea before the President at their meeting the
next day.

According to Walter, Truman listened attentively to the plan. When
Walter finished, he asked the President if he might be willing to go to the
American embassy nearest Russia and warn Stalin himself. "I have been
to Europe twice," Truman answered. "Let the Russians come here and

see me." Then he added, seemingly out of nowhere, "They have a river over there I never even heard of." Walter was shocked. "I couldn't believe this was the President." "The Volga?" Walter offered. "Oh, some river," said the President. Then, his voice rising, Truman declared that he would not go to Europe. "I never kiss anybody's ass." Walter, seemingly more upset by the President's ignorance and mild profanity than by the rejection of his idea, got up and left, "probably the only person who gave a President the back-of-the-neck. . . ."

If it hadn't been before, the breach between the columnist and the President was now irreconcilable. A few weeks after his White House meeting, Walter wrote a column on another imaginary encounter between FDR and his successor. "Every President has the constitutional right to lead as he sees fit," Roosevelt advised, "but we think you lead too often with your chin. No one ever loved good jokes better than I did, but I never, NEVER put them in the Cabinet. It amazes me to see you trust my Wall Street office boys with decisions [. . .] They have given you a splendid Republican administration; but the irony of it is that you face defeat as a Democrat because my office boys were Wall Street Republicans." There was more to say, but, apologized FDR, he had a party to attend, one that his predecessors were throwing for him as thanks for his raising the rank of General Dwight Eisenhower, the supreme Allied commander during World War II and now the president of Columbia University. "I had no notion when I picked Ike as the General for the front in 1942 that I was also picking the Man of the People—for 1948."

Dissatisfied with Truman and mortified at the thought of Dewey or Robert Taft as president, Walter, like many Americans, was longing for Eisenhower as a Presidential possibility, though the general had expressed no interest in the office and hadn't even announced his party affiliation. "I think that if enough of you listeners write to me saying that you want Gen. Eisenhower to run, perhaps the mail response will change the General's mind," Walter broadcast on February 1, 1948, and he called for a postcard poll. "If Gen. Eisenhower really wants to do something for the students at Columbia," Walter pumped again two months later, "he'll take that job in Washington." By June the results of the postcard poll were in. Overwhelmingly Walter's listeners wanted Eisenhower to run. (Walter told *Editor & Publisher* that the general had received eleven million letters after Walter's appeal.) Walter and Klurfeld delivered the tally to Eisenhower personally at Columbia. "He was impressed," Klurfeld remembered. But he still declined to run.

While Eisenhower remained on the sidelines, Walter searched for another Roosevelt and found none. He flirted briefly with Republican Senator Arthur Vandenberg of Michigan. ("The fellow has poise and punch," he wrote *Time*'s Henry Luce.) Another, stranger possibility was Walter's old friend J. Edgar Hoover. When a Connecticut man formed a Hoover for President Committee and tried to enlist Walter's help, Walter sent the appeal on to Hoover with the note "I suggested it first months ago." But there was a stranger possibility yet: Walter himself. "I bet John and I could take over this country," Walter mused to Hoover at a New York Yankee game one afternoon in 1948, and though Hoover had no visible reaction, Walter proceeded to name individuals he would appoint to his administration and continued to solicit Hoover's advice that night at the Stork Club.

These, of course, were delusions. In the real political world, once Eisenhower was out of the race, Walter's heart was no longer in it. Instead he channeled his energies into opposing certain candidates rather than promoting others. On the Republican side, he loathed Taft even more than Dewey; Taft's supporters, he said, were "Taftwits." Taft had consistently opposed Roosevelt's efforts to beef up American defenses after Munich and then Roosevelt's efforts to assist Britain after war had begun. "Hitler must have laughed at these rantings of the Senator from Ohio," Walter sneered on the eve of the conventions.

He was equally opposed to former Vice President Henry Wallace on the left, whom he had once vigorously defended. Wallace was an appeaser as Walter saw it. When a confederate of Wallace's requested a meeting between Wallace and Winchell to discuss what he said was a proposal to "safeguard civil rights," Walter circled the man's name and scribbled on his letter, "This goddamn son of a bastard bitch should have his throat ripped out with a baling hook[,] his body soaked in gasoline[,] set on fire and dragged around the city. This is an attempt to use civil rights for the fifth column." Only now Walter meant the fifth column of the left.

Walter expressed little emotion when Truman confounded the experts and won. There were others, however, who thought the election victory spelled doom. Westbrook Pegler, writing from the right, proclaimed that Truman's election "means that the American Republic . . . is done for." I. F. Stone, writing from the left, later said, "The little piano player in the White House is improvising his country's Götterdämmerung."

Over the next fourteen months one might have been excused for thinking Götterdämmerung was imminent. Six months after Truman's reelection, Shanghai fell to the Chinese Communist forces, and by fall 1949 Mao Tse-tung had taken power. In August the Soviets exploded their first nuclear device, and five months later the Soviet ambassador stalked out of the United Nations, dashing the last fragile hope for collective security that had been launched at San Francisco.

America was convulsing no less than the rest of the world. The summer of the 1948 campaign a rumpled, balding senior editor at *Time* magazine named Whittaker Chambers had testified before the House Committee on Un-American Activities. Chambers, troubled and penitent, told the committee that he had been a Communist agent in the thirties and in that capacity had worked with a mid-level State Department official named Alger Hiss, now the president of the prestigious Carnegie Endowment for International Peace.

With the Hiss revelation, though as yet unproved, the Republicans finally believed they had the smoking gun they had been looking for, and they waved it noisily, especially with the presidential election just a few months away. Richard Nixon, then a young California congressman and one of Chambers's strongest defenders on HUAC, wrote Dewey adviser John Foster Dulles suggesting that Dewey stress "the ease with which communists and their sympathizers were able to get on the federal payroll . . . that under the New Deal communist affiliation was probably the best recommendation possible for a person who wanted to get ahead in government."

Nearly ten years earlier Chambers had confessed his party role and exposed Hiss to a dogged anti-Communist journalist named Isaac Don Levine, and Levine, after vainly lobbying government officials for months to investigate, finally brought the matter of Hiss's treason to Walter's attention. Walter promised to take it up with the President, but Roosevelt was furious when he did. "Leaning closer and pointing a finger in my face, he angrily said, 'I don't want to hear another thing about it! It isn't true!' " For months afterward the President refused to invite him to the White House.

Now that the story had broken, the real import of the Hiss-Chambers affair for Winchell was not that it suggested Communist infiltration in the government or Roosevelt's neglect, but that it handed him a weapon with which to bludgeon one of his sharpest critics, *Time* magazine, which had been skewering him for years. Why, after cordial relations with Clare Boothe Luce, the wife of *Time*'s publisher Henry Luce, had the magazine suddenly turned on him? Late in 1947 when the feud was in full swing, Walter attributed it to a dispute he had had with the Newspaper Guild over Communist infiltration that resulted in his resignation from the union. Afterwards, Walter said, he received a facsimile of a message allegedly sent from the Guild's *Time-Life* unit: "Congratulations on denouncing Winchell. We will take care of him on our end."

But with the revelation that Chambers, a *Time* editor, had once been a Communist factotum, Walter saw a new motive and a new way to retaliate. (That Chambers was now a hero of the right Walter chose to ignore.) Almost every day that December, Walter slipped at least one reference to Chambers's Communist past into the column: "Time mag, which calls Drew Pearson and other columnists names, was edited all these years by Whittaker Chambers, self-confessed Communist, accused perjurer and Russian spy!" "Whittaker Chambers, Russian spy, started as top editor at Time mag in 1939, and not long after that mag could find nothing good about anything this American reporter wrote or said." "We can remember when Time mag was famous for its red cover—instead of its Red face." He devoted his entire column of December 16 to an attack on *Time*, which had asked him to show "a greater sense of responsibility in deciding what is legitimate public news and what is mere trouble-making gossip."

Others may have viewed the Hiss-Chambers confrontation as a micro-cosm of the internal threat to America or of Cold War hysteria. Only Winchell saw it as an opportunity to settle an old score. Chambers's tes-timony was to occasion a great outcry and help trigger a painful, decade-long campaign of Red-baiting. But it was Winchell, using any weapon at his disposal, who Red-baited Chambers himself. And it was Winchell who would find that once he had picked up the weapon, he would have a very difficult time dropping it.

WHILE MUCH of the nation's attention was focused on the high drama of Chambers and Hiss, President Truman, newly elected, was launching his second administration. Among the changes he was pondering was whether to replace Secretary of Defense James Forrestal. A short man, practically chinless with thin lips and a nose prominent only because it had been broken during one of his daily sparring sessions, Forrestal had the grim, unsmiling face of certitude, and it was his certitude that had made him a controversial figure. Because of his fervent belief that the United States could reach no accommodation with the Soviet Union, he had run afoul of more conciliatory figures in the administration, includ-ing the President, who believed that war was avoidable. An advocate of a large military buildup, he found himself frequently crossing swords with the President over the size of the defense budget. A champion, as the first secretary of defense, of the unification of the military services in a strong Defense Department, he had also managed, inevitably, to irritate each branch of the military but especially the Navy, in whose behalf, as its sec-retary, he had once ferociously opposed unification.

Then there was the matter of temperament. The son of a well-to-do building contractor from Matteawan, New York, Forrestal was educated at Dartmouth and Princeton and then, after a brief career in journalism, joined the Wall Street investment house of Dillon, Read. There his rise was meteoric: from bond salesman to head of sales to partner to vice-president and then president in 1938. Though he had been recruited into government by Roosevelt's adviser Harry Hopkins as undersecretary of the navy in 1940, Forrestal remained a steadfast Republican and true believer in the elixir of untrammeled free enterprise. But even if Forrestal didn't subscribe to the New Deal, at least with Roosevelt he had the bonds of class. A man like Truman was incomprehensible to Forrestal, and Forrestal to Truman.

Throughout the 1948 campaign rumors abounded in the Truman camp that Forrestal was covertly supporting Dewey and had made a pact with him to be reappointed to the cabinet should Dewey win as expected. (Forrestal's biographers were to find that he had indeed met privately with Dewey during the campaign.) In any case, Forrestal had sat out the campaign, saying it was unseemly for the secretary of defense to be involved in politicking.

Many in Truman's inner circle distrusted Forrestal, but among the most vociferous of those calling for his scalp that January were Drew Pearson and Walter Winchell. For Pearson, it was a matter of philosophical differences. The liberal Pearson hated Forrestal for being a rich Republican businessman who had opposed the reforms of the New Deal in the past and was now fomenting war with Russia, promoting militarism and creating a powerful intelligence apparatus that Pearson feared would endanger civil liberties. More, he accused Forrestal of supporting policies that would award financial benefits to himself and his Wall Street confreres.

Though a saber rattler himself, Walter claimed he had some of the same problems with Forrestal as Pearson had, and he later traced his opposition to Forrestal's support of the Hopley Civil Defense plan, which called for the suspension of civil liberties, including freedom of the press, should the country be attacked by atomic weapons. But it was unlikely, given the seeming depth now of Walter's animus against Forrestal and especially after Forrestal had courted him as an ally against the Soviets, that Walter had been roused by a civil defense plan. It was far more likely that Walter was incited by Forrestal's attitude toward something much nearer Walter's heart: the Jewish state of Israel.

Since 1946 the Truman administration had been debating the disposition of Palestine, then a British mandate. After the war Truman had pressed the British to admit Jews displaced by the hostilities in Europe, but the British, fearful of angering the Arabs, had refused. Truman then agreed to let an Anglo-American Committee of Inquiry devise a solution, but when the committee recommended a partition of Palestine between Jews and Arabs under a United Nations trusteeship, the Arabs exploded, and the plan was scrapped. Still, Truman urged Jewish resettlement in Palestine and endorsed a plan to grant a hundred thousand visas to European Jews to emigrate there. British Foreign Secretary Ernest Bevin, who impeded the effort, declared that the only reason the Americans were pressing the Jews on the English was that "they did not want too many of them in New York."

While Jewish groups and Zionist organizations pressured Truman to put his weight behind a Jewish state, Forrestal led a countervailing force from within Truman's own administration. Forrestal had never particularly liked Jews and, according to a friend, had never understood how Jews and non-Jews could be intimates. Now he took his anti-Semitism into public policy, arguing that a Jewish state in Palestine would needlessly antagonize Arabs and jeopardize oil supplies, that the Soviets would eventually be pulled into any Mideast crisis and that American troops would eventually have to defend the Jews there. He suggested they settle in Peru instead.

For Walter, this was an old-fashioned fight, lines clearly drawn, just as during the war. The dispossessed Jews of Europe deserved their homeland and only wanted to live in peace with their Arab neighbors, he said. It was the Palestinian Arabs who continually refused to accept a Jewish state, the Palestinian Arabs who, in his view, had committed the grievous sin of collaborating with the Nazis. The Arabs countered that they were victims of an impossible tide of Zionist propaganda and, said one Palestinian official, "the most vicious Zionist writer" was Winchell. Eventually, in November 1947, the UN agreed in principle to the partition of Palestine between Arab and Jewish zones, and the British announced their withdrawal, effective six months hence. Forrestal continued to campaign vigorously against a Jewish homeland, but at midnight on May 14, 1948, in Palestine, the state of Israel was declared, and eleven minutes later the United States awarded it de facto recognition.

Six days later Walter lauded the new nation in a column-length tribute. Though the Israelis were now at war with the Arabs, who rejected the partition, Walter said "they have set an example for the civilized world by fighting without hate. They have not called upon the civilized world to exterminate the Arabs: They have merely asked all decent people to help them defend their homes." He called for the UN to assist Israel in its struggle as a policeman would assist a victim of a crime.

Though more than six months had passed since the battle over recognition of Israel, Winchell had not forgiven Forrestal for leading the anti-Zionist charge. Now Forrestal's post-election vulnerability provided an opportunity for Walter to avenge himself and drive Forrestal from office. He and Pearson maintained a steady tattoo of abuse. In January Pearson accused Forrestal of having established a dummy corporation in Canada in 1929 to avoid American taxes. In his own broadcast on January 9, Walter repeated the story of the alleged tax dodge, denounced Forrestal's plans to arrogate to the National Security Council "dangerous new powers" and predicted that Truman would accept his resignation that week.

But the President, even though he didn't much like Forrestal either, was not going to allow himself to be bulldozed into replacing him. Pearson had learned that "Truman is boiling mad. . . . He has told a friend: 'Pearson and Winchell are too big for their breeches. We are going to have a showdown as to who is running this country—me or them—and the showdown had better come now than later.' " According to Pearson, Truman had ordered the Central Intelligence Agency to investigate Pearson, Winchell and Cuneo. "They have already turned up some amusing alleged facts including one which will not amuse Walter, namely that although his audience is much greater than mine, my influence is much greater than his."

Stepping up the attack and moving from the political to the personal, Walter now repeated another accusation of Pearson's: that Forrestal had run out the back door of his Beekman Place house back in July 1937 when thieves accosted his wife and stole her jewels. "I feel challenged as a newspaperman by the viciousness of this and similar slanders," Westbrook Pegler, no fan of Forrestal's, wrote him after Walter's latest sally. "If our press is worth a damn it ought to destroy these bastards." And he scolded Forrestal for not having taken action against Winchell earlier, when he was still secretary of the navy. "I am telling you, you ought to have terminated Winchell's commission a long time ago. You know damned well he was a coward afraid to take sea duty in the war. . . ." Though deeply distraught by the insults to his personal courage, Forrestal didn't respond to Pegler, but he told a friend, "Pearson and Winchell are a high price to pay for the freedom of the press, but I guess you've got to do it."

In the meantime, he dangled. After a meeting with the President on January 11 Forrestal emerged from the White House denying he would resign and telling the assembled reporters, "I will continue to be a victim of the Washington scene." Two days later Truman reportedly told his chief fund-raiser, Louis Johnson, an American Legion officer and eager aspirant for Forrestal's job, that Forrestal was a "God-damn Wall Street bastard." But he was still not going to be stampeded by Pearson and Winchell into dismissing him. "I want you to distinctly understand," the President told the guests at a dinner honoring White House aide Harry Vaughan, "that any s.o.b. who thinks he can cause any one of these people to be discharged by me, by some smart aleck statement over the air or in the paper, has another think coming."

Friends of Forrestal's implored Walter to desist. They said the secretary was cracking under the strain. He would stare blankly into space, pull down shades in rooms so as not to be a target for assassins, talk obsessively about plots, dip his fingers absently in water glasses and wet his lips while he spoke. In March, when he finally resigned in favor of the bumptious Johnson and flew to Florida to decompress, he was taut and paranoid, repeating over and over again, "They're after me." He spent only three days at Hobe Sound in Florida before flying to Bethesda, Maryland, for psychiatric treatment at the naval hospital there. Drew Pearson reported that he had attempted suicide.

Over the next seven weeks, under the supervision of Dr. George N. Raines, the chief psychiatrist at Bethesda, Forrestal's condition seemed to improve, though Raines noticed a descent whenever the weekend approached. When Raines prodded Forrestal to assess this pattern, Forrestal circled the question for a week before finally admitting that it was the anticipation of Pearson's and Winchell's Sunday broadcasts that agitated him.

By May his mind seemed clear, his spirits high, and he even seemed able to face the onslaughts of Pearson and Winchell without plummeting into depression. Visitors were impressed by the change. But it was deceptive. At 1:45 A.M. on May 22 he sat in his room on the hospital's sixteenth floor copying in longhand Sophocles' "The Chorus" from *Ajax* in which a disconsolate Ajax contemplates suicide. "When Reason's day/Sets rayless—joyless—quenched in cold decay,/Better to die, and sleep/The never-waking sleep, than linger on,/And dare to live, when the soul's life is gone," he wrote. He placed the sheets into the bound volume of Sophocles. Then he apparently dismissed the young naval corpsman assigned to guard his room and walked across the corridor to a pantry. He removed the screen from the pantry window. He tied one end of the silk sash of his dressing gown around a radiator below the sill, the other end around his neck, and leaped through the window. His body landed on a third-floor passageway. He died instantly.

Amid the eulogies came the question of whether Forrestal had been hounded to his death by Pearson, Winchell and other vultures of the media. Arthur Krock of *The New York Times* openly wondered what "part in bringing the tragic climax was played by those who, in the press and on the air, steadily aspersed Forrestal's official record, his courage, his character and his motives while he was Secretary of Defense and followed him to the sick room with every fragment of gossip that could nullify the treatment his doctors hoped would restore him." *Time* concluded, "[I]n the Pearson and Winchell assaults on Forrestal, one thing was clear: both had overstepped the bounds of accuracy and decency," and Pegler flatly accused them of having murdered Forrestal. "I am almost beginning to lie awake nights wondering whether I did," Pearson admitted to his diary.

Walter appeared to feel less guilt. "It is typical of one presstitute," he told *Editor & Publisher*, obviously referring to Pegler, "that one of his articles which piously condemned critics of Forrestal contained another attack on Franklin D. Roosevelt." But twenty years later, in his autobiography, Walter was still attempting to absolve himself from responsibility for the suicide. The real culprit, he wrote then, was a Washington gossip who had hinted that Forrestal's wife was being romanced by young naval officers. He went on to write that in 1967 a member of Forrestal's staff had assured him the secretary had been flung out the window to prevent him from writing his memoirs, which would have indicted "people in the highest government places." Walter was innocent.

Conspiracy theories had circulated at the time of Forrestal's death too, but for once Pegler may have been right in assigning responsibility to Pearson and Winchell, especially after the extent of Forrestal's illness became known. Walter's attack-dog style was predicated on targets who could take it and dish it right back, as Clare Hoffman, John Rankin, Martin Dies, Ed Sullivan, Henry Luce, Truman and Pegler had. That was the sport of it. Forrestal was not such a man. Brittle, sensitive, guilt-ridden, he could never participate in the give-and-take, so Walter *had* overstepped his bounds in bullying him. "Drew Pearson and Walter Winchell killed Forrestal," Dr. Raines told *Time* before asking to have his words deleted. Walter knew that in a sense they had.

VI

At fifty-two Walter Winchell was thinking of his own mortality. Runyon was gone, and his old friend Mark Hellinger had died of a heart attack almost exactly a year later, in December 1947. His aunt Beatty and uncle Billy Koch both succumbed that summer of 1949—Koch, the bookie, had never recovered from the loss he had taken on Truman's election—June was sickly and his mother had suffered a heart attack. Jennie Winchell had spent most of 1949 convalescing in California, then returned that fall with June to New York, where she would sit in her apartment on West 72nd Street across from Central Park, surrounded by clippings on her son.

She was still a handsome woman—small and fair with still-flawless skin—and she had remained active despite her infirmities. But she was increasingly gripped by fear: fear of going outside, fear of contracting an illness, fear even that the Chinese orphans Walter and June had taken in would somehow provoke Chinese officials into attacking her son. On October 25 she was admitted to Doctor's Hospital in Manhattan for lower bowel surgery. At Walter's instruction, Rose Bigman accompanied her. During her hospitalization, Jennie's fears mushroomed. Somehow she had gotten it in her mind that she was suffering from cancer. The doctors, Walter, June, and Rose could not convince her otherwise.

Walter left for Florida early in November assuring his mother that she would be out of the hospital within a week. At 5:45 P.M. on November 14 her relief nurse left to prepare Jennie's dinner. The nurse returned a few minutes later to find the bed empty and the window open. Looking out, she saw Jennie's body crumpled on the pavement ten floors below—an eerie echo of James Forrestal. Paul Scheffels was sitting at the Roney-Plaza bar nursing a martini when Rose had him paged. "Paul, you have to go up and tell Walter that his mother either fell or was pushed out of a window and was killed," she said. Scheffels downed another martini and then headed to Walter's room. Walter had already heard the news. "He never cried," Scheffels recalled. "I just sat around with him and he continued to work."

Work had always been Walter's refuge in times of distress, and his mother's death had affected him far more deeply than Scheffels knew. Reports said that she had "jumped or fell," and Walter's cousin Lola Cowan, believing that she had fallen accidentally, said that Jennie was constantly complaining of the heat when she was in California and begged Lola to open a window even though Lola's house was air-conditioned. Walter knew she had jumped. "I know Mother threw herself out that window," he wrote Rita Greene after she had sent condolences. "She told my wife Sunday afternoon she feared bringing disgrace to the children, me and June and when June said: 'What do you mean, honey?' she looked at the window and said, 'I am afraid I'll go out the window.'" "My consolation is knowing she isn't in agony anymore from fear," Walter confessed in another letter to Rita. "I can't keep from seeing my mother when the lights are out. I have never had such pain before."

At the funeral he put his arm around his brother, Algernon, "as if they were the last survivors," said a family member. Jennie was interred at Mokom Sholem in Queens, New York, where Walter's father, his grandmother Fannie and his grandfather Hyman were also buried, though in death as in life, the family was separated, scattered. Walter understood what Jennie's passing meant. Years before, he had closed a broadcast: [I] "found out long ago that a mother's love—is the greatest of all—

because—it is the first love you have—long before you can stand up—and the only love you are sure of—after you have flopped."

HE WAS getting older and worrying now about aging. Three months after Jennie's death, Louella Parsons said he looked fifteen years younger than his age. Walter amended: "You stop worrying 25 years later when you look around Your Personal Battlefield and Chuckle at All the Pygmies (who used to worry you). . . ." But he knew he looked older than his years. He was particularly sensitive about his baldness, which he usually concealed with his fedora. (He had forsworn a toupee years before after seeing Phil Baker's unceremoniously lifted at Jack White's Club 18 and tossed at the comics onstage.) An interviewer found his eyes "[r]estless and roving" and "straying to your hairline, especially if you've got a fine crop on top."

Even beyond the reminders in the mirror there was constant evidence of how time was passing. "Who is that woman?" he asked Louis Sobol one night at the Stork when he saw a middle-aged matron he didn't recognize; he was shocked to discover that she was an old flame of his. More shocking was his first encounter with Rita Greene since their divorce more than twenty years earlier. Rita had been dunning Walter to increase her stipend again, and Walter had finally "condescended," in Rita's word, to see her. He was nervous. "How will she look to me?" Walter fretted to Klurfeld before the meeting. "How will I look to her?," which was more to the point. They met at Walter's office. "It was like two kids getting together," Rose Bigman said, remembering them chatting and laughing behind closed doors for hours. Walter later told Rose it had been fun seeing Rita again, but Klurfeld had a different recollection. He remembered Walter seeming "morose" afterward. "I could see how old I was getting by looking at her," Walter told him.

He needed to revivify himself. He needed to feel young again. And there was one tonic in particular he felt could renew him: women. He pursued women, young women, chiefly blond showgirls like Mary Lou, avidly. He said he determined a woman's appeal by her scent, but as Klurfeld concluded, a "remarkable number had sex-and-scent appeal." He bragged about his conquests, bragged about his prowess. David Brown, then an executive at Twentieth Century-Fox, remembered Walter's once beaming in the executive dining room over his discovery that a young woman could make an older man potent.

But the sex seemed almost incidental for Walter, proof that he wasn't fading. (Critic John Crosby wrote of one young singer he knew who was using Walter's bed to get notice on Broadway. She told Crosby, "It was terrible. The telephone kept ringing with items for his column.") It wasn't about sex. It wasn't even about power, though there would always be that element in his relations with anyone. It was about restoring his energy, certifying his attractiveness, fending off his loneliness. He needed women to fill his empty nights; he told one acquaintance that he couldn't sleep without a woman beside him but he added, preposterously, that June was actually allergic to him so he had to find others. And it was relationships he sought more than brief encounters. Almost every associate of his thought of him as a "one-woman-at-a-time man," as Ernie Cuneo put it. "He was not promiscuous in sex. He may have had some other encounters . . . and if he went to bed with them sometimes, it was for the same reason that mountain climbers climb peaks—'It was there.' " But conquest was never really the point either; his own peculiar version of love—namely, loving Walter—was.

Of course, there was more to Winchell's search for rejuvenation than sex. There was also the strange belief that if he could somehow relive the triumphs of his youth, he would regain his youthfulness. But for this he needed an opportunity like the ones afforded him by the Hauptmann trial and by Lepke. He needed action. By his luck he got it. In May 1949 an organizer for the International Ladies' Garment Workers Union in New York named Willie Lurye was attacked and stabbed by three men while making a phone call. He died twelve hours later at St. Vincent's Hospital, telling police that he had no enemies. Sixty-five thousand mourners attended his funeral. Meanwhile, police, suspecting mob involvement, launched an intensive manhunt, and the ILGWU offered a $25,000 reward for the arrest of the assassins.

On June 19 Walter, acting on a tip from a friend "on the side of law and order," broadcast the initials of the suspected killers, BM and JG, and suggested they surrender to him with the reward going to the Damon Runyon Fund. They didn't. Two days later Benedicto Macri, a quondam stevedore and former garment manufacturer, and John Giusto were indicted in absentia. Then the story died. Nearly a year had passed when Walter was approached by a party asking if he would like to bring in Macri. "He feels that since he is being accused of taking a life," said the intermediary, "he would be doing a decent thing coming in to you—so that the reward could save lives some day."

Walter obviously realized he was being handed a chance to reenact Lepke's capture, and he happily replayed the scenario. On three successive nights early that June, Walter conferred with associates of Macri's to arrange the surrender. All Macri wanted was for Walter to promise to report that he had never been in trouble prior to his alleged involvement in the Lurye murder. "He has a wife and children," pleaded one of the negotiators. "This might never get in the papers and we thought maybe you would write that."

On June 4, building the drama, Walter called for Macri to surrender and reported the alleged killer's heretofore umblemished record, as he had been requested to do. A caller said that the broadcast had exceeded their expectations. A few nights later, again in a reprise of the Lepke capture, Walter was instructed to meet negotiators at a midtown apartment. Macri's attorney was concerned now that if his client were remanded into Walter's custody, District Attorney Frank Hogan might take it as an affront. Would Walter find out what was on Hogan's mind? Walter resisted, but he wasn't about to lose a good story. He phoned Hogan, who told Walter that he had absolutely no objection to Macri's surrendering to the columnist.

Walter reported Hogan's response to Macri's friends, and he was now told that Macri would surrender that Wednesday, June 14. At sundown on Wednesday, in another page from Lepke, Walter was notified that the surrender was off until Thursday. At 7:00 P.M. Thursday he learned it had been postponed until Friday, and on Friday a caller told him it had been postponed again until Saturday. On Saturday Walter complained that he had a broadcast and column to prepare.

At 8:30 P.M. Sunday he phoned for instructions and was told to call back at 9:15. At 9:15, after the broadcast, he was ordered to go to a midtown address. Walter asked that the actual transfer occur at 20th Street and Eighth Avenue, where *Mirror* photographers could scoop the competition. He was driven to the scene via 27th Street—"the identical route used to meet Lepke 11 years ago"—and then waited ninety minutes in the car. Walter was so nervous one of the emissaries went to the corner bar and brought him a brandy. Finally, at eleven o'clock, his contact walked up the street, talked briefly to an unidentified man and returned. "He's in the black coupe three cars ahead," he told Walter. Walter signaled the photographers and strolled to the auto. "I am sorry to meet you this way," Walter greeted the thin, bespectacled Macri. Then he walked him into the Tenth Precinct station house. "I am a reporter on the Daily *Mirror*," he announced. "This man is wanted for murder."

The story made headlines the next day, and even Walter's rivals saluted him. "As citizens and as newspapermen, we take our hats off to a columnist who has never been comfortable in an armchair," the New York *Post* wrote in precisely the sort of tribute Walter loved. The *Daily News* said, "Nice job, Walter," in what it admitted was "the most uncustomary editorial we could possibly print." At his murder trial the following year Macri said he had hidden out in Ohio, fearing a police frame-up or union reprisals. He surrendered only because "I was looking for someone as big as Winchell to bring me in under safe conduct." In the end he was acquitted—Walter said because the mob had tampered with the jury. Shortly after that Macri's bloodstained car was found but not his body. Walter had heard from a mobster that he had been killed and the body dumped in Gravesend Bay. But by that time Macri no longer mattered to Walter. Walter had gotten his story and a brief taste of what he missed from the old days.

THERE WAS one final similarity between Macri's surrender and Lepke's: Both occurred just before war broke out. Three days after Macri entered the police station, on June 24, 1950, North Korea attacked South Korea. On Friday, June 30, the UN sanctioned collective action against the North Korean aggressors, and the United States, under the UN umbrella, was again at war. Just eight months earlier Walter had waded into the debate over the reorganization of the armed forces, writing an article for *Collier's* that criticized Truman's plan to consolidate the services—one story had *Collier's* buying the piece for $100,000 just to get Walter off its back after its unflattering profile of him the year before—and coming to the defense of a renegade naval officer named John Crommelin who called the military plan "totalitarian" and compared it to "the old Prussian General Staff." The Navy had even enlisted Walter to take up its cause when the Air Force threatened its air arm under the consolidation.

But without a Roosevelt around whom to rally, Walter seemed much more interested in these relatively arcane matters of branch territoriality than in the Korean War itself, and he devoted far less column space to the conflict than he had to World War II or to the prospects for World War III. He seemed distracted. The Runyon Fund was taking more and more of his time, overwhelming not only Walter but Rose and Rose's assistant, Kay Myles. Walter had always boasted that "not one penny" of donations to the fund went to administration, but this was only technically accurate since the American Cancer Society had assumed the operating budget of the fund in return for being allowed to disburse the contributions. Rose and Kay urged him to turn the whole thing over to the ACS. Walter enjoyed cancer fighting too much for that. Instead, early in 1951, he formed a Walter Winchell Foundation and assumed all the administrative costs himself, excluding the ACS entirely, even from allocating the money.

And he had larger designs for his foundation. In May 1951, citing criticism of the Pulitzer Prizes by editor Ralph McGill, Walter announced that he would be awarding prizes of his own for accomplishments in journalism and the arts. Selections would be made by a twelve-person committee of distinguished Americans, including Herbert Bayard Swope, Bernard Baruch and J. Edgar Hoover. Since Walter's foundation would be providing the prize money, $1,000 for each recipient, Walter said he was withdrawing himself from eligibility. The awards would be named after Damon Runyon, and the winners were to be announced on December 10, the anniversary of Runyon's death. In October, though, Walter suddenly dropped his plans, having been convinced that the Runyon Awards would confuse contributors to the Runyon Fund.

Ironically, at the time he announced his awards, Walter had finally been nominated for a Pulitzer Prize himself—by the Minneapolis *Star Tribune*—for another of his attempts to reprise the past. In April 1951 mob leader Frank Costello sat for an interview with Walter in Miami as Al Capone had twenty years earlier. Expatiating for hours, Costello argued that legalizing gambling was the best way to drive the criminal element out of it. "I know a lot about the subject," Walter quoted him, "and that's the only solution. What became of all the bigshots in the gangs when Prohibition was repealed? I think that anybody who isn't a hypocrite and knows that picture would have to agree with me."

It was an unusual exercise—having one of America's suspected gang bosses discourse on how to destroy mob influence—and not everyone in the press was as taken by it as the Minneapolis *Star Tribune*. A Miami *News* reporter named Haines Colbert conducted an interview of his own—with a habitual drunk who delivered a lecture on temperance. *Newsweek* picked up the satire and ran a photo of Colbert and his subject next to one of Walter and Costello. The *News* lacerated him on page one both for a blind item accusing a "Miami newspaper (not the Herald)" of firing its editor after a decline in circulation and for his breach of journalistic ethics in giving a forum to Costello. "We cannot impute a lack of fundamental character to Brother Winchell," the *News* opined. "We will be more generous and assert that the man has gone mad. He couldn't take it when the American public laughed at the Great Winchell."

For someone who had always wanted the respect of his newspaper colleagues, as Walter did, the criticisms rankled. Journalists called him naive and said he had lobbed easy questions to Costello without challenging him or asking about his criminal record. "I'm a reporter, not a district attorney, although some hoodlums think so," Walter answered in his column. "I did not condone anything Costello said or did. I reported what he said." He was even more explicit in a letter to *Time*. "What Time, Newsweek and the Miami Herald critics overlook in the Costello interview when they charge Winchell with going easy on Costello is that I followed orders of my INS [International News Service] editors," he wrote. "They supplied the queries. I supplied the Costello replies. Is there any other kind of reporting?"

Obviously there was another kind of reporting, and Walter was being disingenuous in pretending there wasn't. He was also showing his age. No one had been terribly exercised when he interviewed Capone. No one accused him of breaching journalistic ethics then. Back then, when the mob was part of the romance of the times, mobsters and journalists could openly collaborate, and indeed, Costello had come to Walter, through their mutual friend Curley Harris, precisely to polish his image the way Capone had.

But in thinking he could sell himself as a benign retiree, Costello was being as naive as Walter. In the age of postwar anxiety, Costello was no longer a figure of glamour. He was perceived as a menace, one reason why the interview aroused such hostility. And Winchell was no longer being perceived as a hard-boiled, swashbuckling journalist. For the first time in his life, he was being regarded as an anachronism.

LITTLE MORE than a week after the contretemps over the Costello interview, President Truman dismissed General Douglas MacArthur, the commander of the UN forces in Korea. For ten months after the North Korean invasion, the UN forces had steadily retreated and were facing defeat, until September 1950, when MacArthur landed at Inchon and in a daring maneuver took the offensive. In November he launched what he called the "final offensive," driving to the banks of the Yalu River on the Chinese border. Two days later the Red Chinese entered the war. Once again UN troops were in retreat.

For months after that MacArthur urged the President to widen the war by bombing and blockading China. But under the field command of General Matthew Ridgway, the tide of battle had already begun to turn late in January 1951, and by March Truman had instructed the State Department to draw up a cease-fire agreement. MacArthur was infuriated. Disregarding the President's efforts, he issued his own communiqué to the Chinese: a threat to expand the war unless the Chinese agreed to meet with him. Two weeks later he issued another statement demanding victory in Korea. On April 11 Truman relieved him of his command.

Now Walter had the sort of cause, like the Forrestal campaign, that animated him far more than the war itself ever could. MacArthur's dismissal was part of the "greatest scandal in American history," he wrote in his column the next day. The Chinese were "desperate," doomed to defeat, and MacArthur was perfectly within his rights to defy the commander in chief. "His oath is to the Constitution and to the men under his command," Walter said. "If he deems the orders of his superiors in conflict with them, he is under A DUTY to make known his objections." With his dismissal the country was more divided than at any time since Fort

Sumter, he wrote. On the one side, MacArthur and the United States Senate; on the other side, President Truman and his secretary of state, Dean Acheson. On one side, those who wanted to destroy communism; on the other side, those who wanted to accommodate it.

Walter left no question which side he was on. Containment was unacceptable; America needed victory. In his column the next day he labeled the President "the greatest appeaser in history" for having surrendered Eastern Europe to communist domination. "He didn't intend to oppose Communist Imperialism. If he did, why did he, as recently as one year ago, pigeonhole the 70 group air-force, mothball the fleet, and then tell the American people that 'peace' was near?" On his broadcast of April 15 he went further, accusing the Acheson State Department of actually having backed the Chinese Communists as a native "farmers' movement" until the Korean War.

Later that week a beribboned and defiant MacArthur made his triumphant return to America, greeted by cheering throngs and a cheering Congress. Walter was equally rhapsodic. "MacArthur is not only a military hero," he wrote, "he is the living symbol of a nation's greatness." In another column that same week he crystallized the difference he saw between Roosevelt and Truman: "Truman will go down in history for getting rid of MacArthur. FDR for getting rid of Hitler."

With his defense of MacArthur, Walter had seemed finally to cross a line. It was one thing to denounce the Soviets or to rebuke Truman as he had been doing. Many liberals did that and still retained their bona fides as New Dealers. But supporting MacArthur was something else. MacArthur was anathema to the liberals and had been anathema to Walter too when the general was being courted as a presidential candidate by the America Firsters. He was a hero of the right, promoted by the most reactionary forces in the country even then as a potential presidential candidate in 1952. In defending him, Walter may have been intending to snub Truman, but he had also broken ranks with the entire left, including the moderate leftists.

Nor was it only his defense of MacArthur that seemed to mark a change. There was a new vehemence now both to Walter's anti-Soviet crusade and to his anti-Truman attacks that left even his old supporters wondering whether he was changing his political stripes. "Winchell let loose one of the worst diatribes at the State Dept. and the Truman Administration I have ever heard," Drew Pearson told his diary that May. Surprised, Pearson said he had questioned his former student Ernie Cuneo over Walter's support both for MacArthur and for an increasingly strident new voice against the State Department, Senator Joseph McCarthy of Wisconsin. "Cuneo is frank to say that it's because: 'We are not consulted.' In other words, Roosevelt used to get down on his hands

Another characteristic pose: Walter in Washington spoofs himself as a gossip by cocking his ear on a conversation between J. Edgar Hoover (left) and Vice President John Nance Garner. It was a measure of Winchell's rising eminence that he now hobnobbed with government officials as well as entertainers. *The Bettmann Archive*

Newspaper columnist, radio personality and now movie actor—Winchell made the bizarre leap in *Wake Up and Live*, co-starring (left to right) his radio sparring partner Ben Bernie, Jack Haley and Alice Faye. Louella Parsons predicted stardom. *Museum of Modern Art Film Stills Archive*

With Simone Simon in *Love and Hisses*. Winchell had tried to beg off the picture, pleading overwork, but Twentieth Century-Fox president Darryl Zanuck insisted on exercising his option. *Museum of Modern Art Film Stills Archive*

With the Walter Winchell of the West Coast, Louella Parsons, in a radio studio. The difference between them was that Parsons was part of the Hollywood social establishment, while Winchell saw himself as an antagonist of the elite. *Harry Ransom Humanities Research Center, the University of Texas at Austin*

Suzanne S. Jacobson

Rose Bigman collection

Wide World Photos

The inner circle: secretary Rose
Bigman, the gatekeeper; ghostwriter
Herman Klurfeld (top), of whom a
Winchell confederate once said, "He
was Winchell"; and Ernie Cuneo,
Winchell's political conscience and
his pipeline into the Roosevelt
administration.

Two arbiters of café society: Walter Winchell and Sherman Billingsley, the proprietor of the Stork Club. They ruled café society because as outsiders they had helped fantasize it into existence.
Wide World Photos

The sanctum sanctorum of café society: the Cub Room of the Stork Club. To the left is Table 50, where Winchell held court. *Billy Rose Theatre Collection, The New York Public Library for the Performing Arts*

Walter with Jane, the orphan June took into their home during the war.
Museum of Modern Art Film Stlls Archive

THE
WINCHELLS

December 9, 1946: June and her daughter Walda, obviously grim, outside a Cambridge, Mass., courthouse where they contested the alimony demands of Walda's husband, William Lawless. The marriage had lasted only one day.
Wide World Photos

Texas-born showgirl Mary Lou Bentley, nicknamed the "Long Stemmed Rose," and regarded as one of the most beautiful women in New York. Her long-term relationship with Winchell made her a powerful one as well. *Courtesy of Eddie Jaffe*

Nocturnal sojourners: Winchell and Damon Runyon at the Stork Club. Dying of cancer and deprived of speech, Runyon accompanied Winchell on his nightly rounds, both of them trying to keep loneliness at bay. *Courtesy of Hal Layer*

The great radio debate of March 26, 1944, between Winchell (above) and Representative Martin Dies of Texas, chairman of the House Committee on Un-American Activities. Dies had demanded the time to respond to Winchell's charges that HUAC was soft on fascism, but Winchell bested him.
Harry Ransom Humanities Research Center, the University of Texas at Austin

Lt. Cmdr. Walter Winchell disembarking in Brazil in December 1942 to begin his mission there for Roosevelt. His obsession with joining the military had touched off a firestorm among reactionaries and isolationists in Congress who believed he sullied the honor of the Navy. *Rose Bigman collection*

Walter and Walt, Jr., also known as "Boy." He hated his name, hated the burdens of expectation it placed upon him. *Rose Bigman collection*

Walter and Walda. "What can you expect?" Winchell remarked to Herman Klurfeld when Walda ran off and got married. "Her father is a whore too."
Author's collection

The changing journalistic tides: Winchell's exclusive interview with gang boss Frank Costello in April 1951 drew reproof and derision, whereas his interview with Al Capone twenty years earlier had drawn envy. *Harry Ransom Humanities Research Center, the University of Texas at Austin*

Jane Kean, Winchell's companion in the early nineteen-fifties.
Billy Rose Theatre Collection, The New York Public Library for the Performing Arts

Walter with Grace Appel, the mystery witness in the vice trial of Minot
"Mickey" Jelke. Before testifying, Appel wept that she was in love with Winchell.
Harry Ransom Humanities Research Center, the University of Texas at Austin

James A. Wechsler, editor of the New
York *Post*: Winchell's most vehement
critic, and the target of his most
vicious attacks. *Wide World Photos*

In league with McCarthy: Senator Joseph McCarthy and his journalistic ally at the Stork Club. *Harry Ransom Humanities Research Center, the University of Texas at Austin*

And, in spring 1954, with the counsel for McCarthy's Senate Investigation sub-committee, Roy Cohn (center), and Cohn's assistant David Schine (right) outside the Senate Caucus Room during hearings on charges that McCarthy had used threats to win Schine favors in the Army. *The Bettmann Archive*

ABOVE: Winchell with singer/comedian Jimmy Durante on "The Walter Winchell Show" in 1956. As the program faced cancellation, Winchell began obsessing over criticisms that wearing his trademark gray fedora on television was gauche. *Courtesy of Hal Layer* BELOW: Winchell in Las Vegas in May 1958 with dancer Lita Leon. He was reenacting events from his past and performing a mock broadcast now that he no longer had a real one. *The Bettmann Archive*

ABOVE: Winchell searching for action by touring the Far East with President Eisenhower in 1960. Reporter Bob Considine is on Winchell's immediate left. *Author's collection*

RIGHT: Reconciliations. Winchell with longtime enemy Ed Sullivan (left) and Louis Sobol at El Morocco in 1967. *Bill Mark*

A newsboy again: Winchell early in 1968 hawking the *Column*, the only New York paper in which his column now appeared. *Wide World Photos*

Near the end: Walter in Los Angeles, without his column, his broadcast, his family—or his city. *Author's collection*

once a month so that Walter became his great companion. Now Cuneo can't get near the White House or in to see the Secretary of State." But Pearson had his own suspicions—partly that Truman had once called Walter a "kike" and partly that "Walter sees which way the wind is blowing and wants to get on the bandwagon."

VII

When MacArthur made his valedictory speech before a joint session of Congress, he not only was heard by millions of Americans but was also seen by millions thanks to the new technology of television. In 1946 only six thousand sets had been manufactured in the country, only thirty stations were broadcasting and only fourteen thousand households had had sets. By 1951, when MacArthur spoke, there were over five million sets manufactured, more than a hundred stations in operation and over ten million households with sets.

Though the rapid growth of television alone should have made its impact on radio obvious, surprisingly few foresaw the consequences. Many analysts, including Walter, believed that television would supplement radio without supplanting it, and Walter quoted a 1949 *Variety* survey that "[r]adio listening in TV homes is definitely on the upbeat, particularly among families owning their video sets six months or longer."

It was clearly wishful thinking. After more than twenty years on radio Walter was apprehensive about appearing on television. His first experience, as a commentator on ABC's 1948 election night coverage, had been a miserable one. He had kept on his gray fedora—because, he said, he had a habit of "running my fingers over the brim just like some people rub their lapels"—and then suffered criticism for it. When some viewers phoned to demand he remove the hat, he did. When others called to demand he put it back on because the klieg lights reflected off his balding head, he did. He alternated throughout the night, his hat drawing much more attention than his comments on Truman.

Six months later, on April 9, 1949, Walter deployed television for a sixteen-hour telethon, hosted by comedian Milton Berle, to raise money for the Damon Runyon Fund. (It was the first of the charity telethons.) Though Walter did not appear—he phoned in from Miami—a host of stars, including Jackie Coogan, Jack Dempsey, Sid Caesar and Sir Cedric Hardwicke, did. By the time the telethon ended at 4:00 A.M., it had raised more than $1 million in pledges, nearly half of them after midnight, proving, in Berle's producer's words, that "whether it's late at night or early in the morning, television is here to stay."

That was precisely what Winchell feared. By the second telethon—this time with Walter staying the entire night answering phones on the air—he was being pressured by ABC's Robert Kintner and Mark Woods to move to TV himself. He would, they assured him, continue as the "Number One Star" of ABC. Even so, Walter was hesitant. He understood radio; he had created a persona for it. Television was something entirely different and, as he recognized from his hat experience, something potentially dangerous. On television he couldn't sit there bouncing in his chair and wiggling his telegraph key, his tie loosened, his hat askew, his fly open. It would demystify him. On television he would just be another old man rather than the crusading journalist he had always portrayed himself as being.

Still, Kintner pressed. "[I]t would be good for ABC to have its 'star' on television, and we could certainly sell the time following you. However, in addition, I personally feel you will be a big hit, and don't want to see you lose the market. Television is going to be really hot this season," he promised, and attached a research bulletin to prove his point. But Walter continued to resist.

One reason he did so had nothing whatever to do with television or radio or even his mystique. It had to do with Miami Beach. If he were to simulcast—broadcast simultaneously on radio and television, as ABC wanted—he would have to forgo his annual stay in Miami Beach because ABC did not have television lines running from Florida. This was something Walter was not prepared to do.

He loved Miami Beach. At a time when he was worrying about his age, his health and his popularity, Miami Beach invigorated him. "It's the only place in the world where I get a hard-on like a twenty-one-year-old kid," he told an acquaintance, and he had once even gone so far as to secure a doctor's note advising ABC that he was suffering from "subacute sinuitis, a vasal motor rhinitis and vocal strain," just so he could stay longer in Florida. In Miami Walter was still king. "I went down Lincoln Road in Miami Beach with Walter," recalled one friend. "Now that was like walking down Main Street in Springfield, Illinois, with Lincoln. People stopped and stared, and they couldn't believe they were actually seeing him."

Over the twenty years since Walter had first come to Miami, the Roney-Plaza had remained his Miami Beach command post. He lived in the tower apartment, which occupied the entire top floor—it had been two separate suites until his radio producer, Paul Scheffels, tired of being forced to live next to Walter and be at his beck and call, convinced the Roney to make it one—and he lived alone. June usually arrived with Walt, Jr., sometimes with Walda, for two weeks each winter, but they stayed at another resort north of the Roney, and while Walter visited them, they seldom visited Walter.

Instead he had the girls. "We had our local stable," said Scheffels. "That's the best way of putting it. They were there and willing and eager and fighting to get into the bedroom, so to speak." Yet there was one special girl here too. Her name was Phyllis, and she was a pretty though unostentatious young divorcée from rural West Virginia with a child to care for. "He'd call me up and say, 'I'm horny or whatever,' " Scheffels recalled. "He didn't want the telephone operators listening in. So I would call Phyllis and say, 'The Boss is ready.' And she would go to my room, and the blinds would be closed. And then I would go down to the bar and call him and say, 'The package has been delivered.' A juvenile code." Scheffels would sit in the garden watching his window; when the blinds opened, it meant he could return. "You should see the world's number one columnist making your bed," Phyllis once told him afterward. But Phyllis, like Mary Lou Bentley, eventually got married, and as with Mary Lou, Walter never mentioned her again.

In between these recreations, there was still the column to compose every day and the broadcast to prepare every Sunday. While the waves broke on the shore and guests cavorted in the Roney pool, Walter, in a baseball cap and shorts, kept working the phones as always. But there wasn't the same tension in Miami as there was in New York. He was more playful. He would invite local policemen or military personnel to watch while he broadcast. He would clown. He would sprinkle water on his face, then pour the rest of the glass in announcer Ben Grauer's lap.

And after the broadcast he and Scheffels or Cuneo, if Cuneo happened to be visiting, would cruise Miami nightspots the way Walter cruised the New York streets. Gambling was illegal in Dade County, but the mobsters had nevertheless built gambling palaces, and the authorities generally looked the other way. Out of some peculiar sense of civic duty, Walter wouldn't. He began a campaign against mob infiltration, and the gangsters were not happy. In January 1947 Frank Costello opened the Colonial Inn in Hallandale, Florida. "He knows I'm in this joint down here," Costello complained to Hal Conrad, who was hired as the inn's PR man, "and if he starts to blow the whistle, it might mean trouble." Conrad advised that Costello make a contribution to the Runyon Fund. Costello agreed. So early that February Conrad drove down to the Roney with a $5,000 check for the Runyon Fund.

That night, after delivering another blast on the broadcast against the casinos and scolding the city for having fired a city manager dedicated to stopping illegal gambling, Walter took Cuneo for a drive. As Walter roared down the highway in his Cadillac, Cuneo napped. When Cuneo opened his eyes, he was astonished to find that Walter had driven to the Colonial Inn. Cuneo was afraid they would be killed, but Walter reassured him: "They wouldn't dare." Walter casually sauntered into the establishment and began gambling. When a dozen flashbulbs popped—the great foe of gambling caught in the act—Walter "wasn't disturbed in the least." "He actually held the pose while more pictures were taken," said Cuneo.

If this was hypocrisy, it was also Walter's way of demonstrating that in Miami, at least, he was still above it all. He didn't mute his attacks on illegal gambling, but at the same time he frequently visited the Inn and the other gambling dens, standing on the platform above the gaming tables, watching the action. On rare occasions he gambled himself. Scheffels remembered one evening when Walter—"he was a left-hander and left-handers are supposedly good luck"—threw thirteen passes during a game of craps and won a bettor $40,000 while Walter won only $100 for himself. During these outings he would give Scheffels some money to play and enjoy himself, but when it came time to leave, he instructed Scheffels to lose. "We don't win money in these places," he said. "We don't take their money."

To relinquish Miami would have meant relinquishing his sovereignty, but television was proving an implacable force. In April 1951, at the very time Walter was championing MacArthur, there were rumors that NBC president Joseph McConnell was trying to lure Walter with a long-term television deal of the sort McConnell had recently concluded with Milton Berle. ABC countered with what it called a "life deal," guaranteeing Walter a lifetime contract, but only if Walter eventually agreed to simulcast. Walter rejected the offer on May 22 and signed on for another radio season on ABC under the sponsorship of Warner-Hudnut, a hair products manufacturer, while ABC, then undergoing a complicated merger with United Paramount Theaters, suspended its negotiations.

As the fall 1951 season began, however, Kintner issued a warning. Warner-Hudnut owner Elmer Bobst's "interest in radio only is based on prices very much lower than we are presently paying," Kintner cautioned, "and that any stock options and William R. Warner stock be contingent on your agreeing to do television. My guess is that, on the basis of the feeling that you have to be in Florida, Bobst's interest is quite cold." Kintner asked that Walter have dinner with him before the ABC board of directors' meeting that would be deliberating whether to exercise Walter's option. "As I have told you too many times," Kintner ended, "I feel you are making a great mistake in not entering television now while it is still growing. Even though it will be hard enough to get stations to clear the time, a year or so from now when programs are set to a greater degree, it will be even more difficult to get stations."

Getting stations was Kintner's aim. ABC was a late entry into the network field and was much less well positioned than its more established competitors, NBC and CBS. It needed local stations that would be willing to affiliate, and Walter was one of the keystones in ABC's strategy. Kintner knew that the marquee value of Walter Winchell on Sunday night would lure unaffiliated stations to ABC, and he was not bluffing when he told Walter that time was of the essence. Networks were hovering over stations like hawks.

For Walter, on the other hand, the aim was still security, especially since he doubted he could succeed on television. The "life deal" of the spring would have guaranteed him $1,000 per week for life in addition to any monies he received for his broadcast, which ABC set at $12,500 per week for 1951–52 with $2,500 more for a simulcast and another $7,500 if he were to do a variety program in addition. What it didn't provide was stock—ABC had no provision to give talent stock options—or any way for Walter to lay off his salary in capital gains so he could avoid the 94 percent individual tax rate.

In September Warner-Hudnut addressed one of Walter's concerns by offering him an option for ten thousand shares of its stock to be exercised at any time over the following three years. Further, ABC had reinstated its "life deal," again offering Walter $1,000 per week for life in return for his exclusive radio and television services whether he actually appeared or not. "Under this agreement you will be named by ABC as special consultant to the company on radio and television," Kintner informed him. But the best part was that Walter would not be required to simulcast in 1951 despite ABC's real need to have him do so. He would still receive $8,000 per radio broadcast. "You know all the problems we face as a result of the belief of some advertisers that radio may not be as effective as it has been in the past," Kintner wrote Walter. "You also know, much better than I, of your legitimate reluctance to make any television commitment at the present time. Under these circumstances, I think we have obtained for you, both from Warner-Hudnut and from ABC, the best radio and television deal that any artist has."

Theoretically he was now set for life. Within a month, though, his whole world would begin crashing down on him, and for the first time, he was absolutely powerless to stop it.

PART THREE

WALTER WINCHELL

All is ephemeral—fame and the famous as well.
—MARCUS AURELIUS, *Meditations IV*

CHAPTER 8

A Head for an Eye

THOUGH WINCHELL HAD HAD premonitions of his demise ever since the war's end, the long, torturous descent actually began precisely at 11:15 P.M. on October 16, 1951, in the Cub Room of the Stork Club when Josephine Baker entered. Baker was the illegitimate daughter of a domestic worker and amateur actress who had weaned the young Josephine on the hot music of the Tenderloin district of St. Louis where Josephine grew up. Married at thirteen and again at fifteen, she began traveling the black vaudeville circuit, stealing scenes from the other chorus girls with her comic antics—"doing all sorts of gyrations with her legs, tripping, getting out of step and catching up, playing marbles with her eyes," as composer Eubie Blake recalled.

Eventually she parlayed her comic talents from the chorus line to the Plantation Club in New York. In 1925, then only nineteen, she was invited to join a black troupe touring France. An exotic and bawdy figure in Paris, she caused a sensation in the La Folie du Jour when she descended to the stage in a golden cage and then danced the Charleston garbed only in three bracelets and a girdle of bananas. By the time she opened her own club in Paris the very next year, she was one of the most popular entertainers in the country as well as a symbol of sensuality and fun. Remaining there and claiming to take French citizenship, she became an institution.

Early in 1951, Baker was contemplating returning to the United States for the first time since a disastrous appearance at New York's Winter

Garden Theater fifteen years earlier. Ned Schuyler of the Copa City in Miami had offered her $10,000 per week plus a secretary, chauffeur and limousine. But Baker had two reservations. First, would Winchell attack her for having traded her American citizenship for French citizenship? And second, would Schuyler change Miami policy and admit blacks to her show? In answer to a query by Schuyler on Walter's position toward Baker's citizenship, Walter wrote back: "How's Her Act???" In answer to the second, Schuyler reluctantly agreed to waive his whites-only policy. Opening night Walter sat between Sophie Tucker and former heavy-weight champion Joe Louis. "This is the most important moment of my life," Baker said, moving from table to table, microphone in hand. "Here I am in this city where I can perform for my people, where I can shake *your* hands. This is a very significant occasion for us, and by 'us' I mean the *entire human race.*"

Once the symbol of sexual laissez-faire, Baker, the grande dame, had now become a symbol of racial pride. The NAACP unanimously commended her for breaking racial segregation in Miami. "Such a stand has done much already to expose the vicious nature of segregation based on race and constitutes a magnificent example for your fellow artists and for the public in general," NAACP executive secretary Walter White wrote her. Winchell called her "a real star." Moving on to New York that fall, she received $10,000 a week for appearances at the Strand and then $20,000 a week for a two-week engagement at the Roxy. During her Roxy appearance the NAACP feted her at a block party in Harlem.

On October 16, two days after the block party, Baker arrived at the Stork Club with her husband, Jo Bouillon; Bessie Buchanan, the wife of the owner of New York's Golden Gate Club; one of the stars of *South Pacific*, Roger Rico; and Rico's wife. What happened next depended on who was telling the story. As Josephine told it, she ordered crab salad, a steak and a bottle of French wine. "The looks that the headwaiter gave and his assistants were giving me made me suspect that something was going to happen," Baker later recalled. "But in fact the exact opposite occurred. Nothing happened at all . . . nothing, by which I mean that my friends received their orders but mine did not appear." Baker got the unmistakable impression that she was not wanted there. Sherman Billingsley, who usually fawned over Roger Rico, didn't stop by the table this time. Customers forced to pass them "pointedly turned away." And Winchell, sitting nearby, "looked right through me."

After nearly an hour's wait Rico demanded that the waiter serve Baker's meal immediately. The waiter returned with word that there was neither crab salad nor steak left. Now Bessie Buchanan, assuming that Baker was being snubbed because of race, urged her to inform the NAACP of their treatment. "I went straight to the telephone, where the attendant told me she was much too busy to dial my number," Baker later wrote. So Baker dialed herself and asked Walter White to call an officer to certify that the Stork had refused to serve her. By the time Baker returned to her table, Winchell had left. "A pathetic little steak finally appeared on a platter," according to Baker, but Rico, "his superb voice shaking with anger," asked for the check, and the group departed.

The version Walter's guests gave was significantly different. According to columnist Jack O'Brian, he, his wife, Yvonne, and Walter were sitting at a banquette across from Tables 50 and 51, eating dinner before a screening of *The Desert Fox* at the Rivoli. (Walter was upset at the idea of a film lionizing a Nazi general but out of courtesy to Twentieth Century-Fox head Darryl Zanuck had agreed to see the film before knocking it.) At 11:15, Baker and her party entered the Cub Room, greeted Walter, who introduced them to the O'Brians, and then were seated several tables away from Walter. "They ordered three rounds of drinks in the time we were there," O'Brian remembered. Then Nick Kenny, the *Mirror*'s radio columnist, came in and pulled up a chair. "Nick Kenny was a pain in the ass," said O'Brian. "We had just finished our sandwich, so I looked at Walter and gave him the 'let's go' thing, and we got up and left." He claimed they saw nothing but offered the opinion that a long wait for steak in the Stork was not unusual, and in any case, "it was crowded that night."

Herman Klurfeld, who was also at the Stork that night, was talking to a Chicago newspaperman when he saw Baker storm out. "No one knew what happened," he said, "but we knew something would happen when we saw her go," meaning that he suspected there would be repercussions. Like O'Brian, though, Klurfeld attested to the Stork's leisurely service. "It was not a place where you sat down just to eat. You sat down and spent the whole evening there." Shirley Eder, a syndicated gossip columnist, was in the Cub Room at the time and remembered seeing Billingsley looking "pale and angry." He stopped at Walter's table, whispered something in his ear and then left. Shortly after that Baker arrived. "We saw Winchell greet her, then leave the club, which was not unusual because Winchell never stayed in the club the whole evening." Eder also recalled that the service was particularly slow that evening. Baker rose and left the room. "She was gone for some time. When she returned, there was much whispering and conferring in her party. Then they all got up and left."

Ed Weiner, sitting at the table next to Walter's, said, "Walter Winchell had nothing to do with that whole thing." According to Weiner, "Winchell wasn't there half the time, then came in later and sat in the back of the room with Jack O'Brian. He didn't know what was going on."* By Walter's own account, Billingsley had told him that a "friend of yours is coming in after the theater tonight—Josephine Baker with a party." Billingsley also related that a woman had called that day to make a reservation for the Baker party and had asked if it was all right that she was black. Billingsley told Walter that he had said, "Yes, of course."

In Walter's version, Baker and her party entered the Cub Room a short time later, and she stopped to chat with actress Ann Sheridan and Sheridan's fiancé, publicist Steve Hannagan. "I was seated opposite the O'Brians. Miss Baker didn't see me. I waited a bit for her to stop chatting with Ann and Steve. But she was too busy to be interrupted." Before any of the trouble erupted, Walter said he departed to see *The Desert Fox*. At least that was his story in his autobiography. But a little less than a year after the incident, he told a slightly different story to a CBS radio executive. "When she got up with Mr. Rico," Walter wrote, admitting that he was in the Stork at the time Baker stormed out to make her call, "I turned to friends and said: 'That's nice. They're going dancing.' That's how innocent it all appeared from where I sat—nine tables away from where she said she was embarrassed. Not until the next day did I know from papers that she didn't go dancing with Mr. Rico but to a phone to complain to the NAACP."

Whether Walter was there or not, what happened next was not in dispute. The following morning Baker held a meeting in her dressing room with Bessie Buchanan; Ned Schuyler; Schuyler's attorney; Henry Lee Moon of the NAACP; Billy Rowe, a black deputy police commissioner; New York *Post* reporter Ted Posten; and Baker's press agent, Curt Weinberg, who also happened to be one of Walter's sycophants. "The entire discussion was whether or not Baker could be sued if she picketed—resulting in an attachment of her funds," Weinberg reported back to Walter. Moon contacted NAACP counsel Thurgood Marshall, who believed that Baker's wages could be attached if she picketed. The consensus was that they should picket anyway.

But what disturbed Weinberg was that Walter's name kept cropping up during the discussions. When Weinberg objected, Moon answered, "It's about time we got after Walter Winchell anyhow, to show him up." Weinberg advised them not to anger Winchell, but "they" (Weinberg didn't specify who) said they couldn't understand why there was a fear of making Walter angry. The next day, without authorization from the NAACP or Baker, Moon called a press conference to announce that black

---

*Since Baker arrived at 11:15 and since Walter attended a midnight screening of *Desert Fox*, it hardly seems likely that he could have witnessed much of a snub.

middleweight boxer Sugar Ray Robinson would resign from the board of the Damon Runyon Cancer Fund to which Walter had appointed him. (In fact, this was premature; Robinson didn't resign.) Weinberg begged Baker to repudiate Moon. "She said she couldn't do that—that she had never once mentioned your name in any statement except to answer one question as to whether or not you were in the Cub Room at the time, which she answered by saying the Ricos said you were there but inasmuch as she had only met you once she didn't recognize you herself." Weinberg promptly resigned the Baker account, and a Publicists' Guild official warned fellow publicists that they shouldn't sign on or "it would get them in a jam."

Walter was incensed at having been dragged into a dispute that wasn't even his own. He was also livid over the implication that he was not a true defender of civil rights. As a Jew Winchell had experienced discrimination firsthand, and for years, long before most national journalists, he had been an outspoken champion of civil rights. During the war, when Secretary of the Navy Frank Knox denied a black machine gunner named Dorrie Miller the Congressional Medal of Honor after Miller had courageously stood his ground at Pearl Harbor, Walter campaigned so vigorously to have a medal awarded that Roosevelt was virtually forced to bestow a Navy Cross upon him. He waged an equally impassioned campaign for a black prison inmate named Wesley Wells who had served twenty years in San Quentin for accepting stolen goods and using his employer's car without permission and was then sentenced to death for striking a guard in self-defense. Wells was "stir crazy," Walter said, driven to the brink by guards who called him "nigger." Sentencing him to death "seems a classic example of cruel punishment" forbidden by the Constitution. Thanks largely to Walter's intervention, Wells's sentence was eventually commuted.

And then there were the dozens of ordinary black citizens who petitioned him as their last resort: the black nurse who wrote to complain about discrimination in the armed services ("I am as shocked as you are," Walter wrote back and forwarded the letter to Eleanor Roosevelt for action); or the black soldier stationed at Sioux Falls, South Dakota, who cited only two restaurants off base where blacks were served and who asked Walter as "a man with a lot of prestige" to do something about it (Walter passed the letter on to the President's special executive assistant, Eugene Casey, triggering an investigation).

And there were the simple acts of personal decency: inviting Sugar Ray Robinson to accompany him around Miami at a time when hotels had signs proclaiming NO NEGROES, JEWS OR DOGS ALLOWED. Walter "took me right in," said Robinson. Or taking black friends into Lindy's to integrate it. Or leading the cheers for Josephine Baker in Miami and helping rustle up black notables to integrate the Copa. None of this was done for grandstanding; everyone who knew Winchell knew that there wasn't a discriminatory bone in his body—except when it came to homosexuals. He believed in social and racial equality. No matter how far to the right his old liberal allies might have thought he had moved on anti-communism, this was one issue on which he remained steadfast.

That was why, angered as he was by the sudden suggestion of complicity in the alleged discrimination against Josephine Baker, he was also hurt by it, hurt that anyone would doubt his sincerity. Whether at Walter's request or, as is more probable, on his own initiative, Cuneo, as ardent a proponent of civil rights as Walter, decided to take action to prove that Winchell wasn't culpable. The day after the incident at the Stork, Walter White, attempting to enlist Walter's help against the Stork, wired Cuneo, an old friend of his: WANTED TO DISCUSS TELEGRAM TO WALTER WINCHELL BEFORE SENDING IT . . . IN VIEW OF YOUR MILITANT FIGHT AGAINST RACIAL AND RELIGIOUS BIGOTRY WE HOPE AND ASK YOU WILL USE YOUR POWERFUL INFLUENCE PUBLICLY AND PRIVATELY ON THIS INSTANCE OF SNOBBERY AND BIGOTRY WHICH SHAMES AMERICA BEFORE THE WORLD AND GRAVELY WEAKENS DEMOCRACY. White sent Walter a telegram that same day, but when he failed to receive a reply, he wrote Walter a long letter and forwarded it through Cuneo. "The Josephine Baker–Stork Club incident of Tuesday night has revealed some disturbing and unhealthy attitudes in connection with yourself which, I am sure, are as alarming to you as they are to some of the rest of us," White began.

> For example, on Tuesday night, Sherman Billingsley, I am told, denied you were in the Stork Club, although several persons informed us that they spoke to you there. Mr. Billingsley also, quite amazingly, declared that he had no control over his waiters, which was not exactly the case when an attempt to organize them a few years ago was made. He has also told various people that he did not want Negroes in the Stork Club, which apparently is a hangover from his Southern background. . . .
>
> Everybody knows that Billingsley owes more to you for the success of the Stork Club than any other living human being. He may have forgotten, but he certainly ought to know that the power to destroy is as potent as the one to create.

Now came the real point. "Although I have not yet had a reply to my telegram to you of yesterday, I do trust that you are making effective protest to your friend, Sherman Billingsley. . . ." After pointing out that discrimination here only abetted communism overseas and comparing the Stork Club with the decadent pleasure palaces of Nazi Germany, White closed with a veiled threat: "We have been informed that you were unaware of what was going on. But now that the facts are known we hope you will make your position clear."

Sometime over the next two days Cuneo met with White and arranged a settlement. On his broadcast the following Sunday, Winchell was to denounce the treatment Baker received at the Stork if White would give him a telegram absolving him of any responsibility for the affair and underscoring his long record of civil rights advocacy. As the meeting ended, Cuneo allegedly told White, "As of 9:16 P.M. Sunday night, Billingsley will be just an ex-saloon keeper when Winchell gets through with him."

On October 20, White wired Walter his absolution:

I have examined the facts in the Josephine Baker Stork Club incident. I have learned that you were unaware of what happened and did not know that she had been the subject of discourtesy.

I know your record too well in your opposition to racial and every other kind of discrimination to believe that you would be a party to any insult to human dignity.

But White also wrote and then scratched out a postscript expressing his disappointment that Walter had not yet issued a simple statement that he would thenceforth not patronize the Stork or encourage others to do so. "Such a declaration by you would cause a great tidal wave of joy in the hearts of many millions of people."

The next day Walter broadcast his account of the Baker incident. "I was not in the Stork Club at the time of the alleged discourtesy," he lied. "I saw Miss Baker and her party arrive. I saw them seated six or seven tables from where I sat with newspaper friends. And I was told that they were served at least 2 rounds of drinks before any unpleasantness happened. From where I sat, everything seemed both normal and peaceful. . . ." He left to attend a midnight preview of *The Desert Fox*, he said, and had no idea that anything had occurred at the Stork until he received a telegram (White's apparently) the next afternoon. But rather than indict Billingsley and the Stork, as Cuneo had negotiated, Walter now defended himself. "After 20 years on the radio and almost 30 in the newspapers I thought my record was crystal clear . . . when minorities are getting kicked around. And it irritates me no little now to have to recite that record and disgrace myself with any defense, but apparently I have to do it. To remind some people whose memories are astonishingly short. [. . .] I am appalled at the agony and the embarrassment caused Josephine Baker and her friends at the Stork Club but I am equally appalled at their efforts to involve me in an incident in which I had no part." He then went on to read White's telegram commending him.

Walter White was also appalled. This was clearly not what he had bargained for. Walter had not repudiated Billingsley; he had not even admitted that Baker had been discriminated against. What he had done, in fact, was turn the issue from discrimination against Baker to that of ingratitude toward him. White immediately wired Robert Kintner, ABC's president, asking for airtime. "I gave [a] statement which Winchell read tonight on the promise made that it would be coupled with unequivocal repudiation of Sherman Billingsley's violation of New York Civil rights law and of human decency[.] This he clearly did not do."

Cuneo was no less angry. After the broadcast he and Winchell fought all the way down the elevator and onto 50th Street. "After all I've done for them," Walter shouted, "after all I've done for them! Let me tell you once and for all, butt out. BUTT OUT. *They've lost me, I'm telling you, they've lost me.*" Cuneo said he was "overwhelmed by sadness. Absolute sadness." "No," he quietly told Walter. "Walter, you stupid bastard, you've lost them." And Cuneo turned and walked away. It was, Cuneo believed, the "beginning of the end." He couldn't help thinking of his old friend as a burning bomber about to crash.

Meanwhile, the Baker incident was exploding. The day after Walter's broadcast, NAACP pickets ringed the Stork for an hour—the amount of time Baker said she waited to be served—and the acting mayor, Joseph T. Sharkey, announced that he had instructed every city agency with jurisdiction to investigate the charges of discrimination. Already the Mayor's Committee on Unity, formed to forge harmony in the city, had undertaken its own investigation under its chairman, former police commissioner Arthur Wallander.

Sides were quickly forming. On the one side were all those who had campaigned for civil rights and thought the Stork Club a perfect example of discriminatory practices. On the other side were all those who thought Baker had created a tempest in a teapot. By every political and moral instinct Walter belonged with the NAACP, and if he hadn't been personally involved, he almost certainly would have been in the forefront of its battle. But he *was* personally involved. Billingsley was a friend, and the Stork his own headquarters. To turn on Billingsley now, whether or not Billingsley had acted wrongly, would make Walter the one thing he most detested: an ingrate. More, the NAACP had thrust him in the middle, where he was certain he did not belong; by his analysis, it was using him to settle scores, and he resented it. He had even come to believe that the whole incident had been premeditated by Baker to make the Stork an ex-

ample. So the question boiled down to civil rights versus ingratitude, political allies with no real interest in him versus longtime friends.

By putting Walter on the defensive and pressuring him to renounce
Billingsley or be branded a racist, however, the Baker forces may have finally decided the issue for him. Arnold Forster returned from California
shortly after the Baker incident and advised that Walter have Billingsley
write him a note decrying racism. "I told this to Sherman," Walter wrote
back, "and I agree with him that nothing you can say will please them.
This is their party line and racket. I have been accused, indicted, convicted and almost lynched by the very people who have asked and gotten
me to fight such things." But Forster recollected that Walter for all his
growling was "sick about it, sick about it."

Billingsley, on the other hand, was truculent. Writing White on October 24, he called the incident "exaggerated" and coolly insisted that
"[b]ecause of the exclusive nature of our clientele, we find it necessary to
exclude certain types of persons whom we know would be regarded as
obnoxious by the majority of our patrons." "I am greatly displeased with
the action your organization has taken," Billingsley continued, "particularly with the involvement of Walter Winchell in this matter, since he was
in no way concerned and should never have been drawn in." And as for
the NAACP's pressure, "Be advised that despite pickets and other agitation, the policy of this establishment as regards the exclusion of obnoxious persons will not be altered."

Though Billingsley later insisted that he had not written the letter,
dictated it or had any knowledge of it, to those who knew the Stork Club
proprietor it had the ring of truth. Whether or not he was overtly racist,
Billingsley was still essentially an Oklahoma farmboy, and all his years in
New York hadn't changed that. One patron remembered a longtime customer making a reservation for a party that was to include the maharajah
of Jaipur. Billingsley discouraged him. "I don't want none of those colored men in here," he said. When the customer protested that the maharajah was one of the world's richest men, Billingsley answered, "He's still
colored." Another patron recalled Billingsley recoiling at accusations that
he was racist. "When Yul Brynner was in *The King and I*," he said, "they
had a party for everybody in the cast and I took care of those little pick-
aninnies." His brother Logan also denied any racism on Sherman's part,
chalking up the lack of black patrons to propriety. "You know, he cares
only for the finest people and it wouldn't do him any good to let all the
Niggers in there," Logan told the New York *Post*.

In a sense, Logan Billingsley was right. The Stork was a "snob joint"
where racial prejudice and plain snobbery commingled, but there was still
a presumption against blacks, rich or not, famous or not. Just a few

months before the Baker incident, Sugar Ray Robinson had suggested to Walter that they meet at the Stork. Walter headed him off. "I wish you wouldn't, Champ," he said. "Sherman Billingsley doesn't like Negroes and he doesn't want them in the place and if he came down there and he insulted you, I'd have to break with him although I've known him for 23 years." Robinson didn't go.

If Walter obviously didn't condone this kind of treatment, neither did he stop frequenting the Stork, which gave the NAACP's and Baker's arguments against him some force. He did send Forster to reason with Billingsley and ask him to declare an open policy at the Stork. Billingsley, though, was much more interested in proving that Baker had planned the incident than in proving he wasn't a racist, and Forster, who had spent his life fighting intolerance, felt "queasy" about now defending Billingsley against the NAACP's accusations.

While Billingsley continued to defy White, Cuneo still hadn't despaired of defusing the situation for Walter. Unbeknownst to Walter he paid a secret visit to Baker. She agreed she would make peace with Walter and even suggested they be photographed sitting together at the Stork if he would only publicly denounce Billingsley's policies. Cuneo also convinced White to promise to send another exculpatory letter if Winchell would finally and unequivocally disavow the racist practices of the Stork Club on his next broadcast.

"Ladies and gentlemen," Walter began on his October 28 program, "my statement last Sunday night on the Stork Club incident apparently was not clear enough for minds clouded by anger ... And so I repeat what I said last Sunday night ... in part. I am against all discrimination ... against any person, anywhere ... even when their color is Indian red ... as in Sioux City." That was his plea for racial tolerance. Then he asserted the prerogatives of friendship. "But some people insist that Walter Winchell go further and denounce a café owner who denies their charges ... in short, these peculiar people demand that Walter Winchell use public and private pressure on Sherman Billingsley when they would expect me to fight such pressure against them ... Humph!"

Once again Walter had violated the terms of Cuneo's truce. But by this time he had already decided that he could not sue for peace anyway. This was now war, not war against racism but war against Winchell; making peace would be appeasement. Baker had tried to discredit him. The way he typically met that challenge in the past had been to turn the tables and discredit the offender. In his October 24 column, after suggesting that one of the complainants in the Stork Club incident, presumably Bessie Buchanan, had helped incite a recent riot in Peekskill, New York, when singer and political activist Paul Robeson appeared at a rally there, Walter went after Baker. He cited an Associated Press report dated October 1, 1935, in which Baker had offered to recruit a black army to assist Italian dictator Benito Mussolini in his conquest of Ethiopia. "I am willing to travel around the world," Walter quoted Baker as having said, "to convince my brothers Mussolini is their friend." In the same column he wrote: "The only color line Winchell has always drawn is against those too yellow to tell the truth."

Four days later, after taking "more time to think things over," he declared that "we cannot again fight for Miss Baker, whose record for inciting 'incidents' is obviously a 'plant.' " The next day he ran a long letter from the New York editor of the Pittsburgh *Courier*, a black newspaper, that supported his record of fighting against racism and charged that Baker had Communist sympathies. (That Walter had just accused her of having had fascist sympathies didn't faze him.) "Eleven years ago I made a rule that I would always be completely honest with you, no matter what," Arnold Forster wrote Walter that day, obviously disturbed over this new tack on Baker. "Walter, no one is criticizing you for what is alleged to have happened at the Stork Club. Billingsley is the target and the person charged with unAmericanism. But you have handled the matter in such a way that in the public eye you have allied yourself with Billingsley and it is Winchell versus Baker. Actually, it is Baker versus Billingsley! . . . It is my best advice that you should stop pulling Billingsley's chestnuts out of the fire. I urge you to drop the matter."

Even then, had Walter followed Forster's advice or Cuneo's, he would probably have limited the damage and put the focus back on Billingsley. But he didn't. Perhaps couldn't. The longer the situation festered, the more deeply wronged he felt. He simply could not understand how blacks could impugn his sincerity unless there was some ulterior motive at work—unless they were leftists trying to impugn the American system too. Otherwise why attack *him*, who had always been on their side? More, there were other forces, reactionary forces with their own agendas, that were actively working to convince Walter that the whole Baker incident not only had been premeditated but that it was a Communist plot hatched by the NAACP for propaganda. "Despite White's protestations," a professional anti-Communist named Howard Rushmore wrote Walter, "the communists still swing weight in his gang [i.e., the NAACP]."

All this fed Walter's natural paranoia. When the *Post* quoted Walter White that he had screened the Stork Club pickets for Communist affiliations, Walter circled the item and scrawled, "Haw!," his customary epithet of derision. When *The New Leader*, a respected anti-Communist magazine, ran an article criticizing Walter for his cowardice in the Baker affair and he learned that the magazine's editor was married to black composer Duke Ellington's sister, he scrawled on the report, "Aha. This explains his personal animus." Again Forster advised him "to close the whole problem out of your column and air program," but Walter simply couldn't let go. "I had 7 attacks not counting the entire Negro press," he answered, and vowed, "I haven't started!"

When he did start or, more accurately, when he shifted into his high attack mode, he accused Baker of having aided the Nazi-installed Pétain government in France, of being anti-Semitic, of refusing to patronize black-owned clubs and businesses, of fomenting racial incidents to get attention. He was now firing so many salvos at Baker that *Time* reported the "Champ [of civil rights] was screaming as shrilly as the kind of drunken blonde that Billingsley never, never allows in his club."

But rather than discredit Baker, Winchell succeeded in doing precisely what Forster had feared: He made the attacks themselves the issue and himself, not Billingsley, the villain. Billingsley, after all, had always been a lost cause. Walter, by going after Baker and sparing Billingsley, became a hypocrite and a symbol of white insincerity. "This writer is convinced that Walter Winchell is an arrogant snob and that he plays 'dirty pool,' " the Pittsburgh *Courier* now editorialized. "All negroes have had experiences with white friends like Winchell. They shake your hand, they pat you on the back, they give you a boost so long as they can pose as liberals without too much sacrifice. But they don't want you to move in on them where it's going to cost them something."

Far more hurtful was Sugar Ray Robinson's announcement at the Pal Razor Sports Award ceremony. Robinson had just returned from a Boston fund-raiser for the Damon Runyon Fund to "some very embarrassing news": that his friend Walter Winchell had been at the Stork during the insult to Baker and "did not tend to have a hand in stopping it." "I can't tell you how it makes you feel," Robinson went on, "that you're fighting cancer ... and you have a cancer right there in your own committee." And he promised to make his feelings known even "if I have to resign from the Cancer Fund."

Now that Walter had foolishly made himself the issue, Baker and the NAACP also made him the target. Contemplating legal action against him, Baker engaged famed civil rights attorney Arthur Garfield Hays. Hays, after consulting with Cuneo, convinced her not to file suit. Instead Baker and Hays issued a conciliatory joint press release on December 10, claiming that the incident and its aftermath "involve issues much bigger than either Miss Baker or Mr. Billingsley," absolving Walter of having been at the Stork at the time of the discourtesy and calling "regrettable" the attacks on Baker by Walter, "who is one of our most valiant fighters for minorities." Baker then answered each of Walter's charges against her.

Hays concluded, "I hope that all those who believe in the same ideals will get together for the common good."

Hays, Cuneo and Baker all obviously hoped that this might finally put the matter to rest as far as Winchell was concerned. It was assumed that Walter would air Baker's defense in the column and once more take a stand for civil rights generally, if not against the Stork specifically. Two days later, at Cuneo's suggestion, Hays wrote Walter directly in a further attempt to defuse the situation. "It seems to me that this whole matter is a tempest in a teapot," Hays said, "and I do not see in any way how you are connected with it. At any rate having known you for years as a vigorous fighter for the rights of all minorities, including Negroes, I particularly regret that the matter became in any way a personal one between you and Miss Baker."

For the third time since the Baker incident, Cuneo had given Walter the opportunity to save himself from his own senseless vituperation. And for the third time Walter self-destructively rejected the truce. On December 17, he published Hays's letter to him, but in a repeat of his behavior toward Walter White, he did not include the last sentence or any of Baker's refutations of Walter's plethora of charges. The same day Hays wrote him expressing regret. But anyone who really knew Winchell would have known that he was in far too deep to retreat now, despite Cuneo's valiant efforts; to have admitted that he was wrong about Baker's alleged communism, fascism, anti-Semitism and even racism would have seriously compromised the whole institution of W.W. So he pressed on.

So did Josephine Baker. The same day as Hays's rueful letter, Baker was the featured speaker at a Hanukkah breakfast of the Chicago Women's Division of the American Jewish Committee. "I have been shocked by Mr. Winchell's attitude," she told the guests, "not only because his charges are completely untrue, but because I thought that he would defend the victims of discrimination rather than those who practice it." She closed echoing the lament of Walter White and other black notables now: "For years Mr. Winchell built his reputation on fighting bigotry and injustice. It pained me greatly to see that fight end at the door of the Stork Club."

In the meantime, the police and the Mayor's Committee on Unity had been investigating the incident. On November 29 Police Commissioner George Monaghan issued a six-page report finding no discrimination at the Stork. White was furious and sent Mayor Vincent Impellitteri a long letter listing the investigation's deficiencies, including the report's remarkable acceptance of Billingsley's alibi that he was taking a shower during the entire episode. The Unity report had been submitted to the mayor on November 24, but even its members recognized that Billingsley's response to their investigation was inadequate—he said, "[I]t is our policy to cater to a clientele made up of the people of the world"—and the report sat on the mayor's desk, unreleased, for nearly a month, during which time the committee vainly asked Billingsley for clarification. When the mayor finally issued the report on December 20, it too concluded that there was "nothing to substantiate a charge of racial discrimination," and declared the incident "closed."

It wasn't. By the committee's own admission, the Baker affair had infused the city with "hostility and tension," and the reports hardly dissipated them. White demanded a meeting with the mayor to urge him to reopen the investigation. The mayor refused. On December 21, the day after the Unity Committee report was issued, Josephine Baker gave her response. She announced at the NAACP offices that she had instructed Arthur Garfield Hays to file a $400,000 suit against Winchell, charging him with having embarked on a "public campaign to vilify, libel and damage" her reputation and professional standing.

Ned Schuyler, the owner of the Copa, had warned her against counterattacking. "You don't understand how things work in New York," she said he told her. "The sun rises and sets on that column." Baker ignored him the way Walter had ignored Cuneo and Forster. "I clearly had a fight on my hands," she wrote in her autobiography. "[T]here were ugly stories in the tabloids, aimed at discrediting me morally. Apparently I had led a scandalous life! The number of threatening letters increased. . . . The film contract I had signed the week before which would bring me a quarter of a million dollars, had just been annulled for no apparent reason." But Baker, like Walter, wouldn't capitulate. "Instead of frightening me, they were making me dig in my heels!"

The night she filed her suit Baker did something that, even more than the suit itself, earned her Winchell's everlasting enmity: She appeared on the Barry Gray radio program. Gray, a young disc jockey and interviewer, hosted a popular program from Chandler's Restaurant each night from midnight to 3:00 A.M. over WMCA. As Gray later told it, he was on the air when Baker arrived, offering to tell her story about her abuse at Winchell's hands. Gray was torn. He was starstruck by Winchell. More, Winchell had been an early supporter of his when Gray had first come to radio and had later invited the disc jockey to join him and Runyon on their police radio forays. He knew that putting Baker on the air would infuriate Winchell "unless I called him and asked him to come on to refute the charges." Gray said that he phoned but that Walter had already left for Florida and was unreachable. Though he didn't say that he knew having Baker on the program would be a coup and that he was willing to brave Walter's certain wrath for the attention, he invited her to return the following evening with Arthur Garfield Hays.

Baker appeared for two nights, defending herself and flailing at Walter for both his indifference at the Stork and his attacks on her. When she finished, Gray said, "She left the dais to the cheers of the audience." Gray wired Walter at the Roney on December 24, asking him to appear, but Walter scribbled on the telegram: "Reads like Legal Dept wrote it & is worried." Instead Sugar Ray Robinson and Ed Weiner, obviously without Walter's authority, appeared and offered what Gray called a "pallid" defense.

One engrossed listener of the Baker broadcasts was Walter's old enemy Ed Sullivan. Immediately after Baker had left the air, Sullivan called Gray to praise him for his courage in taking on Winchell and to volunteer to appear on the show himself to tell *his* stories about Walter's misdeeds. Sullivan accepted an invitation for the following night, and as Gray described it, "Chandler's walls seemed bent from the crowd within. There wasn't an inch of space as he walked to the dais."

As it turned out, Baker versus Winchell had been only a preliminary for Sullivan versus Winchell. Among Broadwayites Sullivan had a reputation as kind, loyal and approachable. But however genial he could be to press agents, it was no secret that Sullivan hated Winchell every bit as much as Winchell hated Sullivan. Now, in two appearances on the "Barry Gray Show," all of Sullivan's hate and envy rushed forth in a torrent. "I despise Walter Winchell because he symbolizes to me evil and treacherous things in the American setup," Sullivan announced before launching a long, desultory account of his own efforts on behalf of racial, ethnic and religious tolerance. "I thought a shameful thing had been done," he said, getting back to Baker. "A woman had made a protest of discrimination," and Walter, for all his brave words about defending free speech, had denied her right to make that protest. Instead he made charges against her "recklessly and with great abandon," made them "confident in his power and buoyed by the fact that no New York newspaper except one had taken this thing up, because they didn't want to give him publicity on it. . . . I say that he's a megalomaniac and a dangerous one."

On the second broadcast Sullivan said, "I don't think that Winchell is a great American anymore. I think that something has happened to him. I don't know what it is, but I think that the effects of it are evil." Then Gray came on and admitted that performers might refuse to appear on his program for fear of reprisals but insisted the issue was too important to back down: "Can an individual with power destroy the character of another?"

This was a far cry from the original question raised by the Stork incident. What had happened? How had Billingsley's discourtesy, even his bigotry, toward Josephine Baker evolved into a question of Walter

Winchell's megalomania? Obviously Walter had to shoulder a large part of the blame for deflecting attention from racism to irrelevant questions about Baker's patriotism, but Gray and Sullivan could not have succeeded at making Walter's megalomania the issue if there hadn't already been a host of influential individuals who wanted to make an example out of Walter. Many of them were journalists, celebrities, politicians, artists, socialites who, as St. Clair McKelway had described them a decade earlier in his *New Yorker* profile of Walter, were terrified of Walter's power but despaired of ever having the means of fighting it. Others were liberals who believed that Walter had left the reservation after Roosevelt's death and had become a dangerous voice for irresponsible anticommunism. Still others weren't so much politically opposed to Winchell as culturally opposed to him, just the way *The New Yorker* had been during McKelway's exposé. Both on the left and on the right, they deplored his tactics against Baker, and they mourned the reasonableness that he was helping drive from public discourse.

For all the foes, however, there was one important and inescapable subtext: Senator Joseph McCarthy. McCarthy had been a nondescript Republican senator from Wisconsin until February 9, 1950, when he addressed the Republican Women's Club of Wheeling, West Virginia. Sounding very much like Winchell during the war when Walter was haranguing the fifth column, McCarthy declaimed, "The reason why we find ourselves in a position of impotency is not because our only powerful potential enemy has sent men to invade our shores but, rather, because of the traitorous actions of those who have been treated rather well by this nation, meaning officials of the last two Democratic administrations." In effect, what McCarthy said was no different from what any number of Republicans had been saying even before Whittaker Chambers's revelations. The difference was the specificity and the scale: In his hand McCarthy waved what he claimed was a list of 205 Communists he had identified in the Acheson State Department, and he demanded an explanation from the administration.

Walter took no notice of the speech at the time. In fact, his column the next day chided the Republicans for their new "Statement of Principles" about the spread of communism and fascism. "If you're waiting for them to get specific (and mention Franco)," he gibed, "you'd better take off your shoes and make yourself comfortable." But whether Walter recognized it or not, McCarthy's charges had exploited the same vein of malaise that Winchell was exploiting and provided a ready explanation for the sense of international crisis. As McCarthy's claims of Communist infiltration in the government grew even more grandiose and the numbers and names proliferated, especially after the North Korean invasion, "Mc-

Carthyism" became an acceptable form of anticommunism, marked by recklessness, finger-pointing, innuendo, fabrication, sleight of hand and militancy—marked, in short, by the very tactics Winchell was deploying in attacking Josephine Baker.

The two men had been introduced to each other at the Stork Club during the summer of 1950 by Robert Morris, the counsel for the McCarran Senate committee investigating communism. "I never saw two guys get on so well," said one observer. "They went into a huddle at the corner of the table and it didn't break up for two hours." Walter still wasn't a rabid McCarthy fan in print (he gave him remarkably few mentions), but in conspiratorially minded postwar America, the gossipmonger and the accuser were natural allies, and by 1951 the convergence of their methods was apparent to everyone; indeed, McCarthy may even have learned a thing or two about character assassination from Winchell. It was this affinity between them, the threatened collaboration of the political swordsman with the journalistic one, that scared their opponents and gave the opponents a moral justification to do battle. They saw slaying Winchell as a way to slay McCarthyism.

Walter, of course, always knew that there was an enemy horde poised to destroy him; this conditioned practically everything he did. But so long as he was on the side of angels, fighting intolerance and hate, he had provided no salient of attack to his opponents, save for the reactionaries. Only now, with his seeming indifference to racism at the Stork, with his indulgence in methods strikingly similar to McCarthy's and with Sullivan's scathing denunciation on the Barry Gray program to coalesce the opposition, would all the pent-up resentment and anger finally be unleashed. "I remember that memorable night," then press agent Ernest Lehman said. "Everybody was calling everybody all over New York. 'Turn your radio on.' It was an incredible event. . . . Nobody had ever dared to say that the man blackballed people, kept people from employment, that he had this powerful effect on the lives of other people. . . . That was just the most startling thing for Ed Sullivan to say: 'I want all of you to come out from where you're hiding. Don't be afraid of this man.' "

If Sullivan's tirade was intended to demystify Broadway's Wizard of Oz, Walter was surprisingly unruffled. He was angry, he told Klurfeld, because it had unnerved June, who was ill, but he was not going to respond in kind this time. "I'll get around to all the ingrates," he said. Arnold Forster believed that Sullivan had "clearly" libeled Walter and pressed him to take legal action, but Walter wasn't interested. His only reference in the column to Sullivan's broadcasts was a veiled one, a poem by sportswriter Grantland Rice:

You'll find that most of them around
Would rather knock than boost.
You'll find the poison barbs come thick
The higher that you roost.
But you can gather in this balm
And cherish it as such
They rarely ever knock a guy
Who doesn't matter much.

Even Sullivan's associates were shocked that Walter hadn't promptly unloaded on him. One of them, wanting to know why Walter held his fire, had been told that Sullivan had a document "so devastating that Winchell knew he could never tangle with Sullivan publicly and survive." (In all likelihood the document was Walter's divorce decree, the date of which would have proved Walda's illegitimacy.) The friend asked Sullivan if it was true. "Ed didn't hesitate for a second. 'You'd better believe it. I've got it—and Walter knows I've got it. He also knows that I'll never use it unless he tries to push me too far. That's all I'm ever gonna say about it.' "

Sullivan did seem emboldened. Not only had he publicly attacked Walter, but he frequently went to the Stork now and asked for a table facing Walter's to stare him down. One evening, according to a young production assistant who had accompanied Sullivan to the club, Walter got up to go to the rest room. Sullivan excused himself and followed. Knowing that Walter carried a pistol, Sullivan's wife, Sylvia, asked the assistant if he would go to the rest room and scout. When the assistant peeked inside, he said he saw Sullivan holding Walter's head at the bottom of the urinal and flushing while Walter sobbed. Or so the story went.

However unassailable Ed Sullivan may have been, Barry Gray was not, and Walter may have felt he deserved even worse than Sullivan since he was an ingrate who had recently enjoyed Walter's favor. A few days after the second Sullivan broadcast, Gray and his wife left for a European vacation. By the time their ship docked in New York three weeks later, Walter had already launched a Baker-style campaign against him. Gray later wrote, "I was (and sometimes in the same column) a Fascist, a Communist, a heterosexual, a homosexual, a marital cheater, a deadbeat, a lousy broadcaster, and un-American. . . . It was total war, and Winchell was doing a first-rate job on all fronts." Guests begged off appearing on his program. Friends thanked him for not mentioning their names. Sponsors deserted him. "Where earlier I had walked into Lindy's and greeted friends left and right, now a visit to Lindy's became *High Noon*: conversation would cease as all eyes watched to see who would say hello." At the same time Sullivan, who had promised to defend Gray from Winchell, met Gray's entreaties for help with silence. Gray was totally at the mercy of Walter Winchell.

ONE MIGHT HAVE expected that the Josephine Baker incident, like most of the episodes in Winchell's life, would finally exhaust itself, and the media would turn to another cause célèbre. Indeed, Josephine Baker's slight was largely forgotten, but the war against Winchell continued. No one wanted to let up, no one could afford to let up, realizing that Walter would give no quarter to anyone who did. This had to be a fight to the finish—for Walter's foes, the finish of Walter Winchell.

In late November another combatant entered the battle. Born Lionel Simon but rechristened Lyle Stuart, he was a fast-talking young hustler who had kicked around Broadway working for *Variety, Music Business* magazine, *Mad* magazine, the International News Service, and the National Youth Administration Radio Workshop before joining a publicity office which regularly fed items to Winchell. (When a towering model named Lois DeFay married a midget as a publicity stunt and then got a divorce, Stuart quipped that they didn't see eye to eye; Walter wired Stuart that it was the funniest line he'd had in twenty years.) Whatever he did, according to a fellow press agent, "Stuart always had an angle."

In 1951 he, his wife and an old high school classmate named Joseph Whalen scraped together $1,400, sublet a midtown apartment from an old White Russian sympathizer and began a monthly tabloid called *Exposé* with the guiding principle that there was no such thing as a story "too hot to handle." As Stuart later told it, he and Whalen had been dining at a Chinese restaurant not long after the Baker incident when they began mulling over Winchell's attacks on her. A few years before, while living in Virginia, Stuart had sent Walter a column on the indignities that southern blacks had to suffer. Walter edited the piece, cutting some of the most biting criticisms of Jim Crow—edits that Stuart attributed to Walter's growing conservatism—then declined to publish it. Now Stuart said he was appalled at Walter's racial insensitivity, especially at a black dialect joke that Walter had run. Stuart and Whalen resolved to do something about this hypocrisy. They resolved to run a series on Walter Winchell.

Working through the night, they composed a story headlined THE TRUTH ABOUT WALTER WINCHELL, the "truth" being a litany of charges: that Walter's column was largely written by press agents, that he seldom saw his wife or children, that he had had a relationship with Mary Lou Bentley, that he was cowardly during the Baker incident, that he was moving closer to Senator McCarthy for fear of being attacked by McCarthy himself, that he was vain and egocentric, that he had a "psychopathic streak in his personality" and that he was "probably one of the greatest hoaxes ever put over on newspaper readers."

"I thought you would like to see our issue of Exposé on Winchell," Stuart wrote Walter White early in November. "This issue hits Manhattan newsstands on Thursday and Friday of this week." Or at least Stuart thought it would. But Walter had already gotten wind of Stuart's story and had contacted William Richter, the president of the News Dealers Association, which distributed papers, asking him to prevent *Exposé* from reaching newsstands. I WANT TO ASSURE YOU, Richter telegrammed Winchell, THAT I SHALL NOT DISTRIBUTE THIS PAPER. Stuart immediately objected that the NDA was violating its contract and withholding property and contacted *Time* to get it to run a story. At the same time, Stuart claimed that 3,000 copies had been mysteriously ruined by mimeograph ink before Richter, under the threat of the *Time* investigation, finally agreed to release the papers.

Stuart now worked overtime to produce more copies and established his own distribution system, personally delivering the papers and offering newsdealers four cents per copy, or twice the usual commission. No sooner had he dropped off a bundle and returned to his office than he would get a phone call asking for more. At one Broadway stand alone, in the heart of Winchell country, he said he had sold 1,450 copies. He was even cheeky enough to send a boy to the Stork Club, where copies sold for as much as a dollar, and he was considering sending additional copies to Miami. As of noon, November 15, Stuart was claiming to have sold between 28,000 and 29,000 copies and had orders for 40,000. In the end, by his count, over 85,000 copies were printed.

Again Walter was perplexed. Though he had virtually invented gossip, he simply could not understand the engine of gossip when it was aimed at him, especially since he and Stuart had always had a cordial, even a joking, relationship. So he asked Arnold Forster to investigate why Stuart had turned on him. Forster produced a rap sheet. He learned from a writer named Jake Spolansky that Stuart had been arrested in 1942 for attempted extortion—there were no details—and been given a suspended sentence and two years' probation. Other sources told Forster, wrongly, that Stuart had been fired from the INS where he worked in the Columbus, Ohio, bureau because he was "unreliable"—Stuart claimed he had left after running afoul of his superiors for opposing a state bill full of graft—and that he had been fired from *Variety* as well. (In fact, he had been fired from neither job; indeed, INS had granted him four salary raises in six months, and *Variety* had tried to keep him from leaving.)

Forster closed his report with the information that while Stuart was a member of the American Civil Liberties Union, he "has *no* record of Communist affiliation."

Though deprived of this major weapon, Walter opened fire on Stuart as he had on Josephine Baker. "The so-called exposé on Reader's Digest in a local scandal sheet," Walter broadcast on November 18, careful not to mention the exposé of himself in the same issue, "was written by a person once convicted for attempted extortion. His phoney pen name is Lyle Stuart. STUART. His real name is Lionel Simon. He was arrested in 1942 by detectives from the New York District Attorney's office ... His rogue's gallery photographs are before me now." Thus began his war against Lyle Stuart. "I don't think a week went by when there wasn't a mention of me," Stuart recalled.

Still, Stuart was gloating. "*Exposé* seemed to have opened the floodgates," he said, beaming. Everyone was going after Winchell now. Reporting at the Overseas Press Club on the response to the issue, Stuart said one member remarked, "This could well be the story that will topple Winchell." It was just a few weeks later that Sullivan delivered his screed on the "Barry Gray Show" and brought Stuart's accusations from the sideline to the main arena.

But the worst by far was yet to come.

II

Exposé had barely hit the newsstands when Lyle Stuart received a visitor at his little office on 55th Street. Al Davis was an editor at the New York *Post*. The *Post*, Davis said, had decided to do a series of its own on Winchell, and he wanted to know if Stuart would assist it. Stuart readily agreed on the condition that the paper would credit him and come to his defense when Walter attacked.

Walter heard early of the *Post*'s plans, at least as early as November 15, when Stuart was already bruiting them about. Billy Rose wrote Walter two weeks later to inform him that a *Post* reporter had contacted Rose in connection with the series. "I have been in the ring with the lightweights and the heavyweights for nearly 30 years," Walter wrote back bravely. "This series will revise the New Yorker profiles.... And I'm going to Florida to look tanner."

In December the FBI's Philadelphia office was visited by a journalist who said he had been approached by the *Post* to help write the Winchell series. "The story series is designed to expose Winchell's private life," the man said, "his abilities and lack thereof as a bonafide newspaperman, and to point out what a charlatan and fake Winchell is." The informant was also told that the *Post* would dredge up stories about Winchell's father and Walt, Jr. Hoover wrote on the report, "This is a new low in smear."

Why the *Post*? Owned by Dorothy Schiff—granddaughter of financier Jacob Schiff—who had rescued the paper from certain death in 1939 only because it was the sole evening paper supporting Roosevelt, the *Post* had, with the demise of *PM* the preceding year, become the leading liberal paper in New York. So long as he was blowing Roosevelt's trumpet, Dorothy Schiff had hardly had any grievance against Winchell. She had, in fact, once arranged to meet him through Leonard Lyons, who had told her that Winchell might be amenable to defecting to the *Post*.

"Two things about Winchell surprised me—his appearance and his conversation," Schiff recalled of their meeting. "Wouldn't you expect a gossip columnist who stayed up all night collecting items damaging to so many to be green-faced, ferret-eyed, devilish-looking? Quite the contrary is true. Winchell is a soft-looking, rather handsome, silver-haired man with a pink-and-white baby complexion. He would look rather fatherly except for his restless hands and eyes."

As for his conversation, "I was submitted to a plaintive torrent of grievances against his bosses in the Hearst organization who, he felt, did not appreciate him sufficiently." He respected Hearst, Sr., and told Schiff that if Hearst called him and asked him to stay, he couldn't refuse. As Schiff told it, this routine was repeated several times over the years: Winchell hinting he might leave Hearst and Schiff courting him. The latest overture had occurred about a year before the *Post* series. She closed, "[T]here was something so pitiful about this man—fabulously successful in a worldly sense, abysmally unsuccessful as a human being."

The *Post* had been keeping tabs on Walter for months; long before the Baker incident Earl Wilson, the *Post*'s self-styled "saloon" columnist, wrote a colleague at the Miami *Daily News* inquiring whether Walter spent so much time in Florida to avoid higher New York State income taxes, but Wilson added fearfully, "[Y]ou had better leave my name out of it for the time being." Even so, these seemed to be desultory inquiries. The *Post*'s big guns were trained on Sherman Billingsley, especially after the Baker incident. Curley Harris wrote Walter that Schiff herself had been snubbed at the Stork and "is out to get him" by exposing him in a long series "like the one they did recently on Senator McCarthy." But within weeks of the Baker incident the paper had redirected its fire. "The Post pieces started out to be about Billingsley," Walter wrote Billy Rose, "then they got sore at me for debunking that forged letter they ran 'signed' by Sherman and reminding them (when they denied Baker ever supported Mussolini) that I read it in the NY Post of October 1st 1935."

Perhaps Walter could imagine that these relatively small insults would mobilize the *Post* against him—they would have mobilized *him*—but in assigning seven reporters to a two-month investigation of Winchell, the paper was clearly motivated by more than minor taunts, though exactly what that motivation was was to be the subject of intense speculation. Herman Klurfeld said that the *Post's* managing editor, Paul Sann, a salty little man who had allegedly quit high school for newspapers after seeing *The Front Page*, admitted, "We're just doing it for circulation."

This couldn't be discounted. *PM* and the conservative New York *Sun* were lately dead, and *The Compass*, a liberal paper founded by the *Post's* former executive editor and Schiff's former husband, Ted Thackrey, was on the brink and would soon die. With the *Post* teetering too, Schiff and her editor in chief, James Wechsler, devised a profile for their daily—as Wechsler defined it, "a liberal paper with a large degree of humor and interest, which would include sex as a major phase of the human condition."

But this paper-saving policy posed a dilemma for its editor. Wechsler, a slight man of solemn demeanor whose square face was mounted by dark brows that only accentuated the impression of grimness and whose taste in clothes ran to bow ties and galluses, was a longtime political activist of the left. Though he had departed *PM* in 1946 because he believed the paper was tilting too far toward Stalinism, he maintained his sense of political mission. In begging Schiff to let him take over the *Post*, he had hoped to make it a distinguished and intelligent voice of moderate left opinion. Instead, under the pressures of circulation, he found himself presiding over a schizophrenic publication—divided, as media critic A. J. Liebling put it at the time, "between libidinous and didactic tendencies, Earl Wilson and Max Lerner."

Wechsler was obviously torn too. At one point Schiff asked him if he was ashamed of being editor of the paper. "I could answer no, I really wasn't," Wechsler said, sounding less than convinced. "We had a problem of survival and basically what we were doing was right, even if there were some things which were undistinguished." But like Emile Gauvreau before him, who had negotiated the same dilemma between his better instincts and his baser ones, Wechsler seemed to feel guilty about the compromise, and like Gauvreau, he seemed to need some outlet to let him expiate his sins. Walter Winchell, as the living symbol of journalistic abuse, now provided that outlet. By destroying Winchell, Wechsler might have thought he could purge his own demons.

"Those who are discreet enough to avoid any quarrels with him are permitted to live in peace," Wechsler wrote in a memoir of the period, explaining why he went after Winchell, "and those who violate his rules can expect to be set upon from behind in the journalistic dark alley known as 'Walter Winchell on Broadway.'

"This seemed reason in itself to publish the series. Whatever else might be said about him, it had to be acknowledged that Winchell had achieved a frightening power to bully and browbeat."

Like many of Walter's new enemies, Wechsler had never seemed too concerned about that power so long as it was directed at the right. Writing in 1944 for the house organ of the Newspaper Guild, Wechsler had lauded Walter in his fight against Dies. "He decided that the biggest, most scandalous racket of all time was an outfit called Fascism, an international cartel composed of various wings of Murder, Inc. . . . [H]e decided that this was the time to draw a line and tell the Fascist mob not to cross it.

"He got very mad. He hit hard. He named names," and though few publishers or broadcasters came to his defense, Wechsler believed that "Winchell's fight for democracy on the air waves will be remembered long after Winchell's exposé of Mrs. Smith's illegitimate baby has been forgotten."

But now that Winchell's power was being directed at Truman, now that he had extolled Douglas MacArthur and dined with Joseph McCarthy, he was fair game. "The basic motivation of the vicious series on Winchell was entirely political," press agent Maurice Zolotow complained to a friend later that year. "That anybody should dare to say a good word for MacArthur, McArthy [*sic*] or Eisenhower was too much for Wechsler to bear. . . ."

Wechsler told *Time* that he had long wanted to expose Winchell but that he couldn't find an occasion until the Baker incident. Then he began poring over Winchell's life to find offenses. Lyle Stuart provided more than one hundred names and addresses. "I gave them every press agent, every girlfriend," he said. "And they kept checking with me day by day." Reporters had discovered Klurfeld, one of Walter's best-kept secrets, and stationed themselves outside his Queens home. They even trailed him to his son's school and interviewed his mailman and the owner of the little store where he bought his daily papers. "If you're nice guys," Klurfeld nervously asked them, "you'll tell Winchell when you see him the name of the guy who told you these things. I don't want him to think that I'm the one who's telling you." *Post* reporters had also tracked down Rita Greene, still working as a legal secretary. "I shall get in touch with Mr. Winchell," she said. "I shall tell him to keep you damn people out of my hair."

On December 15 Al Davis and another reporter, Irving Lieberman, traveled to Miami to confront Walter himself and found him outside the Roney. "Well, I hear you've covered my story pretty fully by now," Walter supposedly told them. "Why don't you go ahead without me and print what you have?" When Lieberman protested that they wanted to be fair, Walter grimaced and said, "Aw, stop kidding the kidder."

The series debuted on January 7, 1952, with a front-page article calling Walter "probably the biggest success story in American journalism" but so insecure that "he can be taunted into angry self-defense by a harsh phrase in an obscure Oshkosh weekly," and the man who "made the gossip column a respectable newspaper feature" but who now "spends much of his time justifying the existence of gossip columns and trying to prove he is a heavier thinker than Walter Lippmann." Subsequent installments examined Walter's relationship to J. Edgar Hoover, his alliance with Billingsley (who was called "Winchell's valet"), the roles of Klurfeld and Cuneo and even Rose Bigman.

As with *The New Yorker* series, Walter was outwardly calm. He made no mention of the articles in his column, even when an informant advised him that Wechsler had regularly contributed pieces to the Communist *Daily Worker* between 1934 and 1940. He told Arnold Forster that he wasn't even reading the series. "Everybody in New York was talking about it," Forster recollected incredulously, "and Winchell wasn't reading it!" His attitude, Forster said, was "I don't want to aggravate myself. I long ago stopped reading the crap that's sent to me and Rose doesn't let me have it."

Forster realized that this was a lie and that the *Post* series frightened Walter. "This was a great wall—Winchell was," analyzed Klurfeld. "The *Post* series put an almost imperceptible crack in that wall. For years everything he did turned out right. Even if he was wrong, it turned out right. . . . From this point on, even when he was right, it turned out wrong. . . ."

Now Walter spiraled into depression. According to an FBI report, on January 25 he phoned an NAACP official, most likely Walter White, and unleashed a marathon tirade of over two hours, complaining that he was being "crucified" by the organization and by papers like the *Post* and saying he feared that if he were to visit Harlem, "his blood would flow in the streets." That same day the *Post*, in the eighteenth installment of its Winchell saga, observed that he "frequently acts these days like a man who is just going through the motions. He's lost much of his zest and exuberance."

Two days later Walter was in the lobby of the Roney-Plaza in Miami getting ready for his broadcast when, according to one report, he began to feel dizzy. He called over a doctor he recognized, and the doctor advised him to see a cardiologist. The cardiologist found nothing wrong with Walter's heart but recommended a rest. That night he closed his broadcast with the terse announcement: "I remain your New York correspondent who has been *ordered*—to end all professional activities immediately by my doctors. At least for a month." In his column the next day he explained, "I have been working under terrific pressure. The doctors told me I am on the verge of collapse, that I have to stop at once or there might be some unhappy news—tomorrow, this week or next week. It is a terrific shock to me to know that."

Speculation now was rife over whether he was really physically ill or had actually suffered a breakdown. Earl Wilson, privately tracking Walter's condition for the *Post*, learned from Walter's friend Irving Hoffman that Walter was in bed with a temperature of 104° and was believed to be suffering from a virus. But Paul Scheffels, Walter's radio producer, said the whole thing was a "scheme." "We had two doctors in the adjoining studio," Scheffels remembered. "They were doctors, but they were friends. He had them there to make the veracity of this stunt." By feigning illness and then making his dramatic declaration that he would be leaving the air, Walter hoped to rally listeners to his side and stampede them into demanding his return.

Whether Walter was physically ill, mentally ill or simply scheming for sympathy and support, the *Post* announced it would suspend its series during his convalescence. "We believe in the old journalistic principle," the *Post* editorialized, drawing an implicit distinction between itself and Walter, "that a newspaper should not argue with a man while he isn't in position to answer back." Columnist Joseph Alsop replaced him on the broadcast the first week and reported that Walter had a "virulent virus infection" but was "improving daily." June flew to Miami to be at Walter's bedside, and Elmer Bobst, the president of Warner-Hudnut, wrote Walter to express his sympathies. "I was somewhat fearful of your condition when I talked to you in early January," Bobst wrote, identifying another source of stress.

In my opinion in your case your mind has been troubled for quite a period of time. First of all, you have had to keep thinking of the course which radio is taking. You know that television has cut into radio. . . . You have had to wrestle with the question as to whether or not you should turn to television.

Secondly, you have looked with dread on the New York Post articles. . . . There naturally would be elements of fear coupled with elements of anger, both of which are far from conducive to equanimity.

Walter spent the next five weeks regaining his strength. He returned to the air on March 9, assuring listeners once again that his illness had not been an "ailment of the heart" and that he was feeling a lot better and "lots lazier from all that resting and rusting." *Variety* reported that he had "picked up at exactly the same clip as when last heard . . . with the sharpness and speed of his usual gatling-gun style." The next day the *Post* resumed its series.

Then, a few days before his March 16 broadcast, Walter suffered a relapse. Ernie Cuneo was in Newport, Rhode Island, cross-examining a witness in a libel suit when he got a call from Walter in the hospital saying that he couldn't go on the air Sunday. Cuneo insisted he go on; otherwise he would reveal his vulnerability to his critics. Cuneo would even write the entire broadcast; all Walter would have to do is read it. "I might not be able to finish," Walter worried. Cuneo said he would finish the broadcast for him. "Suppose the doctors won't let me out?" In that case, Cuneo said, he would carry Walter on his back.

Rushing back to the courtroom, Cuneo got an adjournment and then caught a special charter plane from Providence. At the airport he phoned June. She was absolutely determined that Walter not go on the air. "He's *got* to go on," Cuneo insisted. "Take my word for it, June, he's *got* to go on. . . . The battle lines must be held at all costs. They'll say he's quitting under fire and redouble their attack." But June still held firm, telling Cuneo that she had already spoken with Bobst and asked him to suspend Walter's contract. Cuneo said he left the phone booth numb. "I knew that for us it wasn't the Battle of the Bulge, it was a catastrophic Dunkirk. Had I carried him from the hospital and had he died at the microphone, considering what was coming, he would have been better off."

On March 16 announcer Richard Stark, explaining that Walter had fallen ill again, read Walter's script. "Mr. Winchell, against the advice of his doctors and the protest of Mrs. Winchell, prematurely returned to his work following a serious attack of virus infection," his office announced. "He will duly resume after consultation with his physicians." That same day the *Post* ran the last installment of its twenty-four-part series. "No matter how you view the Winchell story," Wechsler summarized, "there are inescapably tragic qualities in any summation of his life and works. At the end as at the beginning of this inquiry, the most striking fact about the man's story is his failure to derive ease and comfort from his extraordinary success. He is still fighting a thousand imagined demons. He still trumpets his petty triumphs. He is still battling and maneuvering for position. And now, just as it was when he began his uphill climb, each of his conquests is viewed with pain by most of his professional colleagues."

. . .

AND SO Winchell's life had become a parable, the lesson of which was: He who operates in the cutthroat world of celebrity where reputations are quickly made and just as quickly broken will have no peace. Already, during the week of his return, said the *Post*, rumors had been flying that Walter had been chastened. "He must still be sick," said one critic. "He was nice to me." "His friends felt he hadn't looked well the past few days," Earl Wilson observed the day after Walter's relapse, and the following day he reported that June had put herself in charge of his recuperation and had made her husband incommunicado to everyone. Now when Walter returned to the Stork, June accompanied him. "W.W. has been going to the movies lately with Mrs. W," another of Wilson's spies reported, "but 'getting home early: not later than one A.M.' "

In the meantime, Cuneo had been meeting with Kintner and Warner-Hudnut to resolve Walter's contract. On March 28 they arrived at an agreement that compelled Walter to return by April 20 and broadcast without his customary vacation or face termination at the sponsor's option. June wasn't pleased. Having finally reclaimed her husband, she wasn't about to surrender him again. Taking matters into her own hands, she phoned Bobst and told him that Walter was "quite ill" and couldn't fix a date for his return; his physician, she said, had recommended that Walter rest for at least four to six weeks and possibly until Labor Day. Cuneo reluctantly phoned Kintner on April 1 to tell him that their agreement was off. Walter had had a "very bad night from anxiety" and "is not sufficiently well enough to proceed with negotiations." He had been spending most of his time undergoing an extensive series of tests. The next day Kintner met with Bobst, who agreed to release Walter from his contract. "I suppose this is the wisest course of action," ABC News President Tom Velotta wrote Walter. "You don't have to return by any specified date and [you get] the elimination of pressure."

On April 7 Jack O'Brian reported in his column that Walter's immediate future didn't include radio but that Walter had denied rumors he was leaving radio for good. "He merely has given the virus six months to get out." As for the column, Walter's editor, Glenn Neville, said, "All we know is there's nothing organically wrong with him. He's fatigued and exhausted. We're just waiting for him to come back, although we've no idea when that will be." It turned out to be only a week later but with a reduced schedule of four columns a week, on Monday, Wednesday, Friday and Saturday.

He was back, but he was still beleaguered, and few defenders were willing to come to his aid. In the past most of his support had been political, not personal. But his old liberal friends were understandably wary of him now, and since most conservatives still didn't trust him either, he was left with the odd, forgiving right-winger who would welcome him to the cause. "I have disagreed with him many times on many things, particularly in years gone by," commentator Fulton Lewis, Jr., a fire-and-brimstone anti-Communist, said after Walter's January breakdown, "but he has my deepest sympathy on this occasion because actually his condition is the result of a war of nerves that has been waged against him by reds and their pinkish friends. . . . We're glad to have him with us."

Nor had Walter cultivated journalistic allies who might rally to him. He had long believed that journalistic feuds were healthy; he had thrived on them, writing once that a "punch on the jaw has saved many a journalistic head from being turned by its own importance." But in the process of socking, he had offended nearly everyone in the press from the right-wing Westbrook Pegler to the left-wing Drew Pearson. The falling-out with Pearson had come, first over clues to a radio quiz called "Stop the Music" (Walter complained that Pearson was stealing Walter's tips and broadcasting them earlier) and then, more seriously, over Senator McCarthy, whom Pearson reviled. As Winchell told it, McCarthy had attacked Pearson in a men's room, and Pearson asked Walter what he was going to do about it. "Not a thing," Walter answered, though he also said that Hearst would have killed any criticism of McCarthy anyway.

But Pearson, as James Forrestal had discovered, was no man to antagonize either. The night of the McCarthy brawl, he broadcast an item linking Walter to Frank Costello. "Drew immediately went on my Ingrate List," wrote Walter. Now Pearson began regularly sniping at Walter while Walter harassed ABC to force him to desist. Though Kintner promised that he wouldn't allow Pearson to insult Walter again, Pearson was not so easily dissuaded. He continued making references to Walter until ABC's Tom Velotta, confessing that Winchell had been "raising hell" with him and making his life "miserable," ordered Pearson to cut them. Under duress, Pearson did—he referred instead to a certain commentator to be heard "later this evening"—but he was now irrevocably lost to Walter.

In times past the Hearst press might have backed Walter, especially against a competitor like the *Post*, but the Hearst empire was itself besieged, slammed by Hearst's own extravagance and by the aftereffects of the Depression. With his company $125 million in debt, Hearst had requested permission from the Securities and Exchange Commission to float $35 million of debentures. The request was denied, forcing the company into trusteeship. Slowly the empire was dismantled: papers sold, employees fired, Hearst's famous art collection auctioned off. Hearst had even been forced to take a $1 million loan from Cissy Patterson. When the downsizing ended, shortly after the war, Hearst's holdings had shrunk by forty percent and the number of papers from twenty-nine to sixteen.

By the time William Randolph Hearst died on August 14, 1951, just two months before the Baker incident, he was already an anachronism. Hearst had been the "last of the dauntless pioneers, the last of the indomitable individualists," as his *Journal-American* eulogized him. He had bulled his way into journalism unfettered by tradition or taste just the way Walter had, and though they had many disagreements over the years, there was a kind of spiritual kinship between them, the kinship of two renegades who had managed to flout all the rules and still survive. Now that Hearst was gone, the "Hearstards" were in control, and they resented Walter as much as the *Post* did.

Finally, he got little support from his own crowd on Broadway, especially from the press agents. For them, as for the celebrities themselves, Winchell had long been both a source and a symbol of their subjugation. "If I didn't get over there [to his office], he'd call me and say, 'Where's your material?'" recalled press agent Leo Guild. "*Demanding* it." One time a press agent named Sid Garfield passed an item to Walter, from what he called an unimpeachable source, that Bette Davis had cancer. When Davis insisted that the report was false, one press agent cracked, "If Bette Davis doesn't have cancer, she better get it." "It's Winchell's world . . . and we're just living in it" was how another press agent described their situation.

Now, with the Baker affair and its aftermath, the agents had their revenge. Nearly all of them rejoiced at Walter's vulnerability; a few of them went further and surreptitiously funneled information to the *Post*. Even some of the stalwarts, like Milt Rubin, who had been one of Walter's cronies in the thirties, defected. "I began criticizing Winchell," Rubin later said, citing Walter's growing conservatism. "I could see he was turning into the negation of what he had stood for—or else [he was] showing his true colors." Certainly no one grieved.

Sooner or later he had fallings-out with even longtime friends like Curley Harris, either by doubting their sincerity or by making preemptive strikes before they could turn on him and hurt him. Klurfeld suspected there hadn't really been any friends to lose. "Not even Ernie was a real friend of Winchell's," said Klurfeld. "I mean, he worked for him. He received two thousand dollars a week when Winchell wanted to pay him. But every once in a while you used to see Ernie standing in front of the St. Moritz in the cold weather hoping he could see Walter because Walter refused to pay him for the last three weeks or something." In the end it was a transaction too.

That left the loyalists: Rose Bigman and Klurfeld. Rose had sacrificed virtually everything for Walter. Back in 1937, over the July Fourth break, she had married an attorney named John Fox. But Fox was a heavy drinker whose stupors spoiled Rose's evenings out, and these diversions were "the only thing that kept me calm working for Walter Winchell." Though Rose offered to quit her job to save her marriage, even she realized it was too late. After ten years of marriage she went to Reno for a divorce. Walter sent her a telegram, joking that she should bring a nightgown and meet him in Las Vegas but adding in commiseration that if there were anything she needed, all she had to do was ask. Rose now was totally his.

At the same time another presumed loyalist was lost. While Walter was recuperating, ABC, without consulting him, had fired Paul Scheffels, his producer and Miami Beach companion, in what it called an economy move. Walter had clearly thought of him as part of his support system. Down in Miami he had once even asked Scheffels to quit ABC and come work for him. What Walter couldn't have known in making his offer was how much resentment Scheffels harbored toward him for having been made a lackey all those years. When Scheffels missed a broadcast because one of his sons had fallen seriously ill, the "old man wasn't decent enough to say, 'Do you need anything?' or 'Good luck' or 'I'm rooting for you.'" When Scheffels left ABC, Walter said nothing either. "He really cared about nobody," Scheffels said. Later, in a retroactive act of revenge, Scheffels melted down a Christmas gift Walter had once given him: a silver cigarette case inscribed, "To Paul, From his assistant Walter Winchell."

As he circled the wagons around himself and his staff, Walter did find one compatriot who was willing to take his side and fight his battle. He had first met Jack O'Brian in 1939, when O'Brian was a reporter for the *World-Telegram* covering a bomb scare at the RCA Building. O'Brian was talking to a police captain when Walter bounced up, identified himself— "Captain, I'm Winchell of the *Mirror*"—and asked what was happening. O'Brian requested that Walter let him finish since he was writing on deadline for the front page. Walter stepped aside. When O'Brian returned from phoning in the story and apologized, Walter invited him to the Stork for a drink. "And that started the friendship," said O'Brian.

O'Brian was a short, pugnacious, ruddy-faced young man who had grown up in the Irish ghetto of Buffalo, New York, with a widowed mother and a large family to feed. He had made his way from the Buffalo docks to a local Catholic newspaper to the Buffalo *Times* and then to the *World-Telegram* for two years before returning to his hometown. In October 1943 he landed again in New York, this time with the Associated

Press. He had been back only a few days when he ran into Ed Weiner, who was then Walter's nightly companion and who remembered O'Brian fondly from the young reporter's first tour. Shortly after their chance meeting Weiner called and invited O'Brian to see Walter. It was a stifling day. "I remember we drove around Central Park to get cool," said O'Brian. "And from that time we got very close." "The secret of my relationship with Walter at the beginning," O'Brian said, reciting Walter's own basis for friendship, "is that I didn't want anything from him. Nothing."

O'Brian was Walter's kind of guy, different from the usual raft of celebrities and hangers-on. "Jack was feisty and bright and full of vim and vigor and often stayed up at night with Walter," recalled another of their frequent cohorts, disc jockey Art Ford. With his working-class roots, his toughness, his self-possession, his seeming honesty, O'Brian may have even reminded Walter of himself as a young man, the way Curley Harris had. He was one of the very few who could tell Walter when he was being a windy bore. He would raise a finger, and Walter would stop, never with anger.

Sharing Walter's lack of political sophistication, O'Brian also shared his politics. He was a remorseless anti-Communist and Red-baiter who happily barreled his way into the postwar debate the way Walter had. More, he had the same instinct for the jugular Walter had. He was a gut fighter, a good man to have in the trenches with you. He didn't care one whit for the sophisticates or the intellectuals or the liberals; he cursed them all. And when he signed on with the *Journal-American* in 1949 as its television columnist, he got something else Walter would need: another public pillar of support.

O'Brian "injected himself into Walter's life," Ford remembered. "He wanted to be Walter Winchell, but since he couldn't be, he wanted to be close to Winchell." And he was. O'Brian was now a frequent tablemate of Walter's at the Stork, and almost every morning at three-thirty, after O'Brian had delivered his column, he and Walter drove down to Ratner's, a dairy restaurant on the Lower East Side, or over to Lindy's. "We never went to bed," O'Brian said.

But if O'Brian was Walter's new protector, snarling at his enemies, his role also convinced fence-sitters that Walter was beyond redemption and drove away what few remaining liberal supporters he might have had. O'Brian was voluble, egocentric and spiteful, but he had none of Walter's charm to leaven these qualities. Many of Walter's old liberal friends detested him, seeing in him the worst excesses of both Hearst and McCarthy and believing he appealed to the worst in Winchell as well. A "very vitriolic and hateful kind of person," said *Variety*'s Nat Kahn of

O'Brian. Klurfeld called O'Brian "the least-liked person I've ever come across." Rose hated him too. Walter heard all the grumbling and ignored it. He signed a photograph to O'Brian and his wife, Yvonne: "Who gave me their hands when others gave me the foot."

THE ONE person who might have launched a successful counteroffensive for Winchell was not there. At the time of the Baker incident Irving Hoffman had been occupied on a round-the-world tour of U.S. military bases for the ostensible purpose of determining what forms of entertainment the servicemen most enjoyed, though anyone who knew Hoffman understood this was just another opportunity for him to enjoy the good life, which always seemed his primary objective.

To the uninitiated, Hoffman hardly seemed a great Rabelaisian figure. He was tall, broad-shouldered and professorially handsome with thick, woolly hair, but he was also disheveled, his hat tilted carelessly back on his head, his tie loose, his face ever in need of a shave, his long, expensive camel hair coat dragging along the ground. (One night Lucius Beebe watched Hoffman dig caviar out of its pockets.) In his back pocket he carried bedroom slippers, which he donned when his feet hurt, and once, as Dorothy Kilgallen put it, he set "a record for informality in a swank café" when he padded into the Stork in the slippers.

On Broadway his nearsightedness was as notorious as his dress. Earl Wilson recalled Hoffman's digging at his dinner plate with his fork, complaining that the peas kept sliding off. "Peas!" replied another diner. "That's the picture design on the plate." Ernie Lehman, who was then working for Hoffman, recalled the two of them sitting in a restaurant waiting for Hoffman's date to arrive. When she walked in, Lehman alerted Hoffman, who, watching her approach, whispered to Lehman, "Is she good-looking?"

Hoffman was a character of mythic proportions, but he was no fool. Born in 1909 to a Bronx high school teacher, he was a prodigy in art and left school at fourteen to sketch participants at the Democratic National Convention for the New York *World*. Attractive and witty, he became both the lover and the protégé of singer Helen Morgan. Meanwhile, he began contributing items to Winchell. By the time he was twenty-two, he had taken over the "Beau Broadway" column in the *Morning Telegraph* and was hosting his own radio interview program, "Tales of Hoffman."

With the sudden surge of public relations in the early thirties, Hoffman decided to open his own press agency and rapidly won himself a sterling reputation as "the best of them all," in the words of one colleague. Hoffman was different from the ordinary press agents foraging for clients and living in terror. No one had better contacts in the press or outside it. He didn't have to solicit clients, they came to him, and he had some of the biggest accounts, including many of the motion-picture studios, which he serviced not only through Winchell's column but by writing a column of his own for the Hollywood *Reporter.* He was never servile. When film producer David Selznick once complained about an item Hoffman had planted, Hoffman fired back that he didn't tell Selznick how to make movies and Selznick shouldn't tell him how to do publicity. Then Hoffman fired him—fired the client.

Whatever tension there was, Hoffman farmed out to his employees— usually four or five harried young press agents, "looking through news- paper clippings to see if they can steal anything from someone else and rewrite it," as one of them put it, and talking on the phones to get news they could then pass on as items. His office, at 247 Park Avenue, was a beehive of activity, but the chaos spilled over wherever Hoffman was—in a restaurant he would immediately spread his papers over the table—and then into his apartment, which was over what had been LaHiff's Tavern in the same building where Walter had once lived. This became one of Broadway's most popular gathering places, a Damon Runyon story come to life.

His sybaritic relationships with an endless stream of women were like his relationship to life generally. "Hoffman I thought was disappointed with life," observed David Brown, challenging the image of him as a happy hedonist. "He had no real relationships. And to that extent I think he empathized with Walter Winchell, who, so far as I know, hid his re- lationships if he had any." In effect, the biggest of the press agents and the biggest of the columnists were partners in cynicism and disenchant- ment. They both understood the system; they both appreciated how silly and fickle it was.

Yet they served it and had no life outside it. Hoffman used Winchell's column to promote his clients, more often than not writing Walter's plugs for movies. He was the most direct link from Hollywood or Broad- way to Winchell, the way Cuneo was the most direct link from Washing- ton. And Walter never begrudged Hoffman his access. He respected him; Gertrude Bayne, Hoffman's more or less steady companion, thought, not without reason, that Hoffman was the only person Walter really re- spected, excepting June. Jack O'Brian might raise his finger during an old story of Walter's, but Walter allowed Hoffman to upbraid him, to tell Walter that he was tired of hearing that same tale again and again. "Irving was the only one I ever heard who used to tell Winchell, 'You're full of shit,'" recalled Klurfeld. He was also the only man who had Wal- ter's permission to look at the holy writ of "The Column" before it went to press.

Walter had long relied on Hoffman for guidance. Now in the wake of the Baker incident and the *Post* series, he needed Hoffman more than ever before to conduct a campaign in his behalf. Hoffman did fire back in his Hollywood *Reporter* column. "[T]o their way of thinking, they could genuinely regard him as a villain who must be struck down," he wrote of the *Post* attacks. "They formed the opinion, I am quite certain, that he had definitely dropped the F.D.R. shield of liberalism, and was flying only the banner of MacArthur, McCarthy and Billingsley." In the meantime, he wrote Hoover warning him that the Los Angeles *Mirror* was going to be running the series which "does not give a true picture."

But Hoffman's counterattack was feeble and futile, only demonstrating his and Walter's impotence once the system had turned Winchell's own tactics against him. In truth, Hoffman hadn't the stamina to fight either, at least not this kind of bloody battle. He was becoming distracted and exhausted. Broadway, as the Baker incident inadvertently showed, was no longer as much fun as it had once been; it was no longer an oasis unaffected by the world outside. By June 1952 Hoffman had decided to quit his agency and his column, announcing he wouldn't return until it was once again a "joy and not a job." Henceforth, he said, he would roam the world as a kind of "gypsy flack." And with Hoffman's departure Walter's last hope had deserted him.

III

All that summer Winchell held his fire. Even Wechsler was surprised at Walter's "almost unprecedented restraint," thinking that perhaps he had been persuaded "that a campaign of retribution could only serve to call attention to the series in many places where the Post did not circulate." But Walter's depression had not dissipated over the summer, and neither had his anger. He seethed. Klurfeld had the "disconcerting sense of something ticking, something that might detonate at any time." The self-deprecating glee in Walter's temper was gone. There was no tweaking now. No fun. "He was like a cornered rat," observed Al Rylander, a publicist for NBC.

All that summer he was possessed by the idea of revenge. All that summer, despite rumors that he had softened and retreated, he kept stoking his anger, fortifying himself for the opportune moment to go back on the offensive and destroy his enemies as he felt they had tried to destroy him. The moment seemed to arrive that August. Wechsler had been preparing a new series on the writers Lee Mortimer and Jack Lait, best known for their *Confidential* books purporting to expose the seamy underside of major American cities. (Lait also happened to be one of Walter's editors at the *Mirror*.) The subjects had gotten wind of the project and had filed a preemptive libel action, accusing the *Post* of wanting to savage them because they were anti-Communists. At a pretrial hearing on August 6 Wechsler testified that he had once been a member of the Young Communist League but had resigned fifteen years earlier.

Acting as if Wechsler's "confession" explained why the *Post* had attacked him, Walter now finally took the offensive, and he used the weapon that was proving so effective in these days of suspicion and recrimination. "Jake Wechsler (the editor of the N.Y. Post) for 3 years was a leader of the Young Communist League here (1934–37)," Walter opened his column on September 8 with a stunning tinge of anti-Semitism in calling Wechsler "Jake." "Time magazine brushed that off by calling him a college radical—and didn't mention that Red group's name . . . But several comrades (who were also 'too young to be communist party members' at the time) grew up to be some of the U.S. Communist leaders, all convicted of Conspiracy to Overthrow the U.S. Gov't by Force and Violence." According to Walter, three of those convicted had sat on the YCL's National Executive Board when Wechsler was a member. "When this 'Ivan' ran his articles 'exposing' me—he prefaced: 'When a man has such a wide audience as Winchell, we believe the people should know his background' . . . Well, Kind Hearts & Gentle People, there's his."

Two days later he was back pressing his case, reporting: "*The New York Post series* attacking Walter Winchell (earlier this year) was in deadly parallel with the warnings in J. Spolansky's book, 'The Communist Trail in America,' " and telling how Wechsler had recently ducked a delegation of war veterans who wanted to ask him about his past political affiliations. Two days later he ran another item: "Bigtown Sideshow: J. Wechsler (the editor of the N.Y. Poo) who is now ducking the dead cats (You Like???), keeps whining that he's a 'former Commy.' " And two days after that he praised the "N.Y. Compost" for running what he called its first "anti-Red editorial." "Prob'ly after reading WW's barrage the night before." The next day, in light of the fact that "there is nothing in his history (that I could excavate) to show that he ever tried to help the U.S. unmask his Comrades in that ratty group," he questioned Wechsler's avowal that the editor had quit the Communists, and he promised to continue his sallies until Wechsler helped the government trap his "former" allies.

Once he began publishing the Winchell series, Wechsler had assumed that his early dabbling with the far left would provide fodder for Winchell's counterattack. He had even told a congressional committee that Walter had "his leg-men trying to dig into my past about when I was a kid with that League," to which Walter riposted, "He means Winchell forced its publication." But if Wechsler had expected the Red-baiting to flow from Walter, he later admitted that he had "underestimated the man's capacity for invention. Our series had recognized his modest talent in that sphere; in his counterattack on the *Post*, he surpassed himself."

Just as he had when he lit out against Whittaker Chambers in 1948, in every column he brought new charges of perfidy, new hints of unrepentance, new descriptions of disaster, and not just against Wechsler but against everyone associated with the *Post*, which was variously called the "Poo," the "Compost," the "Postinko" and the "Postitute." On September 22 he reported that Dolly Schiff was "on the verge" of a breakdown. "The battle (she has confided) 'is wrecking my health' . . . The disclosures here (of the great number of 'former Communists' directing her former newspaper) are said to have hit her ad dept's pocket hard. . . ." The next week he devoted three more full columns to attacks on Wechsler, headed "Memos to the FBI," but on October 6 he steered the attack to a list of the *Post*'s so-called "Presstitutes," including Arthur Schlesinger, Jr., drama critic Richard Watts and columnists Max Lerner and Murray Kempton. ("He hardly has enough pink in his background to qualify as a N.Y. Post Punc," Walter wrote in partial absolution of Kempton.)

"I have no illusions about why I have finally made the honor roll of his targets," Max Lerner answered in his own column on October 15. "It is not because of anything I have written or said about him, which has been almost nil. My inexpungeable crime—which is also the crime of such other targets of his as Arthur Schlesinger Jr., Frank Kingdon, and Murray Kempton—is that I write for the New York Post and that I take pride in counting its editor, James Wechsler, my friend." But Lerner insisted he was not trying to mount a defense for himself against what were, in any event, nonexistent charges. "What interests me most is the tragic deterioration story of what might have been a useful and honorable career in journalism. . . ."

Walter dismissed all this criticism, even from Forster and Klurfeld, who advised him to lay down his arms. Walter couldn't. "They tried to kill me!" he yelled in justification. "Kill me!" He was on a mission now, seemingly political but in reality deeply personal. He was collecting reams of material, his sources ranging from the FBI to disaffected *Post* employees to staff members of the House Un-American Activities Committee who were slipping him reports from executive sessions. One correspondent had even collected material proving that Jacob Schiff, Dorothy's grandfather, had helped finance the Russian Revolution. All this material Walter then fed to Klurfeld, who wrote the actual broadsides. "I figured we'd do one, two or three," he recalled. "We did thirty."

Nearly forty years later, reflecting on the scurrilous attacks he wrote, Klurfeld groped for some explanation for his having consented to do them. "I had no qualms about doing it because in the first place, it was a job," he would say. "In the second place, they [the *Post*] embarrassed me. I was furious at what they did to me: I mean, coming in front of my house when I was taking my son to school and jumping out of the car and taking my picture and following me to school." The *Post* had also harassed his parents. "This old Jewish couple was terrified. They couldn't sleep." But Klurfeld also admitted, "I didn't believe in doing what he [Walter] wanted to do to the Post. I thought it was wrong. I bet if you showed it to me now I'd feel bad about some of the stuff I wrote." Finally he said he did them because he felt sorry for Walter Winchell.

Winchell's own self-pity had vanished with his offensive. Though the syndicate was displeased by the endless attacks on Wechsler, which meant next to nothing to anyone outside New York, Walter was immovable on the subject. (He even offered to write different columns for out of town.) He quoted a Hollywood column that the "WW—NY Post feud is too boring." Walter answered, "Mebbe to you, son, I'm having scads of last laffs." When Gal Friday registered still another complaint about how much "time and space [he] wasted on small-fry," Walter cracked: "A Head for an Eye!"

Now that Walter had loosed his anger, there was also Barry Gray to deal with. In August, even before he began blistering Wechsler, Walter had begun a vendetta against Chandler's Restaurant, where Gray broadcast, citing it for price gouging and overcharging. "One of the bosses is no stranger to authorities," he wrote, accusing the unnamed man of having been investigated for harboring fugitives and of having been caught in "tax trickery." Chandler's owners, Harry and Louis Rubin, promptly sued Walter for a million dollars.

Meanwhile, Jack O'Brian and another *Journal-American* columnist named Frank Conniff began working over Gray himself. O'Brian called him a "fishface" and accused of him everything "from welshing on his debts to collecting graft to finance a trip to Europe." "Mr. Winchell did little to defend himself while one ancient enemy after another was resurrected by Mr. Gray to pour venom on his record," Conniff wrote in his attack. But now the reckoning was near, Conniff warned. "We say to these press agents and producers and personalities who give their support to Mr. Gray: That's just dandy. But surely don't be surprised if we here at the Journal-American invite you to keep getting your plugs from him and not to expect very much from us."

Walter renewed his attacks against Gray on September 10, two days after Walter launched his campaign against Wechsler. "Bernard Yaroslaw, known as B.G., the disc jockey, has been a noisy ally of the 'ex-Commy' editor and that newspaper," he closed the column. And then, referring to a physical assault on Gray by unknown assailants outside a Longchamps restaurant in midtown Manhattan just a few days before, Walter scolded the police for providing him an escort. "[I]f the Commissioner doesn't put an end to this waste of the police at once, we will not tell him or any cop the names of the two Girls who beat him up."

Gray was now "Borey Yellow" or "Borey Lavender" or "Borey Pink," an allusion to Walter's sudden, improbable discovery that Gray, like Wechsler, *might* have once been a member of the Young Communist League and *might* have contributed articles to the *Daily Worker.* (When William Randolph Hearst, Jr., and Hearst lawyer Charles McCabe told Walter that "Borey Yellow" sounded anti-Semitic, Walter entreated them, "This is a name that will stick with him forever so please don't order it killed from the column the next time I use it.") Even friends of Walter thought his feud with Gray was overkill. One called it "one of the most ridiculous and distasteful things ever" and, defending Gray for having merely presented Baker's side of the story and not necessarily having endorsed it, chided Walter to stop his foolishness.

Art Ford, a friend of both Gray's and Winchell's, remembered driving with Walter at the time and advising him to desist. "It's not a battle that does anything for you," Ford said timorously. "He hasn't got a network behind him. He hasn't got a paper behind him. It's like kicking a kid. . . . Even if you're right, you're too big for it." Walter replied evenly: "Arthur, my wife was listening to the Barry Gray Show when Sullivan was on that night. And she got very sick listening to what Sullivan was doing to me. I will never forgive him for it."

Early one October morning Walter, O'Brian and O'Brian's wife were cruising for police calls on 55th Street when they spotted Gray's sidekick Peppy Weiner stepping out of a car parked in front of them. As Walter honked, they recognized Gray leaning against the side. "I'm going to get this sonofabitch," O'Brian announced, but he had only gotten three-quarters of the way out, yelling taunts at Gray, before his wife grabbed his coat and prevented him from going any further. Gray, now realizing he was in peril, jumped back into his car and sped off at what Walter later called "supersonic speed." Walter and O'Brian gave chase. "We chased him in and out of the el like the old movies," O'Brian recalled, but lost him. Then, doubling back to Peppy Weiner's apartment, they caught sight of Gray again. Again he fled. "Our last sight of him was symbolic," Walter wrote in the column the next day. "As he turned tail, he was recklessly passing red light after red light . . ."

. . .

THERE WERE so many feuds, so many scores to settle. And now to the list was added Walter's onetime protégé Leonard Lyons. "You're going to have two enemies, and I can predict them," Paul Scheffels had once told Walter. "They'll be Sherman Billingsley and Leonard Lyons." Walter brushed it off, but time proved Scheffels correct. Years later Lyons wrote that he had had two scrapes with Walter: one when he said Walter blacklisted him from being a summer replacement on ABC and another when Walter accused President Truman of "stew stuff" after the President had written an irate letter to a music critic who had criticized a performance of his daughter, Margaret. According to Lyons, Winchell called him, demanding to know why he dared interfere. And Lyons replied that in challenging the President's sobriety during the Korean War, Walter was himself interfering—"with the welfare of my children, and his own children and everybody's children."

But Lyons was being disingenuous in tracing their feud to these two episodes. In truth their feud had been simmering for years, as much the product of contrasting temperaments as behavior. Lyons was a celebrity hound. "Leonard believed in America, which meant personal success," Seymour Krim observed. "Success was embodied by the famous and talented golden boys and girls free of the scars of immigrant fear. . . . And Leonard pursued them all his life with a passion that could only have come from early pain." Walter's relationship to the elites had been attuned to the thirties, to the sense of envy, anger and revenge that ordinary Americans felt and that he exploited in the column. Lyons was better attuned to postwar America, where celebrity was an aspiration. ("Very simple transaction," *The New Yorker* once said. "Lyons took the eminent down a peg and they took him up one.") Critic John Leonard, then growing up on the West Coast and thinking of New York as some exotic region, thought of Lyons as "our Edward R. Murrow," sending back reports from the celebrity front. "Someday, if we were lucky and good, we might grow up and get our name mentioned in his column, along with Orson Welles and Lillian Hellman." As Krim put it, "He swelled our sensitivity-to-status like a balloon and put the anxiety of being overlooked into our miserable hearts without meaning to, just by following his own fierce needs."

It was those needs that sent Lyons, with what *Time* called his "sparrow eyes and landmark beak," scurrying nervously from table to table—he and Walter were the only columnists without a legman—to collect his anecdotes. Because he invariably said kind things about his subjects—"If you can't say something nice about someone," he told Krim, "don't say anything at all"—most of them welcomed him as *nice* Lenny Lyons, though there were a few who resented his intrusions, resented the presumptuousness of his feeling that he could sit anywhere with anyone without waiting for an invitation, and "21" eventually barred him for his overzealous table-hopping.

Lyons was, a friend said, "the biggest name-dropper this side of the telephone directory." That and the sycophancy, the oscillation between familiarity and obsequiousness, disturbed Walter. Walter "didn't like Lyons's style," said *Post* photographer Art Pomerantz, who sometimes joined Winchell on his police calls. "Lyons was a user." Pomerantz recalled one occasion when he happened to be with Dorothy Schiff's daughter and Lyons treated him "like I was his best friend." Other times Lyons wouldn't acknowledge him. "It was very creepy." Jack O'Brian also observed that Lyons "could high-hat you, if you lost your celebrity."

Above all, it galled Walter that Lyons, the table-hopper and name-dropper, was now considered the liberal and Walter the political Neanderthal, though in the political context of 1951, it wasn't an unfair characterization. While Walter was calling for preparations for World War III, Lyons was risking imprisonment for refusing to reveal his sources for items on the Rosenbergs, the couple convicted of passing atomic secrets to the Soviets. Moreover, Lyons was Truman's boy, the way Walter had been FDR's.

When the tensions finally erupted, however, it wasn't politics that provided the occasion. It was cancer. Lyons was an original member of the Runyon Fund board; he had been put there by Walter. But within a few years he was griping about Walter's autocratic governance of the fund and claiming that Winchell's vaunted assertion that each penny went directly to research was questionable since Walter had allocated money to the Sloan-Kettering Cancer Research Hospital without any provision that the funds be restricted that way. In June 1951 Lyons wrote the fund's president, sportswriter Dan Parker, with a new list of grievances: "recent allocations of Runyon Fund monies without the board passing on them, appointments to the Runyon Fund committee having been made which I learned about only through radio, newspaper and television announcements, special Runyon Awards in journalism, literature, art, music and drama without any consultation, someone being designated administrator of the Runyon Fund without any consultation with me as a member of the Board." He closed, "It is important to bear in mind the fact that a corporation is not an individual and may not be used as a cloak for a one-man operation."

Though Lyons was certainly being difficult, he had a point. Walter seemed to run the fund out of his pockets. Morris Ernst, the fund's attorney, wrote Walter's designated administrator, John Teeter, that the fund's legal affairs were in "deplorable shape." He repeated Lyons's charges that the fund had been run "as a one-man corporation" and "that the affairs of the corporation would never stand up under outside scrutiny." Ernst also urged Lyons and Walter to reach some kind of accommodation, "or there will be trouble that could not be covered up—particularly the irregularity of the membership of Mr. Parker and Mr. Lindy," who seldom attended meetings and who gave their proxies to Walter.

The showdown came at the board meeting on September 6, 1951. Ernie Cuneo, acting as Walter's representative, took the floor. Cuneo put it bluntly. There was clearly a disagreement over how the fund should be run. It would be in the best interests of the fund if either Lyons or Winchell were to resign. If Lyons didn't do so, Walter would. Lyons protested that "such differences could be submerged in the best interests of the corporation," but Walter was staging a coup, and he wasn't about to reconcile. In any case he held enough votes to force Lyons off the board. Reluctantly Lyons submitted his resignation. Leo Linderman was voted the new vice-president, and on October 17, the day after the Baker incident, Sherman Billingsley was asked to fill Lyons's slot on the board. At that same meeting, the takeover was completed when Marlene Dietrich, Joe DiMaggio, Milton Berle and Sugar Ray Robinson were added to the board with their proxies to be held by Walter.

One more ingrate gone, one more false friend showing his true colors. Lyons saw it as one more victory for Winchell's megalomania, and he even briefly tried to withdraw his resignation by claiming that he had never voted to approve the minutes of the September 6 meeting, nor had he signed a waiver of notice, imperative since Walter had neglected to notify him about the meeting as required; therefore, Lyons argued, the actions taken at the meeting were not valid.

By the time of this new squabble the *Post* had launched its series, and Walter had even more cause to feed his enmity, but Lyons, for all his animosity toward Walter, refused to cooperate with his own paper's smear campaign. "He was my friend. I still regard him as my friend," he told *Post* managing editor Paul Sann, "and I will not say anything bad about him. He helped me when I needed it." Walter couldn't believe that Lyons would hold his fire. "Lyons helped the *Post* people trying to destroy me," he insisted when Klurfeld discouraged him from running an attack on Lyons. The two now would not sit in the same room. If Lyons saw Winchell, he would turn and leave, and Billingsley began treating him so shabbily that Lyons stopped going to the Stork altogether.

But for all the backbiting and uneasiness, the feud remained a private matter, restricted to friends of the combatants, until Walter's counteroffensive against the *Post* that fall. Then, oddly enough, the one who made it public was Lyons. He had taken Walter to task for having allegedly disclaimed a responsibility to vote, remarking, "The only adult Americans who never vote are felons, illiterates or those deficient in their concept of the basic responsibilities of American citizenship." Walter had pointedly left Lyons out of his blunderbuss attacks against the *Post*, but he couldn't let an insult like this pass. "Now hold onto your chair," Gal Friday wrote. "Lenny Plotz had such an obvious bit of bunk about you in The Liar's Den that his editor couldn't stomach it—and threw it out of the paper. Hooray for Wechsler, the 'former Commy.' My favorite venomy." By Walter's standards, it was a minor retort for what was relatively minor prey in a fierce hunting season that was about to get even fiercer.

IV

"One of the small but vexing questions confronting anyone in this area with a television set is: 'Why is Ed Sullivan on it every Sunday night?' " asked New York *Herald Tribune* critic John Crosby in 1948 shortly after Sullivan had debuted a variety show called "Toast of the Town." Improbable as it may have seemed, the fact was that Sullivan, who had hosted the *Daily News'* annual Harvest Moon music festivals and had MC'd vaudeville shows in the thirties the way Walter had, was now a television fixture, and his television popularity undoubtedly was one of the major factors that had emboldened him to take on Walter.

TV OR NOT TV? Earl Wilson had wired Walter back in 1949. Ever since, that had indeed been the question for Winchell. Despite enormous pressure from both the ABC network and his sponsors, Walter had managed to resist, but by 1952 the handwriting was on the wall. A Nielsen survey early that year found that ratings for top radio programs had fallen by nearly one million homes over the preceding twelve months. The worse news for Walter was that after registering as the fourth highest rated radio program in 1950, he had fallen out of the top ten during 1951.

That August he signed with the Gruen Watch Company for a radio program at 9:00 P.M. Sundays over the ABC network with its 343 stations and also for a separate television broadcast, scheduled for 6:45 P.M. on Sundays over an ABC hookup that numbered twenty-three stations at the time of the announcement and nearly thirty by the time he hit the air. Significantly, for the first time in Walter's career, his salary was not reported. Also significantly, as it turned out, the contract stipulated that ABC would "use its best efforts to furnish and keep in effect at all times during the entire term thereof " a million-dollar liability insurance policy. Though not a simulcast, the television format was to be identical to that of the radio broadcast. "We bought a photographed version of your radio program," Ben Katz, the Gruen president, stated.

On October 5, 1952, in the midst of his crusade against Wechsler and the *Post*, Walter made his long-awaited, much-resisted television debut. The set was decorated like a cross between the city room of a busy newspaper and a classroom. File cabinets to his right were open, and papers spilled out. Behind him sat a bank of telephones, and behind those, covering the wall, was a stark map of the United States bordered by clocks giving the time in Tokyo, Rome, Honolulu, London and Paris. Directly to his left was a typewriter. His desk was strewn with papers, empty cups and an ashtray. Walter himself was the finishing touch. He wore his gray fedora with a black hatband. His shirt was open at the collar, and his sleeves were rolled up. His tie was loose. His hands held a pair of plastic reading glasses. The effect was that of a working reporter caught in the middle of his labors: Winchell in *The Front Page*.

But did the picture betray the image? Walter approached the broadcast with grave trepidation. Two months later he confessed to Bette Davis, then appearing on Broadway, that after all his years before a microphone he still suffered from stage fright. "I have it every Sunday night (even before television) when I hear the man say: 'And now Walter Winchell.' The breath leaves the body as it used to when I was a hoofer—my last thought every time I go on is My God, where are the fluffs[?]" June, who was ill again with heart trouble at the time of the broadcast and hospitalized under an oxygen tent, was also "breathless with excitement," according to Walter.

On the basis of the first verdicts, Walter's long agony had been unwarranted. Kintner, who was in California, wired Walter: TELEVISION BROADCAST ON COAST WAS TERRIFIC[.] CONGRATULATIONS. Critics seemed to agree. "The entry of the columnist into the video medium . . . promised a performance unlike anything else on the screen," wrote Jack Gould of *The New York Times*. "[T]he promise was fulfilled. On the screen Mr. Winchell is the Hollywood image of the Fourth Estate brought to life. . . .

"Watching Mr. Winchell's emotional intensity, with the muscles of his jaw flexing in rhythm with the torrent of his words, does have a drawback: the scene is so visually absorbing that it is difficult to concentrate on what he is saying." Gould concluded, "Those who were enamored of his radio broadcasts will find him even more fascinating than ever in TV; those who were not so enamored, more disturbing." *Variety* agreed. "The same Winchellian manner which has distinguished him from the orthodox newscasts is accented on his TV debut," it reported, noting that his necktie became increasingly askew as the broadcast proceeded.

But the anticipation over Winchell's television debut may have obscured some deeper truths about his relationship to the medium. In Marshall McLuhan's terms, Ed Sullivan was a cool figure, almost bloodless; his style suited television, which, in the postwar period, allayed anxiety by creating a sense of visual community. Walter was hot. Bouncing in his seat and barking his items in his breakneck staccato, he was almost too much for television, too vivid and intimidating a presence to fit easily in one's living room, especially now that the old charm had curdled into rage. He belonged to radio. He belonged to the era of sound. More, there was something visually disconcerting about Walter. After his telecast the Hollywood *Reporter* described him as looking "oddly like a cross between Harry Truman and Jimmy Durante." He was no longer young and sleek, and his energy seemed incongruous, even misplaced, in a man his age. Years later Walt, Jr., told his wife that he had advised his father not to do television. "I knew that would be his downfall," she quoted him as saying. "The moment they saw this little man on television they would lose all respect for him. And they did."

THE BEGINNING of the telecast coincided with the 1952 presidential campaign, and Walter was in the thick of it. With Truman deciding not to stand for reelection, the Democrats nominated Illinois's intelligent and articulate governor Adlai Stevenson. Remarkably Walter still regarded himself as a liberal Democrat, and when the *Post* lumped him with "Eisenhower . . . and other Republicans," Walter bristled. "Don't call this FDR Rooter a Republican you dirty 'former Communist!' " Stevenson, however, was tarnished in Winchell's eyes. Wechsler and the *Post* were among the Democratic nominee's most vocal supporters, and Wechsler was not only campaigning vigorously for Stevenson, but contributing to his speeches.

Tarnished, perhaps, but not anathema. Walter was relatively easy on Stevenson, even after the Republicans had nominated Eisenhower. He reserved his fire instead for the outgoing President, Harry Truman, who, he believed, had betrayed FDR and subjected Walter himself to humiliation. Somehow Walter had come into possession of sworn affidavits asserting that Truman had once been a member of the Ku Klux Klan back in Missouri. This was an old rumor, first raised by the Hearst press, and Truman angrily denied it, but Walter was undeterred, quite possibly seizing this as apt revenge for the charges of racism against himself in the wake of the Baker incident. Politically, in what was still thought to be a close campaign, the charge could have had a potentially devastating effect on the Democratic core constituencies of Catholics, blacks and Jews. "Ninety percent of the time Winchell and I agreed on political matters,"

Klurfeld said. "But there were times I disagreed with him. Some things I would not do. . . . He wanted me to write a couple of columns attacking Truman, mentioning that Truman was a member of the Ku Klux Klan, and I refused. I said get someone else to write that."

Walter wrote it himself. He broke the story on his October 12 broadcast and telecast and repeated it without elaboration on October 19. The following week he said, "Mr. and Mrs. United States—Last Sunday night I reported the President was once a member of the Ku Klux Klan. That was my answer to the ridiculous comment, later withdrawn, that General Eisenhower had stooped to Nazi tactics. And that the General's guilty of racial prejudice." Drew Pearson, claiming that he had more spies in the Klan than Winchell, had rebutted the charge against Truman, but Walter then dramatically produced his affidavits, one from the Grand Cyclops of the Klan, averring that Truman had attended a Klan meeting in Crandall's Pasture outside Independence, Missouri. (Truman justly insisted these were false.) In his column the next day, Walter wrote: "A series of incredible accidents (plus an historical tragedy) elevated Harry Truman to the Presidency [. . .] As the record certifies—Truman frequently disgraced the dignity of his High Office and his Administration was rotten with corruption [. . .] The infamous sheet [of the KKK] is the moral equivalent of a grafter's mink coat."

But Walter was not about to whitewash the Republican ticket. The Republican vice-presidential nominee, California Senator Richard Nixon, had been accused of having his wealthy supporters contribute to a private slush fund and was now the object of a great debate over whether he should be dumped from the ticket. Walter didn't waffle. "Senator Nixon should get off the ticket," he wrote. "The nation, which completely trusts the heart of the General, shudders to think that ONLY that heartbeat may separate Nixon from the Presidency . . . Nixon's explanation may or may not be sufficient for a U.S. Senator. It certainly is not enough for a possible future President of the United States."

Nixon, of course, stayed, and two days before the election Walter declared his support for Eisenhower. "I have little faith in the brains of any party," he wrote. "But I do have faith in the heart of a man. The General's oath as a soldier was good enough to take us to victory over Hitler. And I regard that as evidence that his oath (as Commander-in-Chief) will be just as effective against Stalin."

This made it difficult for his Democratic friends to accept Walter's professions of Democratic faith, though Walter's own defense was that he wasn't partisan; he was for Eisenhower. (Ernie Cuneo, still a partisan Democrat and a liberal, traveled on Stevenson's campaign train during the last swing, but the campaign kept him at a distance, fearing he might feed pro-Eisenhower material to Winchell.) In Walter's peculiar view, Eisenhower's triumph was not only a repudiation of Truman but a vindication of the New Deal. When the general's supporters gathered at the Stork for a victory party and one thanked Walter for having joined the GOP, Walter snapped, as he had at the *Post*'s earlier and similar charge, "Don't call me a Republican, you Republicans!" He called himself an "FDR guy" but said that "Eisenhower was the nearest thing to him—in Class!" And when the *Mirror* editorialized that the Republican victory represented a rejection of " 'Deals'—New, Fair, or mixed," Walter rejoined that "Truman had rejected New Deal concepts" and that Roosevelt, by appointing Eisenhower the supreme commander during World War II, was actually responsible for his election.

In light of his old postcard campaign to draft Eisenhower, Walter reserved some credit for himself too. "How does it feel to elect a President?" Art Ford had asked him half-jokingly on their way to the inauguration. Walter answered solemnly, "You know, it's really quite something." He attended the inauguration as a correspondent for ABC, racing about with a microphone on a long wire and intercepting dignitaries as if he were at a Hollywood premiere. Afterward his director asked if he had seen the look former President Truman had flashed him. "It was one of those glares," enthused the director. "A real cut dead!" Walter gloated. He now felt he was back from the political wilderness he had roamed since 1946. With the new administration he had a home again.

ON OCTOBER 21, two weeks before the election, Wechsler and the *Post* filed suit against Walter. Wechsler later said it was television that had done it. So long as Walter had confined his attacks to the column and the radio broadcast, the *Post* believed it could parry each thrust. "But television was a different matter," said Wechsler. "For one thing, we had literally no chance to answer back; for another, Winchell's use of the visual technique was far more effective than his use of the written word." By visual implication—holding up photographs in the mendacious fashion of McCarthy—Walter had linked Wechsler to convicts, Communists and ultimately to the Rosenbergs. "Up to a certain point the argument involved simply free competition," Wechsler explained, "but the air introduced a new dimension . . . where failure to sue might finally be construed as an admission of guilt."

Walter obviously assumed that the suit was another frivolous attempt to annoy him, and he met it by escalating his digs at Wechsler and the paper. A Broadway soda jerk was calling a strawberry soda a "Post" because it was all ·pink, Walter wrote the next week. "A cherry-coke, we presume, tch-tch, is called a wexla. . . ." In his snidest attack yet, he answered a *Post* editorial on a schoolgirl who was accused of being a "pink" for continuing to wear her Stevenson button after the election by giving his own highly personal definition of "pink":

> *Virginia, dear,* a Pink is a "former Communist" editor who is too cowardly to admit it . . . A Pink is a person whose logic is based on hypocrisy and his opinions motivated by deceit [. . .] He employs a newspaper as a blackjack against militant anti-Communists while demanding the Bill of Rights as a protective instrument for the Reds . . . A Pink distorts the truth, slants the news and serves as a mouthpiece for liars . . . The clearest definition of a Pink, Virginia, is represented by the N.Y. Post's editorial policy from 1948 to 1952 . . . In conclusion, a Pink is a fraud, a fool, a liar and a louse . . . He can be more dangerous than a Red—since he often deludes those who are ignorant, color-blind—or lack a sense of smell.

These sorts of libels were also stirring other forces to action. At its board meeting on November 10, the NAACP moved to contact Walter's sponsor, the Gruen Watch Company, and King Features "in connection with his scurrilous defamation of the Negro race" and urged its chapters and other black organizations to do the same. The next day Walter White quietly requested an analysis of Walter's broadcasts and columns "as a basis of a story showing definite anti-Negro slant."

Meanwhile, Walter resumed his attacks on Barry Gray, Lyle Stuart and even Josephine Baker, who had long since left the country for France under Walter's earlier barrage. On January 17 Gray was physically assaulted again and badly beaten. Seeing a photo of his bloody face in the *Post,* Walter was deliriously happy. "Headline: 'Borey Pink Lemon Gray Yellow Lavender Beaten Up,' " he chirped in his column. "Police Suspect Fair Play." Klurfeld said Walter chuckled over the *Post's* photo of Gray and remarked that he "never looked more beautiful." (Gray heard Walter had had the photo framed and hung over his bed at the St. Moritz.) Ten days later he questioned whether the assault had even taken place at all. "The phonus-bolonus claimed he was so hurt (after an alleged slugging) that he had to 'rest up over the week-end.' He took the bit of court-plaster off his check (which showed no marks whatsoever) and proceeded to Danny Kaye's premiere and later the Copacabana. What a Fraud-wayite?" In any case Gray obtained a pistol for his protection, prompting one press agent to say, "Take to the sidestreets. Barry Gray has a gun. The King [Winchell] has a gun. It's 'High Noon' at Lindy's!"

Though the press agent was joking, Walter's enemies didn't discount the danger of the gun-toting columnist. To them he now seemed explosive and uncontrollable and possibly deranged. After another flurry of Walter's gibes that spring, one of which had him boasting that he would be acquitted if he were to throw Leonard Lyons in front of a speeding truck, Lyons issued a public appeal to Police Commissioner Monaghan "to pick up his permits and the pistol he carries, or else the city of New York shall be held accountable for any consequences." He suggested that the gun not be returned until Walter underwent a psychiatric evaluation. Two days later, in a retort to Walter's version of Lyons being thrown off the Runyon Fund board, Lyons wrote, "It is obvious one of us must be imagining things. This challenge, therefore, to Winchell: that we both submit to examinations—low IQ pays all."

Walter had become completely unmanageable. Like James Cagney's Cody Jarrett at the climax of the classic gangster film *White Heat*, his youthful drive seemed to have transmogrified into a kind of madness. Like Jarrett, he was shooting wildly and laughing hysterically while everything around him burned. What he didn't realize, what he was too engulfed by hate to see, was that in the process of trying to destroy his enemies, Walter Winchell was also immolating himself.

CHAPTER 9

The Enemy of My Enemy

WHAT SENATOR JOSEPH MC-Carthy had sown in 1950, America was to reap for years, even decades, to come. They would be years of rancor and dread—a time when a toxin seemed to have been released into the American system. By citing scores of alleged Communists and Soviet agents in the administrations of Roosevelt and Truman and by lacerating the educated eastern left-wing elite from which most of them came, McCarthy had not only brought liberalism itself into disrepute; he had tapped his chisel into one of the country's long-standing cleavages—the "jagged fissure," as Whittaker Chambers had called it, "between the plain men and women of the nation, and those who affected to act, think and speak for them."

There was no question on which side of this cultural divide Walter Winchell stood. No matter how he felt about Roosevelt, he stood with those plain men and women and against the intellectuals who now disdained him. And he stood there not only because the plain citizens were his constituents and the intellectuals no longer were, and not only because they believed themselves to be outsiders like him, but because his own wrathful sense of the injustice done him meshed with theirs, at least as McCarthy expressed it for them. "The real function of the Great Inquisition of the 1950s was not anything so simply rational as to turn up spies or prevent espionage," historian Richard Hofstadter wrote in what could have easily served as an analysis of Winchell's own campaigns of hate, "but to discharge resentments and frustrations, to punish, to satisfy enmities whose roots lay elsewhere than in the Communist issue itself."

British journalist Godfrey Hodgson would describe one of those roots as the postwar "frustration of having so much 'power' and then finding that the world refused to be molded by it." Whether that was a source of McCarthy's appeal, it was certainly one of the sources behind Winchell's McCarthyism. Conflating his own growing sense of powerlessness and pessimism with the nation's, Walter constantly invoked the imminent threat of disaster. Conflating his own tormentors with those of the nation, he struck back precisely the way McCarthy had: with accusations of treason. As Richard Hofstadter said of the anti-Communist crusade, "Communism was not the target but the weapon."

But if Winchell practiced McCarthyism, he had not yet fully embraced McCarthy himself. Early on he had feared that the senator was yet another right-wing, anti-Semitic, neo-Nazi of the sort he had spent most of his life fighting, and McCarthy, in courting Walter, was at pains to allay these fears by explicitly disassociating himself from Nazi sympathizers like Gerald L. K. Smith. "As you, of course, know[,] the cabal of smear artists who have objected to my fight against communism in government have been carefully looking into every nook and cranny, hoping they might find something they could label anti-semitic," McCarthy wrote Walter late in 1950. "So far they have been unsuccessful, and as long as they stick to the truth I can assure you they will be unsuccessful."

Yet despite these assurances and despite the fact that McCarthy spoke approvingly of Walter's own anticommunism, Walter was reluctant to give McCarthy his full endorsement. In part he was deferring to his inner circle. Cuneo wanted nothing to do with McCarthy and claimed that he refused even to visit the broadcasts when a source, acting for McCarthy, began sneaking grand jury testimony to Walter in contravention of the law. Arnold Forster was no less disapproving of Walter's relationship to McCarthy. Walter's longtime accountant Harry Geist warned him not to get involved with McCarthy. And even Jack O'Brian, himself a fervid Red-baiter, said he urged Walter to be suspicious of McCarthy's unfounded attacks.

Eventually, though, whatever small resistance Walter harbored was overcome by a young Jewish attorney named Roy Cohn. Walter had first seen him, porcine, erupted in acne and hideously dressed, table-hopping at the Stork Club. Billingsley had signaled to have him barred as an undesirable when Walter said he intervened and told Billingsley that Cohn was in fact the son of a prominent judge. Given the "full treatment" now, Cohn began haunting the Stork nearly every night with his friends, and Walter admitted he struck up a "chumship" with the young go-getter.

In many ways they were an apt pair, both bearing stigmata from their youth. Cohn's maternal grandfather had founded the Bank of United States serving immigrants on the Lower East Side, but the crash wrecked the bank, sending a favorite uncle of Roy's to prison and dragging the family into disrepute. When Dora Marcus married Al Cohn, a Bronx politician who later became a judge and Roy's father, it was, according to one of Cohn's biographers, her attempt to redeem the family honor.

Certainly Roy never forgot the disgrace and, like Walter, he lived to avenge himself. Aggressive, precocious and voluble, he landed his own gossip column in the *Bronx Home News* when he was thirteen and by late adolescence had come to the attention of Leonard Lyons, who occasionally took young Roy on the rounds and became a kind of mentor to him. But unlike Lyons, Cohn staked his destiny on the law, not journalism. After he was graduated from Columbia Law School at the age of twenty, he joined United States Attorney Myles Lane's staff and then stayed on when Lane's successor, Irving Saypol, began prosecuting Communists, among them the Rosenbergs. From there he won promotion to Attorney General James McGranery's staff, "Trapping Reds Coast-to-Coast," as Winchell put it in the column. Walter took credit for having introduced Cohn to McCarthy at the Stork one evening when Walter was dining with McCarthy and Hearst president Richard E. Berlin and Cohn wandered in looking for him.* Shortly after that the senator hired the twenty-five-year-old Cohn as chief counsel to his Subcommittee on Investigations, which would be directing its efforts toward Cohn's specialty: Communist subversives.

If McCarthy was bumptious and unfocused, having seized on anticommunism less out of conviction than convenience, Cohn quickly became his Iago, calculating how best to exploit the issue for maximum political gain. For this, Winchell became a vital ally. As a Jew Cohn persuasively laid to rest Walter's fears of right-wing anti-Semitism, which was, in fact, one of the reasons McCarthy had hired him. As a master self-promoter he ingratiated himself by offering Walter exclusives that effectively gave McCarthy unlimited access to the column and broadcast. Walter later bragged that on Saturdays at 1:00 or 2:00 A.M., Cohn unfailingly provided a batch of memorandums and that "no newspaperman got more 'firsts' than I."

For his part, Cohn bragged about his access to Winchell. "I remember at twelve o'clock on one Friday night," a friend of Cohn's named Neil

---

*Cohn, however, denied that Walter provided his introduction. He would claim that Robert Morris, the chief counsel for the Senate Subcommittee on Internal Security, introduced him to McCarthy after a fundraiser at the Hotel Astor in New York in December 1952. But McCarthy greeted the young attorney by telling him how much he had heard about him, and Morris and Winchell were friendly, so it is likely that Walter had put in a word for Cohn with both the senator and Morris.

Walsh told Cohn's biographer, "Winchell called from the St. Moritz and Roy was in the Stork Club and Winchell came over. He said, 'Only for Roy.' He was tired and didn't feel well. He said, 'Only for Roy would I come over.'" An old classmate of Cohn's, the columnist Anthony Lewis, recalled a dinner at which Cohn got on the phone and demanded to speak to Walter. While the guests listened, "he proceeded to plot out with Winchell how to do something nasty to Jimmy Wechsler. . . . And here was Roy saying, 'Now, Walter, we could play this up and we could do that. . . .'"

Critics and friends alike assumed that Walter must have been insincere in promoting McCarthy and searched for ulterior motives. Most chalked it up to fear—some to Walter's fear of being left behind politically as the country marched rightward, others to his fear that as an old populist he himself might be discredited by McCarthy. "Winchell was an anti-Communist, yes, and he would have continued as the American community became anti-Communist," Arnold Forster asserted years later. "He would *not* have tied up with McCarthy and Cohn, however, because they would have been anathema to him—except for his own protection." Forster said that Walter admitted his political conversion was the product of a kind of blackmail. "He explained it all to me very carefully. There was a fellow who was writing a column for the *Daily Worker*. He was rewriting the same stuff and sending it to Winchell, and it was good information about the Nazis." At the time Walter had no idea that the source was employed by the *Worker*. When he discovered it several years later, he realized the ammunition it would provide opponents. "This tortured him, this haunted him, this worried him. . . . And I think he fell into Roy Cohn's trap partially because of that."

Gary Stevens, a press agent close to Walter, had also been told by a "very big source in Washington" that Cohn had acquired files tying Winchell to the left, especially column material on the pro-Soviet wartime film *Mission to Moscow*, which Walter's friend and Warner Bros. press agent Irving Hoffman had provided to publicize the picture. By this account, Cohn actually threatened Walter, warning he would be brought to Washington to testify. "Walter went completely haywire and fell apart, and Cohn told him what the price was. And that's how he succumbed to McCarthy."

As absurd as it may seem, there *were* rumors at the time of Walter's having closet left-wing sympathies. A California friend had written him in December 1952 of a conversation he had had at a cocktail party. "I remarked that I always made an effort to hear Walter Winchell," wrote the friend. "The couple who sat there beside me [deleted] spoke up. He said, 'Walter Winchell is a communist.' I said, 'No, I can't believe that,' and he said, 'Well, he is, his cell no. is so and so.' " Walter sent the letter on to Hoover to investigate. Meanwhile, Walter's old enemy Westbrook Pegler, poised for another strike at Walter, was collecting information from HUAC on left-wing books Walter had championed during the war and had already boldly accused him of having withheld Chambers's revelations back in 1939.*

In Klurfeld's view, however, it was neither fear of McCarthy's threats nor sympathy for McCarthy's cause that drove Walter into the senator's arms. The explanation for his pro-McCarthy tub-thumping was far simpler, and, to anyone who knew Winchell, far more plausible: in Walter's own words, "You don't shoot somebody who is shooting at your enemies."

To Winchell, Roy Cohn and Joseph McCarthy were instruments of war, just as he himself had been for Roosevelt. Long before Cohn joined McCarthy's staff, he had assisted Walter during the Josephine Baker battle, helping direct anti-Baker information to him. Once Cohn joined the staff, he and Walter immediately began collaborating on a new and far more important objective. They were going to destroy James Wechsler.

Cohn had been chief counsel only four months when Wechsler was suddenly called before the investigations subcommittee on April 24, 1953, and subjected to McCarthy's harangue. The pretext for Wechsler's appearance was that two of his books, written while he had been a member of the Young Communist League, had found their way into United States Information Agency libraries overseas. The real basis for the subpoena was his animus toward Winchell and McCarthy. "I am convinced that you have done exactly what you would do if you were a member of the Communist Party, if you wanted to have a phony break and then use that phony break to the advantage of the Communist Party," McCarthy charged. "I feel that you have not broken with Communist ideals. I feel that you are serving them very, very actively." When Wechsler rebutted that one couldn't fight Communists by shooting them, Cohn yawned showily.

---

*How important the issue was for Walter was demonstrated several years earlier when he had loudly supported Truman's nomination of an oil executive and Democratic fund-raiser named Edwin Pauley as under secretary of the navy despite howls of protest that Pauley was unqualified. Arnold Forster questioned why Walter kept bucking the tide. "Do you know what Joe Kamp [a fascist] has put in my naval intelligence record in Washington?: a twenty-six page memorandum that I'm aware of proving that I'm a Communist," Walter answered. "Do you think I want my grandchildren to see that file and learn that their grandfather was a betrayer, was a Communist? If this guy becomes [under] secretary of the navy I will get that poison out of my file and get it destroyed."

What McCarthy demanded now, as proof of Wechsler's repentance, were the names of YCL members whom Wechsler had known, even though he had broken from the group sixteen years earlier. Wechsler balked, torn, he said, between conflicting obligations. "It was wrong to expose others to McCarthy's wickedness," he later wrote, "but it was equally wrong, in my judgment, to embrace the principle that a former communist should tell nothing to anyone." More, his reluctance was fed by his fear of Winchell. Though Wechsler had testified in executive session where his words were presumably shielded from the public, Walter had obviously been given a transcript by Cohn or Howard Rushmore, an ex-Communist who had been Hearst's resident Communist expert before joining the staff of the McCarthy committee, and Walter had published his own highly editorialized account in the column a few days later, recycling his old charges that Wechsler had yet to recant communism and accusing him of employing Communists at the *Post*. "Not one or two—scads."

As Wechsler later told it, Leonard Lyons now offered to intervene by setting up a meeting with McCarthy at which they could resolve their differences. "His feeling was that I was his friend and Roy Cohn was his friend and therefore how could we be arguing?" Wechsler said of Lyons. Wechsler refused the offer. But by his second session on May 5, while protesting the leaks to Winchell, he agreed to furnish to the committee the names of his YCL colleagues anyway, on the grounds that McCarthy "was still seeking the opportunity to tell the world that I had refused to talk, and thus consign me to the netherworld of silent witnesses." In exchange for the list, Wechsler bargained to have the committee release a transcript of his testimony, which he hoped to use to rally editors to his cause by invoking the threat McCarthy posed to freedom of the press.

"The ultimate in hideous irony has been Wechsler's hammy posturing as a free press martyr," Walter wrote in one of a series of columns that May devoted entirely to attacks on Wechsler. In the meantime, Cohn and McCarthy complained that Wechsler's list had provided them with no new information, triggering more charges of uncooperativeness against him. Through it all, Walter was jubilant. "You know what he said?" Klurfeld recalled. "He said, 'Now he [Wechsler] won't be able to write anything. He's going to be too busy defending himself. . . . Now he won't be able to sleep.' As long as he caused Wechsler trouble, that's all he cared about."

OBSESSED AS he was with avenging himself against Wechsler and the *Post*, Winchell had not forgotten other feuds or forsaken other enemies that winter and spring. The previous August a handsome twenty-two-year-old oleomargarine heir named Minot "Mickey" Jelke III had rocked what remained of café society when he was arrested for running a prostitution ring serving "international café society's well-heeled playboys," in the *Mirror*'s words. "VIP (in Café Sssssiety) now stands for Very Important Pimpressario," Walter joked in his column.

As Jelke's February trial date approached, the public and press seemed to salivate for salacious revelations about the rich and famous in what promised to be the most sensational trial in New York in years. The prosecution's star witness was an attractive nineteen-year-old redhead named Pat Ward. Ward had met Jelke in May 1951 at the Seabright Yacht Club in New Jersey and then again, in September, at a nightclub where she found herself captivated by him. The next day she moved into his apartment. A few days after that a press agent named Ray Russell Davioni suggested that she go into the "racket," as he called prostitution, and her career was launched. Though successful at it, she said she tired of prostitution and headed to Florida to rendezvous with Jelke, who had left. When she got there she discovered that he had already taken up with another girl, and after a brief romance with a nightclub manager, she returned to New York, broke and depressed. A short time later she attempted suicide. It was when the police rescued her that the Jelke story broke.

For the press the tantalizing question was who her clients were. But as she took the stand to testify, her attorney, a histrionic amateur Shakespearean actor and former magistrate named J. Roland Sala, approached the bench and requested that the courtroom be cleared during Ward's testimony. After a half-hour conference and a recess, Judge Francis Valente acceded.

Denied its hot story, the press was outraged, none more so than Winchell. "[T]he evidence is now secondary to the question of whether the trial was conducted according to the Constitution of the State of New York and the U.S.," Walter solemnly intoned in his February 10 column, prompting A. J. Liebling to crack in *The New Yorker*, "I could sense Mr. Winchell's reluctance to add to the volume of the kind of publicity he deplored, but the threat to *two* constitutions had evidently forced his hand."

When Ward did testify—in a closed courtroom—Walter found himself with new ammunition against another old foe of his whom he hated every bit as much as he hated Wechsler. Ward, it seemed, had managed to collect money from her first two "dates" without having had to perform. The third demanded performance, and the fourth introduced her to a long list of prospective customers. His name, as the Jelke legal staff leaked it, was Bill Cahn, the same Bill Cahn who had been Walda's boyfriend. "His right name is Cohen," Walter wrote a few days later. "He has a criminal record. Rogues' Gallery photos etc. Carries a card saying he is with the Henry ('he's my pal') Rosenfeld firm, which is strictly a front in case of another pinch for vagrancy, etc."

While he attacked Cahn, Walter himself briefly grabbed the trial headlines. Grace Appel, a girlhood friend of Ward's, had been called to testify, apparently to show that Jelke was not the one who had led Ward into a life of sin. Appel, however, failed to appear, and Judge Valente charged her mother with delivering the young woman. Walter, acting on a tip, found Appel first. "I assured her she would be doing her civic duty by coming in and taking the stand," he later wrote. That night the wife of Assistant District Attorney Anthony Liebler received a strange phone call from a young woman professing to be the missing Appel. "I'm crying," she told Mrs. Liebler, "because I'm so happy. I've spent almost twenty-four hours with Mr. Winchell. He's going to make me one of his daughters. I'm never going to leave him. I love him."

Liebler assumed the call was a hoax until Appel arrived at the courtroom the next day with Walter and took the stand. Jelke's attorneys questioned her for six minutes, during which she described a wild party she attended with Ward at the Waldorf-Astoria suite of Walter's former brother-in-law, comedian Joey Adams. Then came Liebler. "Did you telephone your lawyer's wife two nights ago and say you were in love with Walter Winchell, that you would never leave him and that you wanted to be one of his children?" he asked, leaving himself out of it. Walter claimed he was "too groggy and too weary to get indiggy or even give Liebler a glare," but his level of indignation soon rose. "If a gossip colyumist did that you'd all yell your heads off," he burned in the column. "Gossip is legal in a court of law but not in a newspaper. Nice going, mister." He concluded, "The fact is, that for a woman to say she loves Walter Winchell is no attack on her credibility. . . ."

The trial, which ended with Jelke's conviction, was treated as cheerful retribution against the excesses of café society, a way of bringing the idle rich to heel by revealing their essential wickedness. But not for Walter, who had been sniping at the idle rich for more than two decades. For Walter, the trial's protagonist had been neither café society nor its tawdry representative, Mickey Jelke. For him, the real protagonist had been Bill Cahn. And Cahn had yet to be brought to justice.

Long before the Jelke trial, Cahn had surrendered to Walter's harassment and broken up with Walda. "Look, kid, when the buzzard dies you'll inherit a couple of million," he was quoted as having told Walda. "But the way things are going he'll cut you out of his will. If I stop seeing you maybe he'll let you alone. And he'll let me make a living." Free of Walda, Cahn landed a job as a salesman for the dress manufacturer Henry Rosenfeld, but if he thought that Walter would now cease hostilities, he was 'mistaken. As soon as the Jelke arrest brought Cahn's name back into the public arena, Walter had not only renewed his attacks on "WC," but throughout the trial, he repeatedly pressed DA Frank Hogan to indict Cahn for procuring.

On March 10, shortly after the Jelke verdict, Cahn was questioned by police from the DA's office about his role in the scandal. A few days later, he made the second biggest mistake of his life after the primary one of hooking up with Walda Winchell in the first place: He got married. So long as there had been even the vaguest prospect that Cahn might become Walda's husband and Walter's son-in-law, he had been spared the very worst of Walter's fury. Married, Cahn became the subject of a new campaign of unrelenting harassment. "He was so mad at him he would have done *anything*," Herman Klurfeld said.

Cahn was en route to Florida for his honeymoon when Walter waved his photograph on the telecast and excoriated him as a "dirty four-letter word." According to law officers, Cahn, apparently fearful that Walter would coerce the authorities into prosecuting him, disappeared and wouldn't be located again by them until August 1954. In fact, he remained in Florida a short time, then headed for California, where he hoped finally to be beyond Winchell's reach. He wasn't. Vacationing in California that May, Walter spotted Cahn at the Beverly Hills Hotel and quickly issued an invitation to Beverly Hills Police Chief Clinton Anderson to attend the May 3 telecast. "Police Chief Clinton Anderson of Beverly Hills is here because I sent for him today," Walter told the viewers. "Two front men and two procurers of the Jelke vice case are at your swankiest hotel. They are up to no good. They may pull a snatch or a murder, you never can tell." On the radio broadcast later that same evening, he added a warning: "I will have to defend myself if any one of these lice get too close to me."

As Walter later told it, the police did collar Cahn during his sojourn in California. But this was just a minor irritation compared with what Walter would soon be engineering against hapless Bill Cahn.

II

What had brought Walter to Los Angeles that spring was neither escape nor revenge but romance. During the Jelke trial, Sherman Billingsley had invited Walter to the Copacabana to catch Betty and Jane Kean, a pair of young singer-comediennes. The sisters routinely introduced celebrities in the audience, and that night, when they came to Walter, he rose and declaimed, "I'm going to tell the world." Afterward he and Jane Kean shared a dance. "He was a wonderful dancer," Jane remembered. "And I think that first night at the Copa that's what struck up an instant rapport."

The next morning, when Jane picked up the *Mirror* she found Walter gushing over the Keans. "Theirs is one of the swiftest-paced routines of all—married to the most comical gags and numbers in seasons," he opened the column. ". . . these talented chicks (Chicks???) rock audiences from the moment they come on until the convulsed spectators reluctantly let them leave. . . ."

Jane Kean, pretty, petite, blond, saucer-eyed and, perhaps above all, young, fit the profile of Walter's amours from Nellie Cliff to Mary Lou Bentley. The Kean sisters had been born in Hartford, Connecticut, to an insurance salesman who was absent most of the time and a determined stage mother who pushed them into show business, Betty, eight years older than Jane, landing roles on Broadway when she was still a teenager. Before the sisters formed an act together, Jane was singing at the Versailles, and it was there she was first introduced to Walter, who was staking out the club while Mary Lou appeared in the chorus.

In the intervening years between their first introduction at the Versailles and their second at the Copa, Walter had lost Mary Lou and Jane had reportedly begun a romance with Ed Sullivan, which may have been what piqued Walter's interest in her. Whatever the motive, the night of his rave Walter invited the sisters to accompany him on his police calls—his own peculiar form of courtship. "In the early stages of our relationship my sister was with us a lot," Jane recalled of what became nightly rounds in Walter's car. But Betty was engaged to be married, and soon it was only Jane and Jack O'Brian and whatever celebrity happened to be visiting. And gradually, as they cruised the streets for action, a relationship developed.

"If he had the hots for somebody, you knew it by reading the column," said Al Rylander, a press agent and later an NBC executive. Walter now constantly trumpeted the Kean Sisters, who found their asking price skyrocketing to four or five times what they had been making—all because of Walter's incessant plugs. "It was day after day after day," Jane remembered. "It got so that I was a little embarrassed about it . . . because I did fall in love with him." By the time the Keans finished their engagement at the Copa, they were signed to headline at the Sands Hotel in Las Vegas. In late April they moved to Ciro's in Los Angeles, and Walter flew out for the opening. "It was the most exciting opening night they ever had because there was every top star from Marilyn Monroe to Lucille

Ball to Betty Grable," Jane happily recalled. "All by his invitation. He bought out the room. Thank God we were a tremendous success because he never liked to stick his neck out if he thought someone was going to bomb." Glowing over Jane's triumph, and his own hand in it, Walter stayed throughout the engagement and composed his column there—he lodging at the Ambassador, Jane at the Beverly Hills Hotel, which is where, leaving her room one morning, he sighted William Cahn.

"It was hard to think of Walter as being married because he did not behave as a married man," Jane said. To her, the thirty-year difference in their ages notwithstanding, he seemed "very romantic"—uncharacteristically lavishing gifts upon her, writing lovelorn "Don Wahn" poems atop the column when she was away, showering attention on her beloved mother. Jane admitted, "All those things were very attractive to a young girl." Equally attractive for a young woman who had grown up without a strong father figure was the very thing Mary Lou had found so appealing: the power Walter emanated. Back in New York, Jane and Walter could walk into the Empire Room at the Waldorf, as a patron there once witnessed, with the band playing and the guests dancing, and the music would suddenly cease. Seconds later the band would break into the "Walter Winchell Rhumba." Walter would grab Jane, and the two of them would dance while everyone else watched silently as if at a performance.

But with the romance came the jealousy. At Ciro's, Jane was dancing with a friend when Walter came in, observed the scene and put his foot through the front glass door. When Jane later appeared in a musical and played a love scene, Walter insisted that it seemed too real. Other times he would phone her apartment to find her whereabouts. "My mother would say, 'Well, she went to the cleaners,' " Jane recollected. "My gosh, I'd be standing at the cleaners and there'd be a call for me. 'Hey, want to have breakfast at Rumpelmayer's?' " That is how it went when Walter Winchell was in love.

California that May had another salutary effect on Winchell besides the invigoration of passion. However much his stock was falling back East now that he had hitched himself to McCarthy, in the West he was still a force to be feared and appeased, and he enjoyed the status more than ever. On May 14, the Friars Club honored him with a "Roastmaster" dinner, ostensibly to commend his efforts for the Runyon Fund but also clearly to win his favor at a time of great apprehension in Hollywood over the wave of Red-baiting. More than four hundred guests attended—the venue had to be changed to accommodate the crowd—and reports noted that the ribbing was unusually tame for this sort of affair.

Standing on the dais with evident emotion, Walter said it took him back to his farewell dinner at LaHiff's Tavern in 1924, when he left *The*

Vaudeville News for the *Graphic* and Jimmy Walker had warned that he would either be a great success and lose his friends or keep them and lose his job. Walter left little doubt which it had been, and he expressed amazement at hearing "praise of any kind. . . . It kind of makes me wince." But rather than accept the orchids gracefully, he went on to launch another intemperate attack on "ingrates" generally and Ed Sullivan specifically, thus putting the lie to any notion that he might be mellowing in his middle age.

He hadn't mellowed. If anything, his pact with McCarthy and his romance with Jane Kean had recharged him to do further battle against his enemies, and in his own mind at least, he seemed finally to have gained the upper hand after nearly eighteen months of defensiveness. Josephine Baker had been floating through Latin America and Europe eroding her martyrdom with anti-American remarks. Her suit against Walter later lapsed when she failed to appear in court. Sullivan, if nothing else, had lost Jane Kean to him. And in June, Barry Gray lost his radio program. Now, as Walter raced back from California at May's end, there remained only James Wechsler to defeat.

Wechsler's attorney, Simon Rifkind, had called Walter to depose him for the upcoming libel trial, and Walter had responded to Rifkind's questions with belligerence. When Rifkind offered that Wechsler had always supported American intervention in Korea, Walter countered sarcastically, "Yankee Doodle Boy." And when Rifkind cited other instances of Wechsler's having taken anti-Soviet positions, Walter attributed them to schisms within the Communist party. At another four-hour session that July, Rifkind baited Walter by accusing him of having used Communist propaganda himself during the war. "I haven't been a dupe for them," Walter bristled. "I've been an officer in the United States Naval Reserve." Later, losing his temper, he yelled at Rifkind, "What am I accused of? Why am I here?"

Writing Ernie Cuneo nearly twenty-five years later, Rifkind, one of New York's most distinguished attorneys, called Walter's performance the "greatest mistake of his life, with respect to his personal reputation." Newsmen had gathered in the reception area outside Rifkind's office seeking permission to attend the deposition. Rifkind had left the option to Walter's counsel, who had sternly refused. But Walter, intoxicated with arrogance that spring and summer, countermanded him. "They did come in," Rifkind told Cuneo. "What they reported concerning these examinations broke Winchell's spirit in my opinion. . . . After that it was all downhill."

It was true that most press accounts portrayed Walter's testimony as childishly cantankerous. But it was hardly true that Winchell's spirit had been broken in these sessions; the notion that Walter was somehow in free fall, which may have been true back in the spring of 1952 when he had suffered his breakdowns, was now wishful thinking by enemies who couldn't possibly allow for Walter's incredible resilience.

The evidence of that resilience was that enemies felt the need to keep battering him. In March, Lyle Stuart resurfaced with another long article in *Exposé* largely devoted to proof of Walter's demise. "Whom the Gods destroy they first make mad," Stuart closed the report, "and at 56, Walter Winchell is an angry little boy, hungry for attention."

"And soon he will be mumbling to himself."

The article itself had less impact than the first one, but three or four weeks later, as he told it, Stuart received a call from a publisher named Samuel Roth, asking if Stuart might be interested in expanding his articles into a book. By Stuart's own description, Roth, who carried a cane, wore a bowler and affected an English accent, was the "most unbelievably unscrupulous person in the history of publishing." But he offered Stuart $1,000 for a Winchell book, and Stuart took on the assignment, admitting it "was really something that I kind of did when I had nothing better to do." Billy Cahn contributed, and Pat Ward of the Jelke case, and Joey Adams, who phoned Stuart nervously when the book was about to be published and begged him to reconsider. Nor was it just the enemies who cooperated. "A good source was Billy Rose, who on the surface was a buddy of Winchell's," Stuart remembered. "But he would give me stuff and I would always be surprised. And he would keep telling me I underestimate him [Winchell]. . . . He said, 'If you get killed, remember I told you.' "

Stuart may have thought that Rose was speaking figuratively. He wasn't. On August 11, just days after completing the manuscript, Stuart was taking a morning walk outside his home in North Bergen, New Jersey. "I heard somebody running behind me," he recalled, "and I figured they were running to catch the bus to Manhattan. And when they didn't pass, I turned my neck, which was very lucky." As he did, a hand slipped around his head, and two men with blackjacks jumped out of the bushes. Fending them off by swinging an attaché case, he managed to break away and run up a small grassy knoll and down to his car, where, seeing the assailants get into an auto, he jotted down their license plate number.

At the station house Stuart identified two of his attackers—waterfront toughs—from a book of mug shots. They were arrested at a New York tavern and were tried and convicted for assault, but the conviction was overturned. "Now everybody assumed Winchell had done this," Stuart later said. "I never in a thousand years considered this as a possibility— never. . . . Winchell doesn't do that stuff. What I had figured was that somebody was going to do this and hire these guys and then sit down at a table with Winchell and say, 'Walter, did you see what happened to Lyle Stuart?' And then Winchell would know."

Walter's own form of revenge, Stuart knew, was different. Once the book, *The Secret Life of Walter Winchell*, was published, Walter scabrously attacked both Stuart and Roth in print, even accusing Roth's son of criminal activity and his daughter of Communist sympathies. ("His troubles are just beginning," Walter wrote ominously after reporting that a Senate committee on juvenile delinquency was interested in Roth.) Stuart believed that Walter also sicced the FBI on Roth; his office was raided, its contents were confiscated and Roth was arrested, convicted and sent to prison once again. Meanwhile, Stuart said he found himself as much a pariah on Broadway as Winchell had been among the liberals. "People I went to didn't want to see me," Stuart recalled. "Or they'd see me two blocks away and [say], 'Please, God, don't tell anybody. After all, I have a wife and two kids.' People were really petrified of him."

If people still feared Winchell, a large part of the terror now derived from Walter's association with a network of unprincipled anti-Communists, not least of whom was a former *Graphic* copyboy named Robert Harrison. Harrison—a born promoter who was once described as a "weird-looking bird with eyes like a hooded falcon" that kept "darting from left to right so you can't eyeball him"—had established a small empire after the war in girlie magazines, including *Wink*, *Titter* and *Flirt*. When competition drove him out of business, he created a new magazine that would push the edge of the gossip envelope far beyond even Winchell's boundaries.

Titled *Confidential* and specializing in saucy tales of celebrity misconduct, the magazine sputtered its first month. But in his second issue, in January 1953, Harrison had a brainstorm. He ran a story called "Winchell Was Right About Josephine Baker." "I took the magazine over to Winchell and showed it to him," Harrison later recounted. Walter liked the piece so much, he held up a copy of the magazine on the telecast. "And I'm telling you, from then on, this thing flew."

Still, Harrison protected his investment. "[W]e started running a Winchell piece every issue," he said. "We'd try to figure out who Winchell didn't like and run a piece about them. One of them was 'Broadway's Biggest Double Cross.' It was about all the ingrates who Winchell had helped to start their careers who turned their backs on him. . . . And he kept on plugging *Confidential*. It got to the point where we would sit down and rack our brains trying to think of somebody else Winchell didn't like. We were running out of people, for Christ's sake!"

Lyle Stuart remembered a *Confidential* piece on him by Howard

Rushmore, who had left the McCarthy committee. "They got a photo-graph of me, colored it very dark," Stuart said. "I mean I looked like somebody I wouldn't want to meet on the street.... He started out say-ing that I was nothing. But in the end of the three-page article I was one of the biggest menaces in America." Walter then showed the issue on his telecast and asked his viewers to read the piece. He did it again the next week, until Stuart finally brought suit against the magazine.

Though *Confidential* was indisputably untrustworthy and quite possibly, as Tom Wolfe later called it, the "most scandalous scandal magazine in the history of the world," it nevertheless had a circulation in the millions and could pose a serious threat to careers; that is how Walter drew power from it. Yet even Walter realized that he had been driven to extremes, as-sociating with the ostentatious and disreputable Harrison, who wore a white polo coat, a white fedora, drove a custom-made Cadillac and was usually adorned with a buxom woman. When the two met one day at Lindy's, Walter asked Harrison, "How the hell did I ever get involved with *Confidential*, I can't figure it out[?]"

He had gotten involved because his only measure of an associate now was whether he was willing to fight alongside Winchell, whether he was on Winchell's "team," as Walter called it. ("When you're on my team, you don't *need* anyone else," he had warned a press agent at the time.) He had gotten involved because he was consumed by anger and vengeance and because he needed every available means to exercise it. And he needed to exercise it because there were plots to destroy him—plots, he told his radio audience that September, hatched in the Soviet Union. "Winchell is high on the list for liquidation," he said.

The paranoia made him increasingly reckless. On the same program on which he revealed the plot to assassinate him, he announced that HUAC was holding secret sessions in California to investigate the entertainment industry. "The most popular of all television stars was confronted with her membership in the Communist Party," he added. Lucille Ball, costar with her husband, Desi Arnaz of the most popular program on television, *I Love Lucy*, was listening to the broadcast that night and mused over whom Winchell could mean. At the same time, Desi was playing poker when a friend called to tell him about Winchell's blind item. "That was not a 'blind' item to me," Arnaz later wrote in his autobiography. "I knew immediately he meant Lucy." Desi phoned her and offered to return home but, realizing that she didn't know about the brewing crisis, re-vealed nothing. MGM publicity chief Howard Strickling also called, as did another friend, Bill Henry of the Los Angeles *Times*, who came right over with what Lucy described as that "death in the family look."

That night the house teemed with friends and supporters calculating how best to limit the damage. Lucy had, in fact, testified twice before HUAC that her grandfather was a devoted socialist and that to pacify him she had once registered to vote as a Communist. Her testimony obviously had been leaked. Strickling recommended they do and say nothing; the whole thing would blow over. But by the morning, when Lucy left to do her first program of the new season, the house was already staked out by photographers, and some action had to be taken.

Lucy spent the week weeping. Desi was furious. He phoned the Stork, trying to get Walter, but wound up with Billingsley instead. "I'm sure he knows the true story," Desi pleaded. "He's a friend of J. Edgar Hoover, so all he has to do is pick up the phone and call Mr. Hoover." In the meantime, Desi prepared to meet the press. He explained the situation and offered that the only thing red about Lucy was her hair. The response was overwhelmingly favorable, and Walter broadcast the next week that the "Lucille Ball story which rocked the nation has had a very happy ending. Congressman [Donald] Jackson [of HUAC] was the very first to give Lucille Ball a clean bill. Newspapers and those who know her best were understanding and sympathetic." What Walter had neglected to mention was that he had been the one responsible for the crisis in the first place.

By then, driven into the arms of the extremists, he had also been driven away finally from his old associates of New Deal days. "This was a very lonely man all his life," Arnold Forster recalled. And when he embraced McCarthy, "we who had been helping him began to drift away from him. . . ." Forster continued to submit material on Jewish matters, but the intimacy was gone. He detested Cohn and had actually engaged in a fistfight with him at the Stork after helping deny him a place on the ADL board. (Cohn had taunted that he was blackballed because he was too anti-Communist for the ADL.) With Cuneo also maintaining his distance from Walter, Walter contemplated replacing him as personal counsel with Cohn. He remained only because Harry Geist, Walter's longtime financial adviser, issued an ultimatum: If Cuneo was replaced, Geist would resign.*

He was in limbo. A young copyboy at ABC, fresh out of college, fre-

---

*When the break finally did come with Cuneo, it was not over McCarthy but over money. With Walter's not getting paid for his summer vacation after his breakdowns, he shut off Cuneo's summer funds. "We never had a profit or loss arrangement," Cuneo wrote him. "Over the years you have repeatedly stated that you get the bows, but you also get the brickbats. It was your enterprise. . . . In any event I am sorry to terminate a long relationship on what I regard as brutal treatment. I have earned more for you in outside activities, actually, than the vacation pay. And even the tough steel barons pay a worker thirty-six weeks when they kick him out."

quently saw Walter that fall of 1953 wandering late Friday and Saturday nights around the empty newsroom on 66th Street and seeming "haunted." "You know what he said to me right off," remembered the copyboy, Neil Toplitzer, forty years later. " 'My life has been threatened by a number of people from Hitler right on down, and I just want you to know, Kid—he always called me Kid—I go, you go too because you'll be a witness.' " Most of those nights Walter sent Toplitzer to get him a sandwich, always with the instruction that he not tell the cook whom the sandwich was for, lest he be poisoned. Some nights he invited Toplitzer to join him in a small lounge off the newsroom where there was a sofa and a television set. Here they would sit, silently, watching old movies on "The Late Show"—the world's most powerful columnist and the copyboy. Alone.

III

Promoting Joseph McCarthy, Walter hadn't spared plaudits for President Eisenhower either. The President had told mutual friends that he and Mamie often listened to Walter's broadcast and appreciated not only Walter's unstinting support but the fact that, as the friends averred, "WW is his best voice and contact with the people." When the friends asked if the President had seen Walter since the inaugural, Eisenhower said he hadn't and promptly invited him to the White House for February 4. "It lasted almost two hours, the longest ever for me with a President," Walter enthused to Walt, Jr., in a letter the same day. The President had given him a personal tour: to the Lincoln Room, where Mamie slept, to the den where Eisenhower hung the canvases he painted, to his own bedroom, where he and Walter engaged in a brief putting contest with a "gadget" the President had installed there. They talked about taxes, economic hardship, the bravery of the Korean people. But Walter closed the letter not with a comment about the President but with a description of a "Yale man" who had recently debated Wechsler on television and bested him by saying he considered a good anti-Communist to be "Anything opposite or contrary to what Mr. Wechsler claims to be! (Haw!)"

Somehow the issue now always returned to Wechsler. In March, after Walter had sought unsuccessfully to have Wechsler's libel suit dismissed, he took up his cudgels again—now for the third time—against the *Post* and its editor. When Dorothy Schiff said she was surprised to hear Walter publicly defend McCarthy's methods, Walter rejoined in the column, "We didn't say that—but on many occasions we think they have been too tame." As for the *Post's* coverage of Walter's seemingly endless pretrial depositions, Walter rebuked the paper for distorting his testimony and devoted several more columns to clarifying the record. In Walter's version, he was driving attorney Rifkind to distraction. "He was feeling out of sorts," Walter wrote. "We felt fine."

There was no such solicitude for Wechsler, but there did seem to be an odd transference occurring when Walter described his rival's alleged psychological state after the *Post* ran a two-part series on McCarthy and Winchell. "The journalistic deviate must inevitably be shaken by inner turmoil," Walter wrote, apparently blind to the application of his analysis to his own situation. "He is constantly endeavoring to reconcile the lofty concepts he pretends to embrace with the cynicism and deceit he practices. The illogic and violent qualities of Wechsler's work is [*sic*] the inevitable consequence of the conflict . . . The downfall of a man is always a sad event . . . Every tenet of humanity seems to crumble with him. His process of deterioration undoubtedly presents a fascinating case study for a psychiatrist. Nothing is more pathetic than a human being clawing to cling to the edges of times which have passed him by."

To most observers, of course, it was Walter who was desperate and irresponsible and clinging to the edges of the times, Walter who was sacrificing every "tenet of humanity."

That April, at the same time he was lashing Wechsler, he engaged in what may have been his most reckless behavior yet. National tests were being conducted on a polio vaccine developed by Dr. Jonas Salk. But on April 4, Walter broadcast that live polio viruses had been discovered in some batches of the vaccine and it "may be a killer" instead of a cure, sending the U.S. Public Health Service and the National Foundation for Infantile Paralysis hurrying to assure the public that the vaccine would not be released unless it was found safe.

"It is nice to have the advice of sidewalk superintendents—like Winchell—and we will give his criticism attention," Dr. Salk announced, attempting to allay fears, "but this is a misrepresentation of what we are doing. The vaccine is tested for effectiveness and margin of safety." Dr. Salk, however, couldn't head off the panic. Already the secretary of the Michigan State Medical Society was withholding approval of the vaccine, and other health boards were soon following suit, one director specifically blaming Walter's "ill-advised television broadcast" for his board's withdrawal.

Oblivious to the fear he had sown and the possible harm he had caused, Walter defended himself by saying he had received the information from a former research director of the National Foundation for Infantile Paralysis who had recently been relieved of his duties. Three weeks later, with the issue still not laid to rest, he invoked Chicago Health Commissioner H. N. Bundesen's warning that all parents "should be made aware of the calculated risk, slight as it may be, to aid them in making up their minds." A week later, he quoted Adlai Stevenson that "Progress always results from persons taking unpopular positions." "That's true," Walter continued. "But so is it true that unpopular positions are taken by a Senator fighting Reds. Or a newsman reporting facts about a vaccine."

FOR JOSEPH MCCARTHY and Roy Cohn, the hearings into alleged subversives in the Army were to be the big show.

Since his opening shot in February 1950, McCarthy had been accusing the Democrats of having harbored Communists, and Republicans, whatever private misgivings some of them might have had about the senator's tactics, had been largely supportive of his efforts. But his months-long campaign in which he accused the Army of sheltering Communists had brought him for the first time into direct confrontation with a Republican administration. He was discrediting the very institution charged with the country's defense, not to mention the one with which the President had so long been associated.

Walter had been joyfully sounding the alarum all that winter and spring: "Senator McCarthy will give the nation another big shudder next week. He will name a very high Army officer as being an out and out Communist, a colonel in the United States Army." "Congressional detectives are now breathing heavily down the neck of a very big man in the Department of Defense. Party card!" "Seven suspects in the Department of the Army—that's Stevens' department—are suspected of being Reds. Seven subpoenas!"

Before McCarthy could get his show trial against the Army, however, a new issue was injected. Roy Cohn had enlisted a wealthy young friend named David Schine for the committee staff. (It was Schine who had accompanied Cohn on a whirlwind tour of USIA libraries in Europe that had served as the pretext for the Wechsler interrogation.) Schine, who frequented the Stork with Cohn and whose father owned the Roney-Plaza, had been eligible for the draft. Now, Army counsel John Adams produced a chronology showing that Cohn had attempted to influence the Army to grant Schine preferential treatment—everything from a commission before he joined the service to special weekend and even midweek passes after he joined—always with the implicit threat that were the favors not granted, McCarthy would proceed with his investigation. Cohn and McCarthy fired back that the blackmail flowed from the Army and produced a sheaf of memorandums proving, they said, that the Army offered to grant the favors to Schine in return for leniency from the committee.

To determine who was telling the truth, the subcommittee agreed to hold hearings that April; for his part, McCarthy agreed to step down from his chairmanship during the proceeding while retaining the right to cross-examine witnesses. Now the issue was joined. It was the Army versus McCarthy. "McCarthy may have been wrong on Schine," Walter broadcast, taking McCarthy's side, "but the real issue is Communism."

Walter observed the first week's sessions from afar in New York, but early in May he arrived in Washington and immediately landed himself in the middle of a controversy. McCarthy had somehow obtained a two-and-a-quarter-page memo from the FBI to a Major General Alexander Bolling of Army intelligence that summarized a 1951 report on alleged Communist infiltration at Fort Monmouth, New Jersey, the U.S. Signal Corps's major research facility. McCarthy had wanted to introduce the top-secret document into the hearings but Secretary of the Army Robert Stevens refused to do so, and McCarthy couldn't unilaterally release it without violating the law. Instead he brandished it. Angry over the Army's refusal to release the memo, Walter grumbled aloud at the May 4 session, "Nothing is personal and confidential to me when it concerns spies and the welfare of our country. I wish I could get a copy of it!"

A short time later in the corridor outside the hearing room, Walter discovered, or so he said, that a copy of the memo had been slipped into his hand while he had been engrossed in conversation. Fearful despite all his public bravado, he contacted Hoover. "Where did you get it?" he quoted Hoover as demanding. "I can't tell you, Mr. Hoover," Walter answered. "I just want to know if I make it public, will you arrest me?" Hoover replied "with the grimmest tones he ever used on me" that he would. So Walter destroyed the document, thinking that settled the matter. He discovered months later that it hadn't.

Meanwhile, the hearings were clearly not going as McCarthy and Cohn had planned. It wasn't only that their crusade had been sidetracked by the Schine matter. For maximum exposure, McCarthy had demanded that the hearings be telecast, and the networks, under pressure, had reluctantly agreed. It was a major tactical blunder. However riveting the hearings ultimately proved as political theater, McCarthy and Cohn were not exactly cut from the cloth of matinee idols. Balding and beetle-browed with tiny eyes and dark jowls, and with a quavering tenor voice, McCarthy looked and sounded more like the rent-collector than the hero. Cohn, his dark hair lacquered to his scalp and his mouth curled in a perpetual sneer, looked even worse. On aesthetic grounds alone, one couldn't have found a better representation of malevolence than these two: the glowering villain and his sniveling young sidekick.

But it wasn't just on aesthetic grounds that McCarthy and Cohn were now being judged. Television showed the public their browbeating, their theatrics, their meanness, their menace and, perhaps most important, their insubstantiality.

They had overplayed their hand, miscalculated the public response, and as the hearings proceeded, with McCarthy boldly announcing he would keep Secretary Stevens on the stand until he had adequately explained his behavior, even McCarthy and Cohn seemed to realize that the tide was turning against them.

"Last week I said that the Army-McCarthy hearings should be continued out in the open," McCarthy's loudest cheerleader, Winchell, announced on his May 9 simulcast. "But since the President has begged for unity because our country is in deadly peril, I believe the hearings should be brought to a prompt conclusion."

They weren't, and the humiliation continued for another five weeks. Now McCarthy and Cohn were lashing out at the Army, the press, even other senators on the committee who, Walter reported, wanted the names of McCarthy's anti-Communist informants. And Walter, who had arrived in Washington in a state of euphoria treating the hearings as if they were the Hauptmann or Jelke trial and writing gossip sidelights, had had his amusement quickly darken to malice as he realized what was happening. " 'We're going to get you,' " Washington journalist Murray Marder remembered hearing in a crowded elevator outside the Senate Caucus Room. "I turned around and it was Winchell. He started to snicker a little. I said, 'What did you say?' He said, 'We're going to get you.' I said, 'Who is "we"?' He said, 'All of us.' . . . There was no prelude or explanation, nothing."

By the time the hearings ended on June 17, with McCarthy shouting to be heard above the din of the departing senators and spectators, these threats had lost their sting. Surveys showed that two-thirds of American households with television sets had tuned into the hearings, and a Gallup poll showed that McCarthy's favorable rating had declined from 50 percent in January to 34 percent in June. Still, Walter, who knew his own fate was closely tied to theirs, continued to act as if McCarthy and Cohn had actually triumphed. "Roy Cohn's fan mail is 2nd only to McCarthy's," Walter wrote in his June 7 column. "The latter's is 95 p.c. pro . . . The McCarthy side is so far ahead they can coast in." Two weeks later Cohn appeared on Walter's simulcast to press his case personally. "If you are voted off the Committee, does that mean your service as a Communist fighter will be lost to the country?" Walter asked. "I intend to do whatever I can to continue in this fight against Communist infiltration, whether on or off the Committee," Cohn assured him. Taking another shot at Wechsler, Walter added that while he was covering the hearings, he had been told "that many anti-McCarthy newspapers in the nation have at least one editorial writer or rewrite slanter, somebody who can re-write the headlines to confuse the people or mislead them." When Cohn confirmed this analysis, Walter called for an investigation of Communist editors. "I think that should come before defense plants."

The next investigation, however, was of McCarthy, not by him. Sena-tor Ralph Flanders, a Vermont Republican, had filed a motion to censure McCarthy, and the Senate had empaneled a select bipartisan committee under Utah Republican Senator Arthur Watkins to weigh the evidence, including the charge that McCarthy had illegally obtained the Bolling memo that had found its way to Walter. Walter was on vacation that summer as the select committee began gathering material, but he re-turned in September ready to carry the fight for the fallen McCarthy, and on his initial broadcast he attacked members of the Watkins committee for "not being the unbiased angels most of them claim."

As it turned out, he was soon part of the investigation himself. On Sep-tember 7, just two days after Walter returned to the air, Watkins subpoe-naed him to testify how he got possession of the Bolling memo, obviously suspecting that it might have been passed to him by Cohn or McCarthy. (Even Robert Collier, the chief investigator for the Mundt committee, which was parent to McCarthy's subcommittee, told Hoover that he was "very concerned that Senator McCarthy may have permitted such a doc-ument to get into the hands of a gossip columnist.") In Watkins's office before his testimony, Walter admitted that his story about someone's slip-ping him the document while he was engaged in conversation sounded improbable. But sitting before the committee itself at 2:30 that afternoon in the same Senate Caucus Room where he had observed the Army-McCarthy drama, Walter was unwilling to elaborate. Asked by associate counsel Guy DeFuria what individual had given him the document, Wal-ter said, "I refuse to tell that." Asked on what ground he refused to an-swer, Walter said, "I will not reveal a source of information." He offered only that people were constantly coming up to him with memos and that he frequently accepted them with little more than a nod; this one he later destroyed, burning it and then flushing the ashes down the toilet at the Shoreham Hotel.

Walter was dismissed after an hour, with the committee no closer to an answer as to whether McCarthy had provided the document. But Walter had already seen how the drama would end. He broadcast the following Sunday that the committee would issue an unfavorable report. On the same broadcast he reported that the McCarthy committee was running out of funds. "The fight to expose 'Reds' will be curtailed," he said. "Several clerks and others on staff will be discharged this week." Roy Cohn had abandoned the committee over the summer. McCarthy himself had been neutralized. If the war wasn't over, at least the general had been cashiered.

But Winchell still could not give up the fight. In November, just days before the Watkins committee's recommendation was to be submitted to the full Senate for debate and days after the midterm election had stripped the Republicans of control of the Senate and McCarthy of his subcommittee chairmanship, Walter reported that McCarthy's supporters were intending to submit an amended resolution praising him for his fight against communism. Two weeks later he accused the committee of having withheld evidence. On the same broadcast he said, "Senator McCarthy's friends bluntly tell his enemies, 'People with glass jaws should not question glass elbows.'"

In the end the committee recommended censure. On December 2 the full Senate voted overwhelmingly to censure after reducing the charges to McCarthy's failure to cooperate with an earlier Senate committee investigating him and to his lambasting the Watkins committee itself, but the reduction in charges mitigated nothing. "As a creature of the same established power [that condemned him], McCarthy had no personal army to overturn the verdict," a victim of McCarthy's later wrote. "He was finished."*

And so McCarthy faded away in a torpor of drink, a symbol of a kind of madness most of the country wished quickly to forget. But Winchell was no less a symbol, and he could not fade away yet. Though in later years he attempted to distance himself from McCarthy—in his autobiography he called him a "madman" and bragged how he had stood up to him when McCarthy's "facts" didn't parse—the truth was that he had defended McCarthy to the last and would be tied to him forever. Henceforth most people would think of Winchell as a crazy reactionary who destroyed careers, exacted revenge, baited alleged Reds, flung lies and half-truths and generally engaged in the worst excesses of this shameful period. And it was all true. No matter how he justified his actions in his own mind, no matter how sincerely he felt that the liberals had cooked

---

*Unregenerate to the end, McCarthy accused the Communist Party of having "extended its tentacles to the most respected of American institutions, the United States Senate," with his censure. When his friend Senator Everett Dirksen pleaded with him to write letters of apology to two Senators he had offended, McCarthy, sounding exactly like Winchell, begged off. "I learned to fight in an alley. That's all I know."

up a conspiracy to ruin him and he was only fighting back, it was true that he had become a right-wing fanatic himself. All that he had done before McCarthy, all that he had represented, would be obliterated. All that would remain was this image of an angry, mean, foolish old man railing at the fates that had betrayed him.

IV

Now ABC wanted to cut its losses. Ever since the Baker incident there had been periodic quarrels between Walter and ABC president Robert Kintner. In January 1953, when Walter missed a broadcast, Kintner threatened him with loss of contract. "I thought I was selling a lot of watches," Walter fired back, referring to his sponsor, the Gruen Watch Company, "but you indicate that if I miss one show I might be fired. So the hell with that. I'm not getting the money I was supposed to get and when I think of all the gain (which took twenty five years to get) I threw away just to be on TV—it makes me realize I need a manager or an analyst." The next contract, he said, he would be demanding $16,000 per week and a simulcast.

In September he had gotten his simulcast, but relations with Kintner hadn't improved. ABC was now demanding to see his script in advance. "Walter being Walter objects strenuously to anyone seeing his copy," Kintner's liaison, Betty Forsling, wrote Rose Bigman. "Unlike radio, the TV show has to be prepared exactly. . . . In radio Walter didn't have to rely on anyone but himself, the announcer and an engineer. In TV the director and ad [assistant director] have to know what's going on[,] otherwise you will louse up the show."

Walter retaliated by gibing at ABC—he once wore a tie with "shit" written in Chinese script—but the network's patience was much thinner than it had been when Winchell was America's favorite commentator. Walter was slipping. His television ratings that fall placed him 111th among programs, his audience of 1.94 million homes far below the 12.97 million homes reached by the top-rated show, *Dragnet*. And his McCarthy crusade hadn't helped matters with advertisers. In December 1954, Gruen decided not to renew its option to sponsor the simulcast, though Bayuk cigars and the American Safety Razor Company, which manufactured Gem razor blades, assumed alternate sponsorship to begin the following February.

It was also in February that a New York court dismissed a libel action filed against Walter by the operators of a cancer clinic he had disparaged. Kintner sent Walter congratulations on the victory and mentioned casually that ABC's insurance would not have indemnified Walter for punitive damages for malice had he lost. If it was Kintner's intent to rouse Walter with this remark, as it almost certainly was, he succeeded.* Walter needed libel coverage. He later claimed that Kintner had advised him to write the ABC board demanding his insurance policy be revised. Instead Walter wrote Kintner a personal letter discussing the situation.

> [T]he shock of learning, as I did only recently, that the insurance people are not going to protect me all the way, has left me unhappy.
>
> So please go before the Board and ask them to allow you to give me a contract that does protect me completely for damages of any kind resulting from my broadcasts. That's what I have at the *Mirror* and I certainly would not have signed a contract with ABC if I thought it did not give me that protection. If the Board refuses to do this—then please release me, as I will not be any good to any of you. The fear would keep me from delivering the broadcasts that have kept me going for 25 years.

Walter obviously assumed—Kintner had probably led him to assume—that ABC would quickly revise the contract rather than risk losing him; he certainly wasn't issuing an ultimatum. He had, in any case, received feelers ·from another network about doing a variety show similar to Ed Sullivan's. He wrote the letter, then, secure in the belief that he was firmly in command of the situation, so secure that he hadn't even consulted Cuneo before sending it.

But Kintner, an ungainly and unattractive man, blubber-faced and beady-eyed, was a Machiavellian who in all likelihood had gulled Walter into a trap. A former Washington correspondent who had coauthored a syndicated political column with Joseph Alsop, Kintner was known at ABC as tough and wholly self-interested, a closet alcoholic who demeaned subordinates and undermined challengers; he once sabotaged a rival by urging him to sign up collegiate football and then instructing the sales force not to solicit ads.

In the Winchell matter, Kintner proved to be equally unscrupulous. "ABC wanted to get rid of him," Cuneo wrote of Walter. "The people hadn't lost him, as he insisted, but he had lost the people, and that's what

---

*In point of fact, Walter *was* covered for punitive damages, and Kintner was either ignorant or lying. ABC general counsel G.B. Zorbaugh wrote attorney Gerald Dunworth, then representing the network in another libel action involving Walter, that a binder issued by Continental Casualty Co. explicitly included punitive damages and explicitly covered any independent contractor, which is what Walter was.

he was getting paid for." Since writing his letter, Walter had been pushing ABC to respond to his request, realizing too late that the revision would not be pro forma. Finally, on March 8, Walter asked Leonard Goldenson, the president of ABC's parent company, to intervene. Goldenson refused. Two days later, a full month after Walter's letter, Kintner finally and bluntly responded to it:

> Referring to your letter of February 10, 1955, in which you asked that the Board of Directors of American Broadcasting-Paramount Theatres, Inc., revise your contract . . . the decision of the . . . Board of Directors was that this revision could not be made.
>
> Referring to your same letter of February 10, 1955, in which, in this event, you request that the Board release you from your contractual commitments for your radio, television, and consultant services to the American Broadcasting Company, the Board of Directors . . . has accepted your offer.

Walter was at first stunned and then angered. His lifetime contract, which Kintner had convinced him to take at the sacrifice of a sweeter deal, was now suddenly gone as well as the $520,000 he was earning from his television-radio broadcasts. Moreover, Walter had given the proceeds of his Warner-Hudnut stock, which was meant to compensate him partially for his sacrifice in salary, to the Runyon Fund. The day he received Kintner's letter Walter announced that he was leaving ABC "as fast as possible," even before his June termination date. The next day he held "informal discussions" with NBC vice-president Manny Sacks about moving to that network.

March 12, 1955, the day after his conversation with Sacks, was to be the blackest day in Winchell's career. As he told it, Hearst executive Charles McCabe and his own *Mirror* editor, Glenn Neville, told him that Dorothy Schiff had agreed to drop the Wechsler libel action if Walter would publicly apologize. If he didn't, the *Post* would drop its suit against his codefendant, the Hearst Corporation. In that event Hearst would not indemnify him for any damages should he lose the case. ABC had apparently also struck a deal with Schiff. Walter had no option but to settle and agree to a retraction. "I signed it to keep my contract and bankroll intact," he wrote in his autobiography, but actually he signed nothing until after his retraction. He did, however, issue a statement through Neville that "he never said or meant to say in The Mirror or over the air that The New York Post or its publisher, or James A. Wechsler, its editor, are Communists or sympathetic to communism. If anything which Mr. Winchell said was so construed, he regrets and withdraws it." His simul-

cast that weekend also began with an apology to Wechsler, though Walter
had the announcer read it. *Time* called it "the most abject retraction of
his career." Worse, the *Post* editorialized that the settlement "constitutes
not only vindication for ourselves but a dramatic setback for what has become known in mid-century America as the practice of McCarthyism."

Walter was devastated. Wechsler had won the three-year war, and he
had won a public humiliation of Walter Winchell. Winchell tried to sal-
vage some small residue of pride by continuing to refuse to sign the
agreement despite entreaties from Neville, Cuneo and Hearst executive
P. J. McCauley. ("We cannot possibly disavow our agreement or pretend
it didn't happen," Neville wrote him.) Finally, nearly three months after
the settlement, Walter relented and signed the releases, though Howard
Rushmore, writing in *Confidential* that fall, contended that Walter "to this
day has never retracted his charge that James A. Wechsler, editor of the
Post, was a former official of the Young Communist League." It was
small consolation for so overwhelming a defeat.

There was more. Just days before ABC terminated his lifetime contract
and the *Post* won its settlement, the Senate Banking and Currency Committee launched an investigation into why stock prices had risen so dramatically from September 1953 to November 1954 while the rest of the
economy stagnated, and it fingered Winchell as a culprit. Walter had
long included stock tips on his broadcast the way he had horse racing
tips. "The next day they would jump two, three points, and if it were a
cheap stock it would jump, say, ten points, and Walter would always
'cock-a-doodle-do,' as he said," recalled Jack O'Brian. For just as long the
Securities and Exchange Commission had been eyeing Walter for violations, and the Federal Communications Commission had been warning
him. Walter answered, according to ABC News President Tom Velotta,
that "as a newsman it is within his prerogative to broadcast any news
items of interest to his listeners. He further said that what he was saying
was true. . . ."

But on his January 9, 1955, broadcast, Walter goaded the SEC into action. He announced a "big piece of advance news": The Pantepec Oil
Company had discovered "substantial oil reserves in the El Roble fields
in Venezuela" and would award a dividend. *The New York Times* had reported the discovery back on November 24 with little effect on the market, but in the week prior to Walter's broadcast heavy volume had pushed
the stock from 5 1/2 to 6 3/4 points. The Monday after the broadcast the
value of each Pantepec share rose 2 points, leading *Time* to say, "There
is no doubt that some speculators are cleaning up on Winchell tips."
That prompted both the New York and American Stock exchanges to begin investigating every stock tipped by Walter in the previous eighteen
months.

As *The New York Times* reported it, on the opening day of Senator William Fulbright's Banking and Currency Committee hearings, "Walter Winchell's stock market tips dominated." Senator Prescott Bush suggested that Congress take action against tipsters, but Edward McCormick, the president of the American Stock Exchange, on which Pantepec Oil was traded, admitted that the *Times* had run substantially the same information as Walter and that he didn't know of "any instance where I could say that there had been a misstatement" by Winchell. (What McCormick didn't say was that Walter made Pantepec *sound* like a revelation.) Walter, while crowing that the stock volume only corroborated his popularity, issued a statement saying he had "no apology to offer for my vast circulation and the confidence of my followers in me." He also begged the committee to call him to testify. But Fulbright refused: "He is not the center of our attention."

Yet it wasn't for lack of trying on Walter's part. If Fulbright wouldn't invite him to testify, then he would invite the committee to his telecast. On his March 13 program—the same one that began with the apology to Wechsler—Senator Homer Capehart, a conservative Republican from Indiana who sat on the committee, served as interrogator, asking Walter the questions Fulbright declined to ask. Should commentators tout stocks? "I never recommend stocks. I never knock them, either. . . . I offer news in advance." Did he violate SEC law by tipping stocks? Walter said the SEC regional director had told the Associated Press that he had violated no regulations. Did he buy stocks himself? "I have never bought a stock—for myself." Over two years ago, he said, he, Marlene Dietrich, Jackie Gleason and several other show business personalities had gone to the exchange to solicit donations for the Runyon Fund. Just before the gong sounded ending trading, Walter told the brokers he wanted to return the compliment. "I'd like to buy something around here. What are you fellows selling in this store?" He came away with $50,000 worth of shares in AT&T, Du Pont and General Electric "for my family's security." While he seemed to be the one under scrutiny, it was the committee, he said, that was frightening the public and driving down stock prices. "When I was Wall Street's best press-agent booster, plus signs were blooming almost everywhere," he boasted, putting in a quick plug for Tri-Continental stock to show he was unbowed. And he closed by telling Capehart that all he wanted was to testify under oath before the committee.

Several days later the committee concluded its hearings without Walter's testifying and without recommending any new regulations, and the matter of Walter's stock manipulations quickly died. What remained, critic Gilbert Seldes wrote several months later, was the issue of television's growing influence: "Suppose that the reason for Winchell's relative potency is precisely the greater authority of the 'friend in the house' (the TV-oracle) and the greater susceptibility of an uncritical audience." In so doing, however, Seldes was implicitly rejecting another explanation which just a few years before would have been the only explanation: Walter Winchell's own power.

V

As Walter's troubles mounted, June Winchell left. She had suffered for years from respiratory problems and heart ailments and had found some relief in the dry heat of Arizona. Now she invited her sister and brother-in-law to help her find a site there for a retirement home for herself and Walter. The spot she chose was as different from the Broadway of which she had so disapproved as one could find: a remote sunbaked foothill on the northeast side of Camelback Mountain, where the ground was parched pinkish clay, coyotes roamed freely and rabbits abounded, the vistas stretched for miles, the silence yawned and the home of the nearest neighbor, Mrs. Maytag of the Maytag appliance fortune, was barely visible.

Here, on an eleven-acre plot largely shielded from the blacktop road by a wall of oleander bushes, June erected a low-slung ranch house of Hawaiian design that stood out among the earth tones. The exterior, of brick with weeping mortar, was painted purple to match a pair of June's favorite shoes; out back was a tree with a purple bloom, and purple flowers rimmed the front. June loved the sound of rain and had sprinklers installed so she could hear the patter. Inside, the master bedroom had been patterned after a hotel room, at Walter's insistence, and there were mirrors everywhere. June's ornate powder room gained local notoriety: Everything in it was glass and marble, and gold braids hung from the ceiling and skylight.

Though it had been intended for retirement, June soon made it her primary residence. She loved the desert; the isolation provided her the more subdued lifestyle she had long desired. Her only complaint was that she saw even less of Walter now than she had in New York when he lived at the St. Moritz and she lived at Twelve Acres. To see him she would have to visit Los Angeles when he happened to be there on one of his periodic forays or she would have to wait for one of his occasional visits when he needed escape or privacy or time to lick his wounds. Then he would stay for a few days, sometimes weeks, puttering around the house, and move on.

The same summer June moved to Arizona, Walda, then twenty-eight and finally divorced from William Lawless, announced her engagement to a forty-year-old twice-divorced banking executive named Hyatt von Dehn, whose father was said to be descended from Danish royalty and often entertained nobility at his posh home in the exclusive Bel Air section of Los Angeles. Walda and von Dehn were married on July 29, 1955, at the Beverly Hills Community Presbyterian Church, but this was to be no more placid a relationship than her first marriage. By mid-October, Walda was announcing divorce plans. By late October, she was announcing a reconciliation and a second honeymoon in Mexico. By the end of the year, von Dehn had reinstated the divorce action, and in January, hearing that Walda was planning to leave Los Angeles and tie up his assets unless he agreed to a substantial settlement, he hired a private investigator named Fred Otash to find her and serve her with the papers.

She was served on February 8, and the divorce became final in April after less than a year of marriage. Walda was terribly distraught. She retreated to Scottsdale for comfort and began taking instruction in the Catholic faith. Later that year she converted to Catholicism. In the meantime, she continued to see von Dehn long after their marriage had dissolved. It was roughly a year after Otash had served her, as the private investigator remembered it, that he received a call from Jerry Geisler, Walda's attorney. Walda was pregnant, *she* said by von Dehn, but he was denying responsibility, and Walter wanted Otash to investigate. Walda greeted her onetime adversary with good humor, agreeing to be wired and then go to bed with von Dehn. (How she carried this off, Otash didn't say.) In Otash's telling, she succeeded, and Geisler eventually reached a settlement with von Dehn.

While Walda drifted in and out of her tempestuous relationship with Hyatt von Dehn, her old boyfriend Billy Cahn had finally been dragooned into court where Walter had wanted him all along. In the official account, the Internal Revenue Service had been investigating a Cincinnati bookkeeper named Louis Rosenbaum who had paid Cahn for a gambling debt, a payment Cahn hadn't acknowledged on his tax return. That oversight turned the IRS onto Cahn himself and the discovery that he had failed to file tax returns for 1951 and 1952, though he had a gross income of $1,574.74 for the first year and $2,100 for the second. Now the U.S. attorney decided to try him for income tax evasion.

That, at least, was the official account. But anyone who knew Cahn's situation also knew that the IRS and the Justice Department weren't going to the trouble of a criminal prosecution over less than $4,000 of unreported income unless there was something else involved. "I'll tell you a concept that I'm ninety-nine percent sure happened," Jack O'Brian later said. "John Edgar Hoover did it all for Walter. He went and dug into it and dug into it and dug into it." Walter, O'Brian said, admitted as much. When Cahn's attorney questioned the IRS over why it was bothering to prosecute so insignificant a case, he was told, "Somebody got hold of Mr. Cahn's file on some kind of a tip and put a big 'R' on it which says 'Racket' and that was a racket file from then on." Subsequently the IRS spent three years scouring Cahn's finances but had only a $600 check from a man who had played gin rummy with Cahn, payments of $954.74 from Cahn's employer, Henry Rosenfeld, a $1,500 check from a garage and another $600 from a company named Display-Rite. "Here is this big racketeer!" Cahn's attorney sneeringly told the court.

Nevertheless, Cahn stood trial in December and was convicted. During his summation Cahn's attorney had asked, "Who is pushing whom? What is going on here? Where does all this come from? I don't know." At the sentencing he seemed to have an answer: "Mr. Cahn has unfortunately run into the ill will of a well-known and perhaps notorious columnist and radio broadcaster." Cahn was sentenced to eighteen months in a federal penitentiary and was refused bail. "[H]e is a very footloose person," said the court. "At least law enforcement agencies have had difficulty picking him up in the past."

Cahn served his sentence, then kicked around California and, as one friend remembered it, finally emigrated to Israel. Only there, at long last, did he escape the implacable vengeance of Walter Winchell.

Whatever Walda had become, Walt, Jr., was perceived as a disaster. Growing up neglected, he had searched vainly for affection and for some niche in which he could comfortably fit. He found neither. What he found instead was the burden of being the son of a famous man. "I can't live with the name of Winchell," he told Seymour Mayer. "I'm tired of fighting, getting beat up." "Walter hated his name," his wife concurred. "He just totally, utterly hated it. Most of the time when he went out, he identified himself as someone else."

But at the same time there was his father's legacy to follow, which, Walt, Jr., seemed to believe, was the only way he could gain his father's attention and his love. Walter encouraged him in this. He asked his friend Art Ford, who had a recording studio in his home on 61st Street, if he would train Walt, Jr., for the radio and then asked WINS to let the boy broadcast the news once a week for experience. Columnist Bob Sylvester, acting on his own initiative, got Walt, Jr., a job in the music library at another station. Radio didn't pan out, so Walt lied about his age and joined the Marines in July 1952, then was discharged later that year when the deception was discovered.

Again at loose ends, he returned to New York. Though he was a high school dropout and an obvious malcontent who loved provocation, he was also handsome and charming and verbally dexterous, and Walter hadn't yet given up on him. He asked his old friend Curley Harris if Harris might get him a job on a newspaper. "Easy enough," Harris told him. "People would hire him because of [his being] Winchell's son."

"Would it have to be that way?" Walter queried. "Well, it would be pretty much," Harris said, "because what can he do?"

Walter left for California, entrusting young Walt to Harris's care. While Walter was gone, Harris imposed upon Gene Pope, the publisher of the New York *Enquirer*, to hire Walt as a columnist. Shortly after his columns began appearing, Harris got a call from Walter. He was steaming. "I want it stopped," he demanded. Taken aback by Walter's reaction, Harris said that in getting Walt the job, he was only doing what Walter had asked him to do. "Well, I don't want him doing it," Walter snapped. "It cheapens me. It's no good for me."

When Harris met Walt, Jr., at Toots Shor's to deliver the ultimatum, he found the young man was surprisingly stubborn. He told Harris he liked the job, and he wasn't going to quit. Deep down, though, Walt knew he couldn't defy his father; instead, he retained the job and then self-destructed on it. Down in the *Enquirer*'s print room there was a linotype machine that used lead bars. As Harris told it, Walt, Jr., drove his MG to the plant and loaded it with bars. "It wasn't worth anything," Harris said. "You couldn't sell it for more than a few dollars. He just wanted to steal something, I guess." But Pope fired him for the theft, and Walt was back on the road to aimlessness.

Having wrecked his son's brief columnar career, as he had wrecked Walda's theatrical career, Walter was still encouraging him. When Walt contributed a short piece to a column in Mexico, his father wrote him enthusiastically that he was "delighted with it and the breezy descriptive style. Oh no! Not another writer in the family!" Then Walter gave some advice: "Seriously, son, I knew you had a flair for writing when you were fifteen and younger. Especially the time you jotted down that excellent report of the visit to General MacArthur. But don't ever write because you think you must. Write only when you feel like you want to. But you have to write a lot to keep in practise [*sic*], I have been told, and there is probably something to that—since you can get rusty when you lay off too long. I know. It has happened to me when the vacations are long."

Walt was, in fact, a talented writer, but he had neither his father's discipline nor his drive, and he frittered away his talent the way he frittered away everything. He much preferred raising hell. Rose Bigman remembered that he liked to pour ketchup over himself and pretend he was wounded. Art Ford remembered walking with him one evening past a cafeteria on Lexington Avenue when Walt said he was going inside and asked Ford to wait for him. Ford waited and then watched as the cafeteria quickly filled with yellow smoke. Walt raced out grinning. "It worked, didn't it?" he beamed over his smoke bomb. On another occasion he took some children for pizza and jokingly pulled a gun on the stunned clerk.

When his antics failed to gain his father's attention, he found father figures to give him what Walter could not: an aged neighborhood friend who took an interest in him; Ernest Cuneo; the old New York newspaper editor Gene Fowler. "He has never set out to deliberately hurt or maim anyone who hasn't deserved it in the extreme," he once wrote Fowler about Walter in one of many letters. "His ethics, Gene, have always been of the highest. People he has boosted and bled for have turned on him down through the years, and it never fails to cause him anguish. . . .

"Dad reveres the newspaper game to the extent that nothing else except patriotism and my mother have ever entered his heart," he continued, pointedly leaving out himself and Walda. "Other men have hobbies: golf, fishing, stamp collecting, watching baseball games, or chorus girls. Dad's relaxation comes mainly from meeting the challenge of a blank piece of paper." He closed: "He's a champion, Gene, and there are damn few like him left around. . . ." How could the son ever live up to that?

VI

These were low days now. That summer of 1955, Walter's obligation to ABC fulfilled, he reached agreement with the Mutual Broadcasting System for a new radio program, but after the McCarthy debacle and the settlement with the *Post*, he was more supplicant than commander. He was having to bargain with Mutual to pick up his libel insurance (Walter proposed to pay the premium himself in return for a slight increase in salary to help defray the cost) and to provide a ten-thousand-share stock option deal along the lines of the one Warner-Hudnut had offered. John Teeter, the Runyon Fund administrator who was advising Walter on the deal, wrote frankly, "It will look better in the trade circles if your salary is higher." (In the event, no salary was announced.)

Walter tried to put the best face on the deal. He boasted in Jack O'Brian's column that he would now be heard on 592 stations and that he could "enjoy some of the luxuries I gave up when I went into TV"— namely, broadcasting from Los Angeles and Miami again. But no matter what gloss he put on it, Mutual was a comedown from ABC, and a six o'clock radio program each Sunday evening hardly compensated for the loss of the television simulcast. And it was television now that obsessed him.

It obsessed him not because he liked the medium any better than he had but because he could not admit to having failed where Ed Sullivan was succeeding and because now more than ever he needed vindication. Already he had petitioned ABC to nullify his own February 10 letter and its March 10 letter and let him fulfill his original contract. When ABC rejected the suggestion, Walter filed a $7-million-dollar lawsuit against the network that September for having misled him about his libel insurance. With ABC ruled out, he approached CBS and NBC, both of which had courted him in the past, but neither leaped for him now.

A meeting with NBC head David Sarnoff was "pleasant," but Sarnoff spent it largely commending Walter for his anti-Communist activities rather than offering a job. At another meeting Walter told the CBS president, Frank Stanton, "I turned you down to stay with ABC seven years ago. Now, here's your chance to turn me down. Would you consider me for things other than commentating—panels, quizzes, variety? I don't want to be off TV." Stanton told him not to worry. "I never heard from Frank after that." Later Walter said he had been told that Sullivan had thrown a "tantrum," hearing that Winchell might join the network. When CBS VP Hubbell Robinson, Jr., issued a statement that the network had never discussed Walter's employment with Sullivan, Walter sent back the release with a note scribbled on it: "Dear Hub This is BULLSH!" "As time went on, I felt like a beggar," he candidly told an interviewer. "Was it possible I was washed up? People were saying I had lost my marbles, that I'd never get my body off the canvas. For a year and a half, I went through agony."

For the first time Walter had also hired an agent, Wallace Jordan of William Morris, to help find him a television outlet, and Jordan was lobbying the NBC-TV president, Sylvester "Pat" Weaver, to let Walter take over the "NBC Comedy Hour" spot from eight to nine on Sunday evening opposite Sullivan. NBC, Jordan reported to Walter, was divided. Weaver wanted to continue the "Comedy Hour" until the fall, at which time he would reconsider putting Walter on the air. Privately, however, Weaver told Jack O'Brian that he "wouldn't have that yapping Winchell voice on the network."

Angered and depressed over the way he was being treated, Walter retreated to Miami with Jane Kean that winter and seemed determined to give others the chance he was being denied. He would become an impresario.

One night Jane took Walter to a club off the beach called Murray Franklin's. The entertainment was a plain, sandpaper-voiced female singer who appeared in a shawl and spectacles. Her name was Roberta Sherwood. "Why don't you tell the world?" Jane's mother, Helen, asked

Walter after he had praised her. So he did. Promoting her daily in the column, Walter made Sherwood, a middle-aged mother of three whose husband was stricken with cancer, a household name. Jules Podell at the Copacabana in New York booked her for three weeks on the basis of Walter's raves. Walter called her debut there that June "the most thrilling in Copa history."

On that same trip Walter was about to return to New York when he missed his flight. This time Jane took him to a shabby hotel called the Golden Nugget, where Rowan & Martin, a comedy act she had seen and enjoyed, were playing. When Walter arrived, there were fewer than a dozen people in the audience. "Well, the proprietor was so thrilled," Jane recalled about Walter's appearance. "Mr. Big, you know. So he invited everybody from the lobby to come in so that there'd be an audience for Rowan and Martin." Dan Rowan said that Walter "roared with laughter" and then waited for the team at the bar afterwards to congratulate them. Driving north to their next engagement, which was in Montreal, the comedians stopped to phone their agent, who was exultant: Walter had devoted an entire column to the act. Now offers were pouring in from nightclubs. Universal and Paramount wanted to test them for the movies, and NBC for television. Their fee zoomed as the Keans' had.

While the campaigns for Sherwood and Rowan & Martin demonstrated that Walter's power hadn't completely dissipated, he seemed powerless to help himself. He returned to New York still desperate for a TV program and despondent over his sudden fall from grace. ("Influence is something you think you have until you have to use it," he told an interviewer.) He spent that spring and summer miserably—lost and lonely. In Las Vegas for the Tournament of Champions golf tournament, which was raising money for the Runyon Fund, Walter invited Al Rylander, a former press agent, to join him for opening night of the Ritz Brothers at the Dunes Hotel.

"There's a line all the way around," Rylander recalled. "He goes up and says, 'My name is Walter Winchell, and you have a reservation for me.' The guy doesn't even look up. He says, 'Get to the end of the line.' Walter says, 'My name is Walter Winchell, and I have a reservation.' The guy still doesn't look up. He says, 'How many times do I have to tell you that I've got a long line and I'm busy?' And Winchell again, for the third time, says, 'There is a reservation in my name.' And the guy throws down the pencil and says, 'Will you get the hell out of here?' "

Walter stormed off, Rylander keeping pace. As they headed toward the parking lot, they ran into Major Riddle, the Dunes's owner, who greeted them effusively and asked where they were going. "And like a viper, he [Walter] turns to him and he says, 'Go and fuck yourself, you cocksucker!' " Leaving Riddle behind confused and speechless, Walter turned to Rylander and said, "Al, you have just seen the beginning of the end of a major columnist."

Now his professional crisis was joined by a personal crisis. "As much as my mother liked Walter," Jane Kean recalled, "she said, 'People are going to say that you're his woman.... You just cannot go on with that. He's married.' " With Mary Lou, marriage had never really been an issue; she understood the terms, understood that Walter wouldn't leave June. Jane did not. She told Walter that she would leave him unless and until he got a divorce.

Walter agonized, no more in control of his romance than of his career. He admitted to Sherman Billingsley that he was deeply unhappy. Billingsley advised that if he was *that* unhappy, he should get a divorce. "And he did go to Phoenix, and he asked her," Jane Kean recounted. "She said, and I quote, 'You think I'm going to divorce you now and let her have you after what I went through in the early years? All the agony that I've gone through? I should just now give you over and get a divorce and hand you over to her?' He told me that. He never lied to me. So I believe that."

Whether or not it was true, whether or not Walter actually had had the fortitude to confront June, he was now going to lose Jane. They met in the lobby that joined the St. Moritz, Walter's residence, to 40 Central Park South, the building where Jane lived with her mother. Sitting with him on the sofa there, Jane explained that her mother had cancer and that Jane's relationship with Walter was torturing the dying woman. "It's not that I don't love you or that I no longer care," she told him, "but I just can't do this to Helen."

Walter cried. But as he had with Mary Lou, he also turned vindictive. Now when they ran into each other, he snubbed her, and the column mentions, which had once been responsible for bankrolling an entire Broadway production for the Kean Sisters called *Ankles Aweigh*, ceased. It was years later that Jane stopped him on the street while he was walking past her again and demanded a truce. Cornered, Walter reluctantly agreed and took her to lunch at Rumpelmayer's.

Occasionally, after she had resettled in California, he called her there when he was in town; once they even went to a baseball game together. But, as with Rita Greene and Mary Lou Bentley, she belonged now to the past, and he never mentioned her publicly again.

As THE 1955–1956 television season entered summer, Walter still had no show, and the prospects for getting one seemed bleak. "He wanted TV so hard he could taste it," said Jack O'Brian. "I thought he was going to be terrific. Walter was never a newspaperman. He was a showman." So O'Brian began campaigning in his column for NBC to sign Winchell, and when Pat Weaver still refused, O'Brian and a press agent named Harry Sobol circumvented Weaver by lining up two sponsors and bringing the package to David Sarnoff's son, Robert, an executive of NBC's parent company, RCA. Robert Sarnoff signed the program for thirteen weeks.

Scheduled for an October premiere, "The Walter Winchell Show" was described vaguely as a half-hour variety program "with not much talk or long introductions." Even though it was evident that Walter, the man who had always prided himself on being an innovator rather than imitator, was imitating Ed Sullivan, he was giddy at the prospect of being back on TV. Everyone noticed the change. Klurfeld said that he was ubiquitous that summer: "At Lindy's he emitted a shrill fingers-in-the-mouth whistle to attract the attention of startled diners and suddenly began introducing celebrities. He walked uninvited onto the Paramount stage, where Frank Sinatra was appearing to launch his new movie, and introduced several performers. He spoke to any newspaperman who would listen, even high school editors." Another observer, remarking on the peculiarity of Walter's sudden accessibility after decades of being unapproachable, thought it hastened the end of his mystique. "One of the things that excited curiosity in Winchell was his unavailability. Now you can find him in any club, just like any Broadway columnist."

And not only in the clubs. With June in Scottsdale and Jane Kean gone from his life, Walter was hanging around Broadway the way he had in the old *Vaudeville News* days. He especially liked mixing with the nightbeat photographers who congregated in and around Lindy's at 51st Street and Broadway. They all parked their cars across the street at Hanson's drugstore while one of them monitored the police radio. At 12:30 a.m. Walter would pull up in front of Lindy's in his Cadillac, have his breakfast, then mingle with the photographers. "He would hang around until one of us would say, 'Do you want to go for a ride?'" remembered one young photographer named Joel Landau. And Landau also recalled that the first thing Walter always did after getting into the car was adjust his fedora as if preparing for a performance.

He drew especially close to Landau that summer, meeting him five or six nights a week and seeming to imbibe the young man's energy. Landau remembered him as paternal. Walter lectured Landau on morality, romance, drink and diet. But mostly they would cruise the streets—stopping off at the Belmore Cafeteria, where the cabdrivers ate, or at DuBrow's, where he would pick the nuts off Landau's Danish pastry, or at the Brasserie, where he would look out at the sunrise and quote Runyon on the "tubercular light of dawn." Sometimes, when he was feeling particularly chipper and didn't want to cruise, he stood on the sidewalk outside Lindy's in the middle of the night and broke into his vaudeville routine. "Right out in the public there, he'd just break into a tapdance," recalled Art Ford. "That was his way of saying: Right now I'm on top of the world. I'm happy."

But Walter's essential loneliness was unmistakable. Landau remembered cruising past a nursing home on Central Park West and Walter commenting wistfully that the very first "three-dot" columnist was lying there now, sick and alone. When one of the photographers told Walter about a recent press party, Walter asked why no one had thought of inviting him. (In fact, everyone had thought he would be too busy.) Coleman Jacoby, then a press agent, also remembered Walter hanging around the Taft Hotel barbershop as he had in the old days, only now he was "jollying up a bunch of guys that were laughing him up or he was laughing them up." Watching him, Jacoby immediately thought of a line in *Death of a Salesman*: "You get a smudge on your hat and it's all over." Now there was a smudge on Walter Winchell's hat.

HE HAD broken with nearly everyone. Finally came Sherman Billingsley's turn. The story, as it circulated in the papers and among the Broadway cognoscenti that summer, was that Walter was dining at the Stork Club with executives from the advertising agency of Walter's new television sponsor, P. Lorillard, when a cigarette girl placed two packages of Old Gold cigarettes, a P. Lorillard product, on the table.

Walter, thinking this was a courtesy of Billingsley's, thanked him. The next day the cigarette girl, Delores Stamkowich, was fired. Billingsley, Walter heard, was paid to promote Chesterfield cigarettes, and Stamkowich had acted on her own in giving Walter the Old Golds.

Walter was shocked. "I can't get over it," he told one reporter. "We've been together over 30 years. At one time he thought I was a wonderful guy." To another he admitted, "I'm sick from it all." But Walter now refused to set foot in the Stork, and Billingsley took down his photo from its place of honor, cracking, "I just didn't want anybody to steal the picture." Meanwhile, Walter got Stamkowich a job addressing envelopes at the Runyon Fund and then passing out cigarettes for his sponsor at conventions.

But the flap over the cigarettes was clearly a pretext for a deeper grievance between the old comrades. "He talked to me about Billingsley quietly, confidentially, as if Billingsley were a man he never trusted," said

Arnold Forster. Al Rylander thought that Billingsley had made a derogatory remark at which Walter had taken umbrage. Sally Dawson, Billingsley's young assistant, thought the feud had something to do with Walter's wanting to bring a guest—she vaguely remembered the transsexual Christine Jorgensen—of whom Billingsley disapproved. Curley Harris traced it to Walter's learning that Billingsley had given information to the *Post* during its series so that the paper would go easy on him. "I'll just have to be more careful picking my friends in the future," Walter had told Harris, adding ominously, "I'll handle his case in my own way."

Walter's own version of the rift, as he told it in his autobiography, was that Billingsley had asked him to attack a woman who had been circulating gossip about Billingsley's private affairs, and Walter had refused. "I can get all the other guys to do it," Billingsley said. Walter was hurt that he would be regarded as another journalist for sale. "Gee, Sherman," he sneered, "thanks for not including me in that dozen." That same summer Billingsley was reported to have said of the press, "I can buy them all for a few neckties or a bottle of perfume." But Winchell was not exactly conciliatory either. That June, a Stork Club employee wrote Walter scolding him for "the way you talked and the remarks you made to my boss in the presence of several very important guests."

For his part, Billingsley attributed it all to Winchell's jealousy over television. While Walter had been agonizing over TV, Billingsley, in 1950, signed with CBS to host an interview program originating from the Stork Club. By every measure the diffident, inarticulate Billingsley was horrendous as a television personality. "Every night was a crisis," claimed his producer, Gary Stevens. "He was totally unprofessional. He didn't know what the hell he was doing." He once asked Admiral William Halsey when Halsey had graduated from West Point, and actress Celeste Holm to send him tickets when her new show opened, even though it had been running for six months. His most serious gaffe occurred on May 8, 1955, when he was shuffling through a stack of photographs with singer Carl Brisson and came to one of the restaurateur Toots Shor. "Want to know something?" Billingsley remarked ingenuously. "I wish I had as much money as he owes." "Owes to you or somebody else?" Brisson asked. "Everybody—oh, a lot of people," Billingsley answered. Shor filed a $1.1 million libel suit.

Still, for all his ineptitude, Billingsley honestly believed he had finally trumped Winchell on television. For one thing, Billingsley's program had been expanded to a half-hour in 1952 while Walter's simulcast was only fifteen minutes. "About all he has time to do with a guest is say, 'Hello, kiss my ass, and goodbye,'" Billingsley bragged to an employee. For another thing, back in March 1955, when Walter was deep in crisis over the

Post suit, his ABC contract and the Senate investigation of stock tips, he had asked Billingsley to cede him the first fifteen minutes of "The Stork Club" so that he might have additional time to answer the committee's charges. Billingsley wired Walter refusing to surrender his time and claiming that press releases had already been issued and commitments to talent made. "Besides all this I just have to think about myself first," Billingsley wrote. Walter circled the comment: "To Mrs. W. Boy, what a revealing statement! The old Run out when a feller needs a friend dept."

When all the rest—the Stamkowich matter, the insinuations about co-operation with the *Post*, the public disdain for the press—was mounted on this ingratitude, the relationship finally broke. Walter had his lawyer advise the Stork that it could no longer display his photo (though it no longer did so anyway), make any reference on the menu to his name or use his name or photo in conjunction with the club.

And so it continued through the fall, long after Billingsley's program had been canceled and Walter's new one had begun; it continued despite the obvious pain both men were suffering—Walter denied his throne, Billingsley denied his mouthpiece. Walter claimed he stayed away for three years, but this seemed an exaggeration to prove his obstinacy. As Jack O'Brian remembered it, O'Brian, his wife, Yvonne, Walter and June, who had returned to New York that fall to lend Walter moral support for his program, had had dinner at Danny's Hideaway and were walking to the St. Moritz. June looked at O'Brian and said, "He still misses the Stork Club." O'Brian said that Walter should make up with Billingsley. "We talked as if Walter weren't there," O'Brian recalled. Finally Walter interrupted. Yes, he would make up with Billingsley. "But I'm going to take my time."

By Walter's own description, he walked into the Stork one night unannounced and was perusing the menu when Billingsley sidled up to him. "He embraced me with a tight little hug and then wept," Walter wrote. With that gesture, the feud was over, the transaction renewed. "We never had a difference of opinion of any import again."

PLEASE REPORT TO THE OFFICE AT ONCE, Walter wired Rose Bigman as the summer of 1956 drew to a close and he prepared for the new TV program: STOP LIVING LIKE A MILLIONAIRE AND START WORKING LIKE A WINCHELL. Walter was still exhilarated. He spent early September touring the fifteen top Trendex rating markets in what *Variety* called "one of the most concentrated premiere buildups in TV." In Washington alone he did twenty-three spots and then phoned the FBI's public relations director L. B. Nichols to expatiate on his plans. NBC

was spending $500,000 to promote the new show, and Old Gold ciga-
rettes another $250,000, he said. He had a thirteen-week contract, and
NBC had already picked up a second option, but he was balking at a
third, preferring to go back to Hollywood to work on a movie, *How the
G-Men Caught Lepke*, which "will do the Bureau much good." He said he
had also attended President Eisenhower's press conference the previous
day and gloated that the President singled him out and shook his hand.

When he returned to New York, he became a dynamo. Journalist Peter
Maas, following Walter for a *Collier's* cover story, found him zipping
manically around Broadway, dropping backstage to invite performers to
appear on his show, tracking down police calls, attending a fund-raiser for
Tammany Hall chief Carmine DeSapio, dancing with Elizabeth Taylor at
El Morocco and offering Deborah Kerr a ride to her hotel before setting
off for more police calls. He even took time to testify before a congressional committee investigating monopolistic practices in television and
charged Kintner with having bullied sponsors into dropping his show. "I
am unhappy because of the double-cross," Walter complained to the congressmen, "which has forced me to go back to be a vaudeville performer
for NBC." And he added in a final swipe at the medium that had rejected
him, "I am a newspaperman first. My second love is radio. TV comes
third."

When Walter met the press the next day to promote the new program,
he hardly seemed a reluctant vaudevillian. "I'll have a great show," he
told the reporters. "It'll be different, but I'm not going to tell you how
different because somebody'll steal it. But you can print this: if the first
one is bad, I won't be around for the second one, and NBC can start su-
ing." Unable to conceal one of the motives that impelled him, he began
attacking Ed Sullivan again. Asked to comment, Sullivan said, "I think
WW is on the verge of a nervous breakdown, and if his first show isn't
good—that may bring it about."

Walter arrived on the set for rehearsals beaming. "This is where I
belong," he told a production assistant. "This is show business." But
as the October 5 debut of "The Walter Winchell Show" approached and
he realized that television wasn't vaudeville, elation turned to anxiety,
just as it had when he made *Wake Up and Live*. "This TV business is
really strange to me," he admitted to an interviewer. "For my news
shows, all I had to do was walk out on camera with my own pitcher of
water, oscillator and script. Now all the talk is about 'markings' and
'spread three minutes.' It's a new world to me."

But it wasn't just about mastering television. It was about proving all
his detractors wrong, and it was about surviving. "All the ingrates were
having the big laugh," he told Peter Maas. "They said I was through."

Initially, at least, Walter seemed vindicated. Though the show was a conventional half hour variety program—the only innovation was a "jury box" on stage with celebrities—Walter was a superb host: dynamic, self-deprecating, seemingly comfortable, confident, even charismatic. Jack Gould, writing in *The New York Times* the day after the premiere, said, "Mr. Winchell seems to be one more example of the old truism that once a person appears before the footlights he never entirely forgets the knowhow. . . . If he could relax even a little more, he could cut quite a figure on TV." Harriet Van Horne in the *World-Telegram and Sun* wrote, "It's probably a redundancy to proclaim the excellence here, since I've a feeling he'll be pretty busy this week proclaiming it in his own column. But there's no gainsaying it, Mr. Winchell has a smart, entertaining show all the way."

There were, however, dissenters. John Crosby at the *Herald Tribune* suspected that Walter's relatively low budget would make it difficult for him to compete with Sullivan for guests. Jay Nelson Tuck at the *Post* believed Walter could compensate what he lacked in budget by what he still retained in column clout, but he chided him for wearing his trademark fedora and for tossing cigarette butts on the stage. Surprisingly, Jack O'Brian, who took responsibility for getting Walter the program, also took him to task. "Walter's premiere would have been far better," he opined, "if his vocal and emotional level had been several decibels below a shout. . . ."

Walter himself seemed entirely satisfied. Herman Klurfeld remembered him at the party at the Plaza Hotel after the debut, mixing with celebrities and once again basking in attention in what Klurfeld called "his last glow." The next day, still flush with excitement, he took an entourage of newsboys to see singer-dancer Sammy Davis Jr. in the Broadway musical *Mr. Wonderful*—Davis had appeared on his program—and then marched them up the aisle in the middle of the performance, took the stage and declared what a great country this is.

Despite the generally favorable reaction to the program, the show was quickly engulfed in tension and chaos—mainly Walter's. His production assistant, Claire Russhon, thought it was a matter of Walter's having overcommitted himself. "[He had] the column, the broadcast and then the variety show, which he was happy doing, but it was just too much to do. . . . We were all having nervous breakdowns." "Nobody knew what they were doing, really," Rose Bigman said. "Until the last minute they didn't know who was going to be the guest or anything like that." Amid the chaos Walter became a "nervous wreck." "He was yelling at everybody."

Thirty years later Alan Handley, the program's director, described

"The Walter Winchell Show" as the "worst experience of my life"—one so traumatic that he hesitated to dredge up the memories. Walter, he said, had definite ideas on what he wanted to do with the program and would not be dissuaded. (One of those ideas was the "jury box," which Handley called "Creepy Peepers" since he thought it was eerie watching celebrities watching a show.) More, Walter would call Handley at all hours of the morning, and when Handley objected, Walter would snap, "If you don't want to talk to me, take the phone off the hook."

But if this was an example of Walter's normal egotism, over the course of the year he was also showing evidence of behavior that could no longer be laughed away as eccentric. Often he seemed manic and paranoid; during the Washington leg of his NBC tour in September, he had phoned the FBI insisting that "Pinkerton men, G-men or cops" had moved across the hall from his hotel room and kept their door open so he could peer in. He wanted to know if the FBI was tailing him. When the ratings for "The Walter Winchell Show" began coming in and he realized that the program was less than the hit for which he had so fervently hoped, his behavior turned so erratic that one had to question his mental stability. Now, Handley remembered, he would call, tell Handley, "I took the big one," meaning a sleeping pill, and drone on unintelligibly; Rose said he was often so heavily sedated on Miltown that she had to have the hotel manager open his door at the St. Moritz and she had to pull him out of bed to ready him for the broadcast. At an Eisenhower rally in Madison Square Garden that October he reportedly forced his way onto the podium the way he had at *Mr. Wonderful* and took over as master of ceremonies. Another night, he was sitting in his Cadillac on Broadway when three teenagers, recognizing him, strolled over to chat. Walter became annoyed, got out of his car, pulled his revolver, lined the teens up against the wall and then marched them to the police station, demanded they be arrested, though the officers could think of no charges on which to book them.

Jane Kean, observing Walter's peculiar behavior from a distance, thought it might have had something to do with their break-up. But Winchell's disintegration that fall was more than the product of romantic disappointment, even if he hadn't already begun ceaselessly promoting a sultry young singer named Lisa Kirk, with whom a romance was rumored. It was a concession of a prideful and wounded man, a concession that he had finally been defeated. Even on the television program, his confidence seemed visibly to ebb by the week; he was edgy, downbeat, his timing and focus were off. He became fixated on criticisms of his wearing his hat on the air; when Jimmy Durante appeared, he made a point of asking if anyone had ever objected to his wearing a hat on stage and ad-libbed, "Chevalier wears his and a couple of other people."

He could not go down peaceably. In the column he attacked a *Daily News* reporter who published his latest and lowest ratings. "She never mentioned them when they led the field. (See???) . . . She and the other 'I hope he flops' brigade (who played up our dive bomb) were not good enough reporters to add that our competition had their ratings taken in 15 cities while WW had his taken in 14 (See???) In other words, decimal points and arithmetic can break you overnight if you let them . . . But we plan to break the heart of the ratings people (and especially the networks and agencies that support them) by writing an exposé about them all for a national magazine. . . ."

In fact, Walter's ratings hadn't been bad at the outset. The A. C. Nielsen survey indicated that his program had a viewership of roughly seven million homes, which made him competitive most weeks with ABC and CBS. But as the season progressed, his ratings kept declining while those of CBS's "Zane Grey Theater" rose, nearly doubling Walter's rating on November 2 and 9 and doing only slightly worse on the two successive weeks. Walter blamed a lack of advertising, an inadequate budget, an inappropriate time slot. Handley blamed Walter's oversized personality: "He couldn't integrate himself into a TV show, and we couldn't feel superior to him the way we could to Sullivan." Whatever the reason for the program's lack of success, by month's end Old Gold and Toni had announced they would not be picking up an option for another thirteen weeks and that the program would terminate with the December 28 broadcast.

Walter publicly declared that he was relieved by the cancellation. "I don't feel like a dead duck," he told reporters at a press conference he called, though he clearly was one now. "My big disappointment is that I don't have my TV newscast. . . . I said that in the first place. I'm a news commentator but they put me on variety. Small time. When it comes to variety, TV is strictly minor league." He swore that his sponsors loved the program. "I've never had a flop. I've never lost a sponsor in my life" (which wasn't exactly true). He vowed again that he would expose the rating system "which devastates and puts performers out of work." And he swore vengeance: "I want to get back at a lot of people. If I drop dead before I get to the Z's in the alphabet, you'll know how I hated to go."

Though canceled, the program still had six weeks to run. In the meantime, Walter had gotten an offer to do the narration for *Beau James*, a film biography of Mayor Jimmy Walker starring Walter's friend Bob Hope; no doubt partly to avoid humiliation in New York, he decided to accept the offer and shift "The Walter Winchell Show" to the West Coast for its swan song. Handley urged him to begin booking guests immediately. Walter boasted that he could get anyone he wanted once he arrived, but he had overestimated his pull. Discovering that guests were reluctant to appear on a failing program, he instructed Handley to book whomever he could, and the show limped to its conclusion, its new theme song, "Give My Regards to Broadway," sounding a knell for a bygone era to which Walter belonged, and its festive New Year's Eve party motif on the final performance forming a strange counterpoint to the depression Walter was suffering.

At the end Al Rylander, now an NBC executive, was present in the studio when an account executive handed Walter a gold lighter as a token of the sponsors' appreciation and mourned the program's passing. Walter took the lighter and threw it hard against the wall. What Rylander remembered then was silence—"absolute silence."

By the time "The Walter Winchell Show" was canceled, Walter had lost his radio sponsor too. In signing with Mutual the previous September, he had thanked Tom O'Neil, the president of Mutual's parent company, effusively: "I will never forget, Tom, that when nobody else wanted me you gave me a microphone." Meanwhile, the Seaboard Drug Company had agreed to underwrite the new broadcast after Walter, under Curley Harris's self-interested prodding earlier that spring, had plugged the company's arthritis drug, Mericin, and its sales soared. (Harris had gotten $1,000 for his efforts.) "I feel free again working for Mutual because you told them you wanted me to be the 'old Winchell,'" Walter wrote the Seaboard president Harry H. Patterson after the September 10 debut.

But Seaboard's enthusiasm for Winchell was short-lived when the "old Winchell" turned out to be not the populist Winchell of the thirties and the war years or even the Winchell of the immediate postwar period but the rabid, vicious, unreliable Winchell of the McCarthy era. Though McCarthy had been discredited and the country was searching for a political consensus, Walter continued to Red-bait, issuing warnings on everyone from a Broadway dance instructor ("alleged secret work for the Red spy network here") to playwright Arthur Miller to *The New York Times*, which became a favorite target of Walter's attacks. He even served notice to his own paper, reporting that the Senate Internal Security Committee had subpoenaed a *Mirror* writer "for possible communist connections."

By the fall presidential election campaign, however, Walter had fastened his sights on Democratic nominee Adlai Stevenson. While Walter was accepting a "Freedom of the Press" award from the Republican administration and accompanying the President on a short campaign swing through Florida and Virginia, he was firing round after round at Stevenson, accusing him of having minimized the Communist threat and then of having surrounded himself with Communist appeasers. For weeks

Patterson of Seaboard, under pressure from Democrats who were threatening a boycott, had been asking Walter to desist. He wouldn't. Instead he committed still another self-destructive act: During Mutual's election night coverage, he compared Stevenson to transsexual Christine Jorgensen and told listeners that Stevenson's election "would mean a woman in the White House." Callers swamped the Seaboard switchboard to complain. The next day Patterson wired Mutual: GENTLEMEN, PLEASE BE ADVISED THAT WE HEREBY CANCEL OUR SPONSORSHIP OF THE WALTER WINCHELL SUNDAY EVENING NEWSCAST FOR CAUSE EFFECTIVE IMMEDIATELY. To the press, Patterson said, "The man has gone mad."*

VII

Winchell had been dragging himself off the canvas for several years now, and he was to try yet again. After most of the guests had left a New Year's Eve party in Desi Arnaz's Palm Springs home, Arnaz asked Walter to reminisce about the days he'd spent chasing police calls. Arnaz seemed spent and drunk, and Walter resisted, but Arnaz persisted. So Walter vividly recalled how he and Runyon once tracked the Park Lane murder gang to a high-rise apartment. At noon the next day Walter got a call from Bert Granet, the executive director of Arnaz's production company, Desilu, requesting a lunch. Despite his apparent stupor at the party, Arnaz not only had heard every word of Walter's recitation but could relate it all verbatim and told Granet that one could construct a series around Walter's memories. Lucy was understandably unhappy about hiring Walter, but Arnaz told her that this was business. On January 15 a deal was struck, with Walter to be paid $7,500 per episode for the first thirteen installments of a series to be called "The Walter Winchell File."

Walter seemed to recognize the poignant irony in his now attempting to make a career out of playing himself at the very time when his career as a broadcaster and even as a columnist was fading. "The trouble is that some of us stay around too long," he had complained just before the 1956 election, when the *Mirror* refused to run a column of his defending Eisenhower. "We don't know when the parade has passed us by. We have to be pushed. So does any paper need a new janitor? Salary no object."

---

*Seaboard itself did not go unscathed. Within months, three creditors had filed a petition for involuntary bankruptcy against the company, and a court-appointed trustee would charge that gross mismanagement and "unjustified extravagance" had depleted $250,000 invested by fourteen hundred shareholders. Walter, rewriting history, told *The New York Times* that when he discovered Mericin was a "phony," he exposed the fraud and fired his sponsor.

While he patched up his quarrel with the Hearst organization, that February he announced he would be leaving the Mutual broadcast on March 3 to devote himself to the new television series. It was the first time since December 1932, when he started the "Jergens Program," that he wouldn't have a regularly scheduled radio series, and he signed off on his final broadcast thanking the Mutual network and "all of you for 28 exciting years." "The manner in which you ended your broadcast Sunday night gave me a feeling of sadness," J. Edgar Hoover wrote him a few days later, "because over the years you have been a Sunday night institution. There is no doubt in my mind that the millions of people who have followed you will certainly miss their weekly sessions with you."

Walter seemed resigned after the program's end. "I am taking it a lot easier," he wrote back to Hoover. "I see too many people I knew fall down." And he told *Herald Tribune* television and radio news columnist Marie Torre, "I was throwing a punch at somebody every night. I saw a girl slip on the street one day and just because the guy next to her didn't help her, I punched him. Well, I'm not looking for trouble any more. I'm not edgy."

TROUBLE STILL found him. That June, while he was fighting for his professional life, United Artists released a film that was to destroy his reputation for posterity the way his association with McCarthy had destroyed it in the eyes of so many of his contemporaries. Its germ was a story by a young writer and former press agent under Irving Hoffman named Ernest Lehman. Lehman had felt frightened at being part of what he called "that dangerous world of aggressive people with healthy egos," but the Broadway world also fascinated him, and he began writing stories about it—not whimsical stories like Runyon's but dark, cold and cynical ones that incriminated the denizens of Broadway in a vast web of deceit.

By the late forties he decided to attempt a novel about the cutthroat symbiosis between columnists and press agents. He began while vacationing in Provincetown and continued that fall in a small rented room in the Hotel Paris near his apartment on 96th Street. He finished one Saturday afternoon and was suddenly struck by an alliterative title: *The Sweet Smell of Success*. The next day he sent it off to his agent. A few days after that *Cosmopolitan* magazine bought it for publication.

"I hadn't worried too much about the implications of what I had done," Lehman recalled, saying he kept writing because he felt the story was so compelling. But someone sent Irving Hoffman the manuscript, and Hoffman was both embarrassed and wounded by what he had read. The novella was an account of an unscrupulous press agent named Sidney

Falco and an all-powerful gossip columnist named J. J. Hunsecker who conspire to destroy a young jazz musician Hunsecker's sister is dating. "The trouble was that a lot of Broadwayites jumped to the conclusion that my fictional columnist was meant to be Walter Winchell," Lehman wrote, passing over the obvious similarities between Hunsecker's crusade against the musician and Walter's against Billy Cahn. "And if that was Winchell, wasn't the press agent inevitably my close friend and former employer . . . Irving Hoffman?"

Hoffman invited Lehman to his office and begged to know what he had done to Lehman to deserve this treatment. "You made me write all those goddamned paragraphs for the [Hollywood] *Reporter* when all I had was time and what was left of my brain to write short stories," Lehman told him, answering for every abused press agent. Lehman and Hoffman didn't speak for a year. Walter, Lehman heard, seemed less distressed. "I don't fool with the Ernest Lehmans of the world," he allegedly said. "I go after the Westbrook Peglers."

But among the press agents and other Winchell acolytes on Broadway, Lehman said it was "nervous time." "Press agents would get up from the table at Lindy's if they saw me approaching. It's like 'Don't go near him. Winchell might see you.'" Meanwhile, out in Hollywood, producer Art Arthur, Walter's old protégé, was working the phones, trying to make certain that no one would consider making a film of the novella. Still, over the next few years producer Walter Wanger approached Lehman about the material, as did MGM producer Charles Schnee, and Harold Hecht, a former agent who had teamed with Burt Lancaster and another agent named Jim Hill to form a production company, kept hounding Lehman to adapt *Sweet Smell.*

By this time Lehman had moved to Hollywood and had become a highly successful screenwriter with credits on *Executive Suite, Sabrina, The King and I* and *Somebody Up There Likes Me.* "I was afraid of it," Lehman admitted about the prospect of adapting *Sweet Smell* into a film. "I was doing very well in Hollywood. Who needs problems?" But Hecht was persistent, his company, Hecht-Hill-Lancaster, was now respectable, having just won the Oscar for its production of *Marty,* and Lehman finally capitulated.

It didn't take him long to realize that if any producers could do justice to the malice in *Sweet Smell,* Hecht-Hill-Lancaster were the ones. Lehman thought them a rapacious and amoral bunch—his introduction to Lancaster came when the actor strode into the office zipping his fly and proudly declaring, "She swallowed it"—who seemed far more concerned with tallying sexual conquests than with filmmaking. To make matters worse, Lehman's agent, the legendary Lew Wasserman, had won

Lehman the right to direct the picture as well as write it, only to have Hecht rescind the offer after Lehman had already scouted locations. (Hecht blamed the studio, which, he said, distrusted a novice.) Upset by losing the right to direct, vexed by difficulties in the script, worried by the risk of offending Winchell and bothered by what he felt was a general air of smarminess at Hecht-Hill-Lancaster, Lehman began developing pains in his lower right quadrant. The diagnosis was a spastic colon— Lehman's colon was clenched so tightly, the doctor had to administer an anesthetic to insert the sigmoidoscope—and the recommendation was that Lehman leave to decompress. So Lehman departed for Tahiti, and playwright Clifford Odets completed the screenplay with Alexander Mackendrick directing.

"Now it's going to open. Now I really started worrying," Lehman remembered. He certainly had reason. On the screen, in ruthless black and white, *Sweet Smell* had become an inventory of Broadway odiousness. Falco services Hunsecker because the columnist is the "golden ladder to the places I want to get," while Hunsecker himself is a charmless, preening demagogue, sitting self-importantly at "21," surrounded by sycophants, giving withering looks and making cutting remarks. Later, watching a drunk being bounced on Broadway, he smiles and says, "I love this dirty town." Everyone is looking for an advantage; when an affable columnist propositions a cigarette girl, who is then fired for rebuffing him, Falco blackmails him into placing a client's name in the column. In the meantime, Hunsecker calls his sister's boyfriend a "marijuana smoking Red" in the column, and when the young man comes to remonstrate, Hunsecker orders Falco to arrange to have him beaten up. Hunsecker's defense: "Don't you see? That boy today wiped his feet on the choice and the predilection of 60 million men and women in the greatest country in the world. . . . It wasn't me he criticized. It was my readers."

The night of the premiere, Lehman was told, Walter lurked across the street, waiting to see the faces of the audience as they left. Irving Hoffman patrolled the lobby afterward collecting intelligence to pass on to Walter and telling everyone who asked that the film was a bore. Other press agents scurried across to Walter to tell him how awful the film was. It wasn't until the end of the year, nearly six months after its run, that Walter acknowledged the film himself, reporting in the column that Hecht-Hill-Lancaster would lose $500,000 on it. (He later revised the figure to $2 million.) "They've had many shocks over their initial defeat at the box office," he wrote. "One of the most agonizing is that co-partner Burt Lancaster plus star Tony Curtis are not strong enough to 'bring them in.'"

But despite Walter's protestations against it, *Sweet Smell* would emerge as a classic—one of the quintessential New York films and one that, rightly or not, definitively established the image of Winchell as a megalomaniac. For Billy Cahn, especially, it may have also provided some small measure of justice, even though he wasn't around to enjoy it. Walter had ruined Cahn's life. Now, by inspiring Lehman's novella and Mackendrick's movie, Cahn had helped sully Walter Winchell's name forever.

WORKING ON "The Walter Winchell File" in Hollywood that year, beyond the pressures of New York and without feuds to wage, Walter seemed chastened, even docile after his bizarre conduct the previous fall. Hollywood gossip columnist Sheilah Graham, interviewing him late that summer just before the premiere of the show, said she had been warned, "He's quite different. He's calm, almost peaceful," and found it to be true. "It's better for me to calm down," Walter told her. "I've put on six pounds and there's nothing for me to get excited about." The California climate, while enervating compared to that of New York, was allowing him to sleep, and he was committed to staying there if his show was renewed. "Funny how everything is for the best," he confessed to Graham.

On the set he was cooperative and complacent. "This is his fourth film and he hasn't exploded yet," remarked a press agent for the show. "He hasn't asked to see a script in advance. He has offered no free advice. He has posed cheerfully for every still picture. He has been the very soul of courtesy and cooperation." And on the program itself, he was "very relaxed and low-keyed," in critic John Crosby's description, "as if he didn't give a hoot what the ratings were."

"The Walter Winchell File" premiered that October. Narrated by Walter and featuring him in cameos playing himself, it was a dramatic series loosely based on episodes from his career, which meant its gaze was primarily backward—toward the old Broadway of bright lights and tough guys. Walter knew that Broadway was long gone, and he admitted as much by his extended stay in California. New York wasn't as lively as it used to be, he said, and Broadway was dead. People were staying home watching television now instead of going club-hopping.

What Walter didn't say is that television was also usurping one of the primary functions of the gossip columnist: rendering judgments on personalities. Where once celebrities had to visit the nightclubs to toady to columnists in order to become celebrities, now they had a means of bypassing the mediator and directly facing their public. The only way for the gossips to seize the initiative once again was to do what Walter had attempted—conduct vendettas so relentlessly that the targets would wither under the assault—or to do what *Confidential* had attempted: expand the purview of gossip beyond romance, infidelity and pregnancy to new and previously unexplored areas like sex and drugs. "Why Sinatra is the Tarzan of the Boudoir," "The Real Reason for Marilyn Monroe's Divorce," and "Mae West's Open Door Policy" were typical of *Confidential*'s pathbreaking, if crass, stories.

For a few years *Confidential*'s tactic had worked, and its circulation, by one estimate, reached four million. But by the spring of 1957 a crackdown had begun. Grand juries in New Jersey, Illinois and California were taking aim on *Confidential* and other so-called scandal magazines for publishing criminally libelous and obscene material. In the meantime, a California state senator named Fred Kraft had launched a probe into whether private investigators were selling information to the magazines, and in May California Attorney General Edmund Brown won an indictment against Harrison and his staff for libel and obscenity.

Harrison was undisturbed. "I love it," he told Harold Conrad, who wrote for *Confidential*. "I've already told my lawyers to be prepared to subpoena every big-name star who ever appeared in the magazine. Can you picture that parade up to the witness stand?" He insisted, in any case, that the stories were true and that many of them had been provided by the stars themselves to generate publicity. Still, Harrison successfully fought extradition from New York and then filed a $2 million lawsuit against Brown for seeking to interfere with the sale and distribution of the magazine.

The trial of *Confidential*'s California staff began on July 29, but with the major defendants absent and the parties looking for a compromise, it quickly adjourned. When it reopened that August, it was not without its own lurid drama. One defendant, who was accused of collecting gossip on a wrist microphone, fled to Mexico and attempted suicide. Another participant, an investigator for the prosecution, succeeded in her suicide attempt, and a subpoenaed witness, Mae West's chauffeur, died mysteriously just before the trial began. What wasn't lurid turned out to be comical: A deputy district attorney, a strict churchgoer, was charged with reading whole articles into the record.

Walter enjoyed the proceedings immensely. "Many writers for respectable slick magazines are suffering from the jitters hoping their names aren't exposed in the Hollywood slimelight," he twitted in the column during the trial. "They have been enjoying a comfortable income (under other names) peddling lowdown on celebrities that their editors deleted." The next week he chortled over the ruckus being raised by the "astounding" fact that "[i]n Hollywood, men and women frequently behave like males and females," and he remarked on how times had changed since he first launched gossip in the twenties when "we were harshly reprimanded for publishing the shocking fact that married folks have babies."

The *Confidential* trial ended, after fifteen days and after what one juror described as "big fights" during deliberations, with the jury hopelessly divided seven to five for conviction. To avoid a retrial, in November the parties agreed that the state would drop all charges against the individual defendants and retain only token charges against the corporation in return for *Confidential*'s changing its editorial policy and announcing these changes publicly in advertisements in New York, Chicago and Los Angeles newspapers. Harrison tried the new, less salacious policy for three issues, then sold the magazine.

In a sense, *Confidential* was a casualty not of its overaggressiveness or its tastelessness but of its success in redefining gossip. When Walter created the gossip column and dozens of imitators followed, it took Walter's nerve, talent, energy and power to prevent himself from being co-opted. *Confidential* had spawned scores of imitators too, but Harrison had to cope not only with them or even with the mainstream press, which was increasingly hospitable to stories it had disdained just a few years earlier, but with the celebrities themselves. "Nearly every high class magazine now offers lowdown articles by well known people, who supply their own skeleton-rattling," Walter wrote shortly after the trial. "In short, they now sell the stuff they once threatened to sue about. . . ."

That was *Confidential*'s epitaph. Whether Walter realized it or not, it was the epitaph for his own gossip column as well.

THAT FEBRUARY, Revlon announced it was canceling "The Walter Winchell File," effective March 28, after only five months on the air. Walter had taken his own informal poll that showed his program was fourth-rated (Ed Sullivan ran twenty-eighth), and he said that just the week before, Charles Revson, the head of Revlon, had sent him a $10,000 check for the Runyon Fund, a pair of diamond cuff links and an assurance that he shouldn't worry about the sponsorship. But whatever Revson had told Walter, he told the press, "We just found it wasn't the right kind of show to sell our product."*

To this indignity was added another. Several years earlier Walter had reported that Jack Paar, a cherubic television personality, and his wife

---

*The previous spring, with "The Walter Winchell File" slotted for ABC, Walter had dropped his breach-of-contract suit against the network. "I don't see how I can sue a network I'm going to work for," he said at the time. Now he felt deceived. "When I agreed to drop the suit at ABC it was because they all made me feel they would continue me there," he wrote his attorney.

"have their pals depressed." Paar insisted there was no marital discord and had a friend ask Walter if he would retract. As Paar later told it, "This self-appointed General Manager of the world sent back word that he could not retract the item but that the source which gave him the wrong information would be 'dead with him.' That was consolation, indeed."

When Paar began hosting "The Tonight Show," a nightly talk show on NBC, Walter was flattering, calling him a "refreshing relief from the usual tight-collar type." But Paar's anger over the old item hadn't subsided. Hostess Elsa Maxwell appeared on the program and began gibing at Walter, accusing him of hypocrisy for waving the flag while never having voted. Paar joined in. He said Walter's column was "written by a fly" and that his voice was so high because he wears "too-tight underwear." From Hollywood Walter called Maxwell a "fat, sloppy, smelly [deleted]" and threatened to sue each of Paar's sponsors for having damaged the Runyon Fund. As for the charge that he hadn't voted, he produced a photograph of himself entering a voting booth in 1956 and demanded that NBC "show that picture of me voting every Tuesday until I got bored. Not until they got bored, but until I got bored." Paar reluctantly displayed the photo and issued a retraction, but he also told the story of the mistaken item about his marriage and cracked that Walter had a "hole in his soul."

Walter as usual professed indifference; he told Klurfeld, "Who really cares about an ingrate and a smelly old cunt?" But as always, Walter did care. Maxwell had called him a "fading star" and said he was "very finished." If these remarks weren't enough to inflict hurt, June's reaction was. Walter later claimed that she was in the hospital at the time, suffering from a heart ailment when a grandmotherly nurse showed her a newspaper with the headline: JACK PAAR ATTACKS WINCHELL. "The shock," Walter wrote, "gave my gravely ill wife her third heart attack."

Once again down. John Teeter, the Runyon Fund administrator, wrote him that April: "It is important to be happy inside because so much inner strength comes from being at peace with yourself. There will always be crises, but it is important to view them in the perspective of the total span of your life." Personally Walter did have things for which to be grateful. June was recovering, Walda had given birth to a little girl, Mary Elisabeth, the previous November and he had accepted an honorary degree from Florida Southern College for his Runyon Fund efforts—his first after having refused honorary degrees for years on the ground that the institutions were only trying to get something from him in return.

But professionally, at sixty-one, he was forced to revive himself yet again, to give the impression that his career was not yet over. And to do so, this time he returned full circle to vaudeville. Remaining in the West, he signed for a two-week engagement at the Tropicana Hotel in Las Vegas at a reported salary of $35,000 per week, which he promised to donate to the Runyon Fund. (That plan was scotched when the IRS ruled that it would consider this *his* income no matter how he disbursed it.) "They'll have three TV cameras in front of me, simulating a newscast, and monitors all over the club so I can be seen on the screen too," he enthused to *Time*, missing the irony of his playing at things he could no longer do for real. "I'll close that part of the show with some advice on the stock market. Then I'll go into a soft shoe with the girls, followed by a hot mambo by one of the girls."

For the finale, he said, "Onstage, you'll see an exact replica of my New York *Mirror* prowl car with me in it. I'll go across the stage—very fast. Then 24 beautiful girls—probably in G strings—come out swinging billies like a bunch of fairies with nothing but a silver badge on their left breast, blowing police whistles."

As it turned out, the show was much more reminiscence than variety entertainment, its mood more melancholic than euphoric. Against huge blowups of Manhattan, Walter strolled onstage toward a mock-up of his *Daily Mirror* office, greeting newsboys, cops, chorines and other Broadwayites while an announcer told the story of his life. Occasionally he paused to reenact a scene: a softshoe from vaudeville or a phone call from Desi Arnaz asking Walter to come to Hollywood for their TV show. During a simulated broadcast on opening night, Walter announced that he had cracked a recent Florida murder case and introduced the victim's family from the audience with the assertion that this might be his biggest story ever because he believed the murderer was paid by someone with political influence. After more dancing by the chorus, Walter returned in a Spanish hat and danced a mambo as promised, despite a torn muscle and a tight corset, grimacing in pain at a high step.

In all, he appeared for only eighteen minutes in the revue, closing with a somber poem he had written and composer Gordon Jenkins had put to music. Its refrain was "I know you miss me." But, for all its nostalgia and eulogistic mood, the engagement seemed to reenergize him—except for the "fifteen days of pain in my back," as he complained to Abel Green. An FBI informant reported that Walter had a "stable" of four or five call girls in Las Vegas and "freely passed out money to all of them," including one "dancer" who asked him to contact the bureau when traveler's checks she had received as a "gift" were returned as stolen. Meanwhile, Walter was telling friends he would be returning to television on ABC with another version of his radio news and gossip program.

This was wishful thinking on Walter's part. In truth, he was having difficulty landing another radio program, much less a prime-time television show. For months John Teeter had been searching for a new sponsor that could put Walter back on Mutual. Negotiations dragged on through the summer, and by early fall Walter had neither the sponsor nor the radio program, despite an announcement by Mutual in September that he would be returning to its airwaves. Finally, on November 16 under the sponsorship of Bon Ami cleanser and a subsidiary of Mutual called Symphonic Electronics, Walter launched his new broadcast. Though he was reportedly earning $1,000 per show, less than one-tenth what he had earned at his peak, the amount was partially offset by a large stock option, and anyway, the point wasn't money or even security anymore. The point now was survival.

It was as a relic, however, that Walter Winchell survived now. According to Burt Granet, Desi Arnaz felt an obligation to Walter after the demise of "The Walter Winchell File" and asked him to narrate a pilot of a new one-hour series based on the Prohibition exploits of a Chicago treasury agent named Eliot Ness. ABC executives, Walter later claimed, had blackballed him from the assignment, but Arnaz and producer Quinn Martin insisted. According to Arnaz, "Walter gave the show a feeling of truth and immediacy. His machine gun delivery was very, very important to the show. Without Walter it wouldn't have been the same."

By the time the first part of the two-part pilot aired in April 1959, ABC had already picked up the series, now called "The Untouchables," and Walter Winchell soon found himself in demand as a narrator; within the year he also narrated a Desilu production called "Lepke," shot a pilot for another Desilu production called "The Crime Commission," signed to narrate a series called "Treasury Agent" (a deal which ABC executives quashed, citing a conflict with "The Untouchables") and was approached to narrate a feature film on Murder, Inc., which, he promised J. Edgar Hoover, would have "considerably more of the Lepke negotiations in it."

His was the voice of history. The "contemporary Walter Winchell has become virtually unrecognizable," reported *Time* magazine, shortly after the airing of "The Untouchables" pilot. "Gentled by the years—or by something—the aging lion has lost most tooth and growl. . . . The famed Winchell legwork has slackened to an amble. His Manhattan prowls are intermittent now; he prefers to let his 40-odd squad of Broadway volunteers pump up the bulk of the gossip. When he does walk abroad, he likes to visit the scenes of old triumphs. . . . He is often alone—an isolation the big game he once stalked is pleased not to invade." A photo accompanying the piece was captioned: "How long ago and far away you seem."

CHAPTER 10

"He'll Wake Up One Day . . ."

THE END CAME "DROP BY DROP," as Aeschylus has described the pain that slowly falls upon the heart and brings wisdom.

In October 1959 Bankers Life and Casualty, which had assumed sponsorship of Walter's Mutual radio broadcast after Bon Ami and Symphonic Electronics pulled out, informed him that it was discontinuing its support as of November 22. On November 23 Mutual notified him that it was "financially not in a position to carry any sustaining programs." So ended his radio career.

A few months later, Jack Paar returned to "The Tonight Show" after a twenty-five-day walkout—NBC had censored a joke of his on the videotape without informing him—and on his first program back launched a new, unprovoked attack on Walter, calling him a "silly old man" and adducing Lyle Stuart's book as evidence of Winchell's wrongdoing. Paar's comments seemed so vicious and gratuitous that according to *The New York Times*, his own friends in the audience "gasped." But Walter was even more defenseless now than he had been in 1958 during Paar's first assault, and the vendetta only underscored how much the balance of media power had tilted toward television and away from the newspaper.

Still, Walter was remarkably intrepid for someone so beleaguered. He kept searching for action. Television critic John Crosby remembered seeing him in Miami Beach that winter looking "very withdrawn, a million miles away" as he shambled into a barbershop despite his nearly bald pate. "Suddenly he came alive for a few moments, the old vital Winchell, and rapped out in that abrasive way: 'Look, Castro has just invited American journalists to fly down and look at his revolution. Let's go,' " referring to Fidel Castro's recent takeover of Cuba. Crosby begged off, and Walter again shambled away—"the alonest man I ever did see."

In June, however, he did get the action he needed to continue playing Walter Winchell. President Eisenhower was making a tour of the Far East, and Walter asked for press credentials. It was to be his first time outside the United States since his mission to Brazil during World War II. Walter described his fellow reporters as "breathless with anticipation." "They know news will be breaking every second of the trip and they cherish their ringside pass." But it was Winchell who was really bursting with excitement. *The New York Times*' Harrison Salisbury said, "It was all we could do to keep up with him." Though sixty-three, Walter stayed up until five each morning, asking questions of the press and conducting interviews with officials. In Seoul, South Korea, where he was named one of the pool reporters for the President's motorcade, he bought himself a camera and snapped pictures "like a veteran," by one account. And in Manila he got a scoop that student protests in Tokyo would force the President to bypass that stop; having to confirm the story at a hastily called press conference, Eisenhower's press secretary, James Hagerty, shot Walter "a look that could kill."

Among the press veterans, Walter, with his *Front Page* style and his endless storytelling, was a curiosity and an entertainment. "What do you mean interrupting me by nodding?" he quipped to a reporter during one of his monologues. Hagerty told him, "I've been around this bunch for a long time. I never heard them applaud anyone before. They all like you," which, for someone who had sought the approval of the working press nearly all his life, was a meaningful accolade. He returned to the United States still wearing his "Welcome Ike!" Korean press badge and asking Hagerty to reserve a spot on the press plane if the President visited Berlin as rumored.

Back in California that summer, he acted as if he hadn't fallen. With a producer-director named Albert Zugsmith, who specialized in exploitation films, Walter formed WW Productions to develop movie projects, the first of which was to be titled *Gyp the Blood* after the old childhood acquaintance of Walter's who had become a notorious murderer. Meanwhile, Walter narrated and appeared in several of Zugsmith's own productions that summer, including *The Private Lives of Adam and Eve* and *Dondi*, based on a comic strip about an orphan. When Sam Wall, a publicist who had brokered the agreement between Winchell and Zugsmith, raised the possibility of a commission, Walter said, "Wouldn't you rather have anything you want in the column?," as if it were the old days when Winchell plugs were worth more than money.

Far more important for Walter than his pact with Zugsmith was the agreement he concluded with ABC television for a news commentary program to run that fall from ten-thirty to eleven Sunday nights under the sponsorship of Hazel Bishop. The contract called for twenty-six weeks at $4,000 per broadcast and options for four additional seasons should the network choose to exercise them. "I'm happy to be back—," Walter told *Newsweek*, adding, not entirely accurately, "but get this straight, I was never fired five years ago. I resigned. And what did it get me? Five years of not being on the air as a commentator. Actually, I was the most overpaid commentator on the air—$16,000 a week. Ninety-one cents of every buck to the government. I said the hell with it."

Again he invoked the mantra of the "old Winchell," as if the reason his popularity had declined was that he hadn't been permitted to assume the persona he once had, as if finding his way back to the old Winchell would make everything well again. Preparing for the new program, Walter did try to summon his past glories. Long before his October 2 premiere, he wrote J. Edgar Hoover asking if the FBI director would provide the "10 Most Wanted List" ("I intend 'dramatizing' why they are wanted, not merely their names and descriptions") and if he would sit for an interview: "I mean you saying what you want the public to know most about the national peril, the Reds, etc.? I could then follow you by displaying your book (Deceit) and tell my viewers to buy it at once and help the FBI in its fight. If you would do this for me—my opening would be auspicious, indeed."

As it turned out, Hoover refused, and Republican Presidential candidate Richard Nixon appeared on the first program instead. Other than that interview segment, the new "Walter Winchell Show" replicated the old radio format right down to its salutation: "Good evening, Mr. and Mrs. North America and all the ships at sea. Let's go to press!" To those who continued to carp at him for freely mixing show business trivia with hard news, Walter answered by reversing his lifelong drift from gossip to political affairs: "Brigitte Bardot is news as well as Nikita Khrushchev. The course of events reflects highlights as well as shadows. News has a capricious quality. Personalities frequently arouse greater public interest than profound issues." And he cited Oscar Wilde's dictum that journalism is " 'organized gossip,' which is where I came in."

To TV critic Nick Kenny in the *Mirror* at least, Walter still "gave off sparks." But what his apologists couldn't admit, what Walter himself didn't seem to realize, was that the old Winchell was *old.* "The Trendex indicates that millions of viewers all over the country have to be made aware and constantly reminded—of the fact that Winchell is back on the air," an ABC executive wrote Hazel Bishop's Raymond Spector after the second telecast, and Spector asked Walter if he could devote a half hour each week to consult with the publicity department to build ratings.

Before the ratings could improve, however, Walter broke down. He had long suffered from dental problems, especially grave to him since he feared that dentures might affect his delivery. Over the years he had spent thousands of dollars on dental surgery, unavailingly. He still agonized with toothaches, and now, scarcely three weeks on the air, he had contracted a staph infection in his gums that forced him off the October 23, October 30 and November 6 broadcasts. ABC kept insisting that he would return shortly, but he claimed to have told ABC's Tom Velotta that they were "fooling the people because I'm just too sick to come back." He knew his appearance and his voice had changed, both evincing his illness, and on November 10, he and ABC agreed to terminate his contract.

Suspending his column as well, Walter withdrew to Twelve Acres to recuperate and spend time with June, who had left Arizona to convalesce there herself. The previous summer she had suffered a series of heart attacks—four in all—and "hovered between life and death," as Walter described her condition in a letter to Rita Greene. Though she had lost weight and aged considerably, she made a miraculous recovery, and a recent cardiogram, Walter wrote Hoover, indicated her "heart is practically new." Now, for the first time since his breakdown in 1952, June had Walter entirely to herself, and she intended to keep it that way. When *Time* phoned to find out how long Walter would be gone and to check rumors that he would be retiring, June, still nursing a grievance against the magazine for past insults to her husband, barked, "It may be in the fall. And it may be never." Walter said he lost fifty papers because of that quote.

In the meantime, William Randolph Hearst, Jr., was also pressing to find out when he might return. "He has not been in the hospital," Rose Bigman wrote back. "It was a matter of viruses, bad gums and then allergy to the antibiotics that weakened him so that the doctor suggested he had to rest for awhile." A few weeks later, Walter wrote Hearst executive Richard Berlin, who had also been inquiring after the columnist's health, that "I am feeling better except for occasional dizzy spells."

The real problem seemed emotional rather than physical. The doctors pronounced him fit, and he flew to Scottsdale, where June said he was "feeling much better, getting out in the sunshine, taking the fresh air, doing some of the shopping, etc." But he had sunk into another funk after his high spirits just six months earlier. "I went to the typewriter from sheer boredom, doing nothing," he told *Time*. "I played around with a column and then tore it up. I'm just not ready to pick up again."

Back at Twelve Acres later that winter he was noticeably depressed. Walt, Jr., told his wife that Walter had drawn the shades and remained largely entombed in the darkness, leaving only to putter about on a little golf green he had installed on the lawn near the front pathway. And Walt, Jr., told his wife that his father had contemplated suicide, had once even attempted it, though there is no evidence of Walter's ever having done so.

He returned to the column in April, after five months, without any acknowledgment of what had happened or where he had been. *Time* found his column the "same mixture as before, but some of the salt was missing. Gone were the public snarls at some particular foe, the three-alarm shrillness, the staccato urgency, the distinctive touch of a man who once polished trifles until they sometimes seemed to gleam." Staying at the Ambassador Hotel in Los Angeles, he admitted he was tired. "In my younger days when I used to hustle, it was a lot more exciting," he told *Time*. "Now the copy comes in by the bushel, and I sit around filling up the wastebasket and staring at the ceiling waiting for an idea to come."

WHILE WALTER Winchell, Sr., was spending his time trying to accommodate himself to the erosion of his fame and power and scheming to recover it, his son, no less a victim of the culture of celebrity, kept trying to find an identity of his own. After his vain attempts to work in radio and in journalism, he had traveled to Europe in the fall of 1956 and then to Africa, where he shot game on safaris, tended bar in Arusha in Tanganyika and observed the local political scene. "Africa was really his love. . . . He loved being away from America and being in a country where he was free from all the things that bothered him," his wife said later. But he had somehow run afoul of the political authorities in Kenya and, his wife believed, had been asked to leave.

He returned to America still without a plan or a hope. For a time he considered joining a treasure-hunting expedition off the Spanish coast, but he found the head of the expedition a "jerk." Instead he departed for California to write a screenplay with a friend. As with his other endeavors, the screenplay never panned out; the collaborators broke up, and when Walt failed to pay the rent, his landlady confiscated a gold-plated typewriter his parents had given him that was to have been the instrument of his success.

But it was while he was bouncing around California early in 1961 that he met Eva von Klebow. Elisabeth Winchell, Walter's granddaughter, described her as "exquisitely beautiful." Eva was tall and blond and elegant with a smoky voice accented in German. The Klebows had come to the United States from East Germany in 1952, when Eva was eighteen. Her father, an engineer who had served in the German army and wore an eyepatch, was an autocrat accustomed to German ways and had a difficult time adjusting. Eva didn't. She loved America.

At the time she met Walt, she was twenty-six, living in a tent near

Oxnard in her own protest against society, and bicycling each week to her apartment in Westwood for provisions and a shower. During her weekly trips she would stop in Malibu at a friend's house, and it was the friend who introduced her to a young neighbor named Walter Winchell who, the friend said, liked all things German. They met on the beach. "And the moment we took a look at each other, he latched on to me. Here was a German girl. A real German girl." Eva was no less taken with him. "Walter had a smile—he would turn his profile and it would come like an image on his face." She described the chemistry between them as "magic."

They made a date for that very evening, Eva rushing home to shower and change. Walt picked her up and took her to the Four Seasons, where he was utterly charming over dinner. Afterward they repaired to the restaurant's piano bar. But by this time Walt, who was a mean drunk, had become inebriated, and before Eva knew it, he had provoked a fight and pulled a gun. Eva "nearly died." In the middle of the fracas he handed Eva the gun and whispered, "Here, dear. You take it some place. Just leave. Get out of here now." So Eva dropped the pistol into her handbag, exited the restaurant and called a friend to pick her up.

She had resolved never to see this strange young man again. But the "moment he got on the telephone he was like a little poodle," Eva recalled. "I am so sorry," he said contritely. "What happened was inexcusable. It will never happen again." For two days they negotiated the return of the gun. Finally, against the advice of her friends, she surrendered the weapon to Walt. The next day he took her to Romanoff's, a famous Hollywood restaurant, to have dinner with Walter, Sr.

Eva had no idea who Walter Winchell was. She only knew that he must be someone important from the treatment he received and that he seemed most perturbed at having to have dinner with her. "All the time that I knew Walter's father he always looked at me with a sour expression on his face," Eva said. Later she attributed it to his hatred of Germans, dating from the war. But that evening he simply seemed testy and out of sorts, complaining at one point that he hated eating in front of other people because it was disgusting to see a person chew.

Two weeks later Walt invited Eva to be his guest at a wedding of a friend in Seattle. She agreed, and the two of them flew up for the festivities, but, Eva remembered, "something always happened when you were with Walter." When the time came to leave, he couldn't pay their hotel bill, and he was phoning friends frantically until one of them wired him money and bailed him out. Eva flew home. Walt decided that he would fly to New York and then send for her.

By this time, despite their misadventures together, Eva had decided,

"This is the man I really wanted to be with. . . . He literally, you know, was like that Prince Charming. He was shy and unassuming. And he was tender and loving and charismatic." But above all, he was painfully vulnerable and appealed to Eva's maternal instincts. "He was lonely for human contact. Even just physical—somebody to be with in the same room. I don't think he liked being alone, and he was always alone. Everybody always had to go home, but of course, I didn't go home."

In January 1961 Eva arrived in New York, and she and Walt moved into a hotel. A short time later New York *Post* columnist Earl Wilson reported that Walt had become a "secret bridegroom." "Not sure how the aspects of subterfuge crept into our marriage," Walt wrote Wilson, "except that we were married out of the country since I'd been to Mexico on business and we neglected to notify any but the immediate and appropriate families. Mexico was our choice, since we'd been invited to stay with some people whose marriage I'd been involved with in the role of best man three years previously in Kenya—and I wanted them on hand for my happiness."

Of course, it was all a tale; Walt loved to confabulate because he loved to entertain. ("Like Hans Christian Andersen," Eva would say. "To him truth had little reality . . . so he would tell a story that he thought you would enjoy hearing.") In fact, they hadn't married—they didn't until much later—though Walter and June naturally assumed they had. They lived happily, wildly, until Walt ran out of money, then moved into a small apartment in the Yorkville section of Manhattan, a predominantly German community.

With no visible means of support, Walt and Eva both went to work for the Runyon Fund in April 1961—Walt as assistant to the administrator, John Teeter. Dorothy Moore, then executive secretary at the fund, said he had been hired to write colorful correspondence. But he would return from lunch, usually drunk, and "this fantasy would come in the door." He would fly out of the office and then fly back in, trying to scare the staff, or he and Eva would sit behind the partition for hours giggling and joking. Finally Teeter had to dismiss him.

Eva later claimed that his misbehavior was frustration at being relegated to a typist's job when what he really wanted was to do something that would win him recognition from his father. When he couldn't get attention from his work, he attempted to get it, again, from his antics. Marrying Eva was itself an act of defiance partly designed to rile his father; papers reported that Eva was the daughter of a former Nazi official, and Walter and June clearly believed it, though there are no records of any Nazi activity on his part. Meanwhile, Walt began goosestepping up the street or affecting a German accent. Once, while getting a shave in a barbershop, he asked whether there were any "Jewish assholes" in there. This behavior elicited phone calls and telegrams from his parents demanding that he stop at once. June was so distressed over his Nazi impersonation that she even called Arnold Forster and asked how she could have her son stripped of his citizenship. Forster told her she couldn't.

In the fall of 1961, out of work and again out of money, Eva and Walt moved to Twelve Acres. June and Walter agreed because Walt could tend the property and presumably stay out of trouble. For Walt's part, he enjoyed the sylvan life. Twelve Acres had become unkempt and wild, so overgrown that Walt had to hack a path through the brush with a machete. It was also isolated, and that was just how Walt wanted it. When a new neighbor packed her two children in a stroller and rolled up the driveway to introduce herself, she remembers being greeted at the door by a gangly youth with a rifle who "allowed as I was not welcome and I should never come back again." It was Walt.

They lived not in the big house where he had grown up but in the gatekeeper's cottage, because Walt couldn't bear being where he had witnessed so many fights and suffered such misery. He had a few friends in the neighborhood whom he visited to play chess or drink or talk. But he suffered from excruciating headaches, for which he took large doses of pain reliever, and much of the time he spent sitting, dazed and uncommunicative, often up all night and sleeping through the day just like his father. "I feel very depressed at times," he had told Eva. "Just let me sit there."

In January, Eva gave birth to a son, Owen Reid. "Walter went wild," Eva remembered. "He bought cigars and he handed them out: I have a son! And he made the announcements and the presents came and it was very, very exhilarating." Walter, Sr., visited to see his new grandson. "Isn't he good-looking?" Walt asked. "All the Winchells are good-looking people," his father answered.

Walter left, never to revisit. But after Owen's birth June decided that she would move back to Twelve Acres and live with her son. Eva thought it was June's last attempt to have the family life that Walter had denied her. Walt saw it as an invasion of his private world. So long as his mother kept to the big house, it was tolerable. When she visited the cottage, though, Walt could barely contain himself. "She would sit there, and she talked in this droning voice. She would talk and talk and talk," Eva recalled. And Walt would pull Eva aside and tell her, "This woman is driving me crazy! Please make her go home." More, upon moving in, June had immediately called in the bulldozers and the mowers to redomesticate and manicure the land, an action that drove Walt to curse her every morning.

After three months she returned to Scottsdale, her experiment a failure. She complained bitterly to her husband that Walt had not taken care of her, a dereliction of duty that further blackened Walt's name with his father. The breach widened when Walt suddenly decided that he wanted to be a doctor and asked for funds to attend college. Walter and June thought the idea ridiculous and refused. "After that he collapsed," said Eva. "After that he started to do drugs. . . . I think he really didn't know what to do. That was the only plan he came up with."

THAT SUMMER of 1962 Walter Winchell was preoccupied with his own future. He had emerged from his funk, as he had from previous bouts of depression, once again stoking his enmity. This time it was directed against the new president, John F. Kennedy. Walter had been surprisingly evenhanded during the 1960 presidential campaign, mainly warning both parties not to relent on American defense. Though he was on his sabbatical during the first months of the new administration, he returned in April with some kind words for President Kennedy—"He has a way of winning over people"—and only a gentle admonition not to rely too heavily on his Harvard-educated aides and not to forget the Soviet threat.

But Walter had long had apprehensions about Kennedy. He had known him fleetingly, from the Stork Club and from various California nightspots, as a charming playboy, not in the Rooseveltian mold, which was still Walter's presidential standard, and his suspicions had only been confirmed when he got the scoop at the Democratic National Convention in Los Angeles that Kennedy was holed up with a woman in a friend's penthouse at the very moment he was receiving his party's nomination.

Once Kennedy had become president he had further corroded his stature with Walter by running afoul of J. Edgar Hoover. Robert Kennedy, the President's younger brother and his attorney general, reportedly believed that Hoover was feeding Winchell gossip to discredit the President, but the antagonism between the attorney general and Hoover would alone have been enough to turn Walter critical. By 1962 Walter was increasingly reproaching the administration for harboring Communists and soft-pedaling the Soviet threat, and Robert Kennedy was increasingly leaning on the Hearst Corporation to censor the column, sending Walter into new paroxysms of anger. "Intimates of the president," he wrote, "have persuaded publishers and editors to 'drop or stop' Winchell."

In June, Walter had had enough. Out in Los Angeles that month he discovered one of his columns had been shorn of seven paragraphs by King Features before syndication, including an item reporting a drop in the New York *Post*'s circulation, an item which Hearst president Richard

Berlin had explicitly approved for the *Mirror*. "This upset me so much," Walter wrote in his autobiography, "I couldn't wait to get to every microphone and teevee camera in Los Angeles so I could pop off."

When he did, he announced that he would be quitting King Features if only he could find someone to whom he could submit his resignation. "I'll be kicking away $150,000 a year," he told the Associated Press, "but I'll do it." Meanwhile, he had taken to submitting his column directly to certain papers rather than route it through King. "Have offers from two New York newspapers, one of the most important newspapers in L.A. and messages from many editors and publishers whose theme is: 'You're not mad at us, are you?' " Walter wrote *Variety* that same week with a touch of hyperbole. "I simply can't understand—nor can many of my editors and publishers—why the Syndicate makes hefty deletions of my fight against Commies and Administration Pinks after the Hearst lawyers, *Mirror* lawyers and editors give it the A-Okay, All Systems Go!"

The only answer he could divine was that William Randolph Hearst, Jr., himself was ordering the cuts. "A long time ago Bill and I had a very rough argument in '21' and then again at the Stork Club," Walter wrote *Mirror* publisher Charles McCabe, "and we both have good reason to dislike each other intensely." Walter was probably correct in blaming Hearst. Hearst had never liked him to begin with—"Walter was a self-centered egomaniac who was small-time in my book. Pop allowed him too much power," Hearst, Jr., was to write—and Hearst's sudden conversion to the Kennedy camp had only intensified the animosity between them and no doubt prompted the cuts. "I'm definitely retaining a lawyer for advice and counsel on how to go about getting out of the King Features prison," Walter wrote McCabe.

Two weeks later he still hadn't cooled down. In San Diego over the July 4 holiday, he held an hourlong press conference at station KFMB during which he once again lashed out at the Kennedy administration's "softness" toward communism, called the White House the "Pink House" and closed by asking what the Kennedy brothers were doing to Hoover—"the number one cop."* The next week, back in Los Angeles,

---

*Reading about Walter's tiff with the Hearst brass, Westbrook Pegler, whose own column of right-wing fulminations was now being highly edited, phoned Walter and flew to San Diego to listen to tapes of Walter's press conference. Emboldened by Walter's criticisms, Pegler addressed a rally of the Anti-Communist Christian Crusade on August 2 in Tulsa, Oklahoma, and excoriated the Hearst organization. Two days later, he was terminated. He latched on with *American Opinion*, the house organ of the extremist John Birch Society, but Pegler proved too outlandish even for them. He ended his career writing for two fringe publications in the South, spewing anti-Semitic bile and calling for the assassination of Robert Kennedy.

Walter repeated the charges on several local television programs. By the end of the week, speaking before the Los Angeles Press Club, Walter was demanding a congressional inquiry to prove his charges that Communist sympathizers had gained key posts in the administration.

While continuing to blast the Kennedys, he temporarily suspended his feud with the Hearst organization, thanks partly to Jack O'Brian's intervention and Richard Berlin's diplomacy, and withdrew his "resignation." (According to reports, he had already closed a handshake deal with the Bell Syndicate.) But whatever his anger at Hearst and whatever his concerns over Communist infiltration, he had already achieved his real objective: He was back on the national scene. To Herman Klurfeld, who had written most of the anti-Kennedy pieces, he gave thanks "for making an old man a big shot again."

THE QUINTESSENTIAL New York figure, the symbol of Broadway, now spent almost all his time in California. Partly it was because he was narrating "The Untouchables" there. But partly it was because New York itself had changed. Not only had it lost its spiritedness, but it had, in a sense, become too real and too dangerous compared with the image of authenticity and danger that Walter had promoted in the twenties and early thirties when hoodlums roamed Broadway and tough detective Johnny Broderick tossed miscreants through plate glass windows. Joel Landau, the young photographer Walter had befriended, remembered one incident when he and Walter were walking near Madison Square Garden and ran into a hulking former prizefighter named Tony Canazari. Walter and Canazari greeted each other effusively. Then Walter teased the ex-lightweight and junior welterweight champion over what would happen if two muggers were to approach him on the street. Canazari answered evenly that he would run. Walter was unsettled by this. He talked about it for days, as if it had taken this remark to drive home the city's violence.

He seemed to prefer the balmy unreality of California to the grimy reality of New York, though his bicoastalism also reflected his restlessness. Landau said that whenever Walter was in New York and felt depressed, he sought Los Angeles as an antidote. "I don't know how he would do it," Landau recalled. The two of them would cruise all night, then retire at 6:00 A.M. Later that day he would call Rose only to find that Walter was in California. "It can't be," he told her. "We went to bed at the same time." Jack O'Brian remembered flying out to Los Angeles to tend to some properties he owned there and getting a call from Walter who wanted the address where O'Brian was staying. O'Brian assumed that

Walter wanted to send him something. "He showed up the next day. He had rented a Cadillac convertible, and at eleven o'clock he was there and we went out to lunch."

Part of California's appeal was that it was easier for Walter to maintain his persona there where appearance counted as much as actuality. In California the press still treated him with deference, even after the cloud of McCarthyism had passed and he no longer seemed a threat. "God, we just sat at his feet," columnist Dorothy Manners said. "Everybody considered him the best, including Louella. . . . I think his ego loved it. He just bloomed like a flower." Everywhere he went he seemed to bring a crowd with him. Los Angeles *Times* sportswriter Jim Murray, writing that summer of 1962, said, "He invites people in car lots. A Winchell entrance in the Coconut Grove looks like an inauguration parade."

On a typical day Walter rose at noon at the Ambassador Hotel, picked up his messages, then went to the hotel barbershop, where he spent an hour or two on the phone. Late afternoons he spent on the Sunset Strip and at his office on the Fox lot, which the studio still maintained as a courtesy. When evening came, he usually attended a baseball game, which was where celebrities could often be found now. "Walter became as familiar a sight and sound around the ball park as the hot dog vendor," wrote Jim Murray. "He flitted from the press box to the owner's box, the locker room to the light tower." And as always, he called attention to himself. "Where the average guy might take his bartender or brother-in-law to the game, Winchell brought the loveliest dolls in show business from Monroe to Lucy Ball and he made sure everyone knew it."

After the game, with a carefree young Los Angeles Angels pitcher named Bo Belinsky usually in tow, Walter went club-hopping. And when the clubs closed, he cruised the streets until 4:00 A.M., when he had a nightly appointment with Agnes Underwood, the city editor of the Los Angeles *Herald-Examiner*, the local outlet for his column. "You have to say this about Walter," columnist Jim Bacon recalled admiringly of Walter's constant foraging. "He really roamed the streets. He really dug for it." What Bacon didn't realize is that there was nothing else for Walter to do but roam.

But buzzing around Los Angeles that summer of 1962, when he was back on the attack, Winchell could still not outrun the tragedy of being a fallen celebrity. The week after his San Diego press conference he wrote his old adversary Robert Kintner, now the president of NBC, boasting that "several famous companies have asked me to return to the air for simulcast" but then abjectly asking Kintner if he might be interested. "Could tape show two three hours before so all concerned at network and agency could delete and edit. No dots and dashes, lots of flashes stuff or material to worry you." Kintner wrote back saying he wasn't interested. Walter made a similar inquiry of Darryl Zanuck when he heard that Fox was planning a new documentary series. "Build me a monument," he told Fox executive Mal Ward. But that project foundered too over a libel waiver when Walter proposed a story about how he had told Roosevelt that Alger Hiss was a Communist agent. Walter wound up denouncing the Fox board of directors as "salami dealers."

Other humiliations, he visited upon himself. Returning to Los Angeles from San Francisco on the Southern Pacific Railroad with his twenty-four-year-old "executive secretary," according to an FBI report, he began drinking, got into an altercation with another passenger, pulled a gun and had to be restrained. At Union Station he allegedly screamed at railway detectives and dared them to arrest him, then drove off in a cab yelling "vile names" at his young companion, whom he left stranded behind.

II

Drop by drop. But through it all there had been one constant, one life-line to which Winchell could always cling: "The Column" in the New York Daily *Mirror*. Now even that was threatened. Throughout 1962 New York Local No. 6 of the International Typographical Union (ITU), which provided the printshop manpower for all of New York's daily newspapers, had been bracing for its biennial negotiation, and this time it was loaded for bear. Between the threat of new technologies, which could put printers out of work, and the relative docility of the rival American Newspaper Guild, whose contract regularly expired five weeks before ITU's, thus setting an industry standard, the ITU was determined to fight to accrue for its members some of the potential savings from automation and to gain a single expiration date for all union contracts—in addition to the traditional labor goals of increased wages and reduced hours.

Against these demands, however, the largely depressed newspapers were equally determined to hold their ground. On December 8, 1962, the ITU president, Bertram Powers, called a strike that was to have devastating consequences for the New York newspaper world. For Walter personally, the loss of his New York outlet, particularly at a time when he was desperately trying to hang on to his celebrity, was terrifying. The *Mirror* sold his column to a rump newspaper called the *Metropolitan Daily*, and he signed on to write a column for *Variety*, but without the *Mirror* he knew he was languishing in the wilderness.

The strike dragged on for 114 days despite enormous pressures to settle, pressures that even emanated from the White House. When it finally ended, under a settlement cobbled by Mayor Robert Wagner and labor negotiator Theodore Kheel, circulation at all the papers plummeted below prestrike levels and the basic price of a daily paper rose from a nickel to a dime at all but the *Daily News* and its morning rival, the *Mirror*; at the *Daily News*, even after the strike the paper with the highest circulation in America, the price was held at a nickel to squeeze further the paper with the second-largest circulation in America, the *Mirror*, and put it out of business.

Burdened by higher labor costs, by declining circulation and advertising revenue and by its five-cent price, the *Mirror* stumbled through the summer of 1963 and was gasping by the fall, though no one on the paper seemed to realize just how close to death it was. At 6:15 P.M. on October 15 managing editor Selig Adler walked down the flight of stairs from his office to the composing room and delivered a sheet of copy to be typeset. "Get it set in type and then go get yourself a job," Adler advised the man in charge of distributing the copy. When the news filtered up to the city room, the employees there had the silent, dazed, grief-stricken expression of attendees at a wake, which was exactly what they were. One man sat at his typewriter tapping out an obituary: "The New York Mirror, 39, a partner in the Hearst Corporation, died yesterday at its home, 235 East 45th Street, after a long illness. It is survived by a sister, The New York Journal-American."

Walter heard the death sentence from Rose Bigman when he arrived at the office that night. "How can a paper with the second largest circulation go out of business?" he asked her. One employee, a nighttime photographer, heard the news on the street and raced back to the city room, where he found Walter staring at the names on the mailboxes. "How do you feel?" the photographer asked, groping for some commiseration. "I'm not really worried about me," Walter said. "I'm really worried about these guys with young children and families. I'll get by." He lingered for hours as the night editor made and remade the last edition. At 2:17 A.M. the *Mirror* rolled off the presses for the last time. The headline read, VALACHI SINGS HERE TODAY, referring to a mob informer named Joseph Valachi. Walter's column concluded: "Broadway's mountain. Tough sledding on the way up—a toboggan on the way down."

"The *Mirror* was no ornament to the profession," *The New York Times* eulogized the next day, "but it did have its own character, it did appeal to nearly a million readers a day and it did add some variety to the city's press." *Editor & Publisher* saw its demise as a "milestone in the period of transition that metropolitan newspapers have been going through for almost 20 years." It cited the basic elements of that transition as suburbanization and the attendant change in retailing from big-city department stores to malls, though it might just as easily have cited the growth of television as a source of news, the expansion of the middle class, which weakened class attachments to newspapers like the blue-collar *Mirror*, and, for the tabloids specifically, the acceptance of sensationalism in the mainstream press and the identification of the tabloid with a bygone era.

If all these things spelled doom for the *Mirror*, they also spelled doom for the paper's most famous columnist. "That was the most crushing blow," Klurfeld remembered of the *Mirror*'s demise. "Losing the broadcast was a tough one to take but . . . the end of the *Mirror* was a crusher for him. That was his flagship. . . . He was the captain of the flagship, and he went down with it. That was the end of him really." Klurfeld felt the signs were even physical. "His voice changed after that. He didn't speak with the same vigor, with the same snap. . . . He spoke more slowly. He spoke in a lower register. He seemed tired." "I died on October 16, 1963," Walter himself wrote just a few years later.

The Hearst organization shifted him to the *Journal-American*, where he was miserable—"like a drowning man trying to get any life preserver that was in his grasp," in Klurfeld's words. When President Kennedy was assassinated a little more than a month after the *Mirror*'s end, Walter was too embittered, too engrossed in his own mourning for the *Mirror*, to care. Klurfeld prepared a column for the occasion in which Walter admitted his feud with the late President but expressed compassion. Walter rejected it. "That's pretty, but it isn't the way I really feel," he told Klurfeld. "I don't want to be a hypocrite." Instead he wrote nothing.

Once again he retreated to Scottsdale and then to California, still acting as if the world of celebrity had not passed him by, still pretending that he was America's foremost columnist. Frank Sinatra, Jr., the son of the famous singer-actor, had been kidnapped the year before, and the perpetrators were on trial in Los Angeles. Walter attended every session as if it were the Hauptmann trial, mingling with the working press, even taking them to lunch and picking up the tab. In the meantime, political correspondents covering Arizona Senator Barry Goldwater's California primary fight against Nelson Rockefeller for the Republican presidential nomination invited him to join their press bus, and he stayed over in San Diego to cover a press conference of former Kennedy press secretary Pierre Salinger, who was then running for the Senate. "I am in San Diego spinning like a top with very little sleep," he cheerfully wrote the Los Angeles FBI office. "I will be 67 on April 7th."

With his birthday approaching, Walter had called columnist Jim Bacon to ask if Bacon might arrange a "surprise" party for him at the Coconut

Grove, all expenses to be paid by Walter. Bacon said he would do what he could, little realizing how responsive the Hollywood crowd would still be. "But came the night and the Coconut Grove was filled," Bacon said, "because Winchell was there." More than one hundred celebrities turned out—even former President Dwight Eisenhower sent a congratulatory telegram—including Jayne Mansfield, Jimmy Durante, Roberta Sherwood and Robert Stack, the star of "The Untouchables." Then Walter arrived, and everyone yelled, "Surprise!" And Walter, Bacon remembered, looked *genuinely* surprised by the tribute and was deeply gratified by it.

Yet he was frightened. He had only the column left—"The Untouchables" had been canceled—and he knew that his position at the *Journal-American* was precarious. Shortly after his birthday he wrote the Hearst high command that he would now "hustle ads for our papers from people who like me, I mean," an act heretofore unthinkable for fear of compromsing his integrity. At the same time, he volunteered to write six columns a week instead of the five for which he had contracted—"to help peddle more papers." But the Hearsts would not be pacified now that they had Walter at their mercy. Shortly after Walter had run the item about the *Post*'s drop in circulation, Dorothy Schiff filed a new libel action. Ten months later, James Wechsler also filed a new libel action after Walter had printed items challenging Wechsler's assertion that he had left the Communist party in 1937. (Walter wrote Hoover deputy Clyde Tolson asking if he could verify a quote from the writer Arthur Koestler that Walter hoped to use in his defense: "[N]ever trust a former communist, including this one.") No doubt with these suits in mind, William Randolph Hearst, Jr., wrote Walter that they would be revoking his indemnification clause, the clause for which he had "struck" in 1935. The only way to do so, however, was for Hearst to cancel Walter's contract—he had been working on a holdover clause since 1946—and make an entirely new arrangement.

Walter complied—he really had no choice—but it was another humiliation. His columns were being drastically edited now, and *Journal-American* editors seemed to enjoy embarrassing him. Returning to the city room one morning after covering a murder, Walter found himself being excoriated by a superior named Paul Schoenstein. "Why don't you give the city desk some help the way Dorothy Kilgallen, Louis Sobol and Jack O'Brian do for our page one, two or three instead of putting it all in your column?" Schoenstein screamed. When Walter remonstrated that he thought he did, "the big mouth added for the edification of his staff, 'I'd fire you in a minute if it weren't for that g———d——— severance!' "

Realizing how little leverage he had with Hearst, Walter began dog-gedly pursuing television again that spring and was pitching ideas to Twentieth Century-Fox and ABC for a documentary series. "Get this," he described one episode of the series to a reporter. "We open—'My name is Walter Winchell. I'm a reporter. Forty-four years on the pap-ers . . . The most exciting case I ever covered was the trial of Bruno Rich-ard Hauptmann of the Lindbergh kidnapping case . . . Wherever I go in the 50 states, newspaper people, police people, people-people ask me, "Walter, do you think he was guilty?" Ladies and gentlemen, we will now prove that he was.' Wham!" But none of these ideas came to fruition ei-ther. One Fox executive remembered taking Walter to lunch with a pro-spective sponsor and Walter's not even mentioning the program. Why? the executive wanted to know. "Oh, I wouldn't want him to sponsor the show," Walter answered. "He's too right-wing."

In July he was at San Francisco for the Republican National Conven-tion, which nominated Barry Goldwater. Ernie Cuneo, seeing him for the first time in years, remembered Walter's isolation even as he was trying to thrust himself back into the center. "In San Francisco, he had a whole bus to drive him around," Cuneo observed, "and the emptiness of the bus and the silence of the phones in his suite was awful—the forerunner of the cool, cool tombs." On the convention floor, when a small ruckus erupted, behind the press bullpen, CBS television reporter Roger Mudd commented, "And in the middle is not Governor Scranton, not Governor Rockefeller, not Senator Goldwater, not General Eisenhower, but Walter Winchell with his felt hat securely on his head."

In August he was in Atlantic City for the Democratic National Con-vention, which nominated President Lyndon Johnson. Walter liked John-son; he remembered the assistance Johnson as a young congressman had provided him during the war when Secretary of the Navy Frank Knox wanted to decommission Walter. He also believed that Johnson was a real liberal: tough on civil rights but equally tough on communism. More, Johnson would woo Walter, though it took far less to do so now than in the Roosevelt days, when Walter was riding high, and it meant much less as well; the President was unfailingly courteous, having his staff process Walter's suggestions and offer him White House press credentials. Finally, even before the massive escalations to come, Walter was a fervent sup-porter of the war in Vietnam, wiring Johnson shortly before the conven-tion: RESPECTFULLY REQUEST ANY ASSIGNMENT (ACTIVE DUTY OR NOT) DURING CRISIS.

But once the campaign began, Walter devoted far less time to politics than to his own peculiar crusades. The daughter of Chicago *Sun-Times* gossip columnist Irv Kupcinet had been murdered the year before, and

Walter promised Kupcinet he would find the culprit. (Walter added, with no apparent awareness of the insensitivity of the boast, that he would win himself a Pulitzer Prize in the process.) Walter snooped around Los Angeles, even obtaining a court order to interview an inmate who apparently had some knowledge of the case, though when the FBI followed up on its own, one of the interviewees said, "Winchell doesn't know what he's talking about." At the same time Los Angeles police chief Walsh begged Kupcinet to get Walter off his back.

By the late fall Winchell had another cause. Word of J. Edgar Hoover's efforts to discredit the civil rights movement had leaked out, and there was growing pressure on the recently elected Lyndon Johnson to replace the aging director with someone who had a greater dedication to civil rights. Walter, in his column, snarled: "It is significant that those who are charging the FBI director with failing to protect civil rights have not offered a single fragment of evidence to support their charges . . . Most of Mr. Hoover's foes are criminals, Communists, Fascists and Nazis." Hoover wrote back gratefully the same day, "Seldom have I read such a well-documented, clear-cut response to critics. . . ." But the exchange only confirmed that they were two old men now, refighting the same old battles, and the bell was tolling for each.

"I WONDER what would happen if I lost my column?" For decades that had been the great underlying fear of Winchell's life. Without the column he was nothing. But now that fear was sharpened by the realization that the Hearst Corporation didn't need much provocation to rid itself of him. Hearst executives knew, and Walter knew, that he never really belonged at the *Journal-American*. He had no allegiance to it, and early in 1965 he moved his office to the Beverly Hotel because there was no room for him at the paper. Though he hung on, by the fall of 1965 he was again tired and unhappy. A new siege of dental surgery forced him to take a leave of absence in late September. This time before he could return, Joe Connolly, the publisher of the *Journal-American*, issued an ultimatum.

"You and I have a problem," Connolly wrote Walter. "For our part, we simply cannot afford what your column is now costing us. However, we would like to continue printing your column in the *Journal-American*, and I am sure you share with us a desire to continue to have your column appear in the *Journal-American*." Walter had been getting 50 percent of the gross revenues King Features earned from syndicating the column in addition to a salary of roughly $1,000 per week from the *Journal-American*. What Connolly proposed was that Walter get $300 per week for three columns of between 600 and 750 words and 100 percent of the gross revenue from syndication. According to Connolly, the new arrangement would gross Walter $57,500 per year minus the $150 weekly service charge to King Features for syndication, less than he had been earning and considerably less than he had earned in his heyday.

Walter accepted the terms—again, he had little choice—but he was more morose than ever, moping around the office, unusually monosyllabic, rebuffing all inquiries because, Rose said, he was "suffering from a gum infection" and was "too upset to think straight." His salary drastically cut, he was now forced to terminate Herman Klurfeld. Klurfeld had long seen the handwriting on the wall and had been doing freelance pieces without Walter's knowledge in anticipation of the day when the column would end, but he was nevertheless stunned by Walter's detachment when their long partnership did end. There was no severance pay—Walter thought the checks Klurfeld had received on the occasions when the column was suspended were compensation enough—and no retirement benefits since Walter's employees were not members of the Newspaper Guild. There was only a letter:

To Whom It May Concern:

Herman Klurfeld of 331 Southwood Circle, Syosset, NY, has been in my employ for 27 years. During that time his duties consisted of research and in some instances help in the preparation of radio and television broadcasts and newspaper themes.

I have always found him to be thoroughly honest, capable and reliable.

No hesitancy in recommending him.

Very truly yours,
Walter Winchell

"I thought you were like a son to Winchell," Klurfeld's wife said, astonished by the perfunctory letter. "And he was like a son of a bitch to me," her husband tartly replied.

THAT FALL of 1965 the Stork Club died. Like Winchell, it had been teetering for nearly a decade. A four-year labor dispute, triggered early in 1957 when Billingsley fired a kitchen employee for union activity, exhausted the Stork Club owner and embittered him, but even before the pickets encircled it, the club had been losing money, and by the time the pickets were finally enjoined, with Billingsley swaggering triumphantly through the club and ordering perfume and cologne for everyone, patronage had fallen precipitously.

"He was acutely aware that the times had changed," said his daughter,

Shermane. "He had very definite ideas of how a lady or gentleman was supposed to conduct herself or himself, and all of a sudden we had the drug scene going, we had the discos, we had the miniskirts and the boys with the ponytails, and he realized he could not relate to this. There was a sense of mourning for that period, a sense of [his] saying, 'I'm so sorry you never experienced what it was really like when people had a sense of style and glamour, and you could get a taxi at four or five in the morning, and the city never slept.' "

Still, he grudgingly tried to keep pace. When musicians refused to cross the picket lines, he took whatever nonunion musicians he could get, including a Dixieland band which ill suited the Stork's image. And early in 1965, after patrons had abandoned the Stork for more youthful and livelier niteries, he converted part of the club into a discotheque, admitting, "We have to keep up with the times. Ninety per cent of our customers want it. If you get a demand for a certain food or liquor you put it on the menu," though this was also a concession that the Stork was now following fashion rather than creating it.

In September 1965 Billingsley suffered what a friend described as a "general breakdown" and checked himself into Roosevelt Hospital. Though neither man knew of the other's convalescence there, Walter was also in the Roosevelt at the time, recovering from his dental surgery. In October a sign appeared outside the Stork Club announcing that it was closed and would relocate. Billingsley did think of opening a smaller club, hoping to catch the cycle again, but he was as forlorn and anachronistic as his old friend Winchell, and over the next year, as he dictated his memoirs into a tape recorder, he seemed to disintegrate. On October 4, 1966, a year to the day he closed the Stork, he complained of a headache to his wife, downed some aspirin and went to sleep at his apartment on East 83rd Street. He never awoke.

Sherman Billingsley was buried as he had lived. His daughter recalled that the atmosphere at the funeral was "like a cocktail party. . . . It was, 'Are you going to Switzerland this winter, dear? Well, where are you staying?' 'How are the Hamptons this summer? Oh, well I missed you!' 'What hairdresser are you going to? Do you still go to Kenneth?' " It turned out that Billingsley had run through his entire fortune. In due course the Stork Club building, which had once accommodated three thousand patrons a day, was purchased by CBS founder William Paley, who razed it and turned the property into a public "pocket park." Now even the lowest-born citizen could sit where only the mighty had once dwelled. Democracy had come at last to the Stork Club.

· · ·

TWO MONTHS after the Stork Club was shuttered, another institution faded. On December 1, Louella Parsons, the queen of Hollywood gossip, resigned the column she had written for more than forty years. Here too the end had been in sight long before it finally arrived. Battered by the death of her beloved husband, "Doc," and by the departure of her daughter, Harriet, Parsons had become increasingly dotty and enfeebled—the dowager of a crumbling empire. "Everything that had been so big and bustling and active just seemed like a house falling down," remembered Parsons's assistant, Dorothy Manners. Though Manners and two secretaries continued to deliver the column under Parsons's by-line, keeping Parsons's condition from the Hearst executives, the pretense finally ended. Harriet placed her mother in a nursing home in Santa Monica where she could receive proper care.

"A very strange thing happened," Manners recalled. "You will not believe this, but for the last ten years of her life, Louella wouldn't speak." Visitors came regularly to see her, but Parsons would sit in her bed and listen, absolutely mute. Manners believed it was an act of defiance: that she still heard and understood but that once relieved of her column, shorn of her power, she refused to engage and instead sat stubborn and sphinxlike until her death on December 9, 1972.

On February 1, 1966, two months after the end of Louella Parsons's column, her rival Hedda Hopper died suddenly from a bout of pneumonia. "Who shall replace the Mmes. Parsons and Hopper?" Associated Press correspondent Bob Thomas asked and then answered, "Probably no one. Their successors are pretenders to thrones that no longer exist. Gone are the days when Hollywood was a tight little town that ruled the entertainment world and hence could be ruled by feminine columnists. . . . Hollywood will continue to be a source of the glamorous, the bizarre and the fascinating. But there will never be another Parsons, nor another Hopper."

III

While Winchell strove to reclaim the world that kept receding from him, his son tried retreating from it. Yet here too Walt, Jr., failed. Back in August 1963 he and Eva were staying in the main house at Twelve Acres with Owen when they heard a ruckus outside. Walt grabbed his rifle and a pistol and raced out the door. He found a band of fifteen rowdy teenagers who had, they later said, driven onto the property by mistake, but Walt instructed Eva to call a friend of his, then fired a shot and ordered the teens to get down on the ground. By the time the police arrived, alerted by neighbors who had heard "strange noises," Walt and his friend were both standing armed over the trespassers, four of whom now required hospitalization for what they said was a pistol-whipping.

The youths and Walt were arraigned, and the incident, much to Walter, Sr.'s displeasure, made all the papers. Walt eventually dropped charges, but he was assaulted late one night a few weeks later by two men who sawed an "instrument" across his throat and chided him for having filed charges in the first place.

Over the next year Walt devised a new plan for his life. Desperate to establish his independence from his father and realizing he could never do so as long as he lived at Twelve Acres, he decided to sell some stock and move to Germany. So early in 1965 Eva, Owen, a new baby girl named Kenya and Walt left Greenburgh and headed to Germany. Eva was to stay with relatives in Dortmund while Walt took off in a Land Rover for Berlin to find himself a job, preferably with a newspaper.

At least that was the plan. But on June 23, he and Eva had a bitter quarrel. Two days later Eva received a call that Walt had been delivered unconscious to the 97th General Hospital in Frankfurt. As he told it, he believed he was going to have an attack of malaria and bought some pills at an apothecary. A short time later he asked a policeman for directions to an auto parts store in Frankfurt, and the officer offered to drive him there. In the car Walt suddenly became dizzy and asked the policeman to take him to an American hospital. Eva knew better. She knew that in Germany one could get Miltown without a prescription and that it was this, not quinine, on which Walt had overdosed.

In any case, Walt was released that night and headed for Munich. Six days later he was admitted to the U.S. Army hospital there, his speech slurred, his thought processes slow, his balance so precarious that he fell to the ground every time he closed his eyes. By the afternoon he was reported in critical condition in a "deep coma" and his recovery was "questionable." Eva was contacted, but she hadn't enough money to go to the hospital and she refused to request assistance from Walter, Sr.

In the end Walt recovered and was released. Eva had been informed that he had suffered a nervous breakdown, but when she saw him, he seemed carefree and refused to speak about the incident. The German adventure, however, was over. Their money gone, Walt's prospects exhausted, they returned to Twelve Acres and their old life there.

Or so they thought. When they returned that fall—the fall that Walter, Sr., was suffering with his teeth and moping about the *Journal-American*—June phoned Walt to tell him that she and his father had decided to sell Twelve Acres and that he would have to find somewhere else to live. Walt was crushed. He had always believed that whatever else happened to him, he would have Twelve Acres the way his father would have "The Column." He relied on it. It was the one constant in his life. He begged his parents to keep one parcel for him. They refused.

June consulted her brother-in-law Seymour Mayer to arrange the sale. By this time there were few large estates in Greenburgh—almost every one had been subdivided—and Twelve Acres could have possibly fetched millions of dollars, even though it abutted a school which had nibbled away several acres over the years. (The Winchells' neighbor had, in fact, earned several millions from the sale of his property.) But neither June nor Walter was wise in the way of finance. June wanted to dispose of the property as quickly and with as little bother as possible. The sale was completed on February 4, 1966, to a development company called Old Scarsdale Farm, which intended to clear the trees and divide the estate into small plots. The sale price was roughly $360,000.

Now Walt and Eva had to move. But before they left that winter, Walt made one last gesture of rage at the betrayal he felt: He took an ax and chopped down a tree near the main house. The felled tree would be the only chattel he could claim. In losing Twelve Acres, he had lost everything else.

DROP BY drop. Walter had spent nearly all of 1966 in Los Angeles, then returned to New York early in 1967 to narrate a documentary and have his teeth examined. His seventieth birthday was approaching and some friends had organized a small celebration at Kenny's Steak House, but Walter, apparently unsure whether this might turn into another humiliation, kept demurring, changing his mind only at the last moment. He arrived flanked by George Raft and Joe DiMaggio to a crowd of nearly three hundred guests. "It was like old times," *Variety*'s Abel Green wrote, "with the sycophants and wellwishers showing up en masse for 'the king.'..." Walter was clearly moved and stayed until after midnight, reminiscing, showing old photographs of June with Gloria and Walda and promising to spend more time in New York.

A short time later, however, he was racing back to Los Angeles, having suffered one of the greatest humiliations of all. Since 1964 the *Journal-American* had been hemorrhaging money, and Richard Berlin had initiated discussions, first with the *Herald Tribune* and then with the *World-Telegram and Sun*, on a possible merger. A disastrous labor settlement with the ITU early in 1965 expedited the talks, and in March 1966 the *Journal-American*, the *Herald Tribune* and the *World-Telegram and Sun* announced the formation of the World Journal Tribune corporation which would continue to publish the *Tribune* as a morning paper, a new entity called the *World Journal* as an afternoon paper and the *World Journal Tribune* as its Sunday paper. On April 24, a day before the merger was to take effect, the final edition of Hearst's old *Journal-American* was published. "I failed the old man, Bob," William Randolph Hearst, Jr., conceded that night to veteran reporter Bob Considine. "I should have kept the paper alive. I failed."

Before the merger could take effect, however, the Newspaper Guild struck the new paper because the union had not been consulted. The strike lasted for more than five months, claiming the *Herald Tribune* as one of its casualties. When the new *World Journal Tribune* was finally launched that September, its editor Frank Conniff, who as a columnist had once defended Walter against Barry Gray, was forced to deny rumors that Winchell's column would not be renewed; the plan, he said, was to alternate Walter with Louis Sobol—Sobol, who had been an amiable lightweight compared with Winchell.

However downcast Walter had been at the *Journal-American*, he was even more despondent at the *World Journal Tribune*. The *WJT*, he felt, was William Randolph Hearst, Jr.'s final revenge. His column kept getting whittled, even chopped entirely, until the *WJT* was running only one of the five he wrote and that on Saturdays, and his name, which once sold so many papers, seldom appeared in the index. Realizing what was happening and hearing that the amusement page editor, Clay Felker, "doesn't think highly of Bway columns," Walter began hunting for another outlet almost as soon as the *WJT* began publishing. But early in May 1967, before he could find one, the *WJT*, a jerry-built publication without a sensibility or an esprit of its own, also disappeared.

"One day they [Walter's employers] will say to me, 'Mr. Winchell, we are sorry, but it's this way,' " Walter had said back in 1934. "I'm all set for that line. It will only get that far, and I'll reach for my hat with a smile."

That day came. On May 13, 1967, G. O. Markuson, the executive vice-president of the Hearst Corporation, informed Walter that his services would no longer be needed on the *WJT*. On June 30, Markuson wrote Walter that his contract was being canceled, effective November 30. So ended his column and his thirty-eight-year association with Hearst.

The week after the end of the *WJT*, Bernard Weinraub of *The New York Times* wrote an obituary for the old Broadway column, now finally put to rest after years of terminal illness. It died, observed Weinraub, because of the "rise of television, a growing sophistication among newspaper readers, the decline of Hollywood and the emergence of an international set of performers who no longer read or care about the Broadway and show business columns, changes in reading taste, a growing uneasiness about the truth of many column items and even changing sexual mores." And he quoted a *WJT* executive: "Frankly, our general feeling is that Winchell was passé. In his genre, I think he was the best but I don't think he has substantial reader appeal anymore."

Walter had said he would go with a smile, but even at seventy he couldn't. Panicky as the November termination approached, he began dunning friends and writing letters, pleading for a job. "Just read August 8 Wall Street Journal discussing various people planning afternoon paper in NYC which includes Time, Inc.," he wired the publisher of *Time* magazine. "This is to apply in case the paper has room for another janitor. I can't get accustomed to not seeing my byline in my hometown where it appeared since 1920 until the *WJT* died."

He was more craven with *Variety*, taking out a full-page ad announcing his availability:

Is the 2nd Largest Newspaper Circulation in America in the market for an extra janitor? ... Women's Wear Daily, maybe?

NY Morning Telegraph? Never claimed being a newspaperman, Mr. Editor. Always called myself a newsboy. Peddling papers.

Why not audition the column for one month? If the answer is 'Nope' how much do you people want to sell the Wall St. Journal to Walter Winchell, former millionaire?

He phoned John Fairchild, the publisher of *Women's Wear Daily*, offering to stand on the corner and sell papers. He even asked his friend Art Pomerantz, a photographer at the *Post*, to intercede on his behalf with Paul Sann, but the *Post* wasn't about to hire Winchell. Meanwhile, in what even he must have realized was a symbolic gesture, he brought a collection of photographs to *Time* magazine to run with his obituary.

And all that fall he continued to plead with the Hearst Corporation. "Who can I talk to at the Hearst Corp. about my future in the newspaper business?" he wrote Richard Berlin or "anyone in authority." "Nearly all the Hearst papers have invited me to remain in their papers in the event I change syndicates." But the Hearst company no longer wanted Winchell, and the contract expired as scheduled. Walter now announced that he would be syndicating the column himself, though two weeks later the McNaught syndicate said that it would be distributing the column nationally. By that time he had also landed the column in weekly *Variety*, *El Diario*, *Film Daily*, a racing sheet called the New York *Morning Telegraph* and a new weekly paper called the Washington–New York *Examiner*, though by December he was writing the *Examiner* asking if he was ever going to be paid.

Walter certainly wasn't unaware of his degradation. He wrote in his autobiography, when his bitterness was fresh, that all his old axioms were now proved: "There's nothing so dead as an ex-critic, columnist, or newspaper publisher. Ex-Anything!" "When they want you, they kiss your ass. When they don't, they kick it!" Celebrities snubbed him (one of the first was Roy Cohn), press agents ignored him; some rivals twitted him. Even Rose received abuse. "You're a has-been," one columnist said when she waved hello. "So's your washed-up boss!"

There were times that summer and fall when Walter was without a New York outlet that he almost seemed to invite abuse if it would keep him in the public eye. One day he leaped onstage at the Palace, where comedian Buddy Hackett and singer Eddie Fisher were performing, just as he used to do, and sat on the apron reminiscing; while the stage manager fretted about overtime, Walter finally got up, did a buck-and-wing and promised to return. Producer David Brown remembered dining with his wife at Danny's Hideaway during this period when Walter, sitting in a banquette, waved them over. He had a brown envelope stuffed with clippings about himself, and he pulled out one after another to read to the captive Browns. Finally he slid the clippings back into the envelope, put up his collar and "went off into the night," as Brown described it. Author Jacqueline Susann remembered him plastering stickers in barbershops along Broadway announcing, "Winchell's Coming Back."

With the degradation had come a peculiar humility. The hate and vengeance that had fueled him for so long were finally dissipating. Feuds were ending rather than beginning, and for all his endless vaunting and snarling, there was a sense of Walter's wanting some closure to his life. Several years earlier he and Leonard Lyons had resolved their differences; after surviving a plane crash in 1954, Hemingway, a friend of each, had scolded Winchell and warned, "If you do not reconcile with him, when I get back I will go straight to the Stork Club and flatten you!" Just before Hemingway died in 1961, they had, and Lyons was the one who phoned Walter with the news of Hemingway's suicide. Walter had also reconciled with Ed Weiner when the two embraced at a party and with Lyle Stuart, now a successful publisher. (Stuart had briefly considered sponsoring a new Winchell radio broadcast.) He had even reconciled with Barry Gray.

And that September he reconciled with Ed Sullivan. Walter was dining at Dinty Moore's restaurant with Runyon Fund executive secretary Dorothy Moore when Moore spotted Sullivan and his wife, Sylvia, across the room. In a recent interview in the *Ladies' Home Journal*, Sullivan had credited Walter with being the first of the Broadway columnists. Taking this as a peace overture, Walter immediately rose, crossed the room, shook hands with Sullivan and invited him to join the Runyon Fund board. (By one account, Walter complained about not having a New York outlet and Sullivan offered to make inquiries at the *Daily News*.) A few nights later they were together at El Morocco when Louis Sobol arrived. Walter "commanded" that Sobol join them for a photograph: three old enemies and rivals now declaring a truce. On Sunday, September 10, Walter appeared in the audience for Sullivan's television program, and the truce went national. Sullivan introduced him now as the "daddy of Broadway columnists," which was the acknowledgment Walter had always wanted. Walter returned the compliment at a Friars Club tribute to Sullivan. "As we both grow older, we found that we were citizens of a kingdom more beautiful than Camelot," Walter remarked. "Not a never-never land, but a very real and magic place called Broadway." Now they were among its last survivors.

WITHOUT A radio broadcast or a New York outlet for his column, Winchell turned his attention to the other institution he had created: the Runyon Fund. He had always kept an eye on the fund; as treasurer he was the only one authorized to sign its checks, and the Walter Winchell Foundation had covered all the fund's administrative costs until 1961, when a separate account was created with monies from dividends and interest on the fund's investment portfolio to be earmarked for administration. And once Leonard Lyons had been ousted, things had run more or less smoothly under the guidance of the fund's executive director, John Teeter.

The trouble started in 1963, when CBS president Frank Stanton donated a dilapidated building at 33 West 56th Street to the fund for its new headquarters. Designed by Stanford White in 1901, the building had, in its better days, once been the Woolworth mansion and had then housed a tony restaurant called Place Elegante. Teeter now seemed determined to restore that lost glory. He asked the board for and received $175,000 from the administrative fund to renovate the premises and then set diligently about the task, including in his plans an apartment for himself.

Before the renovation was completed, however, word reached Walter that Teeter was wildly overspending and turning the new headquarters into a personal fiefdom. Alarmed, Walter dispatched Rose and Harry Geist, his longtime accountant, to tour the building. Both were appalled by what they saw. "Geist and Rose reported to Walter it was too fancy for a charity," Teeter anxiously wrote board member Louis Lurie, a San Francisco industrialist, "and if he moved in[,] the public would feel he was enjoying part of the spoils."

In fact, Walter was so incensed at the extravagance that he ordered all construction stopped immediately and insisted that Teeter and the board, which had approved his plans, submit their resignations. Teeter did—Walter apparently relented on the board—though the board also authorized the president, Dan Parker, to spend an additional $135,000 to complete what Teeter had begun. In the end, the renovation cost $342,000 with an additional $15,900 spent in legal fees to sue the contractors for their overruns.

With Teeter gone, Walter seemed placated, but he was back haranguing the board a year later, demanding space in the refurbished building now that Hearst had cut his contract and he could no longer afford his office at the Beverly Hotel. "He will not speak again," administrative secretary Dorothy Moore wrote the board early in December 1965. He had even threatened to come run the fund himself. With that hanging over it, the board agreed to partition an area for Walter's use, and he was again defused.

But only temporarily. Less than two years later—the same fall of 1967 that Walter was begging for a New York column and was at loose ends—he got word that there was some malfeasance in the operation of the fund. Whether or not the report was true, it was certainly true that Walter's control over the fund had slipped and that other board members, notably Arthur Godfrey, were wielding more power than he. Now, with little else to occupy him, Walter was determined to seize command once again.

He called a meeting for October 20 and wrote other board members asking for proxies "to effect certain changes." When the meeting began, one of the opposition board members, obviously hoping to dilute Walter's power further, moved to increase the board from twelve to twenty members. With six proxies in hand, Walter defeated the motion. When the same board member proposed that the old board be renewed, Walter countered with a new slate of board members. Godfrey asked if these were intended as additions. No, Walter said, they were intended as replacements. The new board was then voted in with Walter again using his proxies. Godfrey expressed his pleasure at having served as a member of the board and, according to the minutes, "excused himself." After Godfrey left, Walter was elected chairman pro tem. The coup attempt had been quashed just as it had been with Lyons. For one brief moment Walter Winchell was back.

MEANWHILE, WALDA disappeared. She and nine-year-old Mary Elisabeth had been staying with June at Scottsdale while Walda tried to get a grip on her life after a botched suicide attempt. One night that October at about nine o'clock, there was a knock at the door. Little Mary Elisabeth, who knew enough to realize how unusual it was to have a visitor, asked who was there. "It's Walt. It's your uncle," came the reply. Mary Elisabeth hadn't seen her uncle in years, and the Winchells never spoke of him, so she got her mother and told her there was a man at the door who was claiming to be her uncle. Walda peeked through the louvers, then opened the door, but rather than greet her brother effusively, she asked what he was doing there. Walt answered that he wanted to stay a few days.

The next day Walt, Walda, Mary Elisabeth and June went to dinner and began arguing heatedly. "In the middle of the night, deep in the night," Mary Elisabeth remembered, "my mother came to me and sat down next to me on the bed and said, 'Honey, do you want to go on a little adventure with Mommy?'" Since Walda seldom paid attention to her daughter, the girl was flattered by the offer, even acceding to her mother's request that she not say good-bye to her grandmother. With Mary Elisabeth carrying only a small stuffed pony, she and her mother drove off into the night. They wound up at a ramshackle motel of plywood cabins furnished with rustic tables and chairs pocked with cigarette holes. There was no heating, and there were no other guests. "We were in hiding," Mary Elisabeth recalled.

They ventured forth only at night for provisions. Mary Elisabeth was not allowed outside to play, and she obviously couldn't go to school. A birthday passed unacknowledged. There was virtually no money; they subsisted on Minute Rice. When Mary Elisabeth asked if they might go home, Walda insisted they could not. Finally, after nearly two months of this internment, Walda fell ill. "She got sicker and sicker and sicker," remembered Mary Elisabeth. "She couldn't even get out of bed. She was so sick she was moaning and crawling to the bathroom to vomit."

One day a doctor arrived. Mary Elisabeth assumed that Walda had somehow contacted a friend—there was no phone—and that when the friend hadn't heard from her again, the woman had alerted the police to Walda's whereabouts. Walda and Mary Elisabeth were both rushed to the hospital: Walda for pneumonia, Mary Elisabeth for malnutrition. When Christmas arrived, Mary Elisabeth was told that her grandparents were visiting and she could see her mother in the intensive care unit. Her mother, she recalled, was lying in an oxygen tent "really frail and sickly." Mary Elisabeth asked if she might go home now with her grandmother and grandfather. Walter and June said that of course she could, but this triggered a new scene in the ongoing Winchell soap opera.

Walda insisted that Mary Elisabeth stay with her. "She looked like she was dead except that she was screaming," said Mary Elisabeth. "She kept falling back on the pillows and gasping for breath." "Mary Elisabeth, I need you. I love you so much," Walda pleaded. "You belong with your mother." Walter was furious. He demanded that Mary Elisabeth choose. When the girl, wanting to go with her grandparents, whom she loved, but feeling that she might be abandoning her mother, asked her grandfather for a reprieve, Walter threw down whatever he was holding, shepherded June to the door and yelled, "You two can have each other because I know when I've been kicked in the pants." A week later Walda and Mary Elisabeth were released from the hospital. Exactly why she had left Scottsdale that night, Walda never said, except to tell her daughter vaguely that June had always tried to keep the children apart, as if that had explained it. A year later they were gone again.

IV

Now came the last hurrah. Over the next year Winchell engaged in a flurry of activity, summoning his energies for one final attempt to recapture the past just as he had done in the early fifties, when he had believed he was facing extinction. An enthusiastic supporter of the war in Vietnam, he accompanied President Johnson that November on a two-day tour of military installations. At the same time he closed the deal with the McNaught syndicate to distribute his column, and he negotiated a five-minute television news insert to air in Washington, but he wrote J. Edgar Hoover hopefully that it would soon be seen throughout the East Coast and Canada. On April 1 he regained a daily New York outlet, albeit a small one, in a new publication called the New York *Column*, which boasted that it "brings together in one daily newspaper more of the nation's leading columnists and cartoonists than have ever been gathered in one publication before." Walter was delighted. "Lou, you wouldn't believe his energy," Dorothy Moore of the Runyon Fund wrote Lou Lurie happily.

A young *Esquire* writer trying to get an interview with Walter found himself waiting weeks. (Rose insisted Walter was just too busy.) When the young man prevailed upon some friends of Winchell's to intervene, Walter finally agreed. The journalist also found him energetic, talking rapidly in slanguage, vaunting about press agents wanting to throw him a birthday party whether he liked it or not and bragging over how many obligations he now had. When the writer said he had to leave for a dinner engagement at his mother's, Walter offered to take him. He drove a blue Rambler now and turned on the police radio as soon as he slid behind the wheel. Sunk in his seat, he could barely see over the dashboard and asked his passenger to call out directions as well as the color of the traffic lights. Somehow they arrived, and the writer noticed Walter lingering as if waiting for an invitation. The writer silently debated whether to tender one—"He might accept . . . seems so lonely"—then decided against it. His mother, an old leftist, wouldn't understand. And so Winchell drove off into the night.

But even if it was only his way of staving off the inevitability of his obsolescence, Winchell greedily sought action. In April, when civil rights leader Martin Luther King, Jr., was assassinated, Walter was in Washington to view the riots there firsthand. A few weeks later he was at Columbia University covering the student protests. A *New York Times* reporter there had edged closer to get a better view of the police apprehending a protester and was knocked back by the officers. "He's a newspaperman," Walter called. "His press card is in his lapel." Now the officers turned on Walter, hitting him in the mouth. "I'm a reporter," Walter yelled. "I know you, Walter," one policeman responded. "You're causing more trouble than anyone." Walter took no offense; rather he took great pride in the scuffle. When a photo in the *Times* showed Walter ministering to the fallen journalist—"Bob Thomas, a casualty, permits another reporter to examine his bandaged hand"—Walter beamed that he had been called a "reporter." "That's better'n a Pulitzer Prize!"

The next day he was in Washington to visit the President. Another round of dental surgery momentarily felled him, but by mid-June he was hectoring the White House to inform him if the President was planning any junkets and asking to be included on a possible trip to Moscow. After a brief visit to June in Scottsdale, he was in Los Angeles for the pleading of Sirhan Sirhan, the accused assassin of Senator Robert Kennedy— Walter linked Sirhan to the communists—and then flew to Miami for the Republican national convention.

Through it all, Walter was also working tirelessly on another project: his autobiography. After decades of deferral, he had signed an agreement with *McCall's* magazine the previous September, when he was at low ebb, to serialize his autobiography and had reached another agreement with Doubleday to publish it. The total contract was reported to be worth $150,000, but the activity was far more important to him than the money. He jumped into the book, dictating to Rose over the phone from California. A month later Doubleday canceled the contract. Walter had been sued by Dr. Sam Sheppard, a Cleveland osteopath who had been convicted in 1954 of having murdered his pregnant wife. Sheppard appealed his conviction on the ground that press reports had created an inhospitable atmosphere for a fair trial, and his attorney specifically cited Winchell as one of the chief offenders. The Supreme Court agreed and ordered a new trial. This time Sheppard was acquitted. Doubleday, believing that Walter would now lose his defamation suit and fearing that it might be culpable in further suits over what Walter wrote in his autobiography, asked for an indemnity. Walter refused.

But the lack of a publisher deterred him no more than the lack of a newspaper had. "There was an almost frantic sense going on with that [autobiography]," Shermane Billingsley Drill remembered. That January Walter wrote Abel Green of *Variety* that he had been up twenty-four hours pounding away at his book because he feared "the heavy load I have been taking on will delay my agreement with McCall's to deliver in the Spring" and boasted that he had over 150 pages written. "The other day I left the typewriter for twenty minutes to go to the corner drugstore for a cup of coffee and a sandwich and wrote almost thirty pages in twelve hours—six P.M. to six A.M." A month later he wrote Green that he was up to 300 pages "and I haven't even looked at the stuff Rose took out of the files a long time ago and put on my desk as reminders."

Written in manic bursts, shuttling back and forth through time, the book was so clipped and frenetic that Shermane Billingsley Drill thought anyone reading it would go "bonkers." But Walter loved it; he would guide visitors into his office and read the manuscript aloud with obvious relish, then race to Rose's office to see if she had finished typing the latest pages so he could read those.

By late June he was done, still without a publisher but nonetheless happy. The book was Walter's grand finale—his chance to have the last word, to settle all the scores once and for all, to demonstrate that while he may have sought closure, he hadn't gone without a fight. When it was finally published, posthumously in 1975, Wallace Markfield, reviewing it in *The New York Times Book Review*, called it a "mean, ungenerous, crudely cynical book, boiling and seething with petty spite and prodigious malice—a love letter to himself, a poison-pen letter to the world." But Markfield recognized as well a poignancy within, "moving in the magnitude of its bitterness and rage and ferocious, obsessed energy, in the alternating tones, sometimes within a single page, of fear and trembling . . . and pompous boasting."

The last public act really came that August at the Democratic National Convention in Chicago. Again Walter made his appearance, decked out in his trademark fedora, a saucer-size ID pin on his lapel, two eyeglass cases in his suit coat pocket and his thick copy pencil aimed like a dagger. When a television crew bulled its way past him, a reporter observed that Walter, "his jaw jutting, let the johnny-come-lately journalistic aggressors know what he thought of them." "It was unmistakable—and heartbreaking—to see Winchell as just one of the crowd," Ernest Cuneo wrote, meeting Walter for the first time since the 1964 Democratic convention. Cuneo wrote a few pieces for Walter about the peace protests during the convention, with Walter characteristically approving police tactics and accusing protesters of Communist sympathies. "I never saw him after that," Cuneo wrote, "and, indeed, I never spoke to him again."

THE LAST hurrah ended in tragedy too.

When Walt Winchell, Jr., disembarked early in 1966 from the bus that took his family from the Los Angeles airport to Orange County, he told his wife quietly and with chilling seriousness, "I know I am going to die here." They had arrived with $5,000 June had given them to relocate but with no more plan than they had had in New York or Germany. They moved into a rented house in Garden Grove, not far from Eva's parents, but Eva soon realized that Walt couldn't integrate himself into a typical suburban community. "It just didn't fit him. He didn't know how to relate to that world at all." Eva said he tried to make friends, but increasingly he withdrew into drugs and books. They lived on credit and from dividend check to dividend check, and when things got terribly rough, Walt sold more stock, leaving smaller dividends and even more distress. "I can't even pay the telephone bill," he might say, but he never seemed desperate, never seemed as if he couldn't make it all turn out right. "He couldn't tell this little girl from Germany that he really was afraid and scared, that he didn't know how to take over," Eva remembered.

Jobless, hopeless, he wandered. By year's end he had gone to Hawaii under the alias of Gehleen Dieter and was said to be impersonating an FBI agent there. (Hoover advised his men only to "admonish him strongly.") He was back in California by April 1967 but was still restless and clearly suffering mental anguish. Finally Eva exiled him until he found a job, and he knocked around La Jolla, staying with friends and looking for construction work. That fall he rented a car and visited his mother—the trip on which Walda left with Mary Elisabeth—yet he found no relief there either. He returned to Orange County so narcotized that he would sit stupefied in his chair, occasionally reaching out to touch the children, unable to do much more.

That Christmas he phoned his mother to tell her he loved her and attempted, unsuccessfully, to talk to his father. Then he drove his car to the ocean, leaving the motor running. The police found him comatose, having overdosed on 140 tablets of Miltown. He was placed in the Patton State mental hospital at San Bernardino, California, where for two months he managed to keep his incarceration from his parents. "I was hostile and resistant to everything concerned," he wrote his mother early in March 1968, when she finally discovered what had happened, "but I have come to realize that 'they' only mean to get people ready to live in and cope with the 'problems' we must all face on the so-called 'outside.' " His doctor, he said, had helped him "readjust some of my thinking. I needed to do that."

The next week, Walt wrote his mother that he and Eva were considering leaving California when he was released, but he admitted that "I just do not have *the plan* I so badly need" and fretted that he was "too old to continue wandering aimlessly." He was released on March 29 into Eva's custody, happy to be back home with his wife and children. But "we did not live very happily together," Eva said, "because I wasn't quite sure whether he was OK or not." The Winchells did not leave Orange County, as he had discussed, and Walt did not devise any scheme to end his aimlessness. Instead he started taking tranquilizers again, and thus lost and befogged, he found a job in a restaurant as the "world's worst dishwasher-fry cook," but only when matters had become so desperate that the family could not survive otherwise.

"*Sikia* (that's Swahili for 'Hear me')," he wrote June in December, "there *are* no panaceas for wasting of the spirit, but 'safe harbors' *do* exist. We must all, at one time, or another, find these refuges: some are mountain tops or isolated beach coves. When geographical ones aren't available[,] take deep breaths or walk in the cool of the evening."

Walt, however, had long had another refuge in mind. On Christmas Day, he invited a friend for dinner. At six twenty-five he rose from the table and said he was going for a walk. Before leaving, he embraced his wife. "Eva, I love you," he whispered to her. A few minutes later, she heard a noise outside in the garage. The friend offered to investigate. (Eva believed that was why Walt had invited him—to spare her.) The friend returned from the garage having found nothing. So Eva now investigated herself. "I turned the light on and I saw he had covered himself [with a tarp]. It muffles the sound. . . . But a gunshot is a gunshot. I know what it sounds like. I lifted up the tarp, and I knew he was there."

Walt had put a .38 caliber pistol into his mouth and fired. He had died instantly. He was only thirty-three years old. "Essentially his plan was always—I know this was something he said to himself—'When the money is gone, I'll just kill myself,' " Eva said.

Eva phoned June to inform her of Walt's death—thirty-six years to the day after the death of Gloria. "She seemed very calm to me . . . motherly and in charge." June offered to make all the arrangements; Walter, who was visiting his wife for the holidays, deferred to her. Like Walt, the casket was simple and roughhewn, a plain pine box, and Walt's friends had written parting words on it before it was flown to Arizona for the services. Only the immediate family and two close friends attended.

"Because of tragedy and illness in his family, Walter Winchell is compelled to temporarily suspend his column," the McNaught syndicate announced early in January, when the storehouse of Walter's columns had been exhausted. "You will be notified promptly when he resumes writing. Walter asks you to bear with him." But a month later, McNaught reported that the column was no longer in syndication. "Due to a series of personal tragedies," ran the press release, "Walter does not feel that he can continue writing his daily column. We naturally hope that he will change his mind, because we've been deluged with requests from newspapers all over the country for more of his copy."

Walter told the press that he was taking a vacation to "get his bearings." "I'm so upset, so distraught," he was reported to have said, "I've got to go away and calm down." But he promised that he would be back. He remained with June in Scottsdale, venturing out to Los Angeles early in February, then quickly returning. He said he was spending his time revising his autobiography and supervising the Runyon Fund, but in truth he did little of anything, speaking to Rose now once a week rather than his usual four or five times each day. By the end of February he gave up the pretense and announced his retirement. "It wasn't so much that he finally quit," the *Daily News* quoted a press agent on the occasion. "The world he lived in and helped shape quit on him."

DROP BY DROP . . . and the death of Walt, Jr., the last of them, was the most painful of them. "Let them have their fun," Walter's friend Mark Hellinger had once written of celebrities. "In their game—as in every game the public watches—the time when they will be placed among the has-beens must surely come. And the pills of bitterness they must then swallow will more than balance the scales." So it had been for Walter Winchell.

He returned to New York shortly after Walt's interment, but he was, in his daughter-in-law's words, "mortally wounded by life." June remained in Scottsdale. "She was just shut down," remembered Mary Elisabeth, who had come out of hiding in California with her mother to attend the burial. "She kept saying she wanted to die too." When Walter tried to comfort his wife, she brushed him away. At one point, she picked up a high wicker stool from the kitchen and threw it across the room.

But if there was no longer anything for Walter in Arizona, there was little for him in New York either. He had outlived several eras and nearly all his friends. "He became old very fast," Klurfeld remembered. "My vision of him was as a vigorous, vivid, exciting, striking man. And a couple of years later I see this old, tired man who could hardly move." Nor was the deterioration only physical. One press agent running into Walter at lunch said he seemed "punchy." "He didn't recognize me. . . . He had me all mixed up with somebody else."

Most of his time he now spent at the Runyon Fund, reminiscing or joking with Dorothy Moore or rooting through his files with Rose or awaiting word from *McCall's* on the fate of his autobiography. So that his sense of self-importance wouldn't flag, Rose recruited press agents to take the "Boss" to dinner. But Walter wasn't fooled; he fully understood what had happened. When Dorothy Moore handed him theater tickets, he waved her off: "I'm not important anymore." And he had even taken to wearing a white tennis cap instead of his fedora, as if to acknowledge that he was no longer "WW," no longer the newsboy.

Later that year, Arnold Forster, his old collaborator, agreed to join him at Montauk Manor at the tip of Long Island. "It is seared into my memory—the picture of him," said Forster. "I walked into the reading room, which was large and airy. And he was sitting there alone with *The New York Times* in his lap and his chin on his chest—sleeping. This was eleven o'clock in the morning. He was all white-haired. And it broke my heart. He was totally defeated. He was totally resigned."

JUNE WINCHELL died in Scottsdale on February 5, 1970. Even before Walt, Jr.'s death she had been remote and careworn, confined largely to the house, confined largely to her bed. She lived in her nightclothes and kept the house dark. She was often heavily sedated. Her beauty long gone, she was painfully gaunt, her cheeks sunken, her straight gray hair pulled back severely in a bun.

After her son's death she had broken down completely. Within the year, she had suffered another heart attack and checked into St. Luke's Hospital in Phoenix under the care of a socially prominent physician named Hilton McKeown. It was there she died three weeks later of coronary thrombosis.

Walter was devastated. "When he answered the door when we came from the airport, he was crying so hard," recalled Mary Elisabeth. "I'd never seen a man cry, and he was just sobbing." The funeral was private. At June's instruction both a minister and a rabbi officiated. The rabbi and Walter had settled upon a passage from the Book of Proverbs that Walter felt described June:

> A woman of valor who can find?
> For her price is far above rubies.
> The heart of her husband doth safely trust in her,

And he hath no lack of gain.
She doeth him good and not evil
All the days of her life [. . .]
She opened her mouth with wisdom;
And the law of kindness is on her tongue [. . .]
Her children rise up and call her blessed;
Her husband also, and he praiseth her:
Many daughters have done valiantly,
But thou excellest them all.

Without realizing it, Eva had chosen a cemetery plot for Walt, Jr., abutting two other plots that were already taken. Since an adjacent plot wasn't available for June, Walter devised a different arrangement to keep the family together: June was buried not beside her son but below him.

Afterward the family returned to the house. During the services Eva had taken the children for an outing, and Walter now took her aside and handed her some money. "I know you're having a rough time," he said. It was the only thing he had ever said to her since Walt's death. But that day, deep in his grief, Walter sat on the floor with his three grandchildren and played with them for the first and only time. "I never would have imagined that he had it in him to be so charming," Eva thought.

It was the last time she was to see him. Walter was the beneficiary of June's will, but he gave the Scottsdale house to Walda—even so, she remained in Los Angeles—and settled into a cabana at the Ambassador Hotel. He had withdrawn from everything. Though he said that at the time of June's death he had been in Scottsdale revising his memoirs, he admitted that he had not been making much headway, and the book was seeming more and more of a justification and less of a project. When Associated Press columnist Bob Thomas wrote him in May 1970 to ask his cooperation in a biography Thomas was writing about him, Walter wrote back: "I have stopped seeing everyone, Bob. The tragedies at my house and various other tragedies have depleted me. There is nothing I want to discuss about my career. I leave it to you historians to deal with it. . . ."

Always a hypochondriac, he dwelled now on illness. That spring he had been plagued by stomach pains and urinary problems. Attorney William Simon, a former FBI agent whom Walter had recruited for the Runyon Fund, found him "very low" that July. Later in the month, Walda, who was now overseeing her father's health, phoned Dorothy Moore frantically asking for a recommendation for a doctor. Through her contacts at the Sloan-Kettering Memorial Hospital, Moore referred Walda to Dr. Joseph Kaufman, chief of urology at the UCLA Medical Center. Walter visited Kaufman on July 31. The diagnosis was the very thing Walter had so long feared and had undoubtedly suspected: cancer.

On August 6 Kaufman performed an orchiectomy, removing Walter's testicles, and immediately put him on a regimen of chemotherapy, radiation and estrogen. These procedures were intended to slow the progress of the cancer and provide relief from the pain, but they could offer no cure. Nothing could. "There was no question about his problem," said Dr. Kaufman. "And of course, he knew that he was going to die."

"He kept the cancer a big secret," recalled Rose Bigman, who was sadly a continent away from her boss. "He was afraid. He was afraid of death. . . . He didn't want anybody to know about it." He left the hospital on August 15 and returned to the Ambassador to recuperate. Dorothy Moore visited him there shortly after the surgery and found him both voluble and contemplative. "He used to sit by the pool in the afternoon and talk—an awful lot about the charity, of course. And he'd reminisce about show business and the heyday of Hollywood." Once he remarked to Moore on the terrible similarities between his life and that of his friend Damon Runyon. Both had unstable daughters, and both had sons who committed suicide. He left unspoken that both would now die of cancer.

Though he was in great pain and walked with difficulty, he returned to New York that fall, no doubt because it was easier for him to seem productive there even though he had nothing to do. As before, he spent much of his time at the Runyon Fund, still tinkering with the autobiography that had no publisher, still ripping fresh pages from Rose's typewriter and reading them aloud. Other times, when his mood darkened, he would sit there silently for hours, doing nothing, seemingly bracing for the end.

But it was not quite over yet. A onetime Broadway columnist for the Brooklyn *Eagle* named Robert Farrell had bought the name New York *Daily Mirror* from the Hearst corporation and was now preparing to revive the paper. He called Walter to invite him to return. Rose was skeptical when Walter told her to prepare a new column; there had been so many false starts over the years. But Walter insisted he was serious, and Rose phoned Clyde Tolson ecstatic over the news and asking to be remembered if the FBI had anything of interest for the column.

On December 10, 1970, Walter appeared at a press conference at the Overseas Press Club to announce the new paper's launching and his own "retirement from retirement." He said that he had gained twenty-five pounds since an operation for what he described as a nonmalignant tumor, but reporters were nonetheless startled by his appearance. His voice, once so loud and sharp that it could cut through any conversation like an icebreaker, was now soft and raspy, and reporters had to strain to hear him despite the microphones. The electricity was gone. He was a shell.

To *Variety* a few weeks later he admitted that the new column was essentially "therapy," and he complained that New York was now too cold and too dead for him. On January 25 he left for Miami, where he rendezvoused with Dr. Kaufman. It was, Walter must have realized, one last nostalgic trip, but even Miami had changed. The once-splendid Roney-Plaza had fallen to the wrecking ball, an apartment complex rising in its place. Still, dining with friends, he kept reminiscing, occasionally blurting, "Good evening, Mr. and Mrs. North and South America, and all the ships at sea," as if the words were an incantation that could summon the past.

In March 1971, he traveled to Los Angeles for more treatment. "He was depressed, irritable and impatient," Dr. Kaufman's notes indicated. "He doesn't want anyone to know he is here." Dorothy Moore had tried coaxing him back east for the twenty-fifth-anniversary celebration of the Runyon Fund, to be held that May at the Waldorf-Astoria. Walter begged off. His energy was too low for the trip, he said. One friend later said, "He didn't want anyone to see him. He went back to the Coast to die."

Moore visited him once again that fall at the Ambassador. "We went out every night. He insisted upon showing me all the places," even though "he was hurting very, very bad" and "wasn't sure he could go to the end with the pain." One day during her stay Walter failed to show for a lunch date. Moore found him sitting on his bed in his cabana, his peak cap pushed back on his head. He began weeping uncontrollably. The day she was leaving for New York she found him in the lobby, sitting in his customary chair near the checkout desk. He told her that she shouldn't really be going. Moore joked that she had a fearsome boss who demanded she return. "What would happen if your boss said you had to stay here?" Walter asked. Moore said she had to get back to the fund business. Walter walked her to the cabstand, and as her cab pulled away, Moore saw him standing there, tears streaming down his cheeks.

The pain had become excruciating. The cancer had metastasized into his bones and all Kaufman could do was administer a pain reliever and a female hormone to slow the progress of the disease. In the meantime, Walter had shrunk to 110 pounds from his usual 165. In October he was admitted to the UCLA Medical Center complaining of pain that radiated from his back down his legs. Even so, he was released after treatment and returned to the Ambassador. A press agent remembered seeking Winchell there. Unable to find him in the lobby or at the pool, he knocked on Walter's cabana door. There was no answer, so the man tried the door and peeked in. The shades were drawn, and Walter was curled in the corner. "Please leave me alone," he said.

On November 19 he checked back into the UCLA Medical Center. Kaufman noted that Walter's "spirits were buoyed and he began to feel slightly better," but he was anorexic and deteriorating, and the pain always threatened. Kaufman put him on morphine. "It was slow. It was a terrible way to go."

He spoke to no one now but Walda and Kaufman. Rose still maintained office hours each day—she left Fridays at two o'clock—dusting the photos and answering what little mail he received. "Wish I didn't have to take it," she wrote him of her paycheck. She sent him information and offers, trying to keep him involved, but Walter only scribbled back brief responses, assuring her that he was feeling fine. Rose was like a soldier's wife, knowing virtually nothing, fearing the worst, waiting for dispatches. Finally the notes stopped altogether.

It wasn't until December—after Rose had written Walda bitterly reproaching her for keeping Walter incommunicado—that she even learned Walter was hospitalized. "Rose, I'm coming along fine. Stop worrying!" Walter wrote her shakily on January 7, 1972, in what was to be their last communication. "I don't respond to any messages etc. Rest most of the time. Best, WW."

And so the master of secrets kept the secret of his illness. In late January UCLA confirmed the rumor that Walter had been hospitalized since November in "serious but not critical condition." A few days later the Associated Press reported that Walter's condition was indeed critical, but *Variety* confirmed only that he had suffered a "serious arthritic attack." On February 15 Kaufman told Walda that Walter would not survive much longer. On February 19 he wrote: "He is deteriorating rapidly," but was still conscious, though heavily sedated. He died in his sleep the next day, Sunday, February 20, 1972.

IN THE end it was Walter and Walda. Just as her mother had reclaimed Walter after his breakdown in 1952, Walda reclaimed him in his death throes from the public to which he had belonged for so many years. Even after his death she would allow no interloper. His body was hastily sent to the Westwood Village Mortuary near UCLA for embalming and then was flown immediately to Phoenix. It arrived at nine-thirteen that night, still February 20. From the airport it was rushed to the Messinger Funeral Home, which had prepared the bodies of Walt, Jr., and June. He was dressed in a blue shirt and sportcoat, his body placed in a plain, cloth-covered cedar casket in accordance with what Walda thought was Orthodox Jewish custom.

The funeral was scheduled for 11:00 the next morning at Greenwood Cemetery, just twenty-eight hours after Walter's death. Walda arrived in a white hearse twenty-two minutes late. "All of Dad's family is here now and I'd like to be alone to show my true emotions," she told a small group of newsmen clustered at the gate. She laid a bouquet of daisies on her mother's grave, carnations on her brother's and roses on her father's. Two funeral home employees served as pallbearers and Rabbi Albert Plotkin, who had co-officiated at June's funeral, conducted the graveside service. Walda crossed herself and knelt throughout the eulogy. "Walter wrote a great chapter in American journalism," Plotkin, who had barely known him, pronounced. "He was part of the American dream because he was the American dream. . . . He left a lasting legacy because he believed in the integrity of America. . . . He gave America a soul to believe in. . . a hope to be achieved. . . . This was his everlasting legacy." Walda was handed an American flag that had draped the coffin. She then placed a posy of bachelor buttons on the coffin while it was being lowered. The entire service lasted ten minutes. Afterward, wrapped in her blue lace mantilla, Walda stopped to tell reporters, "He died of a broken heart. Technically of cancer, but actually of a broken heart."

Much was later made of the fact that no one but Walda attended the funeral; some concluded this was an allegory not only of Winchell's mean-spirited life but of the life of celebrity generally. Walter himself might very well have agreed. But Harry Geist, Ernie Cuneo, Herman Klurfeld, Arnold Forster, had all been poised to attend, and no doubt so had many others, had Walda only let them. In a sense, then, it was Walda's allegory. They would have come to pay their respects to "WW," though he had really died years before. Walda was burying Walter Winchell, the vestige of the man who had lived within the image.

"It twinges me that Walter is buried out on the Arizona desert," Ernie Cuneo wrote, believing that Walter Winchell belonged on Broadway. He rests now on a plot covered by coarse, dry grass, crowded by other gravestones and bordered by conifers and palms. He rests now in utter stillness, broken only by bird calls. He rests now with his family, his flat gray gravestone at the top of the column of Winchells, the epitaph as terse as an item: WALTER WINCHELL 1897–1972. He rests.

Epilogue

They argued over his legacy. Walter had redrawn his will in November during his last illness. He left $35,000 to Rose Bigman, $25,000 each to the Runyon Fund* and to Dorothy Moore, $10,000 to Harry Geist, $5,000 to his sister-in-law, Mary, $500 each to Walt's children, Owen Reid and Kenya, and the manuscript of the still unpublished autobiography to Ernie Cuneo. To Walda, he left the rest of his estate to be held in trust and disbursed each quarter at the rate of $400 a week until her death. "He knew precisely what he was doing," Harry Geist's son Herman claimed. "He was trying to protect Walda by shielding the money from her."

Within days after her father's death, however, Walda contested the will. She claimed that her father was not competent at the time he drafted the revision and that the effective instrument should be the will he had drafted six months earlier, one that left the bulk of the estate to her outright. Eventually Eva joined the challenge, asking for money to continue her children's education, and by late summer both had reached an agreement with the estate, paving the way for probate.

Yet the dispute was finally over relatively little money. The man who had fretted endlessly over his finances, the man who had vaunted over his

---

*Shortly after his death, the fund was renamed the Walter Winchell–Damon Runyon Memorial Cancer Fund.

bankbooks, left an estate of roughly $1.25 million, less than what he made in two years at his peak. Everyone, including his family, had expected much more. Where had it all gone? A good deal had gone to the taxes about which he complained so bitterly. Hundreds of thousands more had gone to the Walter Winchell Foundation to cover the administrative costs of the Runyon Fund. There was the support of Rita Greene, who continued to receive her weekly allowance until Walter's death, and the support of Walda and Walt and then of Eva and her children, however modest the amounts. There was the maintenance of the Scottsdale residence and of the suite at the St. Moritz in New York and the cabana at the Ambassador in Los Angeles. There was also talk of failed investments late in life. And failed investments or not, there was the dramatically reduced salary over the last fifteen years—once the broadcast was gone—that forced Walter to dig into his reserves while his expenses escalated.

Rita Greene wrote Walda a few months after Walter's death asking her to honor his promise that she would always be taken care of and warning, as she had warned Walter years earlier, that she might write a book about him. "I fully realize mortals can no longer hurt June or Walter—but the public still loves gossip." Walda refused, but Rita was only bluffing. Her manuscript remained hidden, and she continued to struggle until the end of her life. In 1962 she had retired and moved to southern Florida with her mother, her sister Charlotte and her old vaudeville partner Jewell Percival, who had performed as Jewell DeVoie. In 1975 her mother died, and Rita joined her sister Dorothy in Ocala in the northern end of the state. There, bent by osteoporosis and wheezing from emphysema, she died on July 31, 1983, her life having been dominated by the man who had left her sixty years before and whom she had scarcely seen since.

If Rita Greene had been fending off poverty, so too was Walda. Since leaving Arizona, she lived in a modest three-room apartment in a shabby building in one of the less desirable sections of Hollywood; her neighbors and friends were largely aging show business veterans who, as her attorney described them, "didn't have much future and were firmly rooted in the past." The inheritance changed little in her life. She still drove a battered Chevrolet, still visited the library to read the newspapers rather than buy them, still spent most of her time in her bedroom, still wrestled with the demons of her past.

A bout with lung cancer had ruined her looks, though she felt compelled to tell everyone, even the checkout girl in the grocery, about her miraculous recovery. As she aged, she shriveled—her cheeks sunken, her arms sticklike. According to her daughter, she eventually narcotized herself with drugs and suffered from pancreatitis. By the summer of

1987 the disease had debilitated her, making her incontinent (she visited the bathroom every few minutes) and frequently incoherent, but she refused to be examined or go to the hospital. Mary Elisabeth had endured her own drug problems and was just five months drug-free when she rushed to her mother's bedside to care for her in the evenings after the day nurse went off duty. For days Walda babbled and hallucinated. She had one last day of coherence, trying to reconcile with her daughter. She died on June 30. Now she too joined the column of Winchells in Greenwood Cemetery.

THEY ARGUED about his legacy. Of course, by the end he was known as the man who abused journalistic trust. He had gone from the people's champion of the thirties and forties, fighting for Roosevelt and courageously against the Nazis, to the cruel, spiteful rumormonger of the fifties, glorifying McCarthy. He had gone from a man who demonstrated the inspiring power of the press to one who demonstrated its terrifying dangers. No one could argue away that politically, at least, he had done good and evil in almost equal measure.

The larger legacy was what he permanently imparted to the culture. It was accepted that he was "the country's best-known and most widely read journalist as well as among its most influential," as the *New York Times* eulogized him in a front page obituary. It was accepted that he had made the journalistic discovery, in Leonard Lyons's words, that "people were interested in people" and that he was credited consequently with the rise of a more lively, personal and personality-oriented media. It was Walter Winchell who rewrote the rules for what was permissible in a major daily newspaper; it was Walter Winchell who first created a demand for juicy tidbits about celebrities and then spent more than forty years attempting to satisfy it. "In the annals of addiction," Michael Herr was to write of the national obsession with celebrity, "nobody ever turned more people on than Walter Winchell."

But that was precisely the problem and the cultural tragedy. If Winchell was responsible for having enlivened journalism, he was also responsible in the eyes of many for having debased it. Once loosed, gossip refused to confine itself to columns. Once loosed, it danced all over the paper, sometimes seizing headlines, sometimes spawning whole publications and television programs, sometimes, and more insidiously, infecting reportage of so-called straight news by emphasizing voice and personalities at the expense of objectivity and duller facts. As Herr said, once gossip had been loosed, *we* would become jaded. We would always want more, and the media would bend to accommodate us.

Long after the gossip column itself had yielded to other, larger and more pervasive vehicles of celebrity, this legacy remained. We would believe in our entitlement to know everything about our public figures. We would believe that fame is an exalted state but suspect that the famous always have something to hide. Above all, we would believe in a culture of gossip and celebrity where entertainment takes primacy over every other value. We would believe long after Walter Winchell, the man who had helped start it all, had been forgotten, another name on the ash heap of celebrity.

Notes

List of Abbreviations

DB	David Brown, producer
EB	Edward Bernays, public relations counselor
GB	Gertrude Bayne, friend of June and Walda
JB	Jim Bacon, columnist
JAB	Jo A. Buckley, relation of June
RB	Rose Bigman
SB	Shirley Bentley, sister-in-law of Mary Lou Bentley
HC	Hal Conrad, press agent
LC	Lola Cowan, cousin of Walter
SBD	Shermane Billingsley Drill, daughter of Sherman Billingsley
AF	Arnold Forster, Anti-Defamation League counsel
MH	Mike Hall, press agent
CH	Robin "Curley" Harris, journalist
CJ	Coleman Jacoby, writer and former press agent
EJ	Eddie Jaffe, press agent
JK	Jane Kean, entertainer
HK	Herman Klurfeld
EL	Ernest Lehman, writer and former press agent

L OF C.	LIBRARY OF CONGRESS, WASHINGTON, D.C.
DM	DOROTHY MANNERS, COLUMNIST AND ONETIME ASSISTANT TO LOUELLA PARSONS
SM	SEYMOUR MAYER, JUNE'S BROTHER-IN-LAW
NYPL	NEW YORK PUBLIC LIBRARY
JO'B	JACK O'BRIAN, COLUMNIST
WMP	WILLIAM MICHAEL PURCELL, SON OF MARY LOU BENTLEY
AR	AL RYLANDER, FORMER PRESS AGENT AND NBC EXECUTIVE
PR	PAT ROSE, NIECE OF RITA GREENE
SR	SETH RUBINSTEIN, WALDA'S ATTORNEY
GS	GARY STEVENS, PRESS AGENT
LS	LYLE STUART, JOURNALIST
NS	NAT SOBEL, FRIEND OF WALDA
PS	PAUL SCHEFFELS, WALTER'S RADIO PRODUCER
MRS. WS	MRS. WILLIAM SCHWARTZ, WIFE OF WALTER'S COUSIN
JT	JACK TIRMAN, PRESS AGENT
EW	EDDIE WEINER, PRESS AGENT
LW	LENORE WINCHEL, WIFE OF WALTER'S COUSIN RUDYARD
RW	ROBERT WILLIAM, PRESS AGENT
W	WALTER WINCHELL
IZ	IRVING ZUSSMAN, PRESS AGENT

INTRODUCTION

PAGE

xi *"like trying to explain Napoleon . . ."* Ernest Cuneo, "The Emperor of Broadway," *Seminar*, June 1972, 30.

By one estimate . . . Ernest Cuneo, Introduction to Walter Winchell, *Winchell Exclusive: "Things That Happened to Me—And Me to Them"* (Englewood Cliffs, N.J.: Prentice-Hall, 1975), iv; Jim Tully, *A Dozen and One* (Hollywood: Murray & Gee, 1943), 199.

"largest continuous audience . . ." Dickson Hartwell, "Walter Winchell: An American Phenomenon," *Collier's*, Feb. 28, 1948, 12.

two hundred thousand readers followed. *Time*, July 11, 1938, 34.

xii *"HE SEES ALL . . ."* Ad for Winchell's column, King Features syndicate, Scrapbook 1933–34, NYPL at Lincoln Ctr.

"It was his contribution . . ." Alexander Woollcott, "The Little Man with the Big Voice," *Hearst's International Cosmopolitan*, May 1933, 142.

"inspired more burlesques . . ." *Vanity Fair*, March 1929.

xiii *"Democracy is where . . ."* Herman Klurfeld int. by author.

"Age of the Two Walters." Woollcott, 142.

"I was astonished . . ." Alistair Cooke, "Walter Winchell: An American Myth," *Listener*, Nov. 20, 1947, 893–94.

xiv *"14-carat son-of-a-bitch."* John Crosby, *The Observer Review*, February 27, 1972, 11.

"He can be as warm . . ." NY *Mirror*, Jan. 25, 1942.

"There are bleeders . . ." Felice Early, int. by author.

xv "*I want them all to know ...*" Winchell, 318.

"*Poor Walter ...*" Quoted in *Variety*, Feb. 23, 1972, 70.

xvi "*Winchell's primary objective ...*" Ernest Cuneo, "Walter Winchell," undated press release, WW—Articles About, Runyon Fund files.

1 THE CURSE

3 "*Life has not always shown me a smile.*" Chayim Weinschel, *Pleasing Plants: Contains Poetry, Letters Written Entirely in Hebrew*, trans. by Judy Fixler for the author (New York: Abraham Ginsberg, [1891]), n.p. and 43.

"*I feel like the human being ...*" Ibid., 89.

"*was loved by everyone ...*" Ibid., n.p.

Baruch Weinschel had sacrificed ... Ibid., 90.

"*cursed the day ...*" Ibid., 96.

4 "*My heart is as ripped ...*" Ibid., 33, 36.

"*Grief stands in front of me ...*" Ibid., 1.

"*Where am I going?*" Ibid., 43.

"*With a happy heart ...*" Ibid., 74.

August 1881. This is the date scrawled on his declaration of intention for citizenship, Oct. 24, 1884, Bundle 385, No. 105, NY County Clerk.

The name Weinschel. Benzion C. Kaganoff, *A Dictionary of Jewish Names and Their History* (London: Routledge Kegan Paul 1978), 206.

Weinschels were scholars. Lola Cowan, daughter of Beatrice Winchel and Walter Winchell's cousin, int. by author.

"*it is justly expected ...*" Weinschel, n.p.

"*You are praised ...*" Ibid., 74.

The Weinschels in New York. The U.S. Federal Census 1900 lists Rebecca Weinschel's birth date as April 1880, which would mean she was born in Europe (E.D. 913, Sheet 3). In an interview with me, her daughter insisted she was born in this country. I have opted to go with the census, since it clearly lists Russia as her place of birth.

5 *East Broadway.* Irving Howe with Kenneth Libo, *World of Our Fathers* (New York: Simon & Schuster, 1976), 69.

"*[T]his isn't the country ...*" Weinschel, 91.

"*the province of only the exceptional immigrant.*" Jeffrey S. Gurock, *When Harlem was Jewish, 1870–1929* (New York: Columbia University Press, 1979), 30.

A "big man on Wall Street." Meyer F. Steinglass, "Broadway's Greatest Scribe," *The Jewish Times*, July 25, 1930, 29.

Hyman Weinschel's death. Hyman Weins[c]hel, Manhattan, NYC, death certificate #131, Jan. 1, 1901.

6 *Anglicizing the name.* LC.

"*Life is a lemon ...*" Lenore Winchel, daughter-in-law of George Winchel, int. by author.

"*The minute you saw Max Winchel ...*" Ibid.

A minor trading infraction. New York Times, July 27, 1945, 52.

Dora Winchel. LC.

Death of Dora. Index 25774—1936, N.Y. County Clerk; Manhattan, death certificate #17055 (1938).

Rebecca Winchel. Carol Dombroff, daughter of Rebecca, int. by author.

6–7 *Beatty Koch.* LC.

7 "*When you talked about Billy Koch ...*" LW.

"*Papa, We Gotta Move Uptown.*" Irving Caesar int. by author.

8 "*The rest of the family wanted nothing to do with him.*" LC.

George Winchel on Jacob. LW.

Jacob's affectations. Winchell, 5; "Winchell for McCall's," 2nd draft, unpub. ms., 12, Cuneo papers.

Rose's marriage. NYC, Manhattan, marriage certificate, #666 [1896].

Morris Bakst. There is some dispute here. In the 1900 Federal Census, Jennie lists her year of immigration as 1890 (E.D. 913, Sheet 3). In the 1905 New York State Census, she states her years in the United States as fifteen, which is consistent with the previous record (A.D. 31, E.D. 17, p. 33). In the 1910 Federal Census, however, she lists her year of immigration as 1882 (E.D. 489, Sheet 2B). I have gone with the 1890 date.

8 *The name Bakst.* Kaganoff, 131.

Morris Bakst never became a citizen. NY State Census, 1925, A.D. 17, E.D. 12, p. 19

Fannie Winchel hunted . . . LC.

Rose never learned how to read. Mrs. William Schwartz, daughter-in-law of Rose Bakst Schwartz, int. by author.

9 *George used to call her* . . . LW.

A neighborhood girl described her . . . Mildred Luber, "His Life Is News," *Radio Mirror* (July 1939), 23.

Jacob and Jennie's marriage. Marriage certificate, NYC, Manhattan, #7957 [1896].

Birth of Walter. Birth certificate, NYC, Manhattan, #18310 (1897).

George provided the name. Winchell, 5.

The Winchels believed he favored their family . . . LC.

First pair of long pants. Photo, inscribed "My first pair of long pants," Rose Bigman coll.

"She used to butter his bread . . ." LW.

"Horrible cruelty was the way of the world." Ernest Cuneo, unpub. ms., 48, Winchell file; Cuneo, "Winchell's Early Background," unpub. ms., 46, Cuneo papers.

10 *Jacob was a shirtmaker. Trow's Directory for the Borough of Manhattan.* These were published every other year.

Moving. U.S. Federal Census, 1900, E. D. 913, Sheet 3; *Bromley's Atlas of the City of New York, Borough of Manhattan*, Vol. 3, (Philadelphia: G. W. Bromley & Co., updated to 1902), plate 38.

Algernon's birth. Birth certificate, NYC, Manhattan, #22299 [1900].

"Walter I like." LW.

106th St. near Central Park. Bromley's Atlas of the City of New York, Borough of Manhattan (Philadelphia: G. W. Bromley & Co., updated to 1905), plate 39.

15 E. 117th St. Ibid., plate 34.

Selling silk. Winchell, 5.

"My pop wasn't much of a businessman . . ." Herman Klurfeld, *Winchell: His Life and Times* (NY: Praeger, 1976), 2.

Jacob's appearing for Sunday dinner. Howard Koch, int. by author.

"Here's Uncle Jake again." Howard Koch int. June 9, 1970, Bob Thomas coll., UCLA.

11 *Humiliation flared into resentment.* See *Weinchell v. Weinchell*, #17639, NY County Clerk, Answer July 3, 1919.

"There was nasty talk." LC.

"He never made the mother a living." Mrs. WS.

"My wife has been most dissatisfied . . ." *Weinchell* v. *Weinchell*, Answer July 3, 1919.

"My father was always attractive . . ." Winchell, 6.

Jennie disappearing. LW.

Walter and Algy were shuttled . . . Ed Weiner, *Let's Go to Press: A Biography of Walter Winchell* (NY: Putnam, 1955), 27. The story is repeated in Lyle Stuart, *The Secret Life of Walter Winchell* (New York: Boar's Head Books, 1953), 14, in Klurfeld, 3, and in Bob Thomas, *Winchell* (Garden City, N. Y.: Doubleday, 1971), 17, though none of Walter's surviving relatives believed it, and Walter never confirmed it.

12 *Danville, Va.* Jane Gray Hagan, *The Story of Danville* (NY: Stratford House, 1950), 145–46.

As Walter recalled it unsentimentally . . . Winchell, 6.

Algy annoyed her. LW.

"Algy was pathetic." LC.

A gap in Walter's education. Pupil's Record: Walter Winchel, P.S. 184, Records P.S. 207; Danville *Register*, Jan. 29 and 30, 1932, which reports that Walter lived in Danville for three years, from age seven through nine, and left when his uncle was transferred back to New York. Also Jefferson Machamer, "Walter Winchell," *Life* [1932], which claims he spent two or three years in Danville. Scrapbook 1930–31, NYPL at Lincoln Ctr.

"delicious chawklit and coconut cakes . . ." Winchell, 6.

Dressing Walter like a "little bitty." Mrs. WS.

55 W. 116th St. Bromley's *Atlas* (Philadelphia: G. W. Bromley & Co., 1911), plate 34.

For the next two years he clerked . . . "Winchell for McCall's," undated, 4, Cuneo papers.

Walter's jobs. N. Y. *Mirror*, April 6, 1958; N.Y. *Journal-American*, September 2, 1964; Klurfeld, 7.

Struck by a trolley. Fred Allhoff, "Walter Winchell—American Phenomenon," *Liberty Magazine* (March 28, 1942), 10. See also Washington *Herald*, n.d. [1934], Scrapbook 1933–34, NYPL, and Stuart, 16–17.

"That is how I became a Broadway columnist . . ." Allhoff, 10.

Another telling. Winchell, 7–8.

13 *First appearance in the papers.* Stuart, 16–17, Klurfeld, 1. A thorough search of the paper over several years, however, failed to turn up the article.

The Imperial Theater. Joe Laurie, Jr., *Vaudeville: From Honky Tonks to the Palace* (NY: Henry Holt, 1953), 240.

"The carpets in its aisles were frayed . . ." Luber, 22.

"I can still remember the way I felt . . ." Klurfeld, 5.

For the McKibbons, the risk was low . . . George Jessel int., March 20, 1970, Thomas coll.; NY *Mirror*, Dec. 29, 1949.

14 *George Jessel.* George Jessel with John Austin, *The World I Lived In* (Chicago: Henry Regnery, 1975), 6.

Photo of Jessel and Winchell. Reproduced in *Vaudeville News*, April 1, 1921, 3.

"Little Men with the Big Voices." Thomas, 17–18.

"a great deal of heavy necking . . ." Jessel, 7.

"the ugliest guy I ever saw." Winchell, 9.

He was the star . . . Jessel, 6.

"dressed in blue serge knickers . . ." Luber, 24.

15 *"heart throb of 116th Street."* Jessel, 6.

"No lady killer . . ." Winchell, 9–10.

"Winchell spent the rest of his life . . ." Jessel, 7; Jessel int., March 20, 1970, Thomas coll.

"I missed the performance . . ." Klurfeld, 6.

[H]*e recalled a girl named Ruthie Rosenberg . . .* NY *Mirror*, December 29, 1949.

"This is your fault." Jessel, 8; Stuart, 19–20.

Auditioning for Gus Edwards. Jessel, 8–12; Winchell, 11.

"Ever since I was a little boy . . ." Clipping, February 17, 19??, Misc., Winchell papers, NYPL at Lincoln Ctr.

16 *"School dunce."* Klurfeld, 3.

He had been left back . . . Pupil's Record, P.S. 184, Records P.S. 207.

A teacher once mildly reprimanded him . . . Klurfeld, 3.

he had secured a pass to the Alhambra Theater . . . Stuart, 18.

To the extent Walter remembered . . . Letter from fifth grade teacher, Mary Petrey, quoted in Klurfeld, 7.

Miss O'Donnell. Walter Winchell, "Things I Never Knew Till Now," *Vanity Fair* (March 1932), 83; *Columbia Jester* (October 1930), Scrapbook 1930–31, NYPL at Lincoln Ctr.

Graduation rates. U.S. Bureau of the Census, *Historical Statistics of the United States to 1870*, Bicentennial Ed., Part 2 (Washington, D.C.: U.S. Dept. of Commerce, 1976), 379.

17 *". . . four inches of scar tissue . . ."* Ernest Cuneo, unpublished ms., 48, Winchell file, Cuneo papers.

"I met the world . . ." NY *Mirror*, April 6, 1958.

Gus Edwards's childhood. Cleveland *Leader*, March 1911, Locke coll., vol. 158, 61, NYPL at Lincoln Ctr.

17–18 *Edwards's song writing.* S. J. Woolf, "Gus Edwards's Academy," *New York Times Magazine*, March 23, 1941, 19.

18 *Edwards's vaudeville acts.* Untitled

clipping, Feb. 8, 1908, Locke coll., vol. 158, 46; NY *Telegraph*, June 14, 1908, Locke coll., 158; Woolf, 19.

18   "*They were talented youngsters . . .*" Mrs. Gus Edwards, "I Like to Remember," in *The Spice of Variety*, ed. Abel Green, (NY: Henry Holt, 1952), 70.

"*Here comes Gus Edwards.*" *Vaudeville News*, Dec. 22, 1922, 22.

"*The Song Revue*" opening. McCall's 4th Draft, unpaginated, Cuneo papers.

"*without a doubt the largest offering . . .*" *Variety*, Sept. 24, 1910, Locke coll., vol. 158, 47.

Description of show. Brooklyn *Eagle*, Nov. 8, 1910, Locke coll., vol. 158, 47; *Variety*, Sept. 24, 1910, ibid., vol. 158, 49.

"*I was one of the kids . . .*" Winchell, 11.

larger agencies had little interest . . . Mrs. Gus Edwards, 71.

19   "*What an ovation on opening night.*" Ibid.

The reception was the same . . . NY *Telegraph*, Sept. 20, 1910, Locke coll., vol. 158, 52.

In Chicago the reaction was so tumultuous . . . Show World, March 18, 1911, Locke coll., vol. 158, 60.

"*It will attract business . . .*" *Variety*, Sept. 24, 1910, Locke coll., vol. 158, 49.

He always remembered playing in Springfield, Massachusetts . . . Ernest Cuneo, "Winchell's Early Background," unpublished ms., 47, Cuneo papers.

Mrs. Edwards always traveled with the company . . . Eddie Cantor, as told to David Freedman, *My Life in Your Hands* (NY: Harper & Bros., 1928), 130–31.

"*You probably never knew it . . .*" Mrs. Gus Edwards to W, June 30, 1942, Edwards file, Winchell papers.

"*Personally, I am in favor of an act of the Legislature . . .*" Cleveland *Plain Dealer*, Oct. 28, 1914, Locke coll., vol.158, 108.

"*the solicitude Edwards showed . . .*" Ibid.

19–20 *Breaking the vase.* Winchell, 12.

20   *Walter could never forgive Georgie Price*

or *Gus Edwards.* Mrs. Gus Edwards to W, June 30, 1942, Edwards file, Winchell papers.

"*Go tell that SOB . . .*" Jay Faygan int., March 28, 1970, Thomas coll.

To get reduced children's fares . . . Woolf, 23.

"*the whole world lighted up.*" Winchell, 13.

Walter cried when they parted. Ibid.

125 W. 116th St. Bromley's *Atlas of the City of New York, Borough of Manhattan* (Philadelphia: G. W. Bromley & Co., 1911), plates 34–35.

21   "*There is not a member of Mr. Edwards' big company . . .*" Toledo *Times*, Dec. 5, 1911, Locke coll., vol. 158, 72.

Edwards was forced to reduce the company. Roy Mack, unpublished ms., Edwards file, Winchell papers.

Singing with Kitty Gordon. Walter Winchell, "Once an Actor—Always?," *Vanity Fair*, May 1928, 106.

"*marvelous material for a second Lieutenancy.*" Ibid.

"*before I got caught stamp collecting.*" *Winchell Exclusive*, 18.

So back he went to the rehearsal hall . . . Mack.

He was so nervous . . . Roy Mack to W, Dec. 6, 1939, S&S file, Winchell papers.

Mack was small and jug-eared . . . Colonial *Bulletin* [Lancaster, Pa.], Feb. 23, 1914, Scrapbook 1933–34, NYPL at Lincoln Ctr.

21–2 *Winchell and Mack.* Mack to W, Dec. 6, 1939; Mack, unpub. ms., unpaginated.

22   *Winchell and Nellie Cliff.* NY *Mirror*, May 30, 1933, 19.

She danced when she walked. Sally Dawson Vandale int. by author.

"*doin' my funny imitation.*" "Diary of Joe Zilch," NY *Graphic*, Oct. 8, 1927.

"*a beautiful time in my young life.*" *Winchell Exclusive*, 16.

22–3 *Vaudeville pay.* Mack.

23   *Walter looked like a vagabond.* NY *Mirror*, May 30, 1933, 19.

"*Either you were pretty broke . . .*" Mack to W, Dec. 6, 1939

Walter's revolt. Mack.

he had decided to marry Nellie.
"Winchell for McCall's," 2nd draft, 42,
Cuneo papers.

"Wear these ..." Winchell Exclusive,
16–17.

He was so pale and haggard ... Mack
to W, Dec. 6, 1939.

24 *Walter and Harry Ruby.* McCall's, rev.,
Sept. 1968, 22, Cuneo papers.

Whoopee Trio. Photo, author's coll.

"[W]hy he even cried." Rita Greene,
unpublished ms., 5, Pat Rose coll.

"Follow the Flag." "Follow the Flag,"
lyric by Walter Winchell, music by Roy
Mack, 1917.

"he would have a stroke." Greene, 6

24–5 *Jacob's silk company.* Certificate of
Incorporation, Jacob Winchel & Co., Oct.
19, 1915, 5478, NY County Clerk.

25 *"[A]s W.W. was a young and handsome
fellow ..."* Greene, 5.

"[h]e couldn't stand the noise ..."
Sullivan Co. Record, August 6, 1931, Scrap-
book 1931–33, NYPL at Lincoln Ctr.;
Mack.

Visiting booking agents. Note, Nat
Lewis, Chamberlain Brown Agency, to Ed
Hopkins, October 5, 1917, B file, Winchell
papers.

The Greene family. Pat Rose, niece of
Rita Greene, int. by author.

26 *"I'm small but mighty."* Ibid.

"sympathy being kin to love ..."
Greene, 5–6; Photo album, Pat Rose.

*"the idea of the thing almost scared him
to death."* Greene, 7.

Trying to boost his sagging confidence.
Ibid.

Rita borrowed money. Winchell, "Once
an Actor," 106.

"which helped us no end ..." Greene,
7; Herbert Baerwitz, son of Samuel Baerwitz, int. by author.

26–7 *The second "l".* Greene, 45; Winchell
Exclusive, 22; Steinglass, 29.

27 *Early bookings.* Greene, 7.

Number of vaudevillians. Pat Casey
test., Federal Trade Comm. 128, Feb. 5,
1919, box 70, 258, 300–01 in Robert W.

Snyder, *The Voice of the City* (New York: Oxford University Press, 1989), 46.

"That's like paying the butcher ..."
"Winchell for McCall's," 13.

At one booking office ... Snyder, 47.

"Small-time." Douglas Gilbert,
American Vaudeville: Its Life and Times (London and New York: Whittlesey House, 1940),
375.

28 *"a dirty crack ..."* New York Graphic,
May 9, 1928.

deuce acts. George Gottlieb in Brett
Page, *Writing for Vaudeville*, (Springfield,
Mass., 1915), 7–10 in Snyder, 66–67.

*"suffered the same agony and humilia-
tion."* Winchell Exclusive, 19.

*"meant that your act wasn't good
enough ..."* "Winchell for McCall's," 2d
draft, 12, Cuneo papers.

Lola thought they were terrible. LC.

"He was a fair actor ..." Andy Talbot
quoted in "Majestic Manager Recalls Appearance of Winchell and Greene," *Houston* ?,
n.d., Scrapbook 1933–34, NYPL at Lincoln
Ctr.

Reviews of Winchell & Greene. Undated, untitled clippings in photo album (Rita
Greene), Pat Rose coll.

"Spooneyville." Variety, March 8,
1918, 19.

The war had decimated the ranks ...
NY Clipper, Aug. 14, 1918, 23; Sept. 18,
1918, 3.

29 *Deciding to enlist.* Greene, 8.

Walter enrolled on July 22. NY Clipper,
June 26, 1918, 19; Enrollment Record, Naval
Reserve Force, Walter Winchell, #164 88 06,
National Personnel Records Ctr.

Accidentally burned his nose. Stuart, 24.

War service. "Columnists as They
See Themselves," *Literary Digest* (July 7,
1934), 10.

Interludes in a period of dull routine.
Greene, 8, 10.

U S S Isis. Paul H. Silverstone, *U.S.
Warships of World War I* (London: Ian Allen,
1970), 180.

Navy uniform. Greene, 9.

"Winchell was probably one of the few

men in the Navy ..." Quoted in Georgiana X.
Preston, "Apology to Winchell the Popgun
Patriot," Washington *Times-Herald*, July 19,
1942, E-8.

29   *Released from active duty.* Enrollment
Record; *Naval Record of Walter Winchell*, rep.
from *Congressional Record*, March 30, 1944
(self-published 1944), 4; *Winchell Exclusive*, 19.

   "*It never dawned upon him ...*"
Greene, 4.

29–30   *One trade paper reported ...* NY
Clipper, Oct. 2, 1918, 3; Oct. 9, 1918, 6.

30   *Influenza in Chicago.* Ibid., Oct. 9,
1918, 6, 13.

   second wave of flu. Ibid., Dec. 4, 1918,
13.

   only drugstores remained open. Ibid.,
Dec. 18, 1918, 13.

   Grand Opera House appearance.
Greene, 10–11.

   "*hoping to meet a friend ...*" Klurfeld,
15.

   " '*Come up to Proctor's ...* ' "
Winchell, "Once an Actor," 106.

31   "*I told him of the great crowds ...*" NY
Mirror, Nov. 10, 1935.

   In later years ... Ibid.; "Walter
Winchell Tells How He Won His Start in
Chicago," Chicago *American*, n.d., NYPL at
Lincoln Ctr.; *Time*, July 11, 1938, 33.

   A press card. John F. Roche, "Walter
Winchell's 'Big Ear' Hears Broadway's Gossip and Slang," *Editor & Publisher* (March 17,
1928), 20.

   His newspaper aspirations had been
"*aroused.*" NY *Graphic*, April 26, 1928.

   "*chairwarming in offices ...*" Winchell, "Once an Actor," 106.

   Fortuitously Walter had no sooner
hatched his scheme ... "Winchell for
McCall's," 8, Cuneo papers.

32   *Chicago act. Winchell Exclusive*, 20–21.
   "*I felt instinctively ...*" Greene, 12.

33   "*where we intended to leave the aches*
of the profession ..." "Walter Winchell Tells
How He Won His Start in Chicago," Chicago *American*, n.d., NYPL at Lincoln
Ctr.

   "*Our knees were shaking ...*" Greene,
13.

   McVickers performance. Ibid., 14.
   "*applause was deafening.*" Winchell,
"Once an Actor," 106.

   "*roof went off the theater ...*" *Winchell*
Exclusive, 22.

   "*[I]t will be the perfect finale ...*"
Greene, 14.

   " '*tallest millinery ...* ' " Winchell,
"Once an Actor," 106.

   "*bewildered with offers.*" Greene, 14.

33–4   *New contract.* NY *Graphic*, April 26,
1928.

34   $250 *a week.* Winchell, "Once an Ac-
tor," 106.

   "*If I would only marry him ...*"
Greene, 15.

   They were married ... Marriage License #837254, Cook County, Ill.

   Rita had been keeping an emergency
fund ... W to Rita Greene, March 12, 1924,
Pat Rose coll.

   The couple's only wedding gift ...
Greene, 16.

   "*The boy is slim ...*" *Variety*, August 8,
1919, 16.

   They spent that fall and winter in the
Midwest ... NY *Clipper*, Sept. 3, 1919, 25;
Oct. 15, 1919; Dec. 31, 1919.

35   "*I had my head almost knocked off ...*"
NY *Graphic*, April 26, 1928.

   Or the time in Salt Lake City ... Ibid.
   Or in Butte, Montana ... Ibid.,
Oct. 8, 1927.

   Or the prostitutes in Missoula ... Ibid.,
April 19, 1928.

   the ferry ride between Oakland and San
Francisco ... Ibid., April 26, 1928.

   "*the fragrance of oranges ...*" NY *Mirror*, May 30, 1933, 17.

   the engagement in Colorado Springs ...
NY *Graphic*, April 26, 1928.

   *In February it published one of his col-
umns ...* Billboard, Feb. 21, 1920.

   In March it published three more ...
Ibid., March 6, 1920; March 20, 1920.

   In April it published two more ... Ibid.,
Apr. 3, 1920; Apr. 17, 1920.

"Most actors are married . . ." Ibid., Feb. 21, 1920.

"Seen outside of Cleveland movie theater . . ." Ibid., March 6, 1920.

"Populace very gloomy." Ibid., March 6, 1920.

Still other items griped about the treatment . . . Ibid., March 6, 1920.

"they will learn something . . ." Ibid., Apr. 17, 1920.

a joke that the Palace was . . . Ibid., Apr. 3, 1920.

"When will I play the 'better houses'? " Ibid., March 20, 1920.

36 *fellow performers . . . began to take note.* Greene, 22.

Some days he even wrote a second edition. Harry Saltpeter, "Town Gossip: A Portrait of Walter Winchell," *Outlook and Independent*, vol. 152, no. 11 (July 10, 1929), 414.

"He used to be pretty good in digging . . ." Fred Johnson, "Winchell's Old Partner Tells Dirt," clipping [Dec. 1931], Scrapbook 1931–33, NYPL at Lincoln Ctr.

Bill J. and Ernestine O' B. Stuart, 26.

By the time the troupe reached the West . . . Greene, 22–23.

Train fare for the Pantages circuit. Herbert Lloyd, *Vaudeville Trails Through the West* (Self-pub., 1919), 25.

The plan was to return to Chicago . . . Greene, 16–17.

"In those days that bank book . . ." Ibid., 18.

Walter gave her his pajamas . . . Ibid., 18–19.

37 *He never bought her gifts . . .* Ibid., 36.

"orphans in a storm." Ibid., 19.

"I got the first taste of W. W.'s temper." Ibid., 21.

United Booking Office. Gilbert, 230.

warfare between UBO and Rats. Snyder, 39.

38 *With Rats' members unable to work . . .* Laurie, Jr., 310–314.

NVA membership swelled . . . Snyder, 79.

"To help cement the relationship . . ." *Vaudeville News*, April 16, 1920.

Walter later claimed . . . Winchell Exclusive, 24.

"We knew of course that you were an actor . . ." Glenn Condon to W, June 23, 1920, Bigman coll.

"That was the start . . ." George Kane, "Friday 13 Good Luck for Veteran Newsman," Tulsa *World*, Oct. 13, 1961.

Walter's "Newssense." *Vaudeville News*, June 11, 1920, p. 2.

39 *Everywhere he went now, he carried a Vaudeville News . . .* Photo album, Pat Rose coll.

"Albee spy." NY *Graphic*, Apr. 26, 1928.

Walter had even been warned . . . Henry Brownlee to W, Jan. 6, 1936, Layer coll. Brownlee had been manager of the Pantages's Grand in San Antonio in 1920 when Winchell & Greene appeared there.

most important departments . . . Greene, 25.

"One wonders how and why actors and actresses . . ." *Vaudeville News*, July 9, 1920, 6.

Though Rita had already determined . . . Greene, 25.

Walter was hedging his own bets . . . *Vaudeville News*, July 9, 1920, 6.

"I wanted to be a newspaperman . . ." Winchell, "Once an Actor," 74.

40 *"I have met many magnates . . ."* *Vaudeville News*, Aug. 6, 1920, 1.

"[Y]ou might be something ten years from now . . ." Winchell, "Once an Actor," 74.

"I felt somehow I wasn't good enough . . ." Ibid.

He doubted that he and Rita would ever advance . . . Ibid.

Declining Pantages's offer. Greene, 25.

One vaudevillian described him as "cocky" . . . Emmett Callahan quoted in Klurfeld, 17.

"What people thought bothered him a great deal." Greene, 9.

41 *"The unpardonable sin . . ."* *Vaudeville News*, July 23, 1920, 6.

41 *Western tour.* Photo album, Pat Rose coll.

"*Her state of mind was low.*" McCall's 3d draft, 55, Cuneo papers.

"*I can't go on . . .*" "Winchell for McCall's," 13, Cuneo papers.

Release from Pantages. Ibid.

"*to postpone the date . . .*" W to Howard Langford [Oct. 1920], W file, Winchell papers.

"*I expect to conduct a news column only.*" Ibid.

42 "*About a week from now send a letter . . .*" W to Langford, Oct. 22, 1920, W file, Winchell papers.

"*new idea.*" W to Langford, n.d. [Oct. 1920], W file, Winchell papers.

"*Winchell & Green* [sic] *are a youthful couple . . .*" *Variety,* July 9, 1920, 6.

"*Winchell & Green* [sic] *stopped proceedings . . .*" Ibid., Oct. 15, 1920, 40.

Even Walter was shocked. W to Langford, n.d. [Oct. 1920].

Letter to Langford. W to Langford, Oct. 22, 1920, W file, Winchell papers.

"*two minds but with a single thought.*" Greene, 27.

"*Walter ('Merciless Truths') Winchell . . . returned to the city . . .*" *Vaudeville News,* Nov. 5, 1920, 8.

43 *Walter visited Condon . . . Winchell Exclusive,* 24.

"*I've got $1,500 . . .*" Steinglass, 29.

Glenn Condon. Obit., Tulsa World, Aug. 24, 1968; Allen Girdler, "Condon Honored," *Tulsa World,* June 19, 1964.

But Walter was persistent. Greene, 27.

"*[H]e was eager and anxious . . .*" Ibid.

"*Sometime ago you told me to look around . . .*" Glenn Condon to Albee, Nov. 17, 1920, Bigman coll.

44 "*a wonderful proposition.*" W to Langford, Nov. 20, 1920, W file, Winchell papers.

"*Mr. Winchell's rise may seem meteoric . . .*" Heywood Broun, "It Seems to Heywood Broun," *The Nation,* vol. CXXVII, no. 3326 (Apr. 3, 1929), 391.

Vaudeville history. Snyder, chap. 1 passim.

"*a kind of theatrical laboratory . . .*" Ibid., 132.

45 "*a kid game for men . . .*" George Jean Nathan, *The World of George Jean Nathan,* ed. Charles Angoff (NY: Knopf, 1952), 464–65.

"*a half-filled house . . .*" Salpeter, 438.

"*when every three days or a week meant 'having to make good' . . .*" NY *Mirror,* May 30, 1933, 17.

"*counting on the mediocre orchestras . . .*" Ibid.

"*cellar dressing rooms . . .*" Winchell, "Once an Actor," 74.

the ones who waited outside the stage door . . . NY *Graphic,* April 26, 1928.

"*gaped up at you . . .*" NY *Mirror,* May 30, 1933, 17.

"*We who were successful . . .*" Quoted in Stuart, 30–31.

"*I would rather click . . .*" Winchell, "Once an Actor," 74.

46 "*It was a good apprenticeship . . .*" "Greetings from Winchell," *Billboard,* Dec. 29, 1934, 65.

2 NEWSBOY

47 *An agricultural country gave way . . .* U.S. Department of Commerce, *Historical Statistics of the United States: Colonial Times to 1970* (Washington, D.C.: Bureau of the Census, 1975), 11.

more than a million immigrants . . . Roderick Nash, *The Nervous Generation, American Thought, 1917–1930* (Chicago:

Rand McNally, 1970; rep. Chicago: Ivan R. Dee, 1990), 144.

"*revolt against dullness.*" Thomas Beer, "Toward Sunrise, 1920–1930," *Scribner's,* vol. 87. (May 1930), 542.

"*If all the Armenians were to be killed . . .*" Quoted in William Leuchtenberg,

The Perils of Prosperity (Chicago: University of Chicago Press, 1958), 150.

48   *Walter Lippmann in* Public Opinion ... Walter Lippmann, *Public Opinion* (NY: Macmillan, 1922; paperback ed., 1961), 310.

"inferior man." Quoted in Nash, 59.

"it is the desire on the part of the peasants ..." Edmund Wilson, *The Shores of Light: A Literary Chronicle of the Twenties and Thirties* (NY: Farrar, Straus & Young, 1952), 293.

He always remembered ... Henry F. Pringle, "Portrait of Walter Winchell," *American Mercury* (Feb. 1937), 141.

"I was office boy ..." Walter Winchell, *Winchell Exclusive: "Things That Happened to Me—And Me to Them"* (Englewood Cliffs, N.J.: Prentice-Hall, 1975), 25.

49   *"Times Square and all of Broadway ..."* Vaudeville News, Feb. 25, 1921, 8.

"if you didn't listen ..." Rita Greene, unpublished ms., 28, Pat Rose coll.

" 'Hiy, Hiy!' yells Harry Burns ..." Vaudeville News, March 11, 1921, 8.

He feared that Condon was going to fire him ... Thomas DeVier, "Winchell's Memories of Condon," Chicago *Tribune*, Aug. 27, 1968.

Condon, later, didn't disagree. Tulsa *World*, Aug. 24, 1968.

He became so discouraged ... Arthur Pomerantz, photographer, int. by author; Don Freeman, "The Emperor of Broadway," *Seminar* (June 1972), 32; Lola Cowan int. by author.

"he could go into minute detail ..." Greene, 29.

50   *Joining the Masonic lodge.* Ibid., 29.

He had resisted asking for a raise ... Ibid., 29.

she resented being treated like a child. Ibid., 31.

"He was kind of a pest." Lyle Stuart, *The Secret Life of Walter Winchell* (NY: Boar's Head Books, 1953), 38.

"later it grew ..." Greene, 33.

51   *"I go the pace that kills ...".* Vaudeville News, Dec. 22, 1922, 33.

"I have always held a hatred ..." Ibid., Dec. 22, 1922, 77.

"What do you know ..." Sam Marx int. by author.

"I saw a young man ..." Bernard Sobel, *Broadway Heartbeat: Memoirs of a Press Agent* (NY: Hermitage House 1953), 301.

Salaries. Greene, 30; NY *Mirror*, July 30, 1940. Study of newspaper salaries by the Association of Teachers of Journalism quoted in Silas Bent, *Ballyhoo: The Voice of the Press* (NY: Boni & Liveright 1927), 118.

"It didn't dawn on me at the time ..." Winchell, 27.

Cheese Club. NY *Star*, Dec. 22, 1920, 17.

American Legion. Vaudeville News, Aug. 17, 1923, 7.

Performing at NVA benefit. Ibid., Dec. 23, 1921, 10.

Singing at Friars Club. Ibid., Dec. 14, 1923, 14.

"Nighthawk of the Roaring Forties ..." Ibid., June 9, 1922. When Bide Dudley, a columnist with the *Evening World*, chided him for rhyming "complain" with "name" and "me" with "me," Walter was contrite. "We'll just fess up that we still have lots to learn" (*Vaudeville News*, June 16, 1922).

52   *Two Sweet Things.* Vaudeville News, Nov. 25, 1921, Dec. 9, 1921.

"I have a wife ..." Ibid., Dec. 23, 1921, 22.

"I was a newspaperman ..." Winchell, 25.

"There was a minor quarrel ..." Ibid., 25–26; "Winchell for McCall's," 13, Cuneo papers.

Rita's description. Greene, 33–35.

53   *He even "appropriated" money ...* W to Rita Greene, March 12, 1924, Pat Rose coll.

that Easter, for the first time Rita could remember ... Greene, 36.

In October he went to Philadelphia ... Ibid., 38–39.

Walter insisted he loved her ... Ibid., 36.

53 *"There's a guy in the heart of Maryland . . ." Vaudeville News*, Oct. 6, 1922.

Meanwhile, Walter's aunt Beatrice . . . Greene, 43.

"you know little Walter . . ." Ibid., 38.

They were strolling up Broadway . . . Ibid., 39.

54 *"I like to think no more my love . . ." Vaudeville News*, Nov. 2, 1923, 14.

"Letters exchanged by two estranged souls . . ." W to Rita Greene, Dec. 2, 1923, Pat Rose coll.

"gave me an opportunity . . ." W to Rita Greene, March 12, 1924, Pat Rose coll.

55 *On January 28, 1919, it finally came apart. Weinchell v. Weinchell*, Filing, June 26, 1919, NY County Clerk's Office, #17639.

"To let out my terrible temper . . ." Ibid., Letter, Jake Winchel to W, Feb. 3, 1919.

Some two years later . . . Weinchell v. Weinchell, Filing, Jan. 3, 1922.

In one version of the story . . . Winchell, 31.

"Sorry. It was rude of me . . ." Cornelia Strassburg, "The True Love Story of Walter Winchell," *Love Magazine* (Jan. 1931), 67–69, 124.

"The parents of little Angeline . . ." Vaudeville News, May 5, 1922, 10.

56 *"he never sat through his meals . . ."* Greene, 32–33.

"grace and beauty . . ." Winchell, 31.

Brookhaven, Mississippi: The WPA Guide to the Magnolia State (NY: Viking, 1938; rep. Jackson, Miss.: Press of Mississippi, 1988), 453–54; Brookhaven-Lincoln County Chamber of Commerce, *Brookhaven: See What We've Got*, n.d.

"where ladies never made calls . . ." WPA, 453–54.

James A. Hoskins. Brookhaven *Leader*, Oct. 12, 1898.

Sawmill burning down. Ibid., Oct. 9, 1884.

"always acting in shows . . ." Jo A. Buckley int. by author; Christine Cotton to author, April 21, 1991.

Another said she had a dry wit . . . JAB.

According to family lore . . . Christine Cotton to author.

"M. C. Magee and Mamie Hoskins . . ." Brookhaven *Leader*, July 22, 1903.

57 *Elizabeth McLaurin.* Ard Matthews, "Brookite Recalls How Local Girl Met and Married Walter Winchell," Brookhaven *Daily Leader*, Feb. 22, 1972, 1, 11.

Earl and His Girls. Brookhaven *Semi-Weekly Leader*, May 4, 1907.

Their theatrical aspirations . . . Sarah Fried, relative, to author, June 7, 1991; Jennie Lee Addison and Jo. A. Buckley to Sarah Fried, May 1991.

"She may have led the family . . ." Christine Cotton to author, June 2, 1991.

"I didn't believe it." Mary Mayer int. by author.

Baby Mary went to Hollywood . . . Vaudeville News, Jan. 26, 1923, 14.

even misreporting in the News . . . Winchell, 32.

"She had such a sweet voice." Mrs. William B. Schwartz int. by author.

"I couldn't eat . . ." Winchell, 32.

58 *Walter insists she kept spurning his advances . . .* Ibid., 37.

"[t]wo popular young members . . ." Vaudeville News, Aug. 4, 1922, 10; Sept. 8, 1922; Sept. 15, 1922.

"If you go for anybody . . ." Strassburg.

The date he always gave was May 11, 1923. Note on *New Yorker* fact checking from Rose Bigman, n.d. [1940], *New Yorker* file, Winchell papers.

"[H]e couldn't afford to fail . . ." Greene, 44.

Bernarr Macfadden. Robert Ernst, *Weakness Is a Crime: The Life of Bernarr Macfadden* (Syracuse: University of Syracuse Press, 1991), 4 passim. Also William R. Hunt, *Body Love: The Amazing Career of Bernarr Macfadden* (Bowling Green, Ohio: Bowling Green State University Popular Press, 1989).

59 *he often stood in front of the mirror . . .* Mary Macfadden and Emile Gauvreau, *Dumbbells and Carrot Strips: The Story of*

Bernarr Macfadden (NY: Henry Holt, 1953), 6.

Macfadden's fortune. Ernst, 88.

Bernays and Macfadden. Edward L. Bernays, *Biography of an Idea: Memoirs of Public Relations Counsel Edward L. Bernays* (NY: Simon & Schuster, 1965), 360.

"Doctors are taboo." Macfadden and Gauvreau, 42.

Byron Macfadden's death. Ibid., 330–31.

"It's better she's gone." Ernst, 70.

"Money is power." Macfadden and Gauvreau, 302–03.

60   *"... there were degrees of sensationalism ..."* Fulton Oursler, *Behold the Dreamer!: The Autobiography of Fulton Oursler,* ed. and with commentary by Fulton Oursler, Jr. (Boston: Little, Brown, 1964), 204.

"all alike, made in the same mold ..." *Editor & Publisher* (Aug. 30, 1924), 5.

"the masses not the classes." Emile Gauvreau, *My Last Million Readers* (NY: Dutton, 1941), 104.

Walter implored him to phone Oursler ... Fred Allhoff, "Walter Winchell—American Phenomenon," *Liberty Magazine* (March 28, 1942), 12; W to Stanley Walker, April 13, 1933, Bigman coll.

Frescott arranged an introduction ... Oursler, 206.

"It was personal." Stuart, 42.

"I knew then he would make a good editor ..." W to Lester Cohen in Cohen, *NY Graphic: The World's Zaniest Newspaper* (Philadelphia: Chilton Books, 1964), 35.

"From my talks with him ..." Oursler, 206; Gauvreau, 118, put the salary at $100 per week. In either case he would be getting less than at the *News.*

61   *"Winchell was scared about it."* George Kane, "Friday 13 Good Luck for Veteran Newsman," Tulsa *World*, Oct. 13, 1961.

"Look, Walter ..." NY *Post*, Jan. 8, 1951, 32.

"Walter, you've had four years experience ..." LC; Don Freeman, "The Emperor of Broadway," *Seminar*, June 1972, 32.

"Are you going to handle the theatrical advertising ..." Walter Kingsley to W, Aug. 22, 1924, W file, Winchell papers.

"proved beyond question of doubt ..." Clipping [Sept. 1924], Scrapbook 1924, NYPL at Lincoln Ctr.

"astonished at the gathering." Oursler, 206.

"Winchell deserves." Clipping, n.d., Scrapbook 1924, Winchell papers, NYPL at Lincoln Ctr.

62   *"Walter, as a dramatic critic ..."* Betty Compton Walker, "WW on Broadway," NY *Mirror*, July 31, 1933, 17.

"We couldn't envisage ..." Frank Mallen, *Sauce for the Gander* (White Plains, N.Y.: Baldwin Books, 1954), 2–3.

After the second dress rehearsal ... Macfadden and Gauvreau, 376.

"A Newspaper with a New Idea ..." Mallen, 5.

"his gestures and bearing ..." Cohen, 5–6.

"We are going to publish a newspaper ..." Ibid., 6–7.

63   *"The common people are the salt of the earth."* NY *Graphic*, Sept. 15, 1924.

First issue of Graphic. Simon Michael Bessie, *Jazz Journalism: The Story of Tabloid Newspapers* (NY: Dutton, 1938), 187–88.

There were other stories that week ... NY *Graphic*, Sept. 16, 17, 18, 19, 20, 22, 1924.

"hardly a newspaper." Ibid., Sept. 24, 1924.

"only three inches ..." *Editor & Publisher*, Sept. 20, 1924, 5.

The New York Public Library stopped carrying ... Stanley Walker, *Mrs. Astor's Horse* (NY: Frederick Stokes, 1935), 305.

"[I]f you're so clever ..." NY *Graphic*, Oct. 23, 1924.

There would be a joke ... Mallen, 56.

"Our advice to young men ..." NY *Graphic*, Oct. 3, 1924.

64   *Walter had the quote ...* Ibid., April 18, 1924.

"the goddam biggest cockroach ..." Edward Anthony, *O Rare Don Marquis* (Garden City, N.Y.: Doubleday, 1962), 142.

64 *"This newcomer ..."* NY *Mirror*, May 19, 1938.

65 *"Other columnists appealed to the high-brows ..."* Emile Gauvreau, *Hot News* (NY: Macaulay Co., 1931), 227–28.

Debut column. NY *Graphic*, Sept. 20, 1924.

"The place vibrated to his gait." Mallen, 148.

65–6 *Walter's office.* Mallen, 150; Cohen, 3.

66 *"a hunched figure ..."* Gauvreau, 118.

"lean hungry look ..." Quoted in Stuart, 44.

He admitted now to "stage fright." Stanley Walker, *The Night Club Era* (NY: Frederick Stokes, 1933), 34.

On Sundays he remained at the Graphic ... Harry Salpeter, "Town Gossip," *Outlook and Independent*, vol. 152, no. 11, July 10, 1929, 438.

To his fellow workers ... J. Eugene Chrisman, "Are the Stars Afraid of Winchell?" Des Moines *Register* [rep. *Screen Play Magazine*], Oct. 1, 1933.

66–7 *Sime Silverman.* Dayton Stoddart, *Lord Broadway: Variety's Sime* (NY: Wilfred Funk, 1941), passim.

67 *"almost paternal."* Ibid., 351.

"My best tipster." Jerry Walker, "Winchell Admits Fluffs; He'd Like a Little Credit," *Editor & Publisher*, Nov. 13, 1948, 46.

"Walter, I give you tips ..." Ibid.

Meeting Guinan. John S. Stein and Hayward Grace, "Hello Sucker!: The Life of Texas Guinan," unpub. ms., 1941, 165, NYPL at Lincoln Ctr.

"A couple of the boys ..." Allhoff, 12–13.

"From that time on ..." Winchell, 2, 49.

Texas's nickname. Stein, 6; See also Louise Berliner, *Texas Guinan: Queen of the Night Clubs* (Austin: University of Texas Press, 1993).

68 *won a following that included President Harding* ... Stephen Graham, *New York Nights* (NY: George H. Doran, 1927), 97.

"I didn't need much coaxing ..." Lloyd Morris, *Postscript to Yesterday: America—The Last Fifty Years* (NY: Random House, 1947), 72.

"It depends on how many quarts ..." Stein and Grace, 147.

"had something that made everyone feel instantly at ease ..." Sophie Tucker, *Some of These Days* (Garden City, N.Y.: Doubleday, Doran & Co., 1945), 102.

"There was something in that 'Hello, sucker!' ..." Jack Lait and Lee Mortimer, *New York Confidential* (Chicago: Ziff-Davis, 1948), 235.

"prodigious woman ..." Edmund Wilson, "Night Clubs," *New Republic*, Sept. 9, 1925, 71.

68–9 *"Let's turn this into a whoopee place ..."* Stein and Grace, 150.

69 *"This little girl is new ..."* Ibid.

"the spirit of after-the-war ..." Nils T. Grandlund, "Gentlemen Gangsters," NY *Mirror*, Nov. 11, 1932, 12.

"It was as if, elevated to fame ..." Morris, 73.

Mark Hellinger. Jim Bishop, *The Mark Hellinger Story* (NY: Appleton-Century-Croft, 1952), passim.

70 *"His conscious effort ..."* Ibid., 15.

"If Hellinger comes ..." Winchell, 50.

Making the rounds together each night ... Bishop, 59–60, 65.

Hellinger once got Walter drunk ... NY *Mirror*, Oct. 19, 1932, 19.

"He is young ..." Percy Hammond, "The Theaters," NY *Herald Tribune*, n.d. [1926], Scrapbook 1924, Winchell papers, NYPL at Lincoln Ctr.

"I was happy." Hellinger to W, April 28, 1926, Hellinger file, Winchell papers.

He wrote a song at Nedick's ... Application for title to Music Publishers' Protective Assn. for "Main Street Rose," by Abel Green, Walter Winchell and Ben Bernie, July 22, 1925, W file, Winchell papers.; clippings, n.d., Scrapbook 1924, NYPL at Lincoln Ctr.

"If Walter Winchell ever gets a flat

tire . . ." Clippings, Scrapbook 1924, NYPL at Lincoln Ctr.

71 *"the dictator of contemporary slang."* Paul Robert Beath, "Winchellese," *American Speech* (Oct. 1931), 44.

Slang. See Irving L. Allen, *The City in Slang: New York Life and Popular Speech* (NY: Oxford University Press, 1993).

slang as protection. Salpeter, 414; "Backstairs Secrets for All," *Literary Digest,* July 27, 1929, 25.

"I'm an alleged representative of Broadway . . ." John F. Roche, "Walter Winchell's 'Big Ear' Hears All Broadway's Gossip and Slang," *Editor & Publisher,* March 17, 1928, 20.

72 *"My idea is to play you . . ."* Sweinhart to W, Dec. 27, 1924, W file, Winchell papers.

"No paper but Macfadden's tabloid . . ." Gauvreau, *My Last Million Readers,* 119.

"the boss wanted sex on every front page . . ." Mallen, 55.

Graphic *contests.* Cohen, 50–51.

Visitors to the office. Gauvreau, *My Last Million Readers,* 105.

Lonely Hearts Balls. Mallen, 19–23.

73 *"Piker!"* John L. Spivak, "The Rise and Fall of a Tabloid," *American Mercury,* vol. 33, no. 127 (July 1934), 310.

The paper was sued by another aggrieved party . . . Ibid.

Composograph. Cohen, 100–101.

"Newspapers have not yet recovered . . ." Spivak, 306.

"on the psychological principle . . ." Walker, *City Editor* (NY: Frederick Stokes, 1934), 69. This notion, in fact, came as a kind of revelation to the journalists themselves, a class who had long been naive empiricists believing in the sanctity of objectivity. When that belief was shaken, it gave rise to "new genres of subjectivity," including the political column. But the tabloid itself was a *medium* of subjectivity. (See Michael Schudson, *Discovering the News: A Social History of American Newspapers* [NY: Basic Books, 1978], 6–8)

74 Daily News *circulation.* Frank Luther

Mott, *American Journalism,* 3d ed. (NY: Macmillan, 1962), 667–69.

The Graphic *by comparison . . .* Gauvreau, *My Last Million Readers,* 132; Oscar Garrison Villard, "Tabloid Offenses, *Forum,* vol. LXXVII, no. 4 (April 1927), 490.

"90 per cent entertainment . . ." Bessie, 139.

"Why do most journalists dislike the N.Y. tabloids?" Clipping, n.d., misc. papers, NYPL at Lincoln Ctr.

The only consolation . . . Bent, 189; *New Republic,* May 25, 1927, 6–7.

"of the people . . ." Martin Weyrauch, "The Why of Tabloids," *Forum,* vol. LXXVII, no. 4 (April 1927), 501.

"semi-literate." Bent, 189–190.

"[O]nly a sharp lowering . . ." Richard G. de Rochemont, "The Tabloids," *American Mercury,* vol. IX, no. 34 (Oct. 1926), 188.

"It is difficult to believe . . ." Samuel Taylor Moore, "Those Terrible Tabloids," *The Independent,* vol. 116, no. 395 (March 6, 1926), 264.

Moral opposition to tabloids. Edward S. Martin, "Editor's Easy Chair," *Harper's Monthly* (April 1927), 664.

"taste of their readers . . ." Silas Bent, "Roller Coaster Journalism," *Saturday Review,* vol. IV, no. 43 (May 19, 1928), 865.

E. E. Cummings . . . blamed them for an infantilism . . . E. E. Cummings, "The Tabloid Newspaper," *Vanity Fair* (Dec. 1926), 83.

"If this appetite is not curbed . . ." Aben Kandel, "A Tabloid a Day," *Forum,* vol. LXXVII, no. 3 (March 1927), 378.

"It is a skirmish in the war . . ." Weyrauch, 492.

75 *"The success of the tabloid . . ."* Quoted in Edmond D. Coblentz, *William Randolph Hearst: A Portrait in His Own Words* (NY: Simon & Schuster, 1952), 263.

"Shaggy Einstein was the symbol . . ." Richard Schickel, *Intimate Strangers: The Culture of Celebrity* (Garden City, NY: Doubleday, 1985), 56.

"There was a time when a reader . . ." Daniel J. Boorstin, *The Image: A Guide to*

Pseudo-Events in America, rev. ed. (NY: Atheneum, 1978), 7.

75–6   *Edward West Browning and Mary Louise Spas*. NY *Daily News*, Aug. 5–9, 1925.

76   *the* Graphic *convinced him to buy a gander* . . . Spivak.

"*Honk Honk. It's the Bonk!*" Walker, *Mrs. Astor's Horse*, 209–212; Cohen, 125. For more on "Daddy" and "Peaches" see Damon Runyon, *Trials and Tribulations* (London: Xanadu, 1946; paperback rep. NY: International Polygonics, 1991), 96–138.

"*Distort the world* . . ." "Tabloid Poison," *Saturday Review of Literature*, vol. III, no. 30 (Feb. 19, 1927), 589.

77   "*drama of life.*" Weyrauch, 496.

Largely working class and . . . *as much as one-third women* . . . John D. Stevens, *Sensationalism and the New York Press* (NY: Columbia University Press, 1991), 120–121.

"*To be seen reading* The New York Times . . ." Meyer Berger, *The Story of the New York Times, 1851–1951* (NY: Simon & Schuster, 1951), 124.

A good, useful definition of "gossip" remains elusive. Dictionaries generally define it variably as a "trivial rumor of a personal nature" or as "casual, chatty talk," but gossip needn't be trivial in its impact while chatty talk is generic and seems to describe something other than the practice of gossip as we know it from tabloids and television. What Winchell and his confreres seemed to mean by gossip was a publicly unverified "fact" about a person or persons that the subject(s) would have preferred to keep private.

Town Topics. Cleveland Amory, *Who Killed Society?* (NY: Harper & Bros., 1960), 123–24.

"*When someone tells us a long story* . . ." *Town Topics*, June 29, 1922.

Broadway Brevities. NY *Times*, Jan. 28, 1925, 21.

78   "*I know of few things* . . ." Ibid., Feb. 1, 1925, 7.

Brandeis on privacy. Samuel D. Warren and Louis D.Brandeis, "The Right to Privacy," *Harvard Law Review*, vol. 4 (December 1890), 193–220.

"*no private scandal* . . ." Quoted in Stevens, 127.

"*Edna Wheaton and Bert Gordon were married last week.*" NY *Graphic*, Oct. 5, 1924.

79   "*tells everything she knows as soon as she knows it.*" Damon Runyon, *Guys and Dolls* (NY: Frederick Stokes, 1931), 123.

"*Why don't you make a note of it* . . ." Winchell, 51; "Winchell for McCall's," 16, Cuneo papers. That there is no record of twins in the Vanderbilt family at that time may throw Walter's memory into question. Unfortunately the columns from that period no longer exist to verify it.

In this account, he had gotten a tip . . . Salpeter; Irving Hoffman, "Things You Never Knew till Now About Walter Winchell," *Radio Guide*, May 1, 1937, 3.

Meanwhile, Walter received two more items . . . Allhoff, 13.

"*If you got a tip* . . ." J.P. McEvoy, "He Snoops to Conquer," *Saturday Evening Post*, Aug. 13, 1938, 45.

"*I was giving them hot news* . . ." Klurfeld, 30.

But he kept collecting the items . . . McEvoy, 45.

"*This news feat* . . ." Walker, *Mrs. Astor's Horse*, 15.

"*People could scarcely believe* . . ." Sobel, 301.

80   "*Winchell reacted almost physically to gossip.*" Herman Klurfeld, 32.

"*every effort not to involve a married man* . . ." NY *Mirror*, Jan. 22, 1935, quoted in Neil MacNeil, *Without Fear or Favor* (NY: Harcourt, Brace, 1940), 296.

81   *Community and society*. Louis Wirth, "Urbanism as a Way of Life," *American Journal of Sociology*, vol. 44 (July 1938), 21.

Gossip as vengeance. Ralph L. Rosnow and Gary Alan Fine, *Rumor and Gossip: The Social Psychology of Hearsay* (NY: Elsevier, 1976), 91.

"*as justice in a corrupt world.*" "The Dish on Nancy," *Nation*, vol. 252, no. 16 (Apr. 29, 1991), 543–44.

"*Gauvreau was opposed to me.*" W to Stanley Walker, Apr. 13, 1933, Bigman coll.

"*I think Gauvreau was jealous of him . . .*" Edward Bernays int., June 15, 1970, Thomas coll.

81–2   *Gauvreau's childhood.* Gauvreau, *My Last Million Readers*, 40–41.

82   *Gauvreau joining the* Graphic. Ibid., 101–02.

"*I was part of that strange race . . .*" Obit., *NY Times*, Oct. 17, 1956, 35.

"*behaved like the sons of clergymen . . .*" Oursler, 205.

"*rebellion against hypocrisy . . .*" Quoted in Cohen, 61.

"*Gauvreau's heart was involved with the paper . . .*" Ibid.

83   "*You are pouring out all your passion . . .*" Gauvreau, *My Last Million Readers*, 130–131.

"*as though he had been a design . . .*" Gauvreau, *The Scandal Monger* (NY: Macaulay, 1932), 187.

"*bludgeoned his way out front . . .*" Ibid., 40.

actually believed he was Napoleon's avatar. Mallen, 55.

"*crowning himself king of Broadway . . .*" Gauvreau, *The Scandal Monger*, 25.

"*He'll smell out the rats . . .*" Ibid., quoted in "Our Own World of Letters," *Editor & Publisher* (Sept. 10, 1932).

"*I was the only one on the paper . . .*" Cohen, 27–29.

84   *Gauvreau's compromising situation.* Mallen, 116–18; Gauvreau, *My Last Million Readers*, 111–113.

"*cripple.*" Winchell, 42.

"*defect . . . accounts for their extreme bitterness . . .*" Walter Winchell, "Tabloid Managing Editors," *American Spectator*, vol. 1, no. 6 (April 1933).

"*it is dangerous in New York . . .*" Ibid.

Gauvreau even hinted . . . Gauvreau, *My Last Million Readers*, 156–58.

"*not terribly amusing.*" A. J. Liebling, "The Boys from Syracuse" in *The Telephone Booth Indian* (San Francisco: North Point Press, 1990), 85.

"*As I do not approve of this system of criticism . . .*" *NY Graphic*, Oct. 29, 1924.

"*to show up the bunk . . .*" Clipping, n.d., Scrapbook 1924, NYPL at Lincoln Ctr.

"*Only those who have been written about . . .*" *NY Graphic*, March 9, 1928.

"*I really don't think any of my regular reviews . . .*" W to John Mason Brown, Sept. 6, 1933, bms 1948 (8411), John Mason Brown coll., Harvard University.

85   "*The greatest and most marvelous . . .*" *Smiles*, draft, Nov. 20, 1930, Winchell papers, NYPL at Lincoln Ctr.

they demanded to be referred to as the "*Messrs. Shubert*" . . . Liebling, 72.

"*One is named Lee and the other Jacob . . .*" C. P. Grenaker to W, Sept. 26, 1925; W to Grenaker, n.d. [1925], W file, Winchell papers.

"*Am I to write what I think . . .*" W to Macfadden, n.d. [March 1926], W file, Winchell papers.

"*we should not allow them to bulldoze us.*" Macfadden to W, March 29, 1926, W file, Winchell papers.

"*I made the terrible mistake . . .*" W to Stanley Walker, April 13, 1933, Bigman coll.

85–6   "*Shuberts feel you are unfriendly . . .*" *Editor & Publisher*, Jan. 14, 1928, 10.

86   "*this paper is staffed by nothing but Winchells!*" Cohen, 35; Clipping, *NY Graphic*, n.d. [1928], Scrapbook 1924, NYPL at Lincoln Ctr.

"*Walter very likely soon will find . . .*" *Winchell Exclusive*, 66.

"*Fun, no end!*" *NY Graphic*, March 16, 1928.

"*You get weary getting barred . . .*" Walter Winchell, "They All Talk Back to Ziegfeld," *DAC News*, n.d. [1929], Scrapbook 1924, NYPL at Lincoln Ctr.

"*A certain critic has been barred . . .*" *NY Mirror*, March 26, 1953.

"*placate them, keep you happy and secure their advertising.*" Memo, Gauvreau to W, March 24, 1928, W file, Winchell papers.

"*Everybody in town is talking . . .*" Clipping, n.d., Scrapbook 1924, NYPL at Lincoln Ctr.

"*You are making a mistake . . .*" Klurfeld, 44.

86 *"I won't crawl."* Philip Schuyler, "Winchell, Disguised as Bearded Hunchback, Sees Shubert Show," *Editor & Publisher*, Nov. 3, 1928, 18.

86–7 *Seeing* Animal Crackers. Ibid. According to *The New Yorker*, Gauvreau refused "in words which should go down in journalistic history": "It would hardly be dignified for the *Graphic.*" ("The Honor of the Graphic," *New Yorker* [Dec. 15, 1928], 25.)

87 *Panning* Wunderbar. NY *Mirror*, March 26, 1953.

Alma Sioux Scarberry and Winchell. Cohen, 41–42.

"He was making Broadway 'mine' . . ." Ibid.

"[E]very race in every age . . ." Gilbert W. Gabriel, "Side Show," NY *American*, May 12, 1931.

88 *"suffusion of floods . . ."* Graham, 13.

"actresses, night club wenches, doctors . . ." Gauvreau, *My Last Million Readers*, 136.

"Broadway was to me where . . ." Eddie Jaffe int. by author.

89 *Comparing Winchell to Mark Twain.* Ernest Cuneo, "Eulogy," Cuneo papers.

Runyon's childhood. Edwin P. Hoyt, *A Gentleman of Broadway* (Boston: Little, Brown, 1964), 11 passim.

Acquaintances called him "Demon." Gene Fowler, *Skyline: A Reporter's Reminiscences of the Twenties* (NY: Viking, 1961), 88.

spent an hour each day dressing himself. Ibid., 213.

"If you happened to meet Damon three different times . . ." Bill Corum, *Off and Running*, ed. Arthur Mann (NY: Holt, 1959), 165.

suspenders bearing his own profile. Walter Winchell, "Things I Never Knew till Now," *Vanity Fair* (March 1932), 110.

"Give a woman a couple of kids . . ." Hoyt, 136.

"fierce fellow." Damon Runyon, Jr., *Father's Footsteps* (NY: Random House, 1954), 42.

Mrs. Runyon's death. Ibid., 82.

a newspaperman's newspaperman. Louis Sobol, *The Longest Street: A Memoir* (NY:

Crown, 1968), 377–378; William Randolph Hearst, Jr. with Jack Casserly, *The Hearsts: Father and Son* (Niwot, Colo.: Roberts Rinehart, 1991), 113.

"Damon Runyon, darnim . . ." NY *Graphic*, Jan. 8, 1927.

90 *"This Waldo Winchester is a nice-looking young guy . . ."* Damon Runyon, "Romance in the Roaring Forties," in *Guys and Dolls* (NY: Frederick Stokes, 1931), 121–122.

"By saying something with a half-boob air . . ." Quoted in Hoyt, 7. See also Chapter Ten in William R. Taylor, *In Pursuit of Gotham: Culture and Commerce in New York* (NY: Oxford University Press, 1992).

91 *"With one hand it bestows . . ."* NY *Mirror*, Jan. 1, 1931.

"It is a hard and destructive community . . ." Walter Winchell, "The Real Broadway," *The Bookman*, vol. LXVI, no. 4 (Dec. 1927), 378–79.

"The popular maxim is . . ." Ibid., 382.

"What can you 'get' on the other fellow?" Ibid.

"The reason why the Broadway character . . ." "Walter Winchell," East Side Evening H.S. *Nocturne*, Oct. 23, 1930, Scrapbook 1930–1931, NYPL at Lincoln Ctr.

"One day he was a nobody . . ." Dave Goldberg quoted in Stuart, 54.

"[Y]ou are a very much admired young man . . ." Ann Ayres to W, Sept. 6 [1928], Winchell papers, NYPL at Lincoln Ctr.

"I hear you widely quoted . . ." O. O. McIntyre to W, n.d. [1928], Winchell papers, NYPL at Lincoln Ctr.

"widely quoted in the big city . . ." Chicago *Evening Post*, Oct. 18, 1928, Scrapbook 1924, NYPL at Lincoln Ctr.

92 *"According to the gossip syndicates . . ."* Louisville *Herald-Post*, n.d. [1929], Scrapbook 1924, NYPL at Lincoln Ctr.

"When he did this he'd put his head . . ." Mallen, 151.

If the criticism were intended seriously . . . NY *Post*, March 16, 1952, 5.

Book contract. Contract, Walter Winchell and Simon & Schuster, Aug. 6, 1928; Max Schuster to Winchell, Oct. 11,

1928, Winchell papers, NYPL at Lincoln Ctr.

Cosmopolitan wanted to talk ... Sol Flaum, asst. to pres., to W, Sept. 1928, W file, Winchell papers.

"young people in picaresque and picturesque situations. ..." Swanson to W, Feb. 6, 1929; Feb. 27, 1929, Winchell papers, NYPL at Lincoln Ctr.

DAC Club News. Charles A. Hughes, publisher *DAC News*, to W, March 19, 1929; March 23, 1929, Winchell papers, NYPL at Lincoln Ctr.

"played me up as being a 'somebody' ..." NY *Mirror*, Oct. 5, 1932.

Walter farmed out the assignments ... Sobel, 303.

93 *"[I]f ever I can find you ..."* John O'Hara to W, n.d. [1928], Winchell papers, NYPL at Lincoln Ctr.

"one of the phenomena ..." Clipping, Robert Benchley, *New Yorker*, in Scrapbook 1924, NYPL at Lincoln Ctr.

Walter had also inspired a two-hour debate ... NY *Graphic*, Dec. 6, 1927.

"A newsboy is a citizen ..." Quoted in John S. Kennedy, "A Bolt from the Blue," in *Molders of Opinion*, ed. David Bulman (Milwaukee: Bruce Pub. Co., 1945), 155.

"[T]o exposing the phoney ..." "The Broad-Wayfarer," *Evening Enquirer*, Oct. 21, 1928, Scrapbook 1924, NYPL at Lincoln Ctr.

"not only to fill my column ..." NY *Mirror*, July 26, 1933, 17.

"looked like an over-grown choir boy ..." St. John Ervine, "Notes on the Way," *Time and Tide*, Sept. 20, 1929, 116.

"Tell me, Winchell." Walter Winchell, "They All Talk Back to Ziegfeld," *DAC News*, n.d. [1929], Scrapbook 1924, NYPL at Lincoln Ctr.

94 *"by the feeling that the clamorous life of the city ..."* Quoted in Leuchtenberg, 240.

"Whether used as a warning ..." "Backstair Secrets for All," *Literary Digest*, July 27, 1929, 25.

he borrowed from the Vaudeville *News's ad income ... Winchell Exclusive*, 37–38.

"Oh, I wish you would." Ibid.

Then she took the baby home ... Ibid.

95 *June's refusal to adopt the child.* LC.

she frequently volunteered ... Winchell Exclusive, 38; LC.

June had taken her to Dr. Curley ... LC.

"I don't recall her ever crying ..." *Winchell Exclusive*, 39.

"Pablum and the other baby food ..." Ibid.

95–6 *LaHiff story.* Ibid., 40.

96 *"I didn't know where the rent was coming from ..."* NY *Mirror*, June 13, 1934.

He made a point of phoning her ... Mallen, 151.

"respectability was Topic A ..." *Winchell Exclusive*, 30.

she and her partner Olive Hill were arrested ... Jo A. Buckley, daughter of June's second cousin, int. by author.

Aunt Beatrice had seen her in a nude revue ... Greene, 43.

96–7 *"Supposing sweetheart, I were lying lifeless" ...* Reprinted in NY *Mirror*, Jan. 7, 1931. Walter scrawled at the top, "I wrote this to June in Vaude News!." Winchell bound columns, NYPL at Lincoln Ctr.

97 *"Don't you remember, I held your baby ..."* Greene, 48.

Daily News photo. NY *Daily News*, final ed., July 20, 1925, 13.

Once again Rita demanded an explanation ... Greene, 50.

98 *His mother still lived in the old Harlem apartment ...* N.Y. State Census, 1925, Manhattan, A.D. 17, E.D. 12, 19.

Jacob and Adlina Laino. N.Y. State Census, 1925, Manhattan, A.D. 23, E.D. 6, 22.

"What did I pay for the divorce for ..." Lenore Winchel, int. by author.

"he was in a position whereby a divorce ..." Greene, 54.

"I felt instinctively from reading his column ..." Ibid., 55–56.

"[T]he more I thought of the situation ..." Ibid., 58.

99 *"His bravado was sickening."* Ibid., 59.

99 *Naming Walda.* "Winchell for McCall's," 2nd draft, n.p., Cuneo papers.

"If you had a new baby girl . . ." NY *Graphic,* May 31, 1927.

A reporter that fall called her Patsy. Hariette Underhill, "How Fine to Be Back to the City," NY *Herald Tribune,* Sept. 18, 1927, Scrapbook 1924, NYPL at Lincoln Ctr.

" 'Bills, rent, bills, rent . . .' " Sobel, 302.

West Indian nursemaid. Underhill.

"In the background of all his first efforts . . ." Alexander Woollcott, "The Little Man with the Big Voice," *Hearst's International Cosmopolitan* (May 1933), 141.

100 *"I do trust it can be done quickly . . ."* W to Mrs. Greene [1928], Pat Rose coll.

Divorce hearing. Winchell v. Winchell, NY Supreme Court, Richmond County, Special Term, Transcript, June 4, 1928; Greene, 66–68.

"I was not in the mood for laughter." Greene, 68.

For Rita it was to be the trauma of her life. Pat Rose, niece of Rita Greene, int. by author.

101 *Mamie Hoskins's death.* Reading *Eagle,* Dec. 16, 1928; *Variety,* Dec. 19, 1928.

3 SURVIVING

102 *When Walter complained that correspondence was stacking up . . .* Memo: W to Gauvreau, n.d.; Gauvreau to W, W file, Winchell papers.

When he asked for a salary increase . . . Frank Mallen, *Sauce for the Gander* (White Plains, NY: Baldwin Books, 1954), 154.

When Walter put in for expenses of $10.80 . . . Ibid., 155.

Suitors. Guylee, NY *Daily News,* to W, n.d., W file, Winchell papers; clipping, March [?] 1928, Scrapbook 1924, NYPL at Lincoln Ctr.; Herbert Bayard Swope, NY *Morning World,* to W, Dec. 12, 1940, Swope file, Winchell papers.

William Randolph Hearst. See Ferdinand Lundberg, *Imperial Hearst* (NY: Modern Library, 1937); W. A. Swanberg, *Citizen Hearst* (NY: Collier/Macmillan, 1961); John Tebbel, *The Life and Times of William Randolph Hearst* (NY: Dutton, 1952).

103 *"the man who introduced the use of big money . . ."* A. J. Liebling, *The Press* (NY: Pantheon, 1981), 492.

In 1920 he owned twelve newspapers . . . Rodney P. Carlisle, *Hearst and the New Deal: The Progressive as Reactionary* (NY: Garland Publishing, 1979), 9–10.

the Graphic *had reneged on a promise . . . Time,* June 17, 1929.

William Curley . . . asked sportswriter Bill Corum . . . Mallen, 156.

104 *Curley's offer . . . Variety,* April 10, 1929.

"reprisal." W to Stanley Walker, April 13, 1933, Bigman coll.

"jubilant." Harry Salpeter, "Town Gossip: A Portrait of Walter Winchell," *Outlook and Independent,* vol. 152, no. 11 (July 10, 1929), 413.

"It is believed to be the first time . . ." *Editor & Publisher,* April 13, 1929, 50.

Gauvreau instructed the "letters to the editor" department . . . NY *Zit's Weekly,* May 18, 1929.

"My secretary has informed me . . ." Memo: Gauvreau to W, May 10, 1929; Arthur Driscoll to Gauvreau, May 11, 1929, W file, Winchell papers.

He began phoning the health faddist . . . Emile Gauvreau, *My Last Million Readers* (NY: Dutton, 1941), 134; Emile Gauvreau and Mary Macfadden, *Dumbbells and Carrot Strips* (NY: Henry Holt, 1953), 394–95.

"daily preparation of unintelligible jargon." Macfadden and Gauvreau, 395.

As Gauvreau told it . . . Gauvreau, *My Last Million Readers,* 134.

"chief claim to dubious prestige." Louis Sobol, *The Longest Street: A Memoir* (NY: Crown, 1968), 15.

"Winchell stared at me in disbelief." Ibid., 12–13.

105 *Hearst decided that the* Mirror *would get Walter . . .* Mallen, 156.

Ballyhoo over defection. Clipping, n.d. [1929], Scrapbook 1924; Advertisement, NY *Daily Mirror,* Scrapbook 1924, NYPL at Lincoln Ctr.; NY *Mirror,* June 10, 1929.

"Not at all." Clipping, n.d. [1929], Scrapbook 1924, NYPL at Lincoln Ctr.

106 *Hellinger leaving* News. Jim Bishop, *The Mark Hellinger Story* (NY: Appleton-Century-Crofts, Inc., 1952), 138–39.

Gauvreau and Hearst. Gauvreau, *My Last Million Readers,* 136–142.

He discovered that Gauvreau had not gotten permission . . . NY *Mirror,* July 30, 1940.

What Walter later heard . . . W to Stanley Walker, April, 13, 1933, Bigman coll.

"Gauvreau sold me out." Quoted in Lyle Stuart, *The Secret Life of Walter Winchell* (NY: Boar's Head Books, 1953), 73–74.

107 *betraying "in a hundred ways . . ."* Salpeter, 415.

"If the gossip doesn't materialize . . ." Edward Churchill, "Okay, Hollywood!" *Motion Picture,* Aug. 1932.

Walter's office. NY *Mirror,* Nov. 16, 1932, 21.

Hiring Ruth Cambridge. Walter Winchell, *Winchell Exclusive: "Things That Happened to Me—and Me to Them"* (Englewood Cliffs, N.J.: Prentice-Hall, 1975), 46–47.

She could neither take dictation nor type . . . Al Rylander int. by author; Winchell, 47.

108 *"tough racket."* Kennedy, 42.

"Edison only slept four hours a night . . ." Jerry D. Lewis, writer-producer, int. by author.

"All over the country people were sitting around . . ." Polly Adler, *A House Is Not a Home* (NY: Rinehart & Co., 1953), 164.

"It was borrowed time anyhow . . ." "Echoes of the Jazz Age," in F. Scott Fitzgerald, *The Crack-Up,* ed. Edmund Wilson (NY: Scribner's, 1931; rep. New Directions, 1956), 21; "My Lost City," Ibid., 33.

"The situation is so terrible . . ." NY *Mirror,* Oct. 29, 1929, 20.

The next day he quoted Cantor again . . . Ibid., Oct. 30, 1929, 20.

"the spirit of this mad jazz age." Harriet Menker, "The Portrait Gallery," *Weekly Radio Dial* (Dec. 23, 1931).

Edward Steichen portrait. Donald Freeman, managing ed., *Vanity Fair,* to W, Nov. 4, 1929, V file, Winchell papers; *Vanity Fair,* January 1930, 49.

109 *"human electricity."* Ben Grauer, quoted by Gary Stevens, int. by author.

"He cursed me . . ." Bernard Sobel, *Broadway Heartbeat: Memoirs of a Press Agent* (NY: Hermitage House, 1953), 305–06.

"You want me, come over here." Sobel, 363.

"unquestionably the town's most conceited peasant." NY *Mirror,* May 9, 1930, 22.

110 *"Gotta have excitement . . ."* NY *Mirror,* Sept. 4, 1930, 21.

"greatest competitor." Robert W. McChesney, "Press Radio Relations and the Emergence of Network, Commercial Broadcasting in the United States, 1930–1935," in *Historical Journal of Film, Radio and Television,* vol. 11, no. 1 (1991), 42–43.

"as Mr. Winchell is very popular . . ." Gauvreau to Bernays, Jan. 10, 1928, W file, Winchell papers.

"more at home before the mike . . ." Clipping, Sept. 13, 1928; Ben Gross, clipping, n.d. [1928], Scrapbook 1924, NYPL at Lincoln Ctr.

"deprecating yet loving gestures." Chicago *American,* Jan. 25, 1929.

Radio appearances. Contract, Judson Radio Program Corp., WABC, March 12, 1929, Winchell papers.

111 *"Let me know as soon as possible what to delete . . ."* Note on Saks script, n.d. [June or July 1930], NYPL at Lincoln Ctr.

"I introduce myself to you . . ." Saks script, NYPL at Lincoln Ctr.

"It is a sad comment on American manhood . . ." NY *World,* April 27, 1930.

"[Y]ou may rest assured that she is in a lather . . ." NY *Mirror,* May 13, 1930, 20.

111 *"[I]t is a pretty good advertisement . . ."* Saks script, May 19, 1930, NYPL at Lincoln Ctr.

112 *"And he isn't going to be seen as the villain . . ."* Saks script, n.d. [June 1930], NYPL at Lincoln Ctr.

Description of Bard of Broadway. *Bard of Broadway*, Vitaphone Pictures, 1930, Library of Congress Motion Picture Collection.

113 *"Maybe if I could get out of the radio deal . . ."* NY *Mirror*, July 10, 1930.

"Daddy loves you so . . ." Ibid.

"I agree with you that you should have a vacation . . ." Kobler to W, July 23, 1930, Old office corr., NYPL at Lincoln Ctr.

"I would advise you to stay here . . ." Gauvreau to W, July 25, 1930, Old office corr., NYPL at Lincoln Ctr.

"for fear I'll miss something." NY *Mirror*, July 31, 1930.

"Walda, 3, was so cute . . ." Ibid., Aug. 7, 1930.

114 *"Maybe if I told everybody where they could go . . ."* Ibid., Aug. 15, 1930.

"I had dinner with Winchell last night." Frank Hause to Joseph Medill Patterson, Aug. 21, 1930, box 17, file 7, Joseph Medill Patterson papers, Donnelly Library, Lake Forest College.

"Winchell is trying to give us the rush act." R. C. Holliss to Patterson, Aug. 28, 1930, box 20, file 10, Patterson papers, Donnelly Library, Lake Forest College.

When Hause contacted him in early September . . . Ibid; Hause to Patterson, Sept. 6, 1930, box 17, file 7, Patterson papers.

"It's a regular Horatio Alger story!" Philip Schuyler, "Winchell: World's Highest Paid Gossip," *Publisher's Service*, Sept. 18, 1930, 5.

115 *The* Mirror's *circulation had climbed . . .* Ibid.

"There is a wallop . . ." NY *Mirror*, Sept. 4, 1930, 21.

"It is a great kick . . ." Wise Shoes script n.d. [Sept. 1930], NYPL at Lincoln Ctr.

"instantaneous, general and sincerely enthusiastic." Quinn Martin, clipping, Scrapbook 1930–31, NYPL at Lincoln Ctr.

The only damper for him was the decision by Wise Shoes . . . Lawrence Schoen, Wise Shoes, to W, Nov. 28, 1930, W file, Winchell papers.

"some of that sunshine . . ." NY *Mirror*, Dec. 5, 1930.

116 *Sometimes he daydreamed . . .* Ibid., Sept. 4, 1930, 22.

"All the years of playing the hick towns . . ." Herman Klurfeld, *Winchell: His Life and Times* (NY: Praeger, 1976), 59.

the Palace was losing as much as $4,000 a week . . . Joe Laurie, Jr., *Vaudeville: From Honky Tonk to the Palace* (NY: Henry Holt, 1953), 495.

117 *Walter was originally scheduled to play the Palace . . .* Editor *&* Publisher, June 21, 1930, 26.

"nervous wreck." Rita Greene, unpublished ms., 75.

"[T]he audience started to howl with glee . . ." *Variety*, Jan. 14, 1931.

"the daily columnist was scared . . ." Ibid.

"His nervousness was not assumed . . ." Ibid.

"another freak attraction." Ibid.

he had dropped four and a half pounds. W to Stanley Walker, April 13, 1933, Bigman coll.

"I'll never do this again . . ." NY *Mirror*, Jan. 14, 1931.

117–18 *Palace records.* Clipping, n.d., Scrapbook 1930–31, NYPL at Lincoln Ctr.

118 *"If you are as good on the stage . . ."* Tel. George S. Kaufman to W, Jan. 8, 1931, Scrapbook 1930–1931, NYPL at Lincoln Ctr.

"They went out of their way to give me a break . . ." NY *Mirror*, Jan. 14, 1931.

Charles D. Dillingham offer. Clipping, n.d., Scrapbook 1930–1931, NYPL at Lincoln Ctr.

E. Ray Goetz offer. NY *Times*, Sept. 21, 1931, 20; clipping, n.d., Scrapbook 1930–31, NYPL at Lincoln Ctr.

"threatened my otherwise placid home

life." W to Kobler, Sept. 27 [1931], Old office corr., NYPL at Lincoln Ctr.

119 *"mandatory."* Dr. Reiser to Kobler, Jan. 30, 1931, Old office corr., NYPL at Lincoln Ctr.

"should leave the city at once." W to Gauvreau, Feb. 1, 1931, Old office corr., NYPL at Lincoln Ctr.

"the matter of your health . . ." Gauvreau to W, Feb. 1, 1931, Old office corr., NYPL at Lincoln Ctr.

"The Mirror shall reserve the privilege . . ." Gauvreau to W, Feb. 4, 1931, Old office corr., NYPL at Lincoln Ctr.

he couldn't leave the city . . . Cambridge to Gauvreau, Feb. 4, 1931, Old office corr., NYPL at Lincoln Ctr.

Steve Hannagan. NY *Mirror*, Feb. 6, 1953, 10.

Roney-Plaza. Arlene R. Olson, *A Guide to the Architecture of Miami Beach* (Miami: Dade Heritage Trust, 1978), 8–9; Roney-Plaza advertisement, Cuneo papers.

"sample of heaven." N. B. T. Roney to W, April 17, 1933, R file, Winchell papers.

120 *"Winchell was very important in making that season there."* Harold Conrad, press agent, int. by author.

Meeting Al Capone. NY *Mirror*, Oct. 28, 1931, 23.

"I am feeling better." W to Gauvreau, Feb. 18, 1931, Old office corr., NYPL at Lincoln Ctr.

La Gerardine contract. Tide, Sept. 1931, Scrapbook 1931–33, NYPL at Lincoln Ctr.

121 *"I want you to feel . . ."* Milton Biow to W, July 2, 1931, G file, Winchell papers.

"I wont [sic] *submit offensive stuff."* W to Biow, Austion or Spech, La Gerardine, n.d. [Sept. 1931], G file, Winchell papers.

"I am now leaving my office at 5:10 A.M.*"* Ibid.

"[W]e insisted that Walter Winchell be sold as 'the world's greatest columnist.'" W. J. Thill, gen. mgr. LaGerardine, to W, Sept. 16, 1931, G file, Winchell papers.

Effect on La Gerardine sales. Tide (Dec.

1931), Scrapbook 1931–33, NYPL at Lincoln Ctr.

"I talked too deliberate . . ." W to Biow, Sept. 29, 1931, G file, Winchell papers.

122 *As Walter later told it . . .* Winchell, 79.

"startled the town." Tel. John F. Royal to W, April 6, 1967, Bigman coll.

Hill's eccentricities. William S. Paley, *As It Happened: A Memoir* (Garden City, N.Y.: Doubleday, 1979), 80.

"first baseball player deal . . ." W to Hy Gardner, n.d., Ed Sullivan file, Winchell papers.

"first commercial air doubler." Clipping, n.d., Scrapbook 1930–31, NYPL at Lincoln Ctr.

Number of radio receivers. U.S. Dept. of Commerce, *Historical Statistics of the United States* (Washington: Dept. of Commerce, 1961), 488, 491, 500; *Editor & Publisher*, Feb. 4, 1933, 20.

"Sound helped mold national responses." Warren I. Susman, *Culture as History: The Transformation of American Society in the Twentieth Century* (NY: Pantheon, 1984), 158–159.

123 *"[M]y skin is thick."* Lucky Strike, Nov. 3, 1931, NYPL at Lincoln Ctr.

"I have been in long trousers long enough to know . . . Lucky Strike Dance Hour, NBC Red, MR 55, Nov. 5, 1931, NBC personnel office.

"one of the greatest steps forward . . ." *Radio Guide*, Nov. 21, 1931, 11; *Zit's Weekly*, Dec. 12, 1931.

first transatlantic broadcast of an English dance band. "O.K. London," clipping, n.d. [Dec. 1931], Layer coll.

"He was continually under wraps . . ." Jerry Wald, "Not on the Air," NY *Graphic*, Dec. 1, 1931.

124 *One visitor said he was so intent on his work . . .* Harriet Menken, "The Portrait Gallery," *Weekly Radio Dial*, Dec. 23, 1931.

"That was certainly third-rate . . ." Sobol, 363.

he would be forced off "The Lucky Strike Dance Hour" . . . Radio Guide, Dec. 24, 1931, 3.

124 *Already he was quibbling with La Gerardine . . . Tide*, Dec. 1931.

"I am glad, Walter, to have done this for you . . ." Spector to W, Oct. 5, 1931, G file, Winchell papers.

Hill . . . lived for one thing. Edward Bernays int. by author.

Walter's new contract. Radio Guide (Jan. 14, 1932; March 17, 1932).

125 *"I don't know how to say what I want to say."* W to Lord & Thomas & Logan, Dec. 20, 1931, A file, Winchell papers.

"I wouldn't be a Winchell imitator . . ." W to Abel Green, *Variety,* June 23, 1967, *Variety* file, Winchell papers.

Sid Skolsky's audition. Winchell, 80. There was, in fact, an additional hurdle. Jacob Winschel, now calling himself Laino after his girlfriend, had been arrested on May 24, 1930, for sodomy. What exactly happened no one seems to know—under the NY Penal Code of the time sodomy included oral and anal sex—and the case was dismissed three days later. But on the eve of his signing with Lucky Strike, Walter was approached by two plainclothes policemen who threatened to release the information unless Walter paid them $1,500. He did, then lamented his mistake. "Pay them off by making known the very things they'd have you fear." Record Bk., City Magistrate Cts., Docket #3592, City Record, Stock #11618, May 24, 1930, Municipal Archives, NYC; NY *Mirror,* Jan. 16, 1937.

$6,000 a week by one estimate. W to Stanley Walker, April 13, 1933, Bigman coll.

126 *Walter bought his suits from Earl Benham . . .* Jack O'Brien int. by author.

Jewelry and Stutz Bearcat. Philip Schuyler, "Winchell: World's Highest Paid Gossip," *Publishers' Service,* Sept. 18, 1930, 5.

Rita's stipends. "Rita Greene Winchell with Walter Winchell: Agreement," July 16, 1931, Pat Rose coll.

Supporting Jacob. Rose Bigman int. by author.

"She went around a lot by herself." Lenore Winchel int. by author.

"Cast your bread upon the waters." Winchell, 44.

when Gauvreau accepted a salary cut . . . Gauvreau, *My Last Million Readers,* 183.

127 *"Hill wanted me to help build a radio audience . . ."* Bernays, 389.

"Lucky Strike Dance Hour." Lucky Strike Program, March 10, 1932, LWO 8420, r3, Sound division, Library of Congress.

"To the thrill furnished by the competition . . ." Portland *Oregonian,* Feb. 21, 1932, Scrapbook 1931–35, NYPL at Lincoln Ctr.

"It sounded monotonous . . ." "I Started the Feud," *Radio Stars,* June 1937, 20–21, MWEZ + n.c. 11, 680, NYPL at Lincoln Ctr.

Missing humor. W to Ben Bernie, n.d., Bernie file, Winchell papers.

128 *He now phoned Bernie . . .* NY *Mirror,* March 9, 1935.

"I just had some swell scrambled eggs." James Frederick Smith, "The Winchell-Bernie Feud," n.d., MWEZ + n.c. 11, 680, NYPL at Lincoln Ctr.

Bernie's success. Gary Stevens int. by author; Ben Bernie to Ruth Cambridge, July 8, 1933, Bernie file, Winchell papers.

"OFFSETTING THIS SMALL MINORITY . . ." Telegram Ben Bernie to Albert Lasker, n.d. [1932], Bernie file, Winchell papers.

"Don't tell me that we've both been that 'deep.' " NY *Mirror,* Jan. 28, 1933, 17.

128–9 *"I am, myself, as great an enthusiast . . ."* George Washington Hill to W, Feb. 8, 1932, A file, Winchell papers.

129 *Walter gratefully acknowledged these letters . . .* Note, March 3, 1932, A file, Winchell papers.

"Okay, America." American Tobacco Co. testimonial, Jan. 25, 1932, A file, Winchell papers.

45,000 billboards of Walter. North Side *News,* April 17, 1932, Scrapbook 1931–33, NYPL at Lincoln Ctr.

"Luckies are kind to your throat . . ." *Time,* May 2, 1932, back cover.

"not only is our program successful . . ." *Printer's Ink,* April 14, 1932.

130 *"His infallible taste in correct pocket-wear ..."* Boulevard Pocketwear ad, *Vanity Fair*, May 1931, 5.

Envelopes bearing nothing but his picture ... NY *Mirror*, July 22, 1932, 19.

"Why do you go into places when I do?" Louis Sobol int., May 20, 1970, Thomas coll.

"getting more use out of a chair ..." Mallen, 159.

He accepted largely because ... Ibid., 162–63.

"It's only fair to warn Eddie ..." NY *Graphic*, May 29, 1931.

131 *"The Maimed Stem."* Ibid., June 6, 1931.

"empty vessels make the most sound." Sobol, 362.

Sullivan ... grabbed Sobol ... Ibid.

132 *"When he finally cooled down ..."* NY *Post*, March 12, 1952, 5, 12.

Walter denied the whole thing ... Winchell, 63.

"Did you mean what you wrote today?" NY *Post*, March 12, 1952, 5.

"Your Monday column still fills me ..." Sullivan to W, July 20, 1931, Sullivan file, Winchell papers.

Yawitz absently said that he was glad. Paul Yawitz int., April 17, 1970, Thomas coll.

"Wonder why it is every time a word becomes popular ..." NY *Mirror*, Dec. 2, 1931.

133 *While he steadily attacked journalistic heavyweights ...* Ibid., Sept. 22, 1930; Nov. 7, 1932.

Feud with M. Glebowitz. Ibid., May 23, 1930, 24.

"The big idea now is to wreck Walter Winchell." W to Sime Silverman, n.d., *Variety* file, Winchell papers.

"Winchell thinks if you mention him ..." Milt Josefsberg int., April 16, 1970, Thomas coll.

134 *"A newspaper should not invade private rights ..."* Quoted in Silas Bent, *Ballyhoo: The Voice of the Press* (NY: Boni & Liveright, 1927), 46.

"[H]e is fond of calling himself a newspaper man ..." Crerar Harris, "The Califor-

nian New Yorker," *The Wasp News Letter*, Sept 20, 1930, 3.

"When Winchell discusses the personal affairs ..." "Says Big Bill," *The Eastern Underwriter*, Oct. 30, 1931, Scrapbook 1931–33, NYPL at Lincoln Ctr.

Incensed by a "swarm of Winchell imitators" ... "Industry Will Fight Gossip Broadcasts," *Motion Picture Herald*, Dec. 26, 1931.

"The talk of the columnists is borrowed ..." Marlen Pew, "Gigolo Journalism," *Editor & Publisher*, Jan. 23, 1932, 22.

135 *Walter served as master of ceremonies* ... W to Stanley Walker, April 13, 1933, Bigman coll.; Broun to W, Oct. 15, 1930, Broun file, Winchell papers.

Walter even carried a wallet ... Inside Stuff, Feb. 27, 1932, 1.

"A great tradition is being smutted over ..." NY *World-Telegram*, Jan. [?], 1932.

"He confuses me with the ladies ..." NY *Mirror*, Jan. 20, 1932, 20.

136 *Betty Compton's marriage.* Gene Fowler, *Beau James: The Life and Times of Jimmy Walker* (NY: Viking, 1949), 290.

"filled with a considerable amount of innuendo." NY *World-Telegram*, Jan. 27, 1932.

"to attack Mayor Walker's private life ..." NY *Mirror*, Jan. 28, 1932.

"As if this or that newspaper cares ..." Draft, NY *Mirror*, Jan. 28, 1932, Misc., NYPL at Lincoln Ctr.

137 *"How they have groaned about me ..."* NY *Mirror*, Jan. 18, 1933, 19.

"While a lot of people say I'm a dirt-disher ..." W to Lord & Thomas & Logan, Dec. 20, 1931, A file, Winchell papers.

"I wish you would call me something else ..." W to Stanley Walker, April 13, 1933, Bigman coll.

he frantically phoned Bernays ... EB.

Walter had learned that Pew had once been jailed ... Memo, Joe Knight to W, n.d. [1932], P file, Winchell papers.

138 *"he is hardly qualified ..."* NY *Mirror*, Jan. 11, 1933.

"A great many people have suffered in-

jury ..." Marlen Pew, "Shoptalk at Thirty," *Editor & Publisher*, Jan. 14, 1933, 40.

138 *"When a man takes more than 5 minutes ..."* NY *Mirror*, Jan. 16, 1933, 17.

"[E]very time a controversy arises about the old-time journalism and the new ..." Ibid., Jan. 18, 1933, 19.

139 *"one of the evils that oozed ..."* *Editor & Publisher*, Dec. 31, 1932, 20.

"nearly plopped." NY *Mirror*, Dec. 7, 1932, 19.

"Alvin Roberts is a curious figure." John W. Perry, "New Play 'Blessed Event' Shows Rise of Bway Columnist," *Editor & Publisher*, Feb. 20, 1932, 20.

140 *"both vulgar and funny."* NY *Times*, Feb. 13, 1932.

"hasn't taken the precaution to have his individuality ..." Arthur Pollack, Brooklyn *Eagle*, Feb. 13, 1932.

"several members of the audience were suffering from conjunctivitis ..." Alexander Woollcott, "The Little Man with the Big Voice," *Hearst's International Cosmopolitan*, May 1933, 48.

Walter sniped that he gave a better performance ... NY *Mirror*, Feb. 5, 1932, 21.

he went to see it at least twice. NY *American*, Feb. 13, 1932.

Scribner's *piece.* Charles W. Wilcox, "Winchell of Broadway," *Scribner's*, Feb. 1931.

he carried it with him in a special binding ... NY *Times*, March 28, 1937; W to Stanley Walker, April 13, 1933, Bigman coll.

"[T]hat's merely a pose on my part ..." NY *Mirror*, Jan. 4, 1933, 19.

story of an irate husband ... Ibid., June 21, 1929.

"Whenever you complained about an item ..." Oscar Levant int., March 24, 1970, Thomas coll.

141 *"The Angel Lad, The Devil Man."* Brochure [1930], NYPL at Lincoln Ctr.

New York Times *internal committee.* NY *Mirror*, July 10, 1930.

"Well, I guess I won't rate a pass to heaven ..." Ibid., Sept. 11, 1930, 20.

Representative William Sirovich. NY *Times*, March 4, 1932; NY *American*, March 2, 1932; clipping, n.d. [1932], Misc., NYPL at Lincoln Ctr.

The roots of the controversy ... NY *Times*, Feb. 25–27, 1926; *Variety*, Sept. 15, 1926.

"No one was ever going to say of me ..." NY *Graphic*, Feb. 3, 1932.

141–2 *"What did you think of Earl Carroll's 'Vanities'?"* W to Stanley Walker, April 13, 1933, Bigman coll.

142 *"[T]he nicest party I ever crashed."* NY *Mirror*, Feb. 3, 1932, 19.

"Mr. Carroll seemed strangely pallid ..." Ibid., Feb. 2, 1932.

"charged to the gills." W to Stanley Walker, April 13, 1933, Bigman coll.

"gracious and charming" remarks. Sidney Skolsky, NY *Daily News*, Feb. 2, 1932.

"Walter, in each gathering there must be a serious note." Mark Hellinger, "All in a Day," NY *Mirror*, Feb. 2, 1932.

"Go ahead, it's OK." W to Stanley Walker, April 13, 1933, Bigman coll.

"There are some wonderful people here." Billy Grady, The Irish Peacock (New Rochelle, NY: Arlington House, 1972), 38.

"Walter, I'm ashamed of that." Hellinger.

"Don't lose your head." NY *Mirror*, Sept. 27, 1940.

appreciative laugh. Grady, 38.

Later that evening he phoned Mayor Walker ... NY *Mirror*, Feb. 2, 1932, 23.

"This important incident in social history ..." Marlen Pew, "Shoptalk at Thirty," *Editor & Publisher*, Feb. 6, 1932, 48.

Solomon announced loudly that he agreed with Carroll ... Ibid.

"Winchell and Hellinger are not fit ..." NY *American*, Feb. 2, 1932.

143 *"As always, he was once more the victim ..."* Hellinger, NY *Mirror*, Feb. 2, 1932.

"If you let me know who's fighting ..." Sullivan to W, Feb. 1, 1932, Sullivan file, Winchell papers.

"If you want to say that he attempted to frame an editor ..." Memo, Gauvreau to W,

Feb. 2, 1932, Old office corr., NYPL at Lincoln Ctr.

"I am trying hard not to get into a spot . . ." W to Gauvreau and Ruth Cambridge, n.d. [Feb. 1932], Old office corr., NYPL at Lincoln Ctr.

"If I wanted to use the gangster people I know . . ." W to Stanley Walker, April 13, 1933, Bigman coll.

"formerly of Pittsburgh . . ." NY *Mirror*, Feb. 2, 1932, 23.

"Mr. Carroll said that I was not fit . . ." Ibid., Feb. 3, 1932, 19.

144 *Kobler even invited . . .* W to Gauvreau and Ruth Cambridge, n.d. [Feb. 1932], Old office corr., NYPL at Lincoln Ctr.

a "new culture." Pew, "Shoptalk at Thirty," 48.

he would always brag that no one had ever won a judgment . . . J. P. McEvoy, "He Snoops to Conquer," *Saturday Evening Post*, Aug. 13, 1938, 44.

Stephen Clow's suit. Editor & Publisher Nov. 22, 1930, 8; Summons, New-Broad Publishing Co., Inc., Nov. 12, 1930, author's coll.

Georgette Carneal's suit. Editor & Publisher, May 14, 1932, 12.

Lady Nancy Cunard's suit. Ibid., Dec. 17, 1932, 8.

"shabbily attired with a sad face." NY *Mirror*, Nov. 25, 1931.

"The word is used in objurgation . . ." *Editor & Publisher*, June 3, 1933, 6; Oct. 13, 1934, 37.

145 *"I wonder if they are in league with the Reds?"* "Lucky Strike Hour," Nov. 19, 1931, NYPL at Lincoln Ctr.

Matchabellis' suit. NY Times, Nov. 25, 1931, 28.

"You had all been afraid I would involve you . . ." W to Gauvreau, Nov. 25, 1931, Old office corr., NYPL at Lincoln Ctr.

The Matchabellis amended their suits . . . Matchabelli Perfumery Co. v. Walter Winchell, American Tobacco Co. and National Broadcasting Co., NY County Clerk, #38323.

"pained me very much." W to Stanley Walker, April 13, 1933, Bigman coll.

Michael Picard's pitch. W testimony, *Fleetwood Fdn v. Daily Mirror and Walter Winchell*, NY Supreme Court, 32019–1930, 297, NY County Clerk.

146 *Hellinger had also badgered him . . .* Winchell, 67.

Nathan Zalinsky stopped by Walter's office . . . Fleetwood v. Winchell, 297.

Walter realized that it wasn't an exclusive club . . . Ibid., 302.

three men entered his office . . . Winchell, 68. The chronology is suspect since, according to his testimony, Walter didn't write his letter until November 20, leading one to believe that much more time had passed between the initial contact by Picard and the conversation with Zalinsky.

"If I were king I would throttle the swift-talker . . ." NY *Mirror*, Nov. 23, 1929.

Visit from Picard and Zack. Fleetwood v. Winchell, 307.

"he writes anything he wants . . ." Ibid., 205.

Walter said the case dragged on . . . Winchell, 69.

147 *"Imagine playing cards at the club . . ."* David Greenstein test., *Fleetwood v. Winchell*, 223.

"Am I not as good as . . ." *Variety*, Dec. 19, 1933.

Snobbery. Ibid., Dec. 26, 1933.

"If you are trying to make me look like a snob . . ." *Fleetwood v. Winchell*, 313.

Walter's testimony. Ibid., 326, 332.

"[T]hese men that write columns on the papers . . ." *Variety*, Dec. 26, 1933.

Walter blamed the histrionics . . . Winchell, 70.

148 *"I just got lost."* Winchell, 71–72; unmailed letter, W to Richard Berlin, Markuson, Hearst, Jr., et al., n.d. [1965], H file, Winchell papers.

149 *His main interests were art and women . . .* Bernard Sobel, *Broadway Heartbeat: Memoirs of a Press Agent* (NY: Heritage House, 1953), 296.

It was Gauvreau who deducted $227.68

... Tel. Ruth Cambridge to W, Dec. 23, 1930, Old office corr., NYPL at Lincoln Ctr.

149 *it was Gauvreau who delivered the message to Walter* ... Gauvreau, *My Last Million Readers,* 154–55.

Walter was so vituperative ... Memo, Gauvreau to W, Jan. 11, 1931, Old office corr., NYPL at Lincoln Ctr.

Walter asked Kobler to ask Gauvreau to read the proof earlier. W to Kobler, Nov. 3 [1931], Old office corr., NYPL at Lincoln Ctr.

"I used to like to annoy him." W to Charles Henry, Hearst legal dept., Jan. 27, 1942, Gauvreau file, Winchell papers.

150 *"look like last year's straw hat ..."* Charles Fisher, *The Columnists* (NY: Howell, Soskin, 1944), 115.

"He told him what he could do ..." *Zit's Weekly,* Nov. 21, 1931.

Kobler then threatened to hit him. Ibid.

Kobler removed Ruth Cambridge from the payroll ... Ibid., Dec. 12, 1931.

Walter responded this time by sending a bill ... W to Gauvreau, n.d. [1931], Old office corr., NYPL at Lincoln Ctr.

"exchanging malevolent glares." Gauvreau, *My Last Million Readers,* 180.

The Sunday column. Clipping, n.d. [Jan. 1932], Scrapbook 1933–34, NYPL at Lincoln Ctr.

"Walter now screamed breach of contract ..." *Variety* galley, n.d. [Feb. 1932], Old office corr., NYPL at Lincoln Ctr.

restricting Walter and his secretary to their own office. Editor & Publisher, March 5, 1932, 8.

"cluttered up the air waves." *Variety* galley, n.d. [Feb. 1932], Old office corr., NYPL at Lincoln Ctr.

"Ignore all silly rumors." Clipping, n.d.; Gauvreau to W, n.d., Old office corr., NYPL at Lincoln Ctr.

151 *"itching to go into court ..."* "Literati," *Variety,* n.d., W file, Winchell papers.

"I am perched for the moment ..." NY *Mirror,* Nov. 1, 1933, 21.

"You get old-looking too fast ..." Ibid., July 11, 1930.

"He thinks his stuff is terrible." Edward Churchill, "Okay, Hollywood," *Motion Picture,* August 1932.

"There must be a time in your career ..." NY *Mirror,* April 19, 1931.

"[O]h the weariness that follows the two hours ..." Ibid., Nov. 16, 1932, 19.

"Dead." Harriet Menker, "The Portrait Gallery," *Weekly Radio Dial,* Dec. 23, 1931.

152 *He would leave the paper in five years* ... Ed E. Pidgeon, "Inner Home Life of Broadway's Boswell," NY *Press,* n.d., Scrapbook 1930–31, NYPL at Lincoln Ctr.

"I want a few more years' time yet ..." Cornelia Strassburg, "The True Love Story of Walter Winchell," *Love Illustrated,* Jan. 1931, 125.

"She's been waiting a decade ..." NY *Mirror,* Feb. 17, 1932, 19.

"She has never, ever done anything ..." Strassburg.

He once recounted an episode ... NY *Mirror,* March 22, 1930.

"Gee! It's that sob column ..." "Brevities Burlesque," *Broadway Brevities,* Aug. 24, 1931, 5.

"dream man." Roberta J. Levy to W, Aug. 22, 1929, Old office corr., NYPL at Lincoln Ctr.

"What particularly depresses me ..." Ruth D. Kent to W, June 21, 1930, Old office corr., NYPL at Lincoln Ctr.

"Why haven't I heard from you?" Helen Fitzpatrick Landry Manning to W, n.d., Old office corr., NYPL at Lincoln Ctr.

152–3 *"Can't golf, fish, swim ..."* "Columnists as They See Themselves," *Literary Digest,* July 7, 1934, 10.

153 *"My family comes first with me ..."* Pidgeon.

forcing himself to get to bed at 3 a.m. ... Hendrick Hudson, Jr., "Making Snoopee," *Pathfinder,* Jan. 24, 1931, Scrapbook 1930–31; NY *Enquirer,* Jan. 4, 1931.

He hated to rush into Childs restaurant ... NY *Mirror,* Oct. 23, 1930.

"Gloria is a beautiful child ..." Ibid., March 17, 1931.

"*That Walda of mine ...*" Ibid., Feb. 10, 1932, 23.

"*I only want to live long enough ...*" Ibid., Feb. 17, 1932, 19.

"*Oh, how I love my beautiful darling wife and kiddies.*" Westbrook Pegler, "Speaking Out on Sports," Chicago *Tribune*, n.d. [1933], Scrapbook 1933-34, NYPL at Lincoln Ctr.

153-4 "*You should be a better writer than the man you parody ...*" Hemingway to Gingrich, March 13, 1933, Ernest Hemingway, *Selected Letters: 1917-1961*, ed. Carlos Baker (NY: Scribner's, 1981), 383.

154 *They were privately educated.* Records, Gloria Winchell & Walda Winchell, Ethical Culture School.

"*If you really care anything about the three of us ...*" NY *Mirror*, Oct. 23, 1930.

"*I guess my own artificial routine of living ...*" NY *Mirror*, July 15, 1931.

Another time he got three columns ahead ... Ibid., Nov. 18, 1931, 23.

"*You might suppose that the thrill of hearing things ...*" FPA, "The Conning Tower," NY *World*, n.d., Old office corr., NYPL at Lincoln Ctr.

155 "*Five planes brought dozens of machinegats ...*" NY *Mirror*, Feb. 8, 1932.

After Demange was ransomed ... Curley Harris int. by author.

Walter insisted on sending the gang leader a check. Allhoff, 56; W to Woollcott, n.d. [1940], bms AM1449 (1797), Woollcott coll., Harvard U.

"*a certain daily newspaper columnist will be bumped off ...*" NY *Mirror*, Nov. 17, 1931, 23.

Walter had placed the names of would-be assassins ... "On the Spot?" *Time*, Nov. 3, 1930.

"DEAR BOB SEE YOU AT THE NEW YORKER THEATER ..." Telegram W to Benchley, May 12, 1930, box 12, folio 19, Benchley papers, Boston U.

156 "*... Winchell could make money for them.*" CH.

"*I turned green.*" Fred Allhoff, "Walter Winchell —American Phenomenon," *Liberty Magazine*, April 4, 1942, 40.

Murder of Coll confederates. NY *Mirror*, Feb. 10, 1932, 3.

Death threats. NY *Times*, Feb. 14, 1932, 21.

Bodyguards. W to Stanley Walker, April 13, 1933, Bigman coll.

"*nervous and in genuine fear for his life.*" NY *American*, Feb. 14, 1932.

George M. Carney subpoenaed Walter. NY *Times*, Feb. 16, 1932, 44.

"*He stayed up all night.*" CH.

"*I'm no heel.*" NY *Times*, Feb. 17, 1932, 6; NY *World-Telegram*, Feb. 16, 1932, 5.

"*I lost seven more pounds ...*" W to Stanley Walker, April 13, 1933, Bigman coll.

"*The members of the grand jury ...*" CH.

156-7 *Walter apologized in his column ...* NY *Mirror*, Feb. 18, 1932, 19.

157 *$90,000 extortion.* Georgiana X. Preston, "Apology to Winchell the Popgun Patriot," Washington *Times-Herald*, July 19, 1942, E-8.

"*They said it would happen ...*" NY *World-Telegram*, April 18, 1932, 8.

Walter was seriously ill and confined to his suite ... NY *Daily News*, April 18, 1932.

One account said his doctor had ordered him ... NY *World-Telegram*, April 19, 1932.

"*He was dragged out of the place ...*" Bill Cunningham, Boston *Post*, n.d. [April 1932], Scrapbook 1931-35, NYPL at Lincoln Ctr.

"*I hope the reports of your illness are exaggerated.*" Swope to W, April 22, 1932, Swope file, Winchell papers.

158 "*was a trick on my part ...*" W to Stanley Walker, April 13, 1933, Bigman coll.

"*painful.*" Ibid.

"*sun cure.*" *Editor & Publisher* May 7, 1932, 12; clipping, LA *Herald*, n.d., misc, NYPL at Lincoln Ctr.

"*It's great to have been ill.*" Churchill, 35.

To George Washington Hill he wrote that he was feeling much better ... George

Washington Hill to W, May 5, 1932, American Tobacco file, Winchell papers.

158 "*I'm utterly amazed by Hollywood's rounds . . .*" Churchill.

"*Nowhere in the East . . .*" NY *Mirror*, June 8, 1932.

"*I'd be handicapped by public opinion . . .*" Churchill.

159 "*He always took the most circuitous route . . .*" Sam Marx int. by author.

"*one of the most famous newshounds . . .*" Clipping, Feb. 24, 1932, Scrapbook 1931–33, NYPL at Lincoln Ctr.

Columbia and Universal were pursuing him . . . Variety, May 9, 1932.

Okay, America. Clipping, n.d. [May 1932], Scrapbook 1931–33, NYPL at Lincoln Ctr.; NY *Times*, May 18, 1932, 25.

if Walter were healthy enough to make a movie . . . Jimmy Starr, clipping, n.d., Misc., NYPL at Lincoln Ctr.

"*They'll forget you.*" Paul Yawitz int., April 17, 1970, Thomas coll.

Rumors. W to Stanley Walker, April 13, 1933, Bigman coll.

He said he wanted $100,000 in advance. Ibid.

He told a reporter in Chicago . . . Chicago *American*, May 23, 1932.

160 "*Walter Winchell. Now—. . .*" NY *Mirror*, May 27, 1932, 10.

"*dull as ever.*" Ibid., June 1, 1932, 19.

Paul Yawitz lost Walter's "famous show-window" . . . Ibid., May 31, 1932, 15.

"*He was in perfect health . . .*" Sobel, 306.

"*I cannot see any reason . . .*" Mike Porter, *Radio Guide*, July 9, 1932, 2.

Kobler, less charitably, insisted Walter had gone out of town . . . NY *Times*, Aug. 14, 1932, sec. 9, 7; *Editor & Publisher*, Aug. 20, 1932, 12.

"*struggle along.*" *Radio Guide*, Aug. 27, 1932, 3.

"*We want Walter Winchell back on the air again . . .*" Ibid., Sept. 17, 1932, 18.

161 *Signing for film shorts.* Contract, William Rowland-Monty Brice Prod., Sept. 1932, Misc. contracts, Winchell papers.

First Jergens broadcast. NBC Blue Network, Dec. 4, 1932, roll 596, NBC records.

Response to Jergens debut. NY *Journal*, Dec. 5, 1932; NY *Daily News*, Dec. 5, 1932. ALL EXECUTIVES IMMENSELY PLEASED . . ." Telegram R. V. Beucus, ad mgr. Jergens Co., to W, Dec. 6, 1932, Scrapbook 1931–35, NYPL at Lincoln Ctr.

Ed Sullivan's dissent. Sullivan to W, Dec. 16, 1932, Sullivan file, Winchell papers.

162 "*Mr. and Mrs. America and all the ships at sea.*" He had first used, "Good Evening Mr. and Mrs. America—dots and dashes and lots of flashes from border to border and coast to coast," on the Saks program, June 9, 1930. "Good evening Mr. and Mrs. America and all the ships at sea," became his standard opening on the Jergens program on October 28, 1934. (NBC Blue, roll 627.)

"*The Big Idea is for sound effect . . .*" "Jergens Journal," Nov. 12, 1939, NBC Blue, roll 742.

"*My voice goes up exactly one octave . . .*" Don Freeman, "The Emperor of Broadway," *Seminar*, no. 24 (June 1972), 32.

163 "*Gloria had walked across the parlor . . .*" Winchell, 88–89.

"*Every time I wake up . . .*" Ibid.

"*Stardust*" *was playing . . .* Press agent Milt Rubin int., Thomas coll.

"*The sympathies of friends are comforting indeed . . .*" W to Hendrik Willem van Loon, Feb. 2, 1933, V file, Winchell papers.

163–4 *she ran frantically to the window and attempted to leap.* "Winchell for McCall's," 2nd draft, 24, Cuneo papers.

164 "*She said her heart was broken.*" Gloria Bayne int. by author.

"*unusually severe and enduring.*" Dr. Lawrence Kubie to Dr. Sophia Kleegman, Nov. 4, 1947, Walda Winchell file, Cuneo papers.

"*Sissy has gone to camp.*" Elisabeth Winchell, granddaughter, int. by author.

Weeks passed before she was finally told the truth . . . Kubie to Kleegman.

"*With my numerous activities . . .*" W to Van Loon.

"I couldn't have said it." Winchell, 89.

"To you, you, you, and you ..." "Jergens Journal," Jan.1, 1933, NYPL at Lincoln Ctr.

"It makes me sad." "Winchell for McCall's," 2d draft, Cuneo papers.

On his desk he kept a small white shoe of Gloria's. Ed Weiner, *Let's Go to Press: A Biography of Walter Winchell* (NY: Putnam's, 1955), 11.

flowers were sent to her crypt. Ed Wei-ner int. by author.

Subsequent Christmases ... Winchell, 89.

"faked." Arnold Forster int. by author.

165 *"He never got over her ..."* HK.

"The only tragedy in my life ..." W to Stanley Walker, April 13, 1933, Bigman coll.

"The Garden of Verses and all of her toys ..." NY *Mirror*, Jan. 4, 1933, 19.

4 FILLING THE VOID

169 *"fresh kid."* Curley Harris int. by author.

170 *"No heroics."* NY *Mirror*, May 2, 1933, 19.

Description of "I Know Everybody." *Variety*, n.d. [Feb. 1933], Scrapbook 1931–35, NYPL at Lincoln Ctr.

"did more to offset the legends about Broadwayites ..." NY *Mirror*, May 2, 1933, 19.

"Poor fellow ..." Ibid., Feb. 1, 1933, 19.

"the Old Copyreader." Walter Winchell, *Winchell Exclusive: "Things That Happened to Me—and Me to Them"* (Englewood Cliffs, NJ: Prentice-Hall, 1975), 90.

"We know the identity of the ambush-er ..." NY *Mirror*, Feb. 22, 1933, 19.

171 *Three days later Hearst wrote Kobler ...* Hearst to Kobler, Feb. 25, 1933, Hearst file, Winchell papers.

The occupant was ... Winchell, 90.

"The scenery between here and Miami Beach is most depressing ..." NY *Mirror*, Feb. 15, 1933, 19.

Walter was leaving the Western Union office ... Ibid., Feb. 17, 1933, 19.

"Where would they put a man in this town ..." J. P. McEvoy, "He Snoops to Conquer," *Saturday Evening Post*, Aug. 13, 1938, 45.

172 *"told him that I'd print his name ..."* Ibid.

"I did it because I don't like rich men ..." Chicago *American*, Feb. 16, 1933.

"terrible burning pain in his stomach." "Jergens Journal," NBC Blue, Feb. 26, 1933, roll 600, NBC records.

"[O]h, the thrill of it ..." Ibid., NBC Blue, Feb. 19, 1933, roll 600, NBC records.

"Oh, I know I didn't help you ..." NY *Mirror*, Feb. 22, 1933, 19.

Hannagan decided to wire its exclusive quotes ... McEvoy, 45.

173 *Damon Runyon's column.* NY *American*, Feb. 23, 1933, 17.

An earthquake damaged the Ambassador Hotel ... Lola Cowan.

"like the world was coming to an end ..." NY *Mirror*, March 15, 1933, 19.

Paramount Theater appearances. Art Arthur, "Reverting to Type," Brooklyn *Eagle*, n.d. [March 1933], Scrapbook 1933–34, NYPL at Lincoln Ctr.; NY *Herald Tribune*, March 18, 1933; Ad, *NY Times*, March 17, 1933.

Beauty on Broadway. Clipping, April 1, 1933, Scrapbook 1931–33, NYPL at Lincoln Ctr.

173–4 *His only complaint ...* NY *Mirror*, May 24, 1933, 21.

174 *"six years young."* "Jergens Journal," NBC Blue, April 2, 1933, roll 602, NBC records.

June returned East in April ... B. L. Wooten, auditor Pocono Hay-ven, to W, May 5, 1933, P file, Winchell papers.

174 *"The struggle that goes with gasping for a breeze ..."* NY *Mirror*, May 30, 1933, 17.

" 'Why, then?' a woman recently queried ..." Ibid.

Chicago trip. Ibid., June 1, 1933, 21.

Hollywood's seeming imperviousness to the Depression. Ibid., June 7, 1933, 19.

"armies" of *"men and women ..."* Ibid., June 28, 1933, 19.

"Fight promoters, fighters, wrestlers, screen stars ..." Ibid.

"Experiencing what it was like ..." Ibid., Sept. 27, 1933, 21.

Offers for personal appearances. Hollywood *Reporter*, June 28, 1933.

"I didn't come out here looking for vaudeville jobs." Hollywood *Herald*, June 29, 1933.

175 *Kobler objected to the guest columns ...* Kobler to W, June 29, 1933, Old office corr., NYPL at Lincoln Ctr.

"The important thing is for you to go ahead ..." Telegram Hearst to W, July 5, 1933, Hearst file, Winchell papers.

Walter told Brand that he had an idea for a movie. Harry Brand int., March 25, 1970, Thomas coll.

"It probably took a half hour ..." "Winchell Through His Own Keyhole," *Family Circle*, n.d., Scrapbook 1933–34, NYPL at Lincoln Ctr.

Twentieth Century Pictures contract. June 23, 1933, Zanuck file, Winchell papers.

other members then demanded the invitation be rescinded ... Variety, June 20, 1933; NY *Mirror*, June 13, 1933, 19.

"gone on a wide open tipping off spree ..." Variety, June 20, 1933.

176 *Writers' Club dinner.* NY *Mirror*, July 19, 1933, 19; Clipping, July 17, 1933, Scrapbook 1931–35, NYPL at Lincoln Ctr.

"tell the truth." J. Eugene Chrisman, "Are the Stars Afraid of Winchell?" Des Moines *Register* (rep. *Screen Play Magazine*), Oct. 1, 1933.

Ruby Keeler and Johnny Costello. NY *Mirror*, Sept. 24, 1928.

176–7 *Jolson's siege of Keeler.* Herbert G. Goldman, *Jolson: The Legend Comes to Life* (NY: Oxford University Press, 1988), 157–159.

177 *Costello greeted her at the train station ...* Billy Grady, *The Irish Peacock* (New Rochelle, NY: Arlington House, 1972), 62–63.

Walter remembered her flashing the diamond ... NY *Mirror*, Sept. 24, 1928.

"This nice man lowered his head ..." Grady, 64.

By one account, he wept ... Goldman, 161.

"I shook hands with him." NY *Mirror*, Sept. 24, 1928.

"She couldn't sleep." NY *World-Telegram*, July 22, 1933, UPI.

By one account, Jolson got up and exchanged words ... Ibid.

By Walter's own account ... NY *Times*, July 22, 1933, 14.

Later Walter claimed he was suckerpunched ... Variety, n.d. [1933], Scrapbook 1933–34, NYPL at Lincoln Ctr.

Melee. Variety, n.d. [1933], Scrapbook 1933–34, NYPL at Lincoln Ctr.

178 *the crowd gave him another ovation.* NY *World-Telegram*, July 22, 1933.

"I hope this will make you feel better." Emile Gauvreau, *My Last Million Readers* (NY: Dutton, 1941), 180.

$500,000 worth of advance bookings. NY *Mirror*, July 24, 1933, 17; NY *Herald Tribune*, July 24, 1933.

"How many fights are you in now?" NY *Mirror*, July 21, 1933, 19.

lawsuit against Jolson. NY *Times*, Aug. 9, 1933, 6.

"To the gentlemen and gentlewomen of the movie colony ..." LA *Examiner*, n.d. [1933], Scrapbook 1933–34, NYPL at Lincoln Ctr.

"where I will be bothered again ..." NY *Mirror*, July 26, 1933, 17.

179 *"elaborate yet tasteful."* NY *Herald Tribune*, Sept. 17, 1933; Gordon Sinclair, Toronto *Star*, Feb. 14, 1934.

"[T]he best picture I've been associated with ..." Telegram Zanuck to W, Sept. 18, 1933, Zanuck file, Winchell papers.

"I want you to get to work immedi-

ately . . ." Zanuck to W, Sept. 18, 1933, Zanuck file, Winchell papers.

Zanuck . . . emerged from a story confer-ence . . . Zanuck to W, Sept. 19, 1933, Zanuck file, Winchell papers.

"worthy successor." Zanuck to W, Oct. 4, 1933, Zanuck file, Winchell papers.

"sick to my stomach a little." W to Zanuck, Oct. 6, 1933, Twentieth Century-Fox file, Winchell papers.

179–80 Keyhole *premiere.* Press release, "Broadway Through a Keyhole" [1933], Scrapbook 1933–34, NYPL at Lincoln Ctr.

180 *"Walter Winchell, the author of this story . . ."* NY *Times,* Nov. 2, 1933.

"[o]rchids, and plenty of them . . ." NY *Evening Journal,* Nov. 2, 1933.

"Broadway's best pal . . ." NY *Herald Tribune,* Nov. 2, 1933.

"I'd encourage newcomers . . ." NY *Mirror,* Feb. 20, 1934.

181 *Walter suffered another collapse . . .* Ruth Cambridge to Chamberlain Brown, Nov. 10, 1933, 8–MWEZ + n.c. 22, 228, NYPL at Lincoln Ctr.

Guinan. NY *Times,* Nov. 6, 1933, 19.

greeted by surprisingly large crowds. John S. Stein and Hayward Grace, "Hello Sucker!: The Life of Texas Guinan," unpub. ms., 1941, 369, NYPL at Lincoln Ctr.

played the "keyhole." Ibid., 372.

McPherson and Guinan. Ibid., 380–85.

"I'm sorry—I—I never cry." NY *Times,* Nov. 6, 1933, 19.

As she lay on her deathbed . . . Stein and Grace, 1–3.

182 *"We learned Broadway from her."* NY *Mirror,* Nov. 29, 1933.

Mrs. Fay heard the news . . . Ibid., Jan. 13, 1933, 19.

"Why do you give his children costly gifts . . ." W to Dayton Stoddart, Silverman biog-rapher, Nov. 3, 1940, *Variety* file, Winchell papers.

"Life is a circus . . ." Quoted in Thomas Kessner, *Fiorello H. La Guardia and the Making of Modern New York* (NY: McGraw-Hill, 1989), 233.

Walker's downward spiral. "Jergens Journal," April 2, 1933.

183 *Demise of* Town Topics *and* Tattler. NY *Times,* Jan. 22, 1932, 21.

Graphic*'s losses. Time,* June 20, 1932, 25; Robert Ernst, *Weakness Is a Crime: The Life of Bernarr Macfadden* (Syracuse, N.Y.: Syracuse Univ. Press, 1991), 106.

"the red light district of journalism . . ." Stanley Walker, *City Editor* (NY: Frederick Stokes, 1934), 73.

Graphic *bankruptcy.* NY *Herald Trib-une,* July 2, 1932.

"Gauvreau tried to make it sensa-tional . . ." Lester Cohen, NY *Graphic: The World's Zaniest Newspaper* (Philadelphia: Chilton, 1964), 231.

"Out of the prevalent business gloom . . ." "Perhaps the Public Has Been Maligned," *Christian Century* (July 20, 1932), 901.

"I never dreamt it would be given me to gaze on the face of an Astor . . ." Jack Lait and Lee Mortimer, *New York Confidential* (Chicago: Ziff-Davis, 1948), 212.

184 *"This place!"* Eve Brown, *Champagne Cholly: The Life and Times of Maury Paul* (NY: Dutton, 1947), 278–79.

"vaulting the barriers of Newport and Fifth Avenue . . ." "The Yankee Doodle Sa-lon," *Fortune,* Dec. 1937, 126.

"We must dispel the idea . . ." Brown, 65, 69.

"Publi-ciety." Cleveland Amory, *Who Killed Society?* (NY: Harper & Bros., 1960), 143.

185 *"Social position is now more a matter of press . . ."* NY *Mirror,* July 6, 1941.

"as players in any good sleazy melo-drama must . . ." Richard Schickel, "The Rise and Fall of Café Society," *Forbes,* Oct. 1985, 40.

185–6 *"It was a fiction . . ."* Ibid.

186 *"The idea of Café Society was all right . . ."* Quoted in Amory, 140.

"frequenters usually attired them-selves . . ." NY *Mirror,* Oct. 2, 1929, 24.

"social grandees feel safe . . ." Brown, 288.

John Perona. Jerome Zerbe and

Brendan Gill, *Happy Times* (NY: Harcourt, Brace, Jovanovich, 1973), 20.

186 *Opening El Morocco.* Robert Sylvester, *No Cover Charge: A Backward Look at the Night Clubs* (NY: Dial, 1956), 98.

186–7 *Oklahoma's governor led a contingent of ministers* ... *Time*, Aug. 7, 1944, 74.

187 *Ora and Sherman struck out on their own* ... Shermane Billingsley Drill int. by author.

Sherman's arrest. NY *Post*, Jan. 21, 1952, 16.

Sherman's prison term. Ibid.

He came to New York ... Quentin Reynolds, "Have You a Reservation?," *Collier's* (Oct. 1, 1938), 41.

Red Pepper or Green Onion. Tex McCrary and Jinx Falkenburg, "New York Close-Up," NY *Herald Tribune*, Jan 12, 1950.

"somebody left a toy bird ..." NY *Daily News*, Jan. 21, 1968.

The club lost money ... SBD.

"Sherman had the instincts of a shithouse rat." Jack O'Brian int. by author.

"I went to work on every customer ..." McCrary and Falkenburg.

188 *"They were all good kids."* Sylvester, 124–25.

Helen Morgan's party. Reynolds, 42.

"there was a nice fellow ..." Frederick Woltman, "Winchell-Billingsley Duet Blow Up in a Puff of Smoke," NY *World-Telegram and Sun*, Aug. 13, 1956.

Billingsley's diffidence. SBD.

First mention of Stork. Clipping, NY *Mirror*, Sept. 1930. Scrapbook 1930–1931, NYPL at Lincoln Ctr.

"The New Yorkiest spot in New York ..." Wise Shoes, Oct. 21, 1930, NYPL at Lincoln Ctr.

"He needed a capitol ..." Jay Faygan int., March 28, 1970, Thomas coll.

"They kept coming in ..." Reynolds, 42.

Billingsley and Costello. JO'B.

"I laughed ..." Sherman Billingsley, "Literary Worm Turns for Sherm," NY *Journal*, June 17, 1959.

189 *Coll kidnapped Billingsley* ... Herman Klurfeld, *Winchell: His Life and Times* (NY: Praeger, 1976), 61; SBD.

"I do not believe that there will be many ..." NY *Times*, Jan. 21, 1932, 23.

Stork innovations. SBD.

"metamorphosis in thinking." Billingsley.

munching an apple. SBD.

"right people." *Variety*, Sept. 15, 1937.

"I decided that my clientele would be strictly carriage trade ..." Billingsley.

Cost of items. Stanley Walker, *The Night Club Era* (NY: Frederick Stokes, 1933), 88.

"ropes are up at the better cabarets ..." "Jergens Journal," Oct. 22, 1933, NBC Blue, roll 610, NBC records.

190 *Rolling back nightclub curfew.* NY *Mirror*, April 17, 1934.

Celebration of rollback. Louis Sobol, NY *Mirror*, May 23, 1934.

getting something for nothing. Brown, 286–87.

"There is only one catch." NY *Mirror*, Dec. 3, 1935.

"like starved men and women ..." Brown, 287.

One-third unemployment. Irving Bernstein, *The Lean Years: A History of the American Worker, 1920–1933* (Boston: Houghton Mifflin, 1960), 316–17.

Hoover Valley. Edward Robb Ellis, *A Nation in Torment: The Great American Depression 1929–1939* (NY: Coward-McCann, 1969), 155.

"man on the street is so gloomy ..." Joseph Mitchell, *Up in the Old Hotel* (NY: Pantheon, 1992), 137–38.

"Poverty and riches side by side ..." NY *Mirror*, Oct. 25, 1933.

191 *"Well, now, isn't that fun and gay?"* Ibid.

"I was in the same predicament ..." Ibid., March 8, 1933.

Joe Kenenan contact. Winchell, 94.

"He said some people voted Republican ..." NY *Mirror*, Nov. 11, 1932, 21.

he speculated that Roosevelt wanted to thank him ... Winchell, 95.

192   *Meeting with FDR.* Ibid., 95.

"the one man who certainly did more for his country ..." "Continuity from Stage of NY Paramount Theater for Week Beginning March 17 [1933]," FDR OF5547, FDR Library.

"the Nation's new hero." "Jergens Journal," March 13, 1933, NBC Blue, roll 601, NBC records.

"Winchell developed a blind adoration ..." Ernie Cuneo, "Introduction," in Winchell, xi.

"He idolized Roosevelt." Rose Bigman int. by author.

"For the first time in my life ..." Quoted in Oliver Pilat, *Pegler* (Boston: Beacon, 1963), 117.

193   *"a tiny column like mine isn't strong enough ..."* NY *Mirror*, May 2, 1933, May 6, 1933.

Announcing President's Day. "Jergens Journal," April 2, 1933, NBC Blue, roll 602, NBC records.

Hearst support for President's Day. W to James Farley, April 10, 1933, FDR OF5547, FDR Library.

Celebration of President's Day. See President's Day, FDR PPF1491, FDR Lib.

"I'd fix matters ..." NY *Mirror*, Feb. 13, 1934, FDR OF5547, FDR Lib.

"Busy as you are, sir ..." W to FDR, Dec. 11, 1933, FDR OF5547, FDR Lib.

"never picks on anyone with influence." NY *Mirror*, Jan.12, 1930.

"people's champion." Glade Valley (Walkersville, MD), *Times*, March 16, 1934, Scrapbook 1933–34, NYPL at Lincoln Ctr.

194   *"It makes me considerably ill ..."* "Jergens Journal," March 11, 1934, NBC Blue, roll 617, NBC records.

"I'll bet that made Dillinger laugh ..." Ibid., May 6, 1934, NBC Blue, roll 619, NBC records.

destitute father who shot a duck ... Ibid., Dec. 9, 1934, NBC Blue, roll 629, NBC records.

"the man you instinctively turn to ..." Sid Weiss, "Mad Manhattan," [?], n.d., Scrapbook 1933–34, NYPL at Lincoln Ctr.

"How many columnists ..." "Winchellism," *Plain Talk*, n.d., Scrapbook 1933–34, NYPL at Lincoln Ctr.

Assisting a newsstand owner. Deputy Commissioner Rainey to Comm. Moss, March 19, 1935; Lester Stone, La G's sec., to Ruth Cambridge, March 20, 1935, Cambridge to Stone, April 2, 1935, Stone to Cambridge, April 6, 1935, Gen. corr.: Winchell file, 1934–38, La Guardia papers, NYC Municipal Archives.

forwarding to the President a letter ... Ltr. Oct. 18, 1934, FDR OF5547, FDR Lib.

learned "early the patter of life ..." Jim Tully, *A Dozen and One* (Hollywood: Murray & Gee, 1943), 199.

195   *"Too bad that a man like Hitler ..."* NY *Mirror*, Feb. 1, 1933, 19.

"when my nose was even more upstartishly Gentile ..." Jean Jaffe, "Meet the Only Walter Winchell," *Jewish Day*, Nov. 9, 1930, Scrapbook 1930–31, NYPL at Lincoln Ctr.

"It is not good for Jews like you ..." Meyer F. Steinglass, "Broadway's Greatest Scribe," *Jewish Times*, July 25, 1930; W to Stanley Walker, April 13, 1933, Bigman coll.

"intuitive" Jew. Steinglass.

"If there was one consistent thread ..." Klurfeld, 129.

he had even fought NBC ... Gary Stevens int. by author; Herbert Polesie, J. Walter Thompson Agency, to W, Aug. 29, 1933, P file, Winchell papers.

"He considered himself a Jew." Arnold Forster int. by author.

"The best way to fight a person like Hitler ..." NY *Mirror*, Feb. 1, 1933, 19.

195–6   *"I cannot refrain from flaunting the fact ..."* Ibid.

196   *"I believe that a man's private life ..."* Ibid., Feb. 7, 1933, 19.

"the most rabid anti-Hitlerite ..." *Variety*, n.d. [1933], Scrapbook 1931–33, NYPL at Lincoln Ctr.; NY *Mirror*, Oct. 13, 1933.

"A recent issue of a Berlin gazette ..." NY *Mirror*, Sept. 27, 1933, 21.

"Down with the Jews." Walter

Winchell, "Down with the Jews," *Jewish World*, August 17, 1934.

196 *American Jewry Hall of Fame.* Meyer F. Steinglass, "The Hall of Fame of American Jewry," *B'nai B'rith Messenger*, Rosh Hashanah ed. [1934], 18–19; Steinglass (Norfolk, Va.), *Jewish Chronicle*, Scrapbook 1931–35, NYPL at Lincoln Ctr.

a friend had sent him a mimeographed newsletter ... Newsletter, Nov. 22, 1933, FDR OF3206, FDR Lib.

Identifying Nazi sympathizers. Memo on Carl Ryoir, n.d., FDR OF5547, FDR Lib.

"Knock Winchell down ..." NY *Mirror*, Feb. 22, 1934.

197 *"When I was in New York last week ..."* Hoover to W, April 23, 1934, Bigman coll.

Hoover's authorization against domestic Nazis. Athan G. Theoharis and John Stuart Cox, *The Boss: J. Edgar Hoover and the Great American Inquisition* (Philadelphia: Temple Univ. Press, 1988), 147–52.

"I am told that there are hundreds of applications ..." W to Hoover, April 24, 1934, Bigman coll.

Hoover wrote an effusive recommendation ... B. E. Sackett, Acting Special Agent in Charge, LA, to Hoover, logged June 11, 1934, FBI: Winchell file, 62–31615–4.

197–8 *Chicago trip.* CH.

198 *"The crowd sounded twelve ..."* Ashton Stevens, Chicago *American*, May 5, 1934.

"With no action save his voice ..." Lloyd Lewis, Chicago *Daily News*, May 7, 1934.

COME OUT VERY SOON. Telegram Walda to W, May 11, 1934, Script file, Winchell papers.

Detroit engagement. Contracts for Chicago Palace and Detroit Fox, April 27, 1934, Misc. contract file, Winchell papers.

"He has been very active ..." Hoover to SAC Dunn, May 28, 1934, FBI: Winchell file, 62–312615–3.

199 *"I had quite a conversation with Mr. Winchell ..."* Sackett, Acting SAC LA, to Hoover, n.d. [logged June 11, 1934], FBI: Winchell file, 62–31615–4.

Rejection of application. F. R. Lackey to W, Aug. 8, 1934, FBI: Winchell file, 62–31615–6.

"Naturally, I am low with disappointment." W to Hoover, Aug. 9, 1934, FBI: Winchell file, 62–31615–6.

When the spotlight fell on him ... Washington *Herald*, Aug. 23, 1934.

the "ovation accorded him as he left the rostrum ..." Washington *Post*, Aug. 23, 1934.

Meeting Hoover. Curley Harris int., July 17, 1970, Thomas coll.

Special correspondents list. Memo to Lester from Hoover, Aug. 25, 1934, FBI: Winchell file, 62–31615–8.

200 *"Someone brought me a note ..."* "Hoover Describes Dossiers," *NY Times*, May 12, 1954, 18.

"federal men are convinced ..." NY *Mirror*, Sept. 14, 1934.

"That was the beginning of my friendship ..." *NY Times*, May 12, 1954, 18.

201 *"It was through him ..."* James J. Waters to Hoover, Oct. 20, 1934, FBI: Winchell file, 62–31516–14.

"Winchell was probably the first ..." William C. Sullivan with Bill Brown, *The Bureau: My Thirty Years in Hoover's FBI* (NY: Norton, 1979), 94.

"did more than any other man ..." Curt Gentry, *J. Edgar Hoover: The Man and the Secrets* (NY: Norton, 1991), 512.

"well known fact that Winchell has 'an in' ..." J. H. Hanson, SAC NY, to Hoover, Sept. 19, 1935; Note, Hoover, on letter. T. H. Tracy, SC, to Hoover, Sept. 17, 1935, FBI: Winchell file, 62–31615–28.

201–2 *"I, of course, knew that you had never made any such statement ..."* Hoover to W, Aug. 8, 1935, Winchell file, Time Inc. archive.

202 *bragging of having escorted Hoover and Tolson around the town.* NY *Mirror*, Sept. 29, 1935.

"There was an expression of agony ..." Emile Gauvreau, *My Last Million Readers* (NY: Dutton, 1941), 199.

203   *Hearst had called in the note . . .* Ibid.

   Mickey Mouse. Paul Yawitz int., Apr. 17, 1970, Thomas coll.

   making noises again about leaving the Mirror . . . Variety, May 8, 1934.

   Arthur Brisbane. Frank Luther Mott, *American Journalism: A History*, 3d ed. (NY: Macmillan, 1962) 526–27.

   "I am paid for doing badly . . ." Quoted in Gauvreau, 203.

   "It annoys many when I talk about blue eyes . . ." Ibid., 214.

   "No matter how vulgarly commercial the topic . . ." Moses Koenigsberg, *King News* (NY: Frederick Stokes, 1941), 337.

203–4   *"Since you came here a few days ago . . ."* W to Brisbane, n.d. [Nov. 1934], Brisbane file, Winchell papers.

204   *"emerged from his rabbit warren . . ."* Gauvreau, 214.

   "I don't understand a word of his jargon." Ibid., 215.

   "That money came fast to him." Ibid., 218.

   "print photographs of as FEW prostitutes . . ." Quoted in Richard Weiner, *Syndicated Columnists* (NY: Richard Weiner, 1977), 75.

   "Four weeks or so have passed . . ." W to Brisbane, Dec. 21, 1934, Brisbane file, Winchell papers.

   the capitulation was less the result of Walter's deference . . . Gauvreau, 269.

   "the biggest scoop . . ." "Jergens Journal," Dec. 9, 1934, NBC Blue, roll 629, NBC records.

   FLASH! NY Mirror, Dec. 9, 1934, 31.

   "Sometime next Summer . . ." Ibid., Dec. 10, 1934, 25.

205   *"[W]hen I imagine . . . NY Mirror*, Jan. 24, 1935.

   "I got the idea that maybe she could help make a better Christmas . . ." NY Post, March 12, 1952, 68.

   Hutton phoned Walter . . . Winchell, 101–02.

   Walter saw an opening . . . NY Post, March 12, 1952, 68.

   "We endorse anybody who helps the poor." NY Mirror, Dec. 18, 1934.

   Brisbane scolded Walter . . . Brisbane to W, Dec. 29, 1934, Brisbane file, Winchell papers.

205–6   *couldn't "dispose" of the Sunday column . . .* Brisbane to W, Jan. 9, 1935, Brisbane file, Winchell papers.

206   *"I learned from our attorneys . . ."* Brisbane to W, Feb. 1, 1935; Brisbane to W, Feb. 16, 1935, Brisbane file, Winchell papers; John U. Reber, J. Walter Thompson Co., to W, March 21, 1935, Layer coll.

   "what is and what is not the right kind of copy . . ." Brisbane to W, Feb. 1, 1935, Brisbane file, Winchell papers.

   Walker liked Walter. NY Mirror, Feb. 20, 1935.

   "The Shoe Must Go On." Gauvreau, 216.

   "Who in hell does he think he is?" Ibid., 216–17.

   "You have neither ethics . . ." Lyle Stuart, *The Secret Life of Walter Winchell* (NY: Boar's Head Books, 1953), 81.

   Evidence of popularity. NY Mirror, Oct. 17, 1935.

   "The Mirror is a mess of newsprint . . ." Richard R. Lingeman, ". . . And with Lotions of Love," *NY Times*, Aug. 23, 1971, 27.

   "There was something about Winchell . . ." Gauvreau, 217.

207   *Dr. Dudley J. Schoenfeld.* Winchell, 104–05.

   A police briefing on September 10 disclosed . . . Gauvreau, 196.

   Walter called bank tellers "yaps" . . . "Jergens Journal," Sept. 16, 1934, NYPL at Lincoln Ctr.

   Walter Lyle and Walter Strum. NY Mirror, Oct. 15, 1935.

208   *"it would soon have to be decided . . ."* Gauvreau, 199.

   Walter said he had had all the information . . . Jerry Walker, "Winchell Admits Fluffs," *Editor & Publisher*, Nov. 13, 1948, 46.

   "I am happy . . ." "Jergens Journal," Sept. 23, 1934, NBC Blue, roll 626, NBC records.

208 *Gauvreau said that Walter had raced ...* Gauvreau, 198; "Jergens Journal," Sept. 23, 1934.

"I pointed out without, of course, mentioning names ..." "The Secret Side of Walter Winchell," *Movie-Radio Guide*, n.d., MWEZ + n.c. 11, 680, NYPL at Lincoln Ctr.

Tickets for Hauptmann trial. W to Brisbane, n.d. [Dec.1934], Brisbane file, Winchell papers.

209 *Walter also requested a police escort ...* Brisbane to W, Dec. 29, 1934, Brisbane file, Winchell papers.

The enterprising sheriff sold tickets ... Stanley Walker, *Mrs. Astor's Horse* (NY: Frederick Stokes, 1935), 150–51, 154, 159.

Witnesses were given vaudeville offers. NY *Mirror*, Jan 16, 1935.

"What a sorry spectacle ..." Ludovic Kennedy, *The Airman and the Carpenter* (NY: Viking, 1985), 257.

Between 100 and 130 photographers ... Ibid., 255.

"If all the famous writers ..." NY *Mirror*, Jan. 16, 1935, 10.

"They had to be things ..." Adela Rogers St. Johns, *The Honeycomb* (NY: Doubleday, 1969), 306.

"I wouldn't let a man like that influence me." NY *Mirror*, Jan. 3, 1935, 17.

210 *Efforts by NBC's legal dept.* Timothy Ropel, "Walter Winchell: The Thirteenth Juror," *Media History Digest*, vol. 5, no. 4 (Fall 1985), 57–61.

"I, too, am world famous." NY *Mirror*, Jan. 5, 1935, 7.

"He should not be allowed here." Ibid., Jan. 7, 1935, 21.

"I have heard it said of me ..." "Jergens Journal," Jan. 6, 1935, NBC Blue, roll 630, NBC records.

"I think your theories and deductions ..." Brisbane to W, Jan. 9, 1935, Brisbane file, Winchell papers.

210–11 *"I can't get into the mood ..."* NY *Mirror*, Jan. 7, 1935, 21.

211 *"You can't eat regularly ..."* Ibid., Jan. 8, 1935, 10.

"Every time we ventured a prediction ..." Ibid., Jan. 9, 1935, 25.

"The big idea is to keep your eyes on Bruno ..." Ibid., Jan. 18, 1935, 13.

"Make sure about my insurance." Ibid., Jan. 16, 1935, 3.

"I could choke her." Ibid., Jan. 19, 1935, 3.

"That spellbinding 40 minutes ..." "Jergens Journal," Jan. 27, 1935, NBC Blue, roll 632, NBC records.

212 *"I said that in October."* Jimmy Breslin, *Damon Runyon* (NY: Ticknor & Fields, 1991), 351.

He had stayed in Flemington throughout the trial ... NY *Mirror*, Feb. 7, 1935.

He had written ... seventy thousand words ... St. Clair McKelway, *Gossip: The Life and Times of Walter Winchell* (NY: Viking, 1940), 61.

lumbago. NY *Mirror*, March 7, 1935.

chewing orange and lime drops. Ibid., Jan. 23, 1935, 10.

He had furiously scribbled notes ... Ibid., Feb. 14, 1935.

"Never thought I'd ever get to the point ..." Ibid., Jan. 23, 1935.

complaining of the "moron" ... Ibid., Jan. 10, 1935, 23.

"Smasho! Flash! Crash!!!" Ibid., Jan 30, 1935, 8.

212–13 *"punch Winchell in the eye."* Ibid., Jan. 6, 1935, 6; Jan. 11, 1935, 4.

213 *"Bruno—was my picture good ..."* Ibid., Jan. 22, 1935, 13.

"He sits in the front row ..." Ibid., Feb. 28, 1935.

"What do you think Hauptmann would rather do?" Breslin, 344–45.

"The same thing would happen again ..." Walker, *Mrs. Astor's Horse*, 159.

"You had to be around at nine o'clock ..." David Brown int. by author.

214 *"strolling one Sabbath evening ..."* Ben Gross, *I Looked and Listened: Informal Recollections of Radio and TV* (New Rochelle, NY: Arlington House, 1970), 166.

Ratings. Harrison B. Summers, *Radio Programs Carried on National Networks,*

1926–1956 (Columbus: Ohio State University Press, 1958). Ratings through 1934–35 are based on the Cooperative Analysis of Broadcasting, which took a single sample either the first week of February or April. From 1935 on, Hooper ratings, which were based on telephone polling in roughly thirty cities, were used.

General Motors offer. NY *Mirror*, May 25, 1934; Brooklyn *Eagle*, May 25, 1934.

New Jergens contract. John U. Reber, J. Walter Thompson Agency, to W, May 21, 1934, Layer coll.

Indemnification. Reber to W, March 21, 1935; Reber to W, Nov. 19, 1935, Layer coll.

"only individual on radio who has held the same job . . ." "Jergens Journal," Nov. 24, 1935, NBC Blue, roll 650, NBC records.

newspaper editors . . . had coerced the Associated Press into withholding its news service . . . Erik Barnouw, *The Golden Web* (NY: Oxford University Press, 1968), 17–22.

"If radio companies want news . . ." *Editor & Publisher*, Dec. 31, 1932, 35.

215 *"the most versatile reporter in America."* "Jergens Journal," March 12, 1933, NBC Blue, roll 601, NBC records.

Art Arthur. Art Arthur int., April 21, 1970, Thomas coll.

Press-Radio Bureau. Edward Bliss, Jr., *Now the News: The Story of Broadcast Journalism* (NY: Columbia University Press,1991), 41–42.

"Get me a good murder . . ." Klurfeld, 101.

"Get your audience . . ." Ibid.

216 *"like a comet."* Ben Grauer int., May 21, 1970, Thomas coll.

"[I]t is as though the whole broadcast were set . . ." Jack Hanley, "Winchell Through a Keyhole," n.d. [1936], MWEZ + n.c. 11, 680, NYPL at Lincoln Ctr.

"voice was not loud." Ben Grauer int., Thomas coll.

"Considering the important issues you discuss . . ." Gross, 167.

"Attention Commissioner Valentine." "Jergens Journal," March 28, 1937, roll 681, NBC records.

"Benny[,] waited for you for two hours . . ." Ibid., Dec. 10, 1939, roll 744, NBC records.

217 *Stories of cynicism.* Ibid., April 29, 1934, roll 619; Sept. 16, 1934, roll 625, NBC records.

Oddities. Ibid., March 22, 1936, roll 657; Dec. 5, 1937, roll 695; July 5, 1938, roll 706; July 9, 1935, roll 706, NBC records.

218 *Walter Jr.'s birth.* NY *Mirror*, July 27, 1935, 3.

Ben Bernie had suggested Lynch. "Jergens Journal," March 3, 1935, NBC Blue, roll 634; Parker Morell, "Mr. & Mrs. Walter Winchell," *Ladies' Home Journal*, June 1940, 63.

"THE SPELLBINDING MAGIC OF NATURE . . ." Brisbane to W, Aug. 1, 1935, Brisbane file, Winchell papers; NY *Mirror*, Aug. 2, 1935, 15.

"the most enjoyable [thrill] I've known." "Winchells Welcome Walter, Jr." NY *Mirror*, July 27, 1935, 6.

"Portrait of a Bundle from Heaven." NY *Mirror*, Aug. 1, 1935, 10.

notes from well-wishers. Ibid., Aug. 3, 1935, 10.

"aversion to men." Records, Ethical Culture School.

219 *she reacted badly to the baby's birth.* Dr. Lawrence Kubie to Dr. Sophia Kleegman, Nov. 4, 1947, Walda Winchell file, Cuneo papers.

"It grabbed Winchell from the time he opened his eyes . . ." Ernest Cuneo, "Introduction," in Winchell, vi.

Winchell "lives his column." Dorothy Kilgallen, "The Cosmopolite of the Month," *Hearst's International Cosmopolitan*, July 1938, 8.

"The truth is . . ." Klurfeld, 26.

"It has long been her contention . . ." NY *Mirror*, Aug. 20, 1937.

"Don't put me in the paper . . ." Ibid., Oct. 10, 1934, 23.

"Don't you dare." Ibid., March 27, 1935, 10.

219 *June had come to disapprove of Walter's lifestyle* . . . CH.

all-wave radio. NY *Mirror*, April 25, 1934.

220 *"the best investment I ever made."* Ibid., Dec. 9, 1934.

Once he and an officer found a murder suspect . . . Art Arthur int., May 5, 1970, Thomas coll.

"She worried that he was going to be murdered . . ." AF.

One mentally unbalanced woman wrote him a letter . . . RB.

Unsigned cartoons. NY *Mirror*, Feb. 8, 1935, 8.

Attack. NY *World-Telegram*, Dec. 18, 1935.

"I am quite ready to admit . . ." Heywood Broun, "Walter Winchell's Tooth," *Nation*, vol. 142, no. 3679, Jan. 8, 1936, 47.

Lucky Luciano vowed to "even things up for you . . ." Fred Allhoff, "Walter Winchell— American Phenomenon," *Liberty Magazine*, April 4, 1942, 42.

221 *"Now I have heard it said . . ."* NY *Mirror*, Oct. 11, 1935.

5 STARDOM

223 *"[I]f you persist . . ."* Note on telegram Bernie to W, Dec. 22, 1934; W to Bernie, n.d., Bernie file, Winchell papers.

"Reliance films have been writing me . . ." W to Zanuck, Oct. 15, 1935, Twentieth Century-Fox file, Winchell papers.

"proper and correct vehicle . . ." Telegram Zanuck to W, Sept. 19, 1936, Zanuck file, Winchell papers.

Moskowitz trailing Walter on his rounds . . . NY *American*, Sept. 30, 1936.

"I hope I haven't been swindled!" W to Zanuck, Oct. 3, 1936, Zanuck file, Winchell papers.

224 *"I will not send for you . . ."* Telegram Zanuck to W, Oct. 5, 1936, Zanuck file, Winchell papers.

"get another couple of paragraphs done." W to Brand, Oct. 14, 1936, Zanuck file, Winchell papers.

Walter departed New York on Dec. 14, 1936 . . . Leonard Gaynor, Twentieth, to Richard Hyman, King Features, Dec. 11, 1936, Zanuck file, Winchell papers.

Cantor thought it would fail. "Jergens Journal," Sept. 11, 1938, NBC Blue, roll 712, NBC records.

"The beautiful part about this story . . ." Zanuck to W, Sept. 19, 1936, Zanuck file, Winchell papers.

"I have just seen the final script . . ." W

to Abel Green, Jan. 4, 1937, *Variety* file, Winchell papers.

"From the office-dressing room windows . . ." NY *Mirror*, Jan. 8, 1937.

225 *The night before his screen test . . .* Ibid.

"very happy." Zanuck to W, Jan. 8, 1937, Zanuck file, Winchell papers.

One rumor had him fainting . . . NY *Mirror*, Jan. 19, 1937.

Walter's nerves. NY *Times*, Feb. 7, 1937.

"We found out it was Winchell's knees . . ." Clipping, n.d., MWEZ + n.c. 11, 680, NYPL at Lincoln Ctr.

"finally got what the authors intended . . ." NY *Mirror*, Feb. 26, 1937.

"TO THINK THAT IT TOOK THE TOUGHEST GUY . . ." Telegram, Lanfield to W, Feb. 26, 1937, L file, Winchell papers.

"Prepare yourself for the kick of your life." Whitney Bolton, "The Stage Today," NY *Morning Telegraph*, Jan. 27, 1937.

226 *"It is sheer entertainment."* Clipping, n.d., Scrapbook 1936–37, NYPL at Lincoln Ctr.

"I HAVE TO ADMIT PREVIEW GREAT." Telegram Lanfield to W, April 7, 1937, L file, Winchell papers.

"My wife is pretty sick." W to Hearst, April 9, 1937, Hearst file, Winchell papers.

"She's a pretty sick girl . . ." W to

Lyons, April 8, 1937, Lyons file, Winchell papers.

"*The W.W.'s anticipate a blessed event . . .*" NY *Mirror*, April 12, 1937.

"*The Walter Winchells aren't that happy.*" Ibid., April 19, 1937.

"WE WOULD RATHER HAVE BABIES . . ." Telegram W to Rose Bigman, April 18, 1937, Bigman coll.

"*the Winchellian personality dominates . . .*" NY *American*, April 24, 1937; April 25, 1937.

227 "*blessed event at the Roxy.*" NY *Times*, April 24, 1937.

Billy Rose's offer. Telegram Billy Rose to W, April 25, 1937, NYPL at Lincoln Ctr.

"*wild horses couldn't drag . . .*" NY *Times*, March 28, 1937.

Louella Parsons's column. NY *American*, April 26, 1937.

6,000 patrons attended . . . Press release, Twentieth Century-Fox, Scrapbook 1936–37, NYPL at Lincoln Ctr.

record of 38,825. Motion Picture Daily, April 27, 1937.

Breaking house records. Harry Brand to W, April 26, 1937; Brand to W, April 28, 1937, Zanuck file, Winchell papers.

"*Walter Winchell is so positive an acting personality . . .*" Quoted in Irving Hoffman, clipping, MWEZ + n.c. 11, 680 in NYPL at Lincoln Ctr.

228 "*I think you're a chump . . .*" Quoted in W to Zanuck, May 5, 1937, Twentieth Century-Fox file, Winchell papers.

"*Whoever wrote you that letter . . .*" Zanuck to W, May 5, 1937, Twentieth Century-Fox file, Winchell papers.

Two months later Joe Moskowitz sent Walter an agreement . . . Moskowitz to W, July 19, 1937, Twentieth Century-Fox file, Winchell papers.

"*Lux Theater*" *appearance. The Front Page,* "Lux Radio Theater," June 28, 1937, Cassette 13646, Sound Div., Library of Congress.

229 OUR INTEREST REQUIRES US . . . Beucus to W, Sept. 16, 1937, Layer coll.

same consideration from the Mirror. *Editor & Publisher* (Sept. 18, 1937), 20.

"*The odds are a good ten to one . . .*" W to Abel Green, Sept. 24, 1937, *Variety* file, Winchell papers.

"*nervous exhaustion.*" Press release, "Love and Hisses," Sept. 22, 1937, Winchell file, Margaret Herrick Lib., AMPAS.

"*All I know is that I sit around . . .*" W to Green, Oct. 1, 1937, *Variety* file, Winchell papers.

230 *he instructed Ruth Cambridge not to put her calls through.* Rita Greene, unpub. ms., 46A–47A, Pat Rose coll.

Rita's career. Ibid., 72–73.

She and her family huddled . . . Pat Rose, niece of Rita, int. by author.

"*Sometime back I found out I had a tumor . . .*" Rita Greene to W, Oct. 2, 1937, Pat Rose coll.

"*[W]e are doing our best to simplify . . .*" Margarie Hockley to Rita Greene, Oct. 4, 1937, Pat Rose coll.

Within a few days Rita got her money . . . Ibid., 52; PR.

231 "*too busy . . .*" Ibid., 52.

"*My hours are never regular.*" W to Rita Greene, Sept. 29, 1938, Pat Rose coll.

"*I am not getting any younger.*" Greene, 52A.

vowing yet again . . . "Jergens Journal," Nov. 14, 1937, NBC Blue, roll 694, NBC records.

"*There's nothing for me to do . . .*" *Time,* July 11, 1938, 36.

232 "*the consensus out here . . .*" Lanfield to W, Dec. 21, 1937, L file, Winchell papers.

"*As sham battles go . . .*" NY *Times,* Jan. 3, 1938.

"*uninspired entertainment.*" *Newsweek,* Jan. 3, 1938, 34.

"*Their continual heckling . . .*" NY *Herald Tribune,* Jan. 3, 1938.

Love and Hisses was actually outperforming Wake Up and Live . . . "Jergens Journal," March 20, 1938, NBC Blue, roll 701, NBC records.

232 *he would have continued making movies
...* Ibid., March 6, 1938, roll 701.

233 *"I have never been able to get far
enough ..."* Alexander Woollcott, "The Little
Man with the Big Voice," *Hearst's International Cosmopolitan*, May 1933, 143.

"The first thing a client did ..." Al
Rylander, int. by author.

"If Winchell says so ..." Lucille Ball
int., Apr. 22, 1970, Thomas coll.

David Brown was shocked to read ...
DB.

*"Other columnists have jocular mo-
ments ..."* Charles Fisher, *The Columnists*
(NY: Howell, Soskin, 1944), 103.

233-4 *"The interests of others concerned
him ..."* Emile Gauvreau, *The Scandal Monger* (NY: Macaulay, 1932), 187.

234 *"Never mind, never mind."* St. Clair
McKelway, *Gossip: The Life and Times of Walter Winchell* (NY: Viking, 1940), 28–29.

*He repeatedly reported that Judge Joseph
Force Crater ...* "Jergens Journal,"
Nov. 17, 1935, roll 650; Sept. 6, 1936, roll
667, NBC records.

*A week after reporting that Douglas
Fairbanks, Jr., had ...* Ibid., Jan. 15, 1939,
NBC Blue, roll 720, NBC records.

"unconfirmed report." NY *Mirror*,
Dec. 3, 1934.

"You give that to Mr. Winchell." Clipping, "Hepburn Home and Happy with Boo
for Walter Winchell," n.d., Scrapbook 1933–
34, NYPL at Lincoln Ctr.

235 *"Now I know why you've been sending
my mail ..."* NY *Mirror*, July 7, 1933, 19.

Rose Bigman's employment. Rose
Bigman to Gordon Van Ark, Nov. 28, 1933,
Bigman coll.

Hired by Ruth Cambridge. Rose
Bigman int. by author.

Sobel was careful not to disparage ...
Bernard Sobel, *Broadway Heartbeat: Memoirs
of a Press Agent* (NY: Hermitage House,
1953), 303.

"Winchell yelled up to Bernie ..." RB.

*"Nobody's Girl Friday, I am sure has
taken so much ..."* Walter Winchell, *Winchell
Exclusive: "Things That Happened to Me—And

Me to Them"* (Englewood Cliffs, N.J.:
Prentice-Hall, 1975), 92.

236 *"bantam rooster."* RB.

"I never went out to lunch." Ibid.

Don't "let the Boss frighten you." Cambridge to Bigman, n.d., Bigman coll.

*"You have found out what a worrier I
am."* Rose Bigman to W, n.d. [1935], Bigman
coll.

"He'd make so many changes ..." RB;
McKelway, 35.

237 *"I'd be so scared ..."* RB.

Walter was furious at being awakened.
Ibid.

"I'm sorry. Mr. Winchell is sleeping."
Ibid.

"Everyone thought I was a battleax ..."
Ibid.

"C'mon, Boss." Ernest Lehman int. by
author.

"Please don't ask him to retract." Ibid.

238 *"I think that contributors to columns ..."* Winchell in intro., Philip Stack,
Love in Manhattan (NY: Liveright, 1932), v.

"Sometimes I'd pick up the column ..."
Curley Harris int. by author.

author Jim Bishop ... made $5 ... Jim
Bishop, Miami *Herald*, Feb. 21, 1972, 14–C.

"It looked like a kindergarten class."
Joel Landau int. by author.

*"He could take any guy's twelve
lines ..."* AF.

239 *"The press agents would send the same
material ..."* Herman Klurfeld int. by author.

Herman Klurfeld. Ibid.

"But I loved it." Ibid.

240 *Walter was in his fedora ...* Ibid.

*The office "didn't look at all the way I
had imagined."* Herman Klurfeld, *Winchell:
His Life and Times* (NY: Praeger, 1976),
72–73.

Winchell courting Klurfeld. HK.

Winchell arranged for Odets ...
Klurfeld to author, Dec. 5, 1992.

"Accountant?" Klurfeld, 73.

241 *"I would write the Sunday column."*
HK.

Working on the lasty. Ibid.

"Psychologically I got the joy ..." Ibid.

242 *Presents to Rose.* RB.

"He was sort of a father image ..." Ibid.

Klurfeld also described his relationship to Walter ... HK.

"If I've made any kind of headway ..." Klurfeld to W, Feb. 14, 1937, Klurfeld file, Winchell papers.

"I want to thank you ..." Klurfeld to W, Nov. 29, 1938, Klurfeld file, Winchell papers.

Sometimes Herman even allowed himself to imagine ... HK.

"We regarded that column as number one ..." Sid White int. by author.

Rates. Maurice Zolotow int., Apr. 18, 1970, Thomas coll.

243 *a single mention would hold a client ...* Leo Guild int., Apr. 13, 1970, Thomas coll.

One press agent recalled rushing his pregnant wife ... Sam Wall int., Apr. 7, 1970, Thomas coll.

"In those days being a press agent ..." Lee Meyers int. by author.

Press agents had first materialized ... Eric F. Goldman, *Two-Way Street: The Emergence of the Public Relations Counsel* (Boston: Bellman Publishing Co., 1948).

Though a bill was introduced in Congress ... Candice Jacobson Fuhrman, *Publicity Stunt: Great Staged Events That Made the News* (San Francisco: Chronicle Books, 1989), 24–26.

Rose Bigman said admiringly ... RB.

"You had to service Winchell ..." Coleman Jacoby int. by author.

"I realized that competing ..." GS.

"USE WHITE PAPER!" Lee Israel, *Kilgallen* (NY: Delacorte, 1979; rep. Dell, 1980), 209.

244 *Milton Berger's schemes.* CJ.

"Marlene Dietrich Award." Eddie Jaffe int. by author.

"if you didn't get in the papers ..." Jack Tirman int. by author.

"We and the other press agents fought ..." EL.

elaborate deception. Bill Doll int., May 29, 1970, Thomas coll.

"We lived in a dangerous world." EL.

"What happened, Art?" CJ.

245 *Walter occasionally sent along a scurrilous item ...* Al Rylander int. by author.

"Look, Walter. I'm enjoying them too." Ibid.

"I'm not listening, Walter." JT.

instinctively checking his car's rearview mirror ... CJ.

"Sometimes people give you a wrong steer." Henry F. Pringle, "Portrait of Walter Winchell," *American Mercury*, Feb. 1937, 143.

Marty Ragaway landed on the DDL ... EJ.

Ben Cohn, under pressure from Walter ... Ben Cohn int., March 25, 1970, Thomas coll.

246 *Gary Stevens and DDL.* GS.

246–7 *"I am sorry that you think ..."* Henny Youngman to W, May 5, 1938, comedian file, Winchell papers.

247 *The only capital crime* ... Milt Josefsberg int., April 16, 1970, Thomas coll.

Robert William and Winchell. Robert William int. by author.

"The press agents were all over him." DB.

"like a shark with little fish ..." Maurice Zolotow int., April 8, 1970, Thomas coll.

"A lot of these guys ..." EL.

248 *Bribes.* Hal Conrad, Gary Stevens, Lee Meyers int. by author.

"cry softly into the beer ..." Stanley Walker, "Playing the Deep Bassoons," *Harper's Monthly Magazine*, vol. 164 (Feb. 1932), 373.

by Eddie Jaffe's estimate ... EJ.

"Publicity is the nervous system ..." Harry Reichenbach, as told to David Freedman, *Phantom Fame: The Anatomy of Ballyhoo* (NY: Simon & Schuster, 1931), 165.

248–9 *"I always believed that a great deal of our news ..."* EL.

249 *He loved to read their columns aloud ...* Ed Weiner, *Let's Go to Press: A Biography of Walter Winchell* (NY: Putnam, 1955), 16.

249 *"I see my rejects ..."* Jack Ellinson int., April 10, 1970, Thomas coll.

David Brown ... was shocked ... DB.

"[M]y impression of the Broadway columnists ..." Danton Walker, *Danton's Inferno: The Story of a Columnist and How He Grew* (NY: Hastings House, 1955), 13.

Danton Walker. Ibid., 48 passim.

250 *"Did you know L. Lyons ..."* NY *Mirror*, May 11, 1934.

Leonard Lyons. Russell Maloney, "Profile," *New Yorker* (April 7, 1945), 30; Mary Braggiotti, "Keeper of the Lyons Den," NY *Post*, Nov. 4, 1947; Warren Lyons int. by author.

Meeting Sylvia Schonberger. Braggiotti.

It was the editor there who renamed him ... Nathan Zalowitz to Lyons, June 19, 1930, quoted in Maloney, 30.

"It was the mad dream." Braggiotti.

Walter claimed to have recommended him. Sid White int. by author.

"Here's a natural for you." Lyons to W, June 13, 1934, Lyons file, Winchell papers.

"Why would a lawyer become a columnist?" WL.

251 *Lyons would admit ...* Braggiotti.

"I just don't like celebrities." J. P. McEvoy, "He Snoops to Conquer," *Saturday Evening Post*, Aug. 13, 1938, 10.

"My father never printed gossip." WL.

"You are the first column ..." NY *Post*, Oct. 8, 1976.

Lyons attacking Sobol. Louis Sobol, *The Longest Street: A Memoir* (NY: Crown, 1968), 367.

"a real gentleman." RW.

"Pleasant." EJ.

"Everyone is Lyons' friend." Maloney.

"There is not a great deal of desperation ..." Ibid.

"Driven, dedicated." EJ.

"The hardest-working newspaperman." AR.

"Lyons never drinks ..." Westbrook Pegler, *Dissenting Opinions* (NY: Scribner's, 1938), 245.

252 *"I pleaded with him by wire ..."* Hause to W, May 5, 1953, Bigman coll.

"Broadway columns are as passé ..." *Variety*, Sept. 15, 1937; Jerry G. Bowles, *A Thousand Sundays: The Story of the Ed Sullivan Show* (NY: Putnam, 1980), 98.

"Well, how shall I start?" W to Danton Walker, Sept. 4, 1937, Walker file, Winchell papers.

253 *"[T]he only word for Ed Sullivan's portrayal ..."* Bowles, 99–100.

"I pointed out to the great Port Chester athlete ..." Hause to W, May 5, 1953, Bigman coll.

Skolsky and Parsons. Sidney Skolsky, *Don't Get Me Wrong—I Love Hollywood* (NY: Putnam, 1975), 42–45.

"I've always claimed a story wasn't a story ..." Louella O. Parsons, *Tell It to Louella* (NY: Putnam, 1961), 13.

Louella Parsons. Parsons, 121; George Eells, *Hedda and Louella: A Dual Biography of Hedda Hopper and Louella Parsons* (NY: Putnam, 1972), 35 passim.

254 *"The only time she would get burned up ..."* Dorothy Manners int. by author.

"She was always in the swim." Ibid.

255 *He filled her station wagon with presents.* RW.

She treated Walter like visiting royalty. Parsons, 126–27.

"Sometimes things break out here ..." Parsons to W, Aug. 30, 1943, Parsons file, Winchell papers.

"hated her guts." DM.

"To him I was a new audience." Hedda Hopper, *From Under My Hat* (Garden City, NY: Doubleday, 1952), 10.

256 *Taking the name Hedda.* Ibid., 13, 20.

"[H]alf the movie colony has gone schizophrenic ..." Quoted in Marlo Lewis and Mina Bess Lewis, *Prime Time* (Los Angeles: J. P. Tarcher, Inc., 1976), 22.

257 *Announced he was a millionaire.* Ben Cohn int., March 25, 1970, Thomas coll.

New Jergens contract. Lennen & Mitchell to W, June 3, 1937; Robert H. Orr to W, May 18, 1938, Layer coll.

One publication estimated his 1937

earnings . . . Screen Book, n.d., MWEZ + n.c. 11, 680, NYPL at Lincoln Ctr.

His actual earnings . . . Harry Scharf, acct., to W: Statement Showing Taxable Income from All Sources, April 13, 1951, Geist file, Winchell papers.

He complained publicly in The New York Times *. . . NY Times*, March 28, 1937.

"I was on the verge of doing it . . ." W to Abel Green, March 2, 1938, *Variety* file, Winchell papers.

"He had never before been so fully seen . . ." "Newspaperman," *Time*, July 11, 1938, 33.

Walter *"seems disconsolate . . ."* Ben Bernie, "Broadway," *Pic*, Nov. 1, 1938, 23.

"May a simple egomaniac . . ." Leonard Lyons, "The Lyons Den," NY *Post*, Feb. 23, 1972, 35.

Walter's own excuses . . . NY *Mirror*, Oct. 17, 1935.

257–8 *"Winchell is a great bore . . ."* Clifford Odets, *The Time Is Ripe: The 1940 Journal of Clifford Odets* (NY: Grove Press, 1988), 142–43, 153–54.

258 *"He said in several thousand words . . ."* Klurfeld, 96.

"compartmentalized." HK.

"TELL LYONS I DIDN'T THINK OR SUSPECT . . ." Telegram W to Rose Bigman, April 22, 1937, Lyons file, Winchell papers.

258–9 *"Mister, I'm almost tempted to believe . . ."* Lyons to W, n.d. [April 1937], Lyons file, Winchell papers.

259 *"His brother Algernon had even come to suspect . . ."* Lenore Winchel int. by author.

"I understand you're worth . . ." Ed Weiner int. by author.

Each evening he phoned her three or four times . . . Parker Morell, "Mr. and Mrs. Walter Winchell," *Ladies' Home Journal*, June 1940, 27.

"Mrs. Winchell is seen in them . . ." NY *Mirror*, July 30, 1940.

History of Walter's estate. Louise Clark, Greenburgh historian, int. by author.

260 *Walter bought it from the town . . .* Deed, Westchester County, Book 3708, 128.

The bed. Eva Winchell.

"When you were in that room . . ." Ibid.

"considerable misgivings." Morrell, 27.

"the way he always does . . ." Ibid.

261 *"I bought a farm for June and the kids."* W to Art Arthur, n.d. [1938], Art Arthur Papers, Folder: Late 30s, Lee Library, Brigham Young University.

To Klurfeld he complained jokingly . . . HK.

the problem of trespassers. Scarsdale *Inquirer*, Sept. 29, 1939, 6.

he took an apartment in the St. Moritz . . . RB, Ed Weiner.

"For him the roses grow and fade . . ." Jim Tully, *A Dozen and One* (Hollywood: Murray & Gee, 1943), 208.

Walter was "sort of a visitor . . ." Seth Rubinstein, atty., int. by author.

"Why do I want to go with a little kid . . ." Eva Winchell.

"Is it your birthday today?" Mrs. Helen Steinman int. by author.

Occasionally, on Thursday nights . . . HK.

262 *"WE LOVE YOU AND ALREADY MISS YOU."* Tel. June to W, Dec. 31, 1938, W file, Winchell papers.

"biggest bankers of New York . . ." "Jergens Journal," April 17, 1938, NBC Blue, roll 703, NBC records.

"as soothing as a nightmare." Cleveland *Press*, Oct. 31, 1941.

"Not to be able to get a table at El Morocco . . ." Jerome Zerbe and Brendan Gill, *Happy Times* (NY: Harcourt, Brace, Jovanovich, 1973), 19.

"a debutante disbarred from the inner sanctum . . ." NY *Times*, Dec. 25, 1938.

"[P]eople must come to the Stork . . ." "Sherm's Place," *Pic*, October 13, 1942, 42.

263 *Differentiating El Morocco from the Stork.* Robert Sylvester, *No Cover Charge* (NY: Dial, 1956), 101–02, 109; DB; Quentin Reynolds, "Have You a Reservation?" *Collier's*, Oct. 1, 1938, 43.

"elegant din." Felice Early int. by author.

"racetrack and the showplace . . ." Er-

nest Cuneo, Introduction in Walter Winchell, *Winchell Exclusive*, xx; Zerbe, 19.

263 *"Is Walter there?"* HK.

"YOU AND YOU ALONE ARE THE STORK'S SANTA." Tel. Billingsley to W, Dec. 25, 1936, Billingsley file, Winchell papers.

Walter never picked up a tab. Winchell, 303.

Headwaiter Jack Spooner personally supervised . . . Weiner, 14.

"Chicken A La Walter Winchell." Stork Club menu, Billingsley file, Winchell papers.

When Walter complained that the noise . . . Milt Rubin int., Thomas coll.

264 *When Walter wanted a place to shave* . . . Shermane Billingsley Drill int. by author.

Hand signals. NY *Mirror*, Nov. 17, 1937.

One reporter compared watching him . . . Russell Whelan, "Inside the Stork Club," *American Mercury*, vol. LIX, no. 249 (Sept. 1944), 357.

"The world is full of drinkers . . ." Sylvester, 123.

"What counts most to the people . . ." Mearl Allen, *Welcome to the Stork Club* (San Diego: A. S. Barnes, 1980), unpaginated.

"by selling the assumption . . ." Ethel Merman with George Eells, *Merman* (NY: Simon & Schuster, 1978), 94.

"If they get tossed out . . ." NY *World Journal Tribune*, Oct. 4, 1966, 46.

264–5 *Billingsley's rules.* Jack O'Brian, "So Long Sherm," NY *World Journal Tribune*, Oct. 5, 1966, 46; "Meet You at the . . . ?" *Newsweek*, Oct. 18, 1965, 42: Sherman Billingsley, "How to Behave in a Night Club," *Good Housekeeping*, July 1947.

265 *When he thought a young press agent was table-hopping* . . . W to Billingsley, Oct. 14, 1938, Billingsley file, Winchell papers.

"A Storker must be at least . . ." Elizabeth Hawes, "If You Want to Be a Stork Clubber, Here's How," *PM's Weekly*, June 1, 1941, 51.

"like a conquering Caesar . . ." Marlo Lewis, 32–33.

"Kremlin for those with blue noses . . ." Weiner, 10.

Ashtrays. SBD.

265–6 *"You'd go into the Cub Room."* DB.

266 *Sometimes Winchell sat with his back* . . . "Sherm's Place," 41.

"He talked through you." Merman, 97.

"[T]here was always the danger . . ." Ibid.

"In his prime, I saw him do a double rhumba samba . . ." Ernest Cuneo, ms. pages, 51, Winchell file, Cuneo papers.

266–7 *"In the pre-war days around the Stork* . . ." Quoted in Ed Wilcox, "Flash!- 30– For WW," NY *Daily News*, March 2, 1969, 2, 25.

267 *he was now increasingly bored by celebrity chitchat.* Pringle.

"My interests are growing." J. P. McEvoy, "He Snoops to Conquer," *Saturday Evening Post*, Aug. 13, 1938, 44.

"Lot's of important things are happening . . ." Gross, 166–67.

"I have said in all seriousness . . ." Heywood Broun, "Shoot the Works," *New Republic*, Vol. LXXXIV, No. 1221, (April 27, 1938), 357–58.

268 *Fortune survey. Fortune* magazine, Jan. 1940, 90.

Aggregate daily circulation. Anon. to W, April 21, 1939, *Time* file, Winchell papers.

Radio audience. W to Frank Norris, *Time*, May 17, 1939, *Time* file, Winchell papers.

"emerged as such an expert on national affairs . . ." Drew Pearson, "Washington Merry-Go-Round," reprinted in NY *Mirror*, May 29, 1938.

part of Washington officialdom. Unpub. ms., "Winchell Broadcasts" file, np., Cuneo papers.

"What Winchell did for FDR . . ." Ibid.

Washington visit. Earl Godwin to McIntyre, May 10, 1938, FDR OF 5547.

269 *Meeting with FDR. Newsweek*, May 23, 1938, 5; Washington *Herald-Times*, May 11, 1938.

"who is sure that America would be a better place to live . . ." "Jergens Journal," Sept. 13, 1936, NBC Blue, roll 667, NBC records.

"I am not a communist . . ." Ibid., Sept. 20, 1936, roll 668.

"There is no room for any ism . . ." Ibid., April 24, 1938, roll 703.

"I took them all on." "Winchell for McCall's," 20, Cuneo papers.

"Walter Winchell is the only . . ." "Winchell Speaks for the Masses of America," *International Teamster*, n.d., NYPL at Lincoln Ctr.

270 *"I personally think Mr. Roosevelt . . ."* Quoted in Rodney P. Carlisle, *Hearst and the New Deal: The Progressive as Reactionary* (NY: Garland Publishing, 1979), 79–80.

"I think we will have to settle down . . ." Edmond D. Coblentz, ed. *William Randolph Hearst: A Portrait in His Own Words* (NY: Simon & Schuster, 1952), 169–70.

"essentially Communism." Carlisle, 100.

"Winchell seems to satisfy the whims . . ." Emile Gauvreau, *My Last Million Readers* (NY: Dutton, 1941), 139.

He had even come to Walter's defense . . . W to Hearst, April 9, 1937, Hearst file, Winchell papers.

promoting Hearst's mistress . . . "Jergens Journal," Sept. 24, 1933, roll 609.

The Milk Fund. Mrs. Hearst to W, March 18, 1932, May 9, 1934, Hearst file, Winchell papers.

called him "Daddy." HK.

Gauvreau's dismissal. Gauvreau, 290–98.

"largely because of the way he treated you." Hearst to W, April 2, 1937, Hearst file, Winchell papers.

"icy atmosphere." Paul Yawitz int., April 14, 1970, Thomas coll.

"Under Brisbane's generalship . . ." Gauvreau, 265.

271 *"You are now getting out the worst paper . . ."* John Tebbel, *The Life and Times of William Randolph Hearst* (NY: Dutton, 1952), 299.

Brisbane raced to San Simeon . . . Ibid., 300.

"I certainly think I should pay them . . ." W to Hearst, March 18, 1937, Hearst file, Winchell papers.

"You have to be a little patient . . ." Hearst to W, April 2, 1937, Hearst file, Winchell papers.

Hearst revised Walter's contract. "From Mike to Type," *Literary Digest*, April 17, 1937, 31.

272 *"They are all the same family."* W to Abel Green, Oct. 1, 1937, *Variety* file, Winchell papers.

"I just dreaded signing . . ." *Variety*, Sept. 29, 1937; W to Abel Green, Oct. 1, 1937, *Variety* file, Winchell papers.

"I told you I never should have signed . . ." W to Art Arthur, n.d. [1938], Folder: Late 30s, Art Arthur Papers, Lee Library, Brigham Young University.

"Controversy, as you know, brings circulation." Reprinted in Winchell, 127.

"I must ask all columnists . . ." Hearst to W, Feb. 7, 1938, Hearst file, Winchell papers.

273 *William Randolph Hearst, Jr., had cornered Walter . . .* W to Ward Green, March 18, 1938, Hearst file, Winchell papers.

"We may as well face it." Note, March 22, 1938, quoted in William Randolph Hearst, Jr., with Jack Casserly, *The Hearsts: Father and Son* (Niwot, Colo.: Roberts Rinehart, 1991), 214.

"Please edit Winchell very carefully . . ." Reprinted in "Walter Winchell Off Broadway," *Ken Magazine* (May 19, 1938), 89.

"I expect to be fired any day . . ." W to Patterson, March 28, 1938, Box 27, File 6, Joseph Medill Patterson Papers, Donnelly Library, Lake Forest College.

Walter himself said only that he had paused . . . W to ed. of "Newsdom," March 30, 1938, Box 27, File 6, Patterson Papers, Lake Forest College.

he made a point of sending Patterson a telegram . . . Tel. W to Patterson, March 30,

1938, Box 27, File 6, Patterson Papers, Lake Forest College.

273 *"My opinions are not for sale."* "Jergens Journal," April 3, 1938, roll 702.

274 *"You say that the Winchell column has become . . ."* W to Hearst, April 7, 1938, Hearst file, Winchell papers.

Newsweek *reported that Hearst was going to retire Walter . . . Newsweek,* April 25, 1938, 8.

Variety *wrote that Walter's contract wasn't up . . . Variety,* June 8, 1938.

"[H]e had as much trouble explaining . . ." NY *Mirror,* Sept. 22, 1938.

"What if I lose my column?" Klurfeld, 78.

"the most dangerous criminal." Quoted in Burton Turkus and Sid Feder, *Murder, Inc.: The Story of "The Syndicate"* (NY: Farrar, Straus and Young, 1951), 331.

274–5 *Louis Buchalter.* Ibid., 332–45.

275 *Reward for Lepke. Time,* Sept. 4, 1939, 12.

Lepke went underground. Turkus, 353–55; Meyer Berger, "Lepke's Reign of Crime," *NY Times,* March 5, 1944, 30.

Hoover had threatened mob heads . . . Klurfeld, 82–83.

Dewey had so disrupted the mob . . . Turkus, 357.

"Don't ask me who I am." NY *Mirror,* Aug. 26, 1939.

As Ernie Cuneo told it . . . Ernest Cuneo, "J. Edgar Hoover and Winchell," unpub. ms., Cuneo papers.

276 *The two FBI officials were sitting next to Walter . . .* Curt Gentry, *J. Edgar Hoover: The Man and the Secrets* (NY: Norton, 1991), 219.

"Your reporter is reliably informed . . ." "Jergens Journal," Aug. 6, 1939, roll 736. It is unclear why W sets the reward at $35,999.

276–7 *Feints and dodges.* Winchell, 136–37.

277 *Lepke was a headline story.* NY *Mirror,* Aug. 15, 1939, 2.

Dewey's agents claimed to have discovered . . . Ibid., Aug. 17, 1939, 5.

Zwillman refused to testify . . . Ibid., Aug. 18, 1939, 10.

Staking out the Stork Club. Ibid., Aug. 17, 1939, 5.

"I am fed up with you . . ." Winchell, 140–41.

"on the verge of tears." Ibid.

278 *"If Lepke doesn't surrender . . ."* NY *Mirror,* Aug. 26, 1939.

"[m]y reputation as a newsman . . ." Winchell, 141.

"Whatzzamatta?" Ibid., 142.

It was a humid night . . . NY *Mirror,* Aug. 29, 1939, 10.

"Oh, nobody will take a shot at the car . . ." Heywood Broun, "The Inside Story of Lepke and Mr. Walter Winchell," *Broun's Nutmeg,* Sept. 2, 1939.

Walter drove slowly . . . Winchell, 144; NY *Mirror,* Aug. 26, 1939.

279 *Lepke complained about his celebrity.* NY *Mirror,* Aug. 29, 1939, 10.

When he phoned June . . . Klurfeld, 85.

Walter said he had lost six pounds . . . "Sherlock Winchell," *Newsweek,* Sept. 4, 1939, 13.

"Without your unselfish and indefatigable . . ." Hoover to W, Aug. 25, 1939, Winchell file, 62–31615, FBI.

Walter refused the reward money . . . Broun.

"How much do you imagine I'd want . . ." Irving Hoffman, "Tales of Hoffman," Hollywood *Reporter,* Sept. 5, 1939, 3.

One report claimed the whole thing had been prearranged . . . Winchell, 146.

Frank Costello had made the arrangements. Leonard Katz, *Uncle Frank: The Biography of Frank Costello* (NY: Drake, 1973), 134.

280 *"Irving Hoffman did the entire thing."* Arnold Forster int. by author.

Walter, he said, had assured him . . . E. A. Tamm to Hoover, Dec. 29, 1939, Winchell file, 62–31615, FBI.

Walter had "double-crossed" him. Foxworth to Hoover, Dec. 29, 1939, Winchell file, 62–31615, FBI.

"very much worried and concerned . . ."

E. A. Tamm to Hoover, Dec. 29, 1939, Winchell file, 62–31615, FBI. In his autobiography Walter blames Lepke's associate Abner Zwillman for relaying a false message to Lepke that the sentence would be light—Zwillman's way of tricking the gang chief into surrendering. Zwillman was later found murdered. (Winchell, 147–48.)

Buchalter's execution. Turkus, 361; Ernest Cuneo, unpub. ms., A430, Cuneo papers.

the editor "groaned." NY *Mirror,* Aug. 26, 1939, 6.

the Mirror *was dominated by a photograph of Hitler . . .* NY *Mirror,* Aug. 25, 1939, 1.

6 AT WAR

281 *"war is not expected . . ."* "Jergens Journal," March 31, 1935, NBC Blue, roll 635, NBC records.

Wall Street bettors were wagering . . . Ibid., March 15, 1936, roll 656.

"it will be up to Russia . . ." Ibid., April 3, 1938, roll 702.

Walter predicted that Hitler would invade Czechoslovakia. . . . Ibid., July 31, 1938, roll 709.

"the most dramatic and hysterical period . . ." Ben Gross, *I Looked & I Listened: Informal Recollections of Radio and TV* (New Rochelle, NY: Arlington House, 1970), 160.

282 *"It is said that Premier Chamberlain flew . . ."* NY *Mirror,* Sept. 18, 1938.

"Trying to make peace with Hitler . . ." Ibid., Sept. 27, 1938.

"Those European nations have given us . . ." Ibid., Oct. 5, 1938.

"squeezing the Russian bear . . ." "Jergens Journal," Dec. 11, 1938, roll 718; May 7, 1939, roll 729.

In May he warned of the imminent German takeover . . . Ibid., May 14, 1939, roll 730; June 18, 1939, roll 733.

"Just as many of us suspected . . ." Ibid., Aug. 20, 1939, roll 737.

"most fateful hour . . ." Ibid., Aug. 27, 1939, roll 737. He followed this solemn pronouncement with: "Maxine Moore, one of the prettiest chorus girls in Lew Brown's big hit, *Yokel Boy,* is now in Chicago to apply for a divorce. If it is granted, Miss Moore will marry Chief Hamilton of the Broadway tribe."

"May I respectfully offer the suggestion . . ." W to Kennedy, Sept. 3, 1939, Chamberlain file, Winchell papers.

Ernest Cuneo . . . thought it took enormous gall . . . Ernest Cuneo, untitled ms., 44, Cuneo papers.

282–3 *"He was grateful for your suggestion . . ."* Kennedy to W, Sept. 4, 1939, Chamberlain file, Winchell papers.

283 *"What absolutely enraged me . . ."* Cuneo, untitled ms., 44.

"I honestly think that the best way . . ." "Jergens Journal," Sept. 4, 1938, roll 711.

"morally bankrupt." Ibid., Sept. 25, 1938, roll 713.

"[T]he future of American youth . . ." Ibid., April 9, 1939, roll 727.

"that it will help keep the United States . . ." Ibid., Sept. 10, 1939, roll 738.

"The total isolation idea . . ." Sherwood to W, Oct. 2, 1938, PPF, Box 1342–1390, File 1356, FDR Library.

"The reason the United States needs a bigger army . . ." NY *Mirror,* May 30, 1938.

283–4 *"Not to be used as tools of Aggression . . ."* "Jergens Journal," Oct. 23, 1938, roll 715.

284 *"A tough-guy world . . ."* Ibid., March 24, 1940, roll 752.

"doing more than anyone . . ." Irving Hoffman, "Tales of Hoffman," Hollywood *Reporter,* Sept. 19, 1939, 3.

Burton Rascoe scolded Walter . . . NY *Mirror,* May 12, 1940.

"I am opposed to another American Expeditionary Force . . ." "Jergens Journal," April 7, 1940, roll 753.

284 *"military experts think that the Na-zis ..."* Ibid., April 21, 1940, roll 754.

"The Allies are going through a per-iod ..." Ibid., May 26, 1940, roll 757.

"continent of Europe is lost ..." Ibid., June 16, 1940, roll 759.

285 *he could and did quote Shakespeare ...* Herman Klurfeld int. by author.

"Ernie looked like what he was." Herman Geist int. by author.

" 'Champagne for everybody ...' " HK.

"a very small school ..." Cuneo, untitled ms., Box G-3, Cuneo papers.

His son believed that a prank ... Jonathan Cuneo int. by author.

"recording the strife of working peo-ple ..." Cuneo, untitled ms., Box G-3, Cuneo papers.

Law school. NY *Post,* Jan. 11, 1952, 5.

286 *Cuneo and Murphy.* Cuneo, untitled ms., Box G-3, Cuneo papers.

"There was only one person ..." Ernest Cuneo, "Introduction," in Walter Winchell, *Winchell Exclusive: "Things That Happened to Me—And Me to Them"* (Englewood Cliffs, N.J.: Prentice-Hall, 1975), ix.

"Necessity is above the gods themselves." Ibid.

"I opened with an amenity." Ibid.

287 *"Lord Lothian, what is Great Britain going to do ..."* Ibid, x.

"I came to a conclusion ..." Ibid.

"I was under the terrific tension ..." Ibid., xv.

Walter quickly became their stalking-horse ... Ibid., xi.

"The President feels the nation needs him ..." "Jergens Journal," July 31, 1938, roll 709.

"The so-called political insiders ..." Ibid., April 9, 1939, roll 727.

287–8 *Steve Early enlisted radio commenta-tor Earl Godwin ...* Early to McIntyre, June 20, 1939, STEP, FDR Lib., in Betty Houchin Winfield, *FDR and the News Media* (Urbana: University of Illinois Press, 1990), 122n.

288 *"Look, Walter."* Cuneo in Winchell, xii.

"I quoted others ..." NY *Mirror,* July 30, 1940.

"dear friend of mine." W to "Peter Carter," May 13, 1938, W file, Winchell papers.

The relationship nearly collapsed ... W to Cuneo, May 13, 1940, Cuneo file, Winchell papers.

"legal services rendered ..." Note, W to Rose Bigman, n.d. [1940], Cuneo file, Winchell papers.

289 *Hull, Berle and Winchell.* Beatrice Bishop Berle and Travis Beal Jacobs, eds. *Navigating the Rapids, 1918–1971: From the Papers of Adolf A. Berle* (NY: Harcourt Brace Jovanovich, 1973), 298.

"help prepare the country for war." Ernest Cuneo, "Fights to the Finish," unpublished ms., A 4–7, Cuneo papers.

"This was interesting." Berle, 298–99.

"mouthpiece of the Nazi movement ..." "Jergens Journal," June 16, 1940, roll 759.

"firmly believes in the fundamental principles of this Republic ..." Ibid.

"Jewish vilifier." Congressional Record, Aug. 12, 1940, 15638.

"alarmist." Variety, July 3, 1940, 3.

"the worst political Pier Sixer ..." Cuneo in Winchell, xiv.

290 *Walter was delighted, ...* Ibid.

"I believe Senator Wheeler is wrong ..." "Jergens Journal," Sept. 21, 1941, roll 804; Sept. 28, 1941, roll 804.

"For five years, American isolation-ists ..." Ibid., Sept. 29, 1940, roll 768.

"appeasement has taught America ..." Ibid., Oct. 13, 1940, roll 770.

Wheeler's accusation. Cuneo, "Fights to the Finish," A2–17; NY *Mirror,* April 24, 1941.

"There should be the closest possible mar-riage ..." Quoted in Curt Gentry, *J. Edgar Hoover: The Man and the Secrets* (NY: Norton, 1991), 265.

BSC. Cuneo, untitled ms., Box G-3, Cuneo papers.

291 *"to do all that was not being done ..."* Quoted in David Ignatius, "Britain's War in

America," *Washington Post*, Sept. 17, 1989, C-2.

BSC schemes. Ibid.

Cuneo was feeding Walter information ... Cuneo, "Fights to the Finish," A2-17, Cuneo papers.

he was secretly feeding Walter British propaganda ... "Winchell" file, 3-15, Cuneo papers.

"If any of our contributors ..." Memo, Jack Lait to W, July 19, 1940, Hearst file, Winchell papers.

"to scrap all the old rules ..." James A. Wechsler, *The Age of Suspicion* (NY: Random House, 1953), 159.

"Willkie for the millionaires." PM, Sept. 20, 1940, 11.

292 *Death of Jacob Winschel.* NY *Mirror*, Aug. 19, 1940; *NY Times*, Aug. 19, 1940; NY *Herald Tribune*, Aug. 19, 1940.

"saw the president often ..." Ernest Cuneo, "Third Term," unpub. ms., 5, Cuneo papers.

asking the President to intercede with Winchell. Averell Harriman to Steve Early, Oct. 29, 1941, OF Box 1, 220, FDR Lib.

"I have a little apartment in New York City ..." Eleanor Roosevelt to W, July 25, 1940; ER to W, Aug. 12, 1940, Box 1585, Eleanor Roosevelt papers, FDR Lib.

293 *"In the war of combat journalism ..."* Cuneo, unpublished ms., 1, Cuneo papers.

Roper poll. Fortune, Jan 1940, 88.

"[S]ome people have wondered ..." "Jergens Journal," Feb. 2, 1941, roll 780.

"And there you are Rip Van Winkles ..." Ibid., May 4, 1941, roll 789.

"blitzkrieging the American people ..." NY *Times*, May 8, 1941, 11.

294 *Arnold Forster.* Arnold Forster, *Square One: A Memoir* (NY: Donald I. Fine, 1988), 19ff.

295 *"Tell that Forster guy ..."* Arnold Forster int. by author.

"I was soon receiving a continuous flow ..." Forster, 58–59.

"I would get a call from Rose." AF.

"We got mountains of stuff." Herman Klurfeld int. by author.

Forster himself drafted whole columns ... Forster, 58.

"We are less in danger today ..." "Jergens Journal," June 23, 1940, roll 760.

"These communists have mercury ..." Ibid., June 9, 1940, roll 758.

295–6 *Walter complained that if they had waited* ... Ed Weiner, *Let's Go to Press: A Biography of Walter Winchell* (NY: Putnam, 1955), 201.

296 *"He shouts a few bits of choice gossip ..."* George Daugherty, "Winchell: J. Edgar Hoover's Man Friday," *Daily Worker*, March 11, 1941.

"When first he tried his hand ..." George Daugherty, "Winchell's Adventures in the Prohibition Era," *Daily Worker*, March 12, 1941.

"This pro-fascist is still the big threat ..." Open letter, Communist Pol. Assn. of NY County, n.d., Sam Weisman, sec., Bigman coll.

"Walter Winchell must be stopped ..." "Jergens Journal," April 27, 1941, roll 789.

"I have never been in so many brawls ..." NY *Mirror*, May 23, 1941.

"If you picked up a column ..." Mike Hall, press agent, int. by author.

297 *"A year and a half ago ..."* NY *Mirror*, Nov. 21, 1940.

"It is the first time in the history of radio measurement ..." Press release, C. E. Hooper, Inc., June 11, 1941.

"the amazing adaptability of the Winchellesque style." "The Secret Side of Walter Winchell," *Movie-Radio Guide*, n.d., MWEZ + n.c. 11, 680, NYPL at Lincoln Ctr.

"The agitated listener waits ..." John S. Kennedy, "A Bolt from the Blue," in *Molders of Opinion*, David Bulman, ed., (Milwaukee: Bruce Pub. Co., 1945), 163–64.

he now spoke for the administration. Ernest Cuneo, "Walter as a Babe in the International Intelligence Game," unpub. ms., 31, Cuneo papers.

"principal daily conduit to the people." Ibid., 34.

"There is today a 100% American ..."

Reprint of ed., Mount Airy [N.C.] *Times* in NY *Mirror*, Oct. 29, 1940.

297 *"the first soldier ..."* St. Clair McKelway, *Gossip: The Life and Times of Walter Winchell* (NY: Viking, 1940), 121.

297–8 *American Legion honors.* Denver *Post*, March 16, 1939 [Amer. Legion Post 139, Arlington, Va.]; Comm. Lewis Landes, Amer. Legion, to J. Edgar Hoover, Sept. 8, 1939, Winchell file, FBI.

298 *Running for Congress.* Winchell, 93.

Cuneo described him three nights before a broadcast ... Cuneo in *Winchell*, xvi.

Cuneo ... often left in tears ... AF.

"for the pure sadistic joy." Cuneo in *Winchell*, xvii.

Cuneo's description of broadcast. Ibid., xvi.

"Gotta go to the bathroom." Bob Hope int., March 31, 1970, Thomas coll.

listen to the transcription ... Weiner, 10.

298–9 *"If June was enthusiastic ..."* Cuneo, unpub. ms., n.p., Cuneo papers.

299 *"He was his own worst enemy."* Rose Bigman int. by author.

"You listen too fast." Clare Russhon, prod. asst., int. by author.

"No one's listening ..." Fred Allhoff, "Winchell—American Phenomenon," *Liberty Magazine*, March 28, 1942, 57.

Ickes on Pegler. Oliver Pilat, *Pegler* (Boston: Beacon Press, 1963), 3.

"Maybe now that I've turned 43 ..." NY *Mirror*, April 11, 1940.

300 *"offended the refinements ..."* Bernays int., June 15, 1970, Bob Thomas coll.

"Would you call Winchell's work serious?" NY *Mirror*, Jan. 24, 1941.

"If the New Yorker does do one ..." W to McKelway, March 4, 1937, *New Yorker* file, Winchell papers.

Ross relented ... Dale Kramer, *Ross and the New Yorker* (Garden City, N.Y.: Doubleday, 1951), 256.

"It will take a long time." McKelway to W, Oct. 18, 1939; Note on letter.: W to McKelway, n.d., *New Yorker* file, Winchell papers.

"beat you to the punch." W to McKelway, May 21, 1940, *New Yorker* file, Winchell papers.

"It just seems a more politic thing ..." McKelway to W, June 7, 1940, *New Yorker* file, Winchell papers.

301 *Walter's accuracy.* McKelway, 53.

"Here's a problem." Ibid., 122.

"When statesmen, novelists, artists ..." Ibid., 138.

"Winchell has no taste ..." Ibid., 149.

302 *"people cannot be hoodwinked ..."* Ibid., 146.

Walter's reaction. Kramer, 256.

"numerous misstatements ..." NY *Mirror*, Sept. 2, 1940.

"so-and-so." Ibid., Sept. 3, 1940.

"One of the prisoners was ..." Ibid., Oct. 15, 1940.

Ross received word ... Kramer, 257.

Walter ... said Ross was barred ... Note on *New Yorker* clipping, n.d. [1940], Billingsley file, Winchell papers.

McKelway had "encountered slime ..." Ross to Billingsley, Sept. 17, 1940, *New Yorker* file, Winchell papers.

"attempt to cut a line ..." Billingsley to Ross, n.d. [Sept. 1940], *New Yorker* file, Winchell papers.

"[F]or godsake let up on me." Note: Ross to W, n.d., *New Yorker* file, Winchell papers.

Walter collected a column's worth of items ... Tel. W to Rose Bigman, Nov. 7, 1940; Jack Lait, ed. NY *Mirror*, to Charles McCabe, Hearst exec., May 20, 1941, *New Yorker* file, Winchell papers.

303 *The Harold Rosses "should hire a hall ..."* NY *Mirror*, April 28, 1941.

"Café Society's first war victim." "Jergens Journal," Jan. 4, 1942, roll 815; NY *Mirror*, Jan. 7, 1942.

"Here is a man ..." W to Lait, June 23, 1942, *New Yorker* file, Winchell papers.

"The American population is electrified ..." "Jergens Journal," Dec. 7, 1941, roll 812.

"I dunno." NY *Mirror*, March 27, 1935.

he had asked to defer his inactive status . . . Note attached to Mike Mulligan, "Walter Winchell Scrutinized," *Atlantan*, n.d., Layer coll.

"breathless week at sea." "Jergens Journal," Aug. 31, 1941, roll 801.

304 *"the rumors of a few years ago . . ."* W to Abel Green, July 16, 1941, *Variety* file, Winchell papers.

"I don't see why I should sign my name . . ." W to Hellinger, Sept. 8, 1941, Hellinger file, Winchell papers.

"because I knew things were going to pop." W to Steve Monchak, *Editor & Publisher* (Jan. 20, 1942), M file, Winchell papers.

"While we all appreciate your desire . . ." Letter from Adm. Arthur J. Hepburn to W, Dec. 17, 1941, quoted in "Winchell Says Hepburn Asked Him to Stay on Radio," *PM*, March 29, 1944, 3.

"How do you do, Mr. Winchell?" W to Saul Price, Jan. 27, 1942, "Lipman [sic] Ketchup Bottle" file, Winchell papers; Winchell, 121.

304–5 *Lindy's fracas.* Winchell, 121.

305 *Lippman's wounds.* NY *Sun*, Jan. 21, 1942.

Lippman had been turned away from the Stork . . . Winchell, 121.

"Now that Lieut. Commander Winchell has won . . ." NY *Daily News*, Jan. 22, 1942, 40.

Attacks on Walker. NY *Mirror*, Jan. 22, 1942.

Cissy Patterson. Ralph G. Martin, *Cissy: The Extraordinary Life of Cissy Medill Patterson* (NY: Simon & Schuster, 1979); Paul F. Healy, *Cissy: The Biography of Eleanor M. "Cissy" Patterson* (Garden City, NY: Doubleday, 1966).

306 *Walter had met her* . . . Winchell, 129.

"It was the first party I had gone to . . ." NY *Mirror*, May 23, 1941.

"imitators steal your act." Ibid.

"Why the hell don't you quit looking under the bed . . ." Winchell, 130.

"couldn't live without a violent hate." Cuneo, untitled ms., 4, Cuneo papers.

"You had some items about Joe Kennedy's son . . ." Hoover to W, Jan. 17, 1942, Winchell file, 62–31615, FBI.

306–7 *Cissy's attacks on Walter.* Martin, 430.

307 *"What is being done . . ."* W to Connolly, Jan. 26, 1942, Washington *Examiner* file, Winchell papers.

Walter decided to sue Patterson . . . W to Connolly, Feb. 22, 1942, Washington *Examiner* file, Winchell papers.

"First time a reporter . . ." NY *Mirror*, Feb. 24, 1942.

he announced he would not re-sign . . . Monchak, 25.

"The omissions are usually . . ." Draft of ad for Washington *News*, March 4, 1942, Washington *Examiner* file, Winchell papers.

"I think we have been too kind . . ." Klurfeld, 109–10.

308 *"I'm not a gentleman . . ."* Cuneo in Winchell, xx.

March 15 attack. "Jergens Journal," March 15, 1942.

Patterson files suit. NY *Times*, March 20, 1942, 24.

Five days a week he hopped the subway . . . W to Steve Monchak, *Editor & Publisher*, Jan. 20, 1942, Misc., Winchell papers.

309 *"He talks navy, navy, navy."* Allhoff, 45.

"Now, I may be wrong about that . . ." *Congressional Record*, House 77:2, March 2, 1942, 1899.

he said he would head to Washington immediately . . . NY *Times*, March 3, 1942, 12.

"My thought would be . . ." *Congressional Record*, House 77:2, March 3, 1942, 1938.

The Navy defended Walter . . . NY *Times*, March 3, 1942, 12.

"How about some active duty . . ." NY *Mirror*, March 3, 1942.

"He is being sniped at . . ." Ibid., March 4, 1942.

"sacrifice of Winchell's life . . ." Ibid., March 6, 1942, 10.

FDR and Walter. Winchell, 187–88.

310 *"I know what I want to do ..."* W to Eleanor Roosevelt, March 12, 1942 [dictated March 8], Box 1669, Eleanor Roosevelt papers, FDR Lib.

Tribune's *anti-Winchell campaign.* R. G. Danner, SAC, to J. Edgar Hoover, March 25, 1942, Winchell file, 62–31615, FBI.

"Is his name Moses Weinstein ..." Joseph Kamp to Frank Knox, sec'y. of navy, March 31, April 10, May 4, 1942; Kamp to Hoffman, n.d. [rec. June 7, 1942], Box 3, Walter Winchell 1942, Hoffman papers, Bentley Lib., University of Michigan. This anti-Semitic taunt apparently originated with Bund leader Fritz Kuhn, who testified before the House Committee on Un-American Activities in 1939 that Walter's real name was "Lipschitz." The untruth persisted in rightwing circles, though Walter had publicly offered $100,000 to anyone who "can back his statement with proof" that Winchell wasn't Walter's real surname. ("Jergens Journal," Oct. 22, 1939.)

"Instead of chasing storks ..." NY *Mirror,* March 17, 1942.

Ben Bernie told Walter ... Winchell, 164–65.

Luther Patrick's support. Congressional Record, House 77:2, March 10, 1942, 2292–94.

311 *Walter decided to return to Washington ...* Monchak, 25.

"Capt. L phoned from Washington ..." NY *Mirror,* March 13, 1942.

the weekend came and went... Ibid., March 12, 1942.

Clare Hoffman was going to be called ... Washington *Times-Herald,* April 21, 1942.

"In nearly every case of alleged subversive activities. ..." Clipping, NY *Mirror,* ? 1942, OF Box 5547, FDR Lib.

"How much longer is Winchell to be permitted ..." Congressional Record, House 77:2, April 20, 1942, 3676–77.

"they might talk too much." Ibid., Dec. 8, 1942, 9729.

312 *"twisted, inferiority-ridden soul ..."* Georgiana X. Preston, "Apology to Winchell

The Popgun Patriot," Washington *Times-Herald,* July 19, 1942, E-1, E-8.

"These publishers refuse to see ..." Radio ed., July 19, 1942, OF Box 144A, Folder: Cartoons & Clippings, 1942, July–Aug., FDR Lib.

"[I]t might refresh him ..." W to Steve Early, Sept. 15, 1942, FDR OF5547, FDR Lib.

"The American people have a right to know ..." Walter Winchell, "Americans We Can Do Without," *Liberty Magazine,* Aug. 1, 1942, 9–11, 44–46.

Walter reported that Kuhn would call his office ... Walter Winchell, "More Americans We Can Do Without," *Liberty Magazine,* Aug. 8, 1942, 12–14.

Third part of series. Walter Winchell, "More Americans We Can Do Without: Even in Congress," *Liberty Magazine,* Aug. 15, 1942, 26.

313 *Rep. Thorkelson had filed a $2 mill. libel suit.* "Jergens Journal," Nov. 22, 1942.

Gerald L. K. Smith was contemplating legal action ... U. S. A. Heggblom, attorney, to Gerald L. K. Smith, Aug. 7, 1943, Box 11, Walter Winchell 1943, Gerald L. K. Smith papers, Bentley Hist. Lib., University of Mich.

"means we're getting down to cases." NY *Mirror,* Nov. 10, 1942.

"... for HE KNOWS WHAT." W to Steve Early, Nov. 10, 1942, FDR OF5547, FDR Lib.

Four times ... Walter had beseeched Washington ... Time, Jan. 11, 1943, 41.

After another of the President's press conferences ... Winchell, 173.

"I report December 1st ..." W to FDR, Nov. 21, 1942, PSF, Box 189, File "W" General, FDR Lib.

Assignment. Time, Jan. 11, 1943, 41.

314 *The night before departing ...* Herman Geist, son of Harry Geist, int. by author.

"Since Walter Winchell got into the navy ..." W to Hedda Hopper, Dec. 19, 1941, Hopper collection, AMPAS.

he vetoed her selection. Winchell, 220.

"When I got off the train ..." W to

Adm. Hepburn, Nov. 29, 1942, PPF, Box 5666, FDR Lib.

At 3:00 A.M. . . . Ernest Cuneo, "Winchell's Early Background," unpub. ms., 52, Cuneo papers.

314–15 *Brazilian mission. Time,* Jan. 11, 1943, 41.

315 *Walter told a friend . . .* Joel Landau int. by author.

"How'd you like to go on a killer group?" Walter Winchell, "Tour of Duty," in *They Were There,* ed. Curt Reiss (NY: Putnam, 1944), 477–79.

As they winged back to the field . . . Winchell Exclusive, 176.

"I daily bless the moment . . ." NY *Mirror,* Dec. 30, 1942.

Walter made one last request . . . Commander Gulf Sea Frontier to Lt. Comm. Walter Winchell, US Naval Reserve, Subject: Anti-Submarine Search, Jan. 21, 1943, Ref: Restricted COMSOLANT for dispatch 192019, Bigman coll.

"most priceless inheritances." W to Rose Bigman, Jan. 2, 1943, Bigman coll.

316 *"You can be sure that while you were out of sight . . ."* Ed Weiner to W, Jan. 13, 1943, "W" articles file, Winchell papers.

"[d]ingy burlesk houses . . ." NY *Mirror,* Jan. 29, 1942.

"Booze is getting scarce." Billingsley to W, Nov. 29, 1943, Billingsley file, Winchell papers.

It was still jammed . . . NY *Daily News,* April 9, 1942.

"a sort of rose arbor . . ." Russell Whelan, "Inside the Stork Club," *American Mercury,* vol. LIX, no. 249 (Sept. 1944), 357.

317 *"It was a gay night . . ."* E. J. Kahn, Jr., "The Army Life," *New Yorker,* March 6, 1943, 56.

the Stork grossed $900,000. "Sherm's Place," *Pic,* Oct. 13, 1942, 42.

1943 grosses and patronage. Time, Aug. 7, 1944, 74.

Breakage and theft alone . . . Whelan, 363.

Refusing the duke and duchess of Windsor. Sherman Billingsley Drill int. by author.

Fritz Kuhn. David Brown int. by author.

Reaction to Westbrook Pegler. SBD.

"I'm getting in trim . . ." Weiner, 13.

318 *"You bet I'm prejudiced . . ."* "Jergens Journal," Jan. 31, 1943.

Hoffman's court-martial resolution. Editor & Publisher, Feb. 6, 1943, 27; House Record Group 233, Papers Accompanying Specific Bills & Resolutions, H.R. 108, Feb. 10, 1943, 78:1, File HR 78A-D23, National Archives.

Clare Hoffman. Obit., *NY Times,* Nov. 5, 1967, 86; Samuel Grafton, "I'd Rather Be Right," NY *Post,* March 31, 1944, 20.

he "established a world record . . ." Grafton.

making it a federal crime to be a member of the B'nai B'rith Anti-Defamation League. Forster, 87.

Hoffman now offered an amended resolution . . . Congressional Record, House 78:1, Feb. 10, 1943, 767–768.

"scandalous conduct." House Record Group 233, Papers Accompanying Specific Bills & Resolutions, H.R. 108, Feb. 10, 1943, 78:1, File HR 78A-D23, National Archives.

319 *Knox acted immediately . . . Congressional Record,* House 78:1, Feb. 9, 1943, 732.

Vinson then quickly forestalled . . . NY *Times,* Feb. 10, 1943, 15.

"I am glad . . ." NY *Mirror,* Feb. 10, 1943.

He admitted that he had erred . . . NY *Times,* Feb. 15, 1943, 4.

Walter went to the White House, his resignation in hand. Cuneo, "Walter as a Babe in the International Intelligence Game," unpub. ms., 33, Cuneo papers.

320 *Roosevelt told him he was needed . . .* W to Irving Hoffman, Dec. 12, 1963, Misc., Winchell papers.

Frank Knox. Cuneo, "Fights to the Finish," A2–17. 58, Cuneo papers.

Meeting with Knox. W to Hoffman, Dec. 12, 1963; *Winchell Exclusive,* 155–56.

"The silence that fell over that spacious room . . ." Winchell Exclusive, 155–56.

320 *"Tell the President I will handle the battle ..."* Memo: EMW [Edwin M. Watson], sec. to the Pres., to FDR, Feb. 17, 1943, PSF, Box 189, File: "W" general, FDR Lib.

"Those who tried to force me off ..." *NY Times*, Feb. 19, 1943 (UPI).

320-1 *"This would seem to mean ..."* NY *World-Telegram*, Feb. 20, 1943.

321 *"Look at this."* Paul Scheffels int. by author.

the real source ... was not Hoover but Cuneo ... Cuneo, "J. Edgar Hoover and Winchell," unpub. ms., 93, Cuneo papers.

Hoover was soon assigning agents to monitor ... Memo for J. W. Cannon, W. S. Crawford from D. M. Ladd, Aug. 31, 1942, Winchell file, FBI.

Tapping Walter's phones. Natalie Robins, *Alien Ink: The FBI's War on Freedom of Expression* (NY: Morrow, 1992), 140. It is unclear from the documents, however, whether Hoover was tapping Winchell's phone or whether Walter was picked up on the tap of someone else's phone.

"I am getting fed up ..." Quoted in ibid., 114.

"You will note that Mr. Winchell from time to time ..." Memo: Hoover to Tolson, Tamm, Ladd, June 22, 1942, Winchell file, FBI.

322 *Mark Woods announced that he was tightening restrictions ...* NY Times, Feb. 10, 1943, 15.

two subordinates of Gen. George Marshall ... Drew Pearson, *Diaries, 1949-1959*, ed. Tyler Abell (NY: Holt, Rinehart, 1974), 132.

he "would fight like hell." AF.

"He would state his grievance ..." Cuneo in Winchell, xv.

"You had a tough time ..." HK.

"My fangs have been removed ..." *Time*, Feb. 22, 1943, 68; *PM*, Feb. 11, 1943.

323 *"frank discussion between businessmen."* *Time*, Feb. 22, 1943, 68.

"What you fellows want me to do ..." Willard Wiener, "Winchell Fights Gag on Pro-FDR Items," *PM*, April 12, 1943, 11.

"All they can do ..." NY *Post*, May 10, 1943.

One report predicted ... Variety, May 12, 1943, 3.

Walter sent the clippings ... NY *Post*, May 17, 1943.

Meeting between FDR and Sarnoff. Edwin Watson to David Sarnoff, May 28, 1943, PPF Box 2, File: Roosevelt, Eleanor, 1943, FDR Lib.

"for finding the time to do something about the Blue Network ..." W to FDR, June 9, 1943, PPF Box 2, File: Roosevelt, Eleanor, 1943, FDR Lib.

324 *"Two men ..."* Fly to FDR, May 5, 1941, PSF, FDR Lib., quoted in Winfield, 110.

NBC's divestiture of Blue. Ned Midgley, *The Advertising and Business Side of Radio* (NY: Prentice-Hall, 1948), 111-35.

Henry Luce refused to buy the Blue ... Luce quoted in Richard Clurman, *To the End of Time: The Seduction and Conquest of a Media Empire* (NY: Simon & Schuster, 1992), 287.

Constitutionality of FCC edict. Variety, May 12, 1943, 3.

324-5 *"in accordance with true democratic principles."* Erik Barnouw, *The Golden Web: A History of Broadcasting in the United States*, Vol. II, 1933 to 1953 (NY: Oxford University Press, 1968), 168-81.

325 *"your courage in risking all your money ..."* W to Edward Noble, Oct. 18, 1943, Blue Net file, Winchell papers.

Walter's deposition. Dep. of W, July 6, 1942, District Court of D.C., Civil Action 15024, Washington *Examiner* file, Winchell papers.

"examine Cissy down to her undies." Quoted in Gentry, 311n.

she had offered to settle ... PM, Feb. 8, 1943.

Patterson's attorneys asked that the case be dismissed. ... Variety, May 12, 1943, 3, 27.

"Shit on Eleanor Patterson!" W to Earl Wilson, n.d. [1944], Wilson papers, Schubert Archive.

she wrote an article ... Eleanor Patterson, "Crazy—Crazy like Foxes," Washington *Times-Herald*, Oct. 28, 1945, D-3.

Walter claimed final victory ... *Winchell Exclusive*, 133.

U.S. Journal. Time, May 26, 1947.

326   *"didn't want to lead the Broadway life."* Art Arthur int., Apr. 21, 1970, Thomas coll.

still waiting for her husband ... Quoted in Marie Torre, "A New Career for Walter Winchell," *Look*, Oct. 30, 1956.

"likes to play with live dolls." Earl Wilson, NY *Post*, March 4, 1944, Irving Hoffman scrapbooks, 21, 185, NYPL at Lincoln Ctr.

Jimmy. NY *Post*, May 7, 1945.

Shopping expeditions. Mike Hall int. by author; Mina Rohm int. by author.

Walt, Jr., ... *found the whole thing inexplicable.* Eva Winchell int. by author.

Rose Bigman said that she adopted babies ... Rose Bigman int. by author.

"They are wards of the state." W note on Harry Scharf to W, Jan. 21, 1947, Geist file, Winchell papers.

Walter later put Jimmy through medical school. Gertrude Bayne int. by author.

327   *Ed Weiner.* EW.

"I like the way you conduct yourself." Ibid.

"He was a garrulous fellow ..." Gary Stevens int. by author.

"lapdog." Jack O'Brian, columnist, int. by author; Martin Burden int. by author.

"If Winchell wanted a drink ..." HK.

"Where's your friend Winchell?" JO'B.

"I would say most of it was jealousy." EW.

"He filled a very important part ..." MH.

328   *"How do you like that bastard* ..." HK.

"I never asked Walter to do me a favor." EW.

"There were seven days and seven nights ..." Ibid.

"must have lost five years ..." Harold Conrad int. by author.

"The minute the word is out ..." Ibid.

"complete illiterate." EW.

"That opened up the doors pretty wide." Ibid.

Congressional investigators tapping Winchell's phones. Phone logs, 1942, attached to letter J. B. Mathews, HUAC, to Westbrook Pegler, April 14, 1949, Box 110, Subj: Winchell, Pegler papers, Herbert Hoover Lib.

329   *"young Lana Turner."* Shirley Bentley, sister-in-law of Mary Lou, int. by author.

"like the little girl next door." Ibid.

"They were dirt poor." William Michael Purcell int. by author.

Tee-Tiny. SB.

"I thought she was beautiful." Irving Zussman int. by author.

One millionaire dept. store magnate ... Lee Meyers int. by author.

"closer than a Princeton haircut." Clipping, NY *Mirror*, [1938], NYPL at Lincoln Ctr.

"Rose advertises ..." NY *Mirror*, Jan. 20, 1938.

a get-together at 3:00 A.M. Ibid., Jan. 25, 1938.

330   *America's most beautiful women.* "The Prettiest Girl," *Look*, Jan. 31, 1939, 14–15.

"It was a very Platonic situation ..." WMP.

he had no choice but to surrender her ... GS. Speir, only 28, died on November 14, 1939, of heart failure, which would seem to suggest that if the legend was true, Mary Lou's relationship with Walter began earlier than some remember.

"That's where a genius ..." EW.

"It's the first time I've ever really been in love." Lyle Stuart, *The Secret Life of Walter Winchell* (NY: Boar's Head Books, 1953), 179.

"Five minutes' conversation ..." Quoted in John Mosedale, *The Men Who Invented Broadway: Damon Runyon, Walter Winchell and Their World* (NY: Marek, 1981), 303.

"could escape the troubles ..." WMP.

331   *giving him change.* Ibid.

he didn't give gifts ... JO'B.

He relented only after press agent ... Eddie Jaffe int. by author.

331 *She would stalk out . . .* HC.
Mary Lou at Empire State Bldg.
WMP.
room service from the Stork . . . HC.
"She was the columnists' favorite . . ."
Jack Tirman int. by author.
"Cute, huh?" HC.
June didn't know about Mary Lou. GB.
Sullivan submitted a column . . . Al
Rylander, press agent, int. by author.
332 *Bodyguard.* Mosedale, *303*; WMP.
"I may say I am a little skittish . . ."
Pamphlet: "Answering Walter Winchell's
Attack—Persecuting Gentiles," [speech by
Rankin, Jan. 26, 1944], Box 110, Subj:
Winchell, Pegler papers, Herbert Hoover Lib.
"Very special $64 question . . ." NY
Mirror, Feb. 1, 1944.
333 *"Consider the time it is."* Ibid., Feb. 8,
1944.
*Rankin introduced a bill . . . Editor &
Publisher*, Feb. 12, 1944, 54.
"that little communistic 'kike' . . ."
Mimeo: WINCHELL STIRS ANTI-
SEMITISM [excerpts from Rankin speech,
Feb. 21, 1944], Box 110, Subj: Winchell,
Pegler papers, Herbert Hoover Lib.
*voters of Michigan ought to keep him at
home . . .* Memo: R. O. Kittelson to Ladd,
FBI, Jan. 16, 1944, Winchell file, FBI.
*Hoffman was moving behind the
scenes . . .* Memo L. B. Nichols to Clyde
Tolson, FBI, March 17, 1944, Winchell file,
FBI.
334 *"I heard about the matter . . ."* "Hoff-
man Smears Winchell," *PM*, March 23,
1944, 5.
*"Congress is hot about the whole
thing . . ."* John T. Flynn to Gen. Robert
Wood, March 23, 1944, Box 5, Flynn corr.,
Wood papers, Herbert Hoover Lib.
So Flynn turned to another ally . . ."
Flynn to Wood, April 7, 1944, Box 5, Flynn
corr., Wood papers, Herbert Hoover Lib.
Winchell had corresponded with Dies . . .
E. K. Gubin, researcher HUAC, to W,
June 10, 1938, Dies file, Winchell papers.
334–5 *Falling out with Dies. Winchell Ex-
clusive*, 155.

335 *Dies harangue. NY Times*, March 10,
1944, 10.
Hoffman repeated the charge . . . Ibid.
(AP), March 14, 1944, 36.
"fully 60% of the statements." Ibid.,
March 14, 1944, 36.
Dies's overture. William Gellerman,
Martin Dies (NY: John Day, 1944) 275; James
Wechsler, "Winchell Says He Rejected
Dies," *PM*, March 17, 1944, 6.
"If Winchell enters that ring . . ." I. F.
Stone, "The Dies Challenge to Free
Speech," *PM*, March 22, 1944, 2.
*Walter . . . suggested that Dies could
even follow . . .* Memo: Arnold Forster to W,
n.d. [1944], Dies file, Winchell papers.
336 *"this drunk-with-power gentleman . . ."*
Willard Edwards, "Winchell Talks Probed by
Dies," Washington *Times-Herald*, March 18,
1944, 1.
Dies immediately accepted . . . Philip
W. Lennen, Lennen & Mitchell, to Dies,
March 18, 1944; Dies to Lennen, March 18,
1944, Dies file, Winchell papers.
"if you invite a guest . . ." *PM*,
March 21, 1944.
*"newspapers are in competition with ra-
dio." Editor & Publisher*, March 25, 1944, 13.
*"The Winchell columns should not be
used . . ."* "Hearst Syndicate Muzzles
Winchell," *PM*, March 22, 1944, 4.
Three drafts. AF.
*On broadcast nights, he parked his car
. . .* Paul Schaffels int. by author.
*He had gotten word of another threat
. . .* AF.
337 *Dies's speech.* Speech, March 26, 1944,
Martin Dies papers, Sam Houston Regional
Lib. & Research Ctr., Texas.
337–8 *Walter's rebuttal.* "Jergens Journal,"
March 26, 1944.
338 *"I thought Walter had made the largest
mistake . . ."* AF.
Aftermath. NY Times, March 27,
1944.
"opening gun in this little offensive . . ."
Flynn to Wood, April 7, 1944; Wood to
Flynn, April 12, 1944, Box 5, Flynn corr.,
Wood papers, Herbert Hoover Lib.

339 *the ratings for the "debate" were actually lower* . . . *Variety*, March 29, 1944, 29.

The NBC switchboard had been clogged . . . Rose Bigman to W, n.d., Dies file, Winchell papers.

Dies "stunk." Note Jack Lait to Rose Bigman [April 1944], James Johnston coll.

a "battle of freedom of speech . . ." *Radio Daily*, April 21, 1944.

calling "attention to persons . . ." "Dies and Winchell," *The New Republic*, vol. 110, no. 14 (April 3, 1944). 454.

"We hold no brief . . ." "Winchell vs. Dies," *Editor & Publisher*, April 1, 1944, 34.

Hoffman and Dies were back in the House . . . NY *Sun*, March 27, 1944.

"[I]t would not only be in the interest of the congress . . ." *Broadcasting*, April 3, 1944, 12.

"Don't you envy just a little . . ." W to J. M. Patterson, March 29, 1944, Box 39, file 4, J. M. Patterson papers, Donnelly Lib., Lake Forest Coll.

"I no longer ask for your subpoena." "Winchell's Answer to Dies Censored," *PM*, April 3, 1944.

Andrew Jergens phoned from Miami Beach . . . Ibid.

340 *Hoffman had claimed that he was responsible* . . . *Editor & Publisher*, April 8, 1944, 16.

"This is libelous." Memo: W to Rose Bigman [for Cuneo], n.d., Cuneo papers.

Walter filed a $250,000 *libel suit* . . . *Winchell* v. *Clare Hoffman*, U.S. District Court, NY Southern District, Summons civ. 25–172, April 10, 1944, Cuneo papers.

HUAC collecting material. J. B. Mathews to Pegler, April 14, 1949, Box 110, Subj: Winchell, Pegler papers, Herbert Hoover Lib. At the time of this book's publication the HUAC files on Winchell had still not been opened to the public. Despite the author's repeated requests over a four-year period to see the material, Donnald Anderson, the House clerk, has refused on the ground that it would not serve the national interest. An archivist, however, has told me that the file is roughly two inches thick.

"last-ditch weapon by the New Deal . . ." Quoted in Weiner, xiii.

"Little did we think . . ." Billy Rose to W, Jan 22, 1944, NYPL at Lincoln Ctr.

340–1 *Eversharp offer.* Milton Biow, Biow Co., to W, May [?], 1944, Misc. contracts, Winchell papers.

341 *"anxious to take it up with us* . . ." Cal Kuhl, Biow Co., to W, June 23, 1944, B file, Winchell papers.

"All Hearst papers using Walter Winchell column . . ." Hearst to W, Dec. 6, 1944, Bigman coll.

"juggling the same flawed glip-glop . . ." Galley, Jan. 7, 1944, PPF 5666, FDR Lib.

the President "looked awful." Klurfeld, 114.

Walter sent Roosevelt a tip sheet . . . Anon. to W, FDR OF 4166 #26, File: Fourth Term Corr., May 17, 1944, FDR Lib.

"feels better than they do." NY *Mirror*, April 26, 1944, ibid.

"The Little Man on the Wedding Cake." NY *Column*, Aug. 20, 1968.

341–2 *Mimeographed report.* W to FDR, Oct. 24, 1944, PSF 189, "W" Gen., FDR Lib.

342 *invitation from the Blue Network* . . . Tel. G. W. John Johnston, dir. of news, Blue network, to W, Jan. 30, 1945, Blue Net. file, Winchell papers.

7 LOST

343 *"The President is dead."* NY *Mirror*, April 13, 1945.

344 "MY DEAR MR. PRESIDENT." Tel. W to Truman, n.d. [1945], Truman file, Winchell papers.

"Victories fought and won . . ." Quoted in Eric F. Goldman, *The Crucial Decade—and After: America, 1945–1960* (NY: Vintage paperback, 1960), 56–57.

"I thought you were . . ." NY *Mirror*, Sept. 11, 1945.

344 *"Americans! Every time you can pray ..."* Ibid., Nov. 21, 1945.

"Neither the American Congress nor the American people ..." "Jergens Journal," June 23, 1946. Walter sent this to Truman [Mathew J. Connelly, sec'y. to President, to W, July 20, 1946, OF, Truman Lib.]

345 *It was Lyons ...* Memo: Re White House Security Survey, May 3, 1945, Leonard Lyons file, FBI.

"Whenever I get my information from Pearson ..." Truman to Hannegan in *Harry S. Truman*, ed. Margaret Truman, (NY: Morrow, 1972), 422.

"I knew that Truman made a remark." Paul Scheffels int. by author.

345–6 *As Herman Klurfeld recalled it ...* Herman Klurfeld int. by author.

346 *Cuneo remembered it a little differently.* Ernest Cuneo int., Thomas coll.

"He's not a President." HK.

"Roosevelt was an awesome giant." Arnold Forster int. by author.

"I'm a little busier ..." "A Current Affair," July 4, 1990, Fox B'casting Network.

Attendance and receipts at nightclubs. Alexander Feinberg, "The Why of Night Clubs," *NY Times Magazine*, May 20, 1945, 23.

"The war years brought a new high ..." Thyra Samter Winslow, "To Eat, Drink and Be Mentioned," *NY Times Magazine*, Feb. 24, 1946, 20.

347 *" 'career girls' at ringside ..."* "Nightclubs," *Life*, Dec. 15, 1947, 109.

"[T]he return to general prosperity ..." Richard Schickel, "The Rise and Fall of Café Society," *Forbes*, Oct. 1985, 46.

"[I]t began to occur to a lot of people ..." Ibid.

Renovating the Stork Club. Mr. Harper, "Free Drink," *Harper's* (Nov. 1948), 107.

"at the top of the world." Clare Russhon int. by author.

Runyon's cancer. Edwin P. Hoyt, *A Gentleman of Broadway* (Boston: Little, Brown, 1964), 286.

"He didn't lend himself ..." Louis Sobol, *The Longest Street: A Memoir* (NY: Crown, 1968), 377.

347–8 *When his son Damon, Jr., asked ...* Damon Runyon, Jr., *Father's Footsteps* (NY: Random House, 1954), 154.

348 *"his great longing to reach out ..."* Gene Fowler, *Skyline: A Reporter's Reminiscence of the 1920s* (NY: Viking, 1961), 72.

"Ha-ha. She'll come back to me." Bill Corum, *Off and Running*, ed. Arthur Mann, (NY: Henry Holt, 1959), 168–69.

"Damon Runyon, now promoted to role ..." NY *Mirror*, Dec.11, 1945.

"He had always scoffed ..." Walter Winchell, "Unforgettable Damon Runyon," *Reader's Digest*, August 1968, 135.

"Any time I make a crack ..." Runyon to W, n.d. [1946], Runyon corr., Runyon Fund.

"I have missed you." Runyon to W, n.d. [1945], Runyon corr., Runyon Fund.

349 *Nightly forays.* Ed Weiner, *The Damon Runyon Story* (NY: Longmans, Green, 1948), 232.

Darryl Zanuck was so fascinated ... Ibid., 241; NY *Mirror*, Sept. 3, 1946.

"Let me tell you a secret." Runyon, Jr., 119.

"I figured out why you like to spend ..." Curley Harris int., May 17, 1970, Thomas coll.

"Winchell was nicer to Damon Runyon ..." Ernest Lehman int. by author.

"I know of no man ..." Tom Clark, *The World of Damon Runyon* (NY: Harper & Row, 1978), 275.

Cuneo's answer for why ... Ernest Cuneo, "Winchell and Runyon," unpublished ms., 88.

Irving Hoffman ... sent Runyon a caricature ... Sidney Carroll, "A Tale of Hoffman," *Esquire* (Nov. 1946).

Leo "Lindy" Linderman and his wife ... NY *Mirror*, Sept. 29, 1957.

350 *"I AM GETTING LONESOME ..."* Tel. Runyon to W, Nov. 19, 1946, Runyon Fund.

Teletypes night of Runyon's death. Teletype, W to Rose, n.d. [Dec. 8, 1946], WW—Corr. about Runyon, Runyon Fund.

"*RUNYON DIED* . . ." Tel. Glenn Neville to W, Dec. 10, 1946, 8:12 P.M., WW—Corr. About Runyon, Runyon Fund.

"*I don't know what I'm going to do.*" (AP).

"*Tell 'em to lay off crying.*" NY *Mirror,* Dec. 12, 1946.

"*When I die if I had one man . . .*" *Variety,* Feb. 5, 1969; Clark, 281.

351 *Runyon had mentioned that he would like to see* . . . NY *Mirror,* Dec. 19, 1946.

"*There I was with the mike . . .*" Albert Q. Maisel, "Runyon's Last Story," *Collier's,* April 22, 1950.

He had made the first contribution . . . "Jergens Journal," Dec. 15, 1946.

people rushed forward to stuff donations . . . Maisel.

Contributions. Tel. W to Arizona Div., American Cancer Society, n.d. [Feb. 1947], History, 1946–Jan./Apr. 1947, Runyon Fund.

First meeting of Runyon Fund Board. Minutes of Bd. of Dirs. meeting, Feb. 28, 1947, Minutes, Runyon Fund.

The next week the same group elected . . . March 5, 1947, Minutes, Runyon Fund.

Walter turned over a check for $250,000 . . . Andrew Tyler, atty., to W, March 24, 1947, History, 1946–Jan/April 1947, Runyon Fund.

352 "*Americans who have interviewed Stalin . . .*" NY *Mirror,* March 31, 1946.

It was much easier for him . . . *Time,* April 14, 1947, 79; NY *Mirror,* April 11, 1947.

"*Tokyo Rose.*" Russell Warren Howe, *The Hunt for "Tokyo Rose"* (Latham, Md.: Madison Books, 1990), 119–27.

353 "*He knew black and white.*" AF.

"*I wish that I could agree . . .*" W to Sherwood, n.d. [Sept. 1946] attached to Sherwood to W, Sept. 27, 1946, bms AM 1947 (1634), Robert Sherwood papers, Harvard Univ.

354 *Vishinsky's address.* NY *Times,* Sept. 27, 1947, 1.

Walter responded that the Soviets . . . NY *Times,* Sept. 27, 1947, 3.

"*Winchell became downright manic.*" Herman Klurfeld, *Winchell—His Life and Times* (NY: Praeger, 1976), 132.

"*Stalin admits in this book . . .*" NY *Mirror,* Oct. 17, 1947.

"*I believe that America . . .*" "Jergens Journal," Oct. 12, 1947.

355 *Trud and Izvestia.* NY *Mirror,* Nov. 28, 1947.

10,000 *letters.* "Winchell vs. Vishinski [*sic*]," *Newsweek,* Oct. 27, 1947.

"*[S]ome state department officials . . .*" Dickson Hartwell, "Walter Winchell: An American Phenomenon," *Collier's,* Feb. 28, 1948, 12.

"*With his suspenders dangling . . .*" Klurfeld, 132.

"*Nutz!*" NY *Mirror,* Dec. 4, 1947.

356 "*You have done such a magnificent job . . .*" Walter White to W, Jan. 29, 1947, NAACP, Group II, A, Box 674, Winchell file, Library of Congress.

"*What the hell are you doing . . .*" Klurfeld, 135.

"*One liberal broadcaster . . .*" NY *Mirror,* April 6, 1947.

"*Good heavens . . .*" W to Arnold Forster, n.d. [Nov. 24, 1947], Klurfeld papers. But six weeks after the Vishinsky episode, when HUAC conducted hearings on Communist subversion in the motion picture industry and Walter was forced to choose between the committee's ham-handed methods and the constitutional rights of alleged Communists, Winchell, under Cuneo's intense prodding, chose the Constitution. "If a government can drive the actors out of a theater, it can drive the people behind barb wire," he wrote with his customary hyperbole. (NY *Mirror,* Nov. 28, 1947.)

357 "*Truth or consequences.*" Tel. Hedda Hopper to W, Jan. 15, 1947, Winchell file, Hopper Coll., AMPAS.

"*There was no need to divorce June.*" AF.

"*She was madly in love with Walter.*" Seymour Mayer int. by author.

357 *"They created their own reality."* Eva Winchell int. by author.

"Never ask him any questions." SM.

"She hasn't been wrong yet." NY Times, Feb. 7, 1970, 29.

"No one was going to push June aside." Ed Weiner int. by author.

"If anyone comes up and tells me ..." Jack O'Brian int., May 20, 1970, Thomas coll.

she once pummeled a Communist sympathizer ... Charles Fisher, *The Columnists* (NY: Howell, Soskin, 1944), 131.

Another time she spit in Ed Sullivan's hand ... Bob Thomas, *Winchell* (NY: Doubleday, 1971), 154.

"She owned him." JO'B.

"She made a little boy ..." Rose Bigman int. by author.

358 *Walter and June acted as if these all were figments* ... Dr. Lawrence Kubie to Dr. Sophia Kleegman, Nov. 4, 1947, Walda Winchell file, Cuneo papers.

"the brightest redhead ..." Nat Sobel, friend of Walda's, int. by author.

"She looked like a girl ..." Felice Early int. by author.

Walda in Hollywood. In the Matter of the Application of June Winchell for Writ of Habeas Corpus, NY State Supreme Court, [1947], 13, Cuneo papers.

"I've seen her face ..." Ibid., 11.

"crazy about her." Curley Harris int. by author.

359 *"I am so happy that we are able to give it to you ..."* In the Matter of June Winchell, 5.

Variety *review.* Variety, March 21, 1945.

"jumped around that auditorium ..." EW.

"She used to complain ..." HC.

"I think he felt that if she had to be ..." HK.

"I was getting so much fighting ..." In the Matter of June Winchell, 9–10.

360 *"I don't want to go home ..."* Gertrude Bayne int. by author.

Later the newlyweds arrived ... Note,

Conversation with William Lawless, Boston, Dec. 20, 1947, Walda Winchell file, Cuneo papers.

"It was then that I thought ..." Interogatory, William Lawless, Dec. 22, 1947, Cuneo papers.

On the ferry Walda had started ... In the Matter of June Winchell, 10.

Lawless filed for divorce ... NY Times, Sept. 7, 1945, 8; PM, Dec. 10, 1946.

June insisted that Walter arrange ... RB.

Forster arranged that they meet ... AF.

"After she ran off ..." HK.

threatened to shoot anyone ... Kubie to Kleegman, Nov. 4, 1947.

William Cohen. Re: William Cohen, Dec. 7, 1947, Cuneo papers. This was a report probably compiled by Arnold Forster for Walter's use.

361 *A friend remembered his driving up* ... Irving Zussman int. by author.

"pretty." NY Times, Sept. 13, 1945.

"attractive." NY Herald Tribune, Sept. 13, 1945.

Reviews of Walda. Variety, Sept. 19, 1945; NY World-Telegram, Sept. 13, 1945; PM, Sept. 13, 1945; NY Sun, Sept. 13, 1945.

"one of the better ingenues." NY Mirror, Sept. 13, 1945.

"It really broke his heart ..." JO'B.

"she is either emotionally or intellectually naive ..." Kubie to Kleegman, Nov. 4, 1947.

362 *"Billy Cahn treated her ..."* NS.

"happy-go-lucky sort." GB.

If Walter had really loved his daughter ... In the Matter of June Winchell, 19–20.

"She was very despondent." NS.

Now Walda was growing as paranoid ... Kubie to Kleegman, Nov. 4, 1947.

"He would run house parties." EW.

"He's going to end up with all our money." CH.

She bounced from the St. Moritz ... In the Matter of June Winchell, 15.

363 *threatened to kill her* ... Lyle Stuart, *The Secret Life of Walter Winchell* (NY: Boar's Head Books, 1953), 190.

"Now here's where I become your best friend." EW.

June invited her daughter to lunch . . . In the Matter of June Winchell, 6.

Dr. Sophia Kleegman and Walda. Ibid.

363–4 *Dr. Kubie's letter.* Kubie to Kleegman, Nov. 4, 1947.

364 *Confrontation at Gotham Hotel.* In the Matter of June Winchell, 4–5.

365 *"very, very ill . . ."* NY *Mirror,* Nov. 28, 1947, 5.

Ed Sullivan . . . also reported Walda's disappearance . . . NY *Daily News,* Nov. 29, 1947.

"I have verbally instructed . . ." Gene McHugh to W, Nov. 3, 1947 [misdated], Walda Winchell file, Cuneo papers.

"Yes, Sullivan knew all along . . ." Ibid.

While she was gone, June had filed . . . Lawless v. Winchell, #35173, Dec. 1947, NY County Clerk; Stuart, 194.

"might press me about Sissy . . ." Tel. W to Cuneo, Dec. 1, 1947, Walda Winchell file, Cuneo papers.

Hearing with Pecora. In the Matter of June Winchell, 23–24.

366 *"It looks like there is blood . . ."* Lawless v. Winchell, 49–51.

Cahn apparently threatened . . . Notes, n.d., Walda Winchell file, Cuneo papers.

Lawless Writ of Habeas Corpus. Lawless v. Winchell, 70–78.

367 *Walter . . . chose his mother.* HK.

June blamed herself. In the Matter of June Winchell, 18.

"I've been very happy . . ." Winchell Exclusive, 206.

Stack never recovered . . . Larry Newman, "The Tragic Path of Genius," American Weekly, May 9, 1948.

"I am incurably ill." NY *Mirror,* March 5, 1948.

368 *"I felt that this man had made . . ."* EW.

After a full day at work . . . Mike Hall int. by author.

"Ed Weiner was a lovely man." AF.

"He opened it up and he says . . ." EW.

Walter's responses. Al Rylander int. by author; AF.

368–9 *"Ed was kind of in a dither."* MH.

369 *"I wish to thank you very humbly . . ."* Weiner to W, March 18, 1948, Weiner file, Winchell papers.

Walter, in his autobiography, said he disapproved . . . Winchell Exclusive, 40.

Jack O'Brian believed . . . JO'B.

"It is such a big plug . . ." Note on INS press release, Nov. 13, [1955], Weiner file, Winchell papers.

"Of course, guys got scared . . ." HC.

"You know what's going to finally kill me?" Jerry D. Lewis, writer-producer, int. by author.

"the party was going to end." William Michael Purcell int. by author.

Mary Lou didn't like being indicted . . . Ibid.

By one story, Walter ended the relationship . . . Jane Kean int. by author; Shirley Bentley, Mary Lou's sister-in-law, int. by author.

370 *Another story had Mary Lou . . .* WMP.

Gallop said that police trailed him . . . HC.

Whenever he auditioned for a job . . . Gary Stevens int. by author.

William Purcell. Shirley Bentley; WMP.

370–1 *Mary Lou's marriage.* NYC Marriage License, vol. 52, A, 5, 14, no. 36156.

371 *"wouldn't dream of saying anything . . ."* Felice Early int. by author.

"It's not the same." SM.

He ate voraciously . . . Weiner, 15.

a favorite family story . . . SM.

chronic diarrhea. Stuart, 237.

"Dead people stay calm." NY *Post,* March 13, 1952, 5.

when a man sneezed . . . Jim Fenton int., March 25, 1970, Thomas coll.

four showers a day. RB.

"Too many anti-Winchell stories . . ." Note, W to Robert Orr, ABC, on telegram Orr to W, Nov. 17, 1947, Cuneo papers.

372 *"Could be."* W to Hooper, Nov. 11, 1947, Cuneo papers.

his rating turned out to be more ... Harrison B. Summers, *Radio Programs Carried on National Networks*, 1926–1956 (Columbus: Ohio State University Press, 1958).

Appeal for type AB blood. Newsweek, Jan. 13, 1947, 55–56; Hartwell. As it turned out, *Newsweek* and *Collier's* were wrong. The donor was a young man named Nathan Dash who had raced to the hospital after Walter's appeal and asked a doctor there if AB blood was needed. When the puzzled doctor questioned Dash on how he knew, Dash told him "the whole country knew it by now." In any case, Dash told Walter that he was AB Rh *positive*. (Nathan Dash to Rose Bigman, Feb. 17, 1948, Dash file, Winchell papers.)

"I call them vomics." "Jergens Journal," Jan. 12, 1947.

"In the course of telling the State Dept. ..." Fort Myers (Fla.) *News-Press*, Jan. 14, 1947, 4, C.L. Brown coll., NYPL at Lincoln Ctr.

Life *magazine called his efforts ...* Allen Grover, VP *Time*, to W, Dec. 22, 1947, Winchell file, *Time* Archive.

"Wonder if Life's *editorial writer ...* NY *Mirror*, Dec. 4, 1947.

"They pay to read me ..." NY *Post*, Jan. 27, 1952, 18.

"Who else will write about me?" Jack O'Brian int., May 20, 1970, Thomas coll.

"If I slowed up ..." Weiner, 8.

"Well, King Canute ..." Ernest Cuneo, "Winchell's Personality," unpub. ms., 75, Cuneo papers.

373 *He made just under* $500,000 *...* Harry Scharf, acct., to W, Statement Showing Taxable Income from All Sources, April 13, 1951, Geist file, Winchell papers.

the friend vaguely recalled the total ... Nat Kahn, *Variety* radio ed., int. by author.

Klurfeld remembered visiting ... Klurfeld, 68.

"A dime didn't mean anything ..." Quoted by Seth Rubinstein, atty., int. by author.

"Listen, you son of a bitch." Al Rylander.

Klurfeld remembered another scene ... Klurfeld, 116.

"He never had enough ..." HK.

Walda had run up a clothes bill ... Florence Lustig to Cuneo, Nov. 8, 1948, Walda Winchell file, Cuneo papers. Lustig owned a clothing shop and was dunning Walter to pay his daughter's bills, as he begrudgingly did.

"Oh my god ..." Scharf to W, Jan. 22, 1948; Note: W to Rose Bigman, n.d. [Jan. 1948], Geist file, Winchell papers.

374 *Even tax deductions were minimized ...* Herman Geist, son of accountant Harry Geist, int. by author.

"That was the only thing I could think of ..." RB.

"because I knew that would be the end." PS.

Offers to leave Hearst. Time, May 5, 1947, 68.

"Your continuation of these attacks ..." Andrew Jergens to W, May 12, 1947, Cuneo papers.

"We're not thinking in terms of five years ..." Robert Beucus, VP advertising Jergens Lotion, to W, July 11, 1945, Misc. contracts, Winchell papers.

375 *"I looked at him indifferently ..."* W to Robert W. Orr, n.d. [1947], Layer coll.

"[T]his is the year ..." W to Robert Orr, n.d. [May 1947], Layer coll.

"Your indifference ..." Ibid.

"I know that before you make any decision ..." Robert Kintner to W, May 24, 1948, Layer coll.

376 *"He said he found talking ..."* Time, June 14, 1948, 82.

"His political and controversial programs ..." Memo: "What Are We Doing to Replace Winchell," Jergens Co., Oct. 19, 1948, Cuneo papers.

Old Gold cigarettes and Lever Bros. NY *Herald Tribune*, July 24, 1948; *Variety*, June 30, 1948.

Kaiser-Frazer contract. NY Times, July 24, 1948.

"the highest paid single ..." Variety, July 28, 1948.

"as a show business entity ..." Variety, March 24, 1948.

377 *"some freak of climate ..."* Alistair Cooke, "Walter Winchell: An American Myth," *Listener,* Nov. 20, 1947, 893–94.

McLuhan on Winchell. Marshall McLuhan, "The Sage of Waldorf Towers," in *The Mechanical Bride: Folklore of Industrial Man* (NY: Vanguard Press, 1951); [rep. London: Routledge Kegan Paul Ltd., 1967], 19.

"Your rating keeps going higher ..." Tom Velotta to W, Nov. 15, 1948, ABC file, Winchell papers.

top-rated on all of radio. Hooper Rating Service, "The Winchell Story," 1948, Winchell file, FBI. Winchell's Nielsen ratings were consistently lower than his Hoopers, Robert Kintner said, because Nielsen was weighted more heavily toward middle-size cities and rural areas, where Walter fared less well than in large urban areas. (Kintner to W, May 28, 1948, ABC file, Winchell papers.)

377–8 *Winchell's listeners.* "The Winchell Story."

378 *"I never listen to Winchell."* John Crosby, NY *Herald Tribune,* Oct. 22, 1948.

"The United States has had a secret history ..." Winchell Exclusive, 208–11.

379 *Shortly before the broadcast ...* NY *Mirror,* April 10, 1951.

fixed a line from Scandinavia through Italy ... "Jergens Journal," March 14, 1948.

Two days later he was back at Forrestal's home ... James Forrestal, *The Forrestal Diaries,* ed. Walter Millis with collab. of E. S. Duffield (NY: Viking, 1951), 399.

"Mr. W. You can't do enough of these!" Note, W to Cleveland *Plain Dealer,* attached to clipping, April 23, 1948, Misc., Winchell papers, NYPL at Lincoln Ctr.

Winchell meeting with Truman. Winchell Exclusive, 214–17; Anon. to W, April 8, 1948, Klurfeld coll.

380 *"Every President has the constitutional right ..."* NY *Mirror,* April 13, 1948.

"I think that if enough of you listeners write ..." "Jergens Journal," Feb. 1, 1948.

"If Gen. Eisenhower really wants to do something ..." NY *Mirror,* April 6, 1948.

Walter told Editor & Publisher ... *Editor & Publisher,* June 26, 1948, 46.

"He was impressed." HK.

380–1 *"The fellow has poise and punch."* W to Henry Luce, Feb. 12, 1948, *Time* file, Winchell papers.

381 *"I suggested it first ..."* Louis Josephson to W, n.d. [Nov. 1947], Winchell file, FBI.

"I bet John and I ..." Klurfeld, 136.

"Hitler must have laughed ..." NY *Mirror,* June 22, 1948.

"This goddamn son of a bastard ..." Note on Milton H. Berger to W, March 6, 1948, Cuneo papers.

Pegler and Stone on Truman. Quoted in A. J. Leibling, *The Press* (NY: Pantheon, 1981), 510.

382 *"the ease with which communists ..."* Nixon to Dulles, Sept. 7, 1948, John Foster Dulles papers, quoted in Roger Morris, *Richard Milhous Nixon: The Rise of an American Politician* (NY: Henry Holt, 1990), 442.

Isaac Don Levine and Winchell. Isaac Don Levine, *Eyewitness to History: Memoirs and Reflections of a Foreign Correspondent for Half a Century* (NY: Hawthorn Books, 1973), 197–98.

"Leaning closer and pointing a finger ..." Winchell Exclusive, 153–54.

"Congratulations on denouncing Winchell." W to Allen Grover, VP *Time,* Dec. 8, 1947, Winchell file, *Time* archive.

382–3 *Attacks on Chambers.* NY *Mirror,* Dec. 8, 12, 14, 20, 1948.

383 *He devoted his entire column ...* Ibid., Dec. 16, 1948.

Forrestal's frictions. Townsend Hoopes and Douglas Brinkley, *Driven Patriot: The Life and Times of James Forrestal* (NY: Knopf, 1992), 423.

383–4 *Forrestal's business career.* Arnold A. Rogow, *James Forrestal: A Study of Personality, Politics and Policy* (NY: Macmillan, 1963).

384 *Forrestal's biographers were to find ...* Hoopes and Brinkley, 422.

Hopley Civil Defense Plan. Editor &

Publisher, Nov. 27, 1948; NY *Mirror*, Dec. 2, 1949.

385 *Still, Truman urged Jewish resettlement* ... Donald R. McCoy, *The Presidency of Harry S. Truman* (Lawrence: Univ. of Kansas Press, 1984), 74–76.

"they did not want too many of them ..." Quoted in Dean Acheson, *Present at the Creation: My Years in the State Department* (NY: Norton, 1969), 173.

Forrestal had never particularly liked Jews ... Rogow, 191.

"the most vicious Zionist writer ..." NY *Times*, June 4, 1947, 5.

"they have set an example for the civilized world ..." NY *Mirror*, May 20, 1948.

385–6 *Pearson accused Forrestal* ... Rogow, 27–29.

386 *Walter repeated the story* ... Forrestal, 544.

"Truman is boiling mad ..." Drew Pearson, *Diaries, 1949–1959*, ed. Tyler Abell (NY: Holt, Rinehart, 1974), 12–13.

"I feel challenged as a newspaperman ..." Quoted in Rogow, 31 fn.

"Pearson and Winchell are a high price ..." *Time*, June 6, 1949, 43.

"I will continue to be a victim ..." Ibid., Jan. 24, 1949, 16.

"God-damn Wall Street bastard." Pearson, 9.

386–7 *"I want you to distinctly understand ..."* Ibid., 24.

387 *Friends of Forrestal's implored Walter* ... Cuneo to W, n.d. [1949], Cuneo papers.

He would stare blankly ... Rogow, 1–18; Hoopes and Brinkley, 455–56.

anticipation of Pearson's and Winchell's Sunday broadcasts ... Hoopes and Brinkley, 461.

Forrestal's suicide. Ibid., 464–66; Rogow, 1–18.

Arthur Krock ... openly wondered ... "Press is Criticized Sharply for Attacks on Forrestal," *Editor & Publisher*, May 28, 1949, 5.

387–8 *"[I]n the Pearson and Winchell assaults* ... *Time*, June 6, 1949, 43.

388 *"I am almost beginning to lie awake ..."* Pearson, 50–51.

"It is typical of one presstitute ..." *Editor & Publisher*, May 28, 1949, 5.

The real culprit ... Winchell Exclusive, 218.

"Drew Pearson and Walter Winchell killed Forrestal." Quoted in Hoopes and Brinkley, 461.

Koch ... never recovered ... Howard Koch int. by author.

she sat in her apartment ... Lenore Winchel int. by author.

389 *At Walter's instruction* ... RB.

Walter left for Florida ... W to Rita Greene, n.d. [1949], Pat Rose coll.

Jennie's death. Death report, Office of Chief Medical Examiner, Manhattan #7021, Nov. 14, 1949.

"Paul, you have to go up ..." Paul Scheffels int. by author.

"jumped or fell." NY *Times*, Nov. 15, 1949.

Jennie was constantly complaining of the heat ... Lola Cowan int. by author.

"I know Mother threw herself ..." W to Rita Greene, n.d. [Nov. 1949], Pat Rose coll.

"My consolation ..." W to Rita Greene, n.d. [1949], Pat Rose coll.

"as if they were the last survivors." LW.

the family was separated. Irma Raskin, Mokom Sholem, to author, March 26, 1992.

"found out long ago ..." "Jergens Journal," Feb. 9, 1936, NBC Blue, roll 654.

390 *"You stop worrying 25 years later ..."* NY *Mirror*, Feb. 19, 1950.

He had forsworn a toupee ... Winchell Exclusive, 48.

"[r]estless and roving." Charles J. Lazarus, "Here's What You Didn't Know About Walter Winchell," *New Liberty*, May 1951, 70.

"Who is that woman?" Louis Sobol int., May 20, 1970, Thomas coll.

Rita had been dunning ... Rita Greene to W, July 18, 1960, Pat Rose coll.

"*How will she look to me?*" Klurfeld, 22.

"*It was like two kids ...*" RB.

"*I could see how old ...*" Klurfeld, 22. Not long after, Walter began boosting the singing career of a twenty-four-year-old physical education instructor named Gloria Warner. When one day in his apartment he made romantic overtures to her, she unthinkingly told him he was too old for her. Walter was shaken and immediately dropped his campaign. (Lloyd Howard int. by author.)

"*a remarkable number had sex-and-scent appeal.*" Klurfeld, 118.

his discovery that a young woman ... David Brown int. by author.

390–1 "*It was terrible.*" John Crosby, *Observer Review*, Feb. 27, 1972, 11.

391 *June was actually allergic ...* Jim Bacon, columnist, int. by author.

"*one-woman-at-a-time-man.*" Cuneo, "Winchell's Early Background," unpub. ms., 53, Cuneo papers.

Lurye's death. NY *Times*, June 19, 1950, 1.

Lurye's funeral. NY *Herald Tribune*, June 19, 1950.

"*He feels that since ...*" NY *Mirror*, June 21, 1950.

"*He has a wife and children.*" Ibid.

392 *Bringing in Macri.* Ibid.

"*I am sorry to meet you this way.*" NY *Herald Tribune*, June 19, 1950.

"*I am a reporter ...*" NY *Mirror*, June 20, 1950.

Tributes. Editor & Publisher, June 24, 1950, 57.

392–3 *He surrendered only because ...* NY *Mirror*, Oct. 26, 1951, 11.

393 *Walter had heard from a mobster ... Winchell Exclusive*, 229.

one story had Collier's *buying the piece* ... Lori Edelman int., n.d., Thomas coll. Another report, in *Time*, put the fee at $12,500, which is probably closer to the truth. (*Time* [June 20, 1949], 66).

John Crommelin. NY *Mirror*, Nov. 20, 1949, 2; Nov. 21, 1949.

The Navy had even enlisted Walter ... Pearson, 87.

The Runyon Fund was taking more ... Rose to W, Dec. 30, 1948, Bigman papers.

"*not one penny.*" M. R. Runyon, ACS, to W, Oct. 10, 1950, Minutes, Runyon Fund.

Forming Walter Winchell Fdn. Memo: W to Dorothy Moore, Aug. 23, 1967, "WW—Corr. about Fund 1967–72," Runyon Fund.

393–4 *Damon Runyon Awards. Editor & Publisher*, May 26, 1951, 14.

394 *Walter suddenly dropped his plans ... Variety*, May 16, 1951; Telegram John Teeter, dir. Runyon Fund, to J. Edgar Hoover, Oct. 11, 1951, Winchell file, FBI.

"*I know a lot about the subject.*" NY *Mirror*, April 2, 1951.

A Miami News *reporter ...* Miami *Daily News*, April 24, 1951, 1.

The News *lacerated him ...* Ibid.

"*I'm a reporter ...*" NY *Mirror*, April 10, 1951.

What Time, Newsweek and the Miami Herald critics ..." W to Dana Tasker, ed. *Time*, n.d. [1951], *Time* file, Winchell papers.

395 *Costello had come to Walter ...* Curley Harris to W, n.d., Costello file, Winchell papers.

"*greatest scandal in American history.*" NY *Mirror*, April 12, 1951.

396 "*the greatest appeaser in history.*" Ibid., April 13, 1951.

On his broadcast of April 15 ... Hudnut program, April 15, 1951.

"*MacArthur is not only a military hero ...*" NY *Mirror*, April 19, 1951.

"*Truman will go down in history ...*" Ibid., April 18, 1951.

"*Winchell let loose one of the worst ...*" Pearson, 161.

397 *Television statistics.* U.S. Bureau of the Census, *Historical Statistics of the United States: Colonial Times to* 1970 (Washington, D.C.: Govt. Printing Office, 1975), 796.

"*[r]adio listening in TV homes ...*" NY *Mirror*, Dec. 12, 1949.

He had kept on his gray fedora ...

Charles Fernandez, "Winchell Arrives," Miami *Herald*, Nov. 5, 1948.

397 *He alternated throughout the night . . .* Edward Bliss, Jr., *Now the News: The Story of Broadcast Journalism* (NY: Columbia University Press, 1991), 215.

"whether it's late at night . . ." Irving Grey quoted in "Program Description, Damon Runyon Cancer Fund Telethon," April 9, 1949, Telethons—Early years, Runyon Fund. One of the featured acts on the third telethon was [Dean] Martin and [Jerry] Lewis, who later applied the same techniques to his own Muscular Dystrophy telethons.

398 *"Number One Star."* Kintner to W, May 8, 1950, ABC file, Winchell papers.

"[I]t would be good for ABC . . ." Kintner to W, Aug. 1, 1950, ABC file, Winchell papers.

"It's the only place in the world . . ." Marlo Lewis and Mina Bess Lewis, *Prime Time* (Los Angeles: J. P. Tarcher, Inc., 1976), 16.

secure a doctor's note . . . Dr. Lewis Kleinfeld to Whom It May Concern, Jan. 7, 1948, ABC file, Winchell papers.

"I went down Lincoln Road . . ." Jerry D. Lewis int. by author.

399 *"We had our local stable."* PS.

He would clown. Ben Grauer int., May 21, 1970, Thomas coll.

"He knows I'm in this joint . . ." Har-

old Conrad, *Dear Muffo: 35 Years in the Fast Lane* (NY: Stein & Day, 1982), 9–12.

Walter casually sauntered into the establishment . . . Ernest Cuneo, "Winchell—Power in Action," unpub. ms., 95–98, Cuneo papers.

400 *Scheffels remembered one evening . . .* PS.

rumors that NBC . . . was trying to lure . . . Variety, April 11, 1951.

ABC countered . . . Robert Kintner to W, Sept. 27, 1951, *Winchell v. ABC,* #11831, 151, NY Supreme Court.

ABC . . . suspended its negotiations Kintner to W, May 29, 1951, Layer coll.

Kintner issued a warning. Kintner to W, Sept. 14, 1951, ABC file, Winchell papers.

401 *Terms of "life deal."* Memo: Cuneo to W, A-2-17, n.d. [1951], Cuneo papers. Cuneo recommended that Walter form his own corporation and then sell its stock to ABC for $1.33 million, giving him the estimated $1 million of the "life deal" in one lump sum. Similarly, he recommended that Walter form his own syndicate to distribute his column, paying the 77 percent corporate tax rate rather than the higher individual one. But Walter apparently rejected both suggestions.

"Under this agreement . . ." Kintner to W, Sept. 27, 1951, *Winchell v. ABC,* #11831, Exhibit A, 151, NY Supreme Court.

8 A HEAD FOR AN EYE

405 *"doing all sorts of gyrations . . ."* Quoted in Lynn Haney, *Naked at the Feast* (NY: Dodd, Mead, 1981), 38.

406 *"How's Her Act???"* NY *Mirror,* Oct. 12, 1952.

"This is the most important moment . . ." Josephine Baker and Jo Bouillon, *Josephine,* tr. by Mariana Fitzpatrick (NY: Harper & Row, 1977), 175.

"Such a stand has done . . ." Walter White to Josephine Baker, Feb. 16, 1951,

NAACP, Group II, A, 98, Baker file, Library of Congress.

"a real star." Walter Winchell, *Winchell Exclusive: "Things That Happened to Me—and Me to Them"* (Englewood Cliffs, N.J.: Prentice-Hall, 1975), 246.

406–7 *Baker's account.* Baker, 179.

407 *O'Brian's account.* Jack O'Brian int. by author.

"No one knew what happened." Herman Klurfeld int. by author.

Shirley Eder's account. Shirley Eder, *Not This Time, Cary Grant!* (Garden City, NY: Doubleday, 1973), 256–57.

"Walter Winchell had nothing to do with that . . ." Ed Weiner int. by author.

408 *Walter's account in his autobiography.* Winchell, 247–49.

"When she got up with Mr. Rico . . ." Note on letter Gertrude Black, CBS radio, to W, Sept. 12, 1952, Baker file, Winchell papers.

The following morning Baker held a meeting . . . Curt Weinberg to W, n.d., Baker file, Winchell papers.

409 *Campaign for Dorrie Miller.* W to Rose Bigman, n.d., Cuneo papers. Cuneo admitted that the President was "embarrassed" by the outcry.

Campaign for Wesley Wells. NY *Mirror*, Feb. 10, 1950.

"I am as shocked as you are . . ." Marguerite Lovell to W, Jan. 8, 1945, ER 150, 9 Misc Req., 1945, S-Z, Box 2541, FDR Lib.

the black soldier stationed at Sioux Falls . . . Cpl. Samuel Taylor to W, July 16, 1943, Box 861, Eleanor Roosevelt papers, FDR Lib.

inviting Sugar Ray Robinson . . . Sugar Ray Robinson int., June 18, 1970, Thomas coll.

410 *"WANTED TO DISCUSS TELEGRAM . . ."* Quoted in "Baker-Winchell," unpub. ms., Cuneo papers.

"The Josephine Baker-Stork Club incident . . ." Walter White to W, Oct. 18, 1951, Cuneo papers.

411 *"As of 9:16 P.M. . . .* NY *Post*, Jan. 11, 1952, 40.

"I have examined the facts . . ." Tel. Walter White to W, Oct. 20, 1951, Group II, A, 98, Josephine Baker, 1951–54, NAACP papers, L of C.

"I was not in the Stork Club . . ." Hudnut program, Oct. 21, 1951.

412 *"I gave [a] statement . . ."* Tel. Walter White to Robert Kintner, Oct. 22, 1951, Baker file, Winchell papers.

"After all I've done for them." Ernest

Cuneo, "Disintegration of Walter Winchell's Power," unpub. ms., 103–04, Cuneo papers.

The day after Walter's broadcast . . . NY Times, Oct. 23, 1951, 35; NY *Herald Tribune*, Oct. 23, 1951.

Mayor's Committee on Unity. NY *Post*, Oct. 23, 1951.

He had even come to believe . . . Winchell, 249.

413 *"I told this to Sherman . . ."* Herman Klurfeld, *Winchell: His Life and Times* (NY: Praeger, 1976), 158.

"sick about it . . ." Arnold Forster int. by author.

"exaggerated." Sherman Billingsley to Walter White, Oct. 24, 1951, Group II, A, 98, Josephine Baker, 1951–54, NAACP papers, L of C.

Though Billingsley later insisted . . . NY Times, Nov. 3, 1951.

"I don't want none of those colored men . . ." Robert Sylvester, *No Cover Charge: A Backward Look at the Night Clubs* (NY: Dial, 1956), 125.

"When Yul Brynner was in The King and I" . . . JO'B.

"You know, he cares only for the finest . . ." NY *Post*, Jan. 22, 1952, 5.

414 *"I wish you wouldn't . . ."* Ibid., Jan. 22, 1952, 5.

He did send Forster to reason . . . AF.

Cuneo's visit to Baker. Herman Klurfeld to author, June 5, 1990.

Cuneo also convinced White . . . Memo [Walter White to W], n.d., Group II, A, 98, Baker file, NAACP, L of C.

"Ladies and gentlemen . . ." Hudnut, Oct. 28, 1951.

415 *Discrediting Baker.* NY *Mirror*, Oct. 24, 1951.

"more time to think things over." Ibid., Oct. 28, 1951.

The next day he ran a long letter . . . Ibid., Oct. 29, 1951.

"Eleven years ago I made a rule . . ." Arnold Forster to W, Oct. 29, 1951, Baker file, Winchell papers.

"Despite White's protestations . . ."

Howard Rushmore to W, Nov. 13 [1951], Baker file, Winchell papers.

415 *natural paranoia.* Memo anon. to W, Nov. 26, 1951, Cuneo papers.

416 *"to close the whole problem out . . ."* Memo Arnold Forster to W, Nov. 9, 1951, Klurfeld papers.

"Champ [of civil rights] was scream-ing . . ." Time, Nov. 12, 1951, 47–49.

"This writer is convinced . . ." "Winchell Caught With His 'Liberal' Trou-sers Down," Pittsburgh *Courier*, n.d., Baker file, Winchell papers.

Sugar Ray Robinson's announcement . . . Text of Sugar Ray Robinson Remarks, Group II, A, 98, Josephine Baker, 1951–54, NAACP papers, L of C.

Hays, after consulting with Cuneo . . . Cuneo, "Baker-Winchell," Cuneo papers.

conciliatory joint press release . . . State-ment from Arthur Garfield Hays, Dec. 10, 1951, Allan Morrison papers, reel 2, no. 9, Schomberg Ctr., NYPL.

417 *"It seems to me that this whole mat-ter . . ."* Arthur Garfield Hays to W, Dec. 12, 1951, quoted in "Baker-Winchell," Cuneo papers.

"I have been shocked . . ." Excerpt from Address by Josephine Baker, Dec. 15, 1951, Group II, A, 98, Josephine Baker, 1951–54, NAACP papers, L of C.

White was furious . . . Walter White to Mayor Vincent Impellitteri, Dec. 5, 1951, Group II, A, 98, Josephine Baker 1951–54, NAACP papers, L of C.

The Unity report. Mayor's Committee on Unity, "Final Report on the Stork Club Controversy," Nov. 24, 1951, Box 24, Dis-crimination 1951–53, Impellitteri papers, NYC Municipal Archive.

418 *"nothing to substantiate . . ."* Mayor's Committee on Unity, "Final Report on the Stork Club Controversy," Dec. 20, 1951, Box 24, Discrimination 1951–53, Impellitteri pa-pers, NYC Municipal Archive.

White demanded a meeting . . . Tel. Walter White to Mayor Impellitteri, Dec. 26, 1951, Box 24, Discrimination 1951–53 file, Impellitteri papers, NYC Municipal Archive.

Baker filing suit. Editor & Publisher, Dec. 29, 1951, 42.

"You don't understand how things work . . ." Baker, 181.

Barry Gray and Josephine Baker. Barry Gray, *My Night People* (NY: Simon & Schuster, 1975), 27–29.

419 *"She left the dais . . ."* Ibid., 31.

Gray wired Walter . . . Tel. Barry Gray to W, Dec. 24, 1951, Klurfeld pa-pers.

"Chandler's walls seemed bent . . ." Gray, 31.

Sullivan had a reputation . . . Irving Zussman int. by author; Gary Stevens int. by author.

"I despise Walter Winchell . . ." Quoted in Gray, 176–89.

420 *Wheeling speech.* Quoted in Godfrey Hodgson, *America in Our Time: From World War II to Nixon* (NY: Doubleday, 1976; pa-perback rep., Vintage, 1978), 37.

"If you're waiting for them to get specific . . ." NY Mirror, Feb. 10, 1950.

421 *"I never saw two guys get on so well."* NY *Post*, Jan. 24, 1952, 5.

"I remember that memorable night." Ernest Lehman int. by author.

"I'll get around to all the ingrates." Note on Arnold Forster to W, Jan. 9, 1952, Cuneo papers.

422 *"You'll find that most of them around . . ."* NY *Mirror*, Dec. 26, 1951.

Sullivan had a document . . . Marlo Lewis and Mina Bess Lewis, *Prime Time* (Los Angeles: J. P. Tarcher, Inc., 1976), 23–24.

Confrontation at Stork Club. Jerry G. Bowles, *A Thousand Sundays: The Story of the Ed Sullivan Show* (NY: Putnam, 1980), 109.

"I was (and sometimes in the same col-umn) . . . Gray, 34–36.

423 *Lyle Stuart.* Lyle Stuart int. by au-thor.

"Stuart always had an angle." Irving Zussman int. by author.

Founding Exposé. Pamphlet: *The Story of* Exposé, n.d., Lyle Stuart.

As Stuart later told it . . . Stuart, 206–07; LS.

THE TRUTH ABOUT WALTER WINCHELL.
Exposé, Dec. 1951.

424 *"I thought you would like to see ..."*
Stuart to Walter White, n.d., Group II, A,
674, Winchell file, NAACP papers, L of C.

"I want to assure you ..." Quoted in
Exposé, Jan. 1952, 1.

Stuart claimed that 3,000 copies ...
Exposé, Jan. 1952; unsigned ltr., Nov. 12,
1951, Klurfeld papers.

personally delivering ... Unsigned letter, Nov. 15, 1951, Klurfeld papers.

At one Broadway stand ... Stuart, 208.

He was even cheeky enough ... Unsigned letter, Nov. 12, 1951, Klurfeld papers.

Stuart was claiming to have sold ...
Ibid.

Over 85,000 copies were printed. Stuart, 208.

Rap sheet. Forster to W, Nov. 13,
1951, Klurfeld papers.

425 *"The so-called exposé ..."* Hudnut
program, Nov. 18, 1951.

"I don't think a week went by ..." LS.

*"Exposé seemed to have opened the
floodgates." Exposé*, Jan. 1952.

Walter heard early ... Unsigned letter, Nov. 15, 1951, Klurfeld papers.

"I have been in the ring ..." Billy
Rose to W, Nov. 29, 1951, NYPL at Lincoln
Ctr.

425–6 *"The story series is designed ..."*
Memo L. B. Nichols to Clyde Tolson,
Dec. 29, 1951, Winchell file, FBI.

426 *New York* Post. Jeffrey Potter, *Men,
Money and Magic: The Story of Dorothy Schiff*
(NY: Coward, McCann & Geoghagen,1976),
161–62.

"Two things about Winchell ..." Dorothy Schiff, "Publisher's Letter," NY *Post*, Jan.
13, 1952, 3.

*"[Y]ou had better leave my name
out ..."* Earl Wilson to Hoke Welch, May
28, 1951, Wilson papers, Shubert Archive.

"is out to get him." Curley Harris to
W, n.d., Baker file, Winchell papers.

"The Post pieces started out to be ..."
W to Billy Rose, Nov. 29, 1951, NYPL at
Lincoln Ctr.

427 *"We're just doing it for circulation."* Art
Pomerantz int. by author; HK.

"a liberal paper ..." Quoted in Potter, 228.

*"between libidinous and didactic tenden-
cies."* A. J. Liebling, *The Press* (NY: Pantheon
paperback, 1981), 358.

"I could answer no ..." Quoted in
Potter, 228.

"Those who are discreet enough ..."
James A. Wechsler, *The Age of Suspicion* (NY:
Random House, 1953), 256.

428 *"He decided that the biggest ..."* James
A. Wechsler, "Winchell Is a Danger," *Guild
Reporter*, April 1, 1944, 1.

"The basic motivation ..." Maurice
Zolotow to Irving Hoffman, Sept. 18, 1952,
Klurfeld papers.

Wechsler told Time ... *Time*, Jan. 21,
1952, 74.

"I gave them every press agent ..."
LS.

They even trailed him ... Klurfeld,
169.

"If you're nice guys ..." NY *Post*,
Jan. 10, 1952, 27.

*"I shall get in touch with Mr. Win-
chell ..."* Ibid., Jan. 8, 1952, 32.

429 *"Well, I hear you've covered my
story ..."* Ibid., Jan. 7, 1952.

The series debuted ... Ibid., Jan. 7,
1952.

"Winchell's valet." Ibid., Jan. 21,
1952, 5.

He made no mention ... Joe Morgan
to W, Jan. 17, 1952, Cuneo papers.

*"Everybody in New York was talk-
ing ..."* AF.

"This was a great wall ..." HK.

he phoned an NAACP official ...
Edward Scheidt to J. Edgar Hoover, Jan. 25,
1952, Winchell file, FBI.

"frequently acts these days ..." NY
Post, Jan. 25, 1952, 5.

430 *"I remain your New York correspondent ..."* Hudnut program, Jan. 27, 1952.

"I have been working under ..." NY
Mirror, Jan. 28, 1952.

Walter was in bed ... Earl Wilson to

Paul Sann, Jan. 28, 1952, Wilson papers, Shubert Archive.

430 *"We had two doctors ..."* Paul Scheffels int. by author.

"We believe in the old journalistic principle ..." NY *Post*, Jan. 28, 1952.

"virulent virus infection." Hudnut program, Feb. 3, 1952.

"I was somewhat fearful ..." Elmer Bobst to W, Feb. 4, 1952, "B" file, Winchell papers.

431 *He returned to the air ...* Hudnut program, March 9, 1952.

"picked up at exactly the same clip ..." *Variety*, March 12, 1952.

Ernie Cuneo was in Newport ... Ernest Cuneo, "Disintegration of Walter Winchell's Power," unpub. ms., 104–07, Cuneo papers.

"Mr. Winchell, against the advice of his doctors ..." NY *Times*, March 17, 1952, 9.

"No matter how you view ..." NY *Post*, March 16, 1952, 5.

432 *"He must still be sick."* Ibid.

"His friends felt he hadn't looked well ..." Note, March 17, 1952; NY *Post*, March 18, 1952, Earl Wilson papers, Shubert Archives.

June accompanied him. NY *Post*, March 16, 1952.

"W.W. has been going to the movies ..." Robert Reud, St. Moritz, to Earl Wilson, n.d., Earl Wilson papers, Shubert Archive.

On March 28 they arrived at an agreement ... Agreement, Warner-Hudnut Co. to W, March 28, 1952, Layer coll.

June wasn't pleased. Memo: Rose Bigman to [Ernie Cuneo], n.d., ABC file, Winchell papers.

"I suppose this is the wisest course ..." Tom Velotta to W, April 3, 1952, Cuneo papers.

"He merely has given the virus ..." NY *Journal-American*, April 7, 1952.

"All we know is ..." *Time*, April 14, 1952, 48.

433 *"I have disagreed with him ..."* Fulton

Lewis, Jr., broadcast, Jan. 29, 1952, Winchell file, FBI.

"punch on the jaw ..." NY *Mirror*, April 8, 1947.

Falling-out with Pearson. Winchell, 256–57.

Though Kintner promised ... Robert Kintner to W, May 29, 1951, ABC file, Winchell papers.

"raising hell." Pearson, 173.

434 *Hearst's holdings had shrunk ...* William Randolph Hearst, Jr., with Jack Casserly, *The Hearsts: Father and Son* (Niwot, Colo.: Roberts Rinehart, 1991), 57–60.

"last of the dauntless pioneers ..." NY *Journal-American*, Aug. 15, 1952.

"If I didn't get over there ..." Leo Guild int. by author.

"If Bette Davis doesn't have cancer ..." Coleman Jacoby int. by author.

"It's Winchell's world ..." Dick Maney quoted in Lewis and Lewis, 16.

"I began criticizing Winchell ..." Milt Rubin int., Thomas coll.

"Not even Ernie was a real friend ..." HK.

435 *Rose's marriage.* NY *Mirror*, June 18, 1937.

Rose's divorce. RB.

ABC ...had fired Paul Scheffels ... NY *Post*, March 13, 1952, 41.

he had once even asked Scheffels ... PS.

Scheffels's resentment. Ibid.

Meeting Jack O'Brian. JO'B.

436 *"I remember we drove around ..."* Ibid.

"The secret of my relationship ..." Ibid.

"Jack was feisty ..." Art Ford int. by author.

He would raise a finger ... JO'B.

"injected himself into Walter's life." Art Ford.

"We never went to bed." JO'B.

"very vitriolic and hateful ..." Nat Kahn, *Variety* radio ed., int. by author.

437 *"the least-liked person ..."* HK.

He signed a photograph ... JO'B.

One night Lucius Beebe watched ...

Rian James, "Names Make News," Brooklyn *Eagle Magazine*, 1931, Hoffman scrapbooks, 21, 283, 150; Louis Sobol, Nov. 21, 1946, and Jan. 16, 1947, 21, 185, NYPL at Lincoln Ctr.

"a record for informality . . ." NY *Journal*, Aug. 1, 1944, Hoffman scrapbooks 21, 185, NYPL at Lincoln Ctr.

digging at his dinner plate. NY *Post*, July 17, 1945, Hoffman scrapbooks 21, 185, NYPL at Lincoln Ctr.

"Is she good-looking?" Ernest Lehman int. by author. Hoffman experimented with contact lenses as early as 1941 but apparently found them too painful. (Hoffman to Norman Krasna, May 7, 1941, Hoffman scrapbooks, 21, 184, NYPL at Lincoln Ctr.)

Hoffman's youth. Sidney Skolsky, "Behind the News," May 26, 1931, Hoffman scrapbooks, 21, 184; Rian James, Brooklyn *Eagle Magazine*; Gertrude Bayne int. by author; Sidney Carroll, "A Tale of Hoffman," *Esquire*, Nov. 1946; NY *Press*, June 8, 1932, Hoffman scrapbooks 21, 185, NYPL at Lincoln Ctr.

"the best of them all." Sid White int. by author.

438 *When film producer David Selznick once complained . . .* EL.

"looking through newspaper clippings . . ." Ibid.

"Hoffman I thought was disappointed . . ." DB.

"Irving was the only one . . ." HK.

439 *"[T]o their way of thinking . . ."* Hollywood *Reporter*, Jan. 29, 1952.

he wrote Hoover . . . Memo Hoover to Clyde Tolson et al., Jan. 23, 1952, Winchell file, FBI.

"a joy and not a job." Herb Stein, clipping, n.d., Hoffman scrapbooks 21, 184, NYPL at Lincoln Ctr.

"gypsy flack." "Pressagentry," *Time*, March 7, 1960, 42.

"almost unprecedented restraint." Wechsler, *The Age of Suspicion*, 256.

"disconcerting sense of something ticking . . ." Klurfeld, 165.

"a cornered rat." AR.

440 *At a pretrial hearing on August 6 . . .* Wechsler, *The Age of Suspicion*, 254–59.

"Jake Wechsler . . ." NY *Mirror*, Sept. 8, 1952.

"The New York Post series attacking Walter Winchell . . . Ibid., Sept. 10, 1952.

"Bigtown Sideshow." Ibid., Sept. 12, 1952.

"N.Y. Compost." Ibid., Sept. 14, 1952.

"there is nothing in his history . . ." Ibid., Sept. 15, 1952.

Walter had "his leg-men . . ." Ibid., Sept. 10, 1952.

441 *"underestimated the man's capacity . . ."* Wechsler, *The Age of Suspicion*, 256.

On September 22 he reported . . . NY *Mirror*, Sept. 22, 1952.

three more full columns . . . Ibid., Oct. 6, 1952.

"I have no illusions . . ." Max Lerner, "The Winchell Case," NY *Post*, Oct. 15, 1952.

"They tried to kill me!" HK.

his sources ranging . . . Arnold Forster; Len [?] to W, Jan. 30, 1953, Cuneo papers. Len was sending Walter HUAC reports on Wechsler "not available to the public."

Jacob Schiff . . . helped finance the Russian Revolution. Memo anon. to W, n.d., Cuneo papers.

"I figured we'd do one . . ." HK.

442 *"I had no qualms . . ."* Ibid.

He quoted a Hollywood column . . . NY *Mirror*, Oct. 5, 1952.

"A Head for an Eye!" Ibid., Oct. 31, 1952.

"One of the bosses is no stranger . . ." Ibid., Aug. 11, 1952.

Chandler's owners . . . promptly sued Walter . . . Editor & Publisher, Aug. 30, 1952, 48.

"fishface." *Time*, Aug. 25, 1952, 37.

"Mr. Winchell did little to defend himself . . ." Frank Conniff, "Barry Gray Yells Foul," NY *Journal-American*, Aug. 13, 1952.

442–3 *"Bernard Yaroslaw . . ."* NY *Mirror*, Sept. 10, 1952.

443 *"This is a name that will stick . . ."* W

to Charles McCabe, Jan. 11, 1953, Misc., Winchell papers.

443 *"one of the most ridiculous and distasteful ..."* Gertrude Black, CBS radio, to W, Sept. 12, 1952, Baker file, Winchell papers.

"It's not a battle that does anything ..." Art Ford.

"I'm going to get this sonofabitch." NY *Mirror*, Oct. 27, 1952; JO'B.

444 *"You're going to have two enemies."* PS.

According to Lyons ... NY *Post*, Feb. 22, 1972, 35.

"Leonard believed in America ..." Seymour Krim, "Mauled in the Lyons Den," *Soho Weekly News*, May 14, 1980, 13.

"Very simple transaction." New Yorker, May 2, 1977.

"our Edward R. Murrow." John Leonard, "Private Lives," *NY Times*, May 21, 1980, C-16.

"He swelled our sensitivity-to-status ..." Krim.

"If you can't say something nice ..." Ibid.

445 *"the biggest name-dropper ..."* Quoted in Stephen Grover, "The Table Hopper," *Wall Street Journal*, April 30, 1968, 29. Writer Goodman Ace once called Lyons with what he said was a hot scoop. Lyons grabbed his pen and raced back to the phone. Ace said simply, "George S. Kaufman," and hung up. [GS]

"didn't like Lyons's style." Art Pomerantz int. by author.

"It was very creepy." JO'B.

Lyons was refusing to reveal his sources ... Washington City News Service, Sept. 18, 1951.

Lyons's complaints. Lyons to W, Oct. 25, 1950, Lyons file, Winchell papers.

a new list of grievances ... Lyons to Dan Parker, June 27, 1951, Cuneo papers.

445–6 *Morris Ernst's assessment.* J. H. Teeter to W, Dan Parker, Sept. 4, 1951, Cuneo papers.

446 *Showdown between Winchell and Lyons.* Minutes, Sept. 6, 1951, Runyon Fund.

he even briefly tried to withdraw ...

Lyons to Morris Ernst, Feb. 1, 1952; Ernst to Lyons, Feb. 4, 1952, Runyon Fund.

"He was my friend." Quoted by Al Rylander.

"Lyons helped the Post *..."* Klurfeld, 173.

If Lyons saw Winchell ... JO'B.

446–7 *he had taken Walter to task ...* NY *Post*, Oct. 31, 1952.

447 *"Now hold onto your chair."* NY *Mirror*, Nov. 20, 1952.

"One of the small but vexing questions ..." NY *Herald Tribune*, Dec. 31, 1948.

"TV OR NOT TV?" Tel. Earl Wilson to W, Feb. 21, 1949, Wilson papers, Shubert Archive. Walter answered then: "Not until its [*sic*] ready."

Falling radio ratings. Variety, Jan. 30, 1952, 23.

signed with Gruen Watch Co. NY *Mirror*, Aug. 13, 1952.

"use its best efforts ..." NY *Post* Corp. v *Winchell*, Points and Cases, Appell. Div., First Dept. NY, NY County Lawyers' Assn., 1954, 218.

448 *"We bought a photographed version ..."* Variety, Oct. 1, 1952.

"I have it every Sunday night ..." W to Bette Davis, Dec. 22, 1952, Misc., Winchell papers.

"breathless with excitement." W to Charles Underhill, camera crew, et al., ABC, Oct. 5, 1952, ABC file, Winchell papers.

"Television broadcast on coast ..." Tel. Robert Kintner to W, Oct. 6, 1952, ABC file, Winchell papers.

"The entry of the columnist ..." NY *Times*, Oct. 12, 1952, II, 11.

"The same Winchellian manner ..." Variety, Oct. 8, 1952.

449 *"like a cross between Harry Truman and Jimmy Durante."* Quoted in NY *Mirror*, Oct. 10, 1952.

"I knew that would be his downfall." Eva Winchell int. by author.

"Don't call this FDR Rooter ..." NY *Mirror*, Sept. 5, 1952.

"Ninety percent of the time ..." HK.

450 *Truman and KKK.* Gruen program, Oct. 19 & 26, 1952; *NY Times*, Oct. 27, 1952.

"*A series of incredible accidents . . .*" NY *Mirror*, Oct. 27, 1952.

"*Senator Nixon should get off . . .*" Ibid., Sept. 24, 1952.

"*I have little faith in the brains . . .*" INS release, Nov. 2, 1952.

Cuneo on Stevenson's train. NY *Mirror*, Nov. 9, 1952.

451 "*Don't call me a Republican . . .*" Ibid., Nov. 7, 1952.

"*Truman had rejected New Deal . . .*" Liebling, 348–49.

"*How does it feel . . .*" Art Ford.

"*It was one of those glares.*" NY *Mirror*, Jan. 22, 1953.

"*But television was a different matter.*" Wechsler, *The Age of Suspicion*, 258–59.

451–2 *A Broadway soda jerk . . .* NY *Mirror*, Oct. 29, 1952.

452 "*Virginia, dear . . .*" Ibid., Nov. 28, 1952.

At its board meeting on November 10 . . . Minutes, Nov. 10, 1952, Group II, A, 674, Winchell file, NAACP papers, L of C.

The next day Walter White quietly requested . . . Memo: Walter White to Miss Baxter, Nov. 11, 1952, NAACP papers, L of C.

"*Headline: 'Borey Pink . . .' *" NY *Mirror*, Jan. 18, 1952.

"*never looked more beautiful.*" Klurfeld, 163.

Gray heard Walter . . . Gray, 37.

"*The phonus-bolonus . . .*" NY *Mirror*, Jan. 28, 1953.

"*Take to the sidestreets.*" Sylvester, 159.

453 *Lyons issued a public appeal . . .* NY *Post*, May 18, 1953.

"*It is obvious one of us . . .*" Ibid., May 20, 1953.

9 THE ENEMY OF MY ENEMY

454 "*jagged fissure.*" Whittaker Chambers, *Witness* (NY: Random House, 1952), 793.

"*The real function of the Great Inquisition . . .*" Richard Hofstadter, *Anti-Intellectualism in American Life* (NY: Knopf, 1963), 41.

455 "*frustration at having so much 'power' . . .*" Godfrey Hodgson, *America in Our Time: From World War II to Nixon, What Happened and Why* (NY: Random House, 1976), 17.

"*Communism was not the target . . .*" Hofstadter, 41.

"*As you, of course, know . . .*" McCarthy to W, Dec. 18, 1950, McCarthy file, Winchell papers.

Cuneo wanted nothing to do with McCarthy . . . Ernest Cuneo, "Disintegration of Walter Winchell's Power," unpub. ms., 107, Cuneo papers.

even Jack O'Brian . . . Jack O'Brian int. by author.

Meeting Roy Cohn. Walter Winchell, *Winchell Exclusive: "Things That Happened to Me—and Me to Them"* (Englewood Cliffs, N.J.: Prentice-Hall, 1975), 253.

456 *When Dora Marcus married Al Cohn* . . . Nicholas von Hoffman, *Citizen Cohn* (NY: Doubleday, 1988), 43–51.

had come to the attention of Leonard Lyons. Ibid., 76.

"*Trapping Reds . . .*" NY *Mirror*, Aug. 25, 1952.

Walter took credit . . . Winchell, 253.

Cohn's Jewishness. John J. Sirica, *To Set the Record Straight: The Break-In, the Tapes, the Conspirators, the Pardon* (NY: Norton, 1979), 254.

Walter later bragged . . . Winchell, 253.

456–7 "*I remember at twelve o'clock . . .*" Quoted in von Hoffman, 94.

457 "*he proceeded to plot out with Winchell . . .*" Ibid., 93.

457 "Winchell was an anti-Communist . . ." Arnold Forster int. by author.

Gary Stevens . . . had also been told . . . Gary Stevens int. by author.

457-8 "I remarked that I always made an effort . . ." [Deleted] to W, Dec. 6, 1952, Winchell file, FBI.

458 Pegler . . . was collecting information . . . Notes of phone conversation with Ben Mandel of HUAC, Jan. 5, [1953], Box 110, Pegler papers, Hoover Lib.

"You don't shoot somebody . . ." Herman Klurfeld int. by author.

Cohn's assistance on Baker. Shirley Eder, Not This Time, Cary Grant! (Garden City, NY: Doubleday, 1973), 259-60. Through a friend Eder had discovered a French book by Baker laced with anti-Semitic taunts. Eder bought the book, had it translated and, after unsuccessfully attempting to get Winchell, contacted Roy Cohn, who arranged a meeting at the Stork Club.

"I am convinced . . ." von Hoffman, 179-80.

459 "It was wrong to expose others . . ." James A. Wechsler, The Age of Suspicion (NY: Random House, 1953), 304.

Walter had obviously been given a transcript . . . NY Mirror, May 3, 1953.

"His feeling was that I was his friend . . ." Quoted in Victor Navasky, Naming Names (NY: Viking, 1980), 64.

he agreed to furnish to the committee . . . Ibid., 61. See also American Society of Newspaper Editors, Comment on the Wechsler Hearings (Washington D.C.: 1953).

"The ultimate in hideous irony . . ." NY Mirror, May 21, 1953.

"You know what he said?" HK.

460 "international cafe society's well-heeled playboys." NY Mirror, Feb. 2, 1953, 3.

"VIP." Ibid., Aug. 25, 1952.

Pat Ward. "What Pat Really Told," NY Enquirer, Feb. 16, 1953.

J. Roland Sala approached the bench . . . "The Jelke Case," mimeo, 2, Cuneo papers.

"[T]he evidence is now secondary . . ." NY Mirror, Feb. 10, 1953.

"I could sense Mr. Winchell's reluctance . . ." A. J. Liebling, The Press (NY: Pantheon paperback ed., 1981), 352-53.

461 "His right name is Cohen." NY Mirror, Feb. 13, 1953.

"I assured her . . ." Ibid., March 2, 1953.

"I'm crying . . ." Quoted in Lyle Stuart, The Secret Life of Walter Winchell (NY: Boar's Head Books, 1953), 231.

Appel's testimony and Walter's retort. NY Mirror, Feb. 26 & March 2, 1953; Stuart, 231-33.

"Look, kid, when the buzzard dies . . ." Exposé, March 1953. Stuart had interviewed Cahn, and this undoubtedly came directly from him.

462 he repeatedly pressed DA Frank Hogan . . . Stuart, 199-200.

On March 10 . . . Cahn was questioned . . . "Stenographer's Minutes," U.S. v William Cohen, C-146-320, Jan. 18, 1956, 5-6, U.S. District Court Southern District of NY.

"He was so mad at him . . ." HK.

"dirty four-letter word." Exposé, March 1953.

Cahn's disappearance. U.S. v William Cohen.

"Police Chief Clinton Anderson . . ." Transcript, May 3, 1953, Winchell file, 62-31615-780, FBI.

"I will have to defend myself . . ." Gruen program, May 3, 1953.

the police did collar Cahn . . . Stuart, 182-183.

462-3 Meeting Jane Kean. Jane Kean int. by author.

463 "Theirs is one of the swiftest-paced routines . . ." NY Mirror, Feb. 25, 1953.

Jane Kean's youth. JK.

"In the early stages of our relationship . . . Ibid.

"If he had the hots for somebody . . ." Al Rylander int. by author.

"It was day after day." JK.

463-4 "It was the most exciting opening . . ." Ibid.

464 "It was hard to think of Walter . . ." Ibid.

Jane and Walter could walk into the Empire Room . . . GS.

Jealousy. JK.

465 *"It kind of makes me wince."* Variety, May 20, 1953.

Deposition with Rifkind. NY Times, April 13, 1953.

"I haven't been a dupe for them." Ibid. July 8, 1953.

"greatest mistake of his life . . ." Simon H. Rifkind to Cuneo, Sept. 29, 1977, Cuneo papers.

466 *"Whom the Gods destroy* . . ." Exposé, March 1953, 12.

"most unbelievably unscrupulous person . . ." Lyle Stuart int. by author. Roth, however, was also responsible for bringing D. H. Lawrence's *Lady Chatterley's Lover*, among other celebrated works of erotica, into this country.

Roth had offered Stuart $1,000 . . . LS.

Attack on Lyle Stuart. Ibid.

467 *"His troubles are just beginning."* NY Mirror, April 16, 1954.

his office was raided . . . M. A. Jones to Nichols, Nov. 20, 1953, Winchell file, FBI.

"People I went to didn't want to see me." LS.

"weird-looking bird . . ." Harold Conrad, *Dear Muffo: 35 Years in the Fast Lane* (NY: Stein & Day, 1982), 96.

"I took the magazine over to Winchell . . ." Thomas K. Wolfe, "Public Lives: Confidential Magazine; Reflections in Tranquility by the Former Owner, Robert Harrison, Who Managed to Get Away With It," *Esquire*, April 1964, 152–53.

"[W]e started running a Winchell piece . . ." Ibid., 153.

468 *"They got a photograph of me* . . ." LS.

"most scandalous scandal magazine . . ." Wolfe, 87.

disreputable Harrison . . . Steve Govoni, "Now It Can Be Told," *American Film*, Feb. 1990, 29.

"How the hell did I ever get involved . . ." Wolfe, 153.

"When you're on my team . . ." Art

Franklin to Eddie Jaffe, Aug. 6, 1991. Author's coll.

"Winchell is high on the list . . ." Gruen program, Sept. 6, 1953.

"The most popular of all television stars . . ." Ibid.

Lucille Ball . . . *was listening* . . . Lucille Ball int., Apr. 22, 1970, Thomas coll.

"That was not a 'blind' item . . ." Desi Arnaz, *A Book*, (NY: Morrow, 1976), 240–41.

"death in the family look." Lucille Ball, Thomas coll.

469 *Desi was furious.* Jim Bacon int. by author.

"I'm sure he knows the true story." Arnaz, 252.

"Lucille Ball story . . . *has had a very happy ending."* Gruen program, Sept. 13, 1953.

"This was a very lonely man." AF.

If Cuneo was replaced . . . Herman Geist, son of Harry Geist, int. by author.

A young copyboy at ABC . . . Neil Toplitzer int. by author.

470 *Invitation and meeting with Eisenhower.* W to Walt, Jr., Feb. 4, 1954, Bigman coll.

470–1 *"We didn't say that* . . ." NY *Mirror*, March 22, 1954.

471 *"He was feeling out of sorts."* Ibid., March 23, 1954.

"The journalistic deviate . . ." Ibid., April 30, 1954.

"may be a killer." NY Times, April 5, 1954, 27.

"It is nice to have the advice . . ." Ibid., April 6, 1954.

"ill-advised television broadcast . . ." Ibid., April 7 & 10, 1954.

Walter defended himself . . . NY Mirror, April 9, 1954.

472 *"should be made aware* . . ." Ibid., April 26, 1954.

"Progress always results . . ." Ibid., May 3, 1954.

sounding the alarum . . . Gruen program, Jan. 31; Feb. 14, Feb. 28, 1954.

473 *"McCarthy may have been wrong* . . ." Ibid., March 21, 1954.

473 *"Nothing is personal and confidential
. . . NY Mirror*, May 6, 1954.

The Bolling memo. Ibid., May 6,
1954.

474 *"Last week I said that the Army-
McCarthy hearings . . ."* Gruen program,
May 9, 1954.

"We're going to get you." Quoted in
von Hoffman, 206.

Surveys showed . . . Cited in David
Oshinsky, *A Conspiracy So Immense: The World
of Joe McCarthy* (NY: Free Press, 1983), 416,
445.

"Roy Cohn's fan mail . . ." NY *Mirror*,
June 7, 1954.

"If you are voted off the committee . . ."
Gruen program, June 20, 1954.

475 *he attacked members of the Watkins
committee . . .* Simulcast, Sept. 5, 1954.

Even Robert Collier . . . Hoover to
Clyde Tolson et al., Sept 7, 1954, Winchell
file, FBI.

Walter admitted that his story . . . NY
Mirror, Sept. 9, 1954.

Walter's testimony. NY *Times*, Sept. 8,
1954.

476 *"The fight to expose 'Reds' . . ."* Simulcast, Sept. 12, 1954.

*Walter reported that McCarthy's sup-
porters . . .* Ibid., Nov. 7, 1954.

*"Senator McCarthy's friends bluntly
tell . . ."* Ibid., Nov. 21, 1954.

*"As a creature of the same established
power . . ."* James Aronson, *The Press and the
Cold War* (Indianapolis: Bobbs-Merrill, 1970),
85.

called him a "madman" . . . Winchell,
255–56.

477 *"I thought I was selling a lot of
watches . . ."* W to Kintner, Jan. 2, 1953, ABC
file, Winchell papers.

"Walter being Walter objects . . ." Betty
Forsling to Rose Bigman, Sept. 4, 1953,
Bigman coll.

he once wore a tie . . . Clare Russhon,
prod. asst., int. by author.

His television ratings . . . Memo L. B.
Nichols to Clyde Tolson, Oct. 29, 1953,
Winchell file, FBI.

Gruen decided not to renew . . . Variety,
Dec. 17, 1954.

478 *"[T]he shock of learning . . ."* W to
Kintner, Feb. 10, 1955, *Winchell v. ABC*,
#11831/55, NY Supreme Court, 154.

he hadn't even consulted Cuneo . . . HK;
Cuneo, "Disintegration of Walter Winchell's
Power," unpub. ms., 108, Cuneo papers.

he once sabotaged a rival . . . Leonard
Goldenson, with Marvin J. Wolf, *Beating the
Odds: The Untold Story Behind the Rise of ABC*
(NY: Scribner's, 1991), 116–17.

"ABC wanted to get rid of him."
Cuneo, "Disintegration of Walter Winchell's
Power," 108.

479 *Walter asked Leonard Goldenson . . . to
intervene.* NY *Times*, March 11, 1955.

"Referring to your letter . . ." Kintner
to W, March 10, 1955, *Winchell v. ABC*, 155.

"as fast as possible." NY *Times*,
March 12, 1955.

"I signed it to keep my contract . . ."
Winchell, 291–92.

"he never said or meant to say . . ." NY
Times, March 13, 1955.

480 *"the most abject retraction . . ."* Time,
March 21, 1955, 59.

the Post *editorialized that . . .* NY *Post*,
March 14, 1955.

"We can't possibly disavow . . ." Neville
to W, May 4, 1955, Wechsler file, Winchell
papers; Cuneo to W, May 5, 1955, Winchell
papers, NYPL at Lincoln Ctr.

Walter relented . . . P. J. McCauley to
W, May 23, 1955, *Post*—Wechsler file,
Winchell papers.

"to this day has never retracted . . ."
Howard Rushmore, "The Truth About the
Walter Winchell Retraction," *Confidential
Magazine*, Sept. 1955.

"The next day they would jump . . ."
JO'B. Amurex Oil opened up six points after
a Winchell tip; Missouri Pacific, 5 1/2 points;
United Consolidated Oil, 5 3/4. (*Time*,
March 15, 1954, 97)

*"as a newsman, it is within his preroga-
tive . . ."* Velotta to Geraldine Zorbaugh,
ABC gen. counsel, n.d. [1954], Cuneo papers.

"big piece of advance news." Time, Jan. 31, 1955, 75.

That prompted both the New York and American Stock Exchanges . . . Editor & Publisher, March 12, 1955, 12.

481 *"Walter Winchell's stock market tips . . ."* NY Times, March 3, 1955, 1.

Senator Prescott Bush suggested that Congress take action . . . U.S. Senate, 84:1, Banking and Currency Comm., *Stock Market Study* (March 3, 1955), 146–47.

"no apology to offer . . ." NY Times, March 5, 1955.

"He is not the center . . ." NY Post, March 8, 1955.

Capehart and Winchell. Stock Market Study, 679–82.

481–2 *"Suppose that the reason . . ."* Gilbert Seldes, "Truth and the TV Tip," *Saturday Review*, June 4, 1955, 28.

482 *she invited her sister and brother-in-law . . .* Seymour Mayer int. by author.

Description of Scottsdale house. Mrs. Bud Brooks, owner, int. by author. Even the address, 6116 E. Yucca, signified it was no real home; it was a pure fabrication, the number bearing no relation to any other number in the vicinity and the "East" contrary to the north-south orientation of the road. Walter had devised it out of his paranoia that someone might try to track him down.

483 *Hyatt von Dehn.* Clipping, Cholly Angelino, Los Angeles *Herald Examiner*, n.d., Elisabeth Winchell coll.

Walda's marriage. NY Herald Tribune, Oct. 18 and 27, 1955.

he hired a private investigator . . . Fred Otash, *Investigation Hollywood* (Chicago: Regnery, 1976), 40.

Walda was terribly distraught. Rabbi Albert Plotkin int. by author.

Walda's conversion to Catholicism. Mutual, Dec. 9, 1956.

It was roughly a year after Otash had served her . . . Otash, 43–45.

In the official account . . . U.S. v. William Cohen, "Stenographer's Minutes," Jan. 18, 1956, 4.

"I'll tell you a concept . . ." JO'B.

484 *"Somebody got hold of Mr. Cahn's file . . ."* U.S. v. Cohen, 22–24. As for the file, it has disappeared from the District Attorney's office—a highly unusual circumstance, I was told.

"Who is pushing whom?" U.S. v. Cohen, 32.

"Mr. Cahn has unfortunately run . . ." Ibid., Jan. 18, 1956, 8–9.

"[H]e is a very footloose person . . ." Ibid., 12–13.

finally emigrated to Israel. Mrs. Henry Rosenfeld int. by author.

"I can't live with the name . . ." SM.

"Walter hated his name." Eva Winchell.

He asked his friend Art Ford . . . Art Ford.

Columnist Bob Sylvester . . . got Walt, Jr., a job . . . JO'B.

joined the Marines . . . Paul D. Gray, asst. dir. for Military Records, Nat'l Personnel Records Ctr., to author, Jan. 31, 1990.

485 *He asked his old friend Curley Harris . . .* Curley Harris int. by author.

his father wrote him enthusiastically . . . W to Walt, Jr., Feb. 4, 1954, Bigman coll.

he liked to pour ketchup . . . Rose Bigman int. by author.

485–6 *Art Ford remembered walking with him . . .* Art Ford.

486 *he took some children for pizza . . .* Elisabeth Winchell int. by author.

"He has never set out to deliberately . . ." Quoted in Bob Thomas, *Winchell* (Garden City, NY: Doubleday, 1971), 276.

"It will look better . . ." John B. Poor, Mutual, to W, June 30, 1955; John Teeter to W, July 15, 1955, Mutual clippings, Winchell papers.

no salary was announced. Note on Harry Trenner, VP Mutual sales, to W, Aug. 1, 1955, Mutual clippings, Winchell papers.

He boasted in Jack O'Brian's column . . . Jack O'Brian, "Winchell Close to Radio Deal," NY *Journal-American*, July 23, 1955.

487 *Walter filed a $7-million-dollar law-*

suit . . . *Winchell* v. *ABC*, NY Supreme Court, #11831/55.

487 *A meeting with NBC head David Sarnoff* . . . Ibid.; HK.

"*I turned you down* . . ." Torre.

Sullivan had thrown a "tantrum" . . . NY *Journal*, Oct. 15, 1956.

"*Dear Hub This is BULLSH!*" Note W to Hubbell Robinson, Jr., exec. VP in charge of network programs for CBS-TV, on press release, CBS, Oct. 15, 1956, Winchell papers.

"*As time went on* . . ." Marie Torre, "A New Career for Walter Winchell," *Look*, Oct. 30, 1956.

Weaver told Jack O'Brian . . . Wallace Jordan to W, Feb. 14, 1956, M file, Winchell papers; JO'B.

Discovering Roberta Sherwood. JK; Roberta Sherwood int. by author.

488 "*the most thrilling in Copa history.*" NY *Mirror*, June 10 & July 4, 1956.

Discovering Rowan & Martin. JK.

"*roared with laughter.*" Dan Rowan int., July 14. 1970, Thomas coll.

"*Influence is something* . . ." Torre.

"*There's a line all the way around.*" Al Rylander int. by author. According to Rylander, Riddle, to the day he died, never understood why Walter Winchell always blasted the Dunes Hotel.

489 "*As much as my mother liked Walter* . . ." JK.

they even went to a baseball game. Ibid.

"*He wanted TV so hard* . . ." JO'B.

490 *Description of "The Walter Winchell Show."* Editor & *Publisher*, June 23, 1956, 44.

"*At Lindy's he emitted a shrill* . . ." Klurfeld, 182.

"*One of the things that excited curiosity* . . ." Quoted in Torre.

"*He would hang around* . . ." Joel Landau int. by author.

490-1 *Landau and Winchell.* Ibid.

491 "*Right out in the public there* . . ." Art Ford.

Walter's essential loneliness . . . Arthur Pomerantz int. by author.

"*jollying up a bunch of guys* . . ." Coleman Jacoby int. by author.

Delores Stamkowich. Torre; NY *Post*, Aug. 14, 1956.

"*I can't get over it.*" Ibid.

"*I'm sick from it all.*" NY *World-Telegram and Sun*, Aug. 13, 1956.

"*I just didn't want anybody to steal* . . ." NY *Post*, Aug. 14, 1956.

Walter got Stamkowich a job . . . Torre; NY *World-Telegram and Sun*, Aug. 13, 1956.

"*He talked to me about Billingsley* . . ." AF.

492 *Billingsley had made a derogatory remark* . . . AR.

Sally Dawson . . . *thought the feud* . . . Sally Dawson Vandale int. by author.

"*I'll just have to be more careful* . . ." Robin Harris, "Winchell Calls Old Pal a Knifer," NY *Inquirer*, Aug. 20, 1956.

Walter's own version . . . Winchell, 302.

"*I can buy them all* . . ." Harris.

A Stork Club employee wrote Walter . . . Tel. Anon. to W, June 25, 1956, Billingsley file, Winchell papers.

"*Every night was a crisis.*" GS.

His most serious gaffe . . . *Shor* v. *Billingsley*, NY Supreme Court, 1956, 158 NY S.2d, 476.

"*About all he has time to do* . . ." Mearl Allen, *Welcome to the Stork Club* (San Diego: A. S. Barnes, 1980), n.p.

493 *Besides all this I just have to think* . . ." Tel. Billingsley to W, March 12, 1955, Billingsley file, Winchell papers.

Walter had his lawyer advise the Stork . . . Sol A. Rosenblatt to Billingsley, Nov. 8, 1956, Billingsley file, Winchell papers.

As Jack O'Brian remembered it . . . JO'B.

"*He embraced me with a tight little hug* . . ." Winchell, 303.

"*PLEASE REPORT TO THE OFFICE* . . ." Tel. W to Rose Bigman, Aug. 28, 1956, Bigman coll.

He spent early September . . . *Variety*, Sept. 12, 1956.

Expatiating to L. B. Nichols. Memo

L. B. Nichols to Tolson, Re: Request of WW to See Dir., Sept. 1, 1956, Winchell file, FBI.

494 *Journalist Peter Maas, following Walter* ... Peter Maas, "Prowling the Night Beat with Walter Winchell," *Collier's*, Nov. 23, 1956.

He even took time to testify ... U.S. House 84:2, House Judiciary Comm., *Monopoly Problems in Regulated Industries*, Part II, Vol. 4, The Television Industry, Sept. 25, 1956, 5712–16.

"*I am unhappy* ..." *Editor & Publisher*, Sept. 29, 1956, 13.

"*I'll have a great show.*" Bill Smith, "Walter Winchell Meets the Press," *Show Business*, Oct. 1, 1956.

"*This is where I belong.*" CR.

"*This TV business is really strange* ..." Torre.

"*All the ingrates were having the big laugh* ..." Maas.

495 "*Mr. Winchell seems to be one more example* ..." *NY Times*, Oct. 6, 1956, 43.

"*It's probably a redundancy* ..." Quoted in *Editor & Publisher*, Oct. 13, 1956, 69.

John Crosby ... *suspected* ... NY Herald Tribune, Oct. 10, 1956.

Jay Nelson Tuck ... *believed* ... NY Post, Oct. 8, 1956.

"*Walter's premiere would have been far better* ..." NY *Journal*, Oct. 6, 1956.

"*his last glow.*" HK.

he took an entourage of newsboys ... *Editor & Publisher*, Oct. 13, 1956, 69.

"[*He had*] *the column, the broadcast and then* ..." CR.

"*Nobody knew what they were doing* ..." RB.

496 "*worst experience of my life.*" Alan Handley int. by author.

Walter would call Handley ... Alan Handley int., Apr. 1, 1970, Thomas coll.

"*Pinkerton men, G-men or cops*" ... Memo L. B. Nichols to Tolson, Re: Request of WW to See Dir., Sept. 1, 1956, Winchell file, FBI.

"*I took the big one.*" Alan Handley int., Thomas coll.; RB.

Erratic behavior. Memo SAC, NY to Hoover, Re: WW, Information Concerning, Oct. 30, 1956, Winchell file, FBI.

"*Chevalier wears his* ..." "Walter Winchell Show," Nov. 30, 1956, Motion Picture Division, L of C.

497 "*She never mentioned them* ..." NY *Mirror*, Nov. 2, 1956.

Nielsen ratings. Nielsen ratings for WW Show, W file, Winchell papers.

"*He couldn't integrate himself* ..." Alan Handley int., Thomas coll.

Old Gold and Toni had announced ... NY *Times*, Nov. 23, 1956.

he was relieved ... Ibid.

"*I don't feel like a dead duck.*" Time, Dec. 3, 1956; clipping, n.d., Lester Sweyd coll., NYPL at Lincoln Ctr.

498 *Walter took the lighter* ... AR.

"*I will never forget, Tom* ..." W to T. F. O'Neil, pres. RKO Teleradio Pictures, Sept. 11, 1956, Mutual file, Winchell papers.

Harris had gotten $1,000 ... Edward Banzal, "Drug Suit Accuses Officials in Losses," *NY Times*, March 19, 1958, 1.

"*I feel free again* ..." W to Harry H. Patterson, Sept. 10, 1956, Mutual file, Winchell papers.

"*alleged secret work* ..." Memo Nichols to Belmont, Re: WW B'cast, April 15, 1956, April 18, 1956, Winchell file, FBI.

Arthur Miller. Memo Belmont to Boardman, Re: WW B'cast, May 6, 1956, May 7, 1956, Winchell file, FBI.

New York Times. Memo Belmont to Boardman, Re: WW B'cast, April 8, 1956, April 9, 1956, Winchell file, FBI.

499 "*would mean a woman* ..." Long John Nebel int., May 21, 1970, Thomas coll.

GENTLEMEN, PLEASE BE ADVISED ... Harry Patterson to Mutual, Nov. 9, 1956, Mutual file, Winchell papers.

"*The man has gone mad.*" Time, Dec. 10, 1956, 47.

Walter and Desi Arnaz. Arnaz, 304. Arnaz places this at the beginning of "The Untouchables," but the context makes it almost certain that this occurred at the inception of "The Walter Winchell File" instead.

499 *On January 15 a deal was struck ...*
Winchell, 267–71; Irving Zussman int. by au-
thor; *Newsweek*, Oct. 14, 1957; Memo W to
Ronald Landers, Oct. 27, 1964, W file,
Winchell papers.

"The trouble is that ..." Note, Oct. 31,
1956, Earl Wilson papers, Shubert Archive.
The note reads, "This was deleted from
WW column of Wed., Oct 31, 1956 (The Ike
Column)" and then includes Walter's lament.

500 *Leaving Mutual. NY Times*, Feb. 5,
1957.

"all of you for 28 exciting years." Mutual program, March 3, 1957.

"The manner in which you ended ..."
Hoover to W, March 7, 1957, Winchell file,
FBI.

"I am taking it a lot easier." W to
Hoover, March 18, 1957, Winchell file,
FBI.

*"I was throwing a punch ..." NY Her-
ald Tribune*, March 15, 1957.

*"I hadn't thought much about the impli-
cations ..."* Ernest Lehman int. by author.

501 *"You made me write ...."* Ernest
Lehman, "If I Say So Myself ..." in *Screening
Sickness and Other Tales of Tinseltown* (NY:
Putnam, 1982), 227.

*"I don't fool with the Ernie Leh-
mans ..."* EL.

*"Press agents would get up from the
table ..."* Ibid.

501–2 *Making* Sweet Smell. Ibid.

502 *The night of the premiere ...* Ibid.

"They've had many shocks ..." NY
Mirror, Dec. 12 and 22, 1957.

503 *"He's quite different."* Ibid., Sept. 22,
1957.

"This is his fourth film ..." "A Few
Notes on Winchell," *TV Guide*, Sept. 28,
1957, 8.

*"very relaxed and low-keyed." NY Her-
ald Tribune*, Oct. 1, 1957.

*New York wasn't as lively ...
Newsweek*, Oct. 14, 1957.

504 *Grand juries ... were taking aim ...*
Gladwin Hill, "Scandal Magazines Face
Trouble in the Courts," *NY Times*, May 5,
1957, IV, 4.

Fred Kraft and Edmund Brown.
Govoni, 32–33.

"I love it." Conrad, 107–08.

*Harrison successfully fought extradi-
tion ... NY Times*, June 14 and July 24, 1957.

The trial of Confidential*'s California
staff ...* Ibid., July 30, 1957.

One defendant ... fled to Mexico ...
Govoni, 33.

Another participant ... NY Times,
Aug. 20, 1957.

a deputy district attorney ... Govoni,
33.

*"Many writers for respectable slick mag-
azines ..."* NY *Mirror*, Sept. 12, 1957.

*"[i]n Hollywood, men and women fre-
quently behave ..."* Ibid., Sept. 19, 1957.

505 *The* Confidential *trial ended ... NY
Times*, Oct. 2, 1957.

To avoid a retrial ... Ibid., Nov. 8 and
13, 1957.

"Nearly every high class magazine ..."
NY *Mirror*, Oct. 18, 1957.

*Cancellation of "The Walter Winchell
File." Time*, Feb. 10, 1958, 86.

506 *"This self-appointed General Manager ..."* Jack Paar, with John Reddy, *I Kid You
Not* (Boston: Little, Brown, 1960), 200–01.

"refreshing relief ..." NY *Mirror*, Oct.
10, 1957.

Paar-Winchell feud. Time, May 5,
1958, 47; *Newsweek*, May 5, 1958, 68.

"Who really cares about an ingrate ..."
Herman Klurfeld, *Winchell: His Life and
Times*, NY: Praeger, 1976, 184.

"fading star." Time, May 5, 1958;
Newsweek, May 5, 1958.

"The shock ..." Winchell, 287.

"It is important to be happy inside ..."
Teeter to W, April 28, 1958, Teeter file,
Runyon Fund.

he had accepted an honorary degree ...
Ted Thackrey, "Walter Winchell's $13,000,-
000 Item," Lakeland (Fla.) *Ledger*, March 2,
1958.

507 *That plan was scotched ... Variety*,
April 23, 1958.

"They'll have three TV cameras ..."
Time, April 21, 1958, 20.

Description of Las Vegas act. Variety,
June 4, 1958; *Time,* June 9, 1958, 75;
Winchell, 284.

"fifteen days of pain . . ." Note on Abel
Green to W, n.d. [June 1958], Bigman coll.

"stable" of four or five call girls . . .
Memo W. C. Sullivan to A. H. Belmont, Re:
Walter Winchell, Information Concerning
Central Research Matter, Sept. 22, 1958,
Winchell file, FBI.

Walter was telling friends . . . D. K.
Brown, SAC LA, to Hoover, April 21, 1958,
Winchell file, FBI.

508 *an announcement by Mutual . . . NY
Times,* Sept. 13, 1958.

reportedly earning $1,000 *per show . . .*

Variety, Nov. 19, 1958, 46; Teeter to W, Aug.
18, 1958, Teeter file, Runyon Fund.

"Walter gave the show a feeling . . ."
Quoted in *Variety,* March 1, 1972. Walter's
cousin Howard Koch, who was assistant director on many of the episodes, said that
Walter was also a significant element in editing the series; using Walter's bridges, one
could easily cut from one segment to another.
(Howard Koch int. by author.)

Narrations. Hoover to W, Nov. 23,
1959, Winchell file, FBI; *Variety,* May 25,
1960; Winchell, 282–83.

*The "contemporary Walter Winchell
has become . . ."* "The Aging Lion," *Time,*
June 15, 1959, 47.

10 "HE'LL WAKE UP ONE DAY . . ."

509 *Termination of Mutual contract.* Rob-
ert L. Finch, VP Phillips & Cherbo advertis-
ing, to Joe Keating, Mutual, Oct. 30, 1959;
A. G. McCarthy, pres. Mutual, to Rose
Bigman, Nov. 23, 1959, Mutual folder,
Winchell papers.

Paar's attacks on Winchell. NY Times,
March 8, 1960, 66.

*John Crosby remembered . . . Observer
Review,* Feb. 27, 1972, 11.

510 *Trip with Eisenhower. Newsweek,*
July 1, 1960.

"a look that could kill." Walter
Winchell, *Winchell Exclusive: "Things That
Happened to Me—and Me to Them"* (Englewood Cliffs, N.J.: Prentice-Hall, 1975),
274–75.

*"What do you mean interrupting
me . . ." Variety,* April 12, 1972.

"I've been around this bunch . . ." NY
Mirror, June 29, 1960.

He returned to the United States . . . W
to Hagerty, July 10, 1960, 8F 135–E, Eisenhower papers, Eisenhower Lib.

Partnership with Albert Zugsmith. Albert Zugsmith to Steve Trilling, WB,
Sept. 12, 1960, W file, Winchell papers.

"Wouldn't you rather have anything you

want . . ." Sam Wall int., April 7, 1970,
Thomas coll.

511 *the agreement he concluded with ABC
television . . . NY Times,* July 20, 1960.

ABC contract. Omar Elder, Jr., VP &
gen. counsel ABC, to W, Aug. 8, 1960, ABC
file, Winchell papers.

"I'm happy to be back." "The Old
WW Himself," *Newsweek,* Oct. 10, 1960, 96,
98.

he wrote J. Edgar Hoover . . . W to
Hoover, Aug. 26, 1960, Winchell file, FBI.

"Brigitte Bardot is news . . ." NY *Mirror,* Oct. 13, 1960.

"gave off sparks." Ibid., Oct. 3, 1960.

"The Trendex indicates . . ." John
Deitrick to Spector, Oct. 10, 1960, ABC file,
Winchell papers.

512 *he claimed to have told ABC's Tom
Velotta . . . Variety,* April 4, 1962; Tel. Velotta
to W, Nov. 10, 1960, ABC file, Winchell papers.

"hovered between life and death." W to
Rita Greene, Sept. 2, 1960, Pat Rose coll.

"heart is practically new." W to Hoover, Aug. 26, 1960.

"It may be in the fall." Time, Feb. 3,
1961, 40.

512 *he lost fifty papers* ... Winchell, 273–74.

"He has not been in the hospital." Rose Bigman to William Randolph Hearst, Jr., Dec. 9, 1960, Hearst file, Winchell papers.

"I am feeling better except ..." W to Richard Berlin, Jan. 5, 1961, Hearst file, Winchell papers.

June said he was ... Neville to McCabe, Feb. 8, 1961, Hearst file, Winchell papers.

"I went to the typewriter ..." Time, Feb. 3, 1961, 40.

513 *he had contemplated suicide* ... Eva Winchell int. by author.

Time *found his column* ... Time, April 14, 1961, 81.

he had traveled to Europe ... Will Fowler int. by author.

"Africa was really his love." Eva Winchell.

For a time he considered joining a treasure-hunting expedition ... John Teeter to W, Jan. 13, 1960, WW—corr. about fund, 1960–72, Runyon Fund.

he departed for California ... Eva Winchell.

"exquisitely beautiful." Elisabeth Winchell int. by author.

514 *"And the moment we took a look ..."* Eva Winchell.

First date. Ibid.

Eva-Walt courtship. Ibid.

515 *"Not sure how the aspects of subterfuge ..."* Walt, Jr., to Earl Wilson, Feb. 1, 1962, Winchell file, Wilson papers, Shubert Archive.

"Like Hans Christian Andersen." Eva Winchell.

"this fantasy would come in the door." Dorothy Moore int. by author.

no records of any Nazi activity ... NY Times, Jan. 30, 1962; David G. Marwell, dir. Berlin Document Ctr., U.S. Embassy, to author, May 28, 1991 (BDC Ref. 1360 1 051).

Walt's Nazi antics. Eva Winchell.

516 *June was so distressed* ... Arnold Forster int. by author.

When a new neighbor packed her two children ... Mrs. Stern int. by author.

"I feel very depressed ..." Eva Winchell.

"Walter went wild." Ibid.

517 *"He has a way of winning ..."* NY Mirror, April 9, 1961.

suspicions had only been confirmed ... Herman Klurfeld int. by author; Jim Bacon int. by author; Winchell, 276.

Robert Kennedy ... believed that Hoover ... Dorothy Schiff quoted in Jeffrey Potter, *Men, Money and Magic: The Story of Dorothy Schiff* (NY: Coward, McCann & Geoghegan, 1976), 298.

Robert Kennedy was increasingly leaning ... HK.

"Intimates of the president ..." NY Herald Tribune, June 21, 1962.

518 *"This upset me so much ..."* Winchell, 310–11.

"I'll be kicking away $150,000 ..." AP wire, June 20, 1962.

he had taken to submitting his column directly ... NY Times, June 21, 1962, 28.

"Have offers from two ..." Variety, June 27, 1962.

"A long time ago Bill and I ..." W to Charles McCabe, June 23, 1962, Hearst file, Winchell papers.

"Walter was a self-centered egomaniac ..." William Randolph Hearst, Jr., with Jack Casserly, *The Hearsts: Father and Son* (Niwot, Colo.: Roberts Rinehart, 1991), 210.

"I'm definitely retaining a lawyer ..." W to McCabe, June 23, 1962.

he held an hour-long press conference ... Memo SAC San Diego to Hoover, July 5, 1962, Winchell file, FBI.

519 *Walter repeated the charges* ... San Diego Union, July 11, 1962, A-19.

By the end of the week ... Beverly Hills Citizen News, July 12, 1962.

revoked his "resignation." Winchell, 311–12.

he had already closed a handshake deal ... Variety, July 4, 1962.

"for making an old man ..." Herman Klurfeld, *Winchell: His Life and Times* (NY:

Praeger, 1976), 189. Publicity seemed to come in bunches. That same July Walter received a call from a "Mr. Smith" who claimed to have masterminded a multi-million-dollar bonds and securities heist for the mob—"bigger than the Brinks case"—and asked Walter to do for him what he had done for Macri. They rendezvoused at 4:30 A.M. in San Francisco and repaired to the Mark Hopkins Hotel, where eighteen FBI agents disguised as hotel employees awaited them. Walter told the FBI that the bellboys looked at him "sympathetically" and two or three expressed apologies—a tip-off, he said, that he was about to be kidnapped or murdered by the mob. (Hoover wrote "Bunk" on the report.) As Walter told it, he made a "fake" phone call to Hoover demanding that Mr. Smith be protected, and Mr. Smith then broke down and revealed the location of the stolen property. Walter received a half-hour break on the story, though the editor at Hearst's San Francisco *Call-Bulletin* had already told him the story was "no damn good and should be thrown out the window." Feeling vindicated, Walter said all he wanted now was a "cup of sleep." ("Skewped," NY *Mirror*, July 21, 1962; Memo: C. D. DeLoach to Mohr, July 18, 1962; Mohr to DeLoach, July 19, 1962, Winchell file, FBI.)

Tony Canazari. Joel Landau int. by author.

"I don't know how he would do it." Ibid.

O'Brian remembered flying out to Los Angeles . . . Jack O'Brian int. by author.

520 *"God, we just sat at his feet."* Dorothy Manners int. by author.

"He invites people in car lots." Clipping, n.d. [1962], Winchell file, Earl Wilson papers, Shubert Archive.

On a typical day . . . "Our Town," *Los Angeles Magazine* (Aug. 1962), 2.

"Walter became as familiar a sight . . ." Clipping, n.d. [1962], Winchell file, Earl Wilson papers, Shubert Archive.

"You have to say this about Walter." Jim Bacon int. by author.

"several famous companies have asked

me . . ." W to Robert Kintner, July 11, 1962; Kintner to W, July 23, 1962, N file, Winchell papers.

521 *"Build me a monument."* Mal Ward int., Apr. 24, 1970, Thomas coll.

Returning to Los Angeles from San Francisco . . . Tel. SAC LA to Hoover, Re: WW, July 20, 1962, Winchell file, FBI.

522 *"Get it set in type . . ."* Jimmy Breslin annotated by James G. Bellows and Richard C. Wald, *The World of Jimmy Breslin* (NY: Viking, 1967), 270.

One man sat at his typewriter . . . Gay Talese, "Forlorn Staff Stands By as Mirror Shuts Down," *NY Times*, Oct. 16, 1963, 31.

"How can a paper with the second largest circulation . . ." Ibid.

"How do you feel?" Art Pomerantz int. by author.

"Broadway's mountain." NY *Mirror*, Oct. 16, 1963.

"The Mirror was no ornament . . ." NY *Times*, Oct. 17, 1963, 34.

"milestone in the period of transition . . ." *Editor & Publisher*, Oct. 19, 1963, 6.

523 *"That was the most crushing blow."* HK.

"I died on October 16, 1963." Winchell, 4.

"like a drowning man . . ." HK.

"That's pretty . . ." Klurfeld, 189–90.

Frank Sinatra, Jr., kidnapping trial. JB.

"I am in San Diego spinning like a top . . ." W to SAC Wesley G. Grapp, March 25, 1964, Winchell file, FBI.

Walter had called columnist Jim Bacon . . . JB.

524 *"But came the night . . ."* JB; San Diego *Union*, April 8, 1964. Bacon mistakenly remembered it as Walter's sixty-fifth birthday.

"hustle ads for our papers . . ." W to Berlin, Markuson, J. Kingsbury Smith, George Hearst, Jr., et al., n.d. [1964], Hearst file, Winchell papers.

he volunteered to write six columns . . . W to William Randolph Hearst, Jr., May 15, 1964, Hearst file, Winchell papers.

524 *Schiff filed a new libel action.* Editor & Publisher, July 7, 1962, 56.

"[N]ever trust a former communist . . ." W to Clyde Tolson, Dec. 3, 1963, Winchell file, FBI.

revoking the indemnification clause . . . William Randolph Hearst, Jr., to W, June 2, 1964, H file, Winchell papers.

"Why don't you give the city desk some help . . ." W to G. O. Markuson, Sept 1967, J file, Winchell papers.

525 "Get this." Don Freeman, "The Emperor of Broadway," Seminar (June 1972), 31.

"Oh, I wouldn't want him . . ." Mal Ward int., Apr. 24, 1970, Thomas coll.

"In San Francisco, he had a whole bus . . ." Ernest Cuneo, "Disintegration of Walter Winchell's Power," unpub. ms., 113, Cuneo papers.

"And in the middle . . ." Roger Mudd to W, Sept. 14, 1964, Radio commentator file, Winchell papers.

RESPECTFULLY REQUEST ANY ASSIGNMENT. Tel. W to LBJ, Aug.6, 1964, WHCF, WW folder, LBJ Lib.

526 "Winchell doesn't know what he's talking about." Teletype SAC, LA to Hoover, Aug. 5, 1964, Winchell file, FBI; Irving Kupcinet with Paul Neimark, Kup: A Man, an Era, a City, Irv Kupcinet's Autobiography (Chicago: Bonus Books, 1988), 187.

"It is significant . . ." NY Journal-American, Dec. 3, 1964; Hoover to W, Dec. 3, 1964, Winchell file, FBI.

"I wonder what would happen . . ." Irving Mansfield int., July 17, 1970, Thomas coll.

A new siege of dental surgery . . . W to J. Kingsbury Smith, Sept. 28, 1965, J file, Winchell papers.

"You and I have a problem." Joe Connolly to W, Nov. 1, 1965, H file, Winchell papers.

527 "suffering from a gum infection." Klurfeld, 191.

To Whom It May Concern . . . Letter, Dec. 1965, Klurfeld file, Winchell papers.

"I thought you were like a son . . ." Klurfeld, 192.

Stork Club labor problems. NY Times, March 5, 1957, Feb. 22, 1961; NY Herald Tribune, May 24, 1957; Variety, Oct. 7, 1959.

"He was acutely aware . . ." Shermane Billingsley Drill int. by author.

528 "We have to keep up with the times." NY Times, Jan. 29, 1965.

"general breakdown." Newsweek, Oct. 18, 1965, 42.

Billingsley's death. NY Times, Oct. 5, 1966.

Billingsley's funeral. SBD.

529 "Everything that had been so big and bustling . . ." Dorothy Manners.

"Who shall replace . . ." AP, Feb. 4, 1966.

Disturbance at Twelve Acres. Eva Winchell; NY Times, Aug. 26, 1963.

530 *he was assaulted late one night . . .* Ibid., Sept. 22, 1963.

he believed he was going to have an attack . . . Memo: Anon. to William Sullivan, June 25, 1965, Walter Winchell, Jr., file, FBI.

Six days later he was admitted to the U.S. Army hospital . . . Memo Anon. to William Sullivan, July 1, 1965, Walter Winchell, Jr., file, FBI.

Eva . . . hadn't enough money . . . Tel. U.S. Consul Frankfurt to sec'y. of state, July 3, 1965, Walter Winchell, Jr., file, Dept of State.

they returned to Twelve Acres . . . Eva Winchell.

531 *He begged his parents . . .* Ibid.

The Winchells' neighbor had . . . The neighbor was named D. J. Bernstein. Lyle Stuart int. by author.

June wanted to dispose . . . Seymour Mayer int. by author.

The sale price . . . Deed, Westchester County, Book 6588, 364–367, Land Records Office.

He took an ax . . . Eva Winchell.

"It was like old times." Variety, April 12, 1967.

Formation of World Journal *and* World Journal Tribune. Richard Kluger, The Paper: The Life and Death of the New York Herald Tribune (NY: Knopf, 1986), 730–31.

532 *"I failed the old man ..."* Hearst with Casserly, 304–05.

the plan ... was to alternate Walter with Louis Sobol. Variety, Sept. 7, 1966.

His column kept getting whittled ... Winchell, 313.

"doesn't think highly of Bway columns" ... W to Paul W. Bensen, n.d. [1966], *WJT* file, Winchell papers.

"One day they will say ..." Clipping, Detroit *Evening Times*, n.d. [May 1934], Scrapbook 1931–35, NYPL at Lincoln Ctr.

On June 30 Markuson wrote Walter ... G.O. Markuson to W, June 30, 1967, H file, Winchell papers.

532–3 *Weinraub's obituary for the Broadway column.* Bernard Weinraub, "Decline and Fall of the Gossip Columnist," *NY Times*, May 14, 1967.

533 *"Just read August 8 Wall Street Journal ..."* Tel. W to publisher, *Time*, Aug. 9, 1967, *Time* file, Winchell papers.

Variety ad. Variety, Sept. 13, 1967, 49.

He phoned John Fairchild ... Quoted in James Brady, NY *Post*, Aug. 28, 1975.

He even asked his friend Art Pomerantz ... Art Pomerantz int. by author.

he brought a collection of photographs ... Richard M. Clurman, *Time*, to W, Sept. 18, 1967, *Time* file, Winchell papers.

"Who can I talk to ..." W to Richard Berlin, Nov. 2, 1967, J file, Winchell papers.

the McNaught syndicate ... Editor & Publisher, Dec. 2, 1967, 49; Dec. 16, 1967, 53.

he was writing the Examiner *asking* ... W to Morris Fox, Washington *Examiner*, Dec. 23, 1967, Washington *Examiner* file, Winchell papers.

534 *his old axioms were now proved.* Winchell, 315.

One day he leaped onstage ... William Doll to Bob Thomas, June 18, 1970, Thomas coll.

Producer David Brown remembered ... David Brown int. by author.

"Winchell's Coming Back." Jacqueline Susann int., July 17, 1970, Thomas coll.

"If you do not reconcile with him ..." Winchell, 273; John Mosedale, *The Men Who Invented Broadway: Damon Runyon, Walter Winchell and Their World* (NY: Marek, 1981), 296.

Lyons was the one who phoned ... Lyons to W, Aug. 24, 1961, Lyons file, Winchell papers.

Reconciliations. Ed Weiner int. by author; LS. Weiner's Winchell biography had finally been published in 1955, temporarily adding to Walter's enmity, but now all was forgiven.

Reconciling with Ed Sullivan. Dorothy Moore int. by author.

535 *Sullivan offered to make inquiries ...* Bob Thomas, *Winchell* (Garden City, N.Y.: Doubleday, 1971), 12–13.

Truce at El Morocco. Louis Sobol, *The Longest Street: A Memoir* (NY: Crown, 1968), 364.

Appearance on "Ed Sullivan Show." *Variety*, Sept. 13, 1967. Sullivan, known for his on-air gaffes, had initially introduced Walter as a "great sports star" before realizing that that introduction was intended for football player Frank Gifford. (W to Sullivan, Dec. 13, 1967, Sullivan file, Winchell papers.)

"As we both grow older ..." Winchell, 320.

a separate account was created ... Administrative Fund (mimeo), Misc. information file, Runyon Fund.

"Geist and Rose reported to Walter ..." Teeter to Louis Lurie, April 3, 1964, John Teeter file, Runyon Fund.

536 *the board also authorized president Dan Parker* ... Teeter to W, April 2, 1964; Geist to W, May 1, 1964; Teeter to board, May 15, 1964, WW—corr. about fund, 1960–72, Runyon Fund.

the renovation cost $342,000 ... Real Estate Acct., Misc. information file, Runyon Fund.

"He will not speak again." Dorothy Moore to bd. of dirs., Dec. 3, 1965, Bigman coll.

he got word that there was some malfea-

sance . . . Arthur Godfrey int., July 17, 1970, Thomas coll.

536 *"to effect certain changes."* W to Bob Hope, Sept. 27, 1967, WW—corr. about fund, 1967–72, Runyon Fund.

October 20 meeting. Minutes of members' meeting, Oct. 20, 1967, Runyon Fund.

536–8 *Walda's disappearance and hospitalization.* Elisabeth Winchell int. by author.

538 *he accompanied President Johnson . . .* Memo Tom Johnson to George Christian, Nov. 14, 1967, WHCF, WW folder, LBJ Lib.

"brings together in one daily newspaper . . ." NY *Column*, April 1, 1968.

"Lou, you wouldn't believe his energy . . ." Dorothy Moore to Lou Lurie, Feb. 20, 1968, Louis Lurie file, Runyon Fund.

A young Esquire *writer . . .* Michael Zwerin, "Flash!. . . . Walter Winchell Is a Reluctant Anachronism," *Esquire*, Aug. 1968, 54–55.

539 *he was in Washington to view the riots . . .* NY *Column*, April 8, 1968.

Covering Columbia riots. Ibid., May 1, 1968; June 13, 1968.

hectoring the White House . . . W to Tom Johnson, asst. press sec'y., June 14, 1968, WHCF, WW folder, LBJ Lib.

he was in Los Angeles for the pleading of Sirhan Sirhan . . . NY *Column*, June 19, 1968.

The total contract . . . Variety, Oct. 4, 1967; *NY Times*, Sept. 28, 1967.

his attorney specifically cited Winchell . . . NY Times, March 1, 1966.

540 *Doubleday . . . asked for an indemnity.* SAC, NY, to Hoover, Nov. 9, 1967, Re: Private Papers of WW, Winchell file, FBI.

"There was an almost frantic sense . . ." SBD.

"the heavy load I have been taking . . ." W to Abel Green, Jan 31, 1968, *Variety* file, Winchell papers.

A month later he wrote Green . . . W to Green, March 6, 1968, *Variety* file, Winchell papers.

"bonkers." SBD.

"mean, ungenerous, crudely cynical . . ." Wallace Markfield, "Winchell Exclusive," *NY Times Book Review*, Nov. 9, 1975, 5.

"his jaw jutting . . ." Thomas BeVier, "Winchell's Memories of Condon," Chicago *Tribune*, Aug. 27, 1968.

"It was unmistakable . . ." Ernest Cuneo, "Disintegration of Walter Winchell's Power," unpub. ms., 113, Cuneo papers.

541 *"I know I am going to die here."* Eva Winchell.

"It just didn't fit him." Ibid.

he had gone to Hawaii . . . Tel. Honolulu to Dir., Feb. 7, 1967; Memo, March 30, 1967, Walt Winchell, Jr., file, FBI

542 *"I was hostile and resistant . . ."* Walt, Jr., to June, March 1, 1968, author's coll.

"I just do not have the plan . . ." Walt to June, March 8, 1968, author's coll.

"too old to continue wandering aimlessly." Walt to June, March 18, 1968, author's coll.

"we did not live very happily . . ." Eva Winchell.

"the world's worst dishwasher-fry cook." Walt to June, n.d. [Dec. 1968], author's coll.

"Sikia . . ." Ibid.

Walt, Jr.'s suicide. Eva Winchell.

Walt's casket. Paul Messinger, funeral dir., int. by author.

543 *"Because of tragedy and illness . . ."* Press release, McNaught syndicate, Jan. 10, 1969, WW—Articles written by, Runyon Fund.

"Due to a series of personal tragedies . . ." Press release, McNaught syndicate, Feb. 7, 1969, WW—Articles written by, Runyon Fund.

"get his bearings." NY *Times*, Feb. 6, 1969.

speaking to Rose now once a week . . . Dorothy Moore to Lou Lurie, Feb. 3, 1969, Louis Lurie file, Runyon Fund.

"It wasn't so much that he finally quit . . ." Ed Wilcox, "Flash! -30- For WW," NY *Daily News*, March 2, 1969.

"Let them have their fun." Quoted in Jim Bishop, *The Mark Hellinger Story* (NY: Appleton-Century-Croft, 1952), 70.

"mortally wounded by life." Eva Winchell.

"She was just shut down." Elisabeth Winchell.

"He became old very fast." HK.

544 *"He didn't recognize me."* Sid White int. by author.

Rose recruited press agents ... Irving Zussman, press agent, int. by author.

"I'm not important ..." Dorothy Moore int. by author.

wearing a white tennis cap ... Frank Rhoades, "The Emperor of Broadway," *Seminar* (June 1972), 31.

"It is seared into my memory ..." Arnold Forster int. by author.

She lived in her nightclothes ... Elisabeth Winchell; Eva Winchell.

June's death. Death certificate, author's coll.

"When he answered the door ..." Elisabeth Winchell.

544–5 *"A woman of valor who can find?"* Proverbs 31: 10–31, *The Holy Scriptures* (Chicago: Menorah Press, 1960), 619–20.

545 *Walter devised a different arrangement* ... Rabbi Albert Plotkin int. by author.

"I know you're having a rough time." Eva Winchell.

he admitted that he had not been making much headway ... *Variety*, Feb. 11, 1970.

"I have stopped seeing everyone ..." Bob Thomas, *Winchell* (Garden City, N.Y.: Doubleday, 1971), 277.

"very low." William G. Simon to Dorothy Moore, July 3, 1970, William Simon file, Runyon Fund.

546 *"There was no question ..."* Dr. Joseph Kaufman int. by author.

"He kept the cancer a big secret." RB.

"He used to sit by the pool ..." Dorothy Moore.

when his mood darkened ... RB.

New York *Mirror. Variety*, Dec. 2, 1970; Tolson to Hoover, Dec. 2, 1970, Re: WW, Walter Winchell file, FBI.

On December 10, Walter appeared ... *Editor & Publisher*, Dec. 26, 1970, 9.

547 *reporters had to strain* ... *Variety*, Dec. 16, 1970.

essentially "therapy" ... Ibid., Jan. 27, 1971.

Miami trip. Charles Whited, "Winchell Showmanship Always Drew Crowd," Miami *Herald*, Feb. 22, 1972, B-2.

"He was depressed, irritable ..." Dr. JK.

His energy was too low. Dorothy Moore.

"He didn't want anyone to see him." NY *Post*, Feb. 21, 1972.

"We went out every night." Dorothy Moore.

"What would happen if your boss said ..." Ibid.

A press agent remembered seeking Winchell there. IZ. The press agent was Sam Wall.

548 *"spirits were buoyed ..."* Notes, Dr. Joseph Kaufman.

"Wish I didn't have to take it." Rose Bigman to W, Oct. 1, 1971, Bigman coll.

"Rose, I'm coming along fine." W to Rose Bigman, Jan. 7, 1972, Bigman coll.

"serious but not critical condition." NY *Times*, Jan. 27, 1972.

Associated Press reported ... *Variety*, Feb. 2, 1972.

"He is deteriorating rapidly." Notes, Dr. Joseph Kaufman.

Preparations of the body. Paul Messinger int. by author; Paul Dean, "Belief in Integrity His Lasting Legacy," Arizona *Republic*, Feb. 22, 1972, 21.

549 *Funeral.* Dean.

"It twinges me ..." Ernie Cuneo, "Winchell's Grave," A-2-17, Cuneo papers.

Epilogue

550 *Walter's will.* Last Will and Testament, Walter Winchell, Nov. 8, 1971, NY Surrogate Court.

"*He knew precisely what he was doing.*" Herman Geist int. by author.

Challenging the will. Seth Rubinstein, atty., int. by author.

551 *Hundreds of thousands more* . . . Ledis & Horowitz, accountants, to W, July 25, 1963, W file, Winchell papers. From its inception in 1952 to the time the Runyon Fund shifted to an administrative account to cover its expenses, the WW Foundation took in $641,269. It is impossible to say how much of this came directly from Walter and how much represents other donations.

"*I fully realize mortals can no longer* . . ."

Rita Greene to Walda, May 30, 1972, Pat Rose coll.

Rita Greene's death. Pat Rose, Rita Greene's niece, int. by author.

she lived in a modest three-bedroom apartment . . . SR.

As she aged . . . Nat Sobel int. by author.

552 *Walda's death.* Elisabeth Winchell int. by author.

"*the country's best-known and most widely read* . . ." NY *Times*, Feb. 21, 1972, 1.

"*people were interested in people.*" NY *Post*, Feb. 22, 1972, 35.

"*In the annals of addiction* . . ." Michael Herr, "Gossip's Forgotten Ancestor," Washington *Post*, May 6, 1990, B-1.

A Note on Sources

One of the central themes of this book is that Walter Winchell helped effect and then came to symbolize a cultural revolution in which control of the American agenda shifted from the mandarins of high culture to the new masters of mass culture. A corollary theme is that he was punished by the intellectual Old Guard for having done so. That victimization, not entirely undeserved, has continued posthumously and creates an imposing hurdle for a serious study of Winchell. Magisterial biographies are generally deemed to concern magisterial subjects: great political figures, military leaders, artists, philosophers. Shunting less august but no less culturally significant figures like Winchell to the historical margins is a way, I think, for high-culturalists to maintain their control over the past even as they have surrendered control over the present. This, indeed, has been Winchell's fate—to be reduced to ephemera.

While the records that magisterial figures leave are usually hoarded for biographical excavation, whatever ephemeral figures leave can be disregarded as insignificant. Walter Winchell left more than a dozen file cabinets of papers and mementos which, had the collection been kept intact, might have served as a record of the culture of celebrity in the mid-twentieth century. With this in mind, Walda Winchell decided to donate the materials to Columbia University, but when the university asked her for a financial contribution to help catalogue the papers, she immediately rescinded her gift. She made another attempt to donate the papers to the University of Southern California, but the offer was snagged by bureaucratic rules, and it too was rescinded.

For the next fifteen years, until Walda's death in 1987, the collection languished in a warehouse, unseen, unused and, frankly, unmissed. Unfortunately Walda, apparently having concluded that no one wanted the papers, made no provision in her will for their disposition. Instead, upon her death the materials were grouped with the rest of her small estate, which was to be divided between her daughter, Elisabeth, and a medical center in Hollywood that had ministered to Walda in her declining years.

When I first learned about the papers early in my research, the collection was being catalogued by the Butterfield & Butterfield auction house in preparation for sale, the proceeds of which were to be shared by Elisabeth Winchell and the medical center. Elisabeth, sensitive to my desire to use the materials, generously permitted me unrestricted access during the cataloguing. The medical center, however, would not, and it remained unmoved after two years of letters, phone calls and trips to California to plead my case. No reason was ever given. It was to remain unmoved even after it had declared bankruptcy and closed its offices.

In the meantime, I attempted to find an institution that might consider buying the collection. This also proved unavailing. Walter Winchell was not the sort of man of whom an academic institution would approve, and I believe this tincture of moralism doomed the effort. In the end the medical center sold the papers piecemeal at auction. My only opportunity, then, to examine the collection was during a preview of the material at Butterfield & Butterfield in Los Angeles. Thanks largely to the efforts of Laura Smissaert there, I was given extended hours and other courtesies.

Working at breakneck speed without pause I managed, by my own rough estimate, to examine 75 percent of the materials and read hundreds of documents into a tape recorder for later transcription. These are the "Winchell Papers" referred to in the notes, though they are now, sadly, a fictitious entity. The auction was held jointly in Los Angeles and San Francisco on December 12, 1990. The materials were scattered among buyers; no one will ever have access to the complete collection again.

At the sale I bought Winchell's own bound volumes of his *Mirror* columns, the complete scripts of his radio programs, from the very first Saks broadcast to his last broadcast on the Mutual network, five large scrapbooks and several crates of miscellaneous material, much of it from the *Graphic* period, including three bound volumes of his *Graphic* columns. I have donated all of this to the Billy Rose Theatre Collection at the New York Public Library for the Performing Arts at Lincoln Center, where it is currently being catalogued (hence the inexactness of many of the citations) and will be made available to scholars. These are the "Winchell Papers in NYPL at Lincoln Ctr." referred to in the notes.

The bulk of this book is based on original documentation in these two "Winchell" collections. But I was also fortunate to have been given access to letters and photographs collected by Winchell's longtime secretary Rose Bigman, including early correspondence between Winchell and Glenn Condon of *The Vaudeville News*. One long letter in her collection dated April 13, 1933, from Winchell to editor Stanley Walker, was particularly valuable in clarifying some of the myths surrounding Walter in the early thirties. I was similarly fortunate to have been given access to letters in the personal collections of Herman Klurfeld, Arnold Forster, Jonathan Cuneo, Elisabeth Winchell and Harold Layer, who bought several lots at the Winchell auction and then kindly shared them with me. Bob Thomas, who had written an earlier biography of Winchell, also granted me permission to examine his notes and interviews for that book. These are listed in the notes as the Thomas collection at UCLA.

The single most valuable document in my research was the manuscript of Rita Greene, Winchell's first wife. Winchell had purged Rita from his life and from his history. In trying to restore her, I was graciously assisted by Rita's niece Pat Rose, whom I found only after a long, persistent search. Mrs. Rose provided me with letters, divorce records, a photo album and Rita's manuscript—all of which proved indispensable in re-creating Walter's vaudeville years, in chronicling his metamorphosis from vaudevillian to journalist and in detailing the end of his marriage.

Other collections I consulted are listed in the notes and in the bibliography. I believe these are self-explanatory. There is, however, one period of my research that deserves special mention. Before acquiring the bound volumes of columns and scripts at the Winchell auction, I began reading the columns in the only way an individual could: by going through each issue of the New York Daily *Mirror* on microfilm at the Newspaper Annex of the New York Public Reference Library. This process took months, and columns were occasionally missing, but reading them this way, within the total environment of the *Mirror*, steeped me not only in Winchell but in the vapors of tabloidia in a way no less intensive search could have. Similarly, the only way to read Winchell's scripts before I acquired them was on microfilm at the NBC Personnel Office, where the logs of the network are kept. This was another months-long process, but the steady barrage of Winchell prose gave me an appreciation for his appeal as well as an understanding of the peculiar cosmology he purveyed on the air.

Beyond the tens of thousands of pages of documents— more than four thousand in Winchell's FBI file alone—this book is based on interviews with more than one hundred individuals who knew Walter Winchell. All but a few of these interviews were conducted in person at the homes of the subjects, and all but one were recorded on tape. These sessions generally lasted several hours, never less than two. In the cases of Rose Bigman and Herman Klurfeld, I spoke with them repeatedly over many years, both in person and on the phone, filling hours and hours of tape. I personally transcribed every interview, each tape. As with my first book, I have used these interviews fully realizing that one must make certain allowances for the vagaries of memory and the biases of the subjects. I like to believe I have made those allowances judiciously.

The bibliography that follows is highly selected. I have not included every source listed in the notes, though I have included several volumes that do not appear in the notes because I believe these books might help an industrious reader understand better the period and culture. Many of them are admittedly meretricious. Yet the range of works, from Edmund Wilson to Earl Wilson, suggests the range of Walter Winchell's own life and the variety that existed within the strange, disjunctive culture he inhabited and which we now perforce all inhabit ourselves: the culture of celebrity.

Selected Bibliography

Manuscript Collections and Private Papers

Art Arthur Papers, Lee Library, Brigham Young University.

Rose Bigman Papers, New York, N.Y. (private collection).

Ernest Cuneo Papers, Franklin D. Roosevelt Presidential Library.

Martin Dies Papers, Sam Houston Regional Library and Research Center, Texas State Library.

Martin Dies Miscellaneous Papers, James Johnston, California (private collection).

Dwight D. Eisenhower Papers, Dwight D. Eisenhower Presidential Library.

Arnold Forster Papers, New York, N.Y. (private collection).

Rita Greene Papers, Brooklyn, N.Y. (author's collection).

Texas Guinan Scrapbooks, Billy Rose Theatre Collection, New York Public Library for the Performing Arts.

Clare Hoffman Papers, Bentley Historical Library, University of Michigan.

Irving Hoffman Scrapbooks, Billy Rose Theatre Collection, New York Public Library for the Performing Arts.

Hedda Hopper Papers, Herrick Library, Academy of Motion Picture Arts and Sciences.

Dorothy Kilgallen Scrapbooks, Billy Rose Theatre Collection, New York Public Library for the Performing Arts.

Herman Klurfeld Papers, Boca Raton, Fla. (private collection).

Time Magazine Collection, *Time* Archive.

NAACP Papers, Manuscript Division, Library of Congress.

National Broadcasting Company Scripts, NBC Personnel Office.

Louella Parsons Scrapbooks, Herrick Library, Academy of Motion Picture Arts and Sciences.

Joseph Medill Patterson Papers, Donnelly Library, Lake Forest College.

Westbrook Pegler Papers, Herbert Hoover Presidential Library.

Franklin Roosevelt Papers, Franklin D. Roosevelt Presidential Library.

M. Lincoln Schuster Papers, Columbia University.

Bob Thomas Papers, UCLA Library.

Harry S. Truman Papers, Harry S. Truman Presidential Library.

Twentieth Century-Fox Script Collection, UCLA Library.

The Vaudeville News, Billy Rose Theatre Collection, New York Public Library for the Performing Arts.

Earl Wilson Papers, Shubert Archive.

Walter Winchell Bound Columns, Billy Rose Theatre Collection, New York Public Library for the Performing Arts.

Walter Winchell-Damon Runyon Memorial Cancer Fund Papers, Runyon Fund Archives.

Walter Winchell File, Federal Bureau of Investigation.

Walter Winchell Miscellaneous Papers, Harold Layer, San Francisco, California (private collection).

Walter Winchell Radio Scripts, Billy Rose Theatre Collection, New York Public Library for the Performing Arts.

Walter Winchell Scrapbooks and Miscellaneous Papers, Billy Rose Theatre Collection, New York Public Library for the Performing Arts.

"The Walter Winchell Show," Motion Picture Division, Library of Congress.

Walter Winchell State Department File, National Archives.

Walter Winchell, Jr., File, Federal Bureau of Investigation.

Robert E. Wood Papers, Herbert Hoover Presidential Library.

Alexander Woollcott Papers, Houghton Library, Harvard University.

BOOKS

Allen, Irving L. *The City in Slang: New York Life and Popular Speech*. New York: Oxford University Press, 1993.

Allen, Mearl. *Welcome to the Stork Club*. San Diego: A. S. Barnes, 1980.

Amory, Cleveland. *Who Killed Society?* New York: Harper & Bros., 1960.

Arnaz, Desi. *A Book*. New York: Morrow, 1976.

Aronson, James. *The Press and the Cold War*. Indianapolis: Bobbs-Merrill, 1970.

Bagdikian, Ben. *Pitchmen of the Press*. Providence, R.I.: [pub. unlisted], 195?.

Baker, Josephine, and Jo Bouillon. *Josephine*, tr. from French by Mariana Fitzpatrick. New York: Harper & Row, 1977.

Barnouw, Erik. *The Golden Web: A History of Broadcasting in the United States*, Vol. II, *1933–1953*. New York: Oxford University Press, 1968.

Bayley, Edwin. *Joe McCarthy and the Press*. Madison: University of Wisconsin Press, 1981.

Bent, Silas. *Ballyhoo: The Voice of the Press*. New York: Boni & Liveright, 1927.

Berle, Beatrice Bishop, and Travis Beal Jacobs, eds. *Navigating the Rapids, 1918–1971: From the Papers of Adolf A. Berle*. New York: Harcourt Brace Jovanovich, 1973.

Berliner, Louise. *Texas Guinan: Queen of the Night Clubs*. Austin: University of Texas Press, 1993.

Bernays, Edward L. *Biography of an Idea: Memoirs of Public Relations Counsel Edward L. Bernays*. New York: Simon & Schuster, 1965.

Bessie, Simon Michael. *Jazz Journalism: The Story of Tabloid Newspapers*. New York: E. P. Dutton, 1938.

Bishop, Jim. *The Mark Hellinger Story*. New York: Appleton-Century-Croft, 1952.

Bliss, Edward, Jr. *Now the News: The Story of Broadcast Journalism*. New York: Columbia University Press, 1991.

Boorstin, Daniel J. *The Image: A Guide to Pseudo-Events in America*, rev. ed. New York: Atheneum, 1978.

Bowles, Jerry G. *A Thousand Sundays: The Story of the Ed Sullivan Show*. New York: Putnam, 1980.

Braudy, Leo. *The Frenzy of Renown: Fame and Its History*. New York: Oxford University Press, 1986.

Breslin, Jimmy. *Damon Runyon*. New York: Ticknor & Fields, 1991.

———. *The World of Jimmy Breslin*, annotated by James G. Bellows and Richard C. Wald. New York: Viking Press, 1967.

Brinkley, Alan. *Voices of Protest: Huey Long, Father Coughlin, and the Great Depression*. New York: Alfred A. Knopf, 1982.

Brown, Eve [Mary Eudora Nichols]. *Champagne Cholly: The Life and Times of Maury Paul*. New York: E. P. Dutton, 1947.

Carlisle, Rodney P. *Hearst and the New Deal: The Progressive as Reactionary*. New York: Garland Publishing, 1979.

Caute, David. *The Great Fear: The Anti-Communist Purge Under Truman and Eisenhower*. New York: Simon & Schuster, 1978.

Chambers, Whittaker. *Witness*. New York: Random House, 1952.

Clark, Tom. *The World of Damon Runyon*. New York: Harper & Row, 1978.

Coblentz, Edmond D. *William Randolph Hearst: A Portrait in His Own Words*. New York: Simon & Schuster, 1952.

Cohen, Lester. *NY Graphic: The World's Zaniest Newspaper*. Philadelphia: Chilton Books, 1964.

Conrad, Harold. *Dear Muffo: 35 Years in the Fast Lane*. New York: Stein & Day, 1982.

Corum, Bill. *Off and Running*, ed. Arthur Mann. New York: Henry Holt, 1959.

Cuneo, Ernest. *Life with Fiorello*. New York: Macmillan, 1955.

Diliberto, Gioia. *Debutante: The Story of Brenda Frazier*. New York: Alfred A. Knopf, 1987.

Driscoll, Charles B. *The Life of O. O. McIntyre*. New York: Greystone Press, 1938.

Eder, Shirley. *Not This Time, Cary Grant!* Garden City, N.Y.: Doubleday, 1973.

Eells, George. *Hedda and Louella: A Dual Biograpy of Hedda Hopper and Louella Parsons*. New York: Putnam, 1972.

Erenberg, Lewis. *Steppin' Out: New York Nightlife and the Transformation of American Culture, 1890–1930.* Westport, Conn.: Greenwood Press, 1981.

Ellis, Edward Robb. *A Nation in Torment: The Great American Depression 1929–1939.* New York: Coward-McCann, 1969.

Ernst, Robert. *Weakness Is a Crime: The Life of Bernarr Macfadden.* Syracuse: University of Syracuse Press, 1991.

Fisher, Charles. *The Columnists.* New York: Howell, Soskin, 1944.

Fitzgerald, F. Scott. *The Crack-Up*, ed. by Edmund Wilson. New York: Charles Scribner's Sons, 1931; reprint, New York: New Directions, 1956.

Forrestal, James. *The Forrestal Diaries*, ed. Walter Millis with collaboration of E.S. Duffield. New York: Viking Press, 1951.

Forster, Arnold. *Square One: A Memoir.* New York: Donald I. Fine, 1988.

Fowler, Gene. *Beau James: The Life and Times of Jimmy Walker.* New York: Viking Press, 1949.

———. *Skyline: A Reporter's Reminiscences of the Twenties.* New York: Viking Press, 1961.

Gauvreau, Emile. *Hot News.* New York: Macaulay Co., 1931.

———. *The Scandal Monger.* New York: Macaulay Co., 1932.

———. *My Last Million Readers.* New York: E. P. Dutton, 1941.

Gellerman, William. *Martin Dies.* New York: John Day, 1944.

Gentry, Curt. *J. Edgar Hoover: The Man and the Secrets.* New York: Norton, 1991.

Gilbert, Douglas. *American Vaudeville: Its Life and Times.* New York: Whittlesey House, 1940.

Goldenson, Leonard, with Marvin J. Wolf. *Beating the Odds: The Untold Story Behind the Rise of ABC.* New York: Charles Scribner's Sons, 1991.

Goldman, Eric F. *The Crucial Decade—And After: America, 1945–1960.* New York: Vintage, 1960.

———. *Two-Way Street: The Emergence of the Public Relations Counsel.* Boston: Bellman Publishing Co., 1948.

Grady, Billy. *The Irish Peacock.* New Rochelle, N.Y.: Arlington House, 1972.

Graham, Stephen. *New York Nights.* New York: George H. Doran, 1927.

Gray, Barry. *My Night People.* New York: Simon & Schuster, 1975.

Gross, Ben. *I Looked and Listened: Informal Recollections of Radio and TV.* New Rochelle, N.Y.: Arlington House, 1970.

Gurock, Jeffrey S. *When Harlem was Jewish, 1870–1929.* New York: Columbia University Press, 1979.

Haney, Lynn. *Naked at the Feast: A Biography of Josephine Baker.* New York: Dodd, Mead & Co., 1981.

Healy, Paul F. *Cissy: The Biography of Eleanor M. "Cissy" Patterson.* Garden City, N.Y.: Doubleday, 1966.

Hearst, William Randolph, Jr., with Jack Casserly. *The Hearsts: Father and Son.* Niwot, Colo.: Roberts Rinehart, 1991.

Hecht, Ben. *A Child of the Century: The Autobiography of Ben Hecht.* New York: Simon & Schuster, 1954.

Hodgson, Godfrey. *America in Our Time: From World War II to Nixon, What Happened and Why.* New York: Random House, 1976.

Hoffman, Frederick. *The Twenties: American Writing in the Postwar Decade.* New York: Viking Press, 1955.

Hofstadter, Richard. *Anti-intellectualism in American Life.* New York: Alfred A. Knopf, 1963.

———. *The Paranoid Style in American Politics and Other Essays.* New York: John Wiley & Sons, 1964.

Hopper, Hedda. *From Under My Hat.* Garden City, N.Y.: Doubleday, 1952.

———, and James Brough. *The Whole Truth and Nothing But.* New York: Pyramid Books, 1963.

Hoyt, Edwin P. *A Gentleman of Broadway.* Boston: Little, Brown, 1964.

Hunt, William R. *Body Love: The Amazing Career of Bernarr Macfadden.* Bowling Green, Ohio: Bowling Green State University Popular Press, 1989.

Israel, Lee. *Kilgallen.* New York: Delacorte, 1979; paperback reprint, New York: Dell, 1980.

Jessel, George, with John Austin. *The World I Lived In.* Chicago: Henry Regnery, 1975.

Kennedy, John S. "A Bolt from the Blue," in *Molders of Opinion,* ed. David Bulman. Milwaukee: Bruce Publishing Co., 1945.

Klein, Alexander, ed. *The Empire City.* New York: Rinehart, 1955.

Kluger, Richard. *The Paper: The Life and Death of the New York Herald Tribune.* New York: Alfred A. Knopf, 1986.

Klurfeld, Herman. *Winchell: His Life and Times.* New York: Praeger, 1976.

Koenigsberg, Moses. *King News.* New York: Frederick A. Stokes, 1941.

Kramer, Dale. *Ross and the New Yorker.* Garden City, N.Y.: Doubleday, 1951.

Kupcinet, Irving, with Paul Neimark. *Kup: A Man, an Era, a City, Irv Kupcinet's Autobiography.* Chicago: Bonus Books, 1988.

Lash, Joseph P. *Dealers and Dreamers: A New Look at the New Deal.* New York: Doubleday, 1988.

Laurie, Joe, Jr. *Vaudeville: From Honky Tonks to the Palace.* New York: Henry Holt, 1953.

Lehman, Ernest. *The Comedian and Other Stories.* New York: Signet, 1957.

———. *The Sweet Smell of Success and Other Stories.* New York: Signet, 1956.

Leuchtenberg, William. *The Perils of Prosperity, 1914–1932.* Chicago: University of Chicago Press, 1958.

Levine, Isaac Don. *Eyewitness to History: Memoirs and Reflections of a Foreign Correspondent for Half a Century.* New York: Hawthorn Books, 1973.

Lewis, Marlo, and Mina Bess Lewis. *Prime Time.* Los Angeles: J. P. Tarcher, Inc., 1976.

Liebling, A. J. *The Press,* 2nd rev. ed. New York: Pantheon, 1975.

Lippmann, Walter. *Public Opinion.* New York: Macmillan, 1922; paperback reprint, New York: Macmillan, 1961.

Lundberg, Ferdinand. *Imperial Hearst.* New York: Modern Library, 1937.

Macfadden, Mary, and Emile Gauvreau. *Dumbbells and Carrot Strips: The Story of Bernarr Macfadden.* New York: Henry Holt, 1953.

MacLean, Albert F. *American Vaudeville as Ritual.* Lexington; University of Kentucky Press, 1965.

Mallen, Frank. *Sauce for the Gander.* White Plains, N.Y.: Baldwin Books, 1954.

Martin, Ralph G. *Cissy: The Extraordinary Life of Eleanor Medill Patterson.* New York: Simon & Schuster, 1979.

McCoy, Donald R. *The Presidency of Harry S. Truman.* Lawrence; University of Kansas Press, 1984.

McCullough, David. *Truman.* New York: Simon & Schuster, 1992.

McIntyre, O. O. *The Big Town: New York Day by Day.* New York: Dodd, Mead and Co., 1935.

McKelway, St. Clair. *Gossip: The Life and Times of Walter Winchell.* New York: Viking Press, 1940.

McLuhan, Marshall. "The Sage of the Waldorf Towers," in *The Mechanical Bride: Folklore of Industrial Man.* London: Routledge Kegan Paul Ltd., 1951; New York: Vanguard Press, 1951.

Mitchell, Joseph. *Up in the Old Hotel.* New York: Pantheon, 1992.

Morris, Lloyd. *Postscript to Yesterday: America—the Last Fifty Years.* New York: Random House, 1947.

Mosedale, John. *The Men Who Invented Broadway: Damon Runyon, Walter Winchell and Their World.* New York: Richard C. Marek, 1981.

Mott, Frank Luther. *American Journalism: A History,* 3rd ed. New York: Macmillan, 1962.

Nash, Roderick. *The Nervous Generation: American Thought, 1917–1930.* Chicago: Rand McNally, 1970; paperback reprint, Chicago: Ivan R. Dee, 1990.

Navasky, Victor. *Naming Names.* New York: Viking Press, 1980.

Odets, Clifford. *The Time Is Ripe: The 1940 Journal of Clifford Odets.* New York: Grove Press, 1988.

Oshinsky, David. *A Conspiracy So Immense: The World of Joe McCarthy.* New York: Free Press, 1983.

Otash, Fred. *Investigation Hollywood.* Chicago: Henry Regnery, 1976.

Oursler, Fulton. *Behold the Dreamer!: The Autobiography of Fulton Oursler,* ed. and with commentary by Fulton Oursler, Jr. Boston: Little, Brown, 1964.

Paar, Jack, with John Reddy. *I Kid You Not.* Boston: Little, Brown, 1960.

Parsons, Louella O. *The Gay Illiterate.* Garden City, N.Y.: Doubleday, 1944.

———. *Tell It to Louella.* New York: Putnam, 1961.

Pearson, Drew. *Diaries, 1949–1959,* ed. Tyler Abell. New York: Holt, Rinehart, 1974.

Pilat, Oliver. *Pegler.* Boston: Beacon Press, 1963.

Potter, Jeffrey. *Men, Money and Magic: The Story of Dorothy Schiff.* New York: Coward, McCann & Geoghegan, 1976.

Reichenbach, Harry, as told to David Freedman. *Phantom Fame: The Anatomy of Ballyhoo.* Introduction by Walter Winchell. New York: Simon & Schuster, 1931.

Robins, Natalie. *Alien Ink: The FBI's War on Freedom of Expression.* New York: Morrow, 1992.

Rogow, Arnold A. *James Forrestal: A Study of Personality, Politics and Policy.* New York: Macmillan, 1963.

Rosenstein, Jaik. *Hollywood Leg Man.* Los Angeles: Madison Press, 1950.

Rosnow, Ralph L., and Gary Alan Fine. *Rumor and Gossip: The Social Psychology of Hearsay.* New York: Elsevier, 1976.

Runyon, Damon. *Guys and Dolls.* New York: Frederick A. Stokes, 1931.

———. *Damon Runyon's Blue Plate Special*. Foreword by Walter Winchell. New York: Frederick A. Stokes, 1934.

———. *Trials and Tribulations*. London: Xanadu Publications, 1946; paperback reprint, New York: International Polygonics, 1991.

Runyon, Damon, Jr. *Father's Footsteps*. New York: Random House, 1954.

Schlesinger, Arthur M., Jr. *The Age of Roosevelt*, vol. I, *The Crisis of the Old Order, 1919–1933*; vol. II, *The Coming of the New Deal*; vol. III, *The Politics of Upheaval*. Boston: Houghton Mifflin Co., 1957–59.

Schickel, Richard. *Intimate Strangers: The Culture of Celebrity*. Garden City, N.Y.: Doubleday, 1985.

Schudson, Michael. *Discovering the News: A Social History of American Newspapers*. New York: Basic Books, 1978.

Skolsky, Sidney. *Times Square Tintypes*. New York: Ives Washburn, 1928.

———. *Don't Get Me Wrong—I Love Hollywood*. New York: Putnam, 1975.

Snyder, Robert. *The Voice of the City: Vaudeville and Popular Culture in New York*. New York: Oxford University Press, 1989.

Sobel, Bernard. *Broadway Heartbeat: Memoirs of a Press Agent*. New York: Hermitage House, 1953.

Sobol, Louis. *The Longest Street: A Memoir*. New York: Crown, 1968.

———. *Some Days Were Happy*. New York: Random House, 1947.

Spacks, Patricia Meyer. *Gossip*. New York: Knopf, 1985.

Stack, Philip. *Love in Mahattan*. Introduction by Walter Winchell. New York: Liveright, 1932.

Steel, Ronald. *Walter Lippmann and the American Century*. Boston: Little, Brown, 1980.

Stevens, John D. *Sensationalism and the New York Press*. New York: Columbia University Press, 1991.

Stoddart, Dayton. *Lord Broadway: Variety's Sime*. New York: Wilfred Funk, 1941.

Stuart, Lyle. *The Secret Life of Walter Winchell*. New York: Boar's Head Books, 1953.

Sullivan, William C., with Bill Brown. *The Bureau: My Thirty Years in Hoover's FBI*. New York: Norton, 1979.

Summers, Harrison B. *Radio Programs Carried on National Networks, 1926–1956*. Columbus: Ohio State University Press, 1958.

Susman, Warren I., ed. *Culture as History: The Transformation of American Society in the Twentieth Century*. New York: Pantheon, 1984.

Swanberg, W. A. *Citizen Hearst: A Biography of William Randolph Hearst*. New York: Charles Scribner's Sons, 1961.

Sylvester, Robert. *No Cover Charge: A Backward Look at the Night Clubs*. New York: Dial, 1956.

———. *Notes of a Guilty Bystander*. Englewood Cliffs, N.J.: Prentice-Hall, 1970.

Taylor, William R., ed. *Inventing Times Square: Commerce and Culture at the Crossroads of the World*. New York: Russell Sage Foundation, 1991.

———. *In Pursuit of Gotham: Culture and Commerce in New York*. New York: Oxford University Press, 1992.

Tebbel, John. *The Life and Times of William Randolph Hearst*. New York: E. P. Dutton, 1952.

Theoharis, Athan G., and John Stuart Cox. *The Boss: J. Edgar Hoover and the Great American Inquisition.* Philadelphia: Temple University Press, 1988.

Thomas, Bob. *Winchell.* Garden City, N.Y.: Doubleday, 1971.

Truman, Margaret, ed. *Harry S. Truman.* New York: Morrow, 1972.

Tully, Jim. *A Dozen and One.* Hollywood: Murray & Gee, 1943.

Turkus, Burton, and Sid Feder. *Murder Inc.: The Story of "The Syndicate."* New York: Farrar, Straus and Young, 1951.

Von Hoffman, Nicholas. *Citizen Cohn.* New York: Doubleday, 1988.

Walker, Stanley. *The Night Club Era.* New York: Frederick A. Stokes, 1933.

———. *City Editor.* New York: Frederick A. Stokes, 1934.

———. *Mrs. Astor's Horse.* New York: Frederick A. Stokes, 1935.

Walker, Danton. *Danton's Inferno: The Story of a Columnist and How He Grew.* New York: Hastings House, 1955.

Walsh, George. *Gentleman Jimmy Walker: Mayor of the Jazz Age.* New York: Praeger, 1974.

Wechsler, James A. *The Age of Suspicion.* New York: Random House, 1953.

Weiner, Ed. *The Damon Runyon Story.* New York: Longmans Green, 1948.

———. *Let's Go to Press: A Biography of Walter Winchell.* New York: Putnam, 1955.

Weinschel, Chayim. *Pleasing Plants: Contains Poetry, Letters Written Entirely in Hebrew.* New York: Abraham Ginsberg [1891].

Wilson, Earl. *Hot Times: True Tales of Hollywood and Broadway.* Chicago: Contemporary Books, 1984.

Wilson, Edmund. *The Shores of Light: A Literary Chronicle of the Twenties and Thirties.* New York: Farrar, Straus & Young, 1952.

Wilson, Jan Hoff, ed. *The Twenties: The Critical Issues.* Boston: Little, Brown, 1973.

Winchell, Walter. *Winchell Exclusive: "Things That Happened to Me—and Me to Them."* Introduction by Ernest Cuneo. Englewood Cliffs, N.J.: Prentice-Hall, 1975.

Winfield, Betty Houchin. *FDR and the News Media.* Urbana: University of Illinois Press, 1990.

Zerbe, Jerome, and Brendan Gill. *Happy Times.* New York: Harcourt, Brace, Jovanovich, 1973.

Zion, Sidney. *The Autobiography of Roy Cohn.* Secaucus, N.J.: Lyle Stuart, 1988.

Articles

Allhoff, Fred. "Walter Winchell—American Phenomenon," Parts I and II. *Liberty Magazine* (March 28, 1942, April 4, 1942).

Beath, Paul Robert. "Winchellese." *American Speech,* vol. 7 ([October] 1931), 44–46.

Broun, Heywood. "The Inside Story of Lepke and Mr. Walter Winchell." *Broun's Nutmeg* (September 2, 1939), 1.

Carroll, Sidney. "A Tale of Hoffman." *Esquire* (November 1946).

Cooke, Alistair. "Walter Winchell: An American Myth." *Listener* (November 20, 1947).

Cort, David. "The Gossip Columnists." *Nation* (October 13, 1956).

Covert, Cathy. "A View of the Press in the Twenties." *Journalism History* (Autumn 1975), 66–67, 92–96.

Crowninshield, Frank. "The New Left Wing in New York Society." *Vogue* (February 1938).

Cummings, E. E. "The Tabloid Newspaper." *Vanity Fair* (December 1926).

Daugherty, George. "Winchell: J. Edgar Hoover's Man Friday." *Daily Worker*, March 11, 1941.

———. "Winchell's Adventures in the Prohibition Era." *Daily Worker*, March 12, 1941.

De Rochemont, Richard G. "The Tabloids." *American Mercury* (October 1926).

Feinberg, Alexander. "The Why of Night Clubs." *New York Times Magazine*, May 20, 1945.

Freeman, Don. "The Emperor of Broadway." *Seminar* (June 1972),

Govoni, Steve. "Now It Can Be Told." *American Film* (February 1990).

Hartwell, Dickson. "Walter Winchell: An American Phenomenon." *Collier's* (February 28, 1948).

Hoffman, Irving. "Things You Never Knew till Now About Walter Winchell." *Radio Guide* (May 1, 1937).

Kandel, Aben. "A Tabloid a Day." *Forum* (March 1927).

Kennedy, John B. "For the Wife and the Kiddies." *Collier's* (October 5, 1929).

Kilgallen, Dorothy. "The Cosmopolite of the Month." *Hearst's International Cosmopolitan Magazine* (July 1938).

Krim, Seymour. "Mauled in the Lyons Den." *Soho Weekly News* (May 14, 1980).

Lazarus, Charles J. "Here's What You Didn't Know About Walter Winchell." *New Liberty* (May 1951).

Luber, Mildred. "His Life Is News." *Radio Mirror* (July 1939).

Maas, Peter. "Prowling the Night Beat with Walter Winchell." *Collier's* (November 23, 1956).

Maloney, Russell. "Profile [of Leonard Lyons]." *The New Yorker* (April 7, 1945).

"Manhattan Night Life." *Fortune* (March 1936).

McChesney, Robert W. "Press Radio Relations and the Emergence of Network, Commercial Broadcasting in the United States, 1930–1935." *Historical Journal of Film, Radio and Television* (1991), 42.

McEvoy, J. P. "He Snoops to Conquer." *Saturday Evening Post* (August 13, 1938).

Menken, Harriet. "The Portrait Gallery." *Weekly Radio Dial* (December 23, 1931).

Moore, Samuel Taylor. "Those Terrible Tabloids." *The Independent* (March 6, 1926).

Morrell, Parker. "Mr. and Mrs. Walter Winchell." *Ladies' Home Journal* (June 1940).

Nathan, George Jean. "Clinical Notes [on tabloids]." *American Mercury* (March 1926).

"Newspaperman." *Time*, July 11, 1938.

"The Old WW Himself." *Newsweek* (October 10, 1960).

Perry, John W. "New Play 'Blessed Event' Shows Rise of Bway Columnist." *Editor & Publisher* (February 20, 1932).

Pew, Marlen. "Gigolo Journalism." *Editor & Publisher* (January 23, 1932).

Preston, Georgiana X. "Apology to Winchell the Popgun Patriot." Washington *Times-Herald* (July 19, 1942).

Pringle, Henry F. "Portrait of Walter Winchell." *American Mercury* (February 1937).

Reynolds, Quentin. "Have You a Reservation?" *Collier's* (October 1, 1938).

Roche, John F. "Walter Winchell's 'Big Ear' Hears Broadway's Gossip and Slang." *Editor & Publisher* (March 17, 1928).

Ropel, Timothy. "Walter Winchell: The Thirteenth Juror." *Media History Digest* (Fall 1985).

Salpeter, Henry. "Town Gossip: A Portrait of Walter Winchell." *Outlook and Independent* (July 10, 1929).

Schickel, Richard. "The Rise and Fall of Café Society." *Forbes* (October 1985).

Schuyler, Philip. "Winchell: World's Highest Paid Gossip." *Publisher's Service* (September 18, 1930).

Spivak, John L. "The Rise and Fall of a Tabloid." *American Mercury* (July 1934).

Steinglass, Meyer. "Broadway's Greatest Scribe." *The Jewish Times* (July 25, 1930).

Strassburg, Cornelia. "The True Love Story of Walter Winchell." *Love Magazine* (January 1931).

Torre, Marie. "A New Career for Walter Winchell." *Look Magazine* (October 30, 1956).

Walker, Jerry. "Winchell Admits Fluffs; He'd Like a Little Credit." *Editor & Publisher* (November 13, 1948).

Walker, Stanley. "Playing the Deep Bassoons." *Harper's Monthly Magazine* (February 1932).

Warren, Samuel D., and Louis Brandeis. "The Right to Privacy." *Harvard Law Review*, vol. 4 (December 1890), 193–220.

Weyrauch, Martin. "The Why of Tabloids." *Forum* (April 1927).

Whelan, Russell. "Inside the Stork Club." *American Mercury* (September 1944).

Wilcox, Charles W. "Winchell of Broadway." *Scribner's Magazine.* (February 1931).

Wilson, Edmund. "Night Clubs." *The New Republic* (September 9, 1925).

Winchell, Walter. "The Wisecrack and the Gag." *The Bookman* (October 1927).

———. "A Primer of Broadway Slang." *Vanity Fair* (November 1927).

———. "The Real Broadway." *The Bookman* (December 1927).

———. "The Merry Magdalens." *Vanity Fair* (January 1928).

———. "Author! Author! Author!" *Vanity Fair* (March 1928).

———. "Once an Actor—Always?" *Vanity Fair* (May 1928).

———. "Hit Him Again—He's Collegiate." *College Humor* (September 1928).

———. "Broadway Novelettes." *College Humor* (November 1929).

———. "Along the Grandest Canyon." *College Humor* (May 1930).

———. "On the Long Lane of Short Careers." *College Humor* (June 1930).

———. "People Who Live in Glass Houses Shouldn't Throw Paragraphs." *College Humor* (September 1930).

———. "These Charming People." *Vanity Fair* (August 1931).

———. "Things I Never Knew till Now." *Vanity Fair* (March 1932).

———. "Tabloid Managing Editors." *American Spectator* (April 1933).

———. "Down with the Jews." *Jewish World* (August 17, 1934).

———. "Americans We Can Do Without." *Liberty Magazine* (August 1, 8, 15, 22, 1942).

Winslow, Thyra Samter. "To Eat, Drink and Be Mentioned." *New York Times Magazine*, February 24, 1946, 20.

Wirth, Louis. "Urbanism as a Way of Life." *American Journal of Sociology*, vol. 44 (July 1938), 21.

Wolfe, Thomas K. "Public Lives: Confidential Magazine; Reflections in Tranquility by the Former Owner, Robert Harrison, Who Managed to Get Away with It." *Esquire* (April 1964).

Woollcott, Alexander. "The Little Man with the Big Voice." *Hearst's International Cosmopolitan Magazine* (May 1933).

"The Yankee Doodle Salon." *Fortune* (December 1937).

Zwerin, Michael. "Flash! . . . Walter Winchell Is a Reluctant Anachronism." *Esquire* (August 1968).

UNPUBLISHED MANUSCRIPTS

Cuneo, Ernest. "Disintegration of Walter Winchell's Power." Cuneo papers, Franklin D. Roosevelt Presidential Library.

———. "Fights to the Finish." FDR Library.

———. "J. Edgar Hoover and Winchell." FDR Library.

———. "Third Term." FDR Library.

———. Untitled. FDR Library.

———. "Walter as a Babe in the International Intelligence Game." FDR Library.

———. "Winchell—Power in Action." FDR Library.

———. "Winchell's Early Background." FDR Library.

———. "Winchell's Grave." FDR Library.

Greene, Rita. Untitled (author's collection).

Mack, Roy. Untitled (private collection).

Mayor's Committee on Unity. "Final Report on the Stork Club Controversy." December 20, 1951. Mayor Impellitteri Papers, New York City Municipal Archives.

Stein, John S., and Hayward Grace. "Hello Sucker!: The Life of Texas Guinan." 1941. Billy Rose Theatre Collection, New York Public Library for the Performing Arts.

Winchell, Walter. *McCall's.* 4th draft. Cuneo papers, Franklin D. Roosevelt Presidential Library.

———. "Winchell for *McCall's.*" 2d draft., Cuneo papers, FDR Library.

Acknowledgments

Though the five and a half years I have devoted to this book have been spent largely in solitary labor, over that time I have been the beneficiary of the kindness of many individuals who encouraged and assisted me and without whom this project would not have been possible. Once again I hope that those who helped will regard the book itself as a form of appreciation. Nevertheless, my deepest gratitude goes with it: first and foremost, to my agent, Elaine Markson, for her patience, her faith and concern; to the Freedom Forum Media Studies Center at Columbia University and especially to its director, Everette Dennis, for nine months of intellectual stimulation; to Rose Bigman for sharing with me her recollections, her papers and her friendship; to Herman Klurfeld for his generosity, his candor and his belief in the value of this project; to Elisabeth Winchell for her unstinting cooperation and enthusiasm; to Eva Winchell for sharing painful memories with me that enabled me to understand better Walter Winchell, Jr.; to Pat Rose for giving me access to her aunt Rita Greene's letters and manuscript; to Jonathan Cuneo for permitting me to examine his father's papers and for his sincere interest in this project; to Alice Davis both for her indispensable help and for the passion she brought to her work during the nine months she assisted me at the Freedom Forum Media Studies Center; to Terry McCabe for lending me his time to examine documents with me at the Franklin D. Roosevelt Presidential Library; to Bob Thomas for kindly granting me permission to use the notes of his own biography of Walter Winchell; to Laura

Smissaert, then of Butterfield & Butterfield auctioneers, for doing everything in her power with no motive other than pure decency to let me examine the Winchell papers; to Shermane Billingsley Drill for reminiscences about her father, Sherman Billingsley, and for her continuing regard for this project; to Sarah Fried for funneling new material about the Hoskins family, of which she is a member, and to Yvonne McGlothing for tracking the Hoskinses and June in Brookhaven, Mississippi; to Rebecca Kry of the Winchell-Runyon Memorial Cancer Fund for giving me access to the fund's archive; to Cathy Lim of the NBC Personnel Office for her unfailing cooperation and good cheer during the many weeks I spent in her office; to Harold Layer for giving me access to his own substantial Winchell collection and allowing me to reproduce photographs from it; to Bruce Abrams of the New York County Clerk's office for unearthing records and documents far above and beyond the call of duty; to Kenneth Cobb of the New York Municipal Archives for meeting each request of mine with graciousness; to the staffs of the New York Public Reference Library, the Billy Rose Theatre Collection at the New York Public Library for the Performing Arts, the Library of Congress Manuscript Division and Motion Picture Division, the Margaret Herrick Library of the Academy of Motion Picture Arts and Sciences, the Franklin D. Roosevelt Presidential Library and the National Archives for their assistance during my visits, and to the staffs of all the libraries and archives I consulted; to my friend David Kehr for reading portions of this manuscript when I needed a reader; to Caomh Kavanagh of the Elaine Markson Agency for expediting matters that needed expediting; to my editor, Jonathan Segal, for his rigorous scrutiny of the manuscript; to his assistant, Ida Giragossian, for performing a multitude of essential and essentially thankless chores; to Brooke Zimmer for her care in the design of this book; to Melvin Rosenthal for his attentiveness as the production editor for the book; to Sonny Mehta for his belief in the value of this project; to John Morahan for his walking tour of Winchell's New York; and to all the individuals who consented to be interviewed for this book. Finally, I owe an enormous, unpayable debt to my wife and children for the many sacrifices they made and the many hardships they endured.

None of these individuals, of course, bears any responsibility for the text of this book. They only bear responsibility for its existence.

Index

A NOTE ABOUT THE AUTHOR

Neal Gabler is the author of *An Empire of Their Own: How the Jews Invented Hollywood*, which won the Los Angeles *Times* Book Prize for History and was named by the Academy of Motion Picture Arts and Sciences as one of the one hundred outstanding books on films. Mr. Gabler holds advanced degrees in film and American culture and has taught at the University of Michigan and Pennsylvania State University. For three years he cohosted the movie review program "Sneak Previews" on public television. He has also held a fellowship at the Freedom Forum Media Studies Center at Columbia University.

Mr. Gabler was born in Chicago and lives with his wife and two daughters in Brooklyn, New York.

A NOTE ON THE TYPE

This book was set in Janson, a recutting made direct from type cast from matrices long thought to have been made by the Dutchman Anton Janson, who was a practicing type founder in Leipzig during the years 1668–1687. However, it has been conclusively demonstrated that these types are actually the work of Nicholas Kis (1650–1702), a Hungarian, who most probably learned his trade from the master Dutch type founder Dirk Voskens. The type is an excellent example of the influential and sturdy Dutch types that prevailed in England up to the time William Caslon developed his own incomparable designs from them.

Composed by Creative Graphics, Allentown, Pennsylvania
Printed and bound by Arcata Graphics, Martinsburg, Virginia
Designed by Brooke Zimmer